SUSAN WEIDMAN SCHNEIDER

◆

JEWISH AND FEMALE

CHOICES AND CHANGES
IN OUR LIVES TODAY

A TOUCHSTONE BOOK
PUBLISHED BY SIMON & SCHUSTER, INC.
NEW YORK

FIRST TOUCHSTONE EDITION, 1985
PUBLISHED BY SIMON & SCHUSTER, INC.
SIMON & SCHUSTER BUILDING
ROCKEFELLER CENTER
1230 AVENUE OF THE AMERICAS
NEW YORK, NEW YORK 10020
TOUCHSTONE AND COLOPHON ARE REGISTERED TRADEMARKS OF
SIMON & SCHUSTER, INC.
DESIGNED BY KAROLINA HARRIS
MANUFACTURED IN THE UNITED STATES OF AMERICA

3   5   7   9   10   8   6   4   2
1   3   5   7   9   10   8   6   4   2   PBK.

LIBRARY OF CONGRESS CATALOGING IN PUBLICATION DATA
SCHNEIDER, SUSAN WEIDMAN.
JEWISH AND FEMALE.
BIBLIOGRAPHY: P.
INCLUDES INDEX.
1. WOMEN IN JUDAISM.   2. WOMEN, JEWISH—UNITED STATES.
3. FEMINISM.   I. TITLE.
BM729.W6S36   1984   296'.088042   84-5344
ISBN 0-671-42103-4
ISBN 0-671-60439-2 PBK.

SOME OF THE ESSAYS CONTAINED IN THIS BOOK HAVE BEEN PREVIOUSLY PUBLISHED
IN LILITH MAGAZINE.

GRATEFUL ACKNOWLEDGMENT IS HEREBY EXPRESSED FOR PERMISSION
TO REPRINT EXCERPTS FROM THE FOLLOWING WORKS:
"THE SHELTERED WORKSHOP" BY AVIVA CANTOR, *Lilith*, NO. 5, 1978.
"THE CASE OF THE RELUCTANT EXOGAMISTS" BY DR. RELA GEFFEN MONSON,
Gratz College Annual, 1976.
"FRIDAY NIGHT" BY DIANNE LEVENBERG, FROM *Out of the Desert*
(NEW YORK: DOUBLEDAY, 1980).
"ARE GOOD JEWISH MEN A VANISHING BREED?" BY BILL NOVAK,
Moment, JANUARY—FEBRUARY 1980.
"MEMOIRS OF A MALE MOTHER" BY DR. ANDRÉ UNGAR,
The Bulletin of Temple Emanuel, WOODCLIFF LAKE, NEW JERSEY, MAY 1980.

ACKNOWLEDGMENTS

The story of this book's evolution cannot be told without first mentioning *Lilith* magazine. The Jewish feminist quarterly, which began publishing in 1976, was conceived by a group of Jewish women journalists and editors in the summer of 1973. My own development in every way has been affected by my experience with *Lilith* and with the women who have been associated with it as editors, writers, advisers, supporters, and subscribers.

In 1973 I was a writer who had just begun to write on explicitly Jewish subjects; I was a woman who was at the first stages of noting how the women's movement gave voice to my own aspirations and fears and anger. For me the magazine was a fusion of professional and personal identities of a profound sort, and the connection with *Lilith*—I was among its founding mothers—felt like a homecoming.

My actual ancestral home, where I spent my childhood and adolescence, is Winnipeg, a Jewish community that gave me security, pride, and a strong sense of myself as a fully participating, valued Jew. Credit for this is due in part to a neighborhood synagogue, where my skills as a junior congregation rabbi and cantor were both praised and accepted as nothing out of the ordinary for a female child. A little reality testing later in life of course convinced me that my earlier feelings of comfort and acceptance as a Jewish woman were illusory, but they did give me a model for creating a genuinely egalitarian Jewish life. Winnipeg and my time there also gave me a freedom to criticize—a freedom I have exercised in the pages of *Lilith* and in this book—yet know I'd still be loved. (The same tension between wanting to be critical and wanting to remain connected with the

Jewish community has characterized many of the choices and changes delineated in this book.)

The need for a book that would attempt to depict the variety and scope of the changes in Jewish women's lives (my own included) over the past fifteen years, and that would look also at the traditions against which some of the changes were taking place, became clear to many of us associated with *Lilith*. The one-room *Lilith* office had become the national address and telephone number of the growing Jewish women's movement. Queries came in every day from women wanting guidance on their path toward integrating feminism and Judaism. Information was needed on how to find speakers for conferences, women serving as rabbis, nonsexist Jewish day care, topics for a dissertation on Jewish women's history, women's groups dealing with midlife crisis, religious support for abortion rights, and much, much more.

A great deal of the information that was conveyed informally by telephone, mail, and personal contacts would, we thought, be useful to larger audiences. We were right, as the increasing demand for speakers testified. But the energy didn't flow only outward. Every time I have addressed an audience on some aspect of our lives as Jews and as women (more than a hundred such talks in the past few years), I have learned as much as I have taught. I want to acknowledge here those women—Jewish and non-Jewish (and some men)—across the United States and Canada who responded not only to the magazine itself but also to the issues raised in my talks. The women who questioned me, challenged my assumptions, shared with me the crises in their own growth and development, are the women whose voices appear throughout this book as a plainsong against which the analysis of religious, social, and political change is articulated. Without these stories there would be no urgency to the struggle for understanding how Judaism and feminism can support one another. To all the women who have called and written and approached me after lectures, often with very painful questions, and to the network of *Lilith* correspondents and authors whose work helped provide the answers, thank you for sharing your experiences and your observations. This book is from you as well as for you.

In the process of developing the idea for this book, the early enthusiasm of three women provided me with the burst of energy I needed to consider undertaking what seemed (and still seems, I must confess) a mammoth task: Nessa Rapoport, who first helped catalyze my diverse thoughts for "a" book derived from the *Lilith* experience; Barbara Grossman, then at Simon & Schuster, who first contracted for the book; and Victoria Pryor, my agent and sounding board, whose initial delight in the project was followed by her chronic optimism and cool thinking, which have been balm throughout the years of the book's making. Erwin Glikes, my editor at Simon and Schuster, and Jill Zimmerman, his assistant, were paradigms of grace and patience; Erwin's gentle instruction and sound judgment helped to shape the book's present form. Bob Bender, who inherited the manuscript, saw it through its final stages with care and enthusiasm.

Vicki Rosenstreich read early drafts of parts of *Jewish and Female* and was always willing to speculate with me on the links between Jewish custom and the psychological dynamics of Jewish women's (and men's) lives today. Nechama Liss-Levinson graciously commented on the sections concerning ritual. Photographer Marilynne Herbert willingly extended herself with skill and good humor to explore "photo opportunities" for the book. Cyma Horowitz and the staff of the Blaustein Library at the American Jewish Committee gave me invaluable assistance in checking references. A great deal of help in preparing the various drafts came from women who originally passed through the *Lilith* office as student interns: Beryl Satter, Liz Leshin, and Joan Friedman. Shebar Windstone helped to prepare the Networking Directory, with care above and beyond the call of duty. My colleagues at *Lilith*, especially Paula Gantz and Reena Sigman Friedman, picked up much of the slack created by my necessary absences to meet the book's deadlines.

Among my friends and coeditors is one person without whom my life and my work would have been much different, and likely poorer, and without whose perspicacity (and files) this book would neither have germinated nor come to fruition. She is Aviva Cantor, my dear friend, and in some ways my teacher, for ten years. According to Aviva, the three most beautiful words in the English language are "You were right," and I've had ample cause to address them to her in our many discussions of the issues in this book. Much of what I hope will be illuminating and useful here is due to her. She helped refine many of my own concepts, shared with me her wide knowledge, and gave invaluable editorial counsel. *Jewish and Female* can in some ways be considered an anniversary offering for a decade of friendship and shared labor in the Jewish women's movement.

The members of my immediate and extended family have given support of another kind. From my mother, Zora Zagrabelna Weidman, physical stamina inherited and dogged determination learned from her example; she also taught me a tolerance that has been immeasurably helpful in looking at the diverse ways in which Jewish women have chosen to express their femaleness and their Jewishness. My late father's loving confidence in my abilities and plans was probably his most valuable legacy. My husband Bruce's unflagging faith in the virtues of doing this book and the loving support system provided by Mort and Toby and Anne Schneider have seen me through the many near-cataclysmic "marker" events—including illness, the birth of our third child and the Bar Mitzvah of our first, career shifts, and a household move—which took place during the years of this book's gestation and labor. Throughout, the support of family and friends has been a rich blessing, which I gratefully acknowledge.

For what I hope are the book's strengths, all of the people named above deserve credit. For any errors of omission or commission I alone am responsible. I hope that many will step in with corrections and additions, so that we can continue together the process of restoring, transforming, and creating options for Jewish women.

For Bruce, Benjamin, Rachel, and Yael,
who have taught me a great deal about choosing and changing.

CONTENTS

THREE—POWER AND PARTICIPATION IN
         THE JEWISH COMMUNITY

JEWISH AND FEMALE

INTRODUCTION

As Jewish women we are in the process of transforming our lives, trying to bring into closer alignment the two poles of our identities—woman and Jew. Since the late 1960s two consciousness-raising movements have carried us farther in this transformation than most of us could then have predicted: the women's liberation movement, which gave us new self-respect as women, and the expansion of Jewish awareness among Diaspora Jews since the 1967 Six-Day War in Israel and the burgeoning of ethnic pride in the 1970s. For Jewish women the two forces seemed to be flowing into each other, carrying many of us in their powerful wake.

But that passive image of women moved by a strong current, adequate perhaps for a backdrop, fails to account for the fact that we women *ourselves* were at center stage, creating the motion even as we felt the changes taking place around us. We have been trying to take charge of events in our own lives and in every area of what we call Jewish life: religion, the community, the family, and all our interpersonal relations. We are learning how to make change and how to cope with change.

Of course, before the present wave of the women's movement there were Jewish women actively lobbying for gender equality in Jewish life, just as there were isolated women trying to change women's status in the larger community. But the recent confluence of a new Jewish and feminist awareness spurred Jewish women on in both struggles—to bring a Jewish dimension to some women's issues and to look at Jewish life through a feminist filter.

Now we see that Jewish women who were until recently strongly identified as *women* but were unconnected with most Jewish activity are bringing the lessons of the general women's movement into Jewish institutions (joining those Jewish women who have been trying all along to reform them), whether working for women's rights in Israel or speaking out against anti-Semitism in the women's movement itself. Similarly, those women who might in an earlier time have identified themselves exclusively with the status quo of the Jewish community are now recognizing what they have in common with all women, acknowledging what has been their own second-class status in much of Jewish life, and are willing to put the influence of the traditional Jewish organizations behind such issues as child care or services for battered Jewish women.

This is not to say that there is now—or ever will be—a seamless meshing of Jewish and feminist issues. There will likely always be certain critical areas in which our first identification will be with one self or the other. For example, when abortion rights are jeopardized by right-wing political forces, most Jewish feminists would probably respond as women first; on the other hand, when Israel's security is threatened or anti-Semitism raises its ugly head, we respond first as Jews.

The existence of this polarity does create a certain dissonance, certain conflicts, for Jewish women attempting to live with the two identities. Yet in the creative resolution of these conflicts—bringing Judaism and feminism into closer alignment—we are making choices and changes in our own lives and in Jewish attitudes and practices which have already transformed aspects of what we know as Jewish life. Women are trying to bring equality into religious and community structures that have heretofore been hierarchical and male-oriented, changing both the institutions and our own lives with them.

Judaism, like most religions and cultures, has been primarily created and dominated by men, with masculine experience and imagery the norm—in short, a patriarchy. Until now men have recorded the religious laws, interpreted them, written the prayers that constitute the traditional liturgy, created most of the institutions, called the shots. For example, there is an entire section of the Talmud entitled *Nashim*, Women; there is no parallel section entitled Men. There was no need for such a designation, since all the rest of Jewish law and lore and practice has to do with men. (In fact, the tractate on women is chiefly concerned with men's relationship to them.)

Until now we have not been considered full Jews. Perhaps, because it has been used so often in criticizing television commercials or pop lyrics, the term "sexism" won't serve our purpose here with sufficient power. To find an analogy to the profound "otherness" of women's status in Judaism, we can transpose the bias of anti-Semitism into a Jewish context; that gives an idea of the distance and dissociation from women's experience that has characterized much of Jewish life in the past. Just as anti-Semitism posits Jews as separate from the rest of humanity, so has much in Jewish law set women apart as a separate caste.

The women's liberation movement has given Jewish women permission, and a vocabulary, to express our agony and revulsion and anger at women's second-class status in Judaism. Jewish women everywhere are responding by challenging the specific forms this patriarchy has taken in religious, communal, and family life. Women are trying to find ways to live as full Jews in a religious and social system that has often used religious strictures as an excuse for limiting women's participation and recognition even in areas we might not consider the province of religion.

The sources of what we recognize today as Jewish religion and Jewish culture are texts, some of which date back thousands of years: the Torah (first five books of the Hebrew Bible), the later Biblical writings, Talmud (the collection of interpretations of Jewish life and law), and writings on the precedent-setting decisions rabbis have made about Jewish law and custom through the years.

Interpretation of these texts and, indeed, rulings on how to live a Jewish life on a day to day basis have until now been made exclusively by Jewish men in a setting usually closed to women: a house of study, court of law, synagogue, or boardroom. These interpretations have had direct bearing on the lives of women, yet we were systematically denied the opportunity to participate when decisions were made. Some women believe that our foremothers, strong Jewish women that they must have been, must surely have contributed to this process in ways unrecorded by male historians, as they cared for the rabbis or scholars or scribes who were their fathers or brothers or husbands, offering a slice of women's experience along with the chicken soup. If this informal participation did exist, we have been denied the knowledge of what is male and what is female contribution to formal Judaism as it has come down to us. Lacking this knowledge, we must assume, as most Jews have, that women were excluded from the process of creating Judaism as we know it today, and therefore were excluded from the partnership with the Divine which Jews believe will bring about the repair of the world. This is an exclusion so profound that it has caused thoughtful people to ask, with Rachel Adler, "Are women also Jews?"[1]

This chronic state of disenfranchisement even impinges on aspects of contemporary Jewish women's experience seemingly unconnected to Judaism as a religion—the dynamics of how Jewish women and Jewish men relate to one another, or how a community agency allots power. Judaism is concerned with every act of every day, very much rooted in quotidian reality. "To the Torah nothing is secular," says Rabbi J. H. Hertz, editor and commentator for the standard English edition of the Torah. The attitudes of religious Judaism have an effect on the ostensibly nonreligious aspects of our lives as well. The membrane between religious Judaism and "secular" Jewish institutions and cultural patterns is highly permeable, with women's status in one sphere affecting the others as well.

With the concept of women's essential otherness so ubiquitous in Jewish law and practice, the tension (and the source of inspiration) for those who are evaluating women's role comes from the desire *not* to cast aside all aspects of Judaism but to move beyond its limited view of women, so that our lives and Jewish life can be richer and fuller. It isn't easy for us to reconcile feminist strivings for equality with the patriarchal historical core of Judaism. A woman feeling herself bound by tradition might choose to deny her feminism, while a more radical feminist might want to move away from Judaism altogether. But for women morally committed to self-determination yet at the same time feeling inexorably linked to something in the very tradition they fault, reinterpreting the tradition itself is the alternative to self-denying acceptance or wholesale rejection.

Among the difficulties for women tackling a revision or a transformation of Jewish life are certain questions that challenge both Judaism and feminism.

• Since men were its early shapers, is Judaism basically too patriarchal a religion for *anything* to be salvageable for women? Or do Jewish women simply need to get back to the "true" meaning of the Torah, in which women and men were *both* created in a holy image? Can both women and men be part of the partnership or covenant with the Divine? And if feminism is an attempt to create a nonhierarchical ideology, and God's relationship to the Jewish people is hierarchical ("I am your God and you shall have no other gods before me"), are feminism and Judaism at some points ideologically irreconcilable?

• Are those women who are returning to or converting to or leaning toward traditional Jewish practice (and there are outreach programs and even special schools for women who want to learn about and experience the tradition) expressing an authentic spirituality by participating in Jewish study and religious practice often closed to women in the past? Or are they selling out by opting for a traditionalism that continues to treat women as less than full members in chosen peoplehood?

• By addressing the nature of *women's* spirituality and encouraging the development of *women's* rituals in Judaism, do we run the risk of maintaining or recreating a division between women and men which feminists deplore in other areas of Jewish life? Or are there real differences—and strengths in these differences—that we can explore and learn from? Perhaps women are, in the words of post-Christian feminist theologian Mary Daly, a "messianic community," whose efforts at true expression can indeed change the world. With this in mind, should we support separateness?

These are conundrums for many of us, and for those who do try their hand at these puzzles the answers, as this book tries to demonstrate, are as varied as the individuals themselves.

The women quoted in *Jewish and Female*, like those women everywhere who are trying to reconcile Judaism and feminism, include those "on the way down" and those "on the way up"—that is, women who are familiar with the tradition and are questioning it from a feminist perspective, and those who knew little about Jewish laws or customs in the first place but who find them fascinating and a source of potential enrichment in women's lives.

The range of answers—and the range of women's accommodation to the dislocations for women present in Judaism—extends from complete rejection to loving rebuke. At one end of the spectrum might be Ann Roiphe (author of *Generation Without a Memory*), who wrote in *The New York Times* of her disgust with Judaism as a patriarchal religion and of her preference for the traditions of Dickens' *A Christmas Carol*. Or, a little closer in, feminist theologian Naomi R. Goldenberg who writes: "I am proud to be of Jewish origin, and want to be identified with my people, but I wish to separate myself from the religion. Actually, I do not have to separate myself from the religion—Jewish sages and rabbis have done that for me."[2]

On the other hand (or, as Talmudic discussions put it, "there are those who say . . ."), there are undisputed links between Judaism and the current movement for gender equality. Judaism is a faith that has stressed social justice, ethical human relations, and good deeds above blind allegiance to a credo. In the words of Batya Bauman, a New York Jewish lecture-bureau manager: "In spite of all, many Jewish feminists are feminists because we are Jews. . . . Stripped of male dominance, the Jewish world view may not be so different from the feminist world view."[3]

Some religious women say that their knowledge and experience of feminism has come between them and their once unshakable faith. Blu Greenberg, author of *On Women and Judaism: A View from Tradition* and for several years the unofficial spokesperson for Orthodox Jewish feminism, talks about the effect of feminism on her own sense of harmony.

> I long to be the deeply devout person I once was, in my more innocent life where everything God said was sacred and everything that was sacred was said by God. I know it has something to do with eating the apple and knowing. Yet I also know I can never go back. I would never want to. . . . All of this enterprise in the area of women and faith during the last decade has made me grow, not only as a woman but as a Jew. So when the dust settles, and women's equality in traditional Judaism becomes all very natural, then I'll be touched by the spirit again.[4]

Strictly religious issues aside, there are some women whom the women's movement has brought closer to their Jewish identity. Many women who had in the past been only marginally Jewish reconnected with their roots through feminist consciousness-raising, self-examination, and a search for bonds with other women. A forty-year-old writer tells how her women's-group discussions in the late 1960s affected her as a Jewish woman:

> As I began to explore what my family life had been, what my socialization had been as a girl, I realized that the fact of my being Jewish was very important to me. Although my family was pretty assimilated (we celebrated Christmas each year with a big tree and a huge family party), I went to the local Reform Sunday school. Discussing my family background in my women's group made me want to take a closer look at Judaism. I went to Israel. I began to look for alternative services and *Jewish* women's groups. Then I began to attend various kinds of services on a regular basis, feeling an identification with some part of myself that had never really gotten expressed before.

For this woman the opportunity to put feminism into action made Judaism an alluring arena.

Another powerful connection between Judaism and the women's movement came through education. Women who were in their twenties and thirties at the start of the contemporary women's movement were the first generation in which most women's Jewish education was likely to have been on a par with that of their brothers. Women who already knew something about Judaism, and who were then exposed to the women's movement, wanted to change things. The women's movement had a catalytic effect: women wanted to use their growing feminist consciousness to alter and improve the ways they could express themselves as Jews.

One woman involved in early agitation for change in Jewish attitudes toward women asked rhetorically, "How could I settle for being less of a person in Jewish life than in the outside world?" Thus was born a wealth of new Jewish liturgical material, explorations of old and new Jewish rituals for women, analyses of methods to overcome the discrimination against women in Jewish law, studies of how Jewish family life has affected women, programs for women in need, Jewish women's studies courses. All these and the other solutions reported on in the pages of *Jewish and Female* are women's own responses to the question of how we can continue to see ourselves as strong, self-respecting people within a religion and a culture that historically have been male-defined.

This book is a guide to the choices and changes Jewish women have been making in our relationship to family and friends, our participation in the Jewish community, and our identification of ourselves as Jews in the wake of the women's movement, a reshaping inextricable from the changes in our own consciousness. These pages map the issues we face—and the resources available to us—as we try to create a synthesis between Judaism and feminism, attempting to harmonize our sometimes dissonant identities, in the process determining how we define ourselves as women and as Jews.

Why do we need a book that sets us apart from other women wrestling with the same angels and demons? How are our experiences different? *Our* patterns of work and family life? *Our* spirituality? *Our* personal expressiveness? What are the "Jewish" issues even for those women who don't consider themselves affiliated with organized Jewish life in any way?

For the past ten years I have been speaking on Jewish women's issues to audiences across the country, audiences as diverse as Jewish women's study groups, feminist college students, social-work students, PTAs of Jewish schools and congregants at gay synagogues, Jewish social-service agency conventioneers and Catskill resort vacationers, to name a few. What is astonishing is not so much the diversity of the audiences eager to hear about Jewish women's issues but the similarity of the questions the women ask. Here is a sampling, questions asked so often they sound like riddles:

I just don't know what to do about my daughter. We encouraged her to get a good education, and we were always proud of her. But now that she's in her late twenties, and we see how she's getting ahead in her law firm, frankly I have another worry. Where are all the terrific Jewish men? She and her friends are bright, attractive, interesting people, and the single men they meet don't seem to be their equals. Are Jewish men turned off by these women because they're too bright or too threatening?

My son says he won't have anything to do with Jewish girls [sic]—he says they're all princesses and very demanding. What can I say to him?

Look, my Jewish upbringing taught me that a woman's role was at home, to provide a good Jewish home for her family. So what am I supposed to do now? I have nobody left to cook for, to care for, to make the holidays for. What am I supposed to do?

Don't you think that the whole women's movement is responsible for all the divorce and unhappiness we're seeing in young people today? I mean, don't you think that all this women's lib stuff is ruining the Jewish family and making real problems in Jewish life?

My mother calls me at least once a day—and I'm a grown woman! Just because I live by myself my parents expect me to visit every Friday night, and preferably stay the whole weekend! A lot of my friends report the same kinds of pressure. What happens in Jewish families that the umbilical cord can never be cut? Is it just Jewish daughters who go through this? And how can I get them to let up a little without making them feel utterly rejected and feeling totally guilty myself?

I'm not observant, so I don't really care too much about the religious aspect of getting a Jewish divorce, but I can't stand the humiliation of knowing that my ex-husband won't give me one—and I feel powerless. I've learned that if I ever decide to remarry I won't be able to have a Jewish ceremony unless he gives me that religious divorce, since under Jewish law I can't divorce him—and I don't even know where he is! Do you know of any rabbis who can help in these situations?

I'm a single Jewish woman and happy with my independence, and I don't see marriage in the cards right now. But sometimes I feel as if I'm just a cog waiting to fit into some future Jewish nuclear family structure. So much of Jewish life revolves around being part of a family— as a child or as somebody's wife or as a parent—that I'm wondering if it's possible to do anything Jewish, either at home or at some community event, if I'm alone. I mean, how can you make shabbos alone? What are the alternatives if I don't want to be part of a family, and I still want to be Jewish?

Jewish women share the goals of most contemporary women—we want equal access to satisfaction in our jobs and personal lives, choices in lifestyles, and alternatives to the overdefined gender roles most of us grew up trying to fit ourselves into (and are still trying to grow out of). There are certainly similarities between the struggles of Jewish women and those of women from other ethnic and religious groups—Black and Italian women, Mormon and Episcopalian women, Catholic nuns.

But there is also a special vision for Jewish women, who look at the world through their own special filter and who, after every rally for equal rights or equal rites, after every reapportioning of the housework, seem to have to answer the question "Is this good for the Jews?"

Jewish life has survived many changes more radical than gender equality, yet Jewish women and men still ask "Is feminism good for the Jews?" The answer is yes, and the reasons are many, as the diverse scope of *Jewish and Female* shows. As Jews we carry the extra burden of concern for the creative survival of our people as a whole even as we strive to satisfy our own needs as individuals. Identifying as a Jew means being part of a peoplehood, sharing a fate and sharing a role in making the world better; here, as in several other places, feminism and Judaism are on the same track.

We are trying to determine the realities of our own lives rather than accepting man-made myths about them. We're looking at where we're similar and where we differ from one another. What do Jewish women have in common that goes beyond differences in age or background—and beyond our common victimization by such negative stereotypes as the Jewish American Princess, the Yiddishe Mama, or the Radical Bitch? What are the cultural, historical, social, and psychological factors we share? What do our *lives* have in common: The family expectations peculiar to Jews as an ethnic group? The "survival techniques" by which many Jewish women were raised by *their* Jewish mothers? The self-image that is the legacy of being raised a Jewish female in a non-Jewish, male-dominated culture in North America?

To unravel some of these threads we first have to move past the stale jokes and stereotypes that limit and insult us. These stereotypes are the first lines of offense and defense when we talk about who Jewish women are, but they tell us only how we appear and reveal nothing about how we really think or how we are. They sometimes even succeed in turning Jewish women into objects to each other.

Jewish women have probably been overrepresented in the movies, books, and magazine articles that constitute our popular culture, and in a consistently negative fashion, especially by male Jewish authors. We have been not so much portrayed as betrayed. Just as previous generations of male rabbis, scholars, and legal authorities created women's codified "excluded" status in religious Judaism (delineated here in the book's first three chapters), today's male comedians, social analysts, and authors claiming to "define" Jewish women have held up a distorting mirror, saying of the resulting image, "This is you."

Who are we really, and why are they saying these horrible things about us? Anthropologists point out that myths and stereotypes—especially negative ones—are the means by which a culture keeps people in line. For Jewish women the popular negative images (posters and "princess" T-shirts included) have become brackets delineating the male expectations for female behavior. The stereotypes cut across the very real individual differences, as all prejudice does. But worse, the very existence of such common negative epithets as the JAP is an inhibiting force, letting women know that if they speak up, assert themselves, or otherwise indicate their refusal to submit to male authority, they run the risk of being categorized in an undesirable way. No matter who we are or how we act, these categories can be applied to "explain" and condemn our behavior and identity. The diversity, originality, and strength of the women who speak out in these pages should help provide American Jewish women with alternative models and a counterweight against the pressure to conform to the expectations of others which is at the center of these stereotypes.

Now women are asking, "Who are we?" and holding up mirrors of our own to see, after all, what's reflected back after a decade and a half of the current women's liberation movement and four thousand years of Jewish history. A few years ago *Publishers Weekly* defined a "new genre of Jewish women's liberation fiction"—and, indeed, just such a genre has emerged, with novels that look at such previously taboo "Jewish" subjects as a wife's marital discontent, the private life of the *rebbitzen*, women's sexuality, and the pressures exquisitely brought to bear on an unmarried Jew of the female persuasion. Films of course also present us with vivid and shared images of real-life Jewish women, and *Jewish and Female* makes reference to these as support for the changes possible in our own lives.

As we grow beyond the stereotypes we begin to see their consequences. They have often prevented us from seeing the Jewish women scholars, activists, shapers of social change, the strong women grappling with issues larger than events in their own lives. Perhaps even more important, we're coming to realize that we've been kept from seeing Jewish women in need, who also don't fit the stereotypes of the bourgeois mother and daughter or the Hollywood radical. These are the women who have until recently slipped through the cracks of our awareness: the elderly, the poor; battered women and alcoholic women; Jewish women suffering in a variety of crisis situations.

All of these changes in our perceptions and the choices we are making in our own lives obviously have an effect on our personal relations as well as on the ways in which we choose to link ourselves in community with other Jews. We have changed the agenda for our own futures and for those of our biological or spiritual daughters.

Some of the issues and conflicts and questions we are raising have no resolutions, at least at present. Is the Jewish mother's involvement with her children different from that of other mothers? Should Jewish women's organizations retain their separate status or should they be planning for their imminent obsolescence? Can religious Judaism stretch to include all women as full participants and still remain Judaism? The purpose of this book is to engage the issues and show how Jewish women have been dealing with them—examining our differences and moving toward new reconciliations of what sometimes seems to be the paradox of being Jewish and feminist. These paradoxes of identity are not new for women. We recall that women in the labor movement in North America in the early twentieth century were pulled between feminism and socialism. The Talmud is even more entrenched a system than Marx (or even Freud), but in the late twentieth century we have the benefit of recent feminist analyses of religion, society, and human relations to help us forge the synthesis of feminism and Judaism rather than having to set up a false dichotomy between them.

The tension for Jewish women today comes from the struggle to stay within the tradition yet not compromise one's identity and integrity as a woman. To this end some women are making radical changes in the way they identify as Jews. Other women are trying to find room for their own needs within some form of Judaism. Some are *rediscovering* aspects of Jewish life that they can feel connected to as women, whether through studying women in Jewish history, or examining source texts for clues to women's input, or through matching aspects of Judaism with aspects of the women's movement. Others are *redefining* certain aspects of Judaism to feminize them, putting women's content and experience into Jewish life by such practices as holding a feminist Passover seder or including women's experiences of liberation into the classic tale of the Jews' liberation from Egypt or giving money to feminist projects in Israel. A third method feminists are using is *transforming* traditional Judaism and Jewish institutions so that they include women, thus equalizing Judaism rather than "feminizing" it.

Jewish and Female attempts to be a clearinghouse of information for all these ways in which Jewish women are creating new realities out of their own changed consciousness (in fact, the original title of the book was "The Ways We Are"). The basic premise is the acceptance of many diverging methods and conclusions. In these pages are tales of women radical and traditional and at every stage in between, all engaged in surveying their lives as Jews from various stations along the frontiers of feminism.

S. W. S.

A NOTE ON USING THIS BOOK

Throughout the book the reader will come across references to organizations and institutions providing relevant resources for Jewish women. In most cases, addresses and other pertinent information appear in the text itself; however, in the case of organizations mentioned frequently this information is not repeated each time; if no address appears with the organization's name, check the Networking Directory for a full listing. The Directory presents a comprehensive compilation of resources, some of which appear also in the text of the book itself, where mentioning them in context would be particularly useful for the reader.

ONE

◆

Women and Religious Judaism: Beyond the Patriarchal Premise

1

•

LAW AND
LEADERSHIP

WOMEN AS DISABLED JEWS: SEEKING EQUAL ACCESS

The basic patriarchal premise of Judaism has been that women and men are essentially different, and that gender differences—extending beyond mere biology—should be sanctioned and sanctified under Jewish law. This concept of difference allowed men (historically the ones assigning the roles) to exclude women unjustly from much that was important in Jewish life—or, rather, to determine that whatever it was that men were doing was defined as important: study, prayer, and communal ritual responsibilities. The role of women was as an essential Other, enabling men and boys to perform *their* roles with greater ease.

The choices and changes women are making in their own lives as Jews today raise some important questions about what we understand as Judaism and its allocation of very different spheres of competence to women and men. We need to look at the traditional role, or place, of women in Judaism, and then move on to see what changes women have wrought in interpretation and practice while still attempting to remain authentically connected to Jewish identity and to some aspects of the tradition.

Judaism is a religion that stresses social justice in law and practice. For example, there are laws requiring that one care for the old and the poor. Yet formal Judaism has in the past held a very limited view of what constitutes justice toward women, beyond seeing women as dependent or inadequate creatures needing special protection. Jewish women's sense of alienation and exclusion from religious life comes from their restricted legal status, from a male bias in prayer, liturgy, and synagogue and ritual activity and from the fact that women's sphere of influence was defined by Jewish law as "domestic affairs."

It may be that in reality individual women can ignore past and present discrimination, or that in real life (as opposed to the dominant mythos) Jewish women are generally powerful beings with a rich spiritual life, even within the constraints of a system that has refused them full access. But the fact that there exist both law and lore that clearly distinguish women's and men's legal and spiritual capacities in Judaism—and define women's as inferior—affects us all. Jewish women have been seen by Jewish men as essentially "other"—different in some basic, radical way, almost as if we didn't share the same human status.

Each morning a strictly observant Jewish man wakes up and prays to God with thanks "that You have not made me a woman." The parallel prayer for women thanks God "for having made me according to Your will." Judaism, which specializes in distinctions, has created or sanctified differences between sabbath and weekday, between kosher and nonkosher, between Jew and Gentile, and between women and men.

Although the majority of Jews do not adhere strictly to Jewish law, with its fine distinctions, its ramifications are crucially important in determining the quality of our lives as Jewish women, whether we know this or not. Jewish law (Halachah), like the Torah from which it is derived, holds nothing to be beyond its province. Halachah has been a kind of constitution-in-exile for the Jewish people for millennia. The laws themselves and the opinions about them have created women's separate status in religious Judaism and, by extension, among all Jews, religious or not.

Halachah is the body of Jewish law derived from the Torah (the five books of Moses thought to be given to Moses in Sinai) and the Talmud, a collection of analyses and opinions on the Torah that was officially closed at the end of the fifth century c.e. (The Talmud is not the codification of the laws themselves but Talmud discussions provided the basis for later codifications.)[1] Under Halachah all Jews are bound to observe certain commandments—for example, to eat only food defined as "kosher," to give charity, to honor parents, to eschew theft and murder. But *women* are exempt (or excluded) from many commandments that are positive and time-bound—those prayers that must be recited at certain times of day, for instance.

At present, according to the strictest interpretation of this law, no Jewish woman can serve as a witness in a religious court, nor can she institute divorce proceedings, nor does she "count" in the quorum of ten adult Jews needed for communal prayer. Her voice is a sexual distraction to men; her body is untouchable for a part of every month; and custom and law have colluded in the past to exclude her from the study of Torah, traditionally the most important activity for Jews.

The various branches of Judaism hold differing views of the power of Halachah. Until the nineteenth century change in Jewish law and practice was made only by Halachic decision-making and precedent. The nineteenth and twentieth centuries have seen the rise of three major Jewish denominations that have challenged the Orthodox interpretation of Jewish law. For Orthodox Jews the traditional laws are binding on all aspects of one's life, whereas Reform Jews believe that Halachah is an appropriate guide but that its rulings are *not* binding. Conservative and Reconstructionist Jews straddle these two positions, viewing Halachah as indeed binding—but believing also that it can be reinterpreted to meet contemporary needs.

Regardless of the position of any denomination on the force of Halachah, the law has almost always been formulated and interpreted by learned male rabbis responding to questions posed to them by lay people and other rabbis (see p. 45). Until such time as we have a body of learned women who rule on questions of Halachic importance, all legal decision-making is out of our hands.

The most profoundly disabling effect of the Halachic distinctions between men and women has been the exclusion of women from many of the obligations that define an adult male as a Jew. Judaism is a religion wherein identification is demonstrated primarily by performance rather than belief or creed. What defines a practicing Jew is the performance of certain ritual obligations—613 in all, if you are careful—from many of which women have been excluded, particularly those that have to be performed at specific times. Under Jewish law, for example, women are "exempted" (that is, excluded) from certain time-bound mitzvot, such as praying three times a day, donning *tfillin* (phylacteries, the black boxes observant men—and now some women—bind to their arms and foreheads in daily prayer). The rationale for this has been that women, busy with child care, couldn't pray at specific times, though the exemption includes *all* women, not just those so occupied.

Inasmuch as performance of the mitzvot (obligations) themselves has been the defining characteristic of a Jew, it is obvious that women's present and historical discomfort or outrage at this exclusion is not the expression of some petty dissatisfaction. Since being a Jew has been defined by specific, public acts—of prayer, dress, appearance at communal worship—a woman's exclusion has been tantamount to prohibiting her from defining herself as a Jew. The gradual movement toward women's greater participation, fueled by women's growing desire to identify fully as Jews, is surely one of the most important events in contemporary Jewish life. Part of the struggle of contemporary Jewish women has been to rectify the exclusionary nature of much Jewish ritual and custom, to challenge the interpretations of Jewish law that have codified women's "different" (second-class) status in Judaism, and to create new ways in which women can express themselves as full Jews.

There are of course options outside of strictly Halachic (or Orthodox) Judaism for those women who want to be equal Jews with men, but the legal inequities present difficulties for *all* Jewish women. Just the fact that there *are* laws that affect women adversely is enough to make some Jewish women uneasy. One observer credits these restrictive laws with a resurgence of interest in studying the law on the part of Reform women rabbinical students, who feel that any law on the books can be brought up in the future and used against all Jewish women.

The demographics: In America very traditional Orthodox families are having many children (families with five and six children are the norm), while non-Orthodox Jews tend to have fewer children, if any. What this means is that in another generation or two the American Jewish community may have a much higher percentage of Orthodox Jews than it now does, and nonobservant Jews will be more likely to encounter the attitudes and laws about women that are tenets of Orthodoxy.

In Israel there is no recognition of non-Orthodox rabbis or a non-Orthodox Halachah, which means that the Israeli rabbinate will not now accept documents signed by their non-Orthodox colleagues. And in America the same situation holds true: Orthodox rabbis consider non-Orthodox marriages, conversions, and divorces "illegitimate." As a result, if you or a family member ever get involved with the Israeli laws of personal status ("Who Is a Jew?"), or if a nonobservant Jew wants to marry an observant Jew anywhere, there might be trouble over divorce proceedings in the past, status of children born to this and other marriages, and other general *tsuris* (trouble). (For an expansion on this, see "Marriage," p. 321.)

For those women who feel pulled toward traditional Judaism the choice is hardest. For those who don't mind taking a step to the left and moving into Conservative Judaism from Orthodox, or into Reform from Conservative, there are always options. But for women who want to maintain an alignment with Orthodox Judaism the problem is severe. It is for these women and also for every Jewish woman who may in the future be affected by the inequities toward women in Halachah that the changes now

Rabbinic Court Judgment *by Jan Styka. What's missing in this picture? There are no women present, either as judges or as witnesses, an exclusion sanctioned by Jewish law.* (Courtesy of Christie's, New York)

being considered are of crucial importance. "The problem is how to attain some justice and some growing room for the Jewish woman if one is committed to remaining *within* Halachah. . . . For too many centuries, the Jewish woman has been a golem [clay creature] created by Jewish society. She cooked and bore and did her master's will, and when her tasks were done, the Divine Name was removed from her mouth. It is time for the golem to demand a soul."[2]

Women are able to make "growing room" in limited ways. While there are laws and customs that have prevented women from participating fully in aspects of Jewish ritual experience, these restrictions are easing as women expand their roles in synagogue and at home (see the section Women and Prayer, p. 61). More difficult to change are the restrictions that spell out women's inferior status in Jewish law. While women are achieving equality in religious participation in some circles, the greatest and most vexing unresolved issues now are those surrounding women's legal infirmities or liabilities. A woman may or may not be a Jew among Jews in her synagogue, but in a *bet din* (court of Jewish law) a woman is always a helpless dependent, with hardly more rights or status than a child.

INFIRMITIES UNDER JEWISH LAW:
REINTERPRETING WOMEN'S "PERSONAL STATUS"

Like the laws governing ritual observance and the giving of testimony before a religious court, the laws concerning marriage, divorce, remarriage and the attendant complications of lineage recognize two kinds of people: men, who suffer no disadvantage under these laws, and women, who potentially can suffer grievous discrimination.

A man "buys" his bride, in the traditional Jewish wedding ceremony, and only he can instigate divorce proceedings.[3] A man who has left his wife is free to form liaisons with any other woman (providing she is not married to another man—that is, not the property of another man), and the children of such a union are in no way tainted or viewed as bastards (*mamzerim*). By contrast, a woman whose husband has left her without giving her a formal writ of divorce is *never* free to remarry, and if she should defy this constraint or enter into a relationship with another man, she would be considered an adulteress. Any offspring of such a union are *mamzerim* under Jewish law, forbidden to marry Jews for ten generations (see also "Marriage," p. 321).

The laws concerning women's marital status are especially cruel when applied (as they can be) to women whose husbands are presumed dead, as in battle, but without witnesses to the deaths. Such women, like those abandoned without a *get* (divorce decree), are *agunot* (bound women)— neither officially widows nor divorced. They cannot remarry. Similarly, a childless widow has an obligation to marry her late husband's brother, if he is single, to keep the family line and must be formally released from this duty. (For more on Jewish laws of personal status as they affect women, see "Marriage" and "Divorce," pp. 318 and 355.)

Women are excluded from positive, time-bound commandments such as regular prayer and are therefore formally excluded from the prayer community of obligated Jewish adults. Similarly, women, who have no obligation to testify before a religious court and cannot be summoned to this court, are not only exempted from testifying (because they might have to be at home with the kids and the kettle) but are in fact excluded from testifying. A child and a slave are also excluded from giving testimony. But a child (male), when grown, becomes able to testify, and when Jews kept slaves, a male slave, when freed, was able to testify. Only women are condemned forever to the status of disqualified persons.

The Lubavitcher Rebbe, Menachem M. Schneerson, explains in one of his publicly distributed pamphlets: "a woman has been gifted with an extra measure of natural emotion. . . . But an overly measure of emotionalism is a hindrance in legal matters. . . . The average woman is more emotional [so] the woman had to be disqualified from judgeship and similar legal matters. . . . Man . . . is less emotional and can be more objective."[4]

Under the Orthodox interpretation of Halachah a woman not only cannot give testimony in court but she also cannot affix her signature to a document as a witness.[5] One Reform woman rabbi says: "A woman wants her best friend to sign her marriage contract as one of the witnesses to the ceremony. I tell her, 'I can't sign and your girlfriend can't sign.' " In Israel, where Halachah is the only personal-status law for Jews, women cannot even witness applications for a wedding document. One Israeli woman recounts: "The rabbi in the office of the rabbinate wouldn't let me be a witness for my friend's wedding license because, as he so nicely put it, 'Women are light-headed.' "

Rabbi Saul Berman of Stern College comments: "The law begins with the desire to exempt women from mandatory public appearances and therefore deprive the courts, in effect, of subpoena power over women."[6] This is considerably more restricting than, say, being excluded from serving on a jury. What this means is that no woman can represent her case to a court for purposes of civil suit, criminal suit, divorce action against her husband, or in other such situations. She is entirely at the mercy of the men around her to look out for her best interests before the law. Dr. Trude Weiss-Rosmarin points out that "Chivalry and tender consideration are not the same as equality before the law."[7]

We see that these exclusions and separations are very real, and we know from American political and social history that "separate but equal" is always unequal. The exclusion is addressed in the very titles of articles and stories that Jewish women are writing: *The Other Half: Women in the Jewish Tradition, The Jew Who Wasn't There, The Woman Who Lost Her Names.*[8]

Among the "excuses"—disguised as "reasons" and mouthed by platitudinous and condescending male rabbis—for women's characteristic exclusion from ritual and from Jewish learning are these:

Women are so in tune with nature's rhythms because of their own biological clocks that they have no need to pray at regular intervals, as men do.

Women's *superior* spirituality best suits them for child care, whereas men's grosser natures need to be tempered by prayer and lots of ritual.

> It's the male who needs the *minyan* more, because his natural tendency is to prove himself in the world. The woman, who is more easily drawn to normative family life, is reinforced by the fruits of her biology. . . . Who needs to *daven* [pray] more—a woman who has been involved with family and with the sensitizing, nurturing syndrome or the man who has been competitive during an eight-to-ten-hour day?"[9]

Here is the old "separate but equal" argument again! Men and women have different biological functions; therefore women under Jewish law have obligations different from men's—not that women are *inferior*, but they are *different*.

A retort to the biology-is-destiny argument so often used to squelch women's strivings for equality in Judaism comes from novelist and social critic Cynthia Ozick. She has said that the salient feature of Torah is that it gives us precepts for living that go against the way the world ordinarily is. She notes that there are laws against theft, adultery, incest, simply because these things do exist in the world. Torah does not counsel that people sit passively by and accept the world as it is but that they act according to supra-natural principles of justice and morality. Similarly with Shabbat: the Torah asserts "the timelessness of the Sabbath as a day set aside for the elevation of humanity. Nature does not recognize the Sabbath; to nature, all days are alike." It's only with regard to women, says Ozick, that Torah gives no precepts for righting the basic injustices of the world. She names *Thou shalt not lessen the humanity of women* the "missing commandment" and calls on halachists—experts in Jewish law—to help repair a lack in Torah, to do for women what has been done in the creation of Shabbat; that is, to counter the "natural" order of things by providing precepts for improving it.[10]

Judaism is not a theology of helplessness in the face of divine authority. Jewish law has always been flexible enough to respond to human needs as they changed with time and place.[11] Consequently, not all the laws of Judaism as they were first formulated are practiced today. For example, at one time Judaism required animal sacrifices; such rituals are no longer in effect. Change has come about because people's own practice has changed, making some observance obsolete.

A *takkanah*, or new enactment, becomes law because of some pressing social need to reflect an already changed social reality. In the tenth century a *takkanah* made polygamy illegal for Ashkenazi Jewish men; polygamy was a practice that was no longer popular at the time of the ruling. By analogy, some Jewish women claim that if women take on full ritual and prayer obligations, the social reality will thus have been changed, making room for a *takkanah* reinforcing the new reality of women as obligated Jews. There have been changes in Jewish law (or the interpretation of the law) based on the decisions of learned people who were the decision-makers—*poskim*—of each generation. When they wanted to make change they were indeed able to do so.

An example of this process of change, analogous to women's struggles to have certain laws reinterpreted, is in the development of the *eruv*, or boundary around a community. Since on Shabbat one cannot carry anything—not even keys, or children too young to walk—except on one's home property, Jews developed the concept of the *eruv*: a fence, either real or symbolic, around a town or section, which makes the whole area "home turf." A walled city is automatically considered to have an *eruv*, and one community of Orthodox Jews living on Staten Island, New York, considers the full circle created by power lines an *eruv*.[12] The concept of the *eruv* is an example of how rabbis found a solution within the law for a problem that faced observant Jews.

Undoubtedly similar creative solutions are available for the inequities women have suffered under Jewish law. The mechanism for change exists. "The real issue" to feminist author Francine Klagsbrun, who was one of the few women whose counsel was sought by the Conservative movement in its decision to ordain women as rabbis (see below, p. 52), is "a deeply disturbing psychological barrier to change in this area."[13] Women are now responding with powerful emotions to feelings of spiritual "entitlement" that, in some instances, they've never had before. And women are struggling to find ways of reinterpreting Jewish law, or of influencing the law's interpreters, so that the inequities can be corrected.

Part of this struggle has involved a reexamination of women's roles as Jewish leaders and decision-makers throughout Jewish history. While that history gives us precious few women of any kind, it does present some women who were active in shaping aspects of Judaism as we now know it. The very existence of such women may help to convince the skeptics that the function of women as religious leaders or as arbiters of Jewish law is not unprecedented. Women have served as religious authorities along with men several times in Jewish history, including the present, though their right to the honorific title "rabbi" has been neither asserted nor accorded. Susan Grossman describes some of these women and their roles as direct shapers of Judaism:

(Gail Rubin)

POWER IN OUR OWN HANDS: WOMEN AS AUTHORITIES ON JEWISH LAW

Twenty-six hundred years ago a scroll written like a scroll of the Torah was found in the Holy Temple in Jerusalem, the center of the Jewish religion at the time. King Josiah, unsure whether to consider this scroll holy, sent his men to inquire of Huldah, the prophetess (II Kings 22:14, II Chronicles 34:22). Upon Huldah's word (speaking for God, as a prophetess would), a fifth book was added to the Torah—Deuteronomy (*Devarim*, in Hebrew), an important book of laws.

The story of Huldah raises two points for us today, reminding us that women have made decisions which have affected Jewish law and observance throughout our tradition, and that such women were more common than popular history would lead us to believe. Most activities of these women were never recorded or, if recorded, did not survive persecutions and dispersions. We generally assume that women like Huldah and Deborah, Bruriah, or Rashi's scholarly daughters were singular women in their generations. However, recent study of rabbinic literature (much of it done by women) is leading to the rediscovery of women from Talmudic times to the twentieth century who learned and taught, who decided law for individuals and even affected the body of Jewish law for future generations. Much of women's historical functioning as religious authorities had been informal, with women answering questions from their own experience. The majority of women who gave these opinions never saw themselves in more formal roles and therefore never moved into such roles.

Maimonides, the great commentator and codifier who lived in the twelfth century, would not permit women to serve as religious authorities. He drew his opinion from the verse in Deuteronomy (17:15), ". . . appoint a king over you . . . ," arguing in his *Mishneh Torah* (Melakim 1:5) that a woman should not be appointed as king or any other officer in Israel. His argument has been used to prohibit women from taking any communal positions of authority—even, in some synagogues, excluding them from voting privileges.

We know that women served as queens during the time of the supreme court of Jewish law, the Sanhedrin (dissolved in the fifth century c.e.). These queens had the same rights and duties as a king's, and they left their mark on Jewish history. The founders of rabbinic Judaism, the Pharisees, were brought to power in 79 b.c.e. by one such queen— Salome Alexandra. The descendants of those rabbis speak in the Talmud of another queen, Helena, of the first century c.e., who set a legal precedent regarding the height of a succah.

Other women now being rediscovered served as religious authorities for the women in their communities. Baile Edels (mid-sixteenth to mid-

seventeenth centuries) also made decisions that have since been incorporated into the body of Jewish law. She was such an expert in the
niddah laws (concerning menstruation and sexual contact) that women
would ask her their questions rather than going to the rabbi. During her
time women lit holiday and Sabbath candles first and then said the
blessing. Baile Edels showed that, according to the law, on holidays
women should say the blessing first and then light candles, following
the general principle of saying a blessing before performing a commandment. (Sabbath candles are lit first, because one is prohibited from
creating a light after saying the blessing, since the blessing begins the
sabbath.)

Baile Edels does not stand as an isolated case. Chana Bat Yohe-
ved, the eldest daughter of Rashi, taught women laws in the twelfth
century. Another descendant of Rashi's, Miriam bat Reb Shlomo
Shapiro, sat in a tent in a yeshiva and taught laws to the best students.
Dulche, the wife of Eliezer Rokeach, taught the laws of keeping
kosher. In Hasidism, Malka, the wife of the first Belzer rebbe, sat with
her husband and they made all decisions together, and the so-called
Maid of Ludomir, Hannah Rachel Werbemacher (1805-92), taught
her followers every Sabbath afternoon.

Until the twentieth century, traditional Judaism was not afraid to
quote women's Halachic decisions when they shed light on an aspect
of Jewish law, nor was it afraid to grant women a degree of legitimacy as
religious authorities. The Enlightenment in Europe had led some of the
more progressive elements of the Jewish community away from Orthodoxy, and women who might have become religious authorities within
the traditional community a century or two earlier became, instead,
leaders in the Reform and Conservative movements. Lily Montagu
helped start the Reform movement in England, Regina Jonas (though
not formally ordained) practiced as a Reform rabbi until she was killed
by the Nazis in Theresienstadt, and Henrietta Szold studied at the
Conservative movement's seminary and argued for broadening women's
involvement in mourning rituals.

Meanwhile the traditional Jewish community felt itself under siege
and withdrew, isolating itself in order to defend the status quo. Aspects
of the tradition which seemed sympathetic to modernization, such as
having women serving as religious authorities, were buried. Communal
authorities feared change as a move toward the dissolution of Judaism
they saw all about them. According to historian Paula Hyman: "In
modern times, the Orthodox community can only be understood in the
context of its fear of the unorthodox community. . . . Women as interpreters of law were [therefore] threatening to their Orthodox notion
of tradition."

How can women achieve formal positions as religious authorities?

They can, have, and should become experts in Jewish law and tradition, and they can become scholars, especially in Talmud. Judith Hauptman, the first woman Ph.D. in Talmud, who teaches Talmud at the Conservative movement's Jewish Theological Seminary, believes that learned women could look at the sources and investigate issues of concern to women which have not until now attracted serious rabbinic attention. According to Hauptman, a decision about a religious issue is not based only upon Halachah but also involves some personal bias, regardless of who is making the decision. Therefore, she says, it is important for women to be involved in such decision-making, as scholars if not as rabbis. Once educated, these women will need to find allies within the rabbinic establishment who will lend credence to the women's comments and decisions. Although Baile Edels originated, proved, and instituted a change in Halachah, a man wrote it down and made it part of the history of Jewish law.

Until women are accepted as independent authorities, men respected in halachically observant communities, such as Saul Berman (an Orthodox rabbi noted for his progressive attitudes on women's issues under Jewish law), can lend their authority and support to decisions made by women. Berman, of Stern College for Women (an Orthodox institution affiliated with Yeshiva University), sees women becoming active participants in the Halachic process in the near future. Although such participation will not be on the institutional level, Berman believes women will be able to influence Halachah by writing scholarly articles, which would, in turn, be used in further discussions by other scholars. Since p'sak Halachah (Halachic decision-making) is mostly a matter of clarification, anyone who has specialized knowledge and competence should be able to serve as a posek (legal decision-maker) in that area.

Today women educated in Judaism have available to them three paths toward a less formal functioning as religious authorities: as a small but growing group of scholars who, through their writing and lecturing, serve as important references and teachers (see "Our Minds for Ourselves," p. 155); as rabbis, campus Hillel directors, and leaders in the Reform, Reconstructionist, and Havurah movements, and as community workers, politicians, and social workers, who function as legal advocates for their constituency or clients.

Among the few contemporary women scholars whose views on Jewish law command some respect is Dr. Trude Weiss-Rosmarin. A Doctor of Semitics, Weiss-Rosmarin has written about a variety of women's and other issues over the past forty-odd years, both in other publications and in The Jewish Spectator, the journal of opinion and ideas that she founded and edits. An example of the kind of creative changes in the interpretation of Jewish law that we can hope for when more women are trained in the field is Weiss-Rosmarin's suggestion that there is Halachic justification for taking the privilege of issuing a Jewish divorce away from the husband and giving that authority to the Jewish court alone.[14]

Since it has been only a little more than a decade since the first woman was ordained in America, we have not yet had the opportunity to see what changes in Jewish law might be wrought by the presence of large numbers of women rabbinical scholars. What has emerged from another area is a small but important group of women, somewhat older than the women newly ordained as rabbis, who function as interpreters of Jewish law in an informal, grass-roots fashion.

Religious women who are community activists are beginning to see part of their role as that of adviser and advocate on religious-law issues. According to New York social worker Sarah Silver Bunim, one of the biggest problems facing women is that they do not know law from lore. Bunim can often help her clients by providing this information. As an Orthodox woman, she is committed to the framework of asking questions of an Orthodox (male) rabbi, yet she serves as a resource for many religiously observant clients by explaining their options within Jewish law and either directing them to a rabbi suited to their needs or approaching the appropriate rabbi for them.

New York City Councilwoman Susan Alter became involved in the issue of Jewish divorce when a growing number of her constituents began coming to her with their problems, sometimes after their husbands had exacted large payments or unfair agreements from them before they would agree to a *get*. She explains her role in correcting inequities in Jewish divorce law: "I'm not saying [to the rabbinate] how to do it, but something must be done."

Both Bunim and Alter function as intermediaries; they are important advocates, parallels to the *rebbetzin* (rabbi's wife), who would counsel women and often present their problems and perspective to the male decision-makers. While functioning in such informal ways is no substitute for having women in actual decision-making roles, it at least allows women some access to the judicial process in religious Judaism.[15]

One of the most successful drives for change in traditional Judaism was led by a group of young, well-educated Conservative women in 1972. These women, ranging in age from nineteen to twenty-four, called themselves Ezrat Nashim (meaning, literally, "the help of women"; the name was also applied to the women's court in the ancient Temple in Jerusalem and to the women's section of an Orthodox synagogue). They went before the annual convention of the Rabbinical Assembly, the organization of Conservative rabbis whose Committee on Jewish Law and Standards is responsible for setting down the legal precepts of Conservative Judaism. Pleading their case often indirectly (to groups of rabbis' wives and others who heard them as one of the convention's "unofficial" programs at a resort hotel), these women brought about an important change in women's rights and rites in Conservative Judaism. They lobbied for—and won—the right for women to be counted in the *minyan* and to be called to the Torah.

Though the final decision was left in the hands of each congregation, a majority of Conservative congregations in the United States have now adopted these two practices. Paula Hyman, historian and dean of the college of the Jewish Theological Seminary and one of the members of Ezrat Nashim, notes: "There have been other, more halachically questionable decisions made in the Conservative movement—such as permitting driving to synagogue on Shabbat," but *none* has caused as much debate as the issue of women's greater participation in worship. Aside from the internal controversy about the decision and its subsequent implementation, there is another problem with the piecemeal solution to women's participation: "Had the Law and Standards Committee [of the Rabbinical Assembly] seem fit to charge women with equal responsibility for prayer, it would not only have achieved their automatic inclusion in the communal rights of minyan and *aliyot* (since the technical, *halachic* exclusion derives from their exemption from obligation) but it also would have come much closer to grappling with the real issues of Jewish feminism: those of religious growth, women's prayer, education, authority."[16]

Not only, then, do we women have to take responsibility for seeing that change is made but we have to make sure that the changes that are made allow for the maximum possible empowerment of women, so that our religious lives are no longer in the hands of men. Even in an Orthodox setting, women can bring about some change by getting onto the synagogue's ritual committee, and onto the powerful search committee that interviews prospective rabbis, making sure that women's drive for full expression in Judaism is noticed and, to whatever extent possible, understood.

An extensive source of information on the whole range of past and current writing on this subject is:

Bibliography on Jewish Women and Jewish Law
by Ora Hamelsdorf and Sandra Adelsberg
Biblio Press
P.O. Box 22
Fresh Meadows, NY 11365

WOMEN AS RABBIS

"There are no theological barriers to women rabbis—only political ones," asserts privately ordained rabbi Lynn Gottlieb in a television interview. This is an opinion borne out by those opposing women's ordination as rabbis. Listen to Conservative Rabbi Richard M. Yellin: "Can a woman become a rabbi? I believe asking a question like that is like asking: Can a Jewish woman become a Jewish man?"[17]

A rabbi is first and foremost a teacher and religious decision-maker, with no "holy" designation separating him or her from the rest of the people—very different from, say, a Catholic priest, who is seen as God's direct representative on earth. There is no Halachic reason why a woman should not be able to fulfill the chief role of the rabbi as a learned authority and guide. The objections to having women serve as rabbis are based both on male chauvinist bias and on a circuitous logic that states that if all women are disenfranchised under Jewish law, it makes no sense to have them in roles in which they are not able to act as full Jews.

Trude Weiss-Rosmarin, longtime advocate of women's rights in Judaism, thinks that the basic legal impediments to women's full equality have to be removed *first*, and arguing over women in the rabbinate still does not remove them. "It seems to me," she says, "that with respect to women's human rights and women's place in the American Jewish Community a great deal is to be done, and my sense of order persuades me that first things come first. Before we tackle the problem of women rabbis we must give women elementary human rights. I want to be respected as an adult, as an adult who can vote, as an adult who can be a witness, as an adult who can demand equal rights before a rabbinic court."[18]

But to bring about equality for women under Jewish law we will need to have women's input into legal decision making, as we have seen. The very presence of numerous women in the rabbinate will certainly mean that more women's voices will be heard arguing for changing women's status under Jewish law. Ultimately, the existence of women rabbis will affect Jewish law (to say nothing of the institutionalized rabbinate itself), even though the decision of whether or not to ordain women as rabbis is not in itself strictly a legal issue.

The dramatic debates over women in the rabbinate highlight the interplay between people's attitudes and political, legal, and social realities. Eighty-four percent of Jewish women support the ordination of women as rabbis, according to one poll.[19] Yet, since Jewish law is not altogether determined by consensus (although some legal positions have evolved out of social realities), what counts most are the religious opinions and attitudes of Jewish legal experts, almost all of them male.

Rabbi Seymour Siegel, professor of theology and ethics at the Jewish Theological Seminary, addressing a street rally supporting the ordination of Conservative women rabbis, argues: "There are those who say that the Halachah does not permit women rabbis because rabbis are judges, and women cannot be judges since women cannot be witnesses. But what about Deborah? If a woman could serve as a judge then, she can serve as a rabbi now."[20]

Another obstacle set before women who want to become rabbis is the precept that a prayer leader (rabbi or cantor) is supposed to function for those members of the congregation who might not be able to pray themselves—for example, an illiterate person. The reasoning here is that since a woman is not bound by the same obligations to pray as a man is, she can't fulfill the mitzvah of prayer for someone else. For the Conservative movement, a way around this would be to take up Blu Greenberg's suggestion of simply declaring women equally responsible with men for the mitzvah of prayer.

Of course the real obstacles to ordaining women have more to do with men's attitudes toward women than with these strictures. The sense of embarrassment or discomfort that tradition-minded men feel when they contemplate having women in rabbinic roles is conveyed in the 1979 minority opinion report of the commission appointed to study the issue of women in the Conservative rabbinate: "We recommend to the leaders of the Conservative Movement that appropriate roles be created for Jewish women short of ordination, so that their commitment and talents may be a source of blessing and not of unnecessary controversy."[21]

Obviously, as more women enter the rabbinate, some of the sex-linked attitudes about rabbis will change, and perhaps the role of rabbi as counselor will be enhanced. One problem with an all-male rabbinate is that rabbis have had an all-male bias in advising their congregants, never having had women as teachers or colleagues in rabbinical school.

Reconstructionist rabbi Sandy Eisenberg Sasso, who has spent more than a decade in the pulpit, defines the ways women rabbis will change Jewish life:

> Does being a woman make essentially any difference in the kind of rabbi I am and can be? I think that it does. Women have a contribution to make to Jewish life as a whole, not "in spite of" or "regardless of" being a woman but precisely because of it. Women in the rabbinate, all Jewish women for that matter, contribute the most to Judaism when they do *not* fashion themselves out of a masculine mold. Women come to the rabbinate with a different set of experiences. The findings of feminist sociologists, psychologists, and moral theorists teach us that we

STEPHEN WISE FREE SYNAGOGUE

EREV SHABBAT, JUNE 10 · 8:15 PM
SPECIAL ADULT B'NAI MITZVAH SERVICE

SHABBAT, JUNE 11
STUDY 11:30 A.M.
WORSHIP 10:30 A.M.

SWFS JEWISH DAY CARE PROGRAM
OPENS IN SEPTEMBER
ENROLLMENT IS NOW OPEN
FULL TIME AND PART TIME PROGRAMS
AVAILABLE

RELIGIOUS SCHOOL REGISTRATION
IS NOW OPEN

BALFOUR BRICKNER   SENIOR RABBI
HELENE FERRIS   ASSISTANT RABBI
ELLEN STETTNER MATH   CANTOR
EDWARD E KLEIN   RABBI EMERITUS
AMY S MADDEN   ADMINISTRATOR
MYRA CARP   RELIGIOUS SCHOOL DIRECTOR

SYNAGOGUE OFFICE 877 4050

(Marilynne Herbert)

come with different priorities, visions of reality, and relationships. Women's center of focus is on people rather than principles. Their primary concern is less with an infraction of a set universal rule than with the failure of relationships. Women's vision of reality is not a hierarchal model where one's goal is to move up, to be alone at the top, but rather a network model where the goal is to connect with others, to be together at the center. We have sustained hierarchies by developing talents for control over others and our environment. We sustain networks by nurturing gifts of facilitation and conservation. Women's voices speak less of dichotomies of good/evil, dominance/subservience and more of a complementary process of interconnections. In this model what is most important is not account-ability, who can be blamed, but response-ability, who can be helped.[22]

In addition to introducing a female perspective in synagogues, the presence of women in the rabbinate will be felt in the community when they occupy nonpulpit roles as well. Some of these positions might be as principals of Hebrew day schools, heads of hospital chaplaincy programs, and directors of Hillel and other campus-based Jewish groups—and in the executive suites of those major Jewish organizations that have always liked to have a rabbi or two on their letterheads.

The Reform and Reconstructionist movements have been ordaining women as rabbis for several years. The Reconstructionist Rabbinical College has admitted women since it opened its doors in 1968, and Reform women rabbis have been ordained since 1972. Almost fifty women had been ordained by the Reconstructionist and Reform movements as of the 1982 graduating classes. Conservative and Orthodox movements have obviously responded quite differently. Here is a current status report on each denomination:

Orthodox
We see that there have been traditional women who have served as rabbis and teachers, even in Hasidic sects (where some preached from behind a curtain or at an open window so as not to violate precepts about men and women praying together). One Orthodox woman has suggested that women could be rabbis in Orthodox synagogues, and men could sit in a separate section, as has happened sometimes when men have come to usually all-women *minyans*. But it is unlikely that this will take place soon,

Facing page: *Rabbi Helene Ferris and Cantor Ellen Stettner Math* (R) *at Friday evening services.*

since among other objections, there is the Orthodox uneasy feeling that having women lead services violates the concept of *kavod hatsibur*—the honor of the community; this is generally interpreted to mean that it would look as if there were no men qualified to lead!

Women in Orthodox Judaism can be ritual slaughterers, ritual circumcisers, and kashrut supervisors (though often excluded from these positions on the basis of custom), so there might be legal precedents for having women serve as rabbis as well. So far, however, few people are searching for these precedents; Orthodox women are largely concerned with issues of participation and equal ritual obligation rather than with religious leadership.

Conservative

Despite open hearings held across the country in the late seventies in which lay people expressed their support for women in the Conservative rabbinate, and despite the recommendation of a specially appointed commission of the Rabbinical Assembly, in 1979 the faculty of the Jewish Theological Seminary (the degree-granting arm of Conservative Judaism) refused to allow women to be ordained. The personal practice and beliefs of most of the senior members of the Seminary faculty responsible for the "nay" votes seem to be mainstream Orthodox, rather than the Conservative Judaism practiced by the majority of Jews in America.[23] After the "nay" vote a group of Seminary students—men and women—joined by lay and faculty supporters, formed an organization, GROW (Group for the Rabbinical Ordination of Women), to continue lobbying for the ordination issue.

In the face of the decision of the Seminary, some women who had enrolled in its graduate school in the hopes of applying their credits toward a rabinical degree left to enroll in Reconstructionist and Reform rabbinical schools. One woman rabbi ordained by the Reconstructionist movement and another ordained by Reform Judaism took pulpits in Conservative synagogues; this was one route for women who had hoped to be ordained as Conservative rabbis.

In October of 1983 the Seminary faculty voted again; this time there was overwhelming support for admitting women to the rabbinical school and from there, presumably, into the pulpits of Conservative synagogues in large numbers. The vote caused jubilation not only among those women already resolved to enter the rabbinate, but also among women who suddenly saw new possibilities in their own lives. The day the news was announced, telephones rang across the country as women called each other to say "mazel tov."

In March 1985 the Rabbinical Assembly—the Conservative movement's organization of rabbis—revised its constitution, permitting *all* rabbis receiving ordination from the Jewish Theological Seminary to become members of the Rabbinical Assembly automatically. Women graduates of other rabbinical schools, like their male counterparts, will have to petition individually for R.A. membership.

While the Seminary was holding hearings and taking votes and stalling female applicants, another path to the rabbinate was followed by Lynn Gottlieb, for several years rabbinical resource to New York City's deaf community. Gottlieb, after studying both at the Seminary and privately with various rabbis and scholars for several years, decided to sidestep the obstacles to her ordination at the Seminary and chose to be privately ordained by two rabbis with whom she had studied.

Reconstructionist

Reconstructionist women rabbis serve congregations and havurot (informal prayer and study groups) across the continent. Perhaps because of the consensus structure of havurot, and certainly because of the consistent acceptance of women in ritual roles throughout Reconstructionism (see p. 73), women rabbis in this movement have probably received the most widespread acceptance in congregational roles. The Reconstructionist Rabbinical School in Philadelphia has been a comfortable environment for many women closed out of the Conservative Jewish Theological Seminary, because Reconstructionism was originally an offshoot of Conservative Judaism.

Reform

Despite the fact that the Reform movement made a decision to accept women as rabbis in the middle of the nineteenth century, it took more than a hundred years until Sally Priesand was ordained as the first American Reform woman rabbi, in 1972. In the words of anthropologist Riv-Ellen Prell, "When the host culture offered feminism, the Reform movement was finally able seriously to consider implementing its 1840's ideology."[24]

Indeed, there have been instances of women serving as Reform rabbis before Priesand. Regina Jonas was privately ordained in Germany in the 1920s, and according to 1951 reports in the Anglo-Jewish press, a woman identified only as Mrs. William Ackerman took over the pulpit of the Reform synagogue in Meridian, Mississippi, when it was vacated on her husband's death.[25] But until Priesand there was no official ordination of women in Reform Judaism.

The problem for Reform women rabbis now (and there will be close to a hundred of them in 1984) is how to get hired. Some of the same psychological barriers to accepting women's ordination in the Conservative movement are at work in subtler ways, preventing the acceptance of women rabbis in the pulpits of Reform congregations. Now that they are ordained, the Reform movement is investigating ways of getting them hired. The early returns from these investigations indicate that the discrimination against women that occurs in the workplace at large also appears in the hiring of women rabbis. When they do make it past the congregational search committees and get job offers, the positions may be accompanied by shorter contracts and salaries lower than those offered male rabbinical-school graduates. (Some male Reconstructionist rabbinical students suggest that men refuse to go out on job interviews to congregations that discriminate against women.) Once hired, women rabbis have reported fierce struggles to get maternity leave from their congregations, according to Trude Weiss-Rosmarin. For Reform women in the rabbinate, then, the obstacles exist too—they are just set up farther along the road.

In fact, even some progressive male rabbis may have difficulty overcoming their resistance to having a female in what is perceived as an authority role—and a young female at that. Aside from men's predictable anxieties about losing power (or granting power) to women, there is an even more subtle reason behind the reluctance of some male rabbis to see women doing "their" job: Reform Rabbi Norman B. Mirsky claims we treat a male rabbi "like a lady." According to Mirsky, the "feminization" of the rabbinate means that American Jews expect their male rabbis to evince no sexuality, no athletic prowess—in short, none of the signs of American masculinity. "It is likely that, in a country that has feminized the clerical role, the actual emergence of a female rabbi represents a very minor shift from mental image to physical reality. On the other hand, to Jewish clergymen who for the first time have found their masculinity impugned by their career choice, the actual existence of a woman rabbi may serve once and for all to confirm what they have often been warned: that being a rabbi is no job for a Jewish boy."[26]

Because Judaism was so late in recognizing women's potential for religious leadership, the women rabbis now being ordained are fairly young women. There is no corps of experienced older women religious leaders (as there is, for example, in Catholicism, with its nuns, or in Protestant denominations, with deaconesses and women preachers). For the women rabbis themselves there are no role models. Reform rabbi Joy Levitt says, "There is no one to turn to with a question." Some of the questions might be trivial—such as how to dress for certain rabbinical functions. Others are more substantive and have to do with relations with congregants and colleagues.

Although, according to some women rabbis, congregants are freer to approach a woman rabbi as a counselor, they have to learn how to accept her in a leadership role: as decision-maker within the congregation, sometimes as authority figure in the congregation's educational structure, and as ritual leader, complete with rabbinic garb, guiding the worshipers through the services.

Reform Rabbi Deborah Prinz has protested that congregants expected her always to act in the role of *woman* rabbi, specifically addressing women's issues in every sermon or lecture. She has said she prefers to be seen as a rabbi, not as a gender representative. Other women rabbis have said that they do see themselves as groundbreakers and feel that if *they* don't speak out on women's issues to the congregation no one will.

An area of greater helplessness for all these women lies in the way they are viewed by Orthodox Judaism, which refuses to accept the ceremonies they perform as halachically valid. One Reconstructionist rabbi, Linda Holtzman, told a women's caucus at a Jewish conference that she warns her congregants that when she performs a ceremony for them, "This will not be acceptable in the eyes of X or Y." "I feel I have to take this position, or the people I marry or convert could be in terrible trouble later on. I think this undermines my effectiveness in certain ways, but I can't honestly do otherwise." It's also awkward for these women when they sit on community-wide rabbinical boards and are ignored or disparaged by other rabbis. One tells of being appointed automatically to her town's board of rabbis but never receiving notices of meetings; the chairman didn't want her presence to offend the more traditional members.

TO BECOME A RABBI

Hebrew Union College-Jewish Institute of Religion
1 West Fourth Street
New York, NY 10012
    (plus campuses in Los Angeles, Cincinnati, and Jerusalem)

Jewish Theological Seminary
3080 Broadway
New York, NY 10027

Reconstructionist Rabbinical College
2308 N. Broad Street
Philadelphia, PA 19132

The rabbi instrumental in performing the private ordination of Lynn Gottlieb was:

Reb Zalman Schachter-Shalomi
Bnai Or Fellowship
6723 Emlen Street
Philadelphia, PA 19119

TO FIND A WOMAN RABBI

Since the names and numbers (to say nothing of the addresses) of women rabbis in the United States and Canada change each year, one source of information is the rabbinical schools listed above (ask for names and addresses of women graduates), and the rabbinical organizations of the Conservative and Reform movements. See also the Networking Directory.

Rabbinical Assembly
3080 Broadway
New York, NY 10027

Central Conference of American Rabbis
(Reform)
790 Madison Avenue
New York, NY 10021

In addition there are the organizations set up by women rabbis themselves:

Women's Rabbinic Alliance
(Reform and Reconstructionist women rabbis and students)
Hebrew Union College-Jewish Institute of Religion
1 West Fourth Street
New York, NY 10012

Women's Rabbinic Network
(organization of Reform women rabbis)
c/o Union of American Hebrew Congregations
838 Fifth Avenue
New York, NY 10021

WOMEN AS CANTORS

Under Halachah, the same strictures prohibiting women from serving as rabbis come into play in keeping them from cantorial roles as well. The issue of a woman's voice as a sensual attraction to men (see *kol ishah*, p. 67) is certainly one of the arguments used against having women cantors in Orthodox Judaism, quite aside from the separate Halachic prohibition against having a nonobligated prayer leader. For both these reasons the cantorial school of the Orthodox movement does not admit women. Because women are not obligated to pray at certain times, they do not qualify as persons who can lead others in prayer or represent other worshipers, as is required in certain of the prayers in the standard liturgy. In fact, in at least one Halachic women's *minyan*, the woman acting as prayer leader does not, as a male would, *repeat* the Amidah (*Shmoneh Esray*) prayer which is the core of the service, but rather she remains silent, not praying while the congregation prays, and then chants her *own* prayer aloud. To the uninitiated observer this would look the same as the procedure in a traditional service, in which the cantor repeats the Amidah aloud after the individual congregants say their prayers to themselves. But the stratagem of having the female prayer leader chant her "own" prayer skirts the issue of having a nonobligated person represent others at prayer.

The Conservative movement admits women to its cantorial program but does not graduate them as cantors. Instead they receive a Bachelor of Music degree. Not only is this issue being ignored at the moment in the Conservative movement, but if it were addressed, it might meet with more opposition than the controversial women-in-the-rabbinate question did, since the Halachic reasons not to have women as cantors seem clear, whereas the objections to women as rabbis now appear to be almost entirely psychological or political. The devotion to Halachah on this issue in the Conservative movement looks like a smoke screen for plain discrimination against women. Dr. Trude Weiss-Rosmarin writes: "Mixed choirs with female soloists sing in . . . many Conservative synagogues. There is no basis, therefore, for the objection to women serving as cantors. . . . One cannot help concluding that the 'Orthodoxy' of the Law Committee of the Rabbinical Assembly and of the United Synagogue with respect to strict adherence to the laws discriminating against women is due to other reasons than concern for 'Tradition.' "[27]

Women graduate as cantors from the Reform movement's cantorial school, and in fact may take over the profession if current trends continue; all but one applicant to the School of Sacred Music of the Reform movement in 1982 was female.

Women do serve as cantors in synagogues of the Reform, Reconstructionist, and Conservative movements even if they have not been formally ordained. As with male cantors, there is a tradition of apprenticeship-training for the cantorate, and some of the women serving as cantors today have prepared for their positions in this fashion. However, there is some enmity between those who have academic degrees (and who insist that the informally trained be called "cantorial soloists") and those who have been apprenticed or studied in other ways (who insist that they are part of a time-honored tradition never questioned when used by male cantors).

For a partial listing of women cantors, see the Networking Directory.

TO BECOME A CANTOR

Cantors Institute
   (Conservative)
Jewish Theological Seminary
3080 Broadway
New York, NY 10027

School of Sacred Music
   (Reform)
Hebrew Union College-
Jewish Institute of Religion
1 West Fourth Street
New York, NY 10012

An alternative to the formal cantorial schools and the apprenticeship method is a master's degree program in Jewish music, which provides a professional track for those students wanting to enter the cantorate:

Gratz College
M.A. Program in Jewish Music
10 Street and Tabor Road
Philadelphia, PA 19141

TO CONTACT WOMEN WHO ARE CANTORS

Women Cantors Network
c/o Cantor Deborah Katchko-Zimmerman
Congregation Beth El
109 East Avenue
Norwalk, CT 06851

American Conference of Cantors
(Reform)
Union of American Hebrew Congregations
838 Fifth Avenue
New York, NY 10021

2

◆

FROM OBSERVER
TO PARTICIPANT

THE CONSEQUENCES OF WOMEN'S
EXCLUSION FROM RELIGIOUS OBLIGATIONS

As we have seen, according to Jewish law, one is not properly fulfilling the
obligations of a Jew if one is merely performing them out of choice, voluntarily. Under this system, free will is *not* a higher state than necessity
(contrary to what most Western philosophy has taught us). Thus women,
not being obligated by law to pray at certain times, are not considered full
participants in communal prayer. The exclusions based on this reading of
the law find their way even into those branches of Judaism that purport to
include women, sometimes as equals. For example, the formula for beginning the grace after meals (Birkat Ha-Mazon) is to say, "Gentlemen,
let us pray" (*Rabbotai nevarech*). Even the Conservative and Reform
"bentschers"—booklets with the prayer, which are usually passed around
just before the grace begins—use this same formula, with nary a token of
recognition for the fact that in non-Orthodox denominations women may
lead the Birkat also. A woman who is often invited to appear as a visiting
scholar before Jewish groups and who lectures at dinner meetings a great
deal says, "Even when I'm the scholar-in-residence, they never change
this formula; they never begin 'Rabbotai and g'virotai'—gentlemen and
ladies—and I don't like to be ignored."

Not only are women systematically and often automatically closed out
of the prayer experience by the very language of the prayer itself, but they
run the risk of being ignored or negated as worshipers also, their presence
a potential distraction to the "real" participants. One Orthodox Manhat-

tan rabbi stood up and announced to his congregation near the close of the Yom Kippur service a few years ago that the women "may want to leave early to prepare the meal to break the fast," but would they please be very quiet when coming down from the women's balcony "so as not to disturb the worshipers."

All these differential patterns of religious observance for women and for men reinforce the notion that women's place is at home raising children, which is the reason commonly given (of the honest reasons) for why women are not obligated to perform all the time-bound mitzvot. How about women who have no small children at home needing their care? How about women who have no children, period? And how about the apparent contradiction that woman *are* required to hear the reading of the *megillah* (scroll) of Esther at Purim, sit in a succah, and attend a Passover seder—all of these taking place at specific times? As Rabbi Saul Berman points out, exemption from certain obligations is "a tool" that Torah uses in order to make it more likely that women will choose to stay out of the public/communal sphere and will choose instead to stay home.[1]

The mitzvot that women *are* to perform include all the nontime-linked obligations, such as keeping kosher, and three special observances: lighting the Sabbath candles, baking challah (Sabbath bread), and following the restraints on sexual contact between wife and husband.[2] (For details on the Sabbath mitzvot, see "Celebrating the Jewish Calendar," p. 84). Although there has been considerable recent interest in mikveh, the ritual immersion in water after each menstrual cycle (see "Our Bodies," p. 203), many feminists believe that the ritual expresses a negative attitude toward women's bodies and that even this "special" obligation for women reinforces their second-class status. Even for women who do observe the special obligations, "the fact that women are excluded from performing certain mitzvot . . . means that they are denied the opportunity to experience the spiritual joy associated with those mitzvot."[3]

WOMEN'S INCREASED PARTICIPATION
IN PUBLIC PRAYER

Some change in women's status is taking place de facto, as women take or make opportunities to participate more fully in worship and other ritual responsibilities once deemed the province of men only. Some of these changes become possible for women willing to move into more liberal branches of Judaism; others are changes available even within Orthodox Judaism to those women who make the effort to explore which exclusions are based on law and which on custom alone. For each woman who is willing to take the risks involved in amending or transforming tradition, there are many more who, with the innovator as role model, are willing to try participating more themselves.

For example, one woman tells of praying in a Conservative synagogue in Washington, D.C., where a woman raised in an Orthodox home, with a yeshiva education, was leading the Yom Kippur morning service for the first time.

> . . . She prayed, chanted, sang, wrapped in the traditional white *kittel* that I'd seen only on male rabbis before. She faced the ark, her back to the congregants the whole time, in the traditional manner. My joy in hearing her pray was mixed with a sense of deprivation that I'd never before heard an adult woman pray like that, in solitude before the congregation. The possibilities, the reservoir of untapped feeling that the experience released in me took me really by surprise. And I was embarrassed to realize that I had never had the sense of spiritual possibility and responsibility, or the visual imagery to go with it, that opened up for me that Yom Kippur. . . .

In the women's section of an ultra-Orthodox shul on another Yom Kippur, I sat with women who were uncomfortable because of the heat in the balcony, restless because they could not hear or see much of the action below, and embarrassed by the presence of a uniformed *male* guard, who from time to time walked over to women to ask them not to chat with their neighbors. Yet I also saw around me women who were praying and beating their breasts, and standing all day, doing what I had associated only with observant men. Despite my own acute discomfort at being where I was (I cried the whole way home Kol Nidre night, humiliated by the seating, the guard, and the rabbi's tone), I was awed by the seriousness of the three or four women who really seemed engaged in repentance.

A Canadian woman says:

> When one of my nephews, a child I feel very close to and who was named after my late father, was about to be Bar Mitzvah in 1975 in my family's Conservative synagogue, I asked if I could have an aliyah to the Torah in honor of the Bar Mitzvah. The rabbi refused. My brother—telling the rabbi that he, too, was conservative on many aspects of ritual practice—asked if I might not have the honor of holding the Torah after the reading, or binding it. No. The honor that was finally accorded me? Pouring tea at the luncheon following the Bar Mitzvah.
>
> Two years pass. Another nephew is about to become Bar Mitzvah. A

(Barbara Gingold)

new rabbi in the congregation is very supportive of complete participation of women in the service, but no women have so far participated. I am given an aliyah. I am very excited. This is my first speaking role at a Shabbat service since my own Bat Mitzvah, twenty years before, on the same *bimah* [platform]. I remember the blessings, with some help from my nephew. I'm going to be the first woman who is not the mother of a celebrant to appear on the *bimah*. Then my nephew informs me that the new ruling is for everyone who has an aliyah to wear a *tallit*. I have never worn one and have no idea what to do! My nephew, himself nervously preparing to enter the synagogue, shows me.

(Marilynne Herbert)

I had always watched men putting on their *tallesim* and felt as if I were watching some special male rite. I had always found it, in fact, rather alluring to watch men take on another dimension as they donned the *tallit*. It felt wonderful to have one on myself. I felt as if I were *preparing* to pray in a way that I'd never felt before, when my preparations for synagogue had revolved (especially in adolescence) around what clothing I was wearing.

With the Bat Mitzvah of my brother's third child, there was a further refinement. Not only was I allowed to have an aliyah (this time without *tallit*—another rabbi had come, and another set of rules prevailed), but at the *kiddush* [festive meal] following the Saturday-morning service the *male* relatives sat at the pastry-laden tables and poured tea! I loved it, and suggest the turnabout as a good consciousness-raising device in all those synagogues which still have the *mothers* of the Bar and Bat Mitzvah celebrants serve at the kiddush, or help cater it, and who rely upon female family members to staff the serving tables. With women and men on the *bimah* it's refreshing to see men *and* women in the shul kitchen. Or, as one man put it, "It's nice to be at a service where the men are holding the babies and the women are holding the Torahs."

The net result of these expanded options for women in both mainstream and "alternative" settings has been that women see themselves in a new way as Jews. One woman, who admits to feeling most comfortable in an Orthodox shul "except for the problem of women," and who now attends egalitarian services only, reports: "I spent all those years in day school and in synagogue, doing *tfillah* [prayers] all the time, and until I got my first aliyah I didn't even bother to follow the service completely. Then—once I was participating—suddenly there was a point to it!"

At Temple Ansche Chesed, a Conservative, egalitarian synagogue on Manhattan's Upper West Side, which has a wide mix of ages among its congregants, the older women—many of them in their seventies and eighties—have been, as one said, "delighted" to have women rabbinical or seminary students lead the Shabbat and holiday services. The free expression of the younger women in prayer and ritual has encouraged the older women to participate actively, many for the first time in their lives.

WHAT TO EXPECT WHEREVER YOU PRAY

Because there is no monolithic structure to religious Judaism (no single, "papal" authority) even within each denomination, women can have problems figuring out what is the custom in any given situation or synagogue at any one time. What follows are some guidelines.

Orthodox

In Orthodox synagogues, where separate seating for women and men is the rule, there are now variations on the traditional "blind" balcony for women. These include cords, waist-high fences, partitions that are movable and can be shifted so that women and men can see the *bimah* equally well, seating in the round, and even—according to report—two-way mirrors, reflective on the men's side but translucent on the women's.[4]

The very existence of a separate section for women in Orthodox synagogues carries a powerful message that women are a breed apart. The separation of men and women by a *mechitza* (partition) in a traditional

(Hugh Smyser, courtesy Brown University News Bureau)

Orthodox synagogue—a practice thought to date back two thousand years at least—makes concrete the attitude that women's bodies are somehow dangerous or tantalizing and that men need to be protected from them (see p. 207). The stated purpose of the *mechitza* is to keep worshiping men from being distracted by women. (It's never suggested that the women might be distracted by the men.)

One argument for the *mechitza* that Orthodox women make (which parallels women's support for all-women's colleges) is that women can pray with greater intensity and powerful feelings of sisterhood without thinking of which men are looking at them. Another positive—and sometimes overlooked—value is to separate a married woman from her husband in such a way as to define her not merely as an adjunct to him and other family members but as a person in her own right (though not, alas, in her own rite).

Among some groups of ultra-Orthodox Jews, physical separation is not enough. Not only the *sight* of a woman is forbidden, lest a man be tempted from holy thoughts, it is even forbidden for him to hear the sound of a woman's voice (*kol ishah*) singing, lest he be distracted or aroused. The Talmud says, "Woman's voice is a sexual enticement, as is her hair and her leg." An Israeli woman, whose daughter has become far more religious than she herself is, protests that she cannot even sing the traditional Sabbath songs on Friday night, either at her own table or in her daughter's home, because her son-in-law would object.

Similarly, religious groups in Israel have been protesting for years the playing of radios on public buses. Their argument is that religious men might accidentally overhear a woman singing on someone else's radio. Once again the theme "woman as temptress." Once again women are cut out of the public sphere. Roslyn Lacks claims that the emphasis on the edict against a man's hearing a woman's voice is "to sanctify the demand for her silence."

Orthodox rabbis sensitive to women's concerns for participation, such as Shlomo Riskin of Manhattan's Lincoln Square synagogue, "permit" separate women's dancing circles (*hakafot*) with the Torah at Simchat Torah; some also permit or even encourage women who want to pray in separate women's prayer groups. In one such women's *minyan*, in New York, a girl recently celebrated her Bat Mitzvah, and the *male* guests sat behind the *mechitza* (see Bat Mitzvah rituals, p. 136). A similar pattern is followed when there are men guests at the women's *minyan* at Brandeis University.

Traditional women whose own rabbis aren't responsive to their desires for a greater role in shul have sometimes taken matters into their own hands. One Orthodox woman says that she wanted to maintain tradition, and was "willing to put up with a lot" in order to do so, but "wondered how I could raise my daughters in a feminist, egalitarian household, teach them the value of egalitarianism, and then ask them to make an exception when it came to Judaism." She learned to *lehn* (read from the Torah with the proper chants or cantillations), and did so in a *minyan* at a college Hillel group.[5]

Women not fortunate enough to find a woman tutor, or even a willing male tutor, can order cantillation instructions and a cassette from:

Chadish Media Press
78 Cortelyou Avenue
Staten Island, NY 10312
(718) 356-9495

Then all you have to do is find a congregation that will permit you to *lehn*.

WOMEN'S PRAYER GROUPS

All-female prayer groups provide a religious alternative for many traditional women who want to remain within an Orthodox definition of
Jewish law and hence do not want to pray in a mixed group, but do want
the participation denied them in a traditional Orthodox synagogue. These
minyans differ from egalitarian ones not only in their single-sex nature but
also in the fact that some do not perform the entire service. For example,
the women who follow the strict interpretation of the law believe that
since they are not obligated to perform the same prayers that men do, they
are in fact proscribed from performing them, and so omit certain parts of
the traditional Shabbat service (for example, the Borchu, Kaddish, and
Kedusha) which some authorities say can be said only in the presence of
a standard *minyan*, a quorum of ten obligated (that is, male) adults.

A caveat about separate women's prayer groups comes from Rachel
Adler, herself a member of the Twin Cities Women's Minyan in St. Paul:
"Some traditionalist rabbis . . . encourage us to pray in separate women's
services, to be 'creative,' to substitute our own liturgy for the prayer book,
to create our own rituals, to develop, in fact, a whole new religion of
'womanism' which would then intersect the male cult of Judaism at
points convenient to the 'Jews.' "[6]

While some women have seen separate prayer groups as damaging to
the cause of women's full participation in public prayer, for the women
committed to staying within Halachah this may be their only opportunity for reading Torah or leading prayers. Arlene Agus says of her early
experiences praying with a group exclusively female: "The first time we
saw the inside of a Torah, our eyes went blind with tears."

For current groups, see the Networking Directory, the National Havurah Coordinating Committee, a rabbi known to be sympathetic to wom-
en's issues, or your campus Hillel. In addition, a "coalition of Orthodox
women devoted to exploring the fullest role of women in Jewish religious practice" is a magnet for women's prayer groups around the country. They are seeking through these groups "a means of religious expression
while remaining true to traditional Jewish law and the observance of
mitzvot":

Task Force on Jewish Woman
Box 1062
Teaneck, NJ 07666

Unorthodox Denominations

CONSERVATIVE JUDAISM

Created in mid-nineteenth-century Europe and America, and now the largest denomination of American Jews, Conservative Judaism has retained much of traditional law but has been slightly more flexible on women's issues than Orthodoxy, now "permitting" Bat Mitzvah for girls and, in some congregations—depending on the will of the rabbi and the ritual committee—"allowing" women to be called to the Torah to recite the blessings and to be counted in the *minyan*.

Conservative Judaism, which sees its place as mediating between tradition and change, has, since its 1973 vote permitting women to be counted in the *minyan* and be called to the Torah (aliyah), tolerated or encouraged a wide range of practice, depending on the individual rabbi and the ritual committee of each congregation (see "Law and Leadership," p. 47). The Conservative Rabbinical Assembly's Committee on Jewish Law and Standards admits, when it makes a decision, that a minority view held by three committee members is a valid option for Conservative Jews. Therefore both the official Conservative views of Jewish law and the practice of these laws may differ widely within the movement.

It may be that Conservative synagogues resistant to including women in the *minyan* and calling them to the Torah may change their policies, not when the congregants change but when the rabbi is replaced. Two Long Island rabbis quoted in the *Long Island Jewish World* in 1980, eight years after the decision to permit women these mitzvot, are very firm in refusing women these options. One says, "A synagogue president has to sit on the bimah and a woman in my synagogue cannot be permitted to sit on the bimah." And the other states: "When my traditional-Conservative group [members] make remarks [to convince me] about women participating in the minyan and receiving aliyot, they do so with humor. They know my position and they respect it. Some rabbis have control and respect, and I feel that I do."[7]

Conversely, some male Conservative rabbis have used "control and respect" to lead the way in integrating their synagogues. Rabbi Sol Landau of Miami has said that after two years of meetings and discussions and educational programs in the mid-seventies his Conservative congregation was able to make a relatively smooth transition to expand women's roles in the synagogue. The most successful transitions, in fact, seem to be those that take a slower, reformist approach, giving time for people to air their anxieties, rather than those effected by unilateral decisions from a rabbi or ritual committee.

Men reluctant to give up power aren't alone in impeding the progress of women into ritual roles. Some women, themselves uneducated or inexperienced, and nervous about their own abilities to perform new ritual responsibilities, sometimes oppose new roles for other women too. How do you respond to someone who says, "The women themselves don't want change"? One woman replies with a little set speech: "Then you need to help these women grow. It's very hard to take on something you feel ill-prepared to do. Some women are afraid to make waves—they prefer not to make change if they think they'll have to face male hostility. But once they're trained in synagogue skills and feel comfortable with new rituals, they'll want to participate in them." Even women learned in Hebrew liturgy have confessed to embarrassing lapses when they have had their first opportunities to participate in services as adults. One woman, herself a distinguished Jewish scholar, says that on the occasion of her first aliyah she forgot the words to the blessing over the Torah; another still trembles when she tells of getting up to lead services and being unable to remember the words to the *Sh'ma*, the prayer she had recited every day of her life.

Women's prior conditioning has to be overcome by education and practice; to this end, one Jewish feminist group sponsored a "Practicum in Synagogue Skills for Women." For some women unaccustomed to the routines of public prayer it comes as a surprise that they are relatively simple to master. An attorney from the Midwest says that she expected "something mysterious, that you had to have gone to *cheder* since childhood to know when to stand up and sit down in synagogue."

Women's participation in synagogue services need not be only in an area in which there's been conflict; women need to feel equal with men in all aspects of ritual. For example, in a city where one woman was visiting she was seated at the early morning service beside a male friend who was a regular member of the congregation. Her husband and her friend's wife were at home readying the children for shul, planning to join them later. The sexton of the synagogue, seeing her beside a "regular" and not knowing her face, correctly assumed that she was a guest. "He approached and offered me an honor, which I knew was traditional in synagogues that want to give guests a special welcome: Would I like to open the ark? I accepted with pleasure, but it wasn't until I was standing on the *bimah* get-

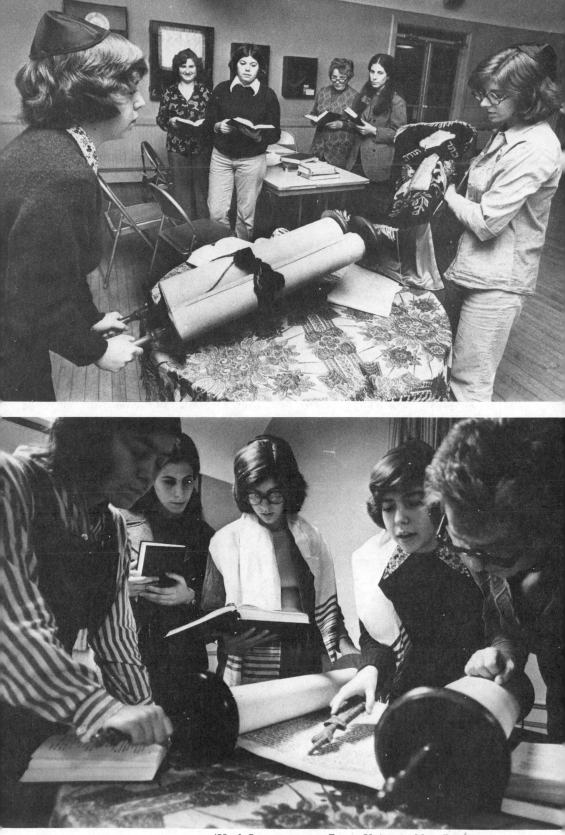

(Hugh Smyser, courtesy Brown University News Bureau)

ting ready to pull the string of the ark curtain that I realized—I had been treated *just like an ordinary Jew!* The honors and approaches that I'd witnessed in strange synagogues over the years had always been made to my father or brother or husband. *I (me!)* was being honored just because I was a Jew who was obviously a stranger in town. It didn't matter that I was a woman (as it had mattered when I had been given a 'token' aliyah in my own synagogue); I was just a visiting *Jew*. That was one of the few times in my life that I felt like a Jew without also feeling that I needed to specify Jewish *woman*."

In fact, some women have protested when male friends or relatives were given ritual honors while they themselves were passed by. Of course it is awkward to challenge the prevailing customs in a synagogue in which one is a guest. But in a situation in which you know it will not offend the prevailing norms, it is not a bad idea to consider what one Miami woman did: "It was *my* relative who was Bar Mitzvah, yet my husband was offered an aliyah to the Torah. He declined graciously, saying that he was sure the family would like me to have the aliyah, since he was related only by marriage to the celebrant, and since the synagogue in question (Conservative) was already giving women aliyot. The father of the Bar Mitzvah had really no recourse but to be equally gracious and say 'Of course.'"

Another woman reports that when there's a routine honor being given out, such as opening or closing the ark, and her husband is approached, they go up to the *bimah* together. The more visible women are on the *bimah* in almost any kind of ritual role the better, because it brings innovation closer to the normative way of running the service. But the "couples" pattern offends both single people and those women who feel, rightly, that their ritual participation should be totally independent of any male they happen to be attached to.

REFORM

The Reform movement, which has always called women to the Torah since its founding in Germany in the middle of the nineteenth century, doesn't require a quorum of ten people for public worship (so there is no issue of women being counted in a *minyan*), and already has women rabbis in pulpits. Here, then, the issues for women revolve more around political than ritual concerns (for example, whether or not all women in the congregation have a vote or whether votes are allocated per "family"). The big push in Reform Judaism in the face of the women's movement has been the elimination of bias in educational programs and of sexist language in the liturgy.

Historically, in the Reform movement women have been given short shrift in a more subtle way than in Conservative and Orthodox Judaism. The very nature of what was considered important and therefore to be retained by Reform when it broke away from Orthodoxy in the 1850s excluded among other things much of what had been women's special domain in Jewish ritual.

Yale historian Ann Braude points out that "The Reform movement and the lack of facilities [in mid-nineteenth-century America] discouraged the traditional religious activities of Jewish women: attending the mikveh, keeping kashrut, and keeping the Sabbath in the home. With some significant exceptions, the shapers of Reform Judaism found that male religious practices were rational and essential, while female religious practices were temporal and superstitious. . . . Women who accepted Reform rechanneled their religious lives into the previously male realm of the synagogue."[8]

RECONSTRUCTIONIST

The Reconstructionist movement, created in the twenties by an American rabbi, Mordecai M. Kaplan, was a breakaway group from Conservative Judaism, with a flexible attitude toward the law but a traditional view of much of ritual and liturgy. Almost from its inception the Reconstructionist movement has had equality for women as a tenet, and women early on participated equally in Torah readings and synagogue ritual. In 1949 New York's Society for the Advancement of Judaism, now the flagship synagogue of Reconstructionism, became the first synagogue to celebrate Bat Mitzvah, count women in the *minyan* and, outside of Reform, to give them aliyot to the Torah. This was also the first of the more liberal movements of Judaism to permit the ordination of women as rabbis and to have them serve in pulpits.

Havurot

Originally an outgrowth of the Reconstructionist movement, havurot have provided, on the whole, the freest setting for women's full participation in prayer, celebration, and communal study. By its very nature antithetical to more formal Jewish religious institutions, the havurah "movement" includes campus groups, urban communelike groups, and even synagogue-based friendship circles.

Equality for women and men as a principle of havurah Judaism has come under fire even at the annual National Havurah Institute, a weeklong session of study, prayer, and good times attended by havurah members from all over the continent. At one institute a group of Orthodox men wanted to have a formally acknowledged separate, men-only traditional prayer service. This traditional separation was opposed by many institute participants, but especially by women, who agreed with *Jewish Catalog* editor Sharon Strassfeld: "First of all, it's time for us to say we're *not* all-inclusive. We'd like to be as open to as many people as possible, but this doesn't mean we're open to everyone. . . . From its inception, the havurah movement has stood for certain things, and one of them is the egalitarian nature of prayer."[9]

To find out about havurot in your area and to receive the quarterly newsletter published by the movement, get in touch with:

National Havurah Committee
2521 Broadway
New York, NY 10025
(212) 316-3011

In Israel an egalitarian setting for worship (aside from the Reform congregations, unrecognized by the Israeli rabbinate) is a traditional service conducted by a group of two hundred or so member families that have been meeting for twenty years and that at one time included the late Rabbi Mordecai Kaplan, founder of Reconstructionism:

Mevakshei Derekh
(Seekers of the Way)
c/o Rehavia Gymnasia
Jerusalem, Israel

WOMEN AND PRAYER GARMENTS

There are three ritual objects, usually worn exclusively by Jewish men for prayer, that women have been adopting and adapting for their own use. (The first terms are in Hebrew.)

tallít, pl. *tallitót* (Yiddish—*tálles*, pl. *tallésim*): fringed shawl, usually striped, worn by observant Jews at morning prayer every day at home and in the synagogue.

tfillín (Yiddish—*tfíllin;* English—phylacteries): small black leather boxes containing scrolls of prayers, with attached straps that are tied onto the left hand and forearm and forehead before the morning prayers on weekdays. (A left-handed person wears *tfillin* on the right arm.)

kippáh (Yiddish—*yarmulke*): skullcap, worn in Orthodox synagogues

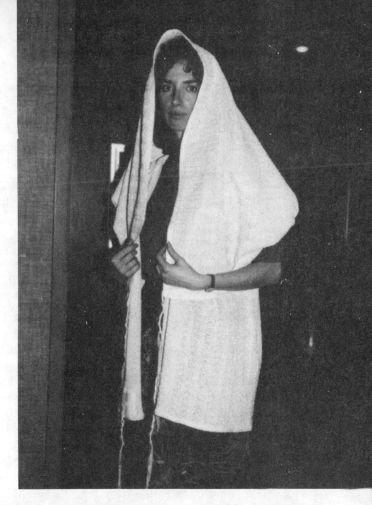

A woman's prayer shawl designed by Arlene Agus.
(Osna L. Haller)

usually by men only; in Conservative and Reconstructionist synagogues by men and women; and in Reform synagogues usually optional for men and women.

While these garments and objects have historically been owned and worn by Jewish males, there is no law against women's wearing them, except for the Biblical proscription against wearing clothing belonging to the opposite sex; nevertheless, the most startling photograph in the 1976 premiere issue of *Lilith* was of a *woman* wearing *tfillin*. (The photo was taken by the late photographer and naturalist Gail Rubin, murdered in 1979 on an Israeli beach by terrorists.) The image was so powerful (and for some so stirring and disconcerting) precisely because *tfillin*, more so than the *tallit*, are considered the exclusive property of men, though it is said that Michal, daughter of Saul, wore *tfillin*, "and the sages did not protest." Perhaps because most American Jews see others at prayer only on Shabbat and holidays, when *tfillin* are not worn, *tfillin* are associated with elderly pious men, pictured in memory or in sentimental paintings. Learning how to don them requires some practice; for instructions, Donin's *To Pray as a Jew* is, again, helpful.

Rabbi Rebecca Trachtenberg Alpert, dean of students at the Reconstructionist Rabbinical College, led a workshop in Philadelphia a few years ago on women's use of these symbolic garments. She comments:

> I raised the issue of whether women should choose to take on "male" symbols such as *tallit, kippah* and *tfillin*. I suggested that experience would really be the best teacher. The workshop participants then proceeded to say the blessing over the *tallit* found in *Siddur Nashim* and, one at a time, wrapped themselves in the *tallit*. . . . One blind woman was moved to tears. She said she could really feel her Jewishness about her for the first time.
>
> Personally, I like an external reminder that I'm involved in a special experience that the *tallit* (actually more than the *kippah*) affords. I've even had a *tallit* woven for me by a friend. Knotting the *tzitzit* [fringes] yourself, and wearing a garment designed for you, really enhances the experience of "feeling your Jewishness around you" during prayer.
>
> *Tfillin* are another story. I've never really felt comfortable praying with them, though I've done it many times. It always feels experimental and inauthentic. That may also be true for my more liberal male friends as well who don't *daven* with *tfillin*.
>
> Whatever anyone's personal final decision, children should participate in the experience of *kippah, tallit* and *tfillin* at the time of Bar/ Bat Mitzvah. It's at that stage that it's important to see that the option is available and sex-neutral.[10]

When a button reading *It's not just tallis envy* was circulated at a Jewish feminist conference in 1974, everyone had a good chuckle. Many of the women who were gathering together in separate prayer and study groups were wearing some variation of a *tallit*. Now, ten years later, in havurot and many other services, you can count on seeing at least a few women wearing the standard *tallit*, the large-size wraparound version or an alternative model—sometimes a fringed shawl or a handwoven serape.

One woman, trying to decide whether to wear a *tallit*, says: "Since praying in public has always been something of an embarrassment for me, I have come to envy those men and women who wear the oversize *tallit* which lets them shroud themselves, head, face and all, while praying. I'm considering doing the same, to create my own space for meditation and prayer while still being part of the community."

Some traditional male rabbis—both Orthodox and Conservative—react with horror or scorn when women wear ritual items commonly associated with men. One has said: *"Tfillin* should be viewed as instruments for channeling male aggression, as most public Judaism is."[11]

While some men have constructed an entire theoretical basis for their prejudice against women's participation, for many men and some women no underpinnings are needed—it's enough that men have "always" worn these symbols and women rarely have. The exclusive nature of prayer, and especially prayer with these garments, is exemplified by one large Conservative synagogue's programming. Its regular Sunday morning prayer and study group, run by the *brotherhood* and assumed to be for men only, is known as the "Tallis and T'fillin Club"—as if that title alone were enough to suggest the exclusively male and religious orientation of the program.

Some feminists would agree with Rabbi Sherwin Wine, creator of an "alternative" movement called Humanistic Judaism, who sets forth steps "to self-esteem" for Jewish women, which include a refusal to use "patriarchal" symbols. Of women who are using these objects he says: "There are certain Jewish symbols so tied into male chauvinistic behavior and clothing styles that their use by women becomes a desperate travesty . . . [honoring] those traditions which were built on the exclusion of women. Self-respecting Jewish women do not seek to rescue the signs of humiliation."[12]

But if we are going to be complete Jews along with our brothers, we are entitled to rewrite the definition of who can make use of these admittedly powerful Jewish symbols, whatever their past usage. Rabbi Wine may see casting off these symbols as part of his own agenda for change, but others have been trying to transform the symbols, both through use (as Rabbi Rebecca Trachtenberg Alpert suggests) and through redesigning the objects themselves.

One such redesigned item is the "kupiah," a kind of *kippah* for women designed by Nita Polay. She says: "Bigger than a *kippah*, it differs from a man's head covering. Smaller than a woman's winter hat, it can't be mistaken for this or assumed to be a sign of marital status." (Married women who are observant often wear scarves or hats to cover their hair out of modesty—see "Our Bodies," p. 236.) Another transformed object is the women's "prayer shawl" designed by Arlene Agus, which has a hood attached.

If you do decide to try wearing a *tallit, tfillin,* or even a *kippah* in a congregation in which it is worn by only a few women—or none—be prepared for comments and questions and challenges, but also be prepared for feeling a degree of self-consciousness about praying that you might not have experienced before. Judith Manelis, a public relations director who decided with a group of friends to begin wearing a *tallit* to Saturday morning services, found when she arrived in her New Jersey synagogue that she was the only woman who had carried through her resolve. She said that she was called up to the Torah that morning, wore her *tallit*, carried her young daughter up to the *bimah* with her, and "went through with it."[13]

"Shul Clothes"

One woman reports that in the 1940s and '50s, in her Conservative synagogue, "many women would rush out in the short break in services before *Ne'ilah* [the concluding service] on Yom Kippur, allegedly to prepare food at home for breaking the fast. When they returned to synagogue for *Ne'ilah*, they would be wearing outfits completely different, right down to the hats and gloves." In contrast to this scene, she now reports: "Last yom tov I saw fancy slacks and trouser suits, sleeveless sweaters, most women's heads uncovered—but very few women left the synagogue until *Ne'ilah* ended."

In an Orthodox setting it isn't permissible for women to wear trousers, very short skirts, or sleeveless tops, and a hat or head covering is required if you are married. In an ultra-Orthodox synagogue stockings and full-length sleeves are probably necessary.

In some Conservative synagogues the no-trousers custom is observed too, but in most you can feel comfortable in normal street clothes. Synagogues that have a policy on women's head covering usually post it near the door to the sanctuary. Where this is required, or customary, there is usually a box of *kippot*, or lace doilies, with which you can cover your head when you enter.

In Reform and Reconstructionist synagogues, dress may be a bit less formal for regular services, unless the Reform temple in question is one of the old and classy ones that dot the country. The fact that one might dress up more for these houses of worship is a function of class and has nothing to do with any ideology about how women should clothe themselves for public prayer.

In havurot and small prayer groups, as in many "alternative" congregations, anything goes. Some women in these groups dress as carefully on the High Holidays as they might if they were going to some "fancy" synagogue, and some wear jeans and sweaters. Head covering is usually optional, though most men wear *kippot* in these groups, so an egalitarian-minded woman might want to, on principle. More casual dressing is not usually considered disrespectful in these settings but as a sign that you take prayer seriously and are at services to worship and not to display yourself as an ornamental object.

PRAYER AND SPIRIT

In the past the transcendence of daily reality in religious worship was not part of many Jewish women's lives. There have been few Jewish women mystics, seers, prophets, or visionaries, at least as far as those men who transcribed the history have told us. Even in popular Jewish writing women are portrayed as practical creatures of the flesh, while men are creatures of spirit. The image of the pious Jewish woman of past generations was of a person with limited education who read psalms or *Tsena-Rena* (women's Bible stories) on Shabbat and other ritual occasions. She wasn't necessarily "holy" or deeply spiritual, but she did have a connection to Jewish religious expression which she felt was her own. With expanding education opportunities, contemporary Jewish women have been trying to stretch their spiritual experience of Judaism as well.

Jewish women are now involved in a great spiritual quest, from rewriting prayers so that they include women's experiences to challenging male definitions of female nature, from exploring the female aspects of God to unearthing the goddess-based religions that predated formal Judaism. The passion of the quest proves that for many of us, long preoccupied with the spiritual needs of the men we relate to and with the practical details of making prayer possible for others (minding the store or the children when they went to synagogue), our own spiritual needs have gone unmet.

In fiction, reminiscence, and even in Biblical tales about Jewish women in which prayer is mentioned at all, the woman praying has been associated with a task that she needs help with: a sick child, a problem in the community. In fact, the stories are often about women turning to men (rabbis) for "intercession" or interpretation of God's will. This is not very serious spirituality in Judaism, which has held that all Jews can communicate directly with God by praying devoutly and with true intention or direction.

The problem for many contemporary Jews—men as well as women—is learning to *pray*, not just to perform the prayers. But how? In Judaism we have had no nuns or female saints as role models, nor is daily religious observance yet incumbent on all Jewish women. (There's no example in Judaism parallel to the figure of a Rose Kennedy going to early Mass every morning.) Yet some women achieve a spiritual intensity regularly in their lives as Jews, through ritual, study or prayer. (See "Our Minds for Ourselves" for examples of how women are engaging in Jewish study.)

LITURGY: THE WORDS WE USE TO APPROACH THE DIVINE

No matter where a Jew prays, and no matter the gender of the worshiper, the Hebrew prayers that she or he says are sexist. Hebrew is a gender-specific language. Unlike English, in which nouns and pronouns may denote male or female (for example, king, queen), in Hebrew the parts of speech in their grammatical form have masculine or feminine endings. So the common beginning of countless Hebrew prayers in the daily and holiday liturgy—*Baruch ata adonai*—all address God as a male being. The pronoun *ata* means "you" (masculine), and *adonai* is a noun (masculine) meaning "master."

The concept these words give us—of a God exclusively male—is theologically false to Judaism, which posits that God has male and female components and that these are made manifest in the male and female humans created in God's own image. However, the exclusively masculine appellations are one reason most of us imagine God as somehow male, and therefore perhaps to imagine human males as next to godliness. If we imagine Moses as Charlton Heston every Pesach, we seem also to imagine God as some spiritual correlative of Michelangelo's Moses. God "looks like" the worshiper—that is, male. Rita M. Gross says: "Though language about God cannot really tell us about the nature of God, because of the limitations of language and the nature of God, it can tell us a great deal about those who create and use the God-language."[14]

In Jewish theology, as in liturgy, there are clear distinctions between male and female. While in prayers God is addressed as exclusively male, in Jewish mysticism the divine presence when it is manifest on earth (for instance, on the Sabbath) is female—the Shekhinah—and one welcomes "the bride of the Sabbath." Rita Gross, quoting Jewish mystical sources, says that one of the reasons Jews are living in *galut* (exile) is that male and female aspects of God have been rent asunder, alienated from each other. "When the masculine and feminine aspects of God have been reunited and the female half of humanity has been returned from exile, we will begin to have our *tikkun*. The world will be repaired."[15] As a first step in this repair, Rabbi Lynn Gottlieb refers to the Shekhinah not as some mystical female presence that comes and goes as God's manifestation on earth but as "She-who-dwells-within" each of us.

In addition to the masculine bias in God language, which is inevitable

(© JEB—Joan E. Biren)

unless the Hebrew prayers themselves are rewritten, there is the masculine bias in the content of the prayers, which is more easily corrected (and often is, by progressive readers and worshipers who just add a female component). For example, when a prayer says, "God of our fathers," the worshiper need only say instead, "God of our mothers and fathers." Similarly, when the God of Abraham, Isaac, and Jacob is called upon, one can say instead, "The God of Sarah, Rebecca, Rachel, and Leah, and of Abraham, Isaac, and Jacob." At least then we can put our foremothers back into history. And until we do, we suffer a deprivation described by post-Christian feminist theologian Mary Daly: "Women have had the power of *naming* stolen from us."[16]

In an attempt to restore the power of naming to Jewish women, a Reform movement Task Force on Equality of Women in Judaism has compiled a glossary of substitute terminology, an English-language listing of masculine terms commonly found in the Reform prayer book, with suggested substitutions, such as: "Heavenly One" for "Heavenly Father," "Ruler" for "King," "kinship" for "brotherhood."

"Glossary of Substitute Terminology"
Union of American Hebrew Congregations
838 Fifth Avenue
New York, NY 10021

Annette Daum, staff person for the task force, says: "As people of the Book, whose most revered prayer is the *Shema* ["Hear, O Israel . . ."]—the command to hear and heed the words which have shaped the religious beliefs of over half the world's population—we Jews cannot underestimate the power of words."

There are other attempts by the major denominations to eliminate (or ameliorate) sexist language in liturgy. One is the change the Conservative movement made in its 1945 *Sabbath and Festival Prayer Book,* in which the traditional prayer an observant man is supposed to say each morning was changed from "Blessed art Thou, O Lord our God, King of the Universe, Who hast not made me a gentile, a slave, a woman" to ". . . Who has Created me in His image, has made me free, and made me an Israelite." God is still "King" and "He," according to the original Hebrew, but at least some of the offense to women has been undone.[17]

The Reform movement's 1975 prayer book for weekdays, Sabbaths, and festivals—*Gates of Prayer*—is introduced by editor Chaim Stern who says:

"Our commitment in the Reform movement to the equality of the sexes is of long standing. In this book it takes the form of avoiding the use of masculine terminology exclusively, when we are referring to the human race in general."

A newer and highly praised prayer book for Shabbat and holidays comes from lay people at Beth El, a Reform congregation in Sudbury, Massachusetts. The *siddur*, entitled V*etaher Libenu* (*Purify Our Hearts*), was published in 1980. God is referred to without gender references or else androgynously, and in both English and Hebrew the anonymous authors have tried to eliminate masculine terminology and exclusively masculine references. Here the matriarchs and the patriarchs get equal billing. The *siddur is* available from:

Congregation Beth El
Hudson Road
Sudbury, MA 01776
$10.00

Women who have written their own liturgies for Jewish prayer have taken an even more radical approach. A college-based study and worship group, the Brown University Women's Minyan, was the setting that in the mid-1970s nurtured a new Shabbat prayer book, *Siddur Nashim* (*Prayer Book for Women*), by Maggie Wenig and Naomi Janowitz, in which God is referred to in specifically female terms. Originally pub lished, in excerpted form, in *Lilith*, the prayers beseech God to "Shelter us in the soft folds of your skirt" and "Cradle us." Many readers were startled by the language, and one reported, "Even though I didn't like to refer to God as a woman at first—it sounded silly, or like goddess worship—the new prayers helped me to see how absurd it is to refer to God in exclusively male terms as well. I had just gotten more used to the other way, but it's no more correct than this, and less interesting!" The prayer book is available from:

M. Wenig
198 St. James Place
Brooklyn, NY 11238
$15.00, including postage and handling

(For more on new prayers Jewish women are writing for specific occasions, see the next chapter.)

3

◆

RHYTHMS
AND CYCLES

CELEBRATING THE JEWISH CALENDAR

Shabbat

Shabbat, coming every week from sunset Friday to sundown Saturday, offers tremendous potential for establishing a rhythm of experiencing Jewish ritual on a regular basis—a whole day during which Jewish law prohibits concerning yourself with workaday cares. Especially as women's lives seem fuller than ever (we're taking on new roles without fully divesting ourselves of the old ones), "making shabbos" may appear at first to be yet another womanly burden, but can instead be a real liberation.

Equalizing the domestic routine of Shabbat is crucial. What kind of preparation is it for a day of rest if the adult females in the household are expected to do all the necessary cleaning, cooking, organizing? A better pattern to establish is to do it on Thursday night, when everyone plans to be home to participate. Or, in the rare household that can do it, everyone takes part of Friday off to cook and prepare. The only danger when you begin to introduce Shabbat—for yourself or for your family—is that you will fall back into roles you may have been conditioned to since childhood. We expect ourselves to do everything and do it perfectly, magically "creating" Shabbat for our significant others. One step at a time, and shared with others if possible, is a good way to ensure that preparing for the Sabbath will be more of a joy than a burden.

A deeper insight into Shabbat comes through a feminist filter: "On Shabbat, you take the model of slave-master, and you say that for one day

a week, you give up using people. You give up putting your image of what they are on them, and you allow them their own existence, their own being. You allow animals their own existence, the earth its own being, and you don't utilize or exploit anyone. There you have an image or relationship which is, I think, the seed for relationships between men and women . . . the sanctification of people, not according to what they do, but who they are."[1]

Since Shabbat includes three ritual meals (Friday night, Saturday lunch and *Se'udah Shlishit*, a third meal or snack late on Saturday afternoon), there are many opportunities for relating to people in a relaxed Shabbat atmosphere, trying not to focus on work-related issues or professional contacts. In addition, the three synagogue services (Friday night, Saturday morning, Saturday afternoon) and two home-based celebrations (*kabbalat* Shabbat, welcoming the Sabbath with candlelighting, and *havdalah*, ushering out the Sabbath's light) can give you so much to do and think about that the combined physical and mental activities really can make the hours of Shabbat feel like an expansion out of time.

HOW TO CREATE SHABBAT: THE BASICS

A woman at a Hebrew school parents' meeting admits: "I just don't know what to do. I have a son in the school and he comes home and he wants to do something for Shabbat and I haven't the vaguest idea what to do. Last Friday night he decided to say the prayers over the piece of whole-wheat bread I was eating. Can somebody tell me how to begin to do Shabbat—for him, but also for me?"

She wants to connect or reconnect with a tradition or a sense of identity that can come through concrete rituals regularly experienced. Fortunately Shabbat, coming so frequently, is a good vehicle for trying out what feels comfortable and what you really want to do. It's not like Pesach, for example, occurring only once a year, so that it's possible to forget from year to year what aspects of the seder you like best. And Shabbat is a great opportunity to retreat into a self you've ignored all week or to extend yourself to people—an ideal twenty-four hours in which to invite friends for a festive meal or an evening or afternoon of relaxation, if you have promised yourself not to work or do errands. *Menuchah,* a special Sabbath peace and restfulness, is achieved only by refraining from the activities that occupy and preoccupy us the rest of the week.

While there is now a prayer book—*Siddur Nashim*—that contains the prayers of the Sabbath service rewritten from the perspective of God-as-a-

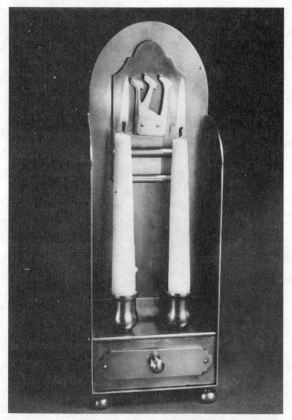

(courtesy In the Spirit gallery, New York)

female (see p. 83), there is only the route of "substitute terminology" for saying the Sabbath prayers at home. Shabbat *is* a celebration strongly associated with the feminine aspects of God. It is supposed to be our taste of paradise on earth, of what life will be like after the Shekhinah and God are reunited, according to Jewish mysticism. Even in the traditional Friday-night prayers and songs, the Sabbath is referred to as a "queen," and songs welcoming her are part of the Sabbath ritual.

Shabbat begins with the lighting of (usually) two plain white Shabbat candles. Women are obliged to light and bless these candles that signify the beginning of the Sabbath; they are thus symbolically credited with bringing on the peace and beauty of Shabbat. The lighting of the candles is supposed to be one of the three mitzvot reserved especially for women, but men living alone or without women are commanded to light candles also. Some single women do not light Shabbat candles, believing, erroneously, that it's a custom or law only for married women. Some families have a tradition of lighting a Shabbat candle for each member, and in some communities unmarried girls and women light only a single candle.

The blessing over the candles, which some women say with their heads covered and/or their eyes shaded, is recited after the candles are lit, just before sundown Friday:

Baruch ata Adonai Eloheynu melech ha-olam, asher kideshanu, be-mitzvotav vetsivanu, lehadlik ner shel Shabbat.

Blessed are you, our exalted God, Ruler of the Universe, who has sanctified our lives through your commandments, commanding us to kindle the Sabbath lights.

Superstition has it that if a woman does not light the candles before sundown (it is forbidden to start a flame after sundown, which is the moment the Sabbath begins), she will be afflicted with pain in childbirth. Similarly, lighting the Havdalah candle on Saturday evening, in the ceremony that marks the conclusion of the Sabbath and the beginning of the new week, is the province of the man of the house. Here the superstition is that a woman who lights the Havdalah candle will grow a mustache. Such superstition must have been very handy for keeping women in line. Since Friday at sundown men were usually in synagogue, engaging in communal prayer, they might not be able to light Sabbath candles on time, so women could have that obligation, and were threatened with an exclusively female curse for failing to honor it. And since men could come home from synagogue at sundown Saturday at Havdalah time, they took for themselves the obligation of performing that ceremony, and warned women away from it with a threat to their "femininity." Yet paradoxically, a woman living alone, or without a man, is commanded to make Havdalah, just as a man alone must light Shabbat candles.

The kiddush (blessing over wine) has been the province of men in most families, but it is increasingly becoming an honor shared by men and women, and is certainly performed by women creating Shabbat alone. Rabbi Irving Greenberg points out that saying kiddush on Friday night is "one of the rare occasions where the Talmud says specifically that the woman can perform the ritual for the man. However, it also says that a curse will strike the man who allows this to happen. (You can't win 'em all.) I can personally testify that a curse never struck me. (Maybe God changed Her mind.)"[2] Interestingly, here a non-obligated person can do a mitzvah for one who is obligated. Herein may lie a precedent that can be marshaled in support of having women as cantors or prayer leaders; women's as yet non-obligated status need not stand in their way even in an Orthodox setting.

The blessing over the wine (in its simple form—there's also a longer version):

(courtesy In the Spirit gallery, New York)

Baruch ata Adonai Eloheynu melech ha-olam, boreh pri ha-gafen.

Praised are you, our exalted God, Ruler of the Universe, who creates the fruit of the vine.

Another of the special mitzvot for women concerns the challah. Women have the formal obligation of remembering the destruction of the Temple in Jerusalem by breaking off a piece of the Sabbath bread dough ("challah" comes from the Hebrew word "to divide") and throwing it into the flames of the oven. Since most women now buy rather than bake their own challahs, merely providing the challah has become the women's Sabbath mitzvah, along with candlelighting.

Kiddush is followed by the blessing over the challah:

Baruch ata Adonai Eloheynu melech ha-olam ha-motzi lechem min ha-aretz.

Praised are you, our exalted God, Ruler of the Universe, who brings forth bread from the earth.

Now the Friday evening meal begins. Traditionally it's the most lavish meal of the week, with choice foods prepared for the occasion. Some people like to save special treats they've stored up during the week for this day—wine, candies, rare fruits. In keeping with the idea of Shabbat as pleasure, mystery, and an escape from time, lovemaking (between wife and husband) is a particularly sanctioned Shabbat eve activity.

"WOMAN OF VALOR"

One of the traditional Shabbat rituals of Friday evening is for the man to praise the "woman of the house," along with blessing the children. Obviously there are some problems related to this issue, especially for women making Shabbat alone. We are accustomed to seeing ourselves as the enablers for others' experience, so that it may be hard to legitimize something we do for ourselves alone. One woman questions, "What do I do when I've lit the Shabbat candles and I look around and there's no one there?"

Yet the Eyshet Chayil (Proverbs 31:10-31) traditionally chanted by the husband—"Who can find a woman of valor? Her price is far above rubies . . ."—has something to recommend it, in that it recognizes woman's competence both at home and in the business world. The problem is that most of the work praised in the verse is directed toward the smooth running of the household, assuming homemaking as women's work, and doesn't leave much room for individual spiritual growth. And there's no parallel song of praise for the man of the house—if there is one—who might even have been the one responsible for the chicken soup.

Some people, especially if they celebrate Shabbat with the same group every week—family or friends—eliminate praise for the woman of the house and substitute a round-robin report of what each person has appreciated about other members of the group that week: what was an especially nice encounter, or an especially appreciated deed. Another possibility is for women celebrating Shabbat together to sing Eyshet Chayil to one another, as praise for womankind in general.

Blessing the children at the Shabbat table has traditionally meant wishing for the boys a future in the path of Abraham, Isaac, and Jacob and for the girls that they model themselves after the foremothers Sarah, Rebecca, Rachel and Leah. More egalitarian would be to have the models less gender linked; some parents do this by blessing the children "In the traditions of our foremothers and forefathers."

Much of the children's books and classroom art we grew up with (and that are still around, alas) shows Mommy and Devorele in the kitchen and Daddy and David going off to services or holding up the kiddush cup to bless the wine on Shabbat. While few Orthodox women attend Friday evening service, real life isn't like this for many other families. The books and images just haven't caught up. Even though sometimes the names may be modernized to Jason and Jennifer, the shadows of Devorele and David loom large.

An encouraging sign is that girls getting a day-school education may be better prepared for these ritual roles than their mothers were. At one modern Orthodox day school in New York City, after a girl recited the blessing over the wine in front of the whole school at a Friday program, a rabbi told the students, "Okay, now I want you all to go home and tell your parents that girls can do it too." (A woman from Jacksonville says she likes to suggest the equalization of ritual roles by giving Bat Mitzvah celebrants both candlesticks *and* a kiddush cup as gifts.) The public statements of those Orthodox rabbis who support expanding girls' and women's ritual options are immeasurably helpful in changing the family politics that might keep females from full Shabbat participation.

HAVDALAH: SHABBAT EXITS

After sundown on Saturday one says goodbye to the departing Sabbath. The Havdalah prayer separates the holy day from the week to come. With a special braided candle one prays that the light of Shabbat will glow into the week ahead. (One tradition is for the Havdalah candle to be held high by a young girl; the height of the candle flame predicts how tall her husband will be.) There's a blessing over the wine, and everybody smells the aromatic spices held in a special Havdalah spice box—so the scents of Shabbat will outlast the day too. The Havdalah ceremony is usually performed by men, and is not a ceremony that many women do by themselves, perhaps because it revolves around the kiddush, a "man's" prayer in popular thinking. Yet a woman making Shabbat needs to usher it out, as she welcomed it in.

SHABBAT RESOURCES

A highly personal moment-by-moment account of making and celebrating Shabbat in a busy home full of children and guests is *How to Run a Traditional Jewish Household* by Blu Greenberg (Simon and Schuster, 1983). The title is in a way too modest, however. The book also includes complete guides for prayer and celebration, not only for Shabbat but for the rest of the Jewish calendar as well. One of the joys of this book is its human and honest tone as the author wrestles with the ambiguities of being a knowledgeable guide through a tradition that has often excluded her sex, suggesting the insights we will all gain as more women scholars examine Jewish subjects heretofore written about only by men. Greenberg's book is important both for the information it contains and for the fact that it is the only traditional Jewish guidebook and reference book written by a woman.

For the basic candlelighting ritual and prayers, plus a chart showing a whole year's worth of candlelighting times (computed on the time of Friday sunset), write or phone:

Lubavitch Women's Organization
770 Eastern Parkway
Brooklyn, NY 11213
(718) 774-2060

A booklet containing prayers and many Shabbat songs with which to increase the joy of Shabbat meals is a *Shiron* (songbook) available from:

National Jewish Resource Center
250 W. 57 Street, Suite 216
New York, NY 10107
$2.50

Despite its sexist title, one book must be recommended as a classic guide to the spiritual resonance of Shabbat: *The Sabbath: Its Meaning for Modern Man,* by Abraham Joshua Heschel (Harper Torchbooks, 1966).

Following the step-by-step plan of a Passover haggada, which describes and explains the order of the service, Michael Strassfeld has compiled a straightforward, easy-to-use handbook, subtitled "For Celebration and Study," which tells in an uncomplicated way what to do and how to do it. The second part of the paperback book contains texts—stories, passages from classical Jewish sources, moral tales (unfortunately, none by women)—followed by questions for discussion. The book is not only comfortable to use but helps to emphasize the blend of study and ritual experience that can fill the whole twenty-four-hour period of Shabbat with enough spiritual richness to carry over into the next six days.

A Shabbat Haggadah
by Michael Strassfeld
Institute of Human Relations Press
American Jewish Committee
165 East 56 Street
New York, NY 10022

Last but not least among Shabbat resources is *The First Jewish Catalog,* edited by Richard Siegel, Michael Strassfeld, and Sharon Strassfeld (Jewish Publication Society, 1973). Its section on observing Shabbat is a basic how-to, with every kind of information (including how to bake challah) for experiencing Shabbat. Aside from a sexism that is, one hopes, dated ("It is generally preferable to pray with a minyan, a quorum of ten men"), it's a very useful chapter on the physical *and* the spiritual dimensions of Shabbat and the connections between them. This is a wonderful guide to how you are supposed to feel and to the mood you are creating for yourself with the various meals and other activities of Shabbat.

Three books on celebrating Shabbat with young children are also a good introduction—*very* basic—for adults with no previous experience or knowledge of Shabbit rituals. The first contains simple musical settings for the prayers and songs, which are hard to find elsewhere.

Come Let Us Welcome Shabbat
by Judyth Robbins Saypol and Madeline Wikler
KAR-BEN Copies
11713 Auth Lane
Silver Spring, MD 20902

The second book, a large-format paperback, not only has prayers for Shabbat but activities for children and a very useful collection of short stories and Bible tales relevant to Shabbat: *The Shabbat Catalogue*, by Ruth F. Brin (Ktav Pub. House, 1978). An adult might like to read the book not only to be able to retell the stories to kids but also to have some midrashic, or story, background for her own understanding.

A third book for children is *Shabbat Can Be* by Raymond A. Zwerin and Audrey Friedman Marcus (Union of American Hebrew Congregations, 1979), which is unusual for its illustrations of women and men, girls and boys sharing Shabbat roles. All the members of the family sing the kiddush, not just the father, and women and men are shown praying and celebrating together.

SHABBAT IN SYNAGOGUE

In Reform and some Conservative congregations Friday-evening services in synagogue usually take place in the late evening, after dinner; in Orthodox synagogues they are held as part of the regular late-afternoon service and precede dinner. Since Shabbat candles must be kindled before sundown, they are lit either before going to synagogue or by someone who stays at home (and we know who that has traditionally been).

Reform and Conservative synagogues have tried to make a special place for women during Shabbat by instituting the Sisterhood Sabbath, through which women participate by leading certain songs or prayers or by lighting candles before the whole congregation. These events may give women a chance to practice their synagogue skills in a safe milieu but smack of tokenism and have the obvious disadvantage of setting women apart from the congregation as a whole. Dr. Trude Weiss-Rosmarin has pointed out that the Sisterhood Sabbath, "like Sisterhood, *is* segregation and discrimination." Why not have them participate as full worshipers and prayer leaders all season long?

Better than this, the New York Federation of Reform Synagogues suggests using a new egalitarian, gender-free service adapted from *Gates of Prayer*, the new Reform Sabbath prayer book. The booklet, *Shabbat Evening Service*, was prepared by the Federation's Liturgy Committee and is available from:

New York Federation of Reform Synagogues
Union of American Hebrew Congregations
838 Fifth Avenue
New York, NY 10021

Kiddush Levana—*a blessing of the moon. Papercut by Deborah Ugoretz.*

For a listing of women's prayer groups that meet regularly to celebrate Shabbat, consult the Task Force on Jewish Woman [*sic*], p. 69.

Rosh Chodesh: Rediscovering Ceremonies for Welcoming the New Month

Like Shabbat, most of the calendar celebrations in Judaism—marking seasonal blessings or remembering historical events—are holidays on which men have traditionally performed most of the ritual. With the exception of candlelighting, most of what women have been expected to do falls into the "enabler" category: preparing the festive meals, giving the home its legendary "special atmosphere," and so on.

An exception to traditional male dominance of holiday ritual is the one holiday especially for women—so it's not surprising that it hasn't received much attention until its recent rediscovery by feminists. This is Rosh Chodesh, the first day of the month—which, since the Hebrew months are computed on a lunar calendar, falls at the new moon, always considered a special day for women.

Legends based on the Talmudic story of the Creation say that the moon, now smaller than the sun, will some day be restored to equality with it. God has rewarded women in this world with the observance of the new moons, and in the next world we are destined to be renewed like new moons. Our monthly cycles are said to renew us just as the moon is new each month, and feminists draw parallels between the moon's future equality with the sun and the equality for women that is to come.[3]

Celebrations of Rosh Chodesh have gained great popularity among women exploring Jewish rituals and spirituality and looking for something especially appropriate to women but fully within the Jewish tradition (as opposed to those women who are exploring witchcraft and goddess cults). The rediscovery of Rosh Chodesh in the past ten years is an example of the blending of a piece of traditional Judaism with women's present needs. The fact that the holiday does come out of the tradition brings women's observation of it into mainstream Judaism and out of the category of what some might consider mere invention.

There are several ways of marking the new month, or new moon. One woman has breakfast in bed and takes time for meditation and private prayer. In a group setting, observances have ranged from the bureaucratic/communal to the mystical/personal/communal.

An example of the incorporation of the Rosh Chodesh ceremony that might have adaptive uses even in Jewish women's organizations occurred at a luncheon meeting of a Task Force on the Role of the Jewish Woman in a Changing Society, sponsored by the New York Federation of Jewish Philanthropies. Arlene Agus gave a *dvar Torah* (short instructive talk on Jewish law) on the holiday and its significance, and all the food served was round (quiche, pies), signifying fertility and femaleness. It's a tradition to eat round food and new fruits at Rosh Chodesh, to refrain from your usual work on at least half of the day of the new moon, and to incorporate certain practices into the celebration itself. These include giving charity (*tzedakah*), which on this occasion might appropriately be earmarked for women's causes or projects; lighting a candle or candles (a candle floating in a dish of water is especially lovely and moonlike); a feast featuring at least some round foods and the recital of special prayers for the new month. A study session or discussion on the holidays or themes of the month ahead might follow.

Though many Jewish feminists speak of Rosh Chodesh as a beautiful opportunity to use expressive ritual that is removed from the male-symbol world of the synagogue, other women disagree. A Florida woman in her fifties, well educated as a Jew, is angry at the renewed popularity of the holiday. She says: "A big deal—a holiday that has not much signifi-cance in the range of Jewish celebrations, so the women get to have it. We get to have a ceremony late in the day—a half holiday is all that it is officially. After we've cleaned the whole house, fed everybody, then we get to have a little holiday all to ourselves. The men have thrown us a little bone."

Women who are drawn to celebrate Rosh Chodesh describe it as a time for renewal, for beginning projects and new books, for wearing new clothes and eating foods that have not yet been sampled that season.

(The different responses to celebrating Rosh Chodesh as a women's holiday are paralleled in other forms of religious observation too, notably in women's positive and negative responses to mikveh. Many women "on

Each year at Rosh Hashanah a group of women gather at a pier in Manhattan to cast bread crumbs into the water to celebrate tashlich, *the traditional sending forth of one's sins. E. M. Broner and Lilly Rivlin write a feminist ceremony for* tashlich, *including prayers for the new moon and for forgiveness and purifica-tion.* (Lilly Rivlin)

the way up"—that is, becoming more informed about Jewish ritual—are attracted to observances that do not have for them the same negative or sexist connotations they might have for women "on the way down"—once observant but no longer so.)

The ceremony itself, usually celebrated in a small group, could be held on a rotating basis as a small monthly party of friends. Independent groups and friendship circles celebrate Rosh Chodesh each month (except at the New Year, when Rosh Chodesh falls on Rosh Hashanah). For information, check the listing of women's *minyans* in the Networking Directory.

A storyteller named Penina Villenchik Adelman who has participated in Rosh Hodesh groups and creative rituals for Jewish women has written a handbook called *Miriam's Well: Rituals for Jewish Women Around the Year*. For more information, write:

BIBLIO PRESS
P.O. Box 22
Fresh Meadows, NY 11365

The article that inspired many women to involve themselves in this special holiday is by Arlene Agus: "This Month Is for You: Observing Rosh Hodesh as a Woman's Holiday," in *The Jewish Woman: New Perspectives* (New York: Schocken, 1976), edited by Elizabeth Koltun.

Rosh Hashanah and Yom Kippur

The traditional "days of awe," when Jews look back over the past year in self-evaluation, are holy days of equal significance to women and to men. The one difference in traditional observance of Rosh Hashanah (the Jewish New Year) is that women are not obligated to hear the shofar blown, since this was considered a time-bound activity that a woman might find it a hardship to attend. In practice, most women do hear the shofar.

The ten days between Rosh Hashanah and Yom Kippur (Day of Atonement) are days of repentance for wrongdoings one might have committed in the past year, and for asking and granting forgiveness for wrongs perpetrated or received. Every year novelist E. M. Broner and filmmaker Lilly Rivlin gather with a group of women on one of New York City's piers to celebrate the new year, to cast off sins, to throw symbolic crumbs upon the waters, to shout: "Our Mothers, Our Queens, forgive us."

This is also a time for resolving to do things differently in the year to come. While the High Holidays have not been marked in any particular way by most women (though some women are taking on responsibility for leading the important High Holiday services in synagogues that accept this), one way women might begin the new year is by meeting in groups during the days of repentance in order to evaluate what progress Jewish women have made in the past year and what advances should be striven for in the months to come. This period could become an important time of agenda-setting by women who often toil for change year in and year out without having specific occasions on which to evaluate their good work, examine their mistakes, and heal any wounds inflicted or received in the struggle for women's liberation.

Like Pesach, which is family-centered, these High Holy Days can be a very painful time for Jewish women alone, whatever their circumstances. Some synagogues and communities provide communal meals and festivities (see "Single, Jewish and Female," p. 300), but the development of women's self-evaluation sessions would be another means for women to define themselves in a Jewish context without being attached to a nuclear family.

Succot

Succot, the fall festival for which one is supposed to build a succah (actually an open-to-the-sky shed) and live in it for eight days, is a holiday that is focused on the natural world, a harvest festival celebrating the bounty of nature and the glories of a not-yet-stifled admiration of the fecund earth, which seems to hark back to a Judaism that isn't dependent on a historical event with exclusively male heroes. The pagan quality may be there, but Succot is also a commemoration of the rough shelters the Children of Israel lived in when they came out of Egypt and wandered forty years in the desert before entering the land of Canaan. The holiday focuses on eating meals in the succah and praying in the synagogue with a *lulav* (set of branches of three specific kinds of plants) and an *etrog* (yellowish, citronlike fruit with a lovely rich scent).

One tension in celebrating Succot may come from the dichotomy between the male/historical provenance of the holiday and its female/harvest-festival origins. Some feminists are eagerly attaching themselves to this holiday as a celebration of Mother Earth, while others object strenuously to a definition of "historical" as quintessentially male and fecundity as female, claiming that this again makes women a group apart.

Meanwhile, the traditional celebrations of Succot can discriminate against women in another way. Owning a *lulav* is one of the mitzvot that is not required of women. In practice, this has meant that while the men's section of an Orthodox synagogue is full of waving *lulavim* (plural), women who want to take on this mitzvah can feel very obtrusive. "It's very hard to be a role breaker," says one, "and to be the only woman in the whole women's section with a *lulav* feels very uncomfortable." Feminist psychologist Nechama Liss-Levinson, herself an Orthodox Jew, suggests that women simply buy their own sets of *lulav* and *etrog*, and make a point of using them, instead of just having a "family" set used by the man. To the objection that the sets are expensive, she counters by pointing out that families assume that it's reasonable, in fact obligatory, to buy them for all boys over the age of thirteen, and that women should insist upon this too. For young children, she proposes that families purchase what she did for her daughters, "starter sets—a *lulav* and a lemon, if an *etrog* is too costly— and let girls experience owning and using them from a very early age."

According to Halachah, women are also excused (read, excluded) from the mitzvah of "dwelling" in the succah.[4] One rabbi in an Orthodox synagogue in the Bronx was reported to have told his congregants a few years ago, "The succah will be very crowded at lunch today, so will the women please not come in." The women and men reporting the story boycotted the synagogue from that day on. Most Orthodox synagogue succot, and of course all those in non-Orthodox synagogues, welcome women and men.

Another aspect of the holiday that girls and women are coming to celebrate more and more is the tradition of inviting guests into the succah for meals and visits. These guests need not be living people; Succot is a time for inviting more mystical guests (*ushpitzin*) as well. Invitees might include Biblical women, political activists from recent centuries, and medieval women poets, invoking their names and describing their special attributes.

For the formula to welcome *ushpitzin* and for a "new-age" guide to Succot and the other holidays, see Arthur Waskow's *Seasons of Our Joy: A Handbook of Jewish Festivals* (Bantam, 1982). To remind yourself of women from the past you might want to invite into your succah, consult *Written out of History*, by Sondra Henry and Emily Taitz. Also useful is a wonderful dramatic reading of prayers and poems written by Jewish women from Biblical times onward composed by Marcia Cohn Seigel; "The Jewish Woman: A Portrait in Her Own Words" is available from

National Federation of Temple Sisterhoods
838 Fifth Avenue
New York, NY 10021

One of the most interesting descriptions of the holiday's background and practices is given in:

(Bill Aron)

A Guide to Sukkot
by Irving Greenberg
National Jewish Resource Center
250 W. 57 Street
New York, NY 10019

An agreeable story for children is Marilyn Hirsch's *The House on the Roof* (Bonim Books, 1976), in which a grandfather who lives alone builds a succah on the roof of his apartment building. He sews for it, decorates it, and cooks meals for his grandchildren to eat in it. The story itself is pleasant, and it's a welcome change to see a man in a domestic, nurturing role.

Simchat Torah
At the end of Succot, Jews begin Simchat Torah, the "rejoicing in the Torah." People dance around the synagogue with the Torah scrolls, and there is much joy in concluding the past year's reading and beginning the

cycle again. Both the night before Simchat Torah (*erev* Simchat Torah, since in the Hebrew calendar days go from sundown to sundown) and during the day's service also, everyone who wants to may take a Torah scroll and march around the synagogue or in the street. Orthodox women or those who belong to very conservative Conservative synagogues have been for the most part closed out of these celebrations because of the traditional separation of women and men during prayers. Their role was to provide the attending children with apples, candy, and colored banners or flags to wave while they accompanied the Torah dancers. Even the banners the girls and boys carry today often show only boys and men—no females at all!

Women have wrought two changes in recent years which have brought them from observer status into the arena (or the street) as direct participants: they have insisted on being fully active in mixed *hakafot* (dancing circles with the Torah) wherever this was possible, and they have organized separate women's *hakafot* in synagogues where mixed participation would not be accepted (in most Orthodox synagogues, for example). In 1980 some sixty strictly observant women in Jerusalem challenged the status quo by staging a " 'women's only' Torah reading and dancing circle in protest against the barring of women from the annual official Simchat Torah celebrations."[5]

In America one woman, a member of a very rigid Conservative congregation with a rabbi who flatly refused to permit women to hold and dance with the Torah scrolls, finally gave up her battle and joined an egalitarian Conservative synagogue where women and men share all ritual honors. "The next Simchat Torah was a watershed for me. I marched around inside the synagogue feeling a little self-conscious but very happy, as happy as I'd been with these 'parades' as a child. When the dancers spilled out into the street, the real excitement began for me. A man, a stranger, who had been dancing with a Torah scroll, came over to me and put the Torah into my hands and put his *tallis* over my shoulders so that I could be completely a *davening*, singing Jew. *That* I had never felt, even as a child."

Chanukah

Chanukah, with its story about a successful revolt against the Hellenistic Syrians who were occupying the land of Israel in the second century B.C.E., is in some ways the quintessentially male celebration of a Jewish historical event. Seven men (brothers, literally) plan, lead, and fight the revolt. They fight in the hills around the town of Modi'in and then go to the Temple in Jerusalem. There they find a cruse of oil intended to last for a day, but it miraculously burns for eight days (thus the eight days of the holiday).

Unlike Passover, for example, which also celebrates a historical event but which has become paradigmatic of many different struggles for liberation, including those of blacks and women, Chanukah has never come to signify more than itself—a historical event in the ongoing struggle of the Jewish people to achieve religious and political feedom in a culture dominated by non-Jews. In fact, this is a festival but not a holy day. Its main significance in our time may have to do more with its calendar location than with any message inherent in the celebration itself. It is the holiday that children say is their favorite, and it gets tremendous advertising and media attention, at least in North America, as a Jewish parallel to Christmas—which, of course, it's not. The holiday, celebrated equally by female and male, includes the lighting of Chanukah candles (often by children), spinning *dreidles* (tops) and playing games of chance, and eating fried foods (pancakes, doughnuts) in commemoration of the oil in the Temple.

Whatever the reasons, Chanukah is one of the few markers on the Jewish calendar that have not proved fruitful ground for Jewish women looking for a usable past. The only traditional Chanukah tale featuring a woman is the story of Hannah and her seven sons. The same forces that were persecuting the Maccabee brothers and other Jews ordered Hannah's children to eat swine flesh (forbidden by Jewish law) or die. After the first six had been put to death for refusing, Hannah was asked to encourage the youngest to spare his own life by eating the nonkosher food; instead she encouraged him to follow the example of his brothers. The story shows a woman willing to die for her faith rather than fighting for it, in contrast to the swashbuckling exploits of the Maccabees.

One of the few attempts to personalize the holiday for girls is a short story for children, "Elektra the Maccabee," by Elizabeth Levy and Aviva Cantor, in *Lilith* #2 (1977).

Tu B'Shevat

The New Year for Trees, Tu B'Shevat, is a planting or sowing festival, parallel in some ways to the harvest festival of Succot in the fall. It occurs on the fifteenth day of the month of Shevat, which puts it in January or February of the Gregorian calendar. In most parts of North America, it's hard to imagine planting anything in the dead of winter, but in Israel at this time of year the first almond blossoms are beginning to appear on the trees.

Present-day holiday observances include eating new fruits (or the first

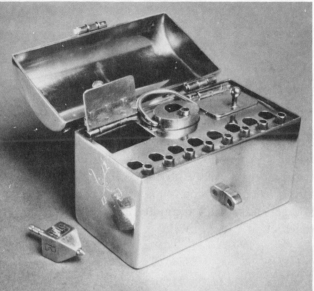

A portable Chanukah kit in miniature, including oil lamp and dreidle, the perfect item for a woman who is traveling during the holiday. (courtesy In the Spirit gallery, New York)

(© Robert L. Kern, 1981)

fruits of the season) and planting trees in Israel by proxy, "buying" a tree or trees through the Jewish National Fund. It's also a holiday that has appeared to some women to be a celebration of fruitfulness, procreation, involvement with "mother" earth and her generative qualities.

Bringing Tu B'Shevat celebrations into a contemporary context, activists have used it as an occasion for teach-ins on respecting the earth, conservation issues, freezing the buildup of nuclear arms, and, in the early seventies, on the refoliation of Southeast Asia. Although no formal celebrations for women have yet evolved, at least one young woman has used this holiday, with its themes of generativity and fecundity, as the basis for her Orthodox Bat Mitzvah celebration. (See p. 137.)

Purim

Purim, which falls on the fourteenth day of the Hebrew month of Adar (usually mid-March), is one of the few Jewish holidays celebrating the actions and role of a woman. The Biblical text in which the Purim story appears is called Megillat Esther—the Scroll of Esther—and is one of the

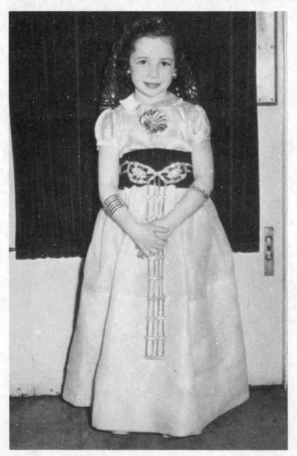

The author as Queen Esther, Purim 1950.

rare books of the Hebrew Scriptures to bear a woman's name. (This is also one text for which women traditionally could be the public readers, sometimes before mixed groups.)

Despite the centrality of Esther to the Purim tale, the story puzzles, intrigues, and angers Jewish women who read it or celebrate it with a critical eye. Briefly, this is the story, which all Jews are instructed to hear read aloud each year on Purim: Persia (the Biblical Shushan) was ruled thousands of years ago by King Ahasuerus, an absolute monarch. To impress a gathering of reveling nobles he sends for his wife, Vashti, commanding her to flaunt her beauty, naked, before the assembly. Vashti refuses (no reason specified), and is sent away; the Midrash, or expanded commentary, adds that she was killed. The king, after an extensive search for a new wife, selects the Jew Esther, the cousin of Mordecai. She becomes queen, never revealing her origins. But when Haman, a "wicked, wicked man," counselor to the king, throws lots (*pur-im* in Hebrew) to determine on what day he will organize a massacre of all the Jews in Persia, Esther takes advantage of her good relationship with the king to ward off disaster. Following instructions from Mordecai, she uses Ahasuerus' love for her to save her people. In the end Haman is hanged, Mordecai is promoted, and the Jews of Persia live.

Esther, in the great tradition of Rebecca and other Jewish heroines, uses power only indirectly and has to rely on sexual stratagems with the king to save her people. It is definitely her intervention that saves the Persian Jews, but she is counseled by Mordecai, and in the end he outshines her. This undercutting of Esther's leadership role is one troubling aspect of the Purim story. Mordecai is much honored at the conclusion of the story, whereas Esther has no ongoing role in the government; after her heroism she is expected to return to her previous cameo role as object to the king.

More exciting than Esther in the disturbance she causes contemporary readers is the character of Vashti, who has been resurrected of late by Jewish feminists combing Biblical writings for female role models. For example, Mary Gendler has contributed "The Restoration of Vashti" to *The Jewish Woman: New Perspectives,* Susan Dworkin has turned Vashti's story into a radio drama with the unbeatable title "The Persian Version," and one educator has developed a feminist approach to studying and teaching the Purim story; see p. 190.

Vashti refused to display herself in front of the king's courtiers. One of the chamberlains comments, "Not against the king alone has Vashti done wrong, but also . . . against all the people. . . . For this deed of the queen will become known to all the women, so that they will despise their husbands in their eyes, when it shall be reported: King Ahasuerus ordered Vashti the queen to be brought into his presence, but she would not come."

So Vashti was banished in order to maintain men's dominance over women! And a decree went out across the land concerning the banishment so that "all wives will show respect to their husbands . . . from the great to the small." Vashti, like Lilith (the woman created simultaneously with Adam and intended as his equal), defied male authority and suffered for her courage. In some ways she is more appealing a character than the obedient Esther, doing her cousin's bidding, though Esther is recognized as "a redeemer."

Traditional joyous Purim celebrations include giving charity and exchanging edible treats with friends. It is a good time to give charity to women's causes, to discuss the contrasting natures of the two women in the story, and to introduce feminist satire via the *Purimspiel*, traditionally the funny and mocking *commedia dell' arte* that in many groups has come to be incorporated into the post-*megillah*-reading revelry.

Purim celebrations often take the form of masquerades, both for children and for adults. The story's message for females reveals itself in the costumes children choose to wear to these parties. With the exception of clowns and other standard types unrelated to the story but found at every costume party, girls dress up only as Esther. No one has ever reported seeing a child come to a Purim party as Vashti. Boys will dress as the foolish king (he may be silly, but he has the crown), as the wicked Haman (a good role for a child who is longing to act up), or as the revered and wise Mordecai. There are at least three roles acceptable for boys, even though one of them is clearly the villain of the piece. But the girls are always Esther.

Storyteller and rabbi Lynn Gottlieb has called the Purim celebration "the time for putting on the mask to speak the truth." For us as adult women, it may be time to consider the truth-telling capabilities in the Vashti role the next time we plan Purim disguises.

Pesach

The emblem of Passover for many women has been plain hard work. One year my mother-in-law, coming out of the synagogue kitchen, where she and the other women of the congregation had been slaving away to prepare a communal seder, asked, "Rabbi, for this we came out of Egypt?"

Passover (Pesach) has been a holiday marked by labor-intensive ad-

*Arlene Agus in costume,
reading the Scroll of Esther.*
(Bill Aron)

vance preparations, including ridding the cupboards of all grain products and leavening and changing everyday china for the particular sets used only at Passover time. A revealing scene in the Joyce Chopra–Claudia Weil film *Joyce at 34* shows Joyce sitting at her mother's Passover seder table, watching as her mother exhausts herself serving everyone—as if this were the natural order of things!

Feminists have begun to use Passover, which is the celebration of the freeing of the children of Israel from their slavery in Egypt, as a model for the liberation of women. And in fact the telling of the story of the liberation from Egypt, which is the central part of the Passover seder, or ritual meal, is a classic tale of oppression and freedom, with obvious parallels to feminism and to other liberation struggles. Like contemporary feminists, the Israelites first had to recognize the nature of their own oppression, after which some of them still would have preferred familiar slavery to a risky, unknown new life.

Greater egalitarianism in many Jewish homes should in time lead to a complete sharing of all the pre-Pesach duties, and this is no minor change in relation to this holiday. Freedom, like charity, begins at home. It may be easier to equalize some of the ritual around the seder table than to try

The Empty Chair, *a film about a woman conducting a Passover seder with her family after her divorce, highlights the uneasiness many women feel when they first take on a ritual role previously played by men only.* (Halcyon Films, a division of Spielman-Magilnick Communications, Inc.)

to equalize the burden of the many hours of preparation for the holiday. Our daughters and sons who see their mothers doing all the laborious preparation won't have that sight erased when Mom raises the kiddush cup. Though it will be harder to do, perhaps making the work force more inclusive this Pesach should be a goal as urgent as making other changes.

Jewish women have experimented with a number of ways to make the Passover experience relevant to their growing consciousness of themselves as liberated people. Some possibilities are: (1) holding separate, women-only feminist seders, sometimes as "model seders" and also on the second or third night of the holiday, after the more traditional "family" seder(s) have taken place; (2) writing alternative, or feminist, haggadot; (3) "mainstreaming," or incorporating "women's" content into the traditional seder: for example, researching and discussing the role of specific women in the Exodus story; (4) developing new rituals connecting Jewish women to their own past, and discussing how they feel connected to and also liberated from those past experiences, much as the Jewish people as a whole feel part of and yet simultaneously freed from the experience of slavery in Egypt.

1. Perhaps the best known (or maybe just the most written-about, because so many writers attend) is the feminist seder convened each year in

New York by E. M. Broner and Phyllis Chesler, where "We honor our mothers and grandmothers. We honor the women who only cooked and served at seders throughout the centuries and in our own lives. We ask four questions about female destiny and deliverance and recite ten plagues of women's oppression [one of these last year was a plague on the publishing industry]. We drink four cups of wine, toasting our own redemption and our daughters' bright futures."[6]

2. Many feminist hagadas are written for use by the small groups that compiled them and are privately circulated. Here are two fine ones that are available to a broader audience. One is the hagada used originally at the Broner/Chesler feminist seders, *The Stolen Legacy*, by E. M. Broner and Naomi Nimrod which will appear with other Broner rituals in *The Ceremonial Woman*. A Xerox copy can be ordered from:

E. M. Broner
40 West 22 Street
New York, NY 10011
$3.00

Particularly noteworthy is a new hagada prepared by Aviva Cantor, who previously authored *The Jewish Liberation Hagada* and *Jewish Women's Hagada*. This one is entitled *An Egalitarian Hagada* and solves several problems of earlier hagadot. First, it has the story told at the Passover seder, eliminating the problem encountered at seders where there are several different hagadot circulating, with few of the "alternative" ones able to be used on their own. More important, this hagada both gives the contemporary relevance of Passover to women and highlights women's role in the original story. It presents both women and men in the Exodus story, so it works well with groups mixed in gender and age. The hagada appeared in a special section of *Lilith* magazine and can be ordered from:

Lilith Magazine
Hagada Department
250 West 57 Street
New York, NY 10019
$4.00

What all the new women-authored hagadas have in common is a desire to move away from the male-biased language and content (for example, the Four Sons) of the traditional Passover hagada and to highlight the participation of certain women in moving along the Passover narrative.

3. It says in the traditional hagada: *Haray zeh meshubach*—Praise is due unto the person who adds to the story. Many hagadas, therefore, now incorporate prayers for victims of the Holocaust or for Soviet Jews. In this tradition, women have taken to adding to the seder readings, songs, prayers, and historical connections about women. These insertions include readings from *The Diary of Anne Frank*; tales of the role that the brave Miriam, sister of Moses, played in saving her brother by setting his cradle into the bulrushes, and dancing after the Israelites crossed to freedom over the Red Sea; and a resurrection of the stories of the midwives Shifra and Puah who were the first to disobey Pharaoh's decree that male infants be slaughtered at birth.

For a selection of some of these and clues as to where they can best be inserted into the traditional hagada, see Reena Sigman Friedman's "Why Is This Passover Different from All Other Passovers," in *Lilith* #3. A reprint is available for $2.50 from *Lilith* magazine.

4. The new rituals surrounding Pesach are those that are unconnected to anything in the Passover hagada as we knew it from the past but that give an added dimension to the holiday. One such practice is to have seder participants describe Jewish women in their lives who have been models for their own freedom. Jacqueline Zeff tells of a recent seder in Detroit: "Degania chapter of Pioneer Women re-created our own feminist seder

Seated on cushions on the floor, washing one another's hands, linking women's liberation and Jewish liberation, a group of women gather in New York each year for a feminist seder led by E. M. Broner and Phyllis Chesler (R). (Lilly Rivlin)

by 'setting a place' for the women special in our lives, in the spirit of Judy Chicago's work. Members and their mothers brought the fish pot, the hand-crocheted tablecloth, the fish knife treasured by a granddaughter in America as it was by the grandmother who brought it from Europe many years ago; some women brought a memory, a photograph . . . a song."[7]

Despite all these joyous additions and innovations, however, there are still special Passover pitfalls for women.

WOMEN ALONE

Because Passover is primarily celebrated at home, with the seder story and a festive meal, it is the most do-it-yourself holiday of the year. For women living alone it can sometimes be uncomfortable to be the perpetual guest, always invited by others. (It's a mitzvah to invite those who have no place to go to share Pesach with you.) One solution: have your own Pesach seder anyway. Invite friends and relatives to your house this year. There is no law that says you have to have a man or a marriage (or grandchildren) to entitle you to make a seder (and to lead it).

One Boston woman, from a traditional family and recently divorced, confessed that she was doing nothing for Passover. "My mother was widowed years ago, I'm an only child, and my husband and I split a few months ago. How can I have Pesach? We don't have a man to be at the head of the table." This woman, despite her knowledge, felt that a man had to lead the seder. She was perfectly serious and perfectly sad. Another woman says she wants to lead the seder but doesn't know how. Do not do this to yourself. You can perform all the seder rituals yourself. Just read through any hagada; even the ones they give away free in supermarkets (look next to the matzah display) have complete instructions. One joy of the seder (which means "order" in Hebrew) is that it's easy to follow.

For mothers who are single parents the situation can be awkward, especially if children have been accustomed to having Daddy at the head of the table doing the whole number, with various family members reading aloud or performing at his bidding—the patriarchal model. A Philadelphia woman, just before the first seder she has prepared as a single parent, says "My table preparations are in order, but my emotions are in disarray."[8]

WOMEN AT A MIXED SEDER

Sue Levi Elwell, a teacher of Jewish women's studies and soon to be ordained as a Reform rabbi, describes a seder with her students: "Like many Jewish women, the women present had always been denied the privilege of leading the seder and had consequently abrogated any responsibility for understanding the power of this ritual."

When women do have ritual skills, they're sometimes not given the opportunity to use them. Aviva Cantor vividly describes her response at a seder of men and women, friends and colleagues: "All the *men* got Hebrew parts to read when we were sharing in the readings from the hagada. No women. The host 'forgot' that I had an excellent Jewish education and speak Hebrew. No offense—he just forgot. Meanwhile the men were breaking their teeth over the readings. But the host's assumption had been, 'You've got male gonads, you can read Hebrew.' "

One way around this is to organize seders yourself so that you have a voice in how things are done. If you want to participate at a mixed seder and you're being overlooked, speak out: "I really like this next passage. I'd like to read it." One of the great things about most seders is their informality, especially as the addition of innovative rituals and passages becomes more common, even among traditionalists.

There are even records and tapes with tunes of the Pesach prayers and songs available through any synagogue gift shop or a Hebrew bookstore (see the Networking Directory).

Some synagogues offer model seders to people preparing for the holiday. Call synagogues in your area or look for announcements in the Jewish press. Check Hebrew schools also, which usually have model seders for the students.

Shavuot

Shavuot, which comes forty-nine days after Passover, is celebrated as the holiday when the Jews received the Torah at Mount Sinai, as a marking of the first (summer) harvest, and as the occasion for reading the Book of Ruth. Women as well as men received the Torah at Mount Sinai and, according to tradition, are specially instructed to be present in synagogue on the morning of Shavuot, when traditional congregations read portions of all the books of the Torah after a night of study.

Since the experience at Sinai is considered the moment of the "giving of the Law," some women have taken Shavuot as the occasion for examining women's relationship to Jewish law. To mark this season a group of women active in the Reform movement published, for International Women's Year in 1978, a feminist *Commentary on the Ten Commandments and the Book of Ruth*. This pamphlet is a useful consciousness-raiser, or trigger for discussion, on the whole issue of equality for women in Judaism. The Ten Commandments may be the only "Jewish" text that most Jews are at least partially familiar with. We usually assume that they

refer equally to men and to women. The comments here indicate otherwise; for example, they reinterpret "Thou shalt not steal" in the light of
the present feeling many women have that their names and sometimes
their very identities have been stolen from them. Similarly, in looking at
the commandment to create a day of rest, the commentary here points out
that the original text frees men—even slaves—and beasts of burden from
work on the Sabbath, yet never mentions women, for whom Shabbat
often means *more* work. The reinterpretation calls for, among other
things, a more equitable reassignment of household tasks. While the text
is sometimes a little heavy-handed, the insights are useful.

We read the Book of Ruth at Shavuot not only because of its link to
harvesting but also because it tells of someone who voluntarily takes on
the laws of Israel. Ruth, a Moabite convert to Judaism, is a childless
widow who follows Naomi, her widowed mother-in-law, to her own land:
"Whither thou goest I will go. Your people shall be my people, your God
shall be my God." Ruth supports Naomi by reaping the grain left over in
the corners of the fields of Boaz, a relative of Naomi's. (The story also
touches on the necessity for giving charity, of leaving some of one's own
harvest for the poor to gather.) Ruth ends up marrying Boaz and becomes

*"So Naomi returned, and Ruth her daughter-in-law with her . . . and they came to
Bethlehem in the beginning of the barley harvest" (Ruth 1:22), from Tsirl Waletzky's
narrative cycle of papercuts illustrating the story which is read at Shavuot.*

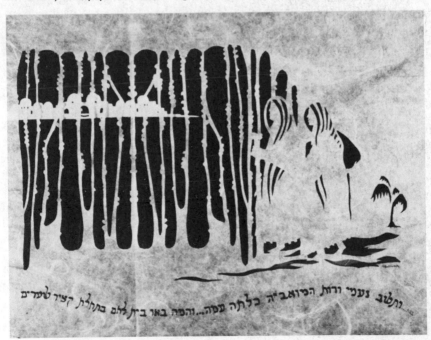

the foremother of King David; from this line the Messiah is supposed to be descended.

The story is an exquisite one of loyalty between women and also of the passion of the convert; because of this story, many women who convert to Judaism take Ruth as their Hebrew name. With insights into the character of the Biblical Ruth as a role model for Jewish women, Nessa Rapoport welcomes a newborn Jewish girl named Ruth, born to her friends Richard and Jeanne Siegel on Shavuot:

> What I saw in Ruth was a woman who chose a path of devotion, who took a risk toward the unknown and uncertain because the certainty of love so filled her that she could carry it with her into foreignness. A stranger to God and to the people she chose, she was no stranger to herself. The Torah is full of examples of people, even righteous people, who hesitate, who lose themselves, who change their minds. Ruth is unswerving. And yet she is never rigid. She in her faith can live in dailiness and find her openings there . . . Her radiant courage transforms not only her own life but all the lives she touches—Naomi's from bitter to sweet, Boaz' in *chesed* [lovingkindness], and ours, in that out of this woman's daily life comes our ultimate vision, the messianic line, the dash into eternity that impels us forward. It pleases me that Ruth's path was through love, through relation to human beings first, because I think that it is an example of a way to transmute what is considered a woman's weakness—living through relationships—into greatness.
>
> The second thing I saw in Ruth was a model for choosing, how this woman who chose us, our people, our faith, was honored by divine history in a way that those born to chosenness were not. . . .
>
> It is traditional to welcome a child into the community and hope that she will be privileged in Torah, the marriage canopy, and good deeds. The Ruth of the Bible chose Torah and it chose her back, she married in its honor, and her *ma'asim tovim* [good deeds], her acts of *chesed* are what earned her her place and brought her a fruitful, blessed life. No matter what path our Ruth chooses, no matter how she creates a way, she has begun her life as a chosen child; she was brought into the world in love, and will learn love by what surrounds her. What greater way to celebrate Shavuot, season of the giving of the Torah, the wedding of the people of Israel with our God, and the traditional birthday of King David and Messiah in his name, than to welcome a new soul into the community of Israel and pray that she in her life of *chesed* will bring us one step closer to *tikkun olam*.

The holiday of Shavuot has taken on yet another layer of meaning for Jewish women in the last century. The Reform movement, with its origins in nineteenth-century Germany and the Enlightenment, decided to do away with Bar Mitzvah entirely and institute a confirmation ceremony at Shavuot for teen-aged girls and boys, usually after they had completed a course of religious education. The ceremony confirms them as responsible Jews. Both Bar and Bat Mitzvah are now celebrated in many Reform congregations (see p. 134), and some non-Reform congregations have adopted confirmation as a graduation ceremony from a Hebrew high school program. But initial connection of confirmation with equality for women in ritual Judaism is something we want to hold on to and perhaps build into contemporary Shavuot celebrations for adults as well as for teen-agers.

In the Northwest, one havurah chose Shavuot as the appropriate time to "ordain" women as spiritual leaders of the community. Havurah members held an outdoor retreat, and complete with ceremony and certificate honored Shonna Husbands Halkin as a leader chosen "by the will of the people." The language used to describe her was that used for the Biblical judge Deborah: *Eshet Chazon, moledet shel neshamah*—woman of vision, midwife of the soul.

Shavuot and its meaning are discussed from a women's perspective in:

Commentary on the Ten Commandments and the Book of Ruth
Task Force on Equality of Women in Judaism
New York Federation of Reform Synagogues
838 Fifth Avenue
New York, NY 10021

For a general commentary on the history and customs of Shavuot, including a discussion of Ruth, see:

Guide to Shavuot
by Rabbi Irving Greenberg
National Jewish Resource Center
250 West 57 Street
New York, NY 10107

Greenberg also has interesting insights into the food we eat on this holiday. We express the connection between the season of the giving of the Law (human historical time) and the season of the finest harvest (nature's time) through food—usually dairy foods, seeds, nuts, and fruits, since the Jews in the desert had little time to slaughter and prepare animals. A parallel explanation for the prevalence of dairy dishes at Shavuot

A ceremony honoring the memory of the six million Jews who were killed during the Nazi Holocaust. (© Robert L. Kern, 1983)

is that they are a physical correlative to the Torah—the milk that nurtures the Jewish people.

Additional Dates on the Jewish Calendar

In our generation two occasions have been added to the cycle of Jewish observances: Yom Ha'Atzmaut (Israel Independence Day) on the fifth of Iyyar and Yom Hashoah (Holocaust Remembrance Day) on the twenty-seventh of Nissan. Since both are newly created events, there may be more chance here than in more firmly established ceremonies to add material about women.

For Israel Independence Day one could arrange to stage biographical sketches of the women involved in founding the State; *The Plough Woman* (see Bibliography) would be a fine resource. Another possibility is to screen films dealing with women in Israel: *I Love You, Rosa*, for example, or Shuli Eshel's feminist critique of women in the Israeli army, *To Be a Woman Soldier*. This would also be an appropriate time to discuss other feminist issues in Israel; for Israeli women's groups and activist groups in America involved with Israeli women's issues, see the Networking Directory, under "Women in Israel."

Holocaust Remembrance Day usually features memorial programs honoring the memory of those who were martyred by the Nazis. This is an appropriate time to read the histories of women who survived, and to familiarize oneself with some of the new research into women's experience of the Holocaust (see p. 189). For an annotated list of women's Holocaust literature, consult the *Bibliography on the Jewish Woman* by Aviva Cantor.

Tisha B'Av

This holiday is a day of fasting and mourning for the destruction of the First and Second Temples in Jerusalem (586 B.C.E. and 70 C.E., respectively). The observances fall equally on men and women on this midsummer day, though Waskow in *Seasons of Our Joy* points out that the blessing of the moon which concludes Tisha B'Av foretells a time, after the Messiah comes, when the moon will be the sun's equal (an event prefigured in some Rosh Chodesh ceremonies as well, as we have seen).

Aside from the moon ceremony and its association with women, the other possibilities for women's special observances on this day are to include special meditations and dirges in the traditional mourning format for those women from our past—known and unknown—who were martyrs for their Judaism, or who suffered for having been women. This is a time also for mourning lost opportunities or wrong paths or times we have been in exile from our true natures (doing what others expected of us, perhaps, and not being true to our own aspirations). Grieving in this way isn't all self-pity, but can be a preparation for the renewal and the energetic resolve to improve our ways that come with Rosh Hashanah and Yom Kippur, as the calendar comes full circle again.

RITUALS FOR THE LANDMARKS OF OUR LIVES

There are many Jewish ceremonies that women and men are resurrecting, transforming, or creating to use in celebrating "marker" events in their lives. These are sometimes special prayers or rituals for secular events—such as when a child leaves home for college—or special Jewish ceremonies that many Jews now interweave into the fabric of their lives, such as having a *chanukat habayit* (consecration of a new house) ceremony to affix the mezuzah to the front door. Even if they would not describe themselves as "religious," many Jews want to reconnect with their Jewish identity at important times in their lives. Aside from holiday observances, these needs are usually expressed around life-cycle events: births, deaths, and all the significant markers in between. (For marriage and divorce, see pp. 318 and 355.)

Given the distinct biological phases of a woman's life, women probably have more occasions to note with prayer or special events than men do: first menstruation, monthly cycle, pregnancy (opening of the womb), birth, weaning, menopause. The recurring paradox, of course, is that while we don't want to be tied only to our biological definition, we are at the same time seeking Jewish rituals to sanctify (or at least reinforce in a positive way) what our bodies experience.[9] Whether public statements or performed privately, such marker ceremonies also give us a legitimate opportunity to focus on ourselves in a way that is, despite the cries of *gevalt* about a narcissistic "me generation," hard to come by for most women, especially those who are trying to juggle many roles and tasks. To sing a song of oneself as a separate person, to borrow from Whitman, yet to affirm that one is a part of the Jewish people at the same time is an important integration for women.

Besides giving a spiritual dimension to daily life, there are other reasons for investing important events in our lives with Jewish symbols: making connections with our collective past as Jews and reinforcing for us a sense of Jewish identity—not necessarily only religious but also ethnic and cultural. Our lives are not value-free or culture-free, and just as many Jewish women are turning to (or returning to) celebrations of Jewish holidays, so they are incorporating a Jewish component into their personal lives as well.

Orthodox or very traditional women who are creating ceremonies around new observances in their lives are careful not to repeat the exact formulations of the blessings used in traditional religious practice, believing that one ought not to use God's name lightly or in an observance that has not been hallowed by centuries of use. Nechama Liss-Levinson says that she has resolved this issue by using "prayers" rather than "blessings" in newly created ceremonies, such as those for naming a daughter or for weaning a child. Critics warn of a certain risk that the women's ceremonies may have in them the seeds of an earlier paganism from which formative Judaism was trying to differentiate itself, there is a retort to this: that so do other Jewish ceremonies that have links, for example, to primitive shamanistic festivals celebrating nature (as on Succot, when one shakes the fronds of the *lulav*). Perhaps this new body- and earth-consciousness will be part of a restructuring of patriarchal Judaism. Yet we ask the question "How Jewish is this?" at the same time, recognizing

One of several amulets to protect a woman in childbirth and her new-born child from evil spirits (including Lilith, who got a very bad press when she was described by some writers as a creature who could endanger babies). Amulets of this sort, suitable for hanging near the delivery table or birthing stool, can still be purchased today.

that for some women these women-based or "new-age"-oriented rituals may be the *only* way into (or back into) a connection with Judaism.

Rachel Adler cautions against other kinds of celebrations based on women's body rhythms: "Creating religious metaphors solely out of our biological experience will tend to make us 'womanists' rather than Jews."[10] Theologians Judith Plaskow and Carol Christ put the question somewhat differently: "Whether these Jewish celebrations for women only are temporary strategies or are intended as a permanent separation of the sexes may depend on the ability of Judaism to integrate the concerns of women into common rituals that women and men celebrate together."[11]

Despite these anxious questions about the implications of building new rituals around female experience, there are clear Biblical precedents for many of the life-cycle events that Jewish women are now honoring. Physicality has always played an important role in mainstream Judaism (see "Our Bodies," p. 198), and even such concerns as fertility and weaning are presented in the Bible, complete with prayers and ceremonies.

After talking of women's need for life-cycle markers as mnemonic devices to remind us of how Judaism can infuse our individual lives as Jews, it seems ironic to begin a section on women's ceremonies with childbirth, thus defining the adult woman by her role as mother rather than as self-sustaining individual, independent of the lives around her. Yet for many women childbearing is their quintessentially female experience.

Conception

In acknowledgment of the Jewish dimension in their decisions about childbearing and child rearing, some Jewish couples are choosing to mark with Jewish rituals their decisions to become parents. Nechama Liss-Levinson, a Long Island feminist psychotherapist, and her husband created a ritual for themselves when they decided to have a child, five years after their marriage.

> We had a private ceremony the evening when we decided to stop using contraceptives. We made a kiddush, and recited the *sheva brachot* [seven blessings traditionally recited at the wedding], because we felt that deciding to have children was a continuation of the marriage ceremony. In past times, when having children usually followed during the first years of marriage, the connection might have been clearer; since we had chosen to wait before having children, we felt that we wanted to recite the *sheva brachot* again, which we also did at the naming ceremony for each of our daughters.

The beauty of ritualizing this occasion is that it makes clear the choice involved in having a child. Rather than the "accidental" or circumstantial pregnancy or conception (methods favored by the ambivalent), a ceremony makes the choice clear and provides an opportunity for the prospective parents to acknowledge their conscious responsibility for the creation of new life.

Giving Birth

Despite the fact that numerous rituals have been developed around the birth and naming of a son, there has been scant traditional ritual around the women in the picture—whether as mothers or as daughters. In the past we had prayers of thanksgiving for the opening up of the womb (for a first pregnancy or subsequent ones) and pleas for good health such as a mother's prayer "for her Pregnated Daughter."[12] Blu Greenberg asks, "Could it be that if men had been giving birth all these centuries, some fantastic ritual would have developed by now?"[13]

Traditionally a woman after childbirth "bentsches gomel"—says the prayer of one who has had a near brush with death. In some communities there are women's prayer groups who will gather together to make the liturgical responses to the woman praying, and they may even go to the hospital or bedside (if there has been a home birth) in order to provide this. Although often it is the husband who has gone to synagogue and said the gomel prayer after the wife has given birth, halachically she can certainly take on the obligation of saying it herself.

Some women and men have extended the experience of childbirth-preparation classes into a Jewish context for the birth itself. A Massachusetts couple had friends construct a mandala (a circular design for meditation) with Jewish symbols, among others, which they hung in the labor room as a focus for the breathing exercises the woman performed in the various stages of labor and delivery.

There are also Jewish rituals for a failed pregnancy (see p. 229). For a stillborn child, certain rituals of burial and mourning are traditionally observed, depending on the age of the fetus. Expanding on tradition, some women are searching for Jewish rituals or a Jewish context in which to mark the loss of a pregnancy (see p. 398). Other women are turning to traditional prayers in pregnancy, labor, and childbirth, especially those that call for the continuing health of mother and child.

Honoring the Birth of a Daughter

If only we could say in this section on birth ceremonies that we were talking about those which surrounded our own births! The truth of the matter is that there are probably few Jewish women reading this book whose own arrival into the world was marked with anything resembling the fanfare that accompanied her brother's appearance.

In the past, fathers were sometimes pitied and consoled on the birth of a daughter—more an occasion for sadness than for celebration. Union activist Lucy Robins Lang wrote of her own birth in the late nineteenth century: "My arrival in this world was a disappointment to a number of people, and especially to my grandfather, Reb Chaim. . . . It was not a boy—only I had come into the world. . . . He hated me from the very first for the disappointment and humiliation I had caused him."[14]

In Kurdistan, at Jewish weddings, the bride would hold a male infant as the guests called out, "May your first be a boy too." There are contemporary manifestations of this wish. One woman reports on a traditional *bris*, or *brit milah* (circumcision ceremony for a newborn Jewish male) held in a progressive academic community in New Jersey in 1981: "The mohel [ritual circumciser] told all the women at the ceremony to take a sip of the kiddush wine, saying, 'I guarantee you'll have a boy if you do.' He repeated this several times to the two or three obviously pregnant women present. My worry was, what were the little girls running around at the ceremony supposed to think when they heard that?"

Sociologist Rela Geffen Monson comments that the two events most likely to startle a Jewish woman into an awareness of her inequality in the tradition are the death of a parent—that is, when the mourning woman cannot participate in the communal *minyan*—and the birth of a daughter, "when all the people who'd planned to come for the *bris* cancel their reservations."

Fortunately this is less true now than it was a decade ago. Now not only is there an array of ceremonies being written to welcome a newborn girl, but also there is greater public expectation that there will be such a ceremony—even for Orthodox families. At a recent naming ceremony for Ilana, the daughter of *Lilith* magazine news editor Reena Sigman Friedman and Aryeh Friedman, one guest commented, "Ten years ago this would have been something extraordinary. Now we expect it."

Other women document the change in their own family lives: "I count myself among those shamefaced parents of ten-year-old girls who must explain to them that, no, there are no pictures of a family party at the time of her birth (as there are for her brother) because *she* was named in a synagogue, one weekday morning when her father was called to the Torah, and the (mostly male) early morning daveners shared a bottle of *schnapps* and that was that. Not that we and other parents weren't delighted with the arrival of a daughter, but it just didn't occur to us that there was any way within the tradition of marking her birth more elaborately."

Ceremonies for newborn Jewish girls have actually existed for centuries; they have just been out of fashion in the Ashkenazi communities. There have always been more elaborate ceremonies—sometimes including amulets for warding off evil spirits—among the Sephardim.[15] In fact, the Celebration for the Gift of a Daughter appears in the Sephardic Daily and Sabbath Prayerbook and includes readings and blessings for family and child.[16]

New ceremonies for naming a daughter have proliferated in the ten years since Jewish women have made a concerted effort toward greater inclusion in Jewish ritual. Booklets describing these ceremonies are much in demand, and the Jewish Women's Resource Center in New York even has a large loose-leaf notebook filled with copies of ceremonies sent in by parents who know that whatever models people can find for such events will be welcome, since there are few formal guidelines.

The central part of the ceremony marking the entry of a baby boy into the Jewish fold is the *brit milah*, or circumcision, performed at the age of eight days, usually by a mohel. Aside from honored guests and relatives, the main participants are the baby, the mohel, the godmother or godfather (or both), and the *sandak*, or person who sits in "Elijah's chair" (and is sometimes also the godparent) and holds the baby (usually bound to a special circumcision palette) for the ceremony. It's useful to keep in mind the details of the ceremony for boys, because those parents—and rabbis—who have struggled to find an appropriate ceremony for girls have debated whether to base it on that of the boy baby or whether to invent something uniquely female.

Even the naming of the ceremony has been problematic to parents. Some popular favorites are Brit B'not Yisrael (the covenant of the daughters of Israel), Brit Kedusha (the covenant of sanctification), Simchat Bat (rejoicing in a daughter).

Whether the ceremonial welcoming of a daughter into the Jewish people (and into the people's covenant with God) should include some physical component, as a sign paralleling the trimming of the foreskin in the circumcision ceremony, is an issue much debated.[17] Most parents would settle for a ceremony that marks the spiritual entry of a Jewish woman into the world, and many build the ceremony not only around prayers but around wishes and dreams for the child and promises about their own roles in the child's development as a woman and as a Jew. Aviva Cantor created a prayer of this sort for the birth ceremony of our daughter Yael Deborah in 1982. Traditionally one wishes that a Jewish daughter will grow up to be like her Biblical foremothers. Here Cantor names some of those role models and the characteristics they embody: "We wish Yael inspiration from the examples of our foremothers: from Lilith swift and unequivocal resistance to tyranny and the fortitude to face the consequences; from Eve (Chava) the hope to choose life and sustain it after Paradise was lost; from Noah's wife the nurturing qualities and patience to be a steward for Earth's creatures; from Sarah the faith to follow a dream into wilderness and to believe the impossible is possible; from Rebecca (Rivka) the wisdom to overcome the dead hand of custom; from Leah endurance and perseverance in the face of loneliness; from Rachel the compassion and love for her sister that spared Leah pain and anguish; from Dina the ability to take risks to break out of confinement (break barriers) to seek friendship with other women; from midwives Shifrah and Puah the courage to defy death to rescue the next generation; from Miriam the ability to be outspoken in her views even when they were unpopular; from Deborah (Dvora) the self-esteem that enabled her to rally and lead resistance and to take pride in her achievements; and from Ya'el, whose name she carries, the courage to do what she knew she had to do. From all these, our foremothers whose actions were recorded in our Torah, and from the countless others in our history both known and unknown to us, may Yael seek and draw insight, inspiration and support."

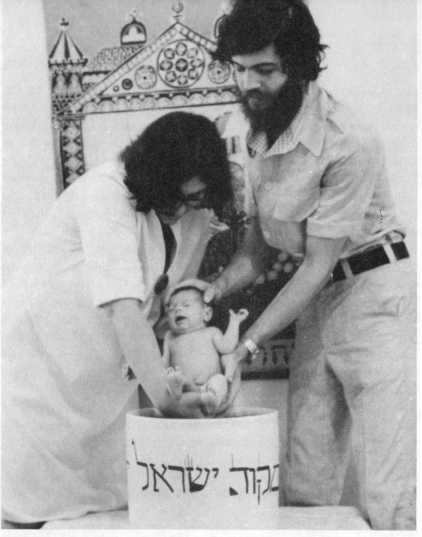

Kayla Strassfeld being immersed in a miniature mikveh created by her parents, Sharon and Michael Strassfeld, for a birth ceremony welcoming her into the Covenant of Israel. (Amy Stone)

Other celebrations have included immersing a daughter in a miniature ritual bath (mikveh).[18] The ceremony offered here, composed by a group of women rabbis, suggests washing the feet of the newborn girl.[19] Here is how they went about creating a ritual naming ceremony, with excerpts from the ceremony, which they call Brit Rechitza.

We all knew that *brit milah* was a powerful ritual, fundamental to Jewish identity, Biblically rooted and psychologically astute. We also knew that it was, by its very nature, a male event. We wanted to find a way to welcome baby girls into the covenant between God and Israel, so nine of us met to review the options currently available for female birth ceremonies.

Many of the ceremonies have, as the central act, the giving of a gift to the infant. These gifts include candlesticks, *kiddush* cups, *tallitot, tefillin*, etc. We were dissatisfied with this because gift-giving seems to ignore the central aspect of the male *brit*: the physical involvement of the child. We wanted to *do* something in which the child would be physically touched, in order to concretize the importance of the passage the baby was undergoing by entering the covenant. The covenant is a gift, but it is also a commitment of mind, soul and body.

We turned to the idea of *mikveh*. This was both practical and Jewish. It was even a ritual of special importance for women [see p. 203]. Ultimately, however, we decided that *mikveh* was a confusing rite to introduce at the time of birth. Its associations were strongly linked with "family purity" [that is, sexual contact]. It would raise an issue about which many of us were ambivalent and which, in any case, was more germane to puberty than to birth.

The idea of water, however, proved to be a compelling one. We wanted something ancient and Jewish, something without diversionary overtones, something physical and something meaningful to the event at hand: a welcoming into the covenant. We recalled that the Bible speaks of more than one covenant. In addition to the covenant with Abraham which is the basis of the *brit milah*, a covenant is also made with Noah after the flood. Surely, we would want to welcome the baby girl into that covenant as well, a covenant that potentially involves all of humanity. With Noah, we were once again drawn to water: the life-giving *"Mayim Hayim,"* that had threatened to destroy, but now preserved human life.

Water. Washing. Welcoming. . . . Someone remembered that when Abraham was recovering from his circumcision, he was visited by three angels of the Lord who promised him that his seed would continue and that Sarah would have a son. Abraham greeted these strangers with the gracious Middle Eastern sign of hospitality—he gave them water to wash their feet. What better way, then, for us to welcome our new members in the family of people and the family of Jews? Feet washing is gentle, loving, and ancient. The ritual grew, as you can see, organically and communally. The end product is not as important in itself as the fact that the process of creating Judaism is far from over.

Today we mark the beginning of your journey, _____, as a member
(name)
of the Jewish people, and we mark this journey's beginning with water. . . .

[Although there is no such reference in the original ceremony, some parents might want to insert at this point some comments about the

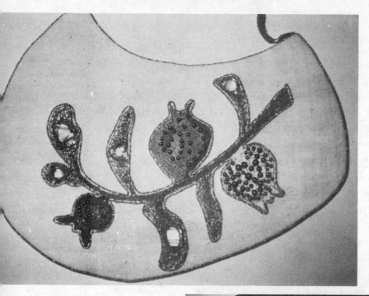

To commemorate the birth of daughters, textile artist Ita Aber has created Torah breast shields of needlework with a design suggested by the Torah portion read on the Shabbat after the baby's birth. The reverse side carries the name and birth date of the child, and can be presented to the synagogue in the girl's honor, to be used on the Torah each year when her portion is read. (Ita Aber)

Biblical associations of water with women: for example, Miriam's song at the Red Sea, or Rebecca at the well.]

When Noah and the others aboard the Ark realized that the flood had abated, the people and animals of the Ark all walked gingerly off the Ark onto the earth, but when they saw the rivers and lakes still full of water, and when they felt gentle raindrops from the heavens, they ran back onto the Ark in fear. "Water still remains in the world," they exclaimed, "we will stay on the Ark lest these waters harm us as did the flood water." Noah prayed to God, asking for help and for a sign of something that would prove to the Ark dwellers that the waters on earth were life-giving and not destructive.

Among God's most precious possessions—among those that God had made on the eve of the Shabbat of creation at twilight (*Pesachim* 54a)—was a luminous bow of multi-colored light. In this bow one could see the very essence of God, the *Shekhinah,* or female aspect of God (*Zohar: Bereishit* 72). God placed this bow in the midst of the cloudy sky. All who saw the bow felt the peaceful presence of God amidst the rain and bowed low in the face of such glory.

God said to the Ark dwellers: "I have set My bow in the clouds, and it shall serve as a sign of the covenant between Me and the earth" (Genesis 9:9,10,13). All the people and animals in the Ark gazed at the rainbow and blessed God saying, "*Barukh atah Adonai Eloheynu, melekh ha'olam zoher habrit.* Blessed are You, Adonai our God, Ruler of the Universe, Who is mindful of the covenant," and they walked bravely from the Ark onto the firm, fresh earth. . . .

Your parent(s) _____ will now wash your feet
(Hebrew names optional)
as a sign of our welcoming you into the *brit,* the covenant between the Jewish people and God. Our prayer for you is that in all your future journeys through life, you will find guidance and sustenance in the waters of Miriam's Well—in God's care, in the words of the Torah, and in the traditions of the Jewish people.

Parents wash the infant's feet and recite: "*Barukh Ata Adonai Eloheynu Melekh HaOlam, Zoher HaBrit B'rehitzat Raglayim.*" Blessed are You, Adonai our God, Ruler of the Universe, Who is mindful of the covenant through the washing of the feet.

We have been blessed with a new life. We have shared love and pain and joy in bringing our daughter into life and have been privileged to participate in the marvel and beauty of creation.

The ceremony concludes with traditional blessings by parents and other family members, giving the child her name, and wishing her a life of "Torah, service, joy and good deeds." The final prayers are the kiddush and Shehecheyanu, giving thanks for having been permitted to reach this day.

Another, more "traditionally" religious ceremony for a newborn daughter is the Brit Bat Tzion (covenant of a daughter of Zion) created in 1979 by Elaine Shizgal Cohen and Stephen P. Cohen for their daughter Maya. This ceremony, which interweaves Chanukah and Rosh Chodesh (new moon) themes (which just happened to be timely) was used as part of a morning Torah-reading service in which friends and relatives participated.

Some aspects of the creation of the Cohens' ceremony may be useful for other parents as well. First, they went to a concordance of the Bible and found passages that seemed to match their ideas about this child and about her name and the name of the ceremony. They included these passages and also a poem, in Hebrew, composed as an acrostic on Maya's name. In addition, the Cohens blessed all three of their daughters at the ceremony, and incorporated a poem to the newborn written by one of her sisters. Theirs is one of the few ceremonies that make a place not only for grandparents and friends but also for siblings.

With or without a formal religious service marking the arrival of a daughter, the tradition has linked whatever ceremonies there have been with the giving of the girl's name. (This is interesting in itself, since women's later lives may include acquiring and divesting themselves of several names.) One of the ways of making the occasion special—and also linking it to the practice in the past of simply calling out the new child's name in the synagogue and letting it go at that—is the inclusion in a ceremony of some description, poem, lesson, or other special association based on the newborn's name—either connecting her to a foremother for whom she is named, with characteristics thought to accompany that name itself, or with the Biblical figure whose name she bears.[20]

The following are additional resources on life-cycle ceremonies for newborn girls:

Call Them Builders
by Sandy Eisenberg Sasso
The Reconstructionist Foundation
2521 Broadway
New York, NY 10025

This booklet gives information about the traditions behind current practices in celebrating the birth of a child and includes special prayers for grandparents and one on weaning the child, in addition to giving the complete text for both a *brit milah* and a *brit b'not Yisrael*.

Blessing the Birth of a Daughter: Jewish Naming Ceremonies for Girls, edited by Toby Fishbein Reifman with Ezrat Nashim is available from:

Ezrat Nashim
c/o T. Reifman
231 Sunset Avenue
Englewood, NJ 07631

This is an extremely practical collection of seven welcoming ceremonies for girls—representing every point on the ideological spectrum, from Orthodoxy leftward. There is a plus: a section on a mother's participation in the *brit milah* ceremony for her son, a sensitive issue for those women who have wanted to participate but who have been forced by custom or an uncooperative mohel into waiting in an offstage bedroom until "the whole thing" was over.

Also useful for introducing children to the process of using, adapting, and creating rituals is a book that explains the basis behind some, especially those surrounding birth, and makes suggestions for how students can invent their own:

The Life Cycle Workbook
by Joel Lurie Grishaver
Alternatives in Religious Education
3945 South Oneida Street
Denver, CO 80237

There are files of original naming ceremonies, most of them unpublished, on the shelves of:

Jewish Women's Resource Center
National Council of Jewish Women
9 East 69 Street
New York, NY 10021
(212) 535-5900

Ita Aber, a textile specialist, custom-makes ceremonial objects for female (and male) baby-naming ceremonies. One is a dress with a Hebrew "inscription" wishing that the child be blessed with a life of Torah, the marriage canopy, and good deeds. Another is a Torah breast-shield (ornamental covering for a Torah scroll) made out of a cloth the baby was wrapped in during her naming ceremony (similar in concept to the Torah ties made from the binder worn by a baby boy at his circumcision). Aber says: "The child may be wrapped in a gorgeous silk fabric from which a Torah breast-shield will be made. The design comes from the Torah portion of the week in which the baby girl was born; the reverse side bears her name and the dedication "On the beginning of her study of Torah." This is then presented to the synagogue when she starts Hebrew school, and may be used to decorate the Torah whenever her portion comes around and especially on her Bat Torah or Bat Mitzvah." These may be ordered from:

Ita Aber
One Fanshaw Avenue
Yonkers, NY 10705
(914) 968-4863

Weaning

Weaning is an event for which women and men have devised striking rituals for the past several years. The weaning ceremony by Shoshana
Silberman and Mel Silberman that appears in *The Second Jewish Catalog* has been widely used, and is one of the "new" rituals for Jewish
women that has a clear Biblical precedent, in the celebration held when
Sara weans Isaac (Genesis 21:8).

Using the themes of feeding and independence from breast or bottle,
Nechama Liss-Levinson suggests that a charitable contribution to an
organization that feeds the Jewish poor, or to a nonsectarian group that
combats hunger worldwide, would be appropriate to mark the occasion
of the child's weaning. She also suggests the gift of a kiddush cup to the
baby girl or boy at this time. Such a ceremony as the Silbermans', which
notes the nurturing roles of the parents and the joys parents and child
feel at the child's new independence, seems particularly appropriate for
families in which the mother will be returning to work after the child is
weaned, or will be resuming a life marked, certainly, by the responsibilities of parenthood, but not entirely structured around her child's dependency.

Puberty and Menstruation

Mary Gendler suggests a Jewish rite of passage into puberty as a correlative to the spiritual and communal nature of a Bat Mitzvah ceremony,
which occurs at approximately the same time as the onset of menstruation. Gendler uses a gift to her daughter as the central point of this
marker event.

> The fact that I have girls makes my encounter with Jewish tradition
> at this juncture not simply academic, but very real and serious. The
> manner in which we welcome our daughters into adult status, the spirit
> with which we acknowledge who they are and who they are becoming,
> can have a profound influence upon how they perceive themselves, per-
> sonally, and how we come to perceive ourselves as a community.
> Puberty presents an especially ripe time to validate our daughters'
> entrance into the community as full, participating, equal members, as
> well as to celebrate their uniqueness, their femininity.

Bat Mitzvah addresses only one aspect of a young Jewish woman's growth, the public acknowledgment of her change of status in relation to the adult community. What is missing is a ritual which marks the important physical changes which occur in young girls' bodies at this time in their lives.

Changes in our bodies, the onset of menstruation—these are very personal events which call for quiet recognition. The only Jewish tradition which I know of relating to the onset of menstruation is that of the mother slapping the girl's face. It is hard to imagine that such an action can cause the girl to feel good about this aspect of herself. If such a basic female biological process is a "curse," then how are we to feel about ourselves as women? The more I thought about this, the more it began to seem absolutely crucial that this moment, a moment in which we show ourselves tangibly to be women, a moment in which we are most different from men, most separate and unique—this moment must be sacralized and celebrated. But how? Anyone who has been around young girls of twelve or fourteen knows that it is an age of acute embarrassment. Our culture, although permissive in many ways, does not talk easily of normal bodily changes. Public acknowledgment is out of the question. The moment must be private but special. Some of my friends have had a celebrative dinner or taken their daughters out to lunch. I was searching for something more formal, more ritualized, more connected, if not to specific Jewish tradition at least tied into ancient imagery and presented in some ritual fashion.

The image that came to mind was that of the moon. As more and more Jewish women are reclaiming and elaborating on the ancient celebration of new moon, Rosh Chodesh [see p. 69], it would appear that

A "moontree" necklace created by Mary Gendler as a Jewish and female symbol for her daughter when the young woman reached puberty. (Mary Gendler)

the moon, and women's special connection to it, may be returning to our consciousness. And nowhere is this connection to her more evident than in our monthly period, our twenty-eight-day cycle which mirrors hers. Waxing and waning, filling followed by emptying followed by filling, we ebb and flow in echo of her rhythm.

The moon, then, was the obvious symbol. It seemed to me that in this instance something tangible might not be out of order, since a lot of fuss and ceremony would only embarrass the girls. Why not make a silver moon necklace which would be symbolic of the occasion, and also a beautiful object in itself? (Ideally it would be made by the mother—it's not hard, I've done it myself with no previous silversmithing experience.) The necklace which I designed is patterned after the ancient moon tree with a six-pointed star added. The bead at the end of the moon is made of coral and symbolizes a drop of blood.

The necklace should be accompanied by a prayer or note, and the occasion could include a special meal. The occasion might be only between mother and daughter, the parents and daughter, or the whole family. Another intriguing idea is to gather together all the female members of the family for a kind of initiation rite into the female clan.

To celebrate our daughters' femaleness, to welcome them as *women* within a Jewish context, is to make the statement to them that we rejoice in who they are. The combination of the public recognition during Bat Mitzvah and the private ceremony for menstruation acknowledges the inner and outer selves which we all have, recognizing our uniqueness as women, and at the same time affirming us as equal, fully participating members of the Jewish community.

Another kind of ritual for menarche is suggested by Rabbi Fishel Perlmutter of Toledo, Ohio. He has designed a ceremony for parents and daughter to conduct together. They declare their gratitude for the "wonder of our bodies"; then parents and daughter each make a silent meditation and a personal prayer for God's blessing, and conclude with the *shehecheyanu*.[21]

In other attempts to counter some of the negative associations with menstruation in Judaism (see "Our Bodies," p. 208), women are developing rituals to provide positive connections with adult women's monthly cycles.

Theologian Ellen Umansky, discussing the blessing for menstruation in *Siddur Nashim: A Sabbath Prayer Book for Women* (see p. 83) notes that blood "is no longer a symbol of death (associated in rabbinic legend with the disobedience of Eve and the expulsion from Eden) but a symbol of the possibilities of life, woven by the Divine through women."[22]

In the early 1970s a group of observant women in New York, calling themselves Bat Kol (Daughter of the Voice, a phrase used for a manifestation of God's Presence), wrote a similar blessing. This can be recited at the first menses or as part of a religious Jewish woman's regular monthly ritual, a counterpart to the blessing "concerning immersion" which a married woman says as she submerges her body in the mikveh each month.

In its Hebrew form the Bat Kol blessing may be said with either male or female appellations for God.

> Blessed are You, O Lord our God and God of our foremothers and forefathers, who has set the moon in its path and has set the order of the cycles of life. Blessed are You, O Lord, who has created me a woman.[23]

Bat Mitzvah

Until this century the marking of a young person's coming of age in Judaism, the formal recognition of the assumption of adult obligations in the community, belonged only to boys. Bar Mitzvah was the authentic rite of passage into Judaism, and girls knew about it only as passive observers. In 1922 Judith, eldest daughter of Rabbi Mordecai M. Kaplan, the founder of Reconstructionism, celebrated the first recorded Bat Mitzvah. It wasn't until the 1950s, however, that Bat Mitzvah became a widespread practice in Reform Judaism and in many North American Conservative synagogues as well.

Bat Mitzvah celebrant blesses the Shabbat wine with her uncle, using a kiddush cup decorated with her name and the date. (David Hechler)

The traditional Bar Mitzvah ceremony usually takes place on a Saturday morning at the Torah-reading service, during which a thirteen-year-old boy is called to the Torah, recites blessings over it, customarily chants the *haftarah* (the selection of writings from the Prophets that accompanies each week's Torah portion), and in some cases reads all or part of the Torah portion as well. His coming of age marks his assuming the obligations (mitzvot) of the adult Jew.

A young woman is considered by the Orthodox automatically to be Bat Mitzvah (Daughter of the Obligations) one day after her twelfth birthday, regardless of what ceremonies mark her ascendancy to ritual adulthood. Non-Orthodox Jews date this one day after her thirteenth birthday. For boys as well, being Bar Mitzvah just means attaining the age to assume adult responsibilities. One is obligated to assume them as soon as one comes of age, regardless of ceremony. In a sense, any ceremonies, for boys as well as girls, are superfluous to defining young people as mature Jews. What the ceremonies do signify is communal recognition of this new, adult status.

Here is how the institution of Bat Mitzvah has evolved in the main denominations of Judaism, although in none of them is a girl's celebration of Bat Mitzvah yet the automatic, unquestioned event the Bar Mitzvah is for boys.

REFORM

Some congregations have dismissed Bar and Bat Mitzvah as anachronistic, instead holding a confirmation service at the end of high school. For those congregations that do have Bar Mitzvah services, there is usually parallelism between that practice and Bat Mitzvah celebrations, with girls being called to the Torah on Saturday mornings.

RECONSTRUCTIONIST

In Reconstructionist congregations there is complete equality for girls and boys (and men and women) in ritual roles, with both chanting a *haftarah* and reading from the Torah.

CONSERVATIVE

Until the late sixties most Conservative congregations held Bat Mitzvah ceremonies as part of a Friday-night service, when the Torah is *not* read. Girls were called to the *bimah*, said the traditional blessings over the Torah, and chanted a *haftarah*. Since women's obligations under Conservative Judaism are still fewer than those of men, it isn't clear which ones a Bat Mitzvah was obligating herself to.

During the past fifteen years many Conservative congregations, in a move toward greater parity, have scheduled Bat Mitzvah ceremonies on Saturday mornings, and girls do read from the Torah.

In those Conservative congregations that have decided to call women for aliyot to the Torah and that count women in the *minyan*, adult women will have an equal role with men in the Bat Mitzvah service—women will be among those honored with aliyot, for example. Some congregations, which do not routinely offer women this equality, make exceptions for the female relatives of the Bat (or Bar) Mitzvah, allowing these women to have aliyot at the ceremony. In general, Bat Mitzvah ceremonies, having a shorter history than those of Bar Mitzvah, allow for greater innovation and flexibility.

In "alternative" Jewish settings, such as in havurot and the Conservative movement's Ramah camps, full equality for girls is the norm, and Bat Mitzvah ceremonies tend to be both traditional and parallel to that of Bar Mitzvah.

ORTHODOX

Since Orthodox synagogues do not allow women to appear on the *bimah* before a mixed congregation, ceremonies marking the coming of age of Orthodox girls are usually held at home; if in a synagogue they take place as a quasi-social event in a room other than the main sanctuary. Even this development—sometimes called a Bat Torah ceremony—in which the girl may give a *dvar Torah* (commentary on the week's Torah portion) or read a poem she has written or make a speech—is still not the norm among most Orthodox Jews but is a fairly recent phenomenon (since the mid-seventies) among "modern Orthodox." In some families there is simply a party to mark the milestone, and in some no notice is taken at all. But the Bat Mitzvah phenomenon has had a snowball effect, so that in some communities Bat Mitzvah is becoming a common practice.

A girl celebrating her Bat Torah or Orthodox Bat Mitzvah may find herself struggling with the negative attitude of Orthodox men, especially some rabbis. While there are rabbis around the country who actively support expanding the role of Orthodox women, others undercut the gains that have been made.

At one Orthodox ceremony recently, held in the reception room of a synagogue in a New York suburb, the Bat Mitzvah celebrant gave a learned explication of certain values expressed in the Torah portion that week in a really illuminating and very mature *dvar Torah*. At the conclusion of her talk the congregation's rabbi rose, congratulated her, and proceeded to make a number of fatuous comments about how fortunate he felt that women could not be Orthodox rabbis, because with young women as capable as this one competing for pulpits, he'd be afraid for his job. He then launched into an apology for women's exclusion from most of the ritual obligations of male Jews on the ground that "women are by nature holier and more spiritual than men and so they don't need these daily reminders through prayer and ritual obligation."

Some Orthodox families, anticipating comments like this if and when a rabbi speaks at a daughter's ceremony, have tried to counterbalance these negative remarks by having the mother of the Bat Mitzvah give a talk to the guests, act as mistress of ceremonies (if one is needed), and in general be as visible and as knowledgeable as possible, giving the girl and the guests a role model.

A more creative solution to the Orthodox dilemma is unfortunately out of reach of all but those families with especially sensitive and responsive rabbis. And that is what was worked out at an Orthodox congregation— The Hebrew Institute of Riverdale—in New York City when, two years apart, two sisters became Bat Mitzvah just as a boy would celebrate Bar Mitzvah.[24] Each read a *haftarah* portion, blessed the Torah, chanted the Torah reading on Shabbat morning. This was permissible under Rabbi Avi Weiss's interpretation of the law, since the services took place in a gathering of women: the Women's Tefila (prayer) Group of Riverdale. A few men were present as invited guests, but they were not participants.

And Deborah Made Ten, *a sculpture by Laurie Gross. More and more girls and women who have celebrated Bat Mitzvah are taking on the obligations of religious Judaism, including praying in a group of ten or more adult Jews.* (Bill Aron)

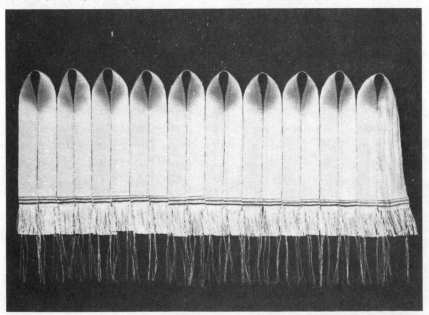

They sat behind the mechitza, where women would usually sit in a mixed gathering at an Orthodox synagogue, and were supposed to have fulfilled their own prayer obligations elsewhere before coming to hear the Torah reading; they were expected to leave immediately following the reading.

While not all girls have the opportunity to celebrate this way in an Orthodox setting, increasing numbers of them are able to participate in some kind of Jewish ritual when they come of age. Arlene Agus, a New York woman long active in the movement to equalize ritual responsibilities for Jewish women, comments: "One big change is the fact that in some Orthodox communities it would now be unthinkable *not* to hold some kind of Bat Mitzvah. The theme has been: within the Orthodox restrictions, how do we expand the possibilities for Bat Mitzvah?"[25]

One innovative Orthodox ceremony in New York City took place in the synagogue (but not in the sanctuary) in the form of a Tu B'Shevat seder, conducted by the Bat Mitzvah girl and her family. It revolved around prayers rediscovered by the girl and her teacher and songs and tales surrounding this holiday's once-common seder, or ritual meal. The celebration was in this case (as it is in many others) much more an occasion for communal recognition of the girl's Jewish knowledge than of any preparedness on her part to take on male-identified ritual responsibility in synagogue.

How to increase the significance of Bat Mitzvah as a young woman's initiation ceremony into Jewish responsibilities? (Some of this applies to *Bar* Mitzvah also, a woman's issue in that it is usually the mother of the celebrant who makes most of the decisions, does most of the planning and the work, and has, as a result, the greatest opportunity to make changes in the way the celebration is perceived.)

• Make sure that the Bat Mitzvah has *role models* in the community. Often the training in Hebrew school and the Bat Mitzvah training in particular is done by men: teachers, rabbis, cantors. Try, if possible, to have your daughter exposed to scholars in the community who are women. Perhaps there is someone who could be a Bat Mitzvah tutor for her, meeting with her a few times before the ceremony—perhaps a student who is herself involved in Judaic studies, or a woman cantor or rabbi if there is one anywhere in your area. Also appropriate would be an adult woman who has been Bat Mitzvah herself.

One model for preparing a girl for her Bat Mitzvah was developed by a Sephardic mother in conjunction with her female cousin. The cousin, who has no daughters of her own, agreed to help the Bat Mitzvah prepare a short speech for delivery during the ceremony (in this case, a routine part of the Bat Torah ceremony of an Orthodox synagogue).

The girl and her tutor decided together that the speech would not highlight only the traditional roles of a Jewish woman—bearer of children and of the tradition in the home—but would also point out the new ways in which women are expressing themselves as Jews (in new ceremonies, new kinds of intellectual endeavors, new career choices within the Jewish community).

The cousin, herself Sephardic, was afraid the girl would see being a Sephardic woman in negative or limiting ways and wanted to help her to see the strengths in her own heritage beyond the cooking that accompanied each ritual occasion. They decided that the girl would take oral histories from the older women of the family, asking them what their lives had been like before they came to America, what their struggles and victories had been. All that she learned she wove into her talk, using real-life examples from her familial past rather than merely the distant, though powerful, Biblical figures of Sarah and Rachel, Rebecca and Leah.

An older woman, other than the girl's mother, is in many ways freer to explore the girl's own feelings about Judaism and womanhood, because she has less invested in how the girl will turn out than the mother herself has. For the girl, having a Bat Mitzvah tutor is often also a chance to see another woman in action and to have a second model for Jewish womanhood.

• It's useful for a group of women committed to Jewish life to meet with a few girls about to be Bat Mitzvah—to talk about their perceptions of what it means to be a woman and a Jew. This shows the girls that there are women who take seriously both parts of their identities, and the experience can give them memories that may sustain them at times in their lives when they feel that it's impossible to be a committed Jew and also have a sense of self-respect as a woman. Discussions about women's issues in the context of Bat Mitzvah may have greater weight as "Jewish" than they would have in a more diffuse setting. This may help women in adolescence and later when Judaism and feminism may seem at odds.

• Along these lines, try to ensure that women will participate in the ceremony itself. Choosing an egalitarian synagogue itself transmits a message. If women are given aliyot to the Torah, try to give them to women your daughter likes—family members or close friends. If aliyah isn't possible, negotiate to have women visible on the *bimah* in other roles—holding and tying the Torah, for instance. At the very least, if there is part of the ceremony that includes the father, make sure you are included as well—whether it's to bless the child, help her don a *tallit,* or make yourself part of the ceremony in some other way. (Of course, these last suggestions hold true as well for the mothers of Bar Mitzvah, but they will be more difficult if not impossible to bring about in Orthodox congregations, which seat the mother of the Bar Mitzvah in the women's section.)

• Make sure that Bat Mitzvah instruction includes, if possible, instruction in synagogue practices (such as how to wear a *tallit*, the practices surrounding Kaddish), so that even if the synagogue the girl presently attends does not include women in these practices, she will be prepared in the event that the rules change, or when she visits a more egalitarian synagogue, or when she goes to college and may have the opportunity for greater participation. In fact, as a tactic for making change, young women should be as familiar with all aspects of ritual as possible, so that Bat Mitzvah can really mark the beginning of a young woman's readiness to seize any opportunity for ritual participation.

• If a synagogue-based Bat Mitzvah is out of the question (for whatever reasons), another course is to hold a ceremony of a different sort altogether. One nominally Conservative family asked Rabbi Lynn Gottlieb to develop a ceremony and a special *siddur* for their daughter's Bat Mitzvah, celebrated at home. The result was a mixture of Hebrew and English, with participation from the girl's friends and many prayers celebrating women in Jewish life.

Although there's more room for creating a "customized" ceremony around Bat Mitzvah celebrations, many who would equalize women's ritual participation feel that these invented ceremonies detract from the seriousness of the endeavor.

A "NONRELIGIOUS" BAT MITZVAH

All but the most devoutly antireligious Jews have felt a commitment to having some kind of marker ceremony around the occasion of Bar Mitzvah. For example, one man now in his thirties describes giving a talk to a gathering of family and friends to mark his thirteenth birthday. The speech stressed his connection to past generations of his family and to "the long march of Jewish history," all in the (secular) context of taking on full identification with the Jewish people.

The women's movement, emphasizing celebration and sharing of important events with circles of friends, who often constitute an extended family and/or a jury of one's peers, has inspired the invention of ways to express a young woman's link with other Jews outside a religious structure. Such secular ceremonies validate the celebrants' Jewishness to themselves and provide a positive expression of Jewish identity for people who might otherwise have none. Sometimes these celebrations take the form of a women-only gathering, where all present make a wish for the Bat Mitzvah celebrant; sometimes the marker event is a family party.

A secular marker like this is significant in showing a girl that her presence in the community is valued and that her future is of concern to a circle larger than her immediate family. However, there's an important factor left out of some of these secular observances which presents a problem for parents trying to unravel their own feelings about Judaism and what elements in it they want to pass on to their children. What's missing is some indication to the child that she has responsibilities also to the community, and not just that the community of friends and relatives are demonstrating their sense of responsibility for her development.

For parents who are struggling with their own uneasiness over issues of religion and/or spirituality, it helps to divide Judaism (and Jewish law and practice) into those aspects that are God-related and those that concern people's relationships with one another (what we might in another context call ethics). Putting aside God questions, it is still possible to put Jewish content into such a "secular" ceremony not only by recalling Jewish grandmothers, as some have, but also by talking very directly about some of the precepts that guide Jews in their behavior toward other human beings and that everyone hopes the Bat Mitzvah will choose to observe. These include the obligation to give charity, to visit the sick, to behave in a just way in dealing with other people, to help those who have fallen, and so on. It's probably also psychologically very important that a girl at this age should feel that she is not only a dependent person, and the object of other people's hopes and good wishes, but that she can be instrumental in her own way, and that the community (smaller or greater) needs her efforts. How better to feel truly grown up and on the brink of adulthood than by having it publicly acknowledged that one has responsibilities to fulfill as well as pleasures to anticipate?

GIFTS

Spread the word around that this is a time for the young person to start building her/his Judaica library and ask that gifts be books with Jewish themes. If it's traditional in your community for a group of friends to get together and buy a large gift, suggest the *Encyclopedia Judaica* if your family doesn't already own one. One can usually get a good price through:

Shaare Zedek Hospital in Jerusalem, Inc.
49 West 45 Street
New York, NY 10036

Giving books as gifts at Bar Mitzvah is a tradition in Israel and one that we'd do well to adopt here. For a girl especially, these gifts signify that she is expected to continue her Jewish education, through the books she'll read if not through formal classes. Good choices would be biographies and history books that deal with Jewish women (see Bibliography, p. 619). These gifts certainly signal different expectations from those suggested by the gold jewelry and facial saunas that have been the vogue in some communities. One of the first girls to be Bat Mitzvah at the Conservative Ramah camps remembers that what she asked for—and received—from her parents as her Bat Mitzvah gift was that they make their house kosher.

Giving is an important concept for the Bat Mitzvah to appreciate even as she is doing all the getting. Especially for children who haven't until this age taken an active role in helping the family make decisions about *tzedakah*—which charities the family members will support—this is a good time to begin. In advance of the Bat Mitzvah ceremony discuss with your daughter the fact that as an adult Jew one of the mitzvot she will now be expected to observe is that of giving charity. Suggest that she set aside a portion of her Bat Mitzvah gift money (or perhaps some of the gifts themselves) to be given away to the causes of her choice. You can suggest that they be specifically Jewish causes, or women's causes, or both. One such list included buying trees in Israel, contributing to the party fund at the local Jewish home for the elderly, and a check to a women's political-action group.

To inquire about the possibility of enriching the Bat Mitzvah ceremony by having the Bat Mitzvah be the proxy for a Soviet Jewish girl who is not free to celebrate, contact your local Committee for Soviet Jewry or:

Student Struggle for Soviet Jewry
210 West 91 Street
New York NY 10024
(212) 799-8900

Some potentially useful books on the Bat Mitzvah experience:

The Jewish Family Book
(Bar/Bat Mitzvah section)
by Sharon Strassfeld and Kathy Green
Bantam, 1981

Bar and Bat Mitzvah
(a workbook/manual)
Alternatives in Religious Education
3945 S. Oneida Street
Denver, CO 80237

ADULT BAT MITZVAH

Largely a phenomenon of the seventies, celebration of Bat Mitzvah for adult Jewish women of course isn't the same kind of biological/social marker event that it is for twelve- or thirteen-year-olds. It represents something else—usually a commitment to catching up on a Jewish education denied them earlier, or an expression of ritual equality for women who did have the education when younger but never had the chance to go public with it. (The Stephen Wise Free Synagogue in New York City also offers catch-up training and a ceremony for men who never celebrated a Bar Mitzvah as children.)

Sometimes adult Bat Mitzvahs are held in a group, an arrangement more comfortable for many women than having an individual public ceremony. (This also makes it easier on congregations with heavily booked Bat and Bar Mitzvah schedules.) Usually adult Bat Mitzvah follows at least one year of Hebrew-language instruction and Judaic-studies classes. An ancillary (and unexpected) consequence of adult Bat Mitzvah ceremonies is that the husbands of women who celebrate them are often prodded to reevaluate their previous views of women's participation in synagogue services and such honors as having aliyot. One man confessed that women's exclusion never bothered him until his wife had a Bat Mitzvah. "Until I saw that my own wife, after two years of study, was still told she couldn't count in a *minyan*, I really didn't care. It was having *her* discriminated against that really made me furious."

Conversion to Judaism

The study and celebration involved in the process of conversion certainly qualify it for inclusion in any listing of life's marker events. Although the major resources on conversion to Judaism are included here following the section on intermarriage (pages 343–354), for many Jews-by-choice the decision to convert is unrelated to a decision to marry a Jew.

Celebrating Midlife

This is the time in a woman's life when the joys and tasks of childbearing and child rearing (if she has experienced these) are winding down. Meeting the needs of the young may be joined by, or supplanted by, meeting the needs of one's own elderly parents. A woman may still feel she is, in Doris Lessing's phrase, "a sponge for small wants," but she may also be experiencing the expansion of vistas that come from knowing one is making a transition from one state to another.[26] We now have rituals for the beginning of life and for its end, but Jewish women are just beginning to create marker ceremonies for this time which is both an end and a beginning.

The most obvious physical sign of midlife is menopause. Nechama Liss-Levinson, who lectures on "From Menarche to Menopause: A Modest Proposal," suggests that women who have been mikveh-observant pay a final visit to the mikveh a year after they have stopped menstruating, as a way of putting closure on what had been a regular monthly practice. She also suggests that some of the prayers women have been composing to celebrate menstruation be adapted for women entering menopause. Rabbi Laura Geller has suggested the *havdalah* service that divides sabbath from weekday as a model for marking menopause. *Havdalah* divides time, and separates two distinct states of being: holy and secular; it would seem, then, to be a very suggestive transition ritual for other passages as well.

Now that most women can expect to live at least into their mid-seventies, menopause doesn't signify the beginning of the end, but the beginning of what Betty Friedan has called "the second third of life." With the energy born of entering a new phase, women in San Diego have written a short book of support and ceremony marking women's midlife in a Jewish manner:

Midlife and Its Rite of Passage Ceremony
by Irene Fine, with a Midlife Celebration by Bonnie Feinman
Women's Institute for Continuing Jewish Education
4079, 54 Street
San Diego, CA 92105
$4.95

Death and Mourning

At few funerals of Jewish women is a eulogy delivered by a woman.[27] Exceptions are those officiated at by a woman rabbi. One of the first women rabbis ordained by the Reform movement reported a few years ago that even families who liked her sermons and classes still preferred not to have her officiate at the funeral of a family member. One woman rabbi says: "When there is a death, people seem to feel that they'd like to do

Visiting the grave of a great-grandmother who is buried on the Mount of Olives, Jerusalem. (Bruce S. Schneider)

the more conservative, traditional thing and have an older, male rabbi officiate. Perhaps because I'm new, or perhaps because they're not sure what the deceased would have thought of having a woman officiate at the funeral."

The survivors of the dead woman might get more meaning from the funeral and might be left with a real sense of who the woman was and what her legacy was if they could hear the words of her friends or women colleagues instead of having to endure the "hired mourner" tone of some professional male funeral speechmakers. At present, at least, it seems that women are more comfortable talking about their feelings and relationships than are most men. So the presence of women eulogists at a woman's funeral might help the mourners by expressing *for them* the feelings of loss on a personal level, as well as by giving them concrete examples of the woman's qualities.

When we ourselves are called upon to plan funerals (as sooner or later we all will probably be) we should consider not only having the rabbi or other public figure speak but also inviting the friends of the deceased to eulogize her. Especially at the funerals of older women, who might never have been known to a young, probably male rabbi, the surviving family and friends would be spared the anguish of hearing a canned eulogy based on information acquired hurriedly from peripheral family members in the hours before the funeral (an especially hectic time because of the Jewish tradition of burying the dead as soon as possible).

It is much easier for a rabbi to eulogize a man he hasn't known or hasn't known well than to do the same for a woman. Until now most men have led lives more public than women's, and the rabbi (or other speech-maker) can always focus on the business and professional accomplish-ments or the organizational activities of the departed. There is *form* to talk about. It's not easy to pick up from an informant at the last minute the sense of what Aunt Sadie was really like. Her most defining charac-teristics may have come out in private, in a family or friendship group, and might require collecting of many anecdotes to convey her essence. The same may be true for the "essence" of many men, but at least, lack-ing that kind of understanding, there's always the public persona to talk about.

As women are becoming more prominent in Jewish life—in both re-ligious and secular roles—they have begun a practice observant Jewish men have followed: chanting a *haftarah*, giving a Torah commentary, or delivering a lecture in memory of a deceased parent on the anniversary of the death, or dedicating some important piece of Jewish-connected work to a dead loved one.

Jewish women across the continent are also becoming involved with the ritual of *chevra kadisha*—the care of the body from death until burial. Of late these rites have been performed by the elderly or left in the hands of paid undertakers, though Jewish tradition has always preferred that they be performed as a mitzvah by members of the community. Atlanta and Toronto are two locations where a cross-section of women have been active in *chevra kadisha* groups.

The traditional Chevra Kadisha performs all the rituals of the under-taker and the funeral director, including the final washing and shrouding of the body. Some groups still do this, but many are not involved with the physical preparation of the body. Instead they act as a support system for the bereaved, making funeral arrangements, calling or sending out notices informing people of the death, and letting friends and relatives know where the traditional *shiva* (seven-day mourning period) will take place. Since according to Orthodox interpretation only women may at-tend the body of a deceased woman, groups engaged in the mitzvah of preparing and accompanying the body are segregated by gender. Usually an Orthodox rabbi will be able to tell you if there is a women's Chevra Kadisha near you. You might want to get in touch with it if you are ar-ranging the funeral for a deceased woman or if you wish to work with the group yourself.

Kaddish—saying the mourner's prayer in a *minyan* each day for the first year of mourning—is *the* synagogue experience that awakens women to their exclusion from an important component of Jewish ritual experience. Many women report that their first desire to be counted in a *minyan* surfaced when they went to say Kaddish at synagogue and were forced to wait until a tenth *man* showed up so that the prayers could begin. For Orthodox women, who at present are not counted in the *minyan*, the discrimination takes other forms: sometimes a family with daughters only will provoke a plaint from the father, "But who will be my Kaddish?" since it usually has been sons who took on responsibility for reciting the remembrance prayers for a deceased parent.

There are women who have taken upon themselves the year-long obligation of saying a daily prayer for a dead parent or loved one, although these duties are obligatory only for men. Henrietta Szold, founder of

(courtesy In the Spirit gallery, New York)

Hadassah, the women's Zionist organization, had no brothers. In 1916 she wrote to a male friend who had offered to say Kaddish for her mother:

> I believe that the elimination of women from such duties was never intended by our law and custom—women were freed from positive duties when they could not perform them, but not when they could. It was never intended that, if they could perform them, their performance of them should not be considered as valuable and valid as when one of the male sex performed them. And of the *Kaddish* I feel sure this is particularly true. . . . When my father died, my mother would not permit others to take her daughters' place in saying the *Kaddish*, and so I am sure I am acting in her spirit when I am moved to decline your offer.[28]

More than sixty years later Rachel Adler wrote:

> The experience which made me a feminist was my grandmother's death. I loved her greatly and wanted her to have a *Kaddish*. Since she had no male relative, I asked if I might assume this responsibility. I was told that I could not say *kaddish* because I was a woman, but that for $350 I could hire a man to say *kaddish* for her. . . . I wondered why the prayer of someone who learned her whole morality from the deceased and helped nurse her through her last illness should be less pleasing to God than that of a man who had to be paid $350 for his services.[29]

For those women who do take on the responsibility of saying Kaddish in synagogue every morning until the first year of mourning is over, the comfort and the difficulties can both be great. Greta Weiner, who with her sister said Kaddish for their mother, tells about some of the awkwardness she was made to feel:

> While our strong attachment to traditional Judaism had led us to believe that the experience would provide comfort, we could never have imagined the spiritual strength we would derive from reciting *kaddish* with members of the Jewish community. On many occasions, total strangers welcomed us into their midst with warm hospitality, and made great efforts to console us.
>
> But we would never have believed either the torment we would feel as a result of the hostility we faced when, on other occasions, we would be treated as "intruders" by male Jews who did not wish to pray with women.
>
> Getting ten men to fulfill their obligation to make a *minyan* was a dilemma facing many of the synagogues which we attended. The huge and elaborate structures were as empty as the one-room places of wor-

ship. And when nine men and I were present, the same scene un-
folded: telephone calls were made, pleas were sent out, services were
missed, and *kaddishes* were not recited.[30]

Another woman, wearing the *tallit* she usually prays in, attended
morning services regularly to say Kaddish during the year after her father
died: "There I was, wearing my father's *tfillin*, in the synagogue where
I'd celebrated my Bat Mitzvah, where I'd read Torah, and when I went
every day to say Kaddish I was made to feel offensive. The *shammes*
[sexton] came up to me and said, 'Please, this is the only part of the synagogue where there is any tradition left. Please don't do it this way.' "
Nevertheless, women have persisted in taking what they feel is their
rightful place in the synagogue for reciting Kaddish, and their presence
is slowly being accepted even by some traditional Jewish men.[31]

RESOURCES

To learn more about the general patterns of mourning and the communal prayers and rituals, see *To Pray as a Jew* by Rabbi Hayim Halevy
Donin (Basic Books, 1980).

Two films explain Jewish burial and the traditions of honoring the
dead:

Bashert
by Brian Kellman
Jewish Media Service
15 East 26 Street
New York, NY 10010
(212) 532-4949

A Plain Pine Box
National Academy of Adult Jewish Studies
United Synagogue of America
155 Fifth Avenue
New York, NY 10010

This is an on-site television documentary produced by ABC which tells
how a Minneapolis congregation formed a Jewish burial society.

The joyful experience of a woman who comes to be recognized as a
true worshiper when she says Kaddish in a *minyan* of elderly men is
recounted in "And Deborah Made Ten," by Deborah E. Lipstadt, in
On Being a Jewish Feminist, edited and with introductions by Susannah
Heschel (Schocken, 1983).

4

•

OUR MINDS
FOR OURSELVES

STRUGGLING AGAINST WOMEN'S
EXCLUSION FROM JEWISH STUDY

Learning is of unparalleled value in Jewish life. Since receiving the Torah at Mount Sinai, Jews have considered themselves—and have been seen by others—as "The People of the Book," and studying Torah is considered superior to observing almost all other religious obligations. Yet free access to books and learning has usually been permitted to men and boys only.

Historically, in accordance with many of the underlying premises and traditional practices of religious Judaism, women have—with few exceptions—been denied the opportunity to study. According to Talmudic law, the exclusion of women from many of the obligations to which Jewish men are bound means that "most significant of all, they are exempt from the important *mitzvah* of studying Torah, a fact that inevitably precludes them from playing a part in Jewish cultural and spiritual life."[1] To be cut off from equal opportunities for study, as most Jewish women were even until very recently, meant being denied both fulfillment as a Jew and personal self-fulfillment as well.

What underlies men's attempts to close women out of the most important area of Jewish study? *Men can maintain control of Jewish law and interpretation if women are ignorant.* "That's why most men don't want us to learn," says one Orthodox woman, who studies Torah every evening with her husband. Men fear that women will begin to challenge male interpretations—for example, that Eve used her sexuality to lure Adam into sin. Or more importantly, that women will develop the skill to enable them to make decisions on Jewish legal matters, challenging male supremacy in divorce legislation, for example.

Jewish study was what engaged men, and therefore study became the ultimate, valued occupation. Study gave men their identity; this was the activity that gave a Jewish man the right to think of himself as a worthwhile human being. Study was also the way he could give himself status within the family. It provided an opportunity to withdraw, to closet himself away; it gave him another sphere in which to operate, removed from the often difficult and/or unpleasant realities of daily life.

Jewish men may not have had the full dose of macho conditioning that has been the birthright of other men, but when it came to learning, the turf was staked out—and it was theirs. "You see it even today," reports an Orthodox woman who has studied family behavior in many Orthodox homes. "The husband is hiding behind his *Gemara*. You shouldn't ask him a question, because of course it will be trivial compared with what he is studying." In a heartrending story of a woman who sees her children starve while her husband studies, the husband says: "Listen woman, do you know what it means not to allow your husband to study? Eh? not to be a believer? . . . Foolish woman, evil woman, not to allow your husband to study. For this you may burn in hell."[2]

Given this exclusion, it is not surprising that there are more historical models for women in support roles than for women scholars. Look at Rachel, the wife of Rabbi Akiva (c. 50–135 c.e.), always praised in Jewish texts. She impoverishes herself to enable her uneducated husband to study. She works and waits for twenty-four years in Jerusalem, supporting Akiva, who is off learning. When he returns as a famous scholar, his wife approaches his entourage, only to be pushed aside by a student. Akiva recognizes her and tells his students that his achievements would have been impossible without her sacrifices. Then he goes off in glory with his disciples (and ultimately marries another woman).

Jewish women have traditionally acquired merit by enabling their husbands and sons to study. A woman who did this was then entitled to be her husband's "footstool in Paradise." And the tradition of vicarious participation exists even today, even among nonreligious women. After interviewing the wives of working-class Jewish men, social worker Mary Cahn Schwartz reports that for many of these women their own intellectual endeavors don't count at all.[3] They want their *men* to read books, be "intellectual," because only what the men do and learn will change the status of the family as a whole. "Her activity could not define the family as an intellectual family; only her husband and perhaps her children could do that."

The typical exclusion of women from Torah study carried into secular realms. Though this study was not always explicitly forbidden to women, it was rarely encouraged. And those few women who defied law and custom to create for themselves a life of the mind were often threatened or punished. Their struggle to become educated was not easy. Even in America, while second-generation Jewish women could assume they would get at least a public-school education, this too was a privilege hard fought for by immigrant women battling entrenched ideas in their families about the propriety of educating females. One woman, for example, queries the advice column of the *Jewish Daily Forward* in 1910: "I ask you to decide whether a married woman has the right to go to school two evenings a week. My husband thinks I have no right to do this. . . . My children and my house are not neglected, but I go to evening high school twice a week. My husband is not pleased and when I come home at night and ring the bell, he lets me stand outside a long time intentionally, and doesn't hurry to open the door. . . . When I am alone with my thoughts, I feel I may not be right. Perhaps I should not go to school. I want to say that my husband is an intelligent man and he wanted to marry a woman who was educated. . . . He is in favor of the emancipation of women, yet in real life he acts contrary to his beliefs."[4]

The force of the Jewish traditions against women's intellectual efforts has often run up against an equally strong force of women's desire to study and to express themselves. Historian Norma Fain Pratt describes the experience of Malke Lee, a turn-of-the-century Yiddish-language poet whose autobiography "revealed with intense bitterness that her father, a pious man, secretly burned her entire portfolio of poetry in the family oven because he believed it was against God's will that a girl write."[5]

THE MIXED MESSAGE FOR JEWISH WOMEN:
"BE SMART—BUT NOT TOO SMART"
(OR, "YOU'LL GET SMICHA ON YOUR KUGEL")

In America, education was an almost certain way for all Jews to move beyond immigrant poverty, so education became a necessity for advancement, if not for survival itself. Jewish women understood this also. In Pittsburgh in the 1920s, for example, records of night-school attendance show that classes were attended largely by Jewish women.

Sociologist Marshall Sklare connects Jewish women's eagerness to learn with a desire for self-fulfillment rather than economic advancement, but asks "why so many of them were given an education. Neither Jewish tradition nor the American culture to which their immigrant parents were exposed encouraged such high educational aspirations for females."[6] Many American Jewish women, when it came to education, turned out to be Jews first. The tales told by the first generation of immigrant women speak of their joy at finding free public-school education; many of them had been starved for learning in the Old Country, and were willing to risk disapproval in order to go to school. Jewish women, being Jews, heard the message about the value placed on education even if it was intended for their brothers' ears alone. A cross-cultural study of American women from different ethnic groups shows that Jewish women continue to value education more than other women do.[7] Reviewing a book about modern women of achievement, Mary Cantwell notes that many of them are Jewish, suggesting that "a passion for education outweighs sexism."[8]

In fact, it is this special tension within a culture that values education and then excludes half its members from full access to that valued activity which creates the atmosphere of ambivalence toward women's intellectual achievements unique to Jewish life. This is more complicated than mere exclusion. Other cultures have also systematically limited women's educational opportunities. For American examples one need look no further than the poetry of Emily Dickinson, which barely saw the light of day while she lived, or the life of Alice James, sister of Henry and William, whose father denied her the fine schooling her brothers had because he flatly opposed education for women. The difference between Jewish women and non-Jewish women who also suffered the oppression of not being educated is precisely the ambivalence that Jewish women experience when limits are placed on their achievements: Be smart (because you're Jewish) but not too smart (because you're female).

As Jewish women we often fear the consequences of being smarter than our brothers or husbands. In fact, several studies indicate that women with no male siblings are the highest achievers. "Playing dumb" may be particularly hard for Jewish women, because we associate dumb with failure, yet a "double bind" exists for us, because being smart may be perilous too. Like the women of other minority groups—most obviously black women—we don't want to put our men in a position of double jeopardy—oppressed in the outside world and made to feel inferior at home. (We're unlike black women in that education in black families is viewed as more appropriate for daughters than for sons.) For many Jewish women, getting an education is an adventure fraught with difficulty, since no-holds-barred all-out academic or occupational success may be failure by another name—failure to be passive enough (and ignorant enough?) to make someone a good wife.

Even Annie Nathan Meyer, the guiding force behind the founding of Barnard College and great-granddaughter of the first Jewish trustee of Columbia College, was discouraged by her own father from continuing her education. "Men hate intelligent wives," he said.[9]

In a Jewish family, and in the community as a whole, there is always a lot of *naches* (pleasure) when a Jewish man does well academically: "My son the doctor . . ." "My son the lawyer . . ." But women's achievements seem dogged by the lurking shadow of failure in the marriage department. Intellectual success is sanctioned only if one is also a success on the domestic front: "My parents have four daughters: a college student, a medical student, a writer, a lawyer. But they aren't content. Though we're all only in our twenties, they're already concerned because there have been no weddings and no grandchildren."

"My mother says to me," reports an unmarried woman in her early thirties, " 'You may have a mind like a steel trap, but not every man you go out with wants to get caught in it. You don't have to express your opinions, or analyze what his problems are.' " And a mother says, "My

Students at the Tonya Soloveitchik Yeshiva High School for Girls of Yeshiva University in New York. (Yeshiva University)

daughter is going to educate herself right out of the marriage market," as if marriage were a job for which one could possibly be overqualified.

Not all Jewish parents have had negative feelings about women's learning, but those who do feel negative about it can find plenty of support, even today, both in Jewish sources and in popular culture. Remember the wife Saul Bellow creates in *Herzog*? Madeline barricades herself in bed with the Russian books she's working on, using her studies literally as a barrier around her, which her husband can't penetrate. Education is blamed for inducing female "frigidity." A 1980 headline in a Jewish newspaper reads: "Bet Din [religious court] Head Blames Wives' Education for Epidemic of Divorces." The thesis here is that women, particularly from very religious backgrounds, are getting a better secular education than their husbands, work outside the home, find out what the rest of the world is like, and therefore want to divorce their parochial husbands. Q.E.D. Education is blamed for inducing marital discontent.

Again and again education and marriage (or marital happiness) are juxtaposed, setting up false choices for women, as if one can be attained only at the expense of the other. The hidden threat behind all the parental imprecations has been: *If you get too smart you'll never get a husband. Jewish men are especially vulnerable and like to be "smarter" (or at least better educated) than their wives. So if you want a nice Jewish husband, you'd better shape down.*

(With this goal in mind, a Brooklyn father is reported to have told his three scholarly daughters, "What are you studying so hard for? Don't worry—you'll get *smicha* [rabbinical ordination] on your *kugel* [pudding].")

In sharp contrast to this view that marriage is the end point for Jewish women, with education merely a small diversion en route, is the attitude among black American women: "So many black girls heard these words, they might have been programmed tapes: 'Girl, get yourself an education, you can't count on a man to take care of you.' 'An education is something no one can take from you.' 'Any fool can get married, but not everyone can go to school.' "[10]

Since in most Jewish families no sacrifice was too great when it came to educating sons, the negative associations with educating women are cast into sharp relief. Even families that support their daughters' Jewish studies, distinguish between "enough" and "too much" education. Blu Greenberg recalls:

During my junior year in college, I studied in Israel for several months at a Hebrew teachers' institute. Nechama Liebowitz was my teacher for Bible. She was the most brilliant, exciting teacher I ever had, and she became an extraordinary model for me. As the time neared to return home, I decided I wanted to take a year off from Brooklyn College where I had been enrolled and just study intensively with Nechama. She was then teaching at fifteen different places, from army camps to kibbutz seminars. My intention was to make Jerusalem my home base, follow Nechama to all the places she taught, and learn from her day and night. "Come home and finish college," said my parents. "You're crazy," said most of my friends. In the back of my mind, I guess I somehow knew that it wasn't the sort of thing a nice Orthodox Jewish girl would do. Not being assertive or terribly independent, I came home. I quietly knew that had I been a young man wanting to stay on and study intensively with a special Israeli rebbe, every encouragement would have been forthcoming.[11]

The greatest conflict arose in those Jewish families in which there was not sufficient money to educate all the children equally and the parents had to make choices. At least in the years preceding the Second World War most families decided to educate their sons, almost regardless of interest or ability. Economic realities made this a sane move: men would work for more years than their sisters and get paid more for every year they worked. Many a family pattern echoed this one, described by a man in his sixties: "My twin sister went out to work and I went to college. The assumption was that she would marry anyway and would never need or make use of her education. So today she is a suburban housewife and I'm the head of a big company." And a woman who got her Ph.D. in her late fifties says: "I was the brightest one in the family, but I went out to work as a bookkeeper so that my brothers could go to college and 'get ahead.'"

BREAKING THE BOUNDARIES:
JEWISH WOMEN AS SCHOLARS

Despite the traditional restriction of much of Jewish learning to men, women have begun to close the gap. Positive changes are the more nearly equal educational opportunities for Jewish women in the world at large; the ways Jewish children are educated; the rising incidence of Bat Mitzvah celebrations (and hence prefatory study); adult education programs; and the emergence of a body of Jewish women as Jewish scholars.

In the postwar years families had more disposable income, and a high proportion of young Jewish women entered college. By the 1950s a college education was in the same category as music lessons: an adornment for a middle-class Jewish woman or the "dowry" she brought her husband.

If the big change since the forties is that Jewish women are going to college at about the same rate as Jewish men, the hot news of the last decade is that since the rebirth of the women's movement in the late 1960s, Jewish women have entered the high-ranking professional schools in astonishing numbers. The prestigious schools of law, medicine, and business all have proportions of women in their classes from 25 to 50 percent, of whom many are Jewish. (For more on this, see "Affirmative Action," p. 492.) According to studies analyzed by the American Jewish Committee in 1969, 3 percent of Jewish women who were college freshmen planned to study for advanced degrees; by 1980 the number was six times as many. (The increase for non-Jewish female college freshmen was only two-and-a-half to one.)

In the 1980s Jewish women are, like all women, receiving secular education approximately equal to what men get; meanwhile parallel changes have been taking place in Jewish education, where the struggle to achieve parity is still joined.

We know very little about the internal intellectual life of the women

(© 1980 by Bonnie S. Geller)

who were assigned the supporting role in Jewish learning and creativity. What we do know is that women were not only excluded from many areas of Jewish—and secular—study but also that those who did manage to sneak into the halls of study, or to study on their own, faced having their accomplishments played down just because they were women.

It was the rare woman who, like the wife of Jacob Mizrachi, a sixteenth-century scholar in Kurdistan, taught in her husband's yeshiva and headed it after his death. (So that she would not be deflected from a life of study, her father, also a scholar, stipulated in a condition of her marriage contract that she was to do no housework!) [12]

One woman who does achieve recognition as a scholar herself is ultimately diminished in stature when she's "revealed" to have been a loose woman. By contrast to Akiva's wife, Bruriah, a third-century woman who was a Talmud scholar in her own right, has until recently had very little coverage in the texts and storybooks.

Stepping outside the traditional role of helpmate (though she was clearly that as well), Bruriah ridiculed the absurdity of those rabbis who instructed men not to talk to women—for example, in the Talmudic injunction "Speak not to women because they are light-headed." The original Talmudic tales of Bruriah stress her insights, fairness, compassion, kindliness. But Rashi, the twelfth-century commentator on the Talmud, invents a tale—eight hundred years after her death—that Bruriah's husband told her she'd pay with her life for going against what the sages had to say about women. According to Rashi, he sent a student to seduce her. The student succeeded after some time, and Bruriah, realizing what she had done, killed herself.

Cynthia Ozick describes the incident: "[Bruriah] was known to speak satirically of those rabbinic passages which make light of the intellect of women. To punish her for her impudence, a rabbinic storyteller, bent on mischief toward intellectual women, reinvented Bruriah as a seductress. She comes down to us, then, twice notorious: first as a kind of bluestocking, again as a licentious woman. There is no doubt that we are meant to see the connection between the two." [13] Rashi's gratuitous besmirching of Bruriah's name is evidence that the presence of a strong, well-educated, intellectual woman in their midst was a threat to Jewish men.

Like Bruriah, there are other Jewish women whose intellectual accomplishments have been distorted, undervalued, or masked in one way or another; and there are, alas, other examples of men devaluing Jewish women's intellectual experience. *Tsena-U'Rena*, the most popular text for Jewish women for the past three hundred years, is not even listed in the 24-volume *Encyclopedia Judaica*, which, since its publication in 1973, has been the standard reference tool for who's who and what's what in Jewish life. The *Encyclopedia Judaica* does, however, give us such important Jewish entries as turtle-dove ("an onomatopoeic word").

A Yiddish book of Bible stories and commentary on them, *Tsena-U'Rena* (literally, go forth and behold) was *the* text for pious Jewish women from its publication in the early seventeenth century. Since reading secular matter was frowned upon for both men and women, *Tsena-U'Rena* became the source of stories also, full of human interest and moral discussion. It was the one sanctioned intellectual resource for Jewish women, the source to which many turned for knowledge and instruction. Through this book women had a chance to find out a little something about the world of scholarship and study that appeared so compelling for men. "What was so captivating about that book that it held women's attention for three hundred years?" a contemporary Jewish educator asks. "My grandmother could sit in a corner of her grocery store with it and take on any visiting rabbi." *Tsena-U'Rena* was for some women a narrow entryway into the male arena of learned disputation.

Of course not all Jewish women have had to restrict their learning to *Tsena U'Rena*. But even those who are learned people by any standards are often denied their full appreciation because they're female. An example is Nechama Liebowitz, the Israeli teacher whose analyses of Biblical texts are so respected that she has been called "one of the world's foremost teachers of Bible."[14] But Nechama Liebowitz, whose name is a household word to those involved in serious Jewish study, is not even mentioned in the *Encyclopedia Judaica*. Nechama Liebowitz may be "renowned," as one recent review of her *Studies in Vayikra* (Leviticus) claims, but she is also invisible. The omission of her name from the *Encyclopedia Judaica* is by no means the worst crime against women's intellectual contributions to Judaism, but it's a measure of how women's work is undervalued, underpublicized, and therefore more prone to be ignored, both now and by future historians.

A benchmark of the sacrifices a woman might be willing to make in order to study is Yentl, title figure in the I. B. Singer story (the basis for a Broadway play and for the Barbra Streisand film). In order to satisfy her thirst for Jewish learning, Yentl, a premodern Eastern European Jew, disguises herself as a young man and lives for the activities in the Bet Midrash, the house of study. She falls in love with a young male student, and the story has a tragic finale. For her there was no successful resolution of the conflict between being a good (therefore studious) Jew and being a "good" ("domesticated") Jewish woman.

But even for women who would study only after fulfilling their traditional roles and obligations the path may be rocky. The male attitude
that women are dangerous (or in danger) sexually (see "Our Bodies,"
p. 207) affects some men's interpretations of Jewish law and hence some
women's opportunities for study. One Brooklyn woman, who was studying recently in a group of other observant women, was forbidden by her
husband to attend classes anymore, because he felt that women should
not be learning *Gemara* (the second part of the Talmud) and other advanced texts that they were analyzing. The woman and her husband
finally took their disagreement to a rabbi, who ruled that it was permissible for the woman to study with her group only when women were teaching other women. When a man was scheduled to teach the group, she was
not to go to class; this mixing of the sexes might suggest impropriety or
immodesty. Since the learning tools for Jewish scholarship have belonged
exclusively to men, how are women to begin to gain access to them if
this rabbi's attitude prevails? *Some* woman has to begin to learn from
men before she can teach other women.

Naturally this rabbi's decision isn't binding on *all* women, nor is it
based on a commonly held view; many learned Orthodox rabbis teach
women. But the story is instructive as an example of the stumbling
blocks still sometimes placed before Jewish women who want to enter
the men's club of Jewish scholarship. More common, however, especially
among Jews who have adapted more to American norms, is the reversal
of the shtetl situation in which the husband studied and the wife earned
a living. Now American Jewish men have become "practical" like their
grandmothers and have entered the economic mainstream, while for middle-class American Jewish women education has become a prime, sanctioned, leisure-time activity.

One example of this turnaround is taking place in the Syrian Jewish
community in Brooklyn, where women who ten years ago took adult-
education courses in crafts are now studying religion. For the first time
religious study has become a women's pursuit. According to anthropologist Faye Ginsburg, who has studied the community, "the new popularity
of religious education for young women . . . ensures that women with
increased leisure time will not threaten the structure of communal life"
(that is, by going out to work).

There are parallels between the shifts in the availability of religious
study for women and their access to secular education, and concomitant
tensions between women's Jewish and secular educations.

When secular learning was devalued, women could acquire it. As a result, there have been times in Jewish history when women were well edu-

cated in secular subjects. An older woman's outrage spills forth in Barbara Myerhoff's study of elderly Jewish women and men, *Number Our Days*:

> The rabbi spoke of scholarship, "the essence of Judaism," and said that the luckiest man among Jews was a retired man who had the freedom to study Torah to his fill.
>
> "That's right—the luckiest man," Hannah leaned over me to tell Nathan. "And what about the girls who were never taught Hebrew? He doesn't speak about what old women are supposed to be doing with all this freedom, you notice. Our rabbi, may he rest in peace, told me an educated woman was a cinder in God's eye. Fortunately he meant educated in religion. So because I was a girl, they let me go to school and study science. For the boys, they got the *real* education."[15]

Jewish women have ridden a kind of seesaw, with secular and religious education throwing each other into relief when the (male) authorities have become concerned that women were receiving either too little religious education (and were therefore likely to assimilate) or alternatively, secular learning was offered as a substitute for the religious education males had. Historian Reena Sigman Friedman writes:

> This process is particularly well illustrated in early nineteenth-century Germany, where a significant number of Jewish women became prominent in German cultural and intellectual circles. The most famous of these were the so-called "salon Jewesses": Henrietta Herz, Dorothea Mendelssohn and Rachel Varnhagen, whose soirees attracted some of the most prominent philosophers and litterateurs of their day. The lives of these salon Jewesses, all of whom eventually converted to Christianity, dramatically illustrated the tendency of many Jewish intellectuals to surrender their Jewish identity in this period, a tendency that was even more marked for Jewish women who had received the benefits of a secular but not a Jewish education.
>
> Educators associated with the Haskalah [Jewish Enlightenment] of this time were alarmed by the growing numbers of young Jewish women who, attracted by Christian Romanticism, abandoned Judaism as a dry, legalistic faith, incapable of satisfying their innermost religious yearnings. In response to what they regarded as a grave threat to Jewish survival, they established schools for girls (with curricula combining traditional Jewish and secular education), separate girls' courses within their schools for boys and columns addressed to Jewish girls in their various educational publications. While these Maskilic [Enlightenment movement] schools pioneered in the field of formal Jewish education for women, their curricula reflected the sex-role

(Gay Block)

stereotypes of their day; boys studied more substantive subjects such as Bible and Rabbinic literature and girls were instructed in domestic science and ethics.

While many argue that Jewish women have traditionally occupied an honored position within the home and family, there is little doubt that they were relegated to second-class status in the central arenas of public prayer and sacred study throughout much of Jewish history. The potential danger inherent in this situation, as the German Maskilim clearly recognized, was that Jewish women who had achieved recognition and a measure of equality in secular society would no longer be content with limitations imposed on them as Jews, and would therefore seek to abandon their Jewish heritage. The efforts of the Maskilim to improve Jewish education for women constituted a vigorous response to that challenge, one that is still very much with us today.[16]

In a situation similar to the one in Germany, young Jewish women in nineteenth-century Russia were also allowed to have (and sometimes encouraged to obtain) a secular education. Many trained in medical specialities—as doctors, dentists, feldshers, nurses. But Jewish study remained closed to them. Daughters were given a secular education, sons a religious education, and the result was that many daughters left the faith, having no sense of rootedness as Jews. As was the case with the "salon Jewesses" of nineteenth-century Germany, secular education with no parallel Jewish education appeared to be the first step in their defection.

Another alarum over the consequences of an exclusively secular education for Jewish women was sounded in the first decades of this century in the Polish Jewish community. Sara Schenirer, concerned that Jewish schools allowed no entry to females, founded a school especially to teach Jewish subjects to girls and young women. Orthodox authorities, seeing that even girls from Orthodox families were straying from tradition as a result of their secular education and exposure to modern life, conceded that it was necessary to offer them some Jewish education. "The Hafetz Hayyim, the outstanding halachic authority of his generation, was to answer critics on the religious right by saying that in view of changing social conditions—widespread assimilation and the breakdown of traditional Jewish family life—the historical prohibitions against women's education were to be disregarded, and that, on the contrary, it would be a *mitzvah* to teach Jewish girls the fundamentals of their faith."[17]

The Bais Yaakov schools founded by Schenirer have expanded to an international network of girls-only religious schools (with many similar schools founded by various religious groups). They now seem very traditional, representing a separatist strain in Jewish education that is anathema to many modern Jewish women. However, the story of the origin of the schools in response to the threat of assimilation has a familiar ring to it as we track the course of present-day waxing and waning efforts for the education of Jewish women.

There's some risk that Jewish education for women may now be seen, particularly by men fearful of assimilation, as an important "emergency" step to Save the Jews. Jewishly educated Jewish women are now, in some circles, thought to be "good for the Jews." This places a very heavy burden on us as women. In a Purim address a Toronto rabbi likens present-day women to Queen Esther, who saved the Jews from the Persians: "Today again our salvation rests in the hands of our women," and he goes on to say that while in the past education of Jewish women had indeed been neglected, now "the trend has changed."[18] There has certainly been improvement in the quality of Jewish education for females, but it would be a heavy price to pay for this education if Jewish women are now going to have to be solely responsible for Jewish salvation!

There's a historical model for this too. Jewish women have been willing to accept the notion that we are responsible for transmitting Jewish culture through the generations, despite the fact that few of us have had the opportunity to learn that culture rigorously. Historian Marion Kaplan warns that women's efforts alone cannot stave off assimilation; she feels, in fact, that women leave themselves open to blame by accepting this overwhelming responsibility. "By concurring with the stereotype of themselves as educators, Jewish feminists [in nineteenth- and early twentieth-century Germany] set themselves up for final failure."[19]

The paradoxical status of Jewish women's education—it was considered necessary if women were going to be able to teach their children, but it was acceptable only if it was of a limited nature—was not exclusively a problem of European or first-generation immigrant women. The paradox continues in somewhat different forms even in Jewish education today.

WOMEN AND GIRLS IN JEWISH SCHOOLS: A STATUS REPORT

Historical evidence supports the view that Jewish women were not meant to be shortchanged. When Queen Salome Alexandra of Judea (139–67 B.C.E.) promulgated a law insisting that Jewish communities educate their children, her intention was to make it incumbent upon them to provide both daughters and sons with a basic education. Somehow, through time, this principle was transmuted into an obligation to educate only male offspring. Even now, in the eighties, complete equality isn't yet at hand. In 1982, only 40 percent of students receiving any Jewish education were female.[20]

In one recent study done by the Reform movement, the most nearly egalitarian branch of Judaism, girls make up only 45 percent of the Hebrew school students. From these enrollment statistics it's clear that parents consider the Jewish education of their sons more important than that of their daughters, despite the commonly held opinion that the mother is supposed to be the primary transmitter of Jewish values to her children. If you believe that the mother is the parent responsible for making the kids Jewish, enlightened self-interest alone would suggest that Jewish girls and young women should, if anything, be given a *better* Jewish education and be taught to feel even *better* about themselves as Jews than their brothers.

Needless to say, this isn't usually the case. Paradoxically, while Jewish women are advancing into the front ranks of the nation's well-educated professional women, whole areas of Jewish study may still be closed off to them. From studies of who gets a Jewish education, what is taught, and who does the teaching to Jewish children and adults, we learn that sexism is rampant, with fewer girls learning, with curricula stressing male achievement, and with most teachers themselves being undervalued and underpaid Jewish women.

Discrimination (for that's what it is) against females in Jewish education cuts across all denominational lines. Orthodox Jews may argue that according to Jewish law women and men should take different roles in the family's ritual practice (with women excluded from communal prayer, for example), but there's a difference between legal distinctions and simple discrimination against women, which has been accorded permanent status by virtue of long-standing custom.

One such "custom" is that women should be the teachers of young children, especially in elementary-level religious schools. Perhaps this is an extension of the idea that only women can provide appropriate nurturing. So, *in loco parentis*, the teachers of young children are women. This fits nicely with the fact that in America most children go to "part-time" or after-school Hebrew schools, which therefore need to hire only "part-time" Hebrew teachers. Who is available (or willing) to work only part of the day? Women. And who wants a son or daughter to grow up to be a Hebrew-school teacher? There's little honor to the job, and a low salary to boot. Doris B. Gold points out: "A community will hire a professional architect for a new synagogue building, a professional caterer for the Bat/Bar Mitzvah, often even a professional choir. But when it comes to teachers, anyone available will do."

A landmark 1979 statistical survey, "Women in Jewish Schools," released by the American Association for Jewish Education (now the Jewish Education Service of North America) seeks to explain why "so few women are engaged in supervisory roles in a field which, as teachers, they dominate numerically." *Less than 10 percent of all the women employed in Jewish education are principals, supervisors, or educational directors.* A clear finding was that these women believe that either direct or indirect sexual discrimination prevents them from advancing to administrative and executive positions.

A large number of them—61 percent—said that traditional concepts of the role of Jewish women held by the male-dominated religious and communal establishment contribute to impeding their advancement. Some of this discrimination may diminish as more women rabbis enter the field of Jewish education. Not all the women now being ordained in the Reform and Reconstructionist rabbinical colleges (and soon to be ordained in the Conservative movement as well) will find their way into pulpits. Some may choose to use their rabbinical degrees as men have for years—as entry passes to certain leadership positions in the Jewish community, which will doubtless include positions of educational leadership.

Until recently (the last twenty years or so), relatively few Jewish girls received a rigorous Jewish education through high school. While in co-ed Hebrew day schools many courses were the same for boys and girls, once study of *Gemara* began in high school, girls were sent off on a different track to learn typing or sewing or cooking. Now even in schools where girls are educated separately the texts studied are usually the same as they have been for Jewish boys. As for typing, which is one of the requirements for getting a high school diploma at one Orthodox girls' high school in New York, the principal of the school, Rivka T. Blau, says: "Yes, I believe that the girls must learn to type. It will come in very handy when they're preparing their Ph.D. theses." Blau also says that she believes that all students—girls and boys alike—should be made more familiar with original texts, so that they can make up their own minds on issues, not deriving their opinions from secondary sources. (Of course, according to a 1977 study by Dr. Geoffrey E. Bock—"Does Jewish Schooling Matter?"—for the American Jewish Committee, boys are more likely than girls to attend schools in which such a rigorous education is provided.)

For a majority of students the hours spent in an afternoon Hebrew school or in Sunday school constitute their only Jewish learning experience. Therefore, what happens there is crucial to the formation of their attitudes—and, for a girl, her self-image too. Moreover, many families rely on the Jewish school to carry the burden (or the responsibility) for establishing the child's Jewish identity. Since there is often little countervailing Jewish reality at home, Jewish schools must be especially careful not to exclude any child, regardless of gender, from any aspect of Jewish life.

We don't want to raise a generation of Jews who see that in the outside world men and women are advancing—albeit slowly—toward more nearly equal opportunities while the Judaism they're exposed to in Hebrew school shows a community making little or no commitment to gender justice. The consequence may be that young Jewish women will see opportunities for themselves in the secular world but few in Jewish life. Having learned well the lesson that Judaism is a men's club, they may vote with their feet and choose not to affiliate with Judaism as adults.

The community as a whole may have made progress toward equalizing female and male roles, especially in the last decade, but Jewish schools have often failed to transmit any sense of that changing reality to students. It's the rare school that exposes its students to the new books, rituals, nonsexist liturgies, and historical studies of Jewish women which Jewish feminist activists have produced.

With premature optimism, some thought that the gains made by women in the Jewish religious and communal spheres in the 1970s would be absorbed by osmosis into all areas of Jewish life. We were wrong.

It turns out that we are going to have to continue the struggle for equality into the next generation, and monitor very closely the ways in which our sons and daughters are being taught to be Jews. Unless we are vigilant, and willing to use the tools the feminist movement has given us for making change, our daughters may have to fight the same battles again. Our challenge as parents and concerned educators is to build on what we already know about how positive change can be made, eliminating sexism from Jewish education and creating instead a Jewish model for teaching gender justice.

HOW TO ERADICATE SEXISM IN
CHILDREN'S JEWISH EDUCATION

Changing the atmosphere begins with having information about what you'd ideally like to see in the classroom. Observe in the school whenever possible, and ask the children questions about what goes on there, not just about the classroom work itself.

• *Are girls enrolled in approximately the same numbers as boys?* This ratio may vary from class to class, but if there is a serious imbalance on a schoolwide level, ask an administrator why s/he thinks it's happened. Sometimes you'll get a plausible "accidental" explanation.

When boys outnumber girls by more than about 10 percent, it may be a sign that the school discourages girls, or it may be that the parents attracted to this particular school don't value a Jewish education as much for their daughters as for their sons.

• *Is the faculty co-ed?* Or are all the teachers women and the administrators men? Some schools say they can "afford" to hire only women.

One faculty structure at a Conservative Hebrew day school in New York had one male—at the top—and women in all other positions. This situation is, alas, hardly unique. According to the 1979 statistical report by the American Association for Jewish Education (now known as Jewish Education Service of North America), women are paid less for the same or comparable work and are promoted much less frequently than men.[21]

Women teachers may need to have a more positive sense of themselves—
and certainly need to achieve pay equity—before they can convey positive images of womanhood to students.

• *Is there a dress code that discriminates against girls?* For example,
skirts always, or on Erev Shabbat? No girl can function comfortably in
the playground in a skirt. There is also a message transmitted when girls
are required to wear skirts each day: that they are to make themselves
into objects, that they are to dress in a way that makes them (and the
boys) conscious of their roles and their gender in what should be a gen-
derless situation. One teacher, protesting the situation in a Hebrew day
school with just such a dress code for the girls, commented: "No matter
how young they are, it doesn't take long before boys in the playground
will tease a girl about seeing her underpants."

Religious Jewish schools can always fall back on a Torah rationale for
keeping girls and boys from "cross-dressing" (see "Our Bodies," p. 240).
But one day school, asked to defend its anticulotte regulation on these
grounds, replied that "culottes aren't *boys'* clothing, but we still don't allow them for girls. Skirts are just our school uniform. Even some nonreligious private schools require uniforms, so just think of it that way."

• *Is there unnecessary segregation of the sexes?* In one school even
class lists were separated according to gender—not even the names could
touch! The underlying reality—and the lists were a clue—was that the social life of the students was also rigidly stratified by sex, as early as the
primary grades. Even at nonreligious functions boys and girls were seated
at separate tables.

• *What hidden curriculum is presented by the images in textbooks and
storybooks?* According to a 1975 study:

> Most women are portrayed as housewives, while men are seen as doc-
> tors, judges, builders, etc. All temple activities are male-dominated,
> with rabbis, presidents, and members of the Boards of Trustees pic-
> tured as men. Men carry the Torah, read from the Torah, etc. Men
> play the more important roles while women, if they are portrayed as
> active in synagogue life at all, serve in the Sisterhood and are shown as
> part of the congregation at worship or opening the Ark, at best.
>
> Males are always shown as brighter and more active than females. In
> too many instances, the majority of main characters are male. Bible
> stories, history books, and Hebrew books neglect the role of women,
> both historically and in story material.[22]

An even more distressing example is the attractive illustrated *Sh'ma*
series of storybooks published by the Union of American Hebrew Con-

gregations. One, entitled *About Learning*, shows 133 males and only 24 females; worse, however, than this numerical imbalance are the positions in which women and girls appear. In the sections "Torah Is for Learning," "A Leader Is for Teaching," and others, the illustrations show men teaching, holding the Torah, being wise; most of those learning are boys and men. But as soon as we get to the section "A Heart is for Caring" we have pictures of girls and women. Playing right into stereotyped notions of women's separate sphere, all the learning pictured here relates to the expression of emotions, rather than showing women engaged in study or leadership as the men are. A mother bends to minister to her little daughter. Another woman kneels in supplication. Worse, the Biblical tale used to illustrate the concept is one in which King Solomon decides who is the real mother of a disputed baby. We finally have a section in which females are shown (stereotyped), and the story told is of competitiveness and manipulation in a situation that had to be resolved by a wise male.

Although the book was originally published in 1971, it is still widely distributed and read, its alluring artwork making it even more damaging than some of the tackier sexist Jewish children's stories on the market. This series looks as good as the best secular children's books and therefore may be taken more seriously by children than some of the other storybooks that sensitive parents would reject outright.

Dr. Gladys Rosen, convener of a "consultation" on the portrayal of girls and women in school materials at the American Jewish Committee in 1978, writes that in most study materials the men have "the most highly prized characteristics such as intelligence, initiative and emotional strength while women have been defined in socio-biological terms with their functions largely limited to the home and family life.[23] The texts that most schools use have few if any portrayals of girls and women in active roles in Jewish communal or religious life. Jewish history, for example, is taught as the history of Jewish men. The few women who've had a role in shaping that history can be counted on one hand—and can be named by even fewer students.

As an exercise, a teacher in a Hebrew high school classroom asked her students, all of whom had had several years of after-school Hebrew school, using standard texts, to name ten famous Jewish men and women. No one could name more than three women. Students had absolutely no sense of what roles women had played in Jewish life, with the exception of Golda Meir.

• *What pictures do the students see?* The informal materials used in Jewish classrooms often reinforce the sexism of the texts. One mother in suburban New Jersey reports: "At Simchat Torah celebrations last year [the holiday when children and adults march with colored flags around and with the Torah], my daughter was handed a flag which showed a smiling male rabbi surrounded by a group of smiling male children. I frantically searched the room for another model I'd seen—one that featured two lions." Similarly, most of the holiday pictures her children bring home from school to color show a father-and-son team entering the synagogue for Shabbat, building the succah, holding the *lulav* and *etrog*.

One school had its corridors lined with oversize emotion-laden photographs of Israeli scenes: men praying at the Western Wall in Jerusalem, soldiers in uniform at prayer, the shofar being blown by an old man with a *tallit* covering his head, men dancing with Torahs on Simchat Torah. Not one picture showed a woman. The message was that women were, and should be, invisible in Jewish life—not heard, and not even seen! Other schools feature drawings and photos of Jewish male role models from Abraham to Herzl, also with no women in sight.

The standard decorations in Hebrew school classrooms fall into the same category: they show no women and girls, or (maybe worse) show them painted into eternal domesticity. In one classroom many drawings of The Jewish Family were posted above the blackboard. Mother was *never* pictured—except when lighting the Sabbath candles—doing anything unrelated to children or cooking: she was holding the baby, setting the table for Shabbat, making latkes. Father studied, went to shul, and blessed the Sabbath wine, with the family looking respectfully on. Mother is never shown studying or even reading, to say nothing of entering synagogue or being out of the house in any role whatever—not even buying the potatoes for the latkes!

• *Try to evaluate individual teachers* on the staff both by sitting in the classroom when possible and by talking with them. Some may not support the institutionalized sexism of the Jewish schools. In one very gender-conscious Orthodox yeshiva, for instance, the male gym teacher insisted that girls participate in the same sports activities as boys. (Of course the two sexes didn't play *together* at gym, and the boys *did* take up the lion's share of the gym space when sharing was necessary!)

Another optimistic report says:

I went into a meeting with my son's new sixth-grade Hebrew day school teacher very suspicious. He looked like a very traditional young man, and I figured that he must be giving the students the party line on roles for men and women in the Bible and in Judaism. (I feel strongly that sexist attitudes are as bad for my son to learn as for my daughter.)

Responding to a question, he said, "We stop and discuss the prayers we're saying. For example, when we come to the prayer that the boys say each morning, thanking God for not having made them a woman, I have told them that some people have interpreted that to mean that Jewish law has divided things up so that men are responsible for some rituals and women for others, or that certain mitzvot are reserved for women and others for men. I tell them that I don't interpret the prayers that way, but that they were written in a time when people did believe that men and women had very different roles to play in Jewish life."

Try to identify those teachers who support your vision of a more nearly egalitarian school. They might be very receptive to having parents present them with hard-to-find material, or welcome any other parental input. (See Resources, p. 173, for where to order some of these.)

Teachers can sensitize students to understand the bias that has left them with such gaps in their knowledge. Annette Daum, a master teacher herself, has designed a course to create such sensitization; even grammar exercises can be used as lessons in the limits of gender-linked associations. The course, "Male and Female in Religion" has two goals for its first session:

1. To have the students examine the school curriculum to see how educational material presents the roles of men and women.

2. To have the students recommend methods of avoiding role stereotyping in the religious school curriculum.

Students draw pictures and write descriptions of the "Jewish mother" and the "Jewish father," so that they see where their own biases are. They go on to explore Biblical stereotyping of men and women and are asked to rewrite some inaccurate but commonly accepted English translations of Biblical Hebrew so as to restore them to their original and more egalitarian meaning.

One session is devoted to Jewish ritual, and the students are encouraged to write new ceremonies—for example, to celebrate the naming of a newborn daughter. Another session focuses on Passover and the need to explore and expand upon the role of women in the Exodus story: Miriam, Jocheved, Zipporah, the midwives. The course includes a session on women in Jewish history, particularly emphasizing the contribution of American Jewish women from Revolutionary times to the present. The names on her list include Ernestine Rose, Rebecca Gratz, and Hannah Solomon. Sometimes just looking for information on these women is a shock—there's almost nothing on any women in standard Jewish reference books.

As their consciousness is raised through an understanding of the paucity of information about women in Jewish history, the students in Daum's course begin to look at the language in which the history and liturgy were written and at who was writing them, and the class prepares a nonsexist service for the entire religious school. Daum says that "the language of prayer, especially language about God, is the most difficult to deal with. Students had difficulty understanding the problem until I substituted 'She' for 'He' in every prayer."

One particularly useful aspect of the course is that it teaches the students to evaluate educational materials for themselves. With this approach, even negative or limiting portrayals of women can be useful: correcting them becomes a good learning device.

• *Ask the teachers to let you bring into the classroom men and women from the community*—women rabbis, cantors, and experts in various fields of Judaica, and men who are engaged in nontraditional pursuits—for example, have a man who's a good cook come in and share his favorite recipes or have a man who's a weaver show how he makes a *tallit.* Your hidden purpose, of course, is to have the children see these figures as role models, shaking loose the images implanted on their retinas by the rigidly defined men's and women's tasks pictured in most books and Jewish posters.

In the process of waging their battle some of the parents learned a lesson that they could apply to other school situations as well: religion is sometimes used as the rationale for the policies that the administrator of a school wants to employ anyway, with no awareness of his/her own hypocrisy.

• *Change the bulletin boards.* In one school—despite walls with posters showing Mommy at home in an apron with Dvoreleh and David and the dog, Daddy going off to work with a briefcase—one single parent head-of-household got the school to recognize the fact that more than 75 percent of its students came from families other than the four-member one shown on the wall.

She suggested that the children bring in and post their own family pictures. The children felt much more comfortable seeing photographs on the wall of their own families at various Jewish celebrations—at weddings, in a succah, or holding a freshly baked challah. The children were better able to feel that Judaism was for them too, not just for the Dick-and-Jane style of nuclear family.

• *Bring in nonsexist books for Jewish children* (see "Celebrating the Jewish Calendar," p. 92, for examples). Suggest that some of these books be ordered for the annual book fair—most schools hold these in conjunction with Jewish Book Month in November.

Protest to the librarian about any book your child brings home from Hebrew school that is especially limiting in its representation of girls and women. Better yet is to shore up the library's holdings by giving it a gift of a nonsexist book (or poster) in honor of your child's birthday or in commemoration of any other event. Offer the librarian a copy of the Union of American Hebrew Congregations' guidelines for authors (see Resources) so that s/he can have a tool with which to evaluate new books.

• *Car-pooling*, or just transporting the children to Hebrew school, is a killer for many parents, especially mothers, upon whom the burden usually falls. (In a set of essays written by Dallas schoolchildren on the theme "What Makes a Jewish Mother?" one child replied, "My mother is a Jewish mother because she drives me to Hebrew school.") [24] Point out to the school that there is no longer a large pool of at-home mothers who can be called upon to chauffeur. Suggest van service, paid for by the parents who use it.

Teaching Your Children to Make Changes

Of course if the weight of the foregoing suggestions comes from home and not from the school—and especially if there seems to be little support for addressing issues of equality in the classroom—you might want to discuss with your child the risks involved in trying to make changes her/himself.

Speaking out or even asking questions about equality may earn short-term disapproval or may earn your child the label "troublemaker." One young woman in an Orthodox high school for girls was warned by a teacher not to be outspoken or the rabbis who directed the school would see her as "a bad match" and withhold introductions to eligible young men; such exaggerated reactions are not common. If queries and even protests about the portrayal of women in the school setting are backed by some information, the student is likely to be respected for her interest, especially if the teacher is a woman—which, as we know, is usually the case.

Our sons as well as our daughters need to be encouraged to speak out when they recognize that a certain course or textbook or picture shows a limited and incorrect view of Jewish women. It may be harder for them, because they see themselves as primarily unaffected by such sexism, and they may be subject to disapprobation or scorn from boys less sensitive to the issues. But this is an opportunity for them to experience at first hand the feeling of speaking out against another's oppression. It also helps them to see their own roles—as males—in the light of traditional male privilege.

Here are some questions you might ask of your child (depending on her/his age) that might also emerge in the classroom: What might *women's* lives have been like in the particular period being studied? (For example, how might Jewish *women* have reacted to the Enlightenment? What were circumstances regarding women's education during the Golden Age of the Jews in Spain?) Even if the history teacher doesn't know the answers when the students bring up questions like these in class, asking is a useful consciousness-raiser in itself.

Relating to classes on Jewish religious practices, ask why traditional liturgy blesses our fathers Abraham, Isaac, and Jacob and not always our mothers Sarah, Rebecca, Rachel, and Leah. Ask why females have been excluded from the *minyan*, from Torah reading, and from other important aspects of public ritual celebration. (This could get the students into an interesting discussion about role definitions for men and women.)

Girls might want to see what happens if they wear a *kippah* or *tfillin* at prayers, or a *tallit* (if the post-Bar Mitzvah boys do in that school). The girls could discover both what it feels like to wear these garments, if they've never worn them, and see the school's reaction and that of the other students. (For more on ritual attire, see p. 74.)

Questions that might be asked about—and in—ethics classes could focus occasionally on the new understanding of equality that the women's movement has given us as Jewish women. Just as we try to live as Jews by having Jewish values inform every aspect of our lives—business dealings, treating our neighbors well, and so on—ask how we can bring feminist values of equality into a Jewish setting.

RESOURCES

A new, independent community Hebrew day school (open 1983), created by a group of concerned educators and parents, tries to meet the issue of sexism head on. The Abraham Joshua Heschel School, which has a commitment to the traditions of Judaism—including observance of Shabbat, holidays, prayer, and dietary laws—has an equally strong commitment to gender equality. The school's board has even produced a statement of their principles on this matter for prospective parents, which may be a unique document in the annals of Jewish education.

The Abraham Joshua Heschel School
30 W. 68 Street
New York, NY 10023

The Reform movement has several aids for combating sexism in Jewish education. Among them are: the summary of a 1976 conference, "How to Avoid Role-Stereotyping in the School Curriculum"; a list, "Guidelines for Authors," compiled by Vicki Friedman, which suggests ways of eliminating sexist bias in books for Jewish children; and a program of in-service consciousness-raising groups for teachers, led by Annette Daum, to help them find ways of using materials they already have in order to promote gender equality in the classroom.

Union of American Hebrew Congregations
838 Fifth Avenue
New York, NY 10021

In the late seventies a group of progressive Jewish educators, many of them women, formed the Coalition on Alternatives in Jewish Education. While not exclusively concerned with women's issues, egalitarianism has been a hallmark of the group's approach. Every summer the coalition (known as CAJE) sponsors a five-day conference for "Jewish educators"—which means parents, professionals, interested lay people. In addition, there are grass-roots outposts of CAJE around the country and a task force on women.

CAJE
468 Park Avenue South
Room 904
New York, NY 10016
(212) 696-0740

For advice on curricula in Hebrew schools of various denominations:

Melton Research Foundation
    (Conservative)
Jewish Theological Seminary
3080 Broadway
New York, NY 10027

Rhea Hirsch School of Education
    (Reform)
Hebrew Union College—Jewish Institute of Religion
3077 University Avenue
Los Angeles, CA 90007

Torah Umesorah—National Society for Hebrew Day Schools
   (Orthodox)
229 Park Ave. South
New York, NY 10003

If you are considering a "formal," traditional school setting for yourself or your daughter, check first with the schools themselves. Even
schools that are attached to specific movements within Judaism don't
necessarily follow the guidelines set up—either for curriculum or even for
teacher certification.
   The Jewish education "establishment" has not been as reluctant to
move away from limiting views of women as one might imagine a traditional Jewish organization could be. In fact, the national umbrella organization for local Boards of Jewish Education around the country conducted the 1979 study of professional women educators in Jewish schools,
predicting that the best and brightest Jewish women would leave the field
if salaries and promotion opportunities didn't improve. The organization
publishes the *Pedagogic Reporter*, useful for lay people who want to find
out what professionals in the field are reading (and who can therefore
speak with greater authority when challenging the practices of a certain
school or teacher).

The Jewish Education Service of North America, Inc.
114 Fifth Avenue
New York, NY 10011
(212) 675-5656

Several local Boards of Jewish Education sponsor resource centers to
showcase new materials for teachers. Most of these are staffed by women,
and if these resource centers are made aware of nonsexist materials (or
of the perniciousness of sexist ones), they can influence the choices of
those who work directly with the students.

Jewish Teachers Resource Center
225 Meramec, Suite 405
St. Louis, MO 63105

Teacher Center
Board of Jewish Education
9325 Brookville Road
Silver Spring, MD 20910

Judith Mars Kupchan, coordinator of the Silver Spring center, says, "We do not promote materials which we might consider to be sexist."

The Kohl Jewish Teacher Center
161 Green Bay Road
Wilmette, IL 60091

A publication that carries reviews of books for children and educators, with a very broad scope and many gifted and sensitive women writing in its pages is:

The Melton Journal
Melton Research Center for Jewish Education
The Jewish Theological Seminary
3080 Broadway
New York, NY 10027

Although the *Journal* focuses on Conservative curricula, its articles and reviews are useful for all classrooms, and it might be a periodical to send to teachers or principals in Orthodox and Reform schools as well.

To prepare yourself with suggestions for a school or synagogue program for children, order a copy of:

Films for Children of All Ages
   (described as "an evaluative guide to materials for use in Jewish
   schools, camps, youth groups")
Jewish Media Service
Jewish Welfare Board
15 E. 26 Street
New York, NY 10010

With this film listing to guide you, you're less likely to give approval to films for children that feature only boys or men or that otherwise give children a limited view of women in Jewish life.

For helpful suggestions about educational sexism in general that can be applied easily to Jewish schools, write for:

TABS: Aids for Ending Sexism in Schools
744 Carroll Street
Brooklyn, NY 11215

A wonderful book that lists questions to ask when monitoring any school situation has been compiled by Dr. Carol Poll, sex desegregation specialist with the New York City public school system:

Sex Equity Resource Guide
Sex Desegregation Program
Board of Education
110 Livingston Street
Brooklyn, NY 11201

And another "secular" resource that can be put to good use in a Jewish context is:

Equal Play
   (a quarterly resource magazine for adults who are guiding young children beyond stereotypes)
Women's Action Alliance, Inc.
370 Lexington Avenue
New York, NY 10017
$10.00 per year

Alyssa Herbert and her Bat Mitzvah tutor. (Marilynne Herbert)

Adult Bat Mitzvah class, Temple Israel, Great Neck, New York. (Len Abrams)

To arrange for speakers of a wide range of Jewish women's issues before a parent-teacher organization or to high school students, get in touch with:

Speakers Bureau
Lilith Magazine
250 W. 57 Street
New York, NY 10019
(212) 757-0818

To help Jewish schools upgrade their curriculum with nonsexist learning materials, send for the catalogue of mini-courses (many dealing with women's issues) prepared by Audrey Friedman Marcus and Rabbi Raymond A. Zwerin of:

Alternatives in Religious Education, Inc.
3945 S. Oneida Street
Denver, CO 80237

For resources on Jewish education for the early years of childhood, see the section on day care in "Responding to the Childbearing Imperative" (p. 394).

STUDYING FOR BAT MITZVAH

One of the crisis points in the education of Jewish girls is the issue of Bat Mitzvah, or, in the case of Orthodox congregations, Bat Torah, as it is sometimes called. To do it or not to do it? (For innovations in the ceremony itself, see Life Cycle Celebrations, p. 133.)

The fact that Bat Mitzvah is "optional" for girls lessens the degree of seriousness with which many of them will view whatever Hebrew or Jewish education they receive. All you have to do is look around at the youngsters at a Bar Mitzvah—girls and boys about the celebrant's age—to see the difference in attitude: the boys are praying with various degrees of involvement, but all of them are "being" Jewish men; often the girls are gossiping and flirting, showing no real interest in the service—not because "women are light-headed" but because there's no percentage in it for them. They have no *real* role, nor had their mothers, who are their role models.

Even though Bar Mitzvah may have become just another rite of passage for assimilated Jews, devoid of much deep religious significance, it is nevertheless a rite that has been almost universally observed. Bat Mitzvah, on the other hand, was for many years (and in some circles still is) an optional event, sometimes just another way to celebrate a birthday. Many women growing up in the fifties, in fact, were given the choice of a lavish Bat Mitzvah celebration or a lavish Sweet Sixteen party. Those who, given the absurd choice, opted for the Bat Mitzvah (for whatever reasons—even if just to get a whole lot of presents sooner) were the lucky ones. The training in synagogue ritual and public prayer, even if exercised only during that one speaking role in synagogue, served them in good stead. At least the learning and the synagogue ritual were made to seem a little less restricted to males.

For young women in an Orthodox milieu, where synagogue-going is part of a weekly routine and isn't perceived as an optional adventure, there's more likelihood that study and prayer will be taken seriously, though less likelihood that self-esteem will derive from such activity.

The sense of deprivation many women feel when denied the logical role their education prepares them for (if they have been fortunate enough to get a Jewish education) is expressed by an adult woman who, along with her twin brother, had studied at home with a private tutor: "In the beginning of our eighth year of study, when our respective Bar and Bat Mitzvahs were but months away, my father informed me that I was not to have a Bat Mitzvah. 'It's not a real ceremony,' he said. 'It's made up.' . . . I wish that I had had a chance to be the daughter of a good deed."

While for this woman her education reached a dead end, others never had the chance to know even as much as she did. The phenomenon of adult Bat Mitzvah is part of the story of Jewish women's education, because it's primarily the undertaking of women who had little or no Jewish background as children and who want the education that precedes the ceremony and not just the ritual itself. For these women, Bat Mitzvah is the culmination of one or two years of intensive training in Hebrew and Jewish subjects, taken very seriously by the students (see p. 142).

BEYOND YENTL: ADULT WOMEN AND JEWISH STUDY

Despite the ambivalence toward admitting women into the mysteries of Jewish study, two factors have combined to create a flowering of Jewish women's learning and creativity: (1) the women's movement, with its advancement of women in general academic spheres, and (2) the profound anxiety over Jewish survival, leading to the understanding that *every* Jewish soul (even one with a woman's body) is worth nurturing.

Before the Messiah comes (may She come soon), we may actually approach a time of the complete empowerment of women as Jews, which will bring along with it a Golden Age of Jewish women's learning and study and scholarship. An information explosion and a teaching explosion (and possibly a spiritual explosion too) have already begun. Jewish women themselves are creating new texts, new courses, new places to learn. And some of the traditional institutions are changing too; for example, the Orthodox Stern College for Women in New York introduced Talmud courses in 1978. Along with caring more about the quality of Jewish education our children are getting, we're at long last focusing on educating ourselves as well.

A different kind of learning for Jewish women takes place in an Orthodox setting and focuses not so much on learning *about* Jewish women as on teaching Jewish women about Judaism in the same rigorous way that young men have been taught. In this context, the return to Judaism (*ba'al tshuva* movement) of previously nonobservant or less observant Jews, many of them women, has spotlighted special houses of study for Jewish women. Some institutions have been around for a long time; some have changed form because of the new demands put upon them; some are new entities that have arisen to meet the special needs of women who either have had little or no previous Jewish education or are already very knowledgeable and want to learn more. Those women who come to the *ba'al tshuva* movement with feminist consciousness have been sparks for igniting interest in expanding women's roles even in the most traditional settings, in ways that range from ensuring child care so that women are freed for study to questioning the reasons behind the restrictions on women's full participation in public worship.

Rachel Ebner, an Orthodox woman, received her graduate degree in advanced Jewish studies simultaneously with her husband from the Bernard Revel Graduate School of Yeshiva University in 1980. She talks about women's role in Jewish learning:

> There have always been women involved in Torah study, but they were the rare exceptions. Archaic resentments and attitudes have subsided

Three students from Yeshiva University's Benjamin Cardozo School of Law were among thirty of their classmates who edited The Women's Annotated Legal Bibliography, *the first bibliography of legal commentary on women's issues to be published in the United States.* (Yeshiva University)

somewhat, and now women with a serious interest in Torah have the opportunity to pursue scholarship on an advanced level. This will enrich Jewish study in general, as women apply their unique perceptions to the study of Torah.

For this and other reasons I believe it's healthy for husbands and wives to learn together; to extend to each other their respective visions. Still, I have to admit that the argumentative side of Torah learning—when men literally scream at each other in the heat of debate, but embrace afterwards as if nothing had happened—remains somewhat difficult for me to deal with. Women new to the "bet midrash" technique may find it difficult to be shouted at. But because its goal is the hammering out of truth, it is a methodology worth acquiring.[25]

A school for young women who have usually had twelve years of Hebrew day school education, Stern College for Women, in New York, a branch of the Orthodox Yeshiva University, is one of the places where changing attitudes have been made visible. Many of the old caveats about educating Jewish women in Judaic studies would have been true of Stern in the past—women's intellectual endeavors were taken seriously, but only to a point. Dean of students Karen Bacon says of teaching those women who want to learn the traditional approaches to Jewish texts that have always been taught to their brothers: "They are motivated to achieve in the secular world and unwilling to live without a Jewish education."[26]

Stern College for Women
245 Lexington Avenue
New York, NY 10016

A women's school for advanced Jewish study (a *kollel*) was formed in 1979 in New York by Rabbi David Silber, who offers intensive courses in Bible and history, plus a *kollel* (advanced, postgraduate) session in the summer. Most students here are women who have had some exposure to Jewish texts in the past. Silber says that "women began to come to me—there's a very great need for a school like this." There aren't facilities for out-of-town students, but the school draws many Orthodox Barnard College students (the college is nearby), and "married women also," according to one student. For a catalogue and further information, write:

Drisha Institute for Jewish Education
122 W. 76 Street
New York, NY 10023
(212) 595-0307

BA'ALOT TSHUVA

WOMEN RETURNING TO TRADITIONAL JUDAISM VIA STUDY

The "new yeshivot," catering to women whose backgrounds have been lacking in intensive (and sometimes even minimal) Jewish content, have attracted women "returning" to Jewish life. One of the best known of these is the Lubavitch-run Bais Chana in St. Paul, which offers short- or longer-term residential study programs for Jewish women. It has been a magnet both for women who have had no Jewish background at all but who are drawn to learning in their college or later years, and for women who grew up in Orthodox homes but are drawn to the practices of Hasidism.

The Bais Chana program is "especially designed for the mature young woman who has had little or no formal Jewish education, but who needs to learn the most elementary principles and precepts on an adult level."

Bais Chana
Women's Institute of Jewish Studies
Lubavitch House
15 Montcalm Court
St. Paul, MN 55116

For general information about the kinds of Jewish-studies programs available for women in Israel, write for the Israel Torah Program Guide to:

Rabbi Yaacov Sprung
Torah Education Department
World Zionist Organization—American Section
515 Park Avenue
New York, NY 10022
(212) PL 2-0600

Two films dealing with the studies and identity changes of Jews studying Torah, and touching briefly on the issues facing women:

The Return
by Yisroel Lifschutz
available from
The Jewish Star
26 Court Street, Suite 1211
Brooklyn, NY 11242
(718) 625-6330

My Father's House
ADL of B'nai B'rith
823 UN Plaza
New York, NY 10017
(212) 490-2525

"LUNCH & LEARN"

One New York synagogue with a very extensive adult education program
has a weekly "businessmen's" lunch-and-learn Talmud study session
which rotates around the participants' office boardrooms. A more egalitarian model is this program in Atlanta: "A semi-monthly luncheon
group designed for businessmen and women to study Talmud. The group
has been in existence for two years and attracts an average of 30 participants to each session." For further information contact:

Atlanta Jewish Community Center
1745 Peachtree Road, N.E.
Atlanta, GA 30309
(404) 875-7881

A FRIENDSHIP CIRCLE TRANSFORMED

A group of friends in Winnipeg, Canada, some of whom went to *cheder*
together more than sixty years ago, have met every Monday afternoon
for nearly three decades. The group began by studying Tanach (Bible)
with the learned wife of a local Conservative rabbi, and moved on
through a succession of teachers of various courses of study, both sacred
and secular. The group now meets without a leader, but the heated debates continue, in a kind of Jewish Great Books format. Named by a
pundit in its early days the Vible Bible Institute (Wives' Bible Institute,
with a nice rhyme in the Yiddish), it has also been a support group, providing a context for the women's interlocking friendships.

CHEVRUTAH

This is an update of the male model of having a study partner with whom
one can discuss the lesson at hand. *Chevrutah* (from the same root as the
word for friend) now can exist without face-to-face contact. For women
who have numerous work and domestic responsibilities but who want to
make time for study without having to leave home, there are tapes available with Bible lessons. After listening to them, women discuss them
with their friends over the phone (as one observer says, "while washing
the Shabbos dishes on Saturday night"). In some Orthodox communities
the telephone *chevrutah* method has been enormously popular.

Julia Wolf Mazow, editor of The Woman Who Lost Her Names, *an anthology of Jewish women's writing.* (Gay Block)

Useful for home-bound students are the tapes of Rabbi Shlomo Riskin's popular series of Wednesday-night lectures, available from:

Adult Education Office
Lincoln Square Synagogue
200 Amsterdam Avenue
New York, NY 10023
$5.00 each; 10 for $45.00

A problem with these ready-made learning programs is that they lack feminist input, and, therefore, learning partners need to maintain a questioning attitude toward what they study.

THE ENTREPRENEURIAL MODEL

Dawn Schuman, the late Chicago educator, exemplified the highly motivated free-lance lecturers who act as resource people for Jewish organizations across the country. Her classes often dealt with women's concerns, but their primary goal was to provide a general Jewish education to adult women who often had very little exposure to Jewish learning. Shortly before her death in 1983, Schuman described the impact of her classes on her students' self-esteem and their Jewish identity:

> Marcia went back to school and started teaching because she says she rediscovered that she had a good mind. Judy enrolled at Spertus College of Judaica in a full program and instituted Shabbat and other observances in her home. A third woman is leaving for Israel to go to an Ulpan [intensive Hebrew language course]. She says her friends now call her a Jewish fanatic because she wants to learn Hebrew and spend that much time in Israel. Two women are planning a rally to protest the visit of the Deputy Mayor of Moscow . . . they had never been active in the organized Jewish community before. . . . Many people have changed synagogues, looking for a richer Jewish life. Others have joined synagogues for the first time.
>
> There are negative aspects to this study also. I have students who have alienated long-time friends and family with their new attitudes about the centrality of Judaism in their lives. They are also beginning to make demands on their families both as women and as Jews that cause a strain in relationships. Change is not without cost, but the joy of this growing awareness of our tradition is well worth the difficulties.

TAKING OURSELVES SERIOUSLY: STUDYING JEWISH WOMEN

One of the enormous changes in the past decade is that we now see *ourselves* as subjects worthy of study. From local groups studying "Jewish Women in Talmud and History" to Ph.D. theses on the history of Jewish women's organizations, on rabbinic responses to rape, and on Jewish women's involvement in the labor movement in twentieth-century America, Jewish women are exploring their own intellectual history. The women's movement has legitimized the study of women, and the heightened Jewish ethnic consciousness of American Jews has made us more interested in studying about Jews.

Some of the study goes on informally through the programming of traditional Jewish women's organizations such as Hadassah or Sisterhood groups, or as an outgrowth of parents' involvement in their children's Jewish education; some is in secular institutions, either under the auspices of women's study programs or Jewish studies' programs; some takes place in special institutions for Jewish women.

The course description of "The Jewish Woman, Then and Now," offered at the Niles Township Jewish Congregation in Skokie, Illinois (and open to men and women), shows the kinds of concerns that Jewish women are now examining in a serious way, with all the legitimacy that a course confers: "In our synagogue we count women in the minyan and include them in the Torah Service. Yet many of us carry ideas about the role of the Jewish woman that were formed from seeing our mothers and grandmothers many years ago. Now we will study the history of the Jewish woman, her place in the community, her contributions to Judaism in ancient and modern times, and then discuss her present status."

No longer are courses in "Slimnastics" or "The kosher way to cook gourmet" the standard offerings for women's programming in synagogues and community centers across the country.

How We Are Learning

SMALL GROUP, LARGE IMPACT

Ezrat Nashim, created in 1971, is one of the best known and certainly most effective of the Jewish women's study groups. (See Jewish women's spirituality, p. 46.) It is now primarily a support and friendship group for its members, whose intellectual lives have merged with the history of the contemporary Jewish women's movement.

Ezrat Nashim (a play on the Hebrew for "help for women" and "area for women"—a reference to the separate seating section for women in traditional synagogues) is the name of a group of Jewish feminists who came mainly from the ranks of the New York Havurah (a co-ed prayer and study group) and who, in the early 1970s formed a study group to explore the status of women in Jewish law. The women of this group— among them historian Paula Hyman and Talmud scholar Judith Hauptman—were able to look at Jewish texts from a feminist viewpoint because its members had had sufficient Jewish learning to be able to study together confidently and completely. A study guide produced and distributed by Ezrat Nashim in the mid-70s is one of the most thorough and provocative guides for creating an independent learning environment for Jewish women.

More current, and with bibliographies that will be especially helpful to a woman studying informally, is a guide which lists such topics as "Jewish Women and Gentile Women Compared" and "Placing Women in Modern Jewish History."

The Jewish Women's Studies Guide
Edited and compiled by Sue Levi Elwell and Edward R. Levenson
Biblio Press, 1982
P.O. Box 22
Fresh Meadows, NY 11365
$6.95

INSTITUTIONALIZING JEWISH FEMINIST STUDY

Since 1976 the Women's Institute for Continuing Jewish Education has offered San Diego women classes in a variety of Jewish topics, workshops, lectures, counseling, and new rituals for Jewish women. The Institute has two major areas of activity—adult education for Jewish women and a "Personal Growth and Directions" program.

There are also two ancillary activities. As a resource for the institute and for the community, a few years ago institute director Irene Fine created the Jewish Women's Network, a support group of "womanpower" in the San Diego area; and the institute has also produced a Jewish women's hagada and a collection of midrashim (stories exploring Biblical themes). While focusing on teaching women at the institute, Fine believes that the most important step in Jewish education will be to "mainstream" women's studies into standard Jewish texts and courses.

Irene Fine, Director of Jewish Studies
Women's Institute for Continuing Jewish Education
4079, 54 Street
San Diego, CA 92105
(619) 442-2666

The midrashim, titled *Taking the Fruit: Modern Women's Tales of the Bible,* attempt to put women back into Jewish religious history by re-visioning or revising that history through women's experience; available from the same address for $5.95.

Midrashim are fanciful stories exploring, explaining, or expanding upon Biblical themes or incidents. The traditional midrashim were usually written down by rabbis and date from about fifteen hundred years ago. Like the women in San Diego, people interested in bringing a female perspective to the Biblical roots of Judaism have begun to construct midrashim of their own as explanations of stories heretofore puzzling, obscure, or misinterpreted by male exegesis.

For example, Rabbi Lynn Gottlieb has composed a midrash about Rachel and Leah, which she performs. In her version of the Biblical tale of the two sisters, Leah, described in the original tale with the phrase "*rakot eynayim*" (weak-eyed—that is, unattractive), becomes a mystic, a seer, whose children will become the people of Israel. Gottlieb translates *rakot eynayim* as "inward-seeing," a metaphor for the woman's visionary quality. We no longer consider her the second-best sister, an object of pity who gets married off through a stratagem of her father's. (Jacob really wanted to marry the younger daughter, Rachel, and subsequently does.) Gottlieb reveals Leah as a strong individual with unique powers and says of her technique, "if you tilt the prism just a little bit, different light comes in."[27]

Midrash-writing classes, and the performances Gottlieb herself gives around the country, are immensely popular, as are the reconstructions of and expansions on stories only suggested in the Bible, such as the reworkings of the Lilith story that have emerged in the past decade. Lilith, considered by Jewish mystical writers to have been the first woman, predating the more submissive Eve, was allegedly created by God at the same time as Adam. "Man and woman created He them" is the line in Genesis that describes the creation of the first humans. Eve isn't mentioned until several verses later. Thus legend has it that the references are to two different women. The first woman, Lilith, considered herself Adam's equal. When she and Adam quarreled over equality (Adam wanting her to "lie beneath" him, according to one story), Lilith fled from the Garden of Eden. Adam begged God for another partner, and this time God created *from* Adam his "help meet," Eve. Replacing Lilith, who, since she was created "from the same dust" as Adam, had claim to equality, Eve represented another female type altogether. The frequent retelling of the Lilith tale is one attempt to find spiritual antecedents for the present-day searchings and yearnings of Jewish women.[28]

THE HOLOCAUST: A SPECIAL FOCUS OF JEWISH WOMEN'S STUDIES

Strength from the new Jewish women's scholarship has led to an approach to Holocaust studies that may alter our understanding of Holocaust victims and survivors. Several historians have begun to explore the special responses of women in the concentration camps, refuting Bruno Bettelheim's statements that the only honorable choice was for Jews to "die like men." The women now investigating women's tales of survival suggest from their preliminary research and from the intuitions of some previous Holocaust scholars that women in the camps and ghettos and resistance movements had special survival skills.

Historian Joan M. Ringelheim, who has spearheaded this new Women and the Holocaust project, says: "There seems to be some evidence that the bonding of women was different from men—that women were able, because of our different material conditions and social relations throughout life, to create or re-create 'families' and so provide networks of survival. Surely we cannot overlook this and simply go on with the ideas about isolation between prisoners or about the destruction of values. It is not so clear how much women's values were destroyed."[29] The scholarship being conducted now by Ringelheim and her colleagues is important not only because of the light it casts on Jewish women's experiences but also because it provides a new perspective on Jewish history as a whole.

Women and the Holocaust Project
The Institute for Research in History
432 Park Avenue South
New York, NY 10016
(212) 689-1931

SECULAR AND RELIGIOUS STUDIES MERGE

Sue Levi Elwell is a scholar in women's studies (soon to be ordained as a rabbi) who has become a nationally known resource person for people planning Jewish women's-studies courses both informally and in a formal academic setting. She involves her students directly and personally—a method that differs considerably from the more "distant" approach to the usual university Judaic-studies curriculum. Here she describes the experience of one group in the process of "rediscovering the Book of Esther."

How can Jewish Women's Studies go beyond the classroom in a way that feminist pedagogy—and, coincidentally, the historical legacy of of participatory Jewish scholarship—are best served?

A group of Jewish women came together to establish an ongoing study group to explore a range of feminist—and Jewish—issues. Several of us had attempted to compensate for our limited Jewish education by pursuing Jewish studies in college, but in most cases, that meant only Hebrew-language study coupled with trips to Israel.

Despite the exceptional background and training of individual group members in secular fields (all had at least M.A. degrees), the median level of Jewish education was low (little formal Jewish education past age twelve). This is particularly interesting when one considers that two of the women are daughters of rabbis, and three are married to men who have both rabbinical and academic Jewish training and teach Jewish Studies at a university.

The group began to meet in June 1979, and by January 1980 we had read and discussed material on a wide range of feminist and Jewish concerns. However, we had tended to stick to areas in which we were comfortable, such as literature and biography, and when we did venture beyond our own areas of expertise, it was into an exploration of feminist politics or philosophy. We eagerly read Maxine Hong Kingston's memoir of growing up as a Chinese American, but were threatened by Anzia Yezierska's exposé of the misogyny of an Orthodox Jewish immigrant patriarch in *The Bread Givers*. And beyond Yezierska lay yet another undiscovered region: the world of Jewish scholarship.

After the first of the year, however, we decided to take a look at the Book of Esther. The Book of Esther, read during the yearly celebration of the Purim festival, depicts the conflict of a Jewish queen, married to a Persian monarch, who is faced with the possibility of witnessing the wholesale destruction of her people. [See Celebrating the Jewish Calendar, p. 104.] The story involves a complex interweaving of subplots, including one involving a former queen (the old/ugly queen . . . remember all those fairy tales?) who disobeys her husband and is consequently banished from the kingdom lest other women emulate her example and defy the authority of their husbands. The ironic juxtaposition of Vashti, the bad queen, and Esther, the good queen, is implicit in the text, and one of the questions we hoped to answer in the course of our inquiry was whether or not any traditional commentators had dealt with the characterizations of the two women.

Thus the impetus to study Esther grew out of an interest in a serious exploration of the images of women in the text, but this became overshadowed by a more difficult to articulate but strongly felt desire to reclaim the text. As Jewish women long denied access to Jewish study, many of us felt a deep sense of alienation from traditional Jewish sources and a sense of inadequacy even in contemplating serious textual study. Exegesis has always been the province of men in the Jewish tradition, and we wondered whether the strength of our feminist convictions would provide us with sufficient chutzpah—and sense of legitimacy—to approach the task. But even with our meager Jewish educations, some of us had proficiency in classical Hebrew, and several were trained in literary criticism, so collectively we possessed some of the tools of interpretation, and finally acknowledged our readiness to confront the tradition.

We divided the preparation among ourselves. Each of us prepared the text and read a commentary. In addition, some of us read midrashic material—material from folktales and legends that is associated with the Esther story. Our intention was to structure a learning session in which each member could participate, in which we could discover together new insights into the ancient text.

We finally came together on Purim afternoon. We had invited our families, and several of us were surprised that our hesitation in confronting the text resurfaced when we faced the patriarchal presence of Jewish scholarship represented by several of the men, the professional Jewish scholars. However, once we began our discussion our own familiarity with the text—and the commentaries—was obvious. And as the text of Esther opened before us, our women's eyes glimpsed the riches that have tantalized our fathers, while eluding our mothers, for generations.

By confronting the text ourselves, we were able to make conjectures about Esther/Vashti, the schizophrenic heroine, the hag/bride who taunts and tempts and proves herself to be more clever—and more powerful—than those who *seem* to hold the power in this ancient kingdom. The tale was revealed to be one that ridicules male prerogative and the excesses of male pride, while celebrating the trickery by which the outsider—woman and Jew—successfully secures a position in the power structure.

The discussion created a forum for women to confront Jewish texts, not as outsiders but as rightful heirs to the tradition, and the opportunity for collective discovery reflected a commitment to both feminist and Jewish pedagogy. In legitimizing women as students and scholars, the experiment also validated women's experiences as relevant—and illuminating—to textual study.[30]

OTHER RESOURCES

If you want to learn on your own, send for the bibliographies listed here (see page 188), get the books that appeal to you, and start reading. For lectures and discussion groups, often free, get your name on the mailing lists of local Jewish women's organizations (see page 566), and on those of general Jewish organizations as well. Visiting speakers, university courses, and synagogue and community centers that sponsor lectures are usually listed in the local Jewish newspaper. (Look in the Networking Guide under Periodicals to find one nearest you.)

If you want to start a class yourself or to turn an existing group into a study group, you can order books listed in the study guides or bibliographies from:

ICI—A Woman's Place
4015 Broadway
Oakland, CA 94611

"We're about the largest feminist bookstore in the country and have always had a largely Jewish collective. We do mail order and we're open every day of the year."

A legendary source for any Jewish book is J. Levine. It is primarily a supplier of textbooks and religious articles, but it also has a very good stock of books on Jewish women, and it carries the complete Nechama Liebowitz Bible commentaries.

J. Levine
58 Eldridge Street
New York, NY 10002

For a listing of colleges and universities offering Jewish studies courses (which should all be open to women, since no institution that receives any government funds can legally discriminate on the basis of sex), write:

Jewish Life on Campus
B'nai B'rith Hillel Foundation
1640 Rhode Island Avenue, NW
Washington, DC 20036

For information about Jewish *women's* studies, try:

Women's Studies Quarterly
The Feminist Press
Box 334
Old Westbury, NY 11568

Two "correspondence" courses on Jewish issues are given by:

National Academy for Adult Jewish Studies
155 Fifth Avenue
New York, NY 10010
and
Academy for Jewish Studies Without Walls
165 East 56 Street
New York, NY 10022

The Academy for Jewish Studies Without Walls also sponsors a week-long summer institute at a university.

Colleges and universities that are primarily devoted to Jewish studies (not listed elsewhere in this section): Jewish Theological Seminary, in

New York; Dropsie College and Gratz College, in Philadelphia; Spertus College of Judaica, in Chicago; Baltimore Hebrew College, and Midrasha College of Jewish Studies, in Detroit. (For places to study if you are a woman and want to become a rabbi, see p. 55. For courses in Jewish community service, see p. 530.)

For women who want to pursue any kind of higher education there's a funding source (nonsectarian but under Jewish sponsorship) for their educational needs exclusively. Grants and loans for undergraduate and graduate study are made by:

The Jewish Foundation for the Education of Women
120 W. 57 Street
New York, NY 10019
(212) 265-2565

WOMEN AS RESOURCES FOR JEWISH
WOMEN'S ACADEMIC SCHOLARSHIP

Just in the past five years a cadre of Jewish women scholars has emerged whose areas of expertise are, basically, the experience of Jewish women. These women, many of whom are mentioned in the pages of this book, not only serve as role models for younger scholars but also illuminate through their work whole areas of Jewish women's history, anthropology, and religious life which have been hidden until now. A contact point for these scholars is:

Women's Studies Section
Association for Jewish Studies
Widener Library
Harvard University
Cambridge, MA 02138
(617) 495-2985

One institution has become a magnet for women scholars working in European and American Jewish history—the YIVO Institute for Jewish Research and its Max Weinreich Center for Advanced Jewish Studies. YIVO's archives contain material, much of it in Yiddish, that documents Jewish settlement in the U.S. and elsewhere, and the Center sponsors seminars and workshops on themes relevant to Jewish women. Historian Deborah Dash Moore, whose field is second-generation New York Jews, Norma Fain Pratt, who has done extensive work with Yiddish-language women writers in America, anthropologist Barbara Kirshenblatt-Gimblett, and Marion Kaplan, specialist in the Jewish feminist movement of nineteenth-century Germany, have all worked at YIVO. Its resources provide documentation for women studying marital desertion in twentieth-century America or shtetl life in Poland a century ago.

YIVO also publishes the "Jewish Folklore and Ethnology Newsletter," which periodically features an extensive directory of researchers in Jewish folklore, ethnography, and related fields. Careful reading of this international directory reveals the diversity of work in areas of interest to women: dance and song patterns of women in Jewish communities around the world, the art forms Jewish women have created, gender symbolism in Jewish ritual, and much, much more.

YIVO Institute for Jewish Research
1048 Fifth Avenue
New York, NY 10028
(212) 535-6700

You can get a good overview of the secular Jewish topics Jewish women are investigating if you check the listings of Ph.D. and Master's theses at several degree-granting institutions.

University Microfilms will do a computer search of dissertations (and Master's theses, if you like) on any subject you want for $15.00. So if you are interested in exploring an aspect of Jewish women's studies—history, religion, current sociology—and want the latest word on the kind of academic work being done in that area (much of which has not yet gotten into print), write for details to:

Datrix
University Microfilms International
300 N. Zeeb Road
Ann Arbor, MI 48106
800-521-3042
In Canada: 800-268-6090

For fairly up-to-the-minute information on dissertations and works in progress on Jewish women's scholarship, consult issues of *American Jewish History*, a quarterly that publishes a list entitled "Recent Dissertations in American Jewish Studies." The periodical is available from:

American Jewish Historical Society
2 Thornton Road
Waltham, MA 02154

A GUIDE TO REFERENCE MATERIAL ON JEWISH WOMEN—
(A DO-IT-YOURSELF KIT FOR LEARNING)

Not only are we learning in formal classes and private study groups, we're learning from each other's writings as well. Women scholars express a strong desire to share their knowledge, working from the assumption, as one woman said, "that we don't have to reinvent the wheel every time."

Some of this sharing has taken the very practical form of just making resources available to one another. In the late sixties Aviva Cantor looked into her own extensive files and library and compiled the first contemporary, annotated bibliography on the Jewish woman, an excerpt from which appeared in the *First Jewish Catalog* and has been widely reprinted. The updated bibliography, which is annotated with the author's precise, perceptive, and highly personal evaluations, is now available from:

Biblio Press
P.O. Box 22
Fresh Meadows, NY 11365

After each issue of the bibliography has appeared, women have written and called the author and publisher to make suggestions for further inclusions. One, Sher Rice, a librarian, sent in a dozen pages of addenda from *her* personal collection. In fact, Rice, a member of the Jewish Librarians' Association, has set up a reference library especially for the Jewish women in her area, where, she says, Jewish materials are often not easy to come by.

Library of the Jewish Woman
190 Apple Drive
Exton, PA 19341

Rice, whose collection is housed in her apartment living room, makes materials available to library members. The archives include "vintage" Jewish periodicals, current ones, and a selection of books on or about Jewish woman. Rice is a good tracker of information and can tell you when a given book was reviewed in Jewish or general periodicals and by whom.

Another self-started collection of writings (and photographs) on Jewish women is the Jewish Women's Resource Center. The collection has books, clippings, and unpublished manuscripts sent in by women around the country since the center opened in 1978.

Jewish Women's Resource Center Library
c/o National Council of Jewish Women—New York Section
9 E. 69 Street
New York, NY 10028
(212) 535-5900

Though it focuses on Jewish life in general, another collection that has
particularly useful materials on Jewish women is the Blaustein Library of
the American Jewish Committee. The committee has been the sociological think tank of the Jewish community for decades, and its library reflects this—with bound copies of Ph.D. theses on intermarriage, population studies, and much other important information. The library has
nearly complete collections of Jewish periodicals in English and other
languages, as well as bound volumes of the Jewish Telegraphic Agency's
daily bulletins of news dispatches. Especially useful are the files of clippings and ephemera pertaining to women. The library usually allows
scholars to use its facilities on Wednesdays. Call first to introduce yourself and make an appointment.

Blaustein Library
American Jewish Committee
165 E. 56 Street
New York, NY 10022
(212) 751-4000

5

◆

OUR BODIES

SEXUALITY

The Pleasure Principle

Traditional Jewish religiously determined attitudes have in the past restricted women's physical activity with laws concerning almost every aspect of women's relationship to their own bodies—from birth rituals to menstrual and reproductive rites and taboos, including Jewish legal positions on everything from abortion to plastic surgery. The laws regulate how a woman is to dress, where her voice may be heard by men, whom she may touch, the timing of her sexual relations, and under what circumstances she may choose to terminate a pregnancy.

While there are laws on rape, prostitution, and adultery (see p. 220) that appear to discriminate against women or to have been formulated without taking women's experience into account, there are also laws and opinions that recognize women as full sexual beings, with none of the Victorian denial of women's sexuality that we have been fighting off in Western culture for the past century, and without the mind/body dualism of Christianity.

Aside from the requirements of modesty, which essentially keep a woman's charms the private pleasure of her husband, there are relatively few limits placed on the free expression of woman's sexuality in Judaism. The Song of Songs, for example, contains love poetry, expressed in the words of women, that is direct, powerful, aggressive, and undeniably sensual, with lovemaking not as a step in propagation but as pure pleasure:

Let him kiss me with the kisses of his mouth—
For thy love is better than wine.
Thine ointments have a goodly fragrance . . .
As an apple-tree among the trees of the wood,
So is my beloved among the sons.
Under its shadow I delight to sit,
And its fruit was sweet to my taste.

Lovemaking on Friday night is especially praiseworthy in the Jewish mystical tradition—for example, a perfect sexual union between husband and wife Erev Shabbat contributes to the process of reuniting God and the Shekhnah. Sex is supposed to be a union of three: woman, man, and God, with two purposes: procreation *and* pleasure.[1] (Sex for pleasure and companionship and not just for procreation is so much a part of a Jew's religious obligation that marriage even to a sterile person is sanctioned.)

The Talmud sets forth that a man must notice his wife's desire and fulfill it, and women's sexual needs are recognized and provided for in Jewish law. Post-Biblical sources even prescribe how many times a week or month are the minimum amounts, depending on the occupation of the man. Whether this encouragement is the source or not, present-day women who see themselves as strongly religious Jews, Protestants, or Catholics report more fulfilling sex lives, better communication with their husbands about sex, and more frequent sexual intercourse than nonreligious women of every faith, according to *Redbook*'s extensive 1975 survey of female sexuality.

Rabbi David Feldman, the contemporary expert on Jewish laws of birth control and sexuality, describes the traditional Jewish view of sex as "the duty of the husband and the privilege of the wife," which he contrasts to the exploitative attitude observed in Western culture by sex therapists Masters and Johnson: "sex as the husband's right and the wife's duty." He also quotes Nachmanides, writing in the twelfth century, who instructs a husband to "win her over with words of graciousness and seductiveness . . . Hurry not to arouse passion until her mood is ready; begin in love; let her 'semination' [orgasm?] take place first."[2]

For all this acknowledgment of women's sexual rights, there are certain aspects of women's sexuality that, not surprisingly, are ignored (or suppressed) both by Hebrew Scriptures and by later and current writings. For example, although it is a mitzvah for a man to satisfy his wife, it is also a mitzvah for him to spare her the embarrassment of voicing her sexual desires by making sure to initiate sex himself. In Rabbinic times a woman

(Marilynne Herbert)

could be divorced without recompense if she was "loud-voiced"—which was interpreted to mean "(1) unashamedly demands sexual intercourse with her husband so someone can hear or (2) disputes intimate sexual matters this way."[3]

While there is talk of the pleasures of heterosexual activity and of the responsibilities of the sexual (that is, marital) partners, Hebrew Scriptures never mention lesbianism or, for that matter, masturbation related to women. Only men are enjoined from "lying with a man as with a woman" and from "spilling seed." The latter ban was primarily intended to hold men to their obligation to inseminate a childless widowed sister-in-law and not because of any ascetic attitude toward masturbation itself. In any case, women aren't included in the ban.

The pleasures of sex are supposed to take place exclusively within marriage. Premarital sex is not looked upon with favor either by Jewish law or by custom. In fact, according to Jewish law, intercourse is one of the ways in which a couple can be considered married (see marriage laws, p. 320). Extramarital sex is a violation of Jewish codes but is considered adultery only if it takes place between a man (marital status immaterial) and a married woman.

The most characteristic aspect differentiating "Jewish" sexual behavior, aside from a Halachic disapproval of celibacy, would be the observance of the *niddah* laws, sometimes euphemistically called the laws of "family purity." These laws dictate a complete separation of wife and husband for approximately half of each month in which the woman has a menstrual period.

Under these laws women have the obligation to immerse themselves in a mikveh (ritual bath made up at least in part of "living" water or rain water) on the evening of the seventh day following the end of the menstrual period. Strictly speaking, the laws concerning abstinence during the "impure" time of the menstrual period and the days that follow it fall equally on men and on women, but the ritual which must be followed before sexual relations can resume is the woman's alone, and is one of the three special ritual obligations of women (see p. 61). The ritual immersion in the bath is not really a mitzvah in itself but is just the prefatory rite before the mitzvah of married sex can resume.

Gila Berkowitz, an Orthodox California writer and one of the few Jewish women to write about sex from a Jewish perspective, gives her view of how the laws govern the sexual experience of a religiously observant married couple.

Why do women and men make love? For pleasure, certainly, and sometimes for procreation. Judaism obligates husbands and wives to please each other physically and also exhorts them to be fruitful and multiply. Yet these are secondary. Sex, like every other action, is primarily a form of spiritual expression. It is one of the rare instances where union with another can be achieved, ideally becoming a metaphor of divine union. It is also the quintessential opportunity to fulfill the commandment "Love your friend as yourself." It is a very pure form of worship. Ancient texts do not hesitate to describe perfect sex as a *ménage à trois*—husband, wife, and God.

Bearing this point in mind—that God is an essential focus of sex, that "good" sex is a basic goal of Judaism—the biblical prohibitions against certain practices begin to assume a logical shape. For example, adultery is "the great sin" because it mocks the love of and perverts the relationship with God, not the spouse. It is true that adultery is defined as an act where the *woman* is married. [See marriage laws, p. 320.] Practically speaking, however, *all* three parties are considered guilty of infidelity, as the Rabbis point out in their lengthy Talmudic discussion of Sotah, the woman accused of adultery without conclusive evidence. In all cases a woman is accountable for her own actions, both legally and morally.

In the case of an adulterous wife, the husband must divorce her and may never remarry her, no matter how much he loves her. Her sin is against God, and it is irrelevant if her husband "forgives" her.

Judaism views other practices as denying the possibility of holiness in sex. Pornography, masturbation, and fetishism are junk food of the spirit, jading the appetite for the sacred nourishment of sex. Unmarried cohabitation is a dead zone of sexuality in the Jewish context; if man and woman cannot pledge commitment to each other, what could they possibly pledge to God? All of us live in a society where there is a lot of pressure to experiment sexually before marriage. But Judaism's advice is based on sound psychology, I believe. The so-called "free" sexual scene really debases the sex act. It now has so little meaning that the standard is not to care about whom or even what you are making love to. Men and women should really ask themselves, "If this person isn't good enough to marry, why is this person good enough to sleep with?"

I have even more sympathy for men who are trying to live up to the Jewish ideal of sexual exclusivity. This culture sees adult women who are not sexually active as prissy and neurotic and cowardly. They see men in the same boat as absolute freaks. Yet Judaism has no double standard for premarital life. Men are enjoined to abstain from premarital sex just as women are.

As a young woman I was much more interested in building my career than in making the kind of commitments necessary to marriage. I had to remind my libido about this frequently. The control of those hot little hormones is not easy. Judaism is not easy. Both control and Judaism are, however, possible.

Yet negative commandments do not define the ideal Jewish sexual life. There is an infinite difference between "Her sexual rights he shall not diminish" and "He shall rejoice with his bride." The former law describes a minimal acceptable behavior, the later describes a goal to strive for.

For all its carping about sex outside of marriage, Judaism loosens the reins within marriage. This or that rabbi may frown upon some esoteric position or play, but the rule is: marriage is the place for experimentation, development and fulfillment. Almost anything agreeable to both partners, as long as it is done at the right time and place, is religiously sanctioned and blessed. I say "almost" anything goes to be on the safe side. Coitus interruptus is forbidden, but it's not what most couples would consider fun. All the usual forms of foreplay are permitted, but you can't get too kinky—Judaism prohibits injuring the body, including your spouse's and your own.

Whatever their feelings about woman's place in society, the rabbis of the Talmud and their successors unanimously championed her rights to satisfaction in bed. Sexual happiness is the one absolute obligation of a husband to his wife (she may waive her rights to support). A woman's sexual obligations are more vague. Women may (and still do, in ultra-Orthodox communities) sue for lack of sexual services, while a man usually has to prove malice on the part of a sexually indifferent wife. For example, an Israeli court recently ruled that a young man had to pay his wife a rather steep sum of money for each day that he delayed consummating the marriage. And rabbinical courts in America and other countries frequently award cash or goods to women in divorce cases where they claim that their husbands were inadequate lovers.

Women have a greater capacity and need for sex, the rabbis claimed. If a man's work keeps him late at the office while his wife waits impatiently, he should change jobs, they recommend. They saw fatigue and stress as the major impediments to sexual satisfaction. The solution is not to settle for less in bed, but to settle for less in the bankbook.

Orgasm is the measure of a woman's satisfaction, and the rabbis ruled that a man must do whatever his wife requires to achieve it. They stress the need for verbal as well as physical foreplay. A man should be available whenever his wife is in the mood, but must never press her to comply with his own. The Talmud and later rabbis do recognize that achieving female orgasm does require some skill in lovemaking on the part of the couple, but there is an assumption that female orgasm is as natural and inevitable as that of the male.

In sharp contrast to much modern law is the attitude toward marital rape. Halachic law sees it as a crime and a sin. Even when force is not involved, coitus is forbidden if one partner is angry at the other, when the woman is asleep or unconscious, when either spouse is drunk. Intercourse must take place in love and respect; it is a moral and religious act.

Total Immersion: The Mikveh Revival, Pro and Con
Gila Berkowitz explains the laws and practices which determine the sexual rhythms of married, observant Jewish couples.

At the heart of the Jewish way of sex are the concepts and practices of the *mikveh*, known also as *taharah* and "family purity." The ethereal mysticism of *mikveh* is hinted at by the fact that the root of the word means "hope" in Hebrew, and that "Mikveh of Israel" is an epithet for God.

The practice of *mikveh* laws today can be summed up briefly. As menstruation begins, a married couple halts all erotic activities. A minimum of five days are considered menstrual, then seven "clean" days are observed with the same restrictions. After nightfall of the seventh day, the woman bathes herself leisurely, removes all traces of cosmetics and jewelry, and immerses herself in a special pool built to exacting specifications. (Most communities with a number of observant families have a *mikveh*; in fact, a community must build a *mikveh*, according to law, even before it builds a synagogue.)

Mikveh, like all Jewish laws, concerns a spiritual concept outlined by a physical boundary. The concept of purity is one of the most complex in all of the Jewish religion; however, only the sexual aspect of purity and impurity routinely applies today. Far from being a singling out of women for the taint of impurity, the *mikveh* laws allow women to be the only people who can regularly achieve a state of ritual *purity*.

Sunday-morning anthropologists love to speculate about the *mikveh* ritual. Some call it a primitive blood taboo. However, these critics seem unaware that there is no blood flow during the major part of the separation period, that the blood itself is not considered a contaminant to the male, or that a woman who has never immersed herself in the *mikveh*—even if she is ovulating, pregnant, or years past menopause—remains in the same state of impurity.

A left-handed compliment to *mikveh* is that it is an early recognition of hygiene. First of all, cleanliness of person, independent of the state of spiritual purity, is required by Jewish law for both men and women. Second, the seven days following menstruation are specifically called *clean* days, in contrast to the *pure* period that follows them. Third, one must be absolutely physically clean before the ritual immersion. Indeed, in the rare case of an ill-kept *mikveh* pool, the woman may choose to shower also *after* the immersion, which nevertheless still renders her pure in the spiritual sense.

The woman in a state of impurity, whether she is menstruating or not, is not the subject of disgust. She may perform all religious functions and touch anything she would otherwise touch. She is simply but unconditionally forbidden to have sex with her husband.

A menstruant may touch and kiss any male that she may routinely touch and kiss. Strictly defined, these include only her father, brothers, and sons. Ultra-Orthodox men do not shake hands with any woman at any time because of the possibility that they may be swept away to erotic acts or thoughts by physical contact. The menstrual status of the woman is irrelevant.

From In Her Hands, *a film on mikveh and its importance in the lives of Syrian-Jewish women in Brooklyn.* (Jewish Media Service)

The idea that a menstruating woman may not touch a Torah is totally fallacious. [See "From Observer to Participant," p. 67.] A woman may touch a Torah scroll at any time. (In many congregations neither men nor women touch the Torah directly but touch a prayer book or other item to the Torah, then kiss the item. This is to avoid the appearance that the Torah is being venerated as an object.)

A bitter accusation, one based on a lack of contact with couples who follow the *mikveh* way, is that it is a means of oppressing women. In fact, the woman suffers no prejudice during the period of impurity. She and, of course, her husband are simply forbidden to relate to each other sexually. They may, indeed must, share communication, respect, love, and all the other aspects of their lives during this time. The husband cannot play the sexual autocrat. He, as well as she, must yoke passion to the dictate of a higher authority. A marriage that cannot withstand this kind of self-control is ipso facto a marriage based on sexual slavery, and is contemptible in the eyes of Judaism.

Says one young woman who keeps *mikveh:* "I like the feeling of 12 days of separation. It's the moment of truth in our relationship, when we have to relate to each other as human beings and we don't have sex to gloss over problems. At that time my body is entirely mine, my bed is mine, my emotions are entirely my own. But after the *mikveh*, wow! That first kiss is as good as a double climax. Even though I'm not yet bored with sex by the time my period rolls around again, I like having that first post-*mikveh* kiss to look forward to. *Mikveh* is like a honeymoon every month—except that our honeymoon wasn't this much fun; we didn't understand each other as well then."

It is absolutely forbidden for either husband or wife to reveal, even hint, to anyone else what the purity status is for them at any time, whether the woman is menstruating, post-menstrually clean, or ritually pure.

Purity, however, is not achieved by rote. The entire ritual is meaningless if the couple is not married, if either partner is not Jewish (non-Jews are not impure, the categories of purity simply do not pertain to them, since they are exclusive features of the Jewish people, "a nation of priests, a holy kingdom"). Children conceived in a state of impurity are, on the other hand, legitimate and even ritually pure at birth.

Is all this non-rational talk of purity and impurity beyond modern sensibilities? Perhaps so. It probably has only a little to do with the current revival in *mikveh* practice. More and more young women, most from backgrounds where *mikveh* was never mentioned, and a considerable proportion who are not otherwise religiously observant, are following the *mikveh* laws, spirit and letter.

One Northern California *mikveh* attendant, who has instructed hundreds of women, has found only a single case of a couple who tried the *mikveh* way and decided not to continue it. The others all seemed to find their sexual energies and their love for their partners refreshed by the *mikveh* experience.[4]

Couples who do not observe other Jewish laws, who don't keep kosher or observe the Sabbath, are reported to be taking up mikveh, with its attendant separation. There are no absolute numbers, but anecdotal reports from both coasts—from "mikveh ladies" and from participating women themselves—reveal that otherwise nonobservant women are observing mikveh as a way of creating space for themselves and a separation from their husbands, providing each partner a measure of autonomy within the marriage. Berkowitz describes mikveh as "a feminist backlash against the so-called sexual revolution." And one Orthodox rabbi claims that under *niddah* a woman can assert her independence from her husband, saying, "I am not your creature."[5] Berkowitz, among others, confirms this. "At the heart of *mikveh* law is the concept that a woman is a complete individual. Every month the practicing woman and her husband are reminded that she is more than an appendage to him, that she does not exist to serve his sexual needs. Yet this system also allows enough time together for the couple to grow sexually."

The husband in a couple who observe the laws of "family purity" says that in his California community there's tremendous interest in mikveh, among feminists especially. He says that their husbands are interested too. When they hear this, New Yorkers invariably quip, "Aha, another variation on the California hot tub." (Not all the resurgence of interest in mikveh comes from nontraditional Jews. The right-wing trend in Orthodoxy has contributed also, with young people more observant of *mitzvot* in general than their parents are.)

Mikveh linked to sexual intercourse is used not only by an already married couple. A bride must go to the mikveh before her wedding, and, under a strict interpretation of the law, she and her husband must then separate for seven days if she was a virgin, on the assumption that blood was shed from her ruptured hymen.

The laws of separation also include a period after the birth of a child, since blood is shed in childbirth. Curiously, there are different periods of separation mandated following the births of daughters and sons: 66 days for the daughter, as opposed to 33 for the son. One Conservative rabbi has said that "everybody" knows people are happier with a son. Therefore a husband rejects his wife more if a daughter is born, so she needs a longer period of recuperation and abstinence after the birth of a daughter. Another rationale is that the period of separation is doubled after the birth of a daughter to emphasize that the mother has just given birth to a baby who herself has the capability of giving birth. (Many women today refuse to accept either explanation, recoiling in anger from a law they see as biased.)

There are two distinct schools of thought on this issue among Jewish women: those who believe that the laws of ritual purity hark back to a primitive blood taboo and reflect male fear and loathing of women; and those who believe that the laws and rituals surrounding mikveh are sensual, spiritual, expressive, allow room for women to experience a symbolic rebirth every month, and, in addition, link them with a traditional Jewish woman's activity that goes back thousands of years.

There is a serious issue here for women. Are the women who are beginning to see mikveh as a way of reasserting women's independence from sex-object status correct? This sounds both possible and very exciting—a feminist thread in traditional Judaism. Or are those women correct who hold that mikveh laws and rituals stem from primitive male fear of female bodily functions and that mikveh should therefore be spurned? Women in the second camp claim that the association of menstruation with something distasteful is an inaccurate overlay onto what is strictly an issue of ritual purity.

A reading of what has been written by a cross-section of contemporary Jewish male "scholars" reveals a misogyny that *does* make the laws of mikveh sound like an expression of some primitive male loathing of women's bodies, with their mysterious reproductive function.

It is certainly true that in writing about the laws concerning menstruation and the avoidance of sexual contact, many religious Jewish men transmit an air of revulsion toward women's menstrual blood. Here are some samples.

Dr. Mortimer Ostow, chairman of the Department of Pastoral Psychology at the (Conservative) Jewish Theological Seminary said in a 1974 speech that women should not be visible in ritual roles in the synagogue not only because their presence on the *bimah* might embarrass men who knew less than they but also because the association of women with menstrual blood might repel some male members of the congregation while encouraging others in "perverse" sexual fantasies linking menstrual blood with "excreta." Choosing to bypass the Halachic consideration, which spells out that the Torah can under no circumstances be contaminated, Ostow says: "Menstrual discharge is repulsive. . . . Among the men who will oppose the presence of women on the *bimah* will be many who fear that a menstruating woman will contaminate them and the sacred objects on the *bimah*, especially the Torah."[6] He also suggests that these men may become sexually impotent at the sight of women in traditionally male ritual roles! Another, self-styled authority writes: "To the Jew [*sic*], the idea of having intercourse with a woman during her menstrual period is revolting; so much so that it is difficult for most Jews to believe that there are people to whom it makes no difference."[7]

There's a great deal being said and written that hardly makes *taharat hamishpachah* sound like a ritual any woman would voluntarily take on, since its proponents sound fanatical. The Lubavitcher rebbe, Menachem Mendel Schneerson, addressed an international gathering of the Lubavitch women's organization in 1980, telling the three thousand women to make observance of the laws of family purity a top priority and to educate others about his belief that strict observance of the law also prohibits contraception. The women mobilized themselves within twenty-four hours and mounted a campaign to carry out the rebbe's wishes.

In keeping with this authoritarian imposition of the observance of this mitzvah is the fact that Israel's all-male rabbínate reportedly sets a couple's wedding date according to the bride's last menstrual period so she won't be "unclean" (that is, menstruating) on her wedding night. In order to be legally married in Israel one must abide by this procedure.

The Jerusalem Religious Council has published materials insisting that "scientifically proven" data show that women who go to the mikveh each month have healthier, brighter children and are themselves much freer from the risk of getting cervical cancer.[8] Despite the fact that Knesset member Chaike Grossman took the council to task for its unscientific publications and for the "psychological damage" they cause, many women, in the United States and in Israel, believe that going to the mikveh will somehow ensure healthy offspring. One otherwise rational (and not strictly observant) thirty-year-old executive says, "I know it's just superstition, but when I am ready to have children, I'm going to start going to the mikveh." Many women who do observe the laws of ritual purity must overcome negative feelings about their own bodies. Rabbi Laura Geller expands on the effects of these negative views on women themselves: "Menstrual taboos are responsible for real damage to Jewish women's views of themselves and their bodies. I have met many women who learned nothing about Torah except that they could not touch the Torah because they menstruate. As adults, when they are told that that is simply folklore, it is already too late. Their sense of themselves as 'inferior' Jews has already permeated their relationship to tradition and to their own bodies."[9]

In response to this and other negative comments on mikveh, Judith Humber supports the tradition: "*Mikveh* and the laws of *taharat hamish-pachah* have been used as instruments of oppression. But this does not mean that they need be, in themselves, oppressive. I believe that we need not to discard this significant part of our heritage but to reclaim it."[10]

One of the most straightforward and unambivalent descriptions of this is Blu Greenberg's "In Defense of the 'Daughters of Israel': Observations on Niddah and Mikveh," in her book *On Women and Judaism: A View from Tradition*.[11] Greenberg says that she observes these laws precisely because they are laws, but that within this context she enjoys the connection with other Jewish women, both in her own family and through history. She also makes a strong case for the salutary effects of a monthly period of sexual abstinence as an opportunity for husband and wife to find other ways of communicating. "In early marriage, when passion and romance dominate, *niddah* allows and encourages a man and woman to develop other techniques of communication. Not every peak emotion may be expressed through sex; nor can every newly married spat be settled

in bed. One also learns quickly that sex cannot be used as a reward or punishment. If sex is being regulated by a force 'out there,' it becomes less a
matter of one or the other partner controlling or manipulating."[12]

An especially useful contribution Greenberg makes is to translate the
seven days following menstruation not as "unclean" days but, in a truer
rendition of the original Hebrew *Levanim*, as "white days," or "whites."

Less personal and more theoretical is the widely reprinted piece by
Rachel Adler, "Tumah and Taharah: Ends and Beginnings," originally
published in *Response* magazine in 1973. Adler argues that the monthly
immersion offers women a chance to experience the nexus of death and
rebirth. "Menstruation is an autumn within, the dying which makes room
for new birth." Immersion after menstruation renders women pure once
again, "having confronted and experienced our own death and resurrection."

Adler traces the various other kinds of ritual purity that once affected
men and women. The only one that now remains in force at all is the ritual
impurity of someone who has been in the presence of a corpse, and who,
like the woman at the end of her "whites," must undergo ritual purifica-
tion (thus the custom of pouring water over one's hands upon returning
from a burial). The point at which menstrual purity became separated,
through time, from other forms of ritual purity, "was the point at which
pathology entered halacha. At that point *tum'at niddah* became divorced
from the symbolism of death and resurrection and acquired a new significance related to its accompanying sexual prohibitions." Adler decries the
fact that women, not having the knowledge to approach Biblical sources
themselves, accepted the medieval view that menstruating women were
revolting and, in the process, turned away from mikveh. (For more positive views of menstruation as the impetus for new rituals, see Life Cycle
Rituals, p. 130.)

Mierle Laderman Ukeles, an artist who has described immersion in the
mikveh as "maintenance art" in which one is "reborn to life," has created
a performance in which a narrator speaks of mikveh as "a square womb
of living waters. She goes in, naked, all dead edges removed—edges and
surfaces that have come in contact with the world. . . . Old surfaces
gone, non-life gone. Life is holy, to be understood as holy and separated
from Death, from dead parts. She is always holy—but she causes a separation to be made between life and non-life." After immersion, "she has a
chance to start again. She moves into another time period. . . . And immerse again. Immerse again. Immerse again. . . ."[13]

Other less well-known functions of mikveh are not linked to women's bodies alone but are general rites of passage. The immersion is not a cleansing in the literal sense. Instead it signifies a division, a *havdalah*, between two states. For example, immersion in a mikveh also marks the final stage of the process of conversion to Judaism. The act of immersion is a physical correlative to an important transition, what anthropologist Faye Ginsburg calls a "sign of consummated passage."

Immersion in the mikveh has been an option for men, who may use it as a preparatory ritual before studying Torah, or to welcome in a Sabbath or holy day. But there is no general legal obligation on men to use the mikveh. Feeling themselves in an exclusive state of impurity for nearly

(Bill Aron)

half of each month, some women acquire in their own minds a pariah status more limiting than the law suggests. To counter this, some husbands and wives both use the mikveh at the end of the impure period. (In the great Jewish tradition of disputation, there are those who say that this detracts from one of the few rituals that are expressly tied to women's own experience.)

That the most significant women-only ritual in Judaism is now being discussed by the participants themselves (rather than by male rabbis, to whom women customarily took their stained undergarments to ask if a spot might be menstrual blood and therefore render them impure) is a tribute to the changing consciousness of women.

RESOURCES

For specific instructions on how to use a mikveh—the process of bathing oneself first, what to expect when you immerse yourself in the small mikveh pool, and other particulars—see the works cited above.

If you are mikveh-observant or would like to become so, you obviously need to know how to find a mikveh. You can order:

International Mikveh Directory
    (compiled by Arlene L. Stern)
Armis Publications
118 W. 79 Street
New York, NY 10024
(212) 595-3161
$2.00 plus postage and handling

A comparison of very different films on mikveh highlights the contrast between the "party line" on a Jewish ritual and the fresh interpretation made possible with a woman's angle.

Mikva, Marriage and Mazel Tov (18 min.)
Alden Films
7820, 20th Avenue
Brooklyn, NY 11214

This is a "traditional" look at mikveh, with the young couple, a rabbi, and a mikveh attendant. The publicity blurb states: "Viewing this film will generate confidence in the Jewish tradition and provide a portrait of time-honored values and culture."

In Her Hands: Women and Ritual (20 min.)
Jewish Media Service
15 E. 26 Street
New York, NY 10010

By Faye Ginsburg, Lily Kharazi, and Diane Winston, this videotape is a woman's look at a woman's ritual, presented from the point of view of two women—one married and one single—in Brooklyn's Syrian Jewish community.

According to this study on the resurgence of interest in mikveh in this community, Syrian women are enthusiastic about mikveh because it gives them respect, power, control, and an authentic religious experience. They seem to observe fixed male and female role definitions much more than other Jews of similar social and economic achievements. The women see mikveh as a way to arrest the trend of "going liberal" into a secular world in which they perceive women's sexuality to be degraded and her role in the home disparaged. Ginsburg reports that "niddah and mikveh provide these women with a powerful means of declaring their status, exercising autonomy within constraints and exerting authority over men."

A book on the social usefulness of *niddah* and similar practices is Karen Ericksen Paige and Jeffery M. Paige's *The Politics of Reproductive Ritual* (Univ. of California Press, 1981). It is an analysis of the social and political reasons behind circumcision, menstrual separation, and other reproductive and sexual rituals among ancient Hebrews and Jews today and in a vast range of other societies. They view these rituals as methods of controlling women's reproductive capacity and of reinforcing group values.

Sexual Ethics

Given the number of Jewish women who (like other women) are staying single longer and not waiting until marriage to begin sexual activity, what difference does it make what Jewish law says, either about women's sexuality or the circumstances in which it ought to be expressed?

There are several answers: The feminist movement, following on the so-called sexual revolution (which robbed some women of their right to decline sex), taught women not to be party to the exploitation of their own bodies. Many women therefore reconsidered how and with whom they wanted to express their sexuality, restoring an element of choice. At the same time, the past fifteen years have seen an upsurge of interest among previously uninvolved or secular Jews in what Jewish laws and traditions have to say on a variety of subjects, including human relations (giving charity, being part of a community, treating other human beings ethically). With this has come a renewed interest in traditional Jewish sexual patterns.

From the other side, Orthodox Jews, especially men, may be adopting more permissive attitudes toward premarital sex. One single man says, "I'm Orthodox above the waist." Susan Grossman analyzes contemporary Jewish views on sexuality: "One gains the impression that many observant males, in particular, do not place pre-marital sex on a par with, say, profaning the Sabbath. (It is possible that what is at work here, aside from the secular influence, is the Orthodox tendency to underemphasize the sanctity of social obligations—those between 'man and his fellow,' *bein adam l'havero*—relative to the importance attached to correct ritual observance.)"[14]

Some people have adopted a sliding scale of values about sex, as Arthur Green does in "A Contemporary Approach to Jewish Sexuality," in the *Second Jewish Catalog*.[15] Ideal sex, a spiritual and physical union, would thus be the "best" kind of sex, with various gradations of declining spiritual and moral content, down to rape as the lowest form of sexual expression. Eugene Borowitz in *Choosing a Sex Ethic*[16] sets forth five "types" of sexual relationships on a similar sliding scale. (Feminists might well object when rape is listed among forms of sexual expression, even if it's only to define the lowest level of sexuality. Rape is a crime of violence against women,[17] and women are justifiably profoundly revolted when men describe it as just another, albeit lower, form of connecting women and men sexually.) (See Rape, p. 220.)

Aside from the opposition to including rape as a category, the "sliding scale" model of sexuality is fine as an intellectual exercise. But for most women, as for most men, sex comes out of a more existential form of decision-making than the calibrated scale suggests. Treating one another with respect would be high on anyone's list of the factors without which sex would be inconceivable. But ethical sexual decisions, for religious *and* for secular Jewish women, may present problems different from those that confront men.

Adultery, for example, is a sexual activity with particular legal consequences for Jewish women (see Marriage, p. 320). The observance of mikveh if one is unmarried but sexually active is another issue that separates women from men. Since sexual intercourse requires no rituals from observant men—other than determining that the woman they're sleeping with isn't "impure" according to menstrual laws—it's observant women who must decide whether or not they will add ritual impurity to the "sin" of premarital sex or whether they will use the sacred mikveh ritual even before they are married.

From her Orthodox perspective, Blu Greenberg suggests that premarital sex should be governed by the same ritual laws covering married sex:

> Unmarried sexual partners observing *niddah* and *mikveh* could learn:
>
> (a) There is more to their relationship than sex, and if there isn't, then perhaps their sex is an abuse.
>
> (b) Real relationships mean commitment and sacrifice, and immediate gratification is an unrealistic expectation in enduring human relationships—a good preparation for real marriage.
>
> (c) *Niddah* would help single men and women to distinguish between promiscuous and authentic sexual relationships. Even logistically, one cannot "sleep around"—male or female—if the laws of *niddah* are observed.[18]

Women, like the men who invented the sliding scale of sexual experiences, are making their own reconciliation between their spiritual needs and their current sexual/marital status. Some of these women have called for a new Halachah on sexuality that will help them resolve conflicts or inconsistencies such as the one presented by an observant single woman in her twenties: "Here I am having lived 'illicitly' with my boyfriend for years, yet I will not pick up the phone if it rings on Shabbos."

Certainly not all Jewish women are concerned with these questions. A large majority of American Jewish women have never even considered using a mikveh—if they even know what it is. The problem is that the attitudes toward sex, formulated by religious Judaism, are transmitted in diluted form even to secular Jewish life.

RESOURCES

Women are still not considered full partners in the formulation of a Jewish sex ethic. Of the "experts" analyzing the subject in public none is a woman, perhaps because of residual feelings that it would be "immodest" for a woman to address such a matter. For example, of the three speakers in a program on Jewish sexuality sponsored in 1982 by one of Manhattan's most progressive lecture series—at Temple Ansche Chesed—none was a woman. Of the half dozen or so books on Jewish sexual ethics that have appeared in the past twenty years none has been written by a woman (although Roland Gittelsohn, in *Love, Sex and Marriage*, brings in a woman to write the chapter "Not to Wait," which runs counter to Gittelsohn's own view opposing premarital sex).

Sad to say, all the books written by men on sexuality have a subtle antifemale bias, as well as a tendency to make pronouncements from a single point of view. Even the analysis that comes out of the Reform movement (considered the most liberal in American Jewry) speaks somewhat disparagingly of the women's liberation movement and of women's desires for a life outside the home.

But, for the record, here are the latest official books on Jewish sex, one from each major denomination:

The Jewish Way in Love and Marriage (Orthodox)
by Maurice Lamm
Harper and Row, 1980

Love and Sex: A Modern Jewish Perspective (Conservative)
by Robert Gordis
Farrar, Straus & Giroux, 1978

Love, Sex and Marriage: A Jewish View (Reform)
by Roland Gittelsohn
Union of American Hebrew Congregations, 1980

A plea for a new Jewish sexual ethic for single women, based on morality and not licit/illicit distinctions, suggests also that single Jewish women could help nurture and educate other people's Jewish children, creating a stronger Jewish community than might have been possible if they were busy raising their own children. See:

"Single and Jewish: Toward a New Definition of Completeness"
by Laura Geller and Elizabeth Koltun, in
Koltun, ed. *The Jewish Woman: New Perspectives*
Schocken, 1976

A very useful discussion guide for issues of human sexuality and one that examines women's role in traditional Judaism and its implications in forming sexual attitudes among young people is:

Course on Human Sexuality for Adolescents in Religious Schools,
    Youth Groups, and Camps
by Annette Daum and Barbara Strongin
Religious Action Department, New York Federation of Reform
    Synagogues
Union of American Hebrew Congregations
838 Fifth Avenue
New York, NY 10021

A short course on Jewish sexual ethics is the theme of an issue of a magazine for Jewish young adults:

"Teenage Sexuality"
Keeping Posted, March 1982
Union of American Hebrew Congregations
838 Fifth Avenue
New York, NY 10021

There has been much interesting writing on women's sexuality coming out of the women's movement, a good portion of it written by Jewish women, but none of it has attempted to formulate a reconciliation with a "Jewish" viewpoint—for example, the ritual separation of women and men—in the context of feminism. Below are two germinal works, the first chosen for its honesty, the other for its scholarly intelligence and eagerness to see women's sexuality as a fit subject for serious inquiry:

The Hite Report: A Nationwide Study of Female Sexuality
by Shere Hite
Macmillan, 1976

Women: Sex and Sexuality
Catharine R. Stimpson and Ethel Spector Person, eds.
Univ. of Chicago Press, 1980

The essays in this volume appeared originally in the summer and autumn 1981 issues of *Signs: A Journal of Women in Culture and Society*.

Hot or Cold? Stereotypes of Jewish Women's Sexuality
The tradition, and the language of the Bible and post-Biblical writings, tell us that sex (in marriage) is a mitzvah, a pleasure, has divine sanction and divine presence, and is as important for women as for men. Reality suggests that sex for many women is something less than this ideal. At a Jewish feminist conference in the seventies, following a session in which women discussed their attitudes about sex, Rabbi Laura Geller gave what one observer called a "glowing report" on Jewish attitudes toward women's sexuality. One participant turned to Geller after her presentation and asked: "If the tradition is so positive about our sexuality, why are Jewish women so screwed up?"

Are they? Are there some generalizations that can be made about Jewish women's sexual responses? Is there something that popular culture—with its jokes about Jewish women's sexuality—has to tell us? And is the "culture" the determinant of our sexual attitudes in the first place?

The jokes that men tell about Jewish women's sexual activity—usually complaining about active rejection or passivity—are an indication that something has gone wrong.

One explanation might be that for many contemporary American Jewish women, brought up to consider the needs of all those around them before considering their own, it has been difficult to move beyond self-sacrifice and amelioration into a recognition that one is *entitled* to be sexual. Lacking the assertiveness to express sexual needs and feelings directly, perhaps Jewish women resort to the passivity the jokes suggest. (The opposite may also be true, of course: that Jewish women are more assertive than non-Jewish women and therefore freer to say *no* to sex, and it's this active rejection that the jokes are about.)

Perhaps some of us really are less tuned in to our own sexuality than our foremothers were. Perhaps the more "proper" Victorian-lady behavior of Jewish women in the recent past means that we have denied something of ourselves—namely, the "earthier," more "natural" behavior of our foremothers. A psychotherapist at a sex clinic in the Northeast says that several of her European-born Jewish patients describe themselves as "hot women" who wanted more sexual activity in their marriages. This phrase, the therapist reports, is never expressed by more Americanized, assimilated Jewish women.

A woman who has spent her professional life analyzing the American Jewish experience claims that "Judaism *is* very physical, not other-worldly. Jewish culture reinforces a lot of physical stuff with talk and ritual. Ritual foods, ritual meals, special prayers you say when you taste the first fruits of a season, or a new fruit or vegetable you've never eaten before. There's lots of attention to physical and sensual things in every-day life—maybe this gets turned into sexuality."

New York psychotherapist Dale Bernstein says that Jews appear to be warmer, earthier, more socially precocious than other people, and that in their social situations there's a lot of emphasis on touching and eat-ing, activities associated with sexuality. Another therapist speculates: "Jewish women are often more involved in political liberalism. Along with this comes more sexual libertarianism and more sexual participa-tion."

Catholic women may in the past (before the Vatican eased its stance) have withdrawn from sexual pleasure out of feelings of guilt that plea-sure itself, even in marriage, is somehow evil. Jewish women don't bear

the burden of this "Madonna complex." There are no stories of parthenogenesis in Judaism and no theologically inspired guilt about sex. Jewish women may hold themselves back from their partners (consciously
or not) because of *anger*. If, as some sociologists have suggested, Jewish
women suffer from overdefined maternal roles and repressed anger (see
"Crisis," p. 443), then lack of desire on the part of these women is not so
surprising. If the woman perceives that an honest expression of her own
feelings would be too threatening to *shalom bayit*—the peace of the
home—then withdrawal may be the only conceivable response to this repressed anger.[19]

Helen Singer Kaplan, head of the New York Hospital sex therapy program, says that Jewish women who come to her from strictly observant
backgrounds have the same psychosexual problems as women who have
been raised in strict, structured, religious Catholic, Mormon, or fundamentalist Protestant families. Which is not to suggest that all observant
women have sexual problems but that those who do seem to have the
same kinds of problems as women from religious homes generally. Despite the fact that Judaism sanctions the pleasurable aspects of sex,
women with sexual problems are tuned in not to the pleasure but to the
guilt about their own desire—or lack of desire.

A Jewish Perspective on Sex Therapy

In the years since Masters and Johnson put "sexual dysfunction" into
the language, therapists have developed special approaches to treating
sexual problems of religiously observant Jewish couples.

Aside from the reluctance of many Orthodox couples to admit that
they are seeing a sex therapist (since traditional modesty prohibits discussing one's sexual activity with others), there are the problems therapists have with Jewish laws pertaining to sex.

Because observant Jewish men are prohibited from "spilling seed,"
and therefore cannot ejaculate sperm except into the vagina of a woman,
they can't masturbate, often an important step in curing some sexual
problems. Therapists now claim to be alert to this situation and don't
contribute even further to the couple's anxieties by insisting either that
the step be taken anyway or that the couple is neurotic in their adherence to religious law. Other difficulties in therapy may be caused by the
prohibition of certain sexual fantasies; one couple actually had to get a
dispensation from their rabbi to indulge in sexual fantasy as part of
therapy.

Articles that may be helpful are: Stuart Ostrov, "Sex Therapy with

Orthodox Jewish Couples," *Journal of Sex and Marital Therapy* (Winter 1978); and Norman Shepard Fertel, M.D., and Esther Gittel Fertel, R:N., "Treating Marital and Sexual Problems in the Orthodox Jewish Community," *Journal of Psychology and Judaism* (Spring/Summer 1981). The latter article has some useful insights into the psychological problems of couples who are unprepared to communicate in nonphysical ways during the monthly period of separation. The authors suggest that a woman's feelings of anger at being "rejected" by her husband at times when there is no sexual or physical contact is sometimes displaced onto the ritual of *niddah* itself.

To find sex therapists who are sympathetic to Orthodox religious views and who won't consider them pathological, consult your local Jewish Family Service or the Jewish hospital in any large city, since now almost all of these have sex-therapy clinics.

VULNERABILITY

Rape

The Jewish laws concerning rape, which derive from a few verses in Deuteronomy, basically view women as helpless creatures, very much the property of their fathers or husbands. A convicted rapist must compensate a father or husband for the rape of his daughter or wife, and only an unmarried orphan is permitted to keep any fine awarded.

There are different Biblical decisions made on a rape, depending on where it took place. In a city, the victim is assumed to be an accomplice, since she could have cried out and had her cries heard, but didn't protest. In the countryside, it is assumed, none would have heard her even if she had cried out.

One of the most appalling consequences of the rape laws, and one that highlighted women's dependent status, was that an unmarried woman who was raped became the bride of the man who raped her. As part of his punishment for dishonoring the woman, the man had to marry her and never divorce her—although some authorities required the woman's consent to the marriage. This is obviously a law intended to protect the dishonored woman from the terrible plight of being alone and rejected by the community all her life, but it's hard to imagine a more horrible situation than being forced to marry a man who has raped you.

The responses of rabbis through the ages to cases of rape provide insights into what happens when men are the only decision-makers in an area in which the primary victims are women. Some rabbinical judgments have decreed that the rapist does not need to compensate the woman's family for "pain," as would be the case if she had been assaulted, because the rabbis could not see how rape would be a different physical experience from sexual intercourse, and, in fact, first intercourse was expected to be painful for women.

Rachel Adler uses a Talmudic discussion of rape as an example of how women's actual experience is "non-data" to the men in power:

Let us turn our attention to some cases in the tradition where there are major discrepancies between the questions answered by the tradition and the questions of concern to women. One such case is brought in Tractate Ketubot (11a,b) and concerns a little girl less than three years old with whom a grown man has intercourse. The tradition's question regarding the case is whether the little girl's virginity is considered to have been destroyed, in which case the [dowry] paid her would be only half that of a virgin. Since the assumption is that the child's hymen would grow back, the ruling is that she receives the full [dowry] of a virgin. Raba declares, "When a grown man has intercourse with a little girl, it is nothing, for when the girl is less than this [that is, three], it is as if one puts the finger into the eye." Being a psychotherapist working with sexual abuse victims, I frequently see women recount, or in some measure relive, their childhood sexual abuse, and I have never heard one compare the experience to putting her finger in her eye. . . . A woman's questions about the case, then, would focus on the pain, injury and terror felt by the little girl. She might ask how the man was to be held morally accountable for his behavior, and what compensation was due the child. . . . The entire area of rape is one in which women's questions differ considerably from men's.[20]

One recent rape case, heard not in a rabbinical court but in Israel's civil courts, attests to the possibilities for the compassionate application of Jewish law, which has often been based on the protection of women. In Israel, in 1980, a man was accused of raping his wife; he based his defense on the provision in English common law that a husband has a right to sexual intercourse with his wife under any circumstances and can even use force to coerce her. The court, which found the husband guilty of marital rape, declared that Jewish law (and hence Israeli law) forbids a husband to have sexual intercourse with his wife against her will.

Not all authorities are that sympathetic or choose to apply the actual protections for women built into certain Jewish laws. Even today women have reported that when they have gone to see a rabbi for counseling or

אונס

אינך לבדך

נשים יושבות ליד הטלפון
24 שעות בימצה
ומוכנות לעזור לך
במרכז סיוע לקורבנות אונס
טל. 220420 - 03
דיזנגוף 228 ת"א

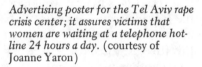

Advertising poster for the Tel Aviv rape crisis center; it assures victims that women are waiting at a telephone hot-line 24 hours a day. (courtesy of Joanne Yaron)

support after being raped, they were greeted with responses that did more harm than good. For example, one Jewish woman in her twenties, raped on the street, went to see a well-known rabbi in her Midwestern city "because I really felt the need to talk to some religious authority about my complicated reactions to this horrible thing that had happened to me. The rabbi said that he thought I should go to the mikveh and purify myself that way."

Norman Mirsky, in *Unorthodox Judaism*, tries to explain Jewish men's feelings of helplessness and collusion over rape:

History reminds us of the frequency of pogroms that left Jewish men unable to defend their wives from rape. . . . Powerlessness led to projection, which led to the defense mechanism of "Jewish humor" . . . that thinly masks the blame incurred by the victim while at the same time eroticizing her. "Let my mother go," a child pleaded with the Cossack. "Shut up," said the mother, "a pogrom is a pogrom!" . . . The oppressed, degraded male and the oppressor work together to create a stereotype, the first in order to de-eroticize his woman while he himself conforms to the degraded image provided by the oppressor, the second in order to dehumanize the object of his oppression and his lust and to render him thereby free from guilt.[21]

Jean-Paul Sartre has attempted to analyze the particular "allure" of the Jewish woman to non-Jewish men, and her "special" role as rape victim, linking violence to non-Jewish men's attraction to Jewish women. Susan Brownmiller expands upon the terrifying idea that Jewish women are especially vulnerable in her landmark book on rape, *Against Our Will: Men, Women and Rape*. Most recently, Andrea Dworkin, in *Pornography: Men Possessing Women*[22] makes the connection between certain kinds of sadistic political behavior (Nazism among them) and the torture, rape, and sexual abuse of Jewish women.

Jewish women have not, however, been raped exclusively by non-Jews. To what should be the shame of Jewish men, rape and sexual harassment were not unknown as a method used by Jewish sweatshop owners to keep Jewish female workers in line in the early decades of the twentieth century. The most visible recent cases of rape involving Jewish women have taken place in the state of Israel. Women there have opened rape crisis centers, and the Tel Aviv center, which tries to staff a twenty-four-hour-a-day hotline for rape victims, reports that Jewish male police officers and doctors do not always understand that a rape victim did not bring about her own fate, and that dress and behavior have nothing to do with inciting rapists.

Similar feelings of guilt and responsibility come out when women from New York's Orthodox communities report that they have been raped. Many say that they feel it's something that has happened because they have not dressed modestly enough or that the rape has come as a punishment from God. For Orthodox women there are Halachic issues involved also—such as whether or not abortion is possible for a pregnancy that results from a rape, and whether the wife of a Cohen need be divorced from him after she has been raped, since a Cohen is forbidden to stay married to a woman who has had sexual relations with another man. An organization now exists—founded by Orthodox women—to counsel rape victims from an Orthodox perspective. It's particularly helpful for those women who fear that they won't receive appropriate support within their own communities, yet fear that their particular concerns will be brushed aside if they turn to secular support groups.

SOVRI
   (Support for Orthodox Victims of Rape and Incest)
c/o Victims Services Agency
54 Nagle Avenue
New York, NY 10040
(212) 567-5008
(Calls will be forwarded directly to SOVRI.)

Prostitution

Since Jewish law forbids sexual contact outside marriage, prostitution is obviously disapproved of. The prophet Hosea warns about women who prostitute themselves and men who "consort with prostitutes and feast with harlots." Originally, however, prostitution was an activity associated with pagan culture, and Jews (women and men) were forbidden to be prostitutes, because this would have meant a religious apostasy.

In the first two decades of this century, in fact, Jewish men were not only feasting with harlots, they were actually engaged in the so-called "white slave" trade, and Jewish women worked as prostitutes in Europe and America. According to historian Reena Sigman Friedman, "It has been estimated that between 1913 and 1920, 17 percent of the prostitutes arrested in Manhattan were Jewish."[23]

As Jews we have sometimes been guilty of a collective denial about the seamier side of Jewish life, naturally preferring to sanitize our image and concentrate on Nobel Prize winners. One of the few serious attempts to deal with the subject of Jewish prostitutes is the remarkable autobiographical account of a Jewish prostitute in America—Maimie Pinzer—told through her own letters, *The Maimie Papers*.[24] Maimie's correspondence with the wealthy Protestant woman who was her mentor tells how she became a prostitute after her father's death left her with much of the responsibility for raising her five younger siblings. Obviously, economic and not sexual needs dictated Maimie's choices. "Maimie's life brings into sharp focus the limited options available to lower-class American women of her time—menial, unskilled labor, marriage, or prostitution. . . . In disowning a daughter who had gone astray, Maimie's relatives reacted in a manner characteristic of many Jewish, Irish and Italian families of the time."[25]

There was some relief for women who might become ensnared in the "white slave" trade when they first came to America. As early as the turn of the century the National Council of Jewish Women positioned Yiddish-speaking women volunteers at Ellis Island to help young women traveling alone and keep them out of the clutches of the men (often Jewish) who would try to entice them into prostitution.

In Europe, Bertha Pappenheim—the real-life analysand of Sigmund Freud known in his writings as "Anna O."—involved herself with the plight of Jewish prostitutes in Germany and Eastern Europe. Both in her work with the Jüdischer Frauenbund, the German Jewish feminist organization she founded in 1904, and in her writings Pappenheim described the numbers and the plight of Jewish prostitutes. According to historian

Marion Kaplan, she discovered prostitutes' hospitals, where a third of the patients were Jewish, and a synagogue in Constantinople where prostitutes donated money to have their pimps called to the Torah on holidays. "As a Jewish feminist, Pappenheim also understood prostitution to be a result of the low status of women in her religion and culture. She maintained that women were seen only as sex objects in the religion and treated as such in Jewish society. Because Jewish women were not educated, they rarely acquired the skills with which they could support themselves and were forced to sell their bodies in order to live."[26]

Pappenheim's analysis would surely hold today for the large numbers of Israeli prostitutes, most from impoverished Jewish Sephardic or Mediterranean families. The only other identifiable group of Jewish women working as prostitutes today are those in the underground drug culture in large North American cities who have turned to prostitution to support a drug habit.

Story of Basha, a film by Dan Wolman based on I. B. Singer's "Out of the Poorhouse," tells the tale of an aging prostitute who tries to leave the ugly realities of her life in the poorhouse by going off with a man she meets in a park. Again we see clearly poverty and limited options for a woman (and also for a Jew in the nineteenth century, when the film takes place). The film is available from:

Jewish Media Service
15 East 26 Street
New York, NY 10010

REPRODUCTION AND CONTRACEPTION

"Be Fruitful and Multiply"

There are two marital obligations concerning sex: *pru u'rvu* (procreation) and *onah* (sexual pleasure), and since pleasure—within marriage—is one of the sanctified reasons for sexual intercourse, contraception is preferable to abstinence. One nineteenth-century rabbi expounds the principle that the more it interferes with pleasure the less acceptable a contraceptive device is.

In contrast to other dogmas, there is considerable elasticity in the interpretation of the contraceptive laws, with the prime objects the preservation of life and the quality of that life. For example, a woman is permitted to drink a "sterilizing potion" (the recipe for which has not come down to us from Talmudic times) if she fears that an extremely painful childbirth experience might be repeated, and she may even overrule her husband's objections to this. "She is not bound to torment herself on account of her submission to her husband," and "one need not destroy oneself in order to populate the world," says Rabbi Moses Schreiber in 1821.[27]

Some authorities say that the sterilizing potion is acceptable because its effects are temporary, and therefore the ban on mutilation is not violated. (Any bodily mutilation, such as castration, is utterly forbidden in Judaism, and it is the only religion to ban the practice outright both for humans and for animals. For this reason a vasectomy would not be an acceptable method of birth control to the observant Jewish man.)

There are laws concerning ways to encourage conception. The Halachic view on artificial insemination permits it for infertile couples as long as the husband's sperm is used. (Some rabbis have equated the use of another man's sperm with adultery.)

One argument against artificial insemination has been that, with the donor unknown, the child thus conceived risks marrying a blood relative and hence (a) committing incest and (b) having a defective child of his/her own. (The same arguments are marshaled against adopting a Jewish baby.) One rabbi, quoted by Sir Immanuel Jakobovits, Chief Rabbi of the British Commonwealth, suggested that a way around this would be to sanction only those artificial inseminations in which the donor was a *non*-Jewish man. The resulting furor was so great, with objections based on the sanctity of Jewish family life and on other such factors, that the rabbi in question later withdrew his decision, and there was subsequently a ban on all artificial insemination using sperm of any donor other than the husband.

If you're not bound by these Orthodox decisions, however, and if you cannot conceive and know you're fertile, you may want to bear a child that has genes from at least one of the parents who will raise her/him. Even with insemination by a non-Jewish donor (and donor sperm is almost always anonymous and can even be a mixture of the sperm of more than one man), the offspring will be Jewish, according to Halachah, if the mother is Jewish.

Controlling Conception

Observing the laws of *niddah* ensures that a couple's sexual contact will take place at the most fertile time of the woman's menstrual cycle—a kind of reverse birth control, or birth encouragement, historically very useful to a people justifiably obsessed with survival in harsh environments.

Preventing conception has its own set of laws and regulations, and while only a small minority of Jews today honor these laws (or the *niddah* laws), the attitudes that shaped the laws or that were shaped by them may well influence Jewish women's current feelings about contraception and abortion.

Pru u'rvu, the Biblical injunction to be fruitful and multiply, is considered to apply only to men. Therefore Jewish laws on birth control usually focus on methods that don't prevent the sperm from meeting the egg. (Today, unfortunately, this means the contraceptive pill—the method most harmful to the woman using it.)

Interpreters of the law permit only those methods that do not interfere with the ejaculation of sperm into the vagina, although in extreme cases in which a pregnancy would imperil the life of a woman and she can use no method of birth control at all—whether because of a physical disability or through fear—the use of a condom may be permitted. In an age of sharing responsibilities for birth control and family planning, the strict interpretation of Jewish law still puts *all* the responsibility and inconvenience onto the woman, because of the interpretation of *pru u'rvu* as a man's obligation.

Women who were pregnant, lactating, or minors (between twelve and thirteen years old) could, according to the Talmud, use a contraceptive tampon of sponge (called a *moch*), so that a pregnancy would not harm either the baby or, in the case of a minor, the woman herself. Even among Orthodox women—for whom the diaphragm, a modern version of this method, might be the preferred one—not all choose to use it. In fact certain Orthodox couples even now will consult their rabbi before considering *any* kind of birth control. Most Orthodox rabbis consider two children—if one boy and one girl—the minimum number one must have. One woman reports counseling her daughter before such an appeal: "She already has five children and she's only twenty-five—I told her to make sure that she told her story in such a way that the decision by the rabbi would come out the way she wanted it to. They don't want to have more children right now, but you have to understand where people like us are coming from. We wouldn't just stop having children. It's not just something you yourselves can decide about. You can't arbitrarily *choose* to stop having children. You have to have a rabbinical decision to stop." This is a far cry from one of the nonnegotiable points of feminists: women have the right to full control over the reproductive powers of their own bodies.

Another woman, who read about contraceptives in a popular women's magazine while waiting her turn at the mikveh one evening, decided to have an IUD inserted without telling her husband. The woman apparently didn't want her husband to have a part in the sin of preventing contraception but thought that somehow the action was less sinful because it was performed by a mere woman and that he would at least not willingly be disobeying the injunction to be fruitful and multiply.

Orthodox social worker Sara Silver Bunim, who recounted the woman's story at a 1979 New York conference on the changing roles of Jewish women, points out that women must see themselves as equally responsible for obeying the Jewish laws concerning contraceptive decisions. She suggests that women speak to their rabbis directly about such decisions rather than sending their husbands to ask for a decision, as is often the practice. Like many Orthodox women eager to see rabbinic responses to women's issues in Judaism, Bunim feels that if rabbis don't get feedback from women themselves, they won't change their attitudes or change the interpretation of the law. She describes the structure of Orthodox Judaism as one of "controlled adaptation," with the individual problems of real people contributing to reinterpretation of Halachah.

The Halachic positions on birth control vary from denomination to denomination, with the strictest view being that no contraception at all should be used unless further pregnancies would harm the mother, and the most liberal being that an ethical position on birth control is one that ensures that only wanted children will be brought into the world.

In reality, regardless of what any religious position on the matter might be, birth control is a way of life for most sexually active Jewish women. In fact, Jewish women use birth control more than other women. On the whole, Jewish women are better educated than other women, and that, more than anything to do with Judaism, probably accounts for their high rate of contraceptive use. According to one study, Jewish couples use the most effective methods, use them the most efficiently, and don't wait until after the birth of their first child to start using contraceptives.[28]

What is widely held to be the definitive compendium of laws on birth control and abortion, which reflects the concern of most rabbis through the ages for women's health and well-being, comes from a Conservative rabbi: *Birth Control and Jewish Law,* by David M. Feldman (New York Univ. Press, 1968). Feldman believes that most decisions under these laws favor women, with rabbinic decision-makers usually taking the most humane stand on an issue. What he *doesn't* deal with is the implication for women of the fact that these decision-makers have always been men.

There is a very real tension between the strictest Jewish position on birth control (even though it may be relatively permissive) and women's strong feelings about the sanctity of self-determination and their right to

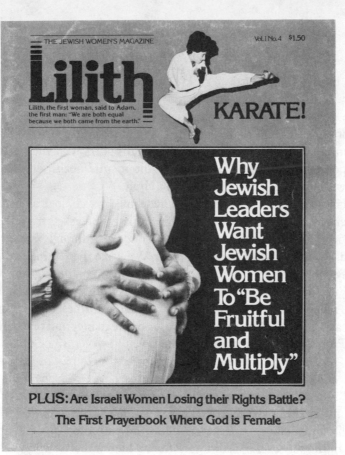

THE JEWISH WOMEN'S MAGAZINE

Vol. I No. 4 $1.50

Lilith

Lilith, the first woman, said to Adam,
the first man: "We are both equal
because we both came from the earth."

KARATE!

Why Jewish Leaders Want Jewish Women To "Be Fruitful and Multiply"

PLUS: Are Israeli Women Losing their Rights Battle?

The First Prayerbook Where God is Female

choose what happens to their own bodies. In fact, these laws and the con-flicts they engender are a microcosm of the tensions between Judaism and feminism. Should some larger than-life (male-dominated) system be permitted to create laws shaping women's lives? (See also "Responding to the Childbearing Imperative," p. 371.)

Abortion

Abortion was known and discussed even in Talmudic times; there were even specified rituals for a woman who had undergone one.[29] While there has been considerable disputation over the circumstances under which abortion was permitted, all agree that the life of the fetus *does not* take precedence over the life of the woman. This is the opposite of the Catho-lic belief that the fetus is alive and must be delivered even if the mother's life is forfeited. Jews believe that if the fetus endangers the mother's life, the pregnancy must be terminated. The strict Orthodox position is that even an abnormal fetus should not be aborted unless it's a threat to the mother. A 1971 statement by the Union of Orthodox Jewish Scientists reflects this view: "Jewish law prohibits abortion when its sole justification is to prevent the birth of a physically deformed or mentally retarded child."

The logic behind aborting a Down's syndrome or Tay-Sachs fetus is then not to spare the child but to spare the parents. In getting a Halachic opinion on whether or not one can seek an abortion in such cases, one must petition in terms of the threat to the mental health of the mother faced with the prospect of raising such a child.

In fact, some rabbis do not even recognize psychological hazards as sufficient reason for abortion. A Philadelphia rabbi, asked his opinion on abortion of an abnormal fetus or a fetus conceived through rape or incest, replied, "We say this is God's way. . . . We leave these things to God."[30] Usually, however, the predominant view prevails, limiting abortion to cases involving hazard to the mother, whether physical or psychological.

The more flexible position, taken by some authorities, distinguishes between an abortion in the first two months of pregnancy and one performed later. Problems arise with these distinctions, however, since often a pregnancy is not discovered in its first month, and amniocentesis—which would determine, for example, if the fetus has Tay-Sachs disease (see p. 249)—cannot be performed until the fourth month of pregnancy.

From a fundamentalist, strictly constructionist Orthodox view that only in a life-threatening situation is abortion permitted, Jewish attitudes range all the way to the Reform position, which is that safe legal abortion should be available to all women, and that the choice to have an abortion is a personal one, not to be legislated. In between are the varying positions of Conservative rabbis, some of whom believe that any psychological stress on the mother is "danger" enough to terminate the pregnancy and that therefore, of course, pregnancies resulting from rape or incest can be terminated also. Because of this range of opinion, Jewish organizations have been aligned both with right-wing and with liberal-centrist groups on the issue of legalizing abortion in the United States and Canada, although a vast majority supports reproductive rights despite the attempt of right-wing Orthodox forces to make the Jewish and Catholic positions appear identical.

In a 1972 statement on United States law and abortion rights American Jewish Congress put forth the position that probably represents the basic opinion of most North American Jews:

Restrictive or prohibitive abortion laws violate the right of a woman to choose whether to bear a child, her right of privacy and her liberty in matters pertaining to marriage, family and sex. . . . Those who find

abortion unacceptable as a matter of religious conviction or conscience
are free to hold and live by their beliefs, but should not seek to impose
such beliefs, by government actions, on others. . . . It is, therefore, the
position of American Jewish Congress that all laws prohibiting or restricting abortion be repealed and that the matter be left to the woman
concerned.[31]

According to *Redbook*'s April 1977 survey of American women and religion, Jewish women are considerably more liberal than Protestants or
Catholics in their views on birth control and abortion. Only 15 percent
of the Jewish women surveyed objected to abortion, compared to 67 percent of Catholics and 50 percent of Protestants.

Jewish support for abortion rights has a long history. Articles on abortion and family planning appeared in the Polish-Jewish press as early as
the 1920s, and the influential *Jewish Daily Forward* supported Margaret
Sanger in her groundbreaking struggle to inform women about birth control and "reproductive freedom." In fact, for women of the immigrant
generation there was little religious stigma attached to abortion. Many of
them spoke to their own daughters about illegal abortions or attempts at
self-induced abortion. One Jewish woman, now in her seventies, raised in
an Orthodox Brooklyn home, recalls being told by her own mother that
she had tried "home remedies" to abort several of the pregnancies that
produced her eight children.

The Jewish position on abortion is particularly relevant now to Jewish
women for two reasons. First, Tay-Sachs disease and other less well-known
Jewish genetic diseases can be detected *in utero* by amniocentesis. This
means that Jewish women have the opportunity to learn in advance if
they will give birth to a child fated to live only four or five suffering years,
at most. Although there are Orthodox women who, knowing that they
were carrying a Tay-Sachs fetus, decide to follow the strictest interpretation of Jewish law and bear the child anyway, since their own lives are not
in danger from the pregnancy, most women faced with this painful choice
would choose to abort the fetus.

The second—and in the long run potentially more important—reason
to become familiar with the Jewish positions on abortion now is that with
right-wing forces in America trying to force their religious view of abortion as a sin into the Constitution, Americans may find themselves with a
Constitution that would deny even the most Orthodox Jews the opportunity to observe Jewish law, which requires abortion in cases where a
woman's life is endangered by a pregnancy.[32]

Abortion is an issue fraught with a peculiar tension for many Jewish women. On one hand, it is intolerable to all feminists that man-made laws, whether religious or civil, should determine such a crucial matter of autonomy as a woman's reproductive choices. On the other hand, for very real historical reasons, "freedom of choice" may bring with it anxieties unknown to non-Jewish women.

Aviva Cantor, in an essay "The Phantom Child,"[33] reconstructs the arguments a woman has with herself before deciding on an abortion. She remembers that barrenness had driven Biblical women (and real-life relatives) mad—while pregnancy was driving *her* mad. Then: "I thought of great scholars, thinkers, leaders. What if Ber Borochov's mother had had an abortion? Or Moshe's mother? Or Emma Goldman's? What if this baby is destined to do great deeds, to be a light unto the world? What if my baby is the Messiah?"

Going on to connect the Holocaust and abortion, Cantor touches an issue that has affected a great deal of modern Jewish thinking and writing about abortion. The Holocaust has been used as justification both for performing abortions and for forbidding them to Jewish women. Montreal physician Henry Morgentaler is a survivor who, when jailed for having performed abortions in Quebec in the 1960s, said that his experiences during the war—seeing women coerced into bearing children against their will and having abortions against their will—convinced him that each woman must be free to choose for herself.

Compare this with the advertising copy for Gloria Goldreich's novel *Four Days* (New York: Harcourt Brace Jovanovich, 1980): "Can a woman who grew up in a Nazi concentration camp ever take a life? . . . Should she abort the unwanted child she is carrying?"

Concern for the depletion of the Jewish people has caused the tightening of abortion laws in Israel, which is estimated to have an abortion rate of sixty thousand per year, in a population of three million Jews. A *Jerusalem Post* editorial supporting more liberal abortion laws is attacked in the letters column as "a national death wish." Immanuel Jakobovits claims that "abortions have depleted the Jewish state of over a million native-born citizens since its foundation."[34]

RESOURCES

"The Jewish Stake in Abortion Rights"
by Annette Daum
Lilith #8

For up-to-the-minute statements on how Jewish organizations are combating restrictive (and often religiously biased) antichoice legislation, contact your local Jewish Community Relations Council (see Networking Directory, p. 543) or:

National Jewish Community Relations Advisory Council
111 West 40 Street
New York, NY 10018
(212) 221-1535

In addition to aligning yourself with Jewish groups interested in keeping the government out of our beds, you may want to get in touch with an ecumenical group trying to keep reproductive choices a personal matter:

Religious Coalition for Abortion Rights
100 Maryland Avenue, NE
Washington, DC 20002

Jewish groups that participate in this coalition are American Jewish Congress, B'nai B'rith Women, National Council of Jewish Women, National Federation of Temple Sisterhoods, Union of American Hebrew Congregations, United Synagogue of America, Women's League for Conservative Judaism.

For further information about abortion rights on a national scale, consult:

National Abortion Rights Action League
   (NARAL)
825, 15 Street, NW
Washington, DC 20005
(202) 347-7774

The Abortion Papers
by Marilyn Braveman and Maureen Schild
Domestic Affairs Department
American Jewish Committee
165 E. 56 Street
New York, NY 10022
$.50

BODY IMAGE

Modesty as a Feminist Issue

Some of the same contradictions associated with mikveh observance arise when we consider other traditional laws and customs concerning women; some women tout the virtue of the traditional concept of modesty as a reinforcer of women's independence, while others claim that it is too closely associated with negative views of women to warrant attention today. The rubric "modesty" in Judaism includes both the restrictions preventing women from singing in public—which in the past have been used to keep women out of the public sphere in rituals (see "Law and Leadership," p. 67)—and also the requirement, more in keeping with some current feminist thinking, that women dress modestly and thereby not present themselves merely as sex objects. (The concept is rarely applied to men.) Of course in one way to assume that a woman's appearance is responsible for the lascivious thoughts of those around her is to blame the victim for a situation that is in the mind of the beholder. However, those women who follow the traditional tenets of Orthodoxy claim that they are not acting in response to some male weakness-of-the-flesh, but are expressing their own strong sense of Jewish self-definition.

Aside from the highly specific legal formulations about women's voices

Left: *Lubavitch women, all wearing long sleeves. The women who are married wear wigs or other hair coverings.* (© 1981 Bonnie Geller)

A wall in the ultra-Orthodox Mea Shearim section of Jerusalem. (Layle Silbert)

(*kol ishah*), the other rules and customs concerning modesty vary from community to community. Less exposed, in every way, usually means more religious.

Gila Berkowitz defends the general Orthodox point of view, yet aligns the feminist and the traditional religious attitude toward "modesty":

> How the word smacks of coyness and prudishness and smarmy Victorians! Nothing could be further from this essential Jewish value. Jewish modesty in speech, dress, and behavior is imperative for both men and women. Its object is to enhance human dignity.
>
> In dress, Judaism requires not dowdiness or unattractiveness but a sense of dignity and respect for one's own body, which, male or female, is the image of God. Women are advised not to treat themselves as male playthings. Wearing suggestive, teasing clothing is a desperate and doomed attempt to wheedle favors from those in power—who tend to be people thoroughly covered from neck to toe.[35]

One aspect of the modesty/morality picture, which includes the rules about expressing sexual desire and about what we wear and how we behave and where we speak and sing, is the matter of hair covering. Covered hair was at one time the most observably "Jewish" part of a woman's appearance. According to Jewish custom, one of the marks of a married woman is that her hair is covered whenever she is in public. (This is aside from the practice of married women—in some settings all women—covering their heads when in synagogue.)

The rule is interpreted in one of several ways. Some authorities say it's sufficient to have a symbolic cover on the hair (paralleling a Jewish man's use of a *kippah*). Others say that all the hair must be covered, because exposed hair equals nudity, and seeing it would therefore be sexually provocative to men.

In America the issue of whether or not women should cover their hair has undergone transformations. The traditional wig or scarf was originally associated with something excessively old-fashioned, and the first generation of immigrant women often experienced tremendous conflict over whether to conform to American practice or to risk being out of the mainstream (a "greener," or "greenhorn") and retain the head covering or wig of Eastern Europe. Remember the scene in *Hester Street*, Joan Micklin Silver's 1975 film about the conflicts when a traditional young wife comes to America to be reunited with her already assimilated husband, in which the heroine and her husband argue over her hair covering? He wants her to be more modern, uncover her hair, and assimilate. In the early years of the twentieth century many young immigrant women longed for their mothers to stop covering their hair or stop wearing wigs, in the fear that their fathers would abandon their mothers because of their Old Country ways.

An ironic sidelight on the issue of hair covering as an expression of modesty is the proliferation of gorgeous wigs that many observant women wear. In resort towns in the Catskills, for example, one sees Hasidic families in which the men, clad in black coats, with hats or *kippot* and side-curls hanging, are accompanied by their wives, out for a summer stroll. The wives, like their husbands, are attired in the halachically approved manner—with long sleeves, dresses, stockings, covered hair. But the difference between the men and the women is astonishing! The women look gorgeous. Their stockinged feet are in high-fashion high-heeled shoes, their long-sleeved dresses are flatteringly cut, and their hair is covered with wigs so stunning that they could appear in shampoo commercials. So much for an observance designed to keep women's attractiveness in the closet!

Giti Bendheim, an Orthodox married woman, describes her feelings about covering her hair and the reasons she does it—reasons that have more to do with her own identity as a Jew than with any reactive response to male sexuality.

There's a story, perhaps apocryphal, told about a new bride on her way to America who threw her *sheytl* [wig] overboard as she approached the port of New York. A wig was something she wouldn't need in this new land. Often, when recalling this emblematic tale, I have been struck by the irony that I, born and bred in twentieth-century America, have willingly chosen to fish that *sheytl* out of the waters.

Like many apocryphal stories, this one has two endings, the second less dramatic, but perhaps closer to reality. In the second version, that new bride simply resolved to wear her wig until it wore out. It seems to me that this latter ending has a more authentic ring. It's more complex, less decisive, and leaves more room for the reluctance and ambivalence that young woman must have felt.

I have to admit that the issue of covering my hair has been both a source of tremendous personal growth and one of occasional anxiety for me in the course of fifteen years of marriage. Covering my hair has added a depth and richness to my married and religious life, while my frustration has been the result, mainly, of my convictions being at odds with the dictates of the society around me.

At one time, the covering of a woman's hair was a clear expression of societal values. Throughout much of the ancient world, hair-covering was a mark of dignity, much as a crown might be today. It was a sign of a woman's self-respect and social status to wear a head-veil, and women of a lower caste of society would often cover their hair to affect a higher standing. In fact, prostitutes who were not permitted to cover their hair in the accepted way often wore a special type of hair-covering in order to create the illusion of respectability.[36]

According to some interpreters the Torah does not have a direct commandment for a woman to cover her hair—simply because it was, at the time, in the woman's self-interest to do so.[37]

Gradually, in response to changing social codes, the practice of hair-covering began to evolve into an expression of modesty, rather than of dignity.[38] During the Mishnaic and Talmudic periods, the sages deal extensively with such issues as the amount of hair that must be covered, and whether this requirement varies in different geographical or functional domains (the home, the courtyard, the marketplace). There is a considerable divergence of opinion as to what constitute the exact requirements of modesty, but, with the passage of time, the practice of hair-covering came to represent the proper behavior expected of the Jewish woman. Thus, by the second century CE, Tertullian, a prominent Church Father, refers to hair-covering as a symbol of Jewish identity, which it remained for centuries.[39]

Within the traditional Jewish community, the head-veil, and much later, the wig, hat, or scarf marked a *rite de passage*, and symbolized the new joys and the attendant responsibilities of married life. Around the time of the Enlightenment in nineteenth-century Europe, however, women began to find this practice increasingly difficult as Jewish life became more intermingled with the secular culture, a dilemma of context which is still a major issue for those women who observe this custom/obligation today.

Whereas all women who classify themselves as "observant" or "Orthodox" adhere to the laws of Shabbat, say, and kashruth, there are a great many modern Orthodox married women who do not cover their hair, except in the synagogue. According to some interpretations, uncovered hair no longer has the same implications it did in earlier centuries, and hair-covering, if required at all, may now be less a direct comment on a woman's modesty than a symbol of her being married and Jewish. On the other hand, many authorities today continue to view hair-covering as a part of a married woman's general expression of *tzniut* or personal modesty, a concept which denotes both a physical sense of privacy about one's body as well as a generally inner-directed spiritual quality of personality.[40]

The exalted position of hair in our society makes the discipline of hair-covering an especially difficult one to maintain. A look through the ads in any magazine will quickly confirm the emphasis on hair as a woman's "crowning glory," reinforcing my sense that hair has been singled out for a particular restriction in Jewish life because of its sensual or provocative quality. Traditional Judaism seems to take the position that this sensuality, left publicly unrestrained, poses a threat to the family and social structure, while that same sensuality, properly channeled, becomes an enriching and stabilizing force. Covering the hair, then, becomes the physical analog of control and restraint, and the affirmation of the sanctity of the marriage bond. In affirming the beauty of a woman's hair, Halachah asks that it be appreciated in the context of marriage or in the privacy of the home.

Certainly, this practice has meaningful, even romantic elements for the married couple, and sometimes sends out an unexpectedly powerful message to the family as well. I remember vividly how one of my children, while still an infant, would begin to cry the moment he saw me put on my scarf to go out, and how he would reach out to pull off my hat (rather than my coat!) upon my return. I think the implication of the body language is striking. For my infant son, hair-covering was clearly something that belonged in the public domain, something that showed my relationship with the world outside our home.

Much of society, however, finds it more difficult than my son did to discern exactly what hair-covering is all about, or sometimes, even that it exists at all. As a symbol, it seems to lack some of the potency it held in the second century. Today a wedding band, for example, announces clearly and almost universally the married status of its wearer. In a more

parochial sense, the *kippah*, worn by observant Jewish males sends out
the immediately obvious message, "I am a Jew." Hair-covering, however, in its many varieties, while a clearly legible symbol in Jerusalem or
parts of Brooklyn, is less easily read in the modern, pluralistic communities in which many of us live.

Among less observant Jews or non-Jewish people, the message may be
not at all apparent. To the uninitiated, for example, my wearing a beret
with a denim skirt, or a sparkly hat to a cocktail party, does not necessarily bespeak a lofty religious commitment. There comes a point when
people you see often, who have assumed that you're an artsy or innovative dresser, begin to suspect that you're covering up some dread disease of the skull.

An obvious way to circumvent some of these bothersome social problems is to wear a wig. Interestingly, wearing a wig was not considered to
be an acceptable form of hair-covering until the same external pressures
of nineteenth-century European life which caused some women to stop
covering their hair made it all but intolerable for women who maintained this practice to wear traditional forms of hair-covering. Because
of the amount of hair it covers, the wig is probably now considered to
be the most acceptable form of hair-covering by strict constructionists
of the law, though to some authorities the wearing of a beautiful and
natural-looking wig still seems to uphold the letter of the law at the
expense of its spirit. To me, wearing a wig feels so unnatural, and so
offends my sense of wholeness, that I prefer to be more straightforward
about my commitment, even at the risk of calling a different kind of
attention to myself.

Depending on the context, then, hair-covering, which began as an
instantly discernible, powerful religious/social symbol, now falls somewhere between a public symbol and a private commitment. I wonder
whether it is this two-directional pull which creates confusion and ambivalence among many women who cover their hair. The practice is perceived differently by different audiences, and is legislated with varying
degrees of strictness by various "poskim" or Halachic authorities. In
fact, it seems to me that one of the few generalizations one can make
about covering one's hair is that it creates a constant personal awareness
of a commitment to dressing according to criteria other than those dictated by vanity, fashion, politics, or mood. A commitment to hair-covering pulls one back, if in only an emotional sense, into the bosom of the
traditional community, where the values may differ from those of the
marketplace, and this may be one reason that hair-covering is enjoying
a rebirth among Jewishly educated young women today.

I think that one of the more subtly significant aspects of hair-covering
is the controlling effect it has, not only over the behavior of others, but
over other aspects of one's own behavior. You think more carefully

about what you wear, the kinds of messages you communicate by the way you look, even where you choose to spend your time. And perhaps that's just the point. Perhaps I'm not supposed to feel so terribly comfortable at that cocktail party. If I perceive my hat as a barrier between myself and the people around me—or if they perceive it in that way—maybe that in itself is a form of self-imposed modesty that would be otherwise unattainable. There are certain limits that Judaism wants me to set, that I want to set for myself, and my consiousness of having deliberately thwarted my own vainer instincts in favor of a higher principle confirms and strengthens my higher expectations of myself and of the people with whom I associate. Perhaps, in a way, my hair-covering challenges people to appreciate me, if they will, for the mind and personality that are under my hat.

Ultimately, for me, the issue boils down to my own sense of humbleness in the face of an ancient tradition. There is a part of me that values hair-covering as an act of faith I share with tens of generations of Jewish women before me. After all, covering one's hair is one of the few observances that can be performed only by women. Like the laws of family purity, its observance links me to a whole tradition of Jewish women in the powerful way that only a concrete observance can.[41]

Just as hair is to be covered, so are most parts of a woman's body. Someone looking in her closet would note that the "traditional" Orthodox woman even today owns no sleeveless or short-sleeved garments, and all her stockings are opaque.

The enforcement of the laws concerning modesty in dress comes from community consensus. In some neighborhoods a woman cannot appear without long sleeves and stockings without eliciting shouts or glances of marked disapproval—as summer visitors to Jerusalem's religious quarters discover. Elsewhere only sleeveless garments may be unacceptable, although women wearing trousers are often frowned upon.[42]

The disapproving attitude toward slacks has to do not with modesty but with Judaism's preoccupation with differences—as between milk and meat, for instance. This concern for distinctions extends to the preservation of differences between women and men. (In fact, perhaps it derives from these gender differences!) And lest these distinctions blur: "A woman shall not wear that which pertaineth unto a man, neither shall a man put on a woman's garments."[43]

What this means in real life is that some Orthodox women will not wear trousers and that some Hebrew day schools forbid girls to appear in them, or even to wear culottes—hardly garments that today "pertaineth unto a man." Most observant Jews resolve this problem in daily life by

(Layle Silbert)

reasoning that "pants designed for women are women's apparel."[44] (For a rundown on appropriate synagogue attire, see p. 78.)

Keeping men and women separate in this fashion extends to separation in social contexts as well. Some Orthodox weddings, especially among Hasidim, for example, have no mixed-sex dancing after the ceremony; instead, women dance with women and men with men, often in separate halls, the bride with the women and the groom with the men. (One heterosexual Orthodox single woman in New York says that she loves to dance and often goes to lesbian bars, because Jewish law says nothing forbidding women to dance with each other. "I can't go dancing with men," she says, "so I dance with women.")

At some resorts in New York State frequented by ultra-Orthodox Jews, women and men do not share the same swimming facilities; there are separate pools or bathing beaches. And in some circles, whether you will appear on a mixed beach or not is another way of distinguishing how religious you are. Several municipal pools in Israel have special swimming hours set aside for women only and for men only, so that those who would be offended by the sight of a member of the opposite sex in a bathing suit can still swim.

Physical Strength

Some of the sexual questions raised by Jewish women have to do with the images we have of our bodies as a whole, not just sexually. As Jews, our physical self-image has been one of passivity. Survival is what counts, not physical prowess. This image persists despite the existence of the much-photographed Israeli army, which has contributed to the American Jewish man's image of himself as a potential tough guy (while photos of Israeli women soldiers show them more as sex objects than as strong defenders of the land).

For American Jewish women there have been no parallel historical images of romanticized physical strength to dilute the picture of the stolid woman bound to a domestic routine, physically strong in a peasant fashion perhaps, but neither swift nor graceful. In America, Jewish boys at least had the streets to play in, where they could try out the New World games. But the streets weren't for the girls, who were still being socialized for the indoors: sewing, cooking, and, if they were among the more affluent, music and artwork.

All middle-class women, especially Jewish women, have been discouraged from *moving* their bodies. One woman describes her childhood summer camp: "The boys played basketball and the girls sat on the sidelines, cheering and crocheting *yarmulkes!*" Some Jewish women (like their brothers) have backed off from physical activity because it seemed safer to concentrate on an area in which success was more attainable: academic

(Bruce S. Schneider)

prowess, verbal acuity. Athletic activity for its own sake was a pursuit Jews felt was better left to others. "All Jews are on a head trip," a Jewish woman complains.

Some of this characteristic physical passivity—or the image of passivity—may be changing. Orthodox women particularly have been drawn to studying karate; perhaps the clue lies in the verb. One *studies* karate; one does not study, for example, tennis. Which is not to say that Jewish women aren't playing tennis too. But for observant Jewish women karate, with the thinking processes and self-defense capabilities that the discipline implies, has become very popular—a kind of kosher version of the women's self-defense movement of the seventies. Karate instructor Lillian Andron says: "Being a woman is like wearing a *yarmulke*; you're constantly being stereotyped as a pushover. As Jewish women, we find it difficult to see ourselves as capable of being aggressive on the street if it becomes necessary, because our traditional role is more family-oriented and sheltered."[45]

For information about about a network of Jewish women's karate classes across the country, write:

Women's Karate Committee
Jewish Karate Federation of America, Inc.
1609 Kings Highway
Brooklyn, NY 11229

Is Jewish Beautiful? How We See Our Hair, Our Noses, Our Shapes

The actual physical strength of our bodies is something we have more control over than how we look—or think we look—in those bodies. "By the third grade, with every other girl in Baybury Heights, I came to realize that there was only one thing worth bothering about: becoming beautiful," says Sasha Davis in Alix Kates Shulman's *Memoirs of an Ex-Prom Queen* (New York: Knopf, 1972).

For women who grow up being told constantly how pretty they are (as Sasha Davis was) the path to parental approval is straight and narrow: keep on looking good.

The dilemma is very clear to a Houston woman, in her late thirties: "My brother was raised to be the family genius. So he worried all his life, and still worries, about how he's doing, and he can never be smart enough, or win enough awards. With me, all I had to be was the pretty little girl." We know from the writings by other contemporary Jewish women novelists (for example: Marge Piercy's *Small Changes* and Susan Fromberg Schaeffer's *Falling*) that if you do not believe you are attractive in the eyes of your parents, you feel forever imperfect. There's nothing you can do to improve things short of surgery or diet. And Jewish women have embraced both these methods of self-improvement. Marc Lee Raphael comments: "This need to feel preoccupied with what Betty Friedan calls 'female economics—beauty and physical appearance,' is widely viewed by [Jewish women] novelists as one of the most oppressive aspects of growing up middle-class and Jewish."[46]

What does it mean to grow up in a culture in which the prevailing standard of what's beautiful is not the way you look? It's true that the Hollywood ideal youth and smooth-skinned blond-haired beauty sets an unrealistic standard for all women, and that all of us grow up in some ways loathing aspects of ourselves: our faces, our bodies, our walk, our smells. Growing up female in America means growing up believing that you have to improve yourself, that you are in error and therefore in constant need of being deodorized, reduced, curled, straightened, finished. Jewish women may be *more* preoccupied with what it means to be "beautiful," since "Jewish" beauty is thought to differ from the American ideal. In an odd kind of dissociation, being part of a minority culture may cause us to come to see our "natural" traits as exotic.

Jewish women in psychologist Judith Klein's ethnotherapy groups in California (see p. 439) describe their "Jewish" appearance as more buxom, darker, hairier, heavier than this ideal. Many believe that Jewish women have certain undesirable physical traits that set them apart from other women. Some of these perceptions may be accurate, but the characteristics are also descriptive of women of European stock generally. Nevertheless there is no literature by Greek women, for example, bemoaning the fact that *they* don't look like "American" beauties. Perhaps it's the thrust of rapid assimilation that caused American Jewish women to want to transmute their very bodies into some other form—assimilation, plus the alleged attraction of Jewish men to non-Jewish women (see p. 290).

Gloria Averbuch, a runner, describes the conflict in being an "atypical" California female: "I am a Jew of Russian descent. I have thick, wavy black hair, dark eyes and olive skin. I spent twenty years as a Californian praying I could be what I was not meant to be: a beach-girl blond."[47]

Phyllis Chesler, feminist psychologist and author of *Women and Madness* (New York: Doubleday, 1972) and other books, says: "Non-Jewish men treated me the way white men treat black women—as more sensual, earthy, sexually accessible; as Rebecca of *Ivanhoe*. I experienced the same treatment from other feminists, when I was singled out by some comrades as somehow fleshier, earthier, sexier, pushier, more verbal: Jewish!"[48]

While the appearance of such ethnically diverse stars as Barbra Streisand and Bette Midler has diluted somewhat the power of the leggy-blonde ideal of American attractiveness, many Jewish women are unaffected by the change and still see their own shapes and selves as less desirable. Rabbi Irving Greenberg reports that while the Black women in his courses at New York's City College wore natural or "Afro" haircuts and talked about "Black is beautiful," the Jewish women were saving every penny for a nose job. "Nose jobs" for middle-class women have become, in fact, a Jewish joke unto themselves.[49] There's a good deal of pathos in a situation in which someone is willing to submit to surgery in order to conform to an alien standard of "appropriate" appearance. Just as in some families a dowry or hope chest was prepared for a daughter, in other families the insurance of a happily wedded future was the nose job. And in some cases, as with dowries for poor girls, the extended family contributed funds toward the surgery.

Granted, there are some cases in which physical characteristics are so markedly different from the norm as to cause almost unbearable psychological torment to their bearer. (The Talmud recognizes this by permitting corrective surgery to help a person overcome grave emotional difficulties or to render a woman more eligible for marriage or to help a person find or keep a job, even though the surgery itself is seen as a mutilation of the body, which is generally forbidden.) But in many of the cases involving Jewish women and their noses, plastic surgery was encouraged by their parents not because the women were hideous with their original profiles but because parents and/or children saw longer-than-pug noses as a Jewish characteristic.[50] If you don't believe that people associate long noses with Jews, look again at what appears in anti-Semitic cartoons: hairy Jews with long, hooked noses. Jews and non-Jews alike have come to believe this stereotype.

A Jewish feminist active in the women's movement tells of an incident in which a Black woman colleague argued: "What do you *mean* you're different and noticeable because you're *Jewish?* Just cut off part of your nose and change your name, and you'll pass."

Assimilation for Jewish women has often meant trying to change the way we look. The "straightening" syndrome has meant straighten your hair, your teeth, your body, your voice, your nose, your house. Our bodies are the tools for creating an assimilated American woman; they are the bearers of our "acceptability." Along with wanting their daughters to assimilate to a WASP model of behavior, parents wanted their daughters to conform to the WASP model in facial structure as well, in what might well have been a capitulation to anti-Semitism. When Fanny Brice had her nose bobbed, the joke was "She cut off her nose to spite her race." Hence the numbers of young women who, over a high-school vacation (especially in affluent suburbs) would enter the hospital allegedly to correct a "deviated septum" or other, often nonexistent nasal problem and emerge with the Dr. Smith nose or the Dr. Jones nose.

It's ironic that, although the ideal of female pulchritude is the non-Jewish Anglo-Saxon or Aryan woman, conformity is to the physical model only. Jewish women are not then expected (by peers or parents) actually to mix with non-Jews because of their new faces.

In *How to Be a Jewish Grandmother*, Sylvia S. Seaman says "Any nose, as long as it's not like that man's, Cyrano's, is all right on a Gentile, or even on an Arab, those other Semites. But on a Jewish girl, a nose has to be short, straight, and turn up a little. In America, that is." Grandmother and granddaughter in this book have nose jobs together: "Now we were two shiksas who still wanted to be Jews, but not to look it."[51]

Running neck and neck (as it were) with the concern for the shape of one's nose is an uneasiness about the shape of one's whole body. Jewish women's preoccupation with being fat—or fatter than some elusive norm—is not based on any reality. According to research in obesity, no ethnic group is particularly prone to being overweight, given comparable socioeconomic status. Whatever the causes of obesity (and opinions vary), nothing about being Jewish predisposes you to being fat.

Perhaps the worry about overweight and dieting comes from another source. The problem may be that Jewish women, led to feel inferior because of their gender in a patriarchal culture anyway, and perhaps feeling self-conscious about being *Jewish* women in a non-Jewish culture, are more prone to see whatever they are—fat, thin, assertive, retiring—as negative.

Just as plumpness (being *zaftig*) is sometimes associated with Jewish women (negatively or positively), some people believe that anorexia nervosa—the disease in which young women starve themselves to near death for the dubious pleasure of being thin—is a "Jewish woman's disease." Since one of the consequences of anorexia is that menstruation stops with the excessive weight loss, young women who want to remain dependent children and not face impending adulthood or sexuality may find that anorexia can prolong their childlike state. Given the pulls both for independence and for continuing dependency in the Jewish family it's not surprising that a high percentage of anorexics are Jewish women.

(Gay Block)

The force-feeding of many Jewish infants and children ("eat this spoonful for uncle, and this spoonful for grandma . . .") makes eating an activity that can involve not only the child herself but the whole family or community. For many women it's hard in adult life to disconnect eating habits and attitudes from their family ties. There is a peculiar double bind here—a confusing message transmitted from many mothers to their daughters (and sometimes from grandmother to granddaughter). It's the "Eat, eat" injunction followed by "Diet, diet."

A college student from Philadelphia tells an odd tale along these lines: My grandmother always was trying to get me to eat. I went through a phase of being a notoriously bad eater—I had been diagnosed as anorexic. Finally, when I was visiting at my grandmother's house, she made a meal that had all my favorites, things I was just dying to eat. Guests dropped in unexpectedly, and for the first time I can ever remember in her house, my grandmother didn't have enough food prepared. So first she served all the men—including her sons, as was her custom—and they all got full portions. On my plate—although she knew that I was looking forward to the meal and she really wanted to "fatten me up"—she put a part of a chicken wing. Her need to sacrifice herself—and me too—to the men in the family was so great that it eclipsed her desire to see me eat!

RESOURCES

There is something that Jewish tradition can teach us about how to evaluate (and de-emphasize) our reactions to our own and others' physical appearance. There are special prayers to be said when encountering a person of startling physical appearance or deformity, and other prayers when seeing a strikingly beautiful person (or natural object). For a discussion of the traditional Jewish attitudes toward responding to physical appearance (particularly helpful as a guide for parents and teachers trying to help support young women in their passage through adolescence) see:

Jewish Perspectives on Beauty and Ugliness
by Danny Siegel and Michael Katz
Leaders Training Fellowship
The Jewish Theological Seminary of America
3080 Broadway
New York, NY 10027

B'tzelem Elohim—In God's Image
by Bernard Novick
United Synagogue Youth
155 Fifth Ave.
New York, NY 10010

The latter book is a guide for teen-agers in making all sorts of decisions about their bodies. The areas dealt with include sexuality, modesty, and general physical appearance.

The women's movement, rather than anything particularly comforting in Jewish tradition, has probably salved our self-consciousness as Jewish women. As we've tried to accept our individual bodies—by looking at them and at the bodies of other women—we have tried to respect our own divergence from some patriarchal womanly ideal that almost no one can match anyway. "I began to see that it wasn't just Jewish women who didn't have movie-star bodies," says a forty-year-old woman of her consciousness-raising swims at the local YWCA.

For a guide to some of the feminist issues surrounding women's concern with beauty (and ugliness), see *Woman in Sexist Society*, ed. Vivian Gornick and Barbara K. Moran (Basic Books, 1971), and Deborah Hautzig, *Second Star to the Right* (Avon, 1982).

The latter is about a fourteen-year-old Jewish girl who becomes anorexic. She tries to stay in control of her life by being thin but sees herself as fat even at seventy-three pounds. The novel deals with the causes of the disease, as Leslie tries to be the "perfect daughter," conforming to her parents' expectations.

HEALTH AND ILLNESS: A SPECIAL
PROFILE FOR JEWISH WOMEN

Not all of our concern with our bodies has to do with how we look. There's also the Jewish emphasis on the importance of physical survival (*ha-icar habriut*—first comes health).[52] Even the sacred laws of the Sabbath and holy days can, and should, be broken in order to save a life, or if health would be seriously endangered by their observance. (For a discussion of Jewish women's mental health, and of alcoholism as a women's health issue, see "Jewish Women in Crisis," pp. 421-44.) Growing up Jewish has meant growing up with a tremendous concern for health and safety. An exaggerated (but true) example of the Jewish preoccupation with good health is a New York radio commercial advertising a Jewish summer camp for girls. It mentions *"two* modern infirmaries" even before it gets to "Olympic-size swimming pool."

By and large, this traditional concern seems to have paid off. Jews have often been healthier and have had lower mortality rates than the surrounding populations, perhaps because of better preventive medicine in general or better care of those who were stricken. Certain Jewish religious practices—such as ritual handwashing before a meal—haven't hurt either. Whatever the etiology, even twentieth-century Jews have an overriding concern with health (and now with fitness too). Along with this concern have come a reverence for the medical profession and a willingness to consult doctors and other "helping" health professionals.[53]

Jewish women have been the big worriers about the health of their families, as all women are expected to be in Western culture. (See the TV ads for pharmaceuticals: wife pushing cold pills, sleeping pills, headache pills on her husband, laxatives on an adult daughter, or toothpaste on the children.) And of particular concern for Jewish women is our predisposition toward certain diseases.

Genetic Diseases
The best-known genetic disease among Eastern European (Ashkenazi) Jews is Tay-Sachs disease, a crippling and soon lethal illness that usually

kills its victims before they reach the age of five. It is a recessive trait, so both parents must be carriers for there to be any possibility that the off-spring will have the disease.

Since the early 1970s a simple blood test has been available to determine if any individual is a carrier of the disease. If both partners in a marriage (or prospective marriage) are carriers, each pregnancy has a one-in-four chance of producing a Tay-Sachs child. Because the testing process is simple, the affected population very distinct, and the accuracy of the re-sults practically unquestioned, Tay-Sachs screening programs have sprung up in Jewish community centers and on college campuses all across the continent. The State University of New York at Stony Brook has monthly screenings for students and their parents, Brandeis University's infirmary will now do screenings on campus, and Hillel groups often ar-range once-a-semester screening programs. In addition, Jewish sororities and fraternities have begun programs to bring testing facilities to their members, and many gynecologists now have signs in their offices asking "Are You Jewish? Planning a Family? Inquire about Tay-Sachs screening."

Some of the early reluctance to encourage large-scale screening, es-pecially among students at all-Jewish institutions (such as New York's Yeshiva University) stemmed from an uneasiness that the young Jews who found themselves to be carriers of the gene would suffer from a loss of self-esteem and/or be viewed by members of the opposite sex as less than desirable marriage partners. Another argument used to limit screen-ing at Orthodox institutions was the end-point possibility of abortion, not an acceptable alternative in this situation for some Orthodox Jews.

Although the traditional attitudes toward marriageability and toward abortion remain, much of the early resistance to Tay-Sachs screening pro-grams has now been overcome.

RESOURCES

To arrange for a screening, call a gynecologist or the genetics depart-ment of any good local hospital, or of a medical school if there is one nearby. Thomas Jefferson University in Philadelphia and Mt. Sinai Hos-pital and Albert Einstein Medical Center in New York are some possibili-ties. Most big hospitals have genetic-counseling departments that do the screenings and will arrange for the amniocentesis if you are pregnant and your husband is found to be a carrier. If you are married to or considering marriage to a Sephardic Jew or to a non-Jew, screening is probably un-necessary.

The other lethal disease found almost exclusively among Jews is Nie-mann-Pick disease, a far rarer condition than Tay-Sachs, which can also be detected by amniocentesis in the first half of a pregnancy. For more information on this and other nonfatal genetic diseases Jews carry, write to:

National Foundation for Jewish Genetic Diseases, Inc.
609 Fifth Avenue, Suite 1200
New York, NY 10017.

The definitive book on the subject, an anthology dealing with all aspects of genetics and Jewish history, was intended for a professional medical audience, but anyone interested in "Jewish" traits (including myopia, inflammatory bowel disease, high intelligence) will learn from it: *Genetic Diseases Among Ashkenazi Jews,* ed. Richard M. Goodman and Arno G. Motulsky (Raven Press, 1979). There are no diseases exclusive to Sephardic Jews.

Nongenetic Diseases

Having the proper genetic makeup isn't enough to keep Jewish women free from non-genetically linked diseases, among them breast cancer and cervical cancer. Breast cancer is reported to be particularly high among Jews.[54] More common among Ashkenazi than Sephardic Jewish women, it is probably linked more to the socioeconomic group than to any Jewish genetic pattern. There is evidence that a diet high in saturated fats may trigger a genetic predisposition to breast cancer or may somehow contribute to tumor formation in the breast's fatty tissues. Good sense and a healthy dose of the Jewish respect for preventive medicine should suggest that every woman learn how to do breast self-examination. Women with a familial history of breast cancer are especially at risk and probably should have a mammography (breast X-ray) at least once, especially if they are past thirty-five.

There is an interesting sidelight on the issue of Jewish women and breast cancer: breast-feeding is correlated with a lower incidence of breast cancer.[55] One study shows that Orthodox women are more likely to breast-feed infants, and for longer periods, than other women, possibly because of the natural contraception breast-feeding sometimes provides, possibly because nursing delays menstruation after childbirth, so observant women can be sexually active all month long (see "Sexuality," p. 204).

RESOURCES

A book on breast cancer that describes not only the medical facts but also one woman's personal trials with the disease: Rose Kushner's *Breast Cancer: A Personal History and an Investigative Report* (New York: Harcourt, Brace, 1975).

To get a chart showing how to do a breast self-examination—which you could do on the first of every Hebrew month, traditionally a woman's holiday (see "Rosh Chodesh," p. 94)—write:

American Cancer Society
4 West 29 Street
New York, NY 10001

Cervical cancer has occasioned one of the many myths that Jewish women have grown up with: somehow, as if by magic, being married (monogamously) to men who are circumcised prevents cervical cancer. Some evidence contradicts this: Moroccan-born Jewish women have a higher rate than Ashkenazi women; so do women from countries such as Turkey, where men are routinely circumcised.

Since cervical cancer may turn out to be transmitted by a virus (possibly herpes II), the risk of getting cervical cancer increases with the number of sexual partners. The traditionally monogamous sexual behavior of Jewish women was probably the chief reason for the previous low incidence of cervical cancer, along with an inherited genetic makeup that may have given them a low predisposition for the disease.

However, new evidence shows that the incidence of cervical cancer is rising among Jewish women, partly because of a shifting genetic pool through intermarriage and partly because of an increase in nonmonogamous couplings, a distinct change from the "highly unpromiscuous" sexual behavior of Jewish women in the past.

For further information, consult Baruch Modan, "Cancer" (see n. 54), and Sharon Lieberman, "Circumcision Is No Insurance," *Lilith* #3 (Spring/Summer '77), p. 21.

Lieberman, a feminist health writer, concludes:

> Clearly, as Jewish women living in a secular environment, we must look beyond the comforting myth of the protection afforded us by male circumcision, and consider the responsibilities and risks that accompany lifestyles divergent from our Jewish traditions.
>
> In demystifying the role of circumcision in cervical cancer, we have also established the sexual autonomy of the Jewish female. For if we believed that our circumcised men provided a cancer prophylaxis, we would rather arbitrarily enhance their desirability as sexual partners. But if we can acknowledge that, in fact, we control the risk of disease through our sexual behavior, we take on a responsibility for our sexual and reproductive lives, for our health, our bodies, our selves.

TWO

◆

DEFINING AND TRANSFORMING OUR RELATIONSHIPS

◆

6

♦

JEWISH WOMEN IN THE NUCLEAR FAMILY AND BEYOND

JEWISH WOMEN AND THE JEWISH FAMILY

Feminism and the Family

The Jewish family has been labeled pathogenic and supportive, cruel and kind; the women in it have been the butt of jokes, the material of stereotypes, and the basis for invective and caricature. Any attempt to demythologize the lives of Jewish women must talk about the institution in which we relate to those we live with most intimately and whose expectations shape both our identity and our behavior. Though so-called "family issues"—marriage, childbearing, and child rearing, the division of domestic labor, and so forth—should certainly not be the exclusive concern of women, at present they occupy more space in the lives of women than of men.

How Jewish women see themselves in the context of their own families—and how Jewish men and women interact in families—is important beyond the confines of the immediate family itself. All members of the group—in this case, Jews—are perceived as extended family. A New York editor, asked why he works in a Jewish institution, replies, "It's *mishpocha* [family]." This means that our relationships with other Jews, even outside any connection with our "real" families, are colored by the roles and the expectations we learn in our family interactions.

No matter how "the" Jewish family has been defined, the traditional role of the wife/mother has been fairly constant: she is responsible for the management of the household, for the socialization and "domestic" education of the girl children, and sometimes for part of the family's income as well. Although fewer and fewer Jewish daughters, wives, or mothers are living in anything resembling the two-parent nuclear families of previous generations, the families we were born into or which we've chosen to create with spouses, children, friends, or lovers remain the context for relating to those we're closest to. Examining these changing forms of family life and their implications for all Jews, Jewish organizations have for the past decade sponsored numerous conferences and publications and brainstorming sessions on issues that relate to how Jews live in families.[1] And while they have been active for more than a hundred years in some communities, the numerous Jewish organizations which exist to counsel and provide support services for families and children (see Networking Directory, p. 537) find themselves now in the limelight. Suddenly Jewish family life (by which is usually meant Jewish *women*'s role in family life) is hot news.

The uncertainty of Jewish life (threatened from without by oppression and from within by assimilation) contributes to the heavy emphasis on "family." Because the historical threat has been so real, it's hard for women to redefine roles in the family, or redefine the family itself, without encountering a great deal of resistance from those who would create a false polarization between feminism and the family. Thus the women's movement, with its reevaluation of traditional male-female roles within the family, may have been perceived as a special threat to some Jews, despite (or because of) the fact that many Jewish women were highly visible in the movement.

In contrast, there are those who actually see Jewish identity endangered by any further changes in the definition of the Jewish family. Sociologist Chaim I. Waxman says that the family "is the *central institution* for defining and transmitting the identity and identification without which the Jewish ethnoreligious community could not exist."[2] And Blu Greenberg gives family life more credit than it usually receives, except when under attack. She says, "The Jewish home has been more significant in transmitting religious values than the synagogue."[3]

While it's tempting to believe that women's domestic role (which is what's usually meant by the euphemism "home") has been an important vehicle for Jewish continuity, this belief also puts an immense burden on Jewish women who are eager to move into other spheres of influence as well.

Why all the emphasis *now* on the importance of family in Jewish life? With appropriate uneasiness, Jewish feminists suggest that the hue and cry is a reaction to the emergence of Jewish women into the labor force from their typical roles in the American Jewish family of the past forty

The powerful, mythic quality of the mother in the Jewish family is conveyed by this larger-than-life masked figure in The Last Yiddish Poet, *written and performed by A Traveling Jewish Theater.* (Marvin Lichtner, courtesy of Naomi Newman, TJT)

years. They point out that when Jewish men moved into the mainstream of American life from the 1920s to 1945, no one called a conference to examine how *their* actions were subverting the traditional Jewish male values of study and religious observance. "This talk of 'family' all sounds to me like a push to keep women at home having babies," says Ann G. Wolfe, a New York social worker long active as a professional in Jewish life.

Aside from the legitimate accusation that the present concern for Jewish families is a backlash against the women's movement and has to do only with wanting to keep Jewish women at home (well shod but pregnant), there is another factor explaining the potent mythology of Jewish family life. Family may be much more important to a group that per-

ceives itself as easily threatened by outside forces. We suspect that because "Jews, more than any other group of white Americans, are . . .
more apt to be discriminated against; feelings of security and well-being
may entail greater emphasis on family ties . . . than is generally true of
others."[4]

In the 1970s the contemporary women's liberation movement sparked
redefinitions of what women's roles could be. Jewish women's discussion
groups, for instance, focused on new roles and new directions: entry or
reentry into the workplace, greater options for women in religious Judaism, a reevaluation of volunteerism. By contrast, the action in the 1980s
is in the family arena.

Now the conferences are entitled "Jewish Family Network" and "The
Effect of the Women's Movement on the Jewish Family," and so on.
The issues are the same so-called "women's" issues, but the difference in
focus is very important. With the rubric now "family" and not "new
roles for Jewish women," we return to an analysis of a woman's behavior
based on her relation to others. Her needs as an individual are no longer
at center stage. And yet even though the current focus on "family" issues
is troublesome, it may not be all bad, especially if it prefigures the provision of more services to women, men, and children.

Attacking the hardy myth that the Jewish family is the one institution
that keeps us all happy and Jewish, psychologist Phyllis Chesler speculates on the frailty of the family as it tries to service the needs of all its
members:

> Ask yourself, how effective is the Jewish family in dealing with Jewish
> poverty in America—and in Israel? With the problems of the Jewish
> aged, of Jewish youth and with the problems of the Jewish woman?
> Has the Jewish family been able to eliminate wife-beating, wife aban-
> donment, female depression, sexual frigidity, insecurity and a patho-
> logical degree of female dependency and self-sacrifice for men and
> small children? Has the Jewish family been able to teach women how
> to mother and nurture daughters and each other as they do sons? To
> show compassion for female suffering?[5]

This is not only the radical feminist position; Rabbi Gerson Cohen,
Chancellor of the Jewish Theological Seminary, concurs:

> . . . the Jewish family never sustained the Jew. That is a myth that is
> being perpetrated by people who are dissatisfied with the synagogue
> and find themselves failures. The family, as a unit in a strongly orga-

The real role of the Jewish woman in the family is often more that of the classic enabler than that of some archetypal transmitter of Jewish culture. (Layle Silbert)

nized community, had very little to do except to generate, feed, and clothe kids. The community educated them. Where? In the street, in the marketplace, in the synagogue, in the house of study, in the assembly hall. The family today is being asked to do things which it can't possibly do. It is called upon to replace community, to provide leisure, love, respect, satisfaction, fulfillment. But that's impossible, because we can't do these things in isolation. We can do them only as a community.[6]

Perhaps the very structure of Judaism as a communal religion helped create and sustain what was in premodern times an extended family for Jews almost everywhere they lived. The community was another extension of the family. After all, with most prayers requiring the minimum of ten adults (all male in those days, and in many places today), Jews *could not* live in isolation from one another. Even where civil law would

Early conditioning.
(Bruce S. Schneider)

have permitted Jews to own tracts of land and live on isolated farms, the religious structure of Judaism mandated proximity to other Jews, fostering communities that were geographically as well as spiritually close. Understanding this, we have already driven one wedge into the myth that it was the tireless effort of the Jewish mother, with her enabling and her cooking, that held Jews together. The *minyan* (prayer quorum), and not the nuclear family, may have been the cell for Jewish continuity.

Historian Paula Hyman has analyzed the myths surrounding the Jewish family: "It can be argued that . . . the nature of the Jewish community served to preserve the traditional Jewish family rather than that the Jewish family preserved Judaism. . . . The theory that women are culture bearers is one which many women are inclined to accept without challenge, despite its inaccuracy, because it is flattering. It connotes power and a recognition of the value of the mothering role."[7]

Aside from the classic association of the mother with the survival and transmission of Jewish values, there are other characteristics unique to the Jewish family. Change, in the form of improvement of life from generation to generation, is what most of us have come to see as the "Jewish" way. Jews "want better" for their children. It's hard to imagine a situation in a Jewish family that would echo the story of one Italian-American family. Joe Brancatelli tells that his father gave up a promising legal career to return to the family shoe-repair business because *his* father said he was needed there. He was a "good son." The author describes himself as the "bad son" in the story, because he aspired to something different. He quotes his father: "You can't be a writer. You're a Brancatelli, you sell shoes."[8] It's almost impossible to imagine this scene being played out—or accepted as the norm—in an American Jewish family, where children who have before them the prospect of "bettering" themselves are held up as models for all to admire.

Upward economic mobility, in addition to geographic mobility, has left Western Jews with the sense that it's natural for children to live lives different from their parents'. The problem with this is ensuring religious and cultural continuity within the change. The essence of this concern comes through in a conversation overheard after a conference on Jewish women and the family. One woman said, "I wasn't religious, but I raised my kids with Jewish values and good politics. They're Jewish now, but who knows what the future will bring?" Her companion answered, "Look, I raised my son to understand that he's Jewish because of his connection to Jewish history. But do I know if my grandchildren will be Jewish?" Neither woman had any faith at all in her own role as a transmitter of Jewish identity to her children. The myth of the Jewish mother's infallibility in this regard was obviously no comfort.

RESOURCES

Some realistic comments on how the Jewish family was perceived in the past come from those familiar with Yiddish literature. There was, it seems, always conflict within the Jewish family, but with all its faults the home scene was the metaphor for Jewish survival. For an interesting tour through the family themes in Yiddish literature, especially the role of women, see Bibliography: Sol Gittelman, *From Shtetl to Suburbia: The Family in Jewish Literary Imagination*, and Karl Zborowski and Elizabeth Herzog, *Life Is with People: The Culture of the Shtetl*.

An anthology that gives an overview of women's, men's, and children's roles in families also includes material on Jewish women in an essay by Beverly Gray Bienstock, "The Changing Image of the American Jewish Mother": *Changing Images of the Family*, ed. Virginia Tufte and Barbara Myerhoff.

For many examples of how the Jewish family has changed through history, look at an excellent "mini-course" for Jewish students in seventh grade and older:

The Jewish Family: Past, Present and Future
by Paulette Benson and Joanne Altschuler
Alternatives in Religious Education
3945 S. Oneida Street
Denver, CO 80237

The Jewish Community and Jewish Families

With the planning for the White House Conference on Families in 1980, Jewish organizations and feminist groups became involved in discussions and analyses of family life that are still going on. For feminist groups, the White House conference, like the National Organization for Women Assembly on the Family, held in New York in 1980, represented an opportunity—in the words of NOW founder Betty Friedan—"to take back the family from the right wing."

From the evidence that Jewish women are themselves presenting, it's clear that the "traditional" Jewish family of mid-twentieth-century America—with two parents, one of whom is a stay-at-home mom—is fading

(*from* Leaving Home: A Family in Transition, *a film produced and directed by Ilana Bar-Din*)

fast, with only 20 percent of families now in this category. To serve the needs of whatever the new, pluralistic definition of the "Jewish family" is, agencies and special services have sprung up like mushrooms after a rain. Here are some examples.

• The American Jewish Committee has created a Jewish Family Center, whose original logo showed the traditional ma-and-pa-and-two-kids family and a Star of David. The center, now logoless, has published a number of studies on the impact of social change on the Jewish family, including a study of Jewish working women with three or more children, and a newsletter that lists Jewish child-care facilities nationwide. It acts as a clearinghouse for other information that might appropriately fall under the broad rubric of Jewish "family" concerns.

The National Jewish Family Center Newsletter
Jewish Communal Affairs Department
American Jewish Committee
165 E. 56 Street
New York, NY 10022
$2.50 per year

From the same address you can order a pamphlet entitled *Sustaining the Jewish Family*, which discusses Jewish family policy and makes several original suggestions: that communal agencies provide housing grants to needy Jewish families and scholarships to Jewish schools and day-care programs, and reach out to single people and single parents. The pamphlet justifies its concern with all the varieties of Jewish families, stating that for a minority group "the family plays a more central role in insuring group continuity than it does in the American society as a whole."

• *Medium*, the Jewish Media Service newsletter featuring film reviews on Jewish subjects, devoted its fall 1979 issue to "The Jewish Family." A healthy dose of realism infuses the issue, including these comments in the introduction: "The world of our grandparents and even our parents has changed. As the extended family with its tentacles reaching across time and space disappears, we need not elevate its memory to a romanticized ideal. Everything was not perfect then; nor is it now."

• The Melton Research Center for Jewish Education at the Jewish Theological Seminary, which publishes a quarterly newsletter, produced a special feature in the fall of 1980, "The Family in Our Time." (For ordering address and information, see "Our Minds for Ourselves," p. 176.) In this issue David G. Roskies asks a fascinating question about havurot, those small circles of Jews who pray, study, and celebrate together: "Is the family really our last and only hope, or is the Havurah movement and its like not the next step in the Jewish dialectical response to modernity?"

In the magnetic field created between the poles of tradition and modernity other Jews ask, "If we recognize a certain 'untraditional' way of life as legitimate in a Jewish context, are we going to make it easier for others to choose to live like this person [homosexual, single parent, unmarried couple living together], instead of opting for a more traditional Jewish nuclear family?" Yet it's especially these Jews who are not living in "traditional" nuclear families who most need the community's strength, which has become for some a surrogate extended family. ("The Jewish community is where they have to let you in when you knock," says one such nontraditional Jew.)

• Jewish Family Life Education hopes to prevent family dysfunction with an interweaving of mental-health principles and education. Groups discuss predictable, normal life phases or changes and how to grow with them and resolve them, often in the context of Jewish agencies and support services.

The best place to start looking for JFLE is at your local Jewish Family Service Agency or local Board of Jewish Education. (See Networking Directory, p. 537, for names and addresses.)

• For further information about how the community can meet the needs of a range of Jewish families, see a book edited by Gerald B. Bubis, the director of the influential School of Jewish Communal Service at Hebrew Union College-Jewish Institute of Religion in Los Angeles: *Serving the Jewish Family* (Ktav, 1977). For services useful to women in a state of family dislocation, such as widows, displaced homemakers, and victims of domestic violence, see "Jewish Women in Crisis: Community Resources," p. 401. For resources for families with children, including single-parent families, see "Responding to the Childbearing Imperative," p. 371.

Keeping the Kinship Ties Tied

In Jewish family structure the extended family has always been important. For example, in Yiddish there are specific words to denote the relationship between the sets of parents of a married couple. They are *machutunim* to one another, the mother-in-law on the other side is the *machuteneste*, and the father-in-law on the other side is a *machutan* to the father-in-law on your side. A network of family ties is drawn tight even through language. The close connection between the present generation and any and all recorded ancestors is known in Yiddish as *yichus*, or proud family line.

(courtesy Zora Zagrabelna Weidman)

Jewish families have many more kinship ties than other families, with relatives often staying in or near the same geographic area. In one study, 78 percent of the Jews (as compared to 14 percent of the Protestants) say that they have "regular interactions" with at least five households of these relatives.[9] What may be a uniquely Jewish way of keeping the kinship ties tied is the "cousins' club," meeting regularly to create a family network that reinforces every member's sense of belonging, of having a reference group or "home room" even in adulthood.[10]

For women the security that can come from having a sense of belonging to a family is especially valid. We've been accustomed to taking on the names of the men we are married to, sometimes losing even our first names in the process. Cousins' clubs serve the purpose for women of providing a kind of primary identity—family are the people who will love you—or at least stand by you—no matter what you do and no matter what your name.

And being cousins, members of the extended family circle are less likely to drive you crazy than siblings, parents, or children, while still pro-

From The Tribe, *a film by Lilly Rivlin which documents the history of the Rivlins, now numbering ten thousand members and the largest extant Jewish family in the world.* (© 1983 from *The Tribe*)

viding the warm glow—or backbiting or blood feuds—of family connectedness. Especially when family ties are becoming more complicated because of divorce and remarriage, and at a time when women with children worry about how/when the children will connect with *their* families, it's good to remind ourselves that *we* count too, and that the people we were once connected to in a primary way (as daughters, nieces, cousins) can be a source of pleasure in our lives again, regardless of our marital status. Especially now that Jewish families are having fewer children, relationships with cousins are very important—for adults and for kids—as a substitute for friendship with siblings.

The very practical advantages of family kinship networks have been explored too. Contrary to commonly held beliefs of social scientists that close family ties are most often associated with lower-class populations, for Jewish families there's a correlation between extended family ties and middle-class status.[11] The sharing of resources—skills or cash—among family members who had similar values and social and residential bonds was instrumental in bringing the family to this status and in maintaining it.

Cousins' clubs, and especially the kinds of storytelling and reminiscences they encourage, also give us a chance to figure out the lives of some of the women in our families. Often our family histories, like history generally, tend to be economic (that is, male) rather than domestic. Where did the men get work? Where did they move their families to when they could afford something better than the old neighborhood? What professions did the male children enter? For historical data gathering and to provide some psychological context and stability, the ritualization or formalization of getting together with relatives is useful and important.

With changing circumstances, the ways in which Jews relate to their extended families may change also. Smaller families mean fewer siblings and, later, fewer cousins, while the rising incidence of Jewish events for females (such as baby-naming ceremonies and Bat Mitzvahs) provide new opportunities for ritual celebrations where family members can meet.

In the Jewish extended family, women's nurturing role has meant that women spend a great deal of time as cooks and organizers, which has at least one advantage. Since Jewish life-cycle events and holiday celebrations often feature special foods, women, almost always the providers of the food, have had a private realm for *schmoozing* and intimacy, a context in which they can get to know one another.

For Jewish women, especially Orthodox women, even synagogue life is an opportunity to be in a collectivity of women—in the women's gallery, usually totally divided from the men's section. This division of women and men takes place in some home-bound ceremonies and gatherings as well, with women not eating with men in the succah, or staying in a separate room during the *brit milah*, or during the Saturday night *melave malke* (ushering out of the Sabbath). At Orthodox weddings there may be separate dancing rooms for men and for women, and in Syrian Jewish homes, even in America, a Saturday-afternoon *sibbit* (a praying, studying, singing, feasting celebration of a birth, engagement, or other simcha) has the men all sitting at a large table with all the women serving them.

These separations from men do create an opportunity for women to support one another, at least momentarily free from other obligations. The question logically arises as to how much of our admiration of female bonding in this context is appropriate, and how much is mere apology for a caste system which defines women as enablers and shunts them aside.

MOTHERS AND DAUGHTERS FROM
A FEMINIST PERSPECTIVE

When we consider relationships within the Jewish family, we risk getting caught in a tangled web of myths and damaging stereotypes about Jewish women. The contradictory myths—that the second-generation American Jewish mother appears to be all self-sacrifice while covering a hard core of manipulation; that her daughters are demanding and aggressive and are eternally tethered to a shallow materialism—don't take into account the historical realities that have shaped these stock characters. Some mothers may fit the Yiddishe Mama stereotype, just as some daughters cannot feel that they are worthwhile people without the trappings of material success. But the constant associations of "Mama" and "Princess" with being Jewish deny the history behind the stereotypes (the survival value of Mama's concern for her children; the ornamental value of having a dolled-up daughter as a symbol of the newly successful American Jewish man) while perpetuating the ugly implications of the stereotypes themselves.

Even if we are never mothers, we have all been daughters sometime. And although we learn about mothers and sons in the Torah—starting with Eve and Cain and Abel, going on to Sarah and Isaac and many more—mothers and daughters are markedly scant, both in the Torah and in subsequent Jewish writings. The traditional Jewish material on mothers and daughters comes from folklore rather than serious literature, leaving women to the mercy of the popular culture.

The unattractive, ubiquitous and essentially anti-Semitic stereotyping of Jewish women[12] either as Yiddishe Mamas or Princesses has a message for anyone trying to understand Jewish mother–daughter relations. These stereotypes are really opposite sides of the same coin. The all-sacrificing mother, denying her own needs while intrusively involved in the perceived needs of her children, contrasts vividly in every way with the selfish daughter, self-absorbed, demanding, too interested in the events of her own life to be sympathetic to others, and certainly unwilling to submit to male authority. There are many ironies in this juxtaposition, not the least of which is that the Princess is expected to become the Mama as soon as possible after she marries and/or has children of her own.

Two jokes (of the seemingly endless number) contrast the "types": The Demanding Princess joke: A man goes out in a raging blizzard, walks for blocks, and enters a bakery. He orders two rolls. Baker: "My God! Did your wife send you out on a night like this?" Man: "Would my *mother* have sent me out on a night like this?" The classic Jewish Mother joke: How many Jewish mothers does it take to change a light bulb? None. "That's okay, I'll just sit here in the dark."

This Jewish mother is strictly a creation of American Jewish writing (and thinking) and the manifestation of the leap into prosperity that allows women the luxury of being "overinvolved" with their children, even if only in myth. Some of the realities behind the stereotype were there all along—the self-sacrifice of the mother who did without in order to feed her children, for example, or the mother's concerns for her children's safety during sieges, pogroms, and famines. But when the same behavior is expressed in less straitened circumstances, we get the light-bulb joke, making the woman's suppression of her own needs ridiculous.

It's time to move beyond these images—noting first that they originated in certain needs that Jews have had—and look at the realities of Jewish family life for women.

Dr. Rose Oliver, exploring mental health and achievement among Jews, concludes that "we are forced to discount the 'Jewish mother' as a destructive agent in her offspring's development. . . . In fact, she may have done something right!"[13] At the top of her form this mother gives her children—even her daughters, to some extent—emotional support at home that frees them from being overly dependent on peer pressure, thus

(Layle Silbert)

freeing them also to be more creative (to the point where her sons can even produce an oeuvre of anti-Jewish-mother literature).

Oliver posits ageism and general misogyny as the twin roots of the negative "mama" stereotype, but there's an economic basis as well. When American Jewish men began to enjoy a degree of financial success, many tried to assimilate to a more "American" style of behavior and thinking. This included accepting the prevailing neo-Victorian notion that women's place was in the home, that she was a fragile creature who needed protection from the outside world. Thus upward social mobility caused the world of the American Jewish woman to shrink![14] What a shock this must have been to women whose image of themselves, and of their mothers and grandmothers before them, had been of hardy, active people. The real roles of Eastern European Jewish women included helping support the family, making decisions, and having (at least in much of family and community life) shared responsibilities with their husbands.

Some patterns from the past remained after immigration to America, in the form of marriages often more egalitarian than those of other ethnic groups. But for the Jewish woman living through the changing expectations of her husband, father, or sons, the strains must have been enormous, since she had no models in her own cultural past for the passive, ladylike image she was now supposed to emulate. And because Jews assimilated into mainstream American life much faster than many other groups (they did in one generation what in other groups sometimes took three), the accelerated rate of change must have created enormous confusion for women, who had to learn to see themselves as no longer instrumental, even in the family setting.

For women finding themselves suddenly remanded to the home front because new prosperity made their wages unnecessary and their husband's status required an at-home wife, there was no other choice but to put the same energies into the raising of children that previously had gone into paid labor *plus* home responsibilities. Like their non-Jewish sisters, many Jewish women (especially after the Second World War, with prosperity and a houseful of labor-saving devices), threw themselves into their maternal role. The difference for Jewish women was the tremendous influence of the family in Jewish life (or at least the perception of its influence) and the sense that the children were both a way of ensuring Jewish continuity and one of the only sanctioned ways in which the mother could express herself. It was also through her performance of the maternal role that the Jewish woman was judged and judged herself.

What effect has this Jewish mother's involvement with home life had on her daughter? The daughter seems more distressed by Mama's self-sacrifice than by her manipulative power—seeing her, for example, deprive herself and give to her offspring. The mama who is rumored to have no drives of her own isn't a useful role model for the daughter who today is trying to synthesize the work and achievement goals of her father and brothers (and perhaps her grandmother) with her mother's investment in the domestic scene.

When our mothers are also our models for future versions of ourselves, their feeding us and starving themselves presents a terrifying, sacrificial model that may have nothing to do with present-day cupboard realities, where abundance is more likely than want, but may reflect the vivid psychological reality of a woman who can't afford to have any needs of her own. This sacrificial feed-the-others mentality of Jewish women is not a matter of individual pathology—it is so widespread that we have to recognize it as a vestigial survival skill.

Mimi Sheraton, formerly the *New York Times* restaurant critic, titles her book of recipes and reminiscences *In My Mother's Kitchen*. The de-

(Gay Block)

scription of a family meal served by Sheraton's Jewish mother is recognizable immediately. ". . . by the time she served herself, those who had been fed earliest were ready for seconds. My vision of my mother eating at those happy, noisy, groaning boards is of a woman jumping up and sitting down, cutting off bites that she chewed on the run to the kitchen to get more for the rest of us, a woman whose plate always seemed to contain what looked like trimmings and odd pieces and quarter portions, who finished what others left."[15]

The messages we picked up about women, the image transmitted to us, was often of self-sacrifice and self-abnegation. Many of us also learned that no parallel sacrifices were ever expected of men. "There were seven children in my family, plus my parents," reminisces a woman now in her late sixties. "When we were growing up on the Lower East Side of New York my mother would go down every morning and buy eight rolls for breakfast. She would cut and butter them all, giving one to each child and one to my father. Then she would gather up the crumbs on the board, sweep them with one hand into the cupped palm of the other, and put the crumbs into her coffee. That was *her* breakfast."

Another, older woman, recounting her years as the young daughter of a large family to her creative writing class at a Jewish Senior Citizens' Center, recalled that for years she had believed that her mother's favorite piece of chicken was the bony neck, because that was the piece she served herself every Friday night at the Sabbath meal. "Later I realized that she felt the better parts should go to the children. And I don't think that's wrong—I gave to my children too."

One classmate asked: "But even if it's O.K. to sacrifice for the children, don't you think that both parents should do it equally? Maybe your father could have eaten the neck every second Friday night." And the reply was: "I never thought of that. Sacrificing for the children was always my *mother's* way."

This isn't universally true, despite the fact that Jews sometimes feel that sacrificing for one's children is a part of every culture. In non-Jewish small-town American life another pattern prevailed: "Formerly children were fed at the second table or later and often found the choice foods and choice portions of food already gone. Older people sometimes say, 'I was nearly grown up before I knowed chicken *had* any other pieces except wings and necks.' "[16]

E. M. Broner, the novelist whose works include *Her Mothers*, describes in a unique anthology a generation of Jewish mothers living "a life of nurturing, of feeding others and starving one's self."[17]

(Gay Block)

No wonder a common image in literature is of the all-consuming Jewish mother. She's hungry. In fact, she's starving—starving herself, in many ways. Reflecting this is an extraordinarily moving analysis by Erika Duncan in *The Lost Tradition*, entitled "The Hungry Jewish Mother." Duncan notes: "The mother's starvation is, needless to say, scary for the child, who has no choice but to take. . . . So many male writers have turned the one who endlessly spoons out chicken soup into a mad devourer from whom they have to flee lest their identities be eaten up. . . . But for our Jewish women writers the journey is far more complicated, for they are both the takers of the food their mothers do not really have to give, and the future providers."[18]

The Talmud says, "Ewe follows ewe; a daughter's acts are like those of her mother." The Yiddish equivalent, with much more flavor, goes: *Meshugene ganz, meshugene grievene*—loosely, "If you have a crazy goose, the cracklings fried in the goose fat will also be crazy." Echoing this is the Jewish mother's common "curse" on her daughter: "May you grow up to have children just like you." What these sayings suggest is that there is something potentially hazardous in the transmission of values from mother to daughter.

Daughters are afraid not merely of having children like themselves but of the implications of the curse—that they, in adulthood, will become like the mother.

In *Of Woman Born,* Adrienne Rich defines "matrophobia" as "the fear not of one's mother or of motherhood but of *becoming* one's mother."[19]

A writer in her twenties who has been living in an egalitarian relationship with her boyfriend for several years says that she still gets nervous around noontime, thinking, Dinner, dinner. Provide, provide. "Yet I know," she says, "that he doesn't expect that I'll plan or cook dinner. But that part of my mother that provided, not always happily, for other people's needs is still the voice inside me."

Our earliest identification suggests that we will base much of our behavior on that of the adults present in our childhood, most likely our mothers. We sometimes see this as a frightening model. Perhaps because we know that, despite the pseudopowerful image of a Sophie Portnoy, our mothers, like most women, have been largely powerless to shape their own lives, to make their own choices. Psychiatric and popular literature abound with references to women of achievement who identify with their fathers' power rather than with what they perceive as their mothers' passivity. Despite the emergence of a feminist analysis of family roles which recognizes some of our mothers' strengths, we must still contend with our early perceptions that our mothers are simultaneously all-powerful in our juvenile world and often victims of circumstance in the larger sphere.[20]

And so we grow up—all women, and not just Jewish women—torn between the passive model (waiting to be *chosen,* whether by husbands or employers) and striving for a more active role in shaping our own lives. With self-sacrifice the dominant mode for at least some Jewish mothers, Jewish daughters seeking to assert themselves must first understand the anger and disappointment many feel toward their most important role models. "I still have an enormous amount of anger towards my mother for the fact that she hasn't asserted her needs or her rights all these years. I understand her feelings of helplessness, but they make me angry, and frighten me. I think that that's why I'm so outspoken myself. I'm not going to let anyone make a *shmatte* out of me," says a woman of forty who is still trying to overcome the desire to fight her mother's battles for her.

With all the negative feelings about Jewish mothers in the culture (see p. 269), it's not surprising that daughters fear creating for themselves a persona that is too similar to their mothers'. Adrienne Rich has taught us that it is "easier by far to hate and reject a mother outright than to see beyond her to the forces acting upon her." And when Jewish men ridicule Jewish mothers, "Jewish daughters are left with all the panic, guilt, ambivalence and self-hatred of the woman from whom they came and the woman they may become. . . . The mother stands for the victim in ourselves, the unfree woman, the martyr."[21]

A somewhat complicitous helpmeet/ally relationship between many Jewish daughters and mothers may derive from the fact that the women shared an exclusion from aspects of Jewish ritual life, may have sat together and away from the men in synagogue, and shared also a domestic reality that men—even within the same family—often had no part in. Many mothers who didn't work outside their homes felt a companionship void that they looked to their daughters to fill. Older women, speaking honestly, admit that they didn't want to tell any "secrets" to anybody—even close friends—outside their family circle. Their daughters, presumably witnesses to some of the secrets anyway, were safe ears.

The anecdotes of these Jewish daughters reveal both closeness and conflict with their mothers and a tension between an intimate dependency and the yearning for independence continuing unresolved even into adulthood. A New York journalist in her forties describes her own relationship: "My mother always wanted to be my best friend, and always criticized every friend I ever had, letting me know that She could be counted on for undying loyalty, but not Them."

The emotional closeness of Jewish families was certainly echoed in the family structures of the other two groups of women (Slavic and Italian) that Dr. Corinne Azen Krause has studied.[22] But Jewish women tend not to live in the same houses, or even in the same neighborhoods, as their mothers. There seems to be a conscious effort for daughter to get some distance from mother (and mother from daughter), despite expressed feelings of closeness.

Responding to Krause's study, a business manager in her thirties describes how she plans to deal with her own mother's aging: "She isn't going to be able to lay a guilt trip on me. I would tell her, 'Look, Mother, I'll be happy to provide care for you at any expense, to arrange for whatever is necessary. But it is just *impossible* for you to come and live with me.' "

There are exceptions to this pattern, of course. One clear difference is among daughters of Holocaust survivors, who, like their brothers, tend to maintain very close geographic bonds to their parents, often living at home long after their peers have struck out on their own. Another is in both Orthodox and Syrian American Jewish communities, where daughters marry young and often deliberately choose to live in the same neighborhood as their mothers. But both Orthodox and Syrian families tend to have many more children than the Jewish average, so the relationship between mother and daughter may not be perceived as so close, or so confining, as that between mothers and daughters in smaller families.

Not only geography, but also significant life-style differences between adult Jewish daughters in the 1980s and their mothers have created a veritable "tradition of change" over the past three generations:

1. The way the daughter generation interprets life is different from what came before. *Grandmothers*, whether Jewish Italian or Slavic, according to Krause's study, acted out of survival needs. Whatever they did, occupationally or within the family, they knew they were ensuring sheer physical survival and comfort for their families and themselves. Their daughters (the *mother* generation of the study) did what was expected of them by others. For Jewish women, especially, this conclusion must ring true. Remember that middle generation of Jewish women who were told that if they worked outside their homes it would bring shame upon their husbands, impugning the men's reputations as adequate providers? For the *daughter* generation there are choices. Serve one's own needs? Serve the needs of one's own family? Work full time? Part time? In short, the social climate, at least for middle-class women, has changed in such a way as to place very different meanings on the ways we live.

2. The shape of the lives of the daughter generation is different. Jewish women, if they do choose to have children, are having them later in life than women of other ethnic groups. Perhaps this reflects our greater level of education and consequently our greater career opportunities (see "Responding to the Childbearing Imperative," p. 374). Whatever the cause for the postponement, as Jewish women put off childbearing or don't have children at all, the pattern of the daughters' lives differs radically from those of their mothers and grandmothers; at certain ages we are in different phases from those of previous generations at the same ages. For example, the norm for Jewish women in the 1980s may well be to postpone childbearing until the early or middle thirties, at the earliest. The mothers of these women were probably mothers themselves by their early twenties. The very different shapes of the lives of these two generations follows inevitably, and the reconciliation between the generations

that typically occurs with the birth of the first grandchild now occurs much later, if at all.

3. Different generations may have very different goals for their own offspring. The at-home, nonworking mother may prolong her children's dependency, so she will be raising children who are different in certain ways from the generation of sons and daughters produced by working mothers. Current realities—with the majority of mothers of preschool children out to work—are producing offspring in some ways more self-sufficient than their parents.

Has the women's movement changed any of our negative feelings toward our own mothers? Has it healed any of the wounds we've received or inflicted? In the safe context of the women's movement many women have begun to examine for the first time the complexities of this relationship—as daughters still connected to our mothers by a knot tied with love, pain, and guilt.

Part of the new respect women are showing their mothers is in recording oral histories of older women. Certainly part of the search and discovery is the quest for our *own* usable past, but some is—especially for Jewish women—homage to a generation of women (particularly immigrant women) whose own lives gave them opportunities for courage and fortitude, flexibility and strength, that we, largely middle-class daughters, haven't had the opportunities to be tested on.

The women's movement has given us some of the intellectual tools and the support necessary to effect a reconciliation with our mothers which might in earlier generations have taken place almost biologically, as a natural evolution from being daughters to being mothers ourselves. But for a daughter faced with caring for an aged mother the situation may be especially poignant. With earlier conflicts sometimes still unresolved, the daughter must become care-giver to her mother. Women, whether as daughters or daughters-in-law, have traditionally been the ones responsible for care of the elderly and infirm, a situation now causing enormous pressure in the lives of middle-aged daughters, caught between the often irreconcilable demands of younger and older generations.

Judging from anecdotal material alone, Bart and other diagnosticians of the Jewish family may be correct in saying that Jewish women are more devoted to their children than to their parents.[23] Corroborating this, one woman with three adolescent children and a mother in her seventies confesses that "when my mother is in my house and her needs conflict with what I see as crucial needs or demands of my children, I answer to the kids' needs first. Always."

The characteristic plaint of the older woman—"I would rather die than be a burden to my children"—bespeaks a terror at an impending loss of control over one's own life in the face of a world turned upside down, a world in which someone whose own life has been devoted to caring for others now needs caring for. There is a more chilling aspect of the Jewish mother's expressed reluctance to be a burden to her children: perhaps the mothers feel that the burden won't be shouldered! In her studies of depressed middle-aged women Pauline Bart discusses the phenomenon of older Jewish parents who live frugally in order to make sure they'll have a nest egg to use if illness or disability should strike. Bart comments that these parents are reluctant to be in need of help from their children for fear of putting the relationship "to the test which it may not survive."[24]

Part of the way this is enacted may be in the willingness of older Jewish parents to relocate to "Sun Belt" communities, leaving their *children* behind. (In fact, this southward shift in the population of older Jews is, along with the declining birthrate, the most crucial Jewish demographic finding of the early 1980s.)

One theme sounded again and again by professionals who counsel the aged and their children is that old conflicts don't disappear with old age. A mother's lifelong patterns of behavior—whether self-sacrificing or demanding, for example—will continue as she ages, as will the essential aspects of the daughter's personality. They also point out that the caregivers (or potential care-givers) are entitled to lives of their own. "Don't give up your own life, and don't feel guilty—it's not your *fault* that your mother is growing older. But do honor your responsibility to be there for her in times of need," says one social worker who counsels Jewish families. (See also "Jewish Women in Crisis: Community Resources," p. 414.)

"Respect" is the key word for daughters as they and their mothers age—respect for the older woman, and for the reasons behind behavior that might otherwise be puzzling. The Jewish concept of *Derech Eretz* (literally, the way of the land) means that an extra measure of understanding is due to those who are much older than we. To our mothers it may mean that we question them sympathetically about their own lives, that we try to show that their experience, however radically different from our own, has value. (Sometimes this is impossible for daughters but possible between granddaughter and grandmother, in which case the ties of guilt and responsibility are not drawn so tightly.)

Some of the recent analytical writing on Jewish women that has emerged from the women's movement has helped daughters to view their mothers lives with renewed (or original) respect. See Gail M. Rudenstein, Carol Farley Kessler, and Ann M. Moore, "Mothers and

Daughters in Literature: A Preliminary Bibliography," in *The Lost Tradition*; Aviva Cantor, *The Jewish Woman: 1900–1980: A Bibliography*; Sonya Michel, "Mothers and Daughters in American Jewish Literature: The Rotted Cord," in Elizabeth Koltun, ed. *The Jewish Woman: New Perspectives*; and Charlotte Baum, Paula Hyman, and Sonya Michel, *The Jewish Woman in America*. Also see Aviva Cantor Zuckoff, "The Oppression of the Jewish Woman," *Response* (Summer 1973).

And for a thorough exploration of second-generation Jews, which does *not* condemn their desire for material comfort, see Deborah Dash Moore, *At Home in America: Second Generation New York Jews*.

One way of opening up a new relationship between daughters and older mothers is by discussing—if you can—the idea of an ethical will. Judaism has always had a tradition of passing along parental values to children in the form of a written will, setting out what values, what ethical precepts, what spiritual guidance parents want to leave children. Needless to say, most of these in the past were written by men. In fact, the *Encyclopedia Judaica* describes them as "a *father's* last words to his children" (italics added). You or your mother may at first consider this ghoulish, but there's a case to be made for helping your mother to see that she has given more to her children—and therefore has more to leave them—than an accumulation of property.

If you have children yourself, or anyone close to whom you want to leave a spiritual "legacy," you could prepare an ethical will *with* your mother. It can be very illuminating for you both to see how much of what you would pass along to your own children comes from her, and where your values differ. You might gain new respect for some of the differences between you and learn a lot about where you're similar. A good guide to the subject is:

Ethical Wills
by Jack Reimer
The National Jewish Resource Center
250 W. 57 Street
New York, NY 10019
$1.75

The conflicts between mother and daughter in Jewish families take a different turn in the relationship between daughters-in-law and mothers-in-law. The focus here is usually not so much on the dynamics between the two women as on the man who connects them. An exception to this is the classical Biblical tale of mother-in-law and daughter-in-law: Naomi

(from the collection of Zora Zagrabelna Weidman)

and Ruth. These women nurture each other when the men in the family have died; the story highlights not only the special friendship and love between the women but also the fact that it takes place in the conspicuous absence of the son/husband who provides the link between them.

When the son is present we certainly have examples of hostility in the traditional mother-in-law/daughter-in-law relationship. One of these is the "broiges-tants"—the "dance of enmity" that the bride and her mother-in-law would perform at an Eastern European Jewish wedding. The dance and some of the proverbs about the relationship between these two women are precursors to the mother-in-law jokes (always told by men), an expression of the fear men have of a bonding between these two women.

Some of the hostility women express has to do with shifting expectations. The mother-in-law expects that her son will marry and continue to be taken care of as she has taken care of him. After his marriage she fears that the treasure she has cherished will not be as highly valued by his wife as he is by his mother. Now that daughters-in-law (like daughters) have aspirations of their own, they aren't able to give the kind of care to their husbands that many mothers-in-law would like to think is their sons' due.

Many cultures have anti-mother-in-law jokes and tales. What is particularly problematic in the relationship between Jewish mothers- and daughters-in-law is the higher value traditionally placed on Jewish male offspring. The mother-in-law really does believe that she is turning over a treasure to a stranger's keeping. One woman tells, with some anger: "My mother-in-law is always telling me to remind my husband to get a haircut, to dress warmly, to have his good suit cleaned before the family Bar Mitzvah. This man is past fifty. But my mother-in-law still feels that if he looks untidy it reflects badly on *her*."

Empirical evidence suggests a kind of infantilization of the son/husband, in which both his mother and his wife are complicitous. Both women have a great deal invested in what the man does. Miriam, the wife of Rabbi Small in the *Friday the Rabbi . . .* mystery-story series, worries about what he will eat and recalls that his mother warned her that it was best to keep the courses coming without interruption, otherwise David would stop eating. How many times have you heard a woman say of her husband, "It's like having another child"? Some wives, and some mothers, feel more comfortable in the role of maternal care-giver to a man; it's one way of seizing, or taking back, power in the dyad.

DAUGHTERS AND FATHERS

An essay contest with the subject "My Jewish Mother" elicits entries from Hebrew school students who have very clear ideas about what makes their mothers Jews:[25] "She always cooks a lot of food for the holidays," wrote one. It's hard to imagine a parallel essay contest on the Jewish father; there's very little to differentiate him from "Jew" since we have been taught to respond to the word "Jew" by thinking of a man.

Unlike the image of the Jewish mother in popular culture, there's no single, stereotyped view of the Jewish father. This is not to say that we don't have certain notions about Jewish fathers too. We are accustomed to thinking that there are certain things he is *not*, among them that he is not selfish in regard to his children. When *Ms.* magazine ran an article in the late seventies about fathers and food—fathers holding the family purse strings; men deciding what kind of food the family would eat and what eating-out relief the mother would get; and, in primitive cultures, which teeth women would have removed or sawed down in the name of beauty (leaving them unable to chew the choice meats, which the men then ate)—Jewish women responded: "Well, that's certainly not the Jewish model. Jewish fathers aren't like that. Jewish fathers *sacrifice* for their children."

However, the writings of Anzia Yezierska and others remind us that this benevolent stereotype is not necessarily true. Anzia Yezierska's painful, acid-etched 1925 autobiographical novel *Bread Givers* (subtitled *A Struggle Between a Father of the Old World and a Daughter of the New*)[26] tells of a father who takes the very food his daughters yearn for and eats it while they look on, starving, who takes over the front room for his books while the family lives cramped in the back of the apartment, who cares more for study than for the well-being of his daughters. "We sat down to the table. With watering mouths and glistening eyes we watched Mother skimming off every bit of fat from the top soup into Father's big plate, leaving for us only the thin, watery part." A match for this father is the scholar in "A Woman's Wrath" by I. L. Peretz; he, like Yezierska's father, speaks to his wife about the world to come and ignores the real, physical needs of his starving, suffering children in this world.[27]

Certainly not all Jewish fathers behave in this way toward their children. But it is the nature of patriarchy that fathers do have a measure of control over daughters. (In Biblical times girls were sold into marriage—or "given" in marriage for the payment of a bride-price—by their fathers; the current practice of a father's "giving away" his daughter as a bride bespeaks the same kind of control.) Even if the popular image of the Jewish daughter is that she can wrap Daddy around her little finger, we have to ask why it is that scheming and manipulation of the father seem to be the ways she gets what she wants, rather than by stating her needs and desires in a more direct way.

The modern-day parallels to the controlling father might be Mr. Patimkin in *Goodbye Columbus* and the father in the film *Private Benjamin*. Both are willing—even happy—to provide for their daughters' material needs but close themselves off (as do the mothers in these two portrayals) from recognizing emotional need.

With growing prosperity after the Second World War and the passing on of the immigrant generation, whatever pathos helped create the nice-guy "shlemiel" image of the Jewish father—well-meaning but a little incompetent in the real world—passed on too. What was left was either the father who was an economic failure (about which we see very little in fiction) or the father as a power broker.

The Father and the Princess

With material success in America, Jewish men's distance from their children increased. No longer a figure sitting in synagogue or in a study hall, or working in the neighborhood and appearing regularly for three meals

(from *Leaving Home: A Family in Transition,* a film produced and directed by Ilana Bar-Din)

a day in the family kitchen, he removed himself from the domestic scene by hard work, hard play, and plenty of male bonding. Sociologist Rela Geffen Monson notes: "Thus, the father who was concerned with *kashrut* in the home, the quality and quantity of Jewish learning of his children and in their emotional, ethical and intellectual growth as Jews, was replaced by the one who provided the money so that secondary institutions and surrogate teachers and models could do this job for him, under the direction and coordination of the mother."[28]

The one single trait in any composite portrait of the assimilated, non-Orthodox North American Jewish father would be desire for his daughters to reflect his success. In a horrible poster of the "JAP" advertised in stationery-store windows across the country in 1979, a conspicuously consuming young woman is pictured in diamond stud earrings, a gift from Daddy when she stopped smoking. (The poster also shows her with a cigarette in one hand the warning "Don't tell Daddy.") She is his pride and joy, his ornament. Legend has it that he can refuse her nothing.

Always younger and sometimes more attractive in an "American" way than her mother, embellished with material goods and even cosmetic surgery (see "Our Bodies," p. 245), this daughter can be the most successful female object in the house, the best symbol of the father's having made it. If his son goes to an Ivy League school, perhaps the son's own efforts have been involved in some way. If a daughter dresses well and wears costly ornaments, only the father's wealth is responsible. Unlike what the popular wisdom posits, a young woman's father may be more responsible for the indulged-princess image than her mother.

Fathers without sons appear to be more supportive of their daughters' academic and other accomplishments. Those women—and there are a few—who describe sitting and studying Talmud with their European-born scholarly fathers are all women without brothers! Parallel to this are the women who learned business skills from their fathers, or were groomed to take over a family business (a more recent phenomenon).

With Jewish women having access to first-rate professional training now (see "Our Minds for Ourselves," p. 156), perhaps a daughter's career achievements will be the new pride-and-pleasure factor for fathers, making their daughters even better ornaments. Careerist daughters often describe their fathers as crucial models and their mothers as more shadowy, background figures to the drama on center stage.[29]

Redefining Jewish fatherhood may help wean Jewish men from a tendency to see and treat their daughters as objects—*naches* machines of one sort or another. Perhaps if feminism can teach Jewish men to balance careers and family life, and free themselves from some of their narcissistic involvement with their own work, they'll be able to relearn those genuine nurturing skills long ascribed to Jewish parents of both sexes.

FEMALE AND MALE

In every patriarchal society there are marked differences in the way male and female children are raised, since parents assume that they are socializing them for very different roles as adults. Girls of almost every ethnic and religious group thus lead lives that are more circumscribed than those of their brothers.

As we know, in the relations between Jewish brothers and sisters two messages are transmitted very early. The first is that sons are valued more than daughters. The second is that the education of sons is more important than that of daughters (see "Our Minds for Ourselves," p. 155).

From the very birth of a male child there's rejoicing and ritual celebration. Until recently (the past ten years or so) a girl child, at best, got her name called out in synagogue the Sabbath after her birth—if her parents were regular synagogue-goers. (Things are being equalized somewhat now with the proliferation of welcoming ceremonies for newborn Jewish daughters: see "Honoring the Birth of a Daughter," p. 121.)

In every Jewish family there seem to be tales not only of ritual inequities such as these but also of very real sacrifices that sisters were expected to make for their brothers. One woman relates that her mother and uncle had both shown musical promise when they were young and each had a flute. The young boy was tricked out of his by a thief. When he went home and told the family, the parents took away the sister's flute and gave it to her younger brother. There was never money to buy her another. "My uncle grew up to be a good—though not great—flutist. From what I know of my mother's ability, *she* would have been a soloist!"

In some societies it's assumed that the children will sacrifice for the parents. Jewish families, among others, expect that parents will usually be willing to sacrifice for children. However, a dimension unique to the Jewish family, and to the relationships fostered within it, is the assumption that sisters will sacrifice themselves for their brothers. A non-Jewish Bostonian married to a Jewish doctor puts it this way: "My husband was raised like a pasha. His sisters were expected to wait on him hand and foot. Everything he did was important. And my sisters-in-law were raised to believe that they themselves were worthless." Another woman says:

My mother yells only at *me*. She has *never* raised her voice to my older brother. All his sins are overlooked completely. All they pick up from him is *naches*; the disappointments fade. I'm the one who does everything for my parents, yet I get no credit. When *he* walks in their door their faces light up, and when *he* speaks at the dinner table there's rapt silence—everybody assumes that whatever *he* has to say is worth listening to. It was years after I left home before I felt secure enough to open my mouth in any intellectual discussion; I expected to be ignored, the way my parents had always passed over my dinner-table conversation in favor of my brother's.

In light of situations like these, it is no wonder that the studies of high-achieving women show that they almost invariably come from families in which there were no male siblings and in which they were treated like the missing son.

Yet somehow, despite the documentation that boys are favored in Jewish families, Jewish daughters are the children thought of as spoiled or demanding or self-absorbed. Why, since Jewish sons are raised with material advantages comparable to those of their sisters, is there no comparably widespread "prince" stereotype? The answer is that the daughter is still a two-dimensional object, whereas the son has a real, authentic life. It's acceptable for a Jewish young man to think well of himself, to feel worthy of all that he possesses or achieves, to strive openly for excellence. The core anxiety for his sister, often victimized by the demanding-princess stereotype, is that she is only the sum of her parts: what she possesses or wears or achieves, or whom she marries. There is no parallel objectification of her brother.

RESOURCES

For general documentation of the phenomenon of differential child rearing for girls and boys—and how absurd this is in light of what we know about child development—see Letty Cottin Pogrebin, *Growing Up Free: Raising Your Child in the 80's*.

For comments by older Jewish women about their experiences as sisters expected to sacrifice their own aspirations so that their brothers could succeed, see *Jewish Grandmothers*, ed. Sydelle Kramer and Jenny Masur, and Barbara Myerhoff, *Number Our Days*.

Sisters and brothers of the next generation will benefit, we hope, from more nearly egalitarian upbringing. For data on nonsexist child rearing, see "Responding to the Childbearing Imperative," p. 383; to correct sexism in Jewish education for children, see "Our Minds for Ourselves," p. 166.

7

◆

WHOM WE CHOOSE
AND WHY

JEWISH WOMEN AND JEWISH MEN

The different attitudes toward boys and girls in the Jewish family have consequences in the ways adult Jewish women and men relate to one another, each sex projecting onto the other some less-than-flattering attributes. While the Jewish woman, as mother or daughter, is pictured by Jewish men as having great power to manipulate or affect others, Jewish women say Jewish men are often anxiety-ridden—always worried about bones in the fish, expecting peril around every corner, trapped in history and unable to take pleasure in the moment. (This image may not seem to hold for all the Adidas-wearing Jewish jocks and joggers that the seventies produced, but seems true enough for earlier and more traditional models.)

Going along with this is the stereotype of the Jewish male as still not fully formed, not fully adult. "The Prince is not taught to stand on his own two feet. It is not a materialistic thing as with the Jewish American Princess: the Prince is just demanding, not only of his wife, but of everyone. It is immaturity . . ."

This Baltimore woman put it very succinctly. The Jewish man, she said, "does not want to marry a JAP. He wants to marry a *shiksah* because he wants the type of wife who caters to his ego."[1] Sometimes the conflicts are addressed by the mothers of single women: "My daughter is so talented and attractive. She's in her late twenties, doing well in her law firm [or other great job], and I want to know where are all the nice Jewish boys her age? Why are they all marrying non-Jewish women?"

There are obviously many Jewish men who would prefer to see the old roles remain—with male superiority in the world (whether the world of study or of business) and women safely tucked away in their homes, nurturing and replenishing others while the men demand and deplete.

Despite the fact that the New World saw many sweet *zaydes* (grandfathers) become hardheaded businessmen, the image of male helplessness persisted. Did women have to see their men as inept in certain ways in order to strengthen their own roles at home and in the work world? If a man cannot so much as slice a piece of bread for himself, then the woman's role as nurturer (bread-slicer if not breadwinner) becomes necessary to survival.

Are Jewish men really different from other men? A historical view of Jewish male and female roles suggests that Jewish men have a wider range of expressiveness available to them than other men, which makes for fewer distinctions between "male" and "female" behavior:

> Deprived of political independence and, in most places, the right to bear arms, Jewish men denigrated physical prowess as a cultural ideal. Instead, they cultivated intellectual and spiritual pursuits. They expressed their masculinity in the synagogue and in the house of study, not on the battlefields and not through the physical oppression of their women. The absence of the macho mystique also freed Jewish men and women—until they assimilated into modern Western societies—from the sharpest differentiation of gender characteristics: the strong, emotionally controlled, yet potentially violent male versus the weak, emotional, and tender female. Jewish culture "permitted" men to be gentle and emotionally expressive, and women to be strong, capable, and shrewd.[2]

Jewish men (like Black men and men of other oppressed groups) may lash out at "their" women in their pain at being excluded from the ruling class. Jewish women have taken the attitude that injustices of all sorts were "permissible" or at least understandable coming from Jewish men, because there has been so much oppression heaped upon them. Until very recently, Jewish women didn't speak out about their own double oppression, as Jews and as women—as if all the suffering of Jews affected Jewish men alone.

If you want to call to mind a suffering Jew, the image of an old, bent, bearded Jewish *man* flashes onto your inner eye. The broken or stunted dreams of elderly Jewish women never enter our imaginations in the same way. Humiliation, too, seems worse for Jewish men than for women.

(Bill Aron)

Male pride must be assuaged, whereas women have no pride to speak of anyway. We are the flexible ones, the ones capable of bending to fit the situation, not the stiff-necked ones of the Jewish people. It's our job to make life softer for the stiff-necked men. Part of our job description is to understand and forgive their oppression of Jewish women as necessary for Jewish survival.

Andrea Dworkin (the feminist theorist of *Our Blood, The New Woman's Broken Heart,* and *Pornography: Men Possessing Women*) says of the Jewish man: "He uses his hurt to justify his hurting her." And when women go along with this, Dworkin says, we are not being understanding people providing support for someone who has suffered, but we are "victims of male supremacy."

The oppression of Jewish women by Jewish men takes many forms. Although the myth that Jewish men are not violent toward their women is being shattered by the awful realities in reports of domestic violence in Jewish families (see p. 426), most of the unpleasantness between Jewish women and Jewish men is, as we'd expect from a verbal people, in words.

The verbal hostility between Jewish men and Jewish women goes back far. Even the Talmud has tales of verbal sparring, though no jokes. Just look at old jokebooks, and you will see that there's plenty of animosity between the sexes, usually directed by men at women. In a study of jokes told about Jewish women in various roles (mother, mother-in-law, wife) the researcher—Gladys Weisberg Rothbell of the State University of New York at Stony Brook—found so many nasty cracks dating back as far as the 1920s, that she asks, "When are feminists going to retaliate?"[3]

The jokes Jewish men tell about Jewish women have no parallel in other cultures; there's no comparable *oeuvre* of jokes about Greek or Baptist or Irish women. The jokes about Jewish women (of the "In a coma? I thought she was Jewish!" variety) told with impunity in social gatherings and on television talk shows reflect Jewish men's uneasiness about their relationships with Jewish women, characterized here by feelings of hostility and rejection. They fall into two categories: Jewish women withholding sex, and Jewish women passive and unresponsive sexually. In Category I would be:

Q: How do you get a Jewish woman to stop screwing?
A: Marry her.

In Category II would be:

Husband to ex-wife: Let's make love one last time.
Ex-wife: Over my dead body.
Husband: Isn't that how we always used to do it?

If we agree with Freud that jokes contain repressed wishes, then perhaps the Jewish men telling the jokes are saying that they wished Jewish women would be less sexually active. (Joke one suggests that Jewish women are promiscuous—at least before marriage.) The jokes themselves suggest that any woman who says what she really wants (whether it's more sex or less sex) runs the risk of being thought demanding or being made the object of ridicule on late-night television. In any case, there seems to be a lot of ambivalence on the part of Jewish *men* about sex, and women themselves are left with what psychiatrist and sex therapist Helen Singer Kaplan has called "desire problems."

Of course, if the jokes are not true, and Jewish women are no different in bed from other women (who knows?), why are the men saying these nasty things about us?

Jewish men are caught between trying to define their manhood in front of Jewish women ("their" women) and trying to define it before non-Jewish men. The shlemiel image is one safe mask to hide behind. Alexander Portnoy says in the Turkish bath: "There are no women here. No women and no *goyim*. Can it be? There is nothing to worry about!"

Remembering strong mothers or foremothers, American Jewish men fear the reemergence of this strength in Jewish women, sexually and in other ways. They don't want competition from their women, they want (intelligent) support. Or, as a woman tells a Boston newspaper reporter, "Jewish men want intellectual sex objects." The title of one Woody Allen short story plays on this controllable intellectual titillation—"The Whore of Mensa."

Jewish men, in their attempt to succeed in the American style, compete with the handsome non-Jews who are the prototypical male sex objects in a culture in which Jews are in a minority—in which Robert Redford is sexier than Dustin Hoffman. In this competitive context the jokes about Jewish women and sex may function as a beacon to warn non-Jewish men that Jewish women aren't worth the trouble. The jokes disparage the women *and* try to keep them the exclusive property of Jewish men. Oppressed men typically have no physical protection to offer their women against rape and abuse; historically this was certainly true of the Jews. The jokes may be a perverse kind of protection, a barrier against the attentions of other men: "Don't Patronize These Premises. Lousy Merchandise Within."

The jokes about Jewish women are also an attempt by Jewish men to ingratiate themselves with their non-Jewish competitors. Jokes about women bind men together—but it would be unthinkable for Jews to joke about WASP women, for example, so Jewish men tell "secrets" about a safer subject: their "own" women. The jokes are a cop-out, pretending that the conflict is sexual, when it's political. The Jewish woman has become the paradigm for all Jews, and Jewish men do to her in the jokes what overt anti-Semites do to Jews.

Obviously there's a strong element of anti-Semitism in the jokes. The joke tellers, and perhaps the audience as well, want to distance themselves from Jewishness but may not feel comfortable about doing this overtly. So both Jewish men and non-Jewish men are able to denigrate the Jews in the guise of striking out "only" at Jewish *women*. The jokes are a way of expressing anti-Jewish feelings under a cover of misogyny.

And the misogyny runs deep, affecting the way some Jewish men see all Jewish women. As Jews we're justifiably suspicious when a non-Jew says, "You're not like other Jews I've known." But Jewish men have been known to express the same prejudice. One woman recounts:

> When I was 17, an older Jewish man I was dating looked into my eyes and said with a miraculous tone in his voice, "You are only the second Jewish girl I have ever liked!" I didn't know whether to laugh, walk out, or kiss his hand for the "compliment." Four years later, certain lessons being obviously difficult to learn, I sat patiently listening to another Jewish man tell me that I was the first Jewish woman, since his unbearable first wife, that he had even considered dating. Much to his astonishment, he even liked me!
>
> Now . . . I see the incidents with these men as the truly dangerous signs of potential shame and oppression that they actually are.[4]

The negative views Jewish men have of Jewish women are reinforced (or perhaps even shaped) by the attitudes in the popular novels written by American Jewish men. Barbara Quart, a critic and English instructor, speaks about her disenchantment with these views of Jewish women:

> I came out of college in the late 1950's, head full of literary loves and fantasies of a real-life one. That one always had a Jewish face in my imagination, and the rumpled, articulate intensities of a Jewish intellectual or artist—my idea of a beautiful man. Looking back on those years, what puzzles me now is how come I never noticed—as I excitedly read the new Malamud or Roth or Bellow, or Mailer's latest shocker in the *Village Voice*—that women characters were generally very unpleasant in those books; that Jewish women characters were inordinately unpleasant; that more often than not, the pointedly Jewish men at the center of the novels sought Christian women to love, screw, marry—and, in short, that a woman like myself was to a remarkable extent a *persona non grata* in the fantasies, the fiction, of these men. The face in my dreams resembled Norman Mailer's, but *his* dream girl was a long-legged blonde starlet from Georgia named Cherry or Lulu, who in no way resembled me or anything I wanted to be.[5]

In fact, Jewish men are often telling that they like non-Jewish women better (in everything from *Cosmopolitan* articles to the film *Heartbreak Kid*). There's even fiction by Jewish men projecting their own attitudes toward Jewish women onto non-Jewish men. (One such example is Mailer's story "The Time of Her Time," in which the heroine is a Jewish woman who can have orgasms only with her non-Jewish lover, and then only when he calls her a "dirty little Jew.")

Another example of anger and projection are the comments of a Midwestern rabbi on the crises facing the Jewish family. For the conflicts between *klal Yisrael* (the Jewish people, with all its variants) and the narcissism of the me generation, he blamed "Jewish girls [*sic*] seeing themselves as the center of the universe," expecting to be showered with love and gifts.[6] The easy way in which this man scapegoated Jewish women echoes the reasoning some Jewish men use to avoid or blame Jewish women: the women are going to care more about their own comfort than about the needs of others. This rabbi—who is responsible for shaping the "Jewish" opinions of his congregants—bought the demanding-princess package outright! No wonder so many Jewish women and men don't like or even understand each other.

Perhaps some of the bitterness comes from failed expectations. If Jews tend to see other Jews as kindred ("like," rather than "other"), then Jewish women and men may see each other as "family." Incest taboos aside, this identification may create disappointment when the man or woman fails to be Daddy or Mommy—or represents Daddy or Mommy.

Jewish men and women have very high expectations of one another and of themselves. After all, haven't we been told that we should have the best in life, or at least that we should do better than our parents did (regardless of how high that standard is)? Jewish men, then, expect that Jewish women will provide what their selfless mothers did: unconditional love, total approval. No wonder they say they fear Jewish women—they expect more from them and therefore have more to lose if the expectations are disappointed. Are Jewish men afraid of being judged by Jewish women and found wanting?

In a unique research project that examines the negative attributes Jewish women and men project onto one another, Berkeley psychologist Judith Weinstein Klein has found a way to break down some of the barriers between them. She notes that for some Jewish women, Jewish men call forth negative associations with physical weakness and intellectual bravado. For some Jewish men, Jewish women are assertive princesses, demanding more than Jewish men feel they will be able to give, setting up expectations the men fear they won't be able to meet, and their own feelings of inadequacy then turn into anger at all Jewish women. Klein practices "ethnotherapy," in which she brings together groups of Jewish women and men to work through some of the negative associations they have with being Jewish and with one another. (See also "Jewish Women in Crisis," p. 439.)

The perception of conflict between Jewish men and Jewish women is so widespread that the advertisement for a communitywide discussion group in Boston announces the topic: "Jewish Men and Jewish Women: Why We Love and Hate Each Other." Similar events are drawing overflow crowds all across the country.

Jewish women have always reassured themselves that their men were different; yet even with the tenderness and emotional expressiveness many Jewish men permit themselves, there is another kind of male feeling of superiority at work—this time a superiority based on precisely the spiritual and intellectual capacity that Jewish men declared as their specialty. In fact, the Jewish men whom Jewish women have traditionally valued and found attractive were those who had a lot of intellectual weight—"My idea of a beautiful man," as Quart puts it. Just as in Eastern Europe the scholar was the most desirable *chussin*, or bridegroom, a group of Jewish women, in a straw poll taken by a single woman in her twenties, showed that none of the women reported wanting a man who was not as smart as she was.[7]

California philosophy instructor Harry Brod, in a lecture to a group of progressive American Jews, delivers a *mea culpa* on this issue: "The emphasis on mind over body in many areas of Jewish culture is one reason why the kind of unconsciously sexist behavior which predominates in the Jewish community often looks different. . . . While many Jewish men do not fall into the more boisterous stereotypes of male sexist behavior, many do fall into a common male intellectual intimidation of others."[8]

Male Jewish intellectual dominance, at least among the middle class, is a stance very familiar to anyone able to observe Jews in action with a little of the anthropologist's distance. He who is better able to command the rapt listening attention of the other diners at a dinner party ranks higher on the special scale of Jewish power. Intellectual rather than physical prowess is the determinant of the Jewish male's value or his place in the pecking order.

One form of Jewish machismo is some men's scorn for women's struggles. One such man always jokes, "Well, I guess I'm just an old sexist, just a male chauvinist pig." Perhaps we can rationalize away his scorn by telling ourselves that those having power will relinquish it only reluctantly. But the insult here is great, particularly because this man and many like him would never permit someone to say casually, "Well, I guess I'm just an old anti-Semite [or racist]." But the deeply felt and casually expressed misogyny of some very bright Jewish men doesn't even strike them as bad manners, let alone bad politics. They utterly fail to see that for some women their feminist identity is as nonnegotiable as their being Jews.

Men like this are still caught between Lilith and Eve.[9] Lilith, remember, was the first woman. After a fight over equality, Lilith flees the Garden of Eden. Eventually Adam gets himself the more tractable Eve. Some Jewish men believe that they want a lively, intelligent companion, a woman who will be an intellectual peer; yet these same men also want a traditional, male-dominated relationship of the Adam-and-Eve variety.

For these men there is a list of remedial reading, at least some of which should help to awaken a recognition of their own male chauvinism and of the oxymoronic nature of what they claim to desire in a Jewish woman.

Bob Lamm, active in many movements for social change but especially visible as a Jewish man opposing gender-role stereotyping among Jews, suggests "One concrete step for men—one vivid sign of respect for feminism—would be a *serious* effort to study feminist literature. Many progressive Jewish men have spent years studying the Talmud, or socialist Zionism, or Marxism, or other traditions of male political and religious thought. It is time for men to make this type of commitment to the study of feminist thought."[10]

Despite the strong endogamous ties between Jewish women and Jewish men, there are very distinct differences in their orientation which may indeed make them implacable opposites. While the men Lamm was addressing were reading Marx and Freud (not to say that women weren't reading them too), women of the same generation were most likely also reading *The Feminine Mystique* or *Women in Sexist Society*, or even *Marjorie Morningstar*, and therefore were imagining a very different world from their male counterparts—a world based more on personal politics than on theory. As a result of these different male/female worlds of experience and learning, Jewish women and Jewish men have been on the opposite sides of certain controversial political issues.[11]

On a more profound level, what these political disagreements can mean is that some women for the first time are willing to risk taking a stand different from that of their male protector—husband, lover, father, colleague. It's no wonder that women activists are now trying to connect themselves with role models of independence from the Jewish past, particularly with such women as Ernestine Rose, Emma Goldman, and the other Jewish women involved in the suffragist and labor movements. Remembering historian Gerda Lerner's observation that women live in great intimacy with, essentially, their oppressors (or at least their "superiors"),[12] we have to commend those women willing to take risks to dissolve patriarchy—not in an abstract sense but by direct confrontation with the men they encounter in classes, at home, and on the job and risk their negative reactions or ego-bruising stereotyping.

Many Jewish women fear that they will "turn off" the Jewish men they hope to attract (or to "keep") by being too outspoken on the issues that they deem vital. If Jewish men fear feminism, many Jewish feminists say that they fear rejection because of their feminist views. Anti-feminism has in some cases become another weapon in the arsenal of Jewish men who may be looking for ways to dissociate themselves from women they see as too threatening or too smart.

JEWISH WOMEN AND NON-JEWISH MEN

Partly as a result of their conflicts with Jewish men, some Jewish women have turned to non-Jewish men, who may see their characteristic outspokenness and assertiveness in a far more favorable light than Jewish men claim to. By the same token, some of the negative characteristics Jewish women and men project onto each other (see preceding section) lead them to believe that *non*-Jewish partners embody the opposite characteristics and hence are more desirable love objects. As a *pattern* of involvement for some Jewish women, it may illuminate some of their problems with Jewish men.

The growing literature on intermarriage (see p. 334) emphasizes the implications of this social phenomenon for the future of the Jewish people, but there's been very little written about Jewish women who are involved in relationships with non-Jewish men, and about the causes for such relationships. One woman, a Missouri teacher in her mid-thirties, tells of her first such experience:

> At first I thought I'd find the whole experience very alien, but I'll tell you, he's very competent in the real world, very sure of himself, doesn't have the same difficulties making decisions as the Jewish boyfriends I've had. But I think that the most striking contrast is that he's a very warm, giving person, yet without all the leaning, and the constant neediness, of the Jewish men I've been involved with. I don't know if it's just his non-Jewish background, but there's something very appealing about this man because he hasn't sacrified caring, loving feelings, though he seems to be a mature adult. He also doesn't fear my strengths, my assertiveness, or my willingness to open my mouth about the things that bother me.

A Midwestern woman asserts that her non-Jewish boyfriend "*lowers* my level of anxiety, rather than turning it up. He isn't afraid of my emotions, and he doesn't seem to need to dominate me. My being a strong woman seems to be no problem for him." Despite the appeal, both these women, interestingly, ended their relationships when they suspected their boyfriends of covert anti-Semitism.

One woman reports a very different response from a formerly religious Christian man she had been dating: "It seemed that I could share my Judaism with him in a way I couldn't with the Jewish men that I met, who seemed terribly threatened by my keeping kosher, my refusal to date on Friday night, and the fact that my children were in a Jewish day school."

Doubtless Jewish women *are* seen differently by non-Jewish men. Perhaps the same kind of sexualization takes place here as between Jewish men and non-Jewish women; the incest taboos on in-group women are lifted. It's ironic that Jewish men, in fact, tend to characterize Jewish women as unresponsive, whereas non-Jews see Jewish women in the opposite light. Non-Jews viewing Judy Chicago's *Dinner Party* have responded that this work had to have been the creation of a Jewish woman because it is "so sensual."[13]

Any exogamous relationship may be freer of guilt than a relationship with a member of one's own group. For instance, a Brooklyn-born man who has lived in Israel for ten years reports that Israeli men find American Jewish women sexier (which may mean more available for sex) than Israeli women; American men report Israeli women sexier and more available than their American Jewish counterparts. This is the *greene felder* theory (loose translation from the Yiddish: "The grass is always greener . . .") . Anyone unfamiliar acquires an exotic attractiveness.

Non-Jewish men may associate Jewish women's allegedly greater expressiveness with sexuality. This escalates: there is also always the ugly threat of rape in the attraction of non-Jewish men to Jewish women. (See also "Our Bodies," p. 223.) Jean-Paul Sartre describes this situation in his discussion of La Belle Juive in *Anti-Semite and Jew*: "There is in the words 'a beautiful Jewess' a very special sexual signification, one quite different from that contained in the words 'beautiful Rumanian,' 'beautiful Greek,' or 'beautiful American,' for example. The 'beautiful Jewess' is she whom the Cossacks under the czars dragged by her hair through the streets of her burning village."[14] Author Andrea Dworkin says that "Jewess" is an "eroticized term"—condescending, but sexual.

The Jewish woman has, in fact, been something of a stock character in the writings of non-Jewish men, from essayist Charles Lamb's anti-Semitic comments to the sexualization in Thomas Wolfe's *Of Time and the River,* or *The Web and the Rock,* in which he describes Jewish women's bodies as the "living rack" on which the backs of Christian lovers had been broken. Commenting on the complex portrait of "the" Jewish woman in American drama, Ellen Schiff pinpoints the peculiar amalgam of danger and appeal this woman comes to represent to non-Jewish men: "a provocatively ambiguous composite of carnality and special wisdom, of Lilith and the Virgin Mary."[15] And of course there is writing by non-Jewish men about Jewish women, such as William Styron's *de rigueur* depiction of the spoiled Jewish daughter in *Sophie's Choice.*

Some non-Jewish men describe Jewish women as exotic, not quite human, interesting, warm, troubled, mysterious because different, "earthy." And some women, getting these signals, respond positively. "I remember my first, friendly encounters with all-American non-Jewish boys at college: even in a casual conversation I would begin to think of myself as what I then termed, to myself, "an almond-eyed Jewess." I knew that they saw me as an exotic, and were surprised to discover that I was human too."

A similar theme is played out in a short story by Enid Levinger Powell:

> I dated happily until a golden basketball player focused his attention on me . . . I masked my anxiety to please with attempts at humorous self-deprecation. He introduced me to his fellow players as a "brain," grinning to show how illogical it was to find one housed in me. "You know," he finally said, after an evening in which we emptied ourselves of every detail of our past, "you don't seem Jewish." . . . A contemptuous laugh broke out of my throat: "I don't consider that a compliment."[16]

Being seen as very attractive by the men of the majority culture can at times work to our advantage and is sometimes a terrible liability (for example, when Jewish women fear "losing" Jewish men to the women of the majority culture, who now have *The Shikse's Guide to Jewish Men* by Marsha Richman and Katie O'Donnell to help them).

Jewish women sometimes feel that if they do not conform to some stereotyped image of non-Jewish women they'll lose their magnetism for Jewish men. ("Blondes have more fun.") At the same time their "Jewishness" is described as especially alluring both by those Jewish men so far from their own Jewish identity that Jewish women seem exotic and by some non-Jewish men—the "status" males in this culture.

Walking down the aisle is a scene most young girls expect to experience—which is why staying single makes some women feel that they are not following the script. (Frederic Perry)

The message is very confusing. Both in religious law and to some easily threatened nonreligious Jewish men a woman who's had a relationship with a non-Jewish man is considered to be little better than a whore, a betrayer of her people. Fewer sanctions exist for Jewish men attracted to non-Jewish women. In fact, one of the popular, "daring" Jewish fraternity songs of the 1950s had to do with a "nice Jewish boy" who "takes out *shiksas* on Yom Kippur night."

In the fifties, as earlier, heaven help the Jewish woman who went out with a *shaygetz* (Yiddish slang for non-Jewish male). Some of the social disapprobation of these liaisons is gone now, but what remains is the multiple risk to the woman: being seen as some distant, exotic "other" by the non-Jewish man and feeling disloyal for having trespassed across an uncertain boundary between the Jews and potentially hostile strangers.

The uncertainty itself makes the situation harder for Jewish women. The old dichotomy between a narrow particularism and looser, universalist human connections makes parents uncomfortable about wanting children to date only Jews. Without religious justification for such exclusivity, what plausible reasons can they give? Thus many single Jewish women sense parental and communal disapproval of their relationships with non-Jews, yet aren't clear about the source of the negative feelings.[17] (For the responses of Jewish women who intermarry, see p. 337.)

TO BE SINGLE, JEWISH, AND FEMALE

Whatever your "object choice" when you are unattached, marriage (preferably to a "nice Jewish man") is often assumed to be your goal. According to Jewish law, interpretation and tradition, marriage is the normative state for adult Jews. Unlike Catholicism, which sanctions and even praises a life of "single blessedness," there has never been an approved role in Jewish life for celibacy. Even postponing marriage past the age of twenty is frowned on by some rabbinic sources (see "Marriage," p. 318).

A single Jewish woman is often a nonperson, whether she is single by choice or by circumstance, and whether she is never-married, widowed, or divorced. While a Catholic woman can sing the praises—and advantages—of the single life, a Jewish woman who does so is considered akin to a heretic.[18]

This disapproval is hardly restricted to commentary in dusty tomes. One prominent East Coast (male) rabbi, commenting on the large number of single Jews in New York City (estimated conservatively at 125,000), says, "It's disgusting." And a panelist at the largest annual Jewish gathering in North America—the General Assembly of Jewish Federations and Welfare Funds—focused an entire session on the singles "problem."

Contemporary pressures to marry—even in the free-choice-of-life-style atmosphere of the 1980s—are very real. They are directed primarily at never-married Jewish women, who are accused of being selfish, narcissistic, and disloyal to the continuity of Jewish life, as if all of them were single by choice. Rabbi R. M. Yellin, writing in *Conservative Judaism*, announces that "anyone who feels that getting married or having children is oppressive or gets in the way of realizing identity reflects a posture that cannot exist normatively within the Jewish system." In one sentence he excommunicates single women! And he is talking about women, not men—make no mistake about it. Men are not the ones who are accused of saying that having children "gets in the way of realizing identity."

This attitude is counterproductive to the existence of a flourishing Jewish community. With American Jews marrying even later than other Americans, there are more women spending more years single than ever before. Therefore they have more time in which to feel alienated from a "couples only" Jewish life. This attitude of distance or estrangement may not change even if the women ultimately do marry. Their feelings of rejection by the community may be so powerful that they may be the ones doing the rejecting when given the chance.

What is a single, heterosexual Jewish woman to do when Jewish opinion-makers describe her status as loathesome, problematic, and embarrassing? One of the most painful and disabling aspects of life as a single woman in a couples-oriented community is the sense of not being a legitimate person, a full citizen. A single woman is seen as less than human—someone who is only in a holding pattern, *waiting* to marry.

The heroine of Gail Parent's *Sheila Levine Is Dead and Living in New York* finds out that she can't even buy a single cemetery plot in which her body can rest after she kills herself! "The problem is, dear, we don't cater to single people. All our plots are double." Sheila, and every other single Jewish woman (and any married woman with a degree of consciousness on the issue), has her very personhood devalued by this attitude.

Women who are single by choice—whether temporarily or permanently—are justifiably outraged by such treatment. With slowly awakening consciousness, some synagogues and community centers offer memberships on an individual basis; others have "professional women's" divisions, with an emphasis on group activities and not couples programming. Yet even a decade or more of exposure to feminism hasn't helped some Jews to accept an unmarried woman. The headline on a press release describing a recent United Jewish Appeal "mission" to New York City reads "Southwest couples to explore Jewish roots." There are no unmarried Jews in the Southwest? Or maybe they have no roots? Or was the intent to keep single people away from the safely married? With similar bias, the membership application forms of many synagogues ask for "date of wedding anniversary" along with "name of spouse" right at the top of the application blank.

Whether never-married, widowed, or divorced, women may miss the reflected glory of a husband's position, or money, often required for full acceptance into the community. Single men are "eligible bachelors" regardless of occupation or personality or sometimes even sexual preference, so the situation is less difficult for them.

Additionally painful, aside from the special disapproval directed at all Jewish women who haven't produced children, is a "blame the victim" mentality behind the criticism of never-married Jewish women, even those who are actively looking for what one woman describes as "a *mentsch* to marry." Single women are blamed for being "too choosy" or "too involved with a career."

The Talmud says, "A man should build a house, then plant a vineyard and after that marry." Jewish women aren't entitled to arrange their lives in this order. Even with the marriage age of most educated Americans rising into the late twenties, in Jewish families anxieties about "spinsterhood" surface very early, sometimes as soon as a woman is out of college. Women's career goals still appear to some parents more of a threat to marriageability than an essential part of the life pattern of a mature adult of either gender.

The basic asymmetry in men's and women's lives—their roles and their biology—makes being single a much more poignant situation for women than for men. Men still get to do the asking in many circles. More desirable as they get older, and more powerful, they have an increasing pool of younger women to choose from. None of this is news, nor is the observation that women's biological clocks are ticking so fast that the woman in her mid-thirties who would like to have children feels she cannot afford the luxury of exploring any relationship that seems to lack "marriage potential." Often Jewish men's response to this neediness is scorn. "Oy," says one jaded single man speaking of Manhattan's "Jewish" singles bars, "another girl looking for a serious relationship."

Even if they believe on an intellectual level that "A woman without a man is like a fish without a bicycle" (the adage attributed to Florynce Kennedy), a majority of Jewish women doubtless would like to marry, and they would prefer to marry Jewish men, despite the hostilities that often exist between them. In fact, finding a partner who is Jewish is the goal of single men as well, if the ads specifying "J" in personals columns are a valid indicator.

The *Metropolitan Almanac*, New York City's weekly newspaper listing diverse events, most of them for singles, features such ads as:

SJM 28, seeks SJW of similar description: 25-31, lotsa brains, good looks, ample wit and warmth, who enjoys modern art, Szechuan cuisine, *Scientific American*, classical music, and prolonged intellectual discussions.

A very special Jewish widow, 5'7", wants to meet that very special man. Young 50+, 5'9"+, NJ resident, unencumbered.

SJF 36, good fig., MA Eng seeks SJM prof or bus. 40-45, big and tall, very hairy body.

The "intellectual" national magazines or "journals of opinion" are also good places to read about "J" singles, including *The New York Review of Books*, with a personals column that has finely calibrated shorthand for every body type, race, religion, and sexual preference.

Sadly, some of these advertisements serve to highlight the pariah status of the single woman in Jewish circles. She is often not entitled to appear alone, even at simchas, as if reminding others of the imperfections in this world. The *Long Island Jewish World* regularly runs a classified ad from a fifty-five-year-old Jewish man who advertises himself as an "escort service" for "weddings, Bar Mitzvahs, etc." Despite the apparent willingness of Jewish women to seek Jewish partners, the demographics of Jewish life have shrunk the pool of available candidates. In the title of a much-discussed article, journalist Bill Novak asks a question with which single Jewish women have been tormenting themselves: "Are Good Jewish Men a Vanishing Breed?"

Very simply, roughly 20 percent of all young Jewish women are not going to marry a Jewish man, because there just isn't one available.

Here's why: First, in the 20-34 age bracket, there are 92 Jewish males for every 100 Jewish females. That's just a 4 percent difference, but then we have to take account of the intermarriage statistics. Out of every 92 male Jews who marry, roughly 24 are going to marry "out," a choice which only 12 out of every 100 Jewish women will make. And that reduces the number of Jewish males who are available as husbands from 92 to 68, as against 88 Jewish women who are available as wives. Sixty-eight men, 88 women, or 20 women who are a kind of remainder: 20 out of every 100.

These numbers are rough estimates. Maybe they're off, maybe the figure is not 20 percent, but only 15 percent. Still, there is a very large group of Jewish women who are, for all practical purposes, stuck. They could intermarry, of course, but they don't. It's not clear why they don't; perhaps they agree with my friend who says, "I sometimes think I could marry a Buddhist, if he were a genuinely nice person, but that's only a passing thought. I'm so socialized against marrying somebody who isn't Jewish that I really can't take my desperate thought seriously. I refuse to imagine Shabbas as a solo affair, or one in which my sweet Buddhist will indulge me."

There are, in short, not enough men to go around. When all the sorting is done, some women are going to be left over, and they will most likely blame themselves, because nobody has bothered to tell them the harsh statistical truth.

A truth which gets worse: According to Noreen Goldman, a population researcher at Princeton University's Woodrow Wilson School, there are several other factors involved. Let's consider the case of a woman born in 1947—we'll call her Fran—who will turn 33 in 1980. If Fran is single, and if she ever wants to have children, she had better find a man pretty soon—unless, of course, she decides to have children outside of marriage. But even then, Fran understands that she must act relatively soon. At her age, if she waits too much longer, there may be real and significant pregnancy risks.

But even if Fran doesn't want to have children, she is still, like other women, statistically likely to marry a man who is older than she is. Noreen Goldman calls this "societal pressure," but whether or not it's perceived in these terms, it's a fact of life that the overwhelming majority of women marry men who are older than they are. In Fran's case, she is most likely looking for a man who was born before 1947. And here comes the crunch: Because she was born near the beginning of the baby boom, Fran is going to have a hard time finding such a man. There were, it turns out, more than 400,000 fewer babies born in 1946 than in 1947, the year of Fran's birth, and there were more than *half a million* fewer babies born in 1945 than in 1946. And so, by definition, the men that Fran would find appropriate are in short supply and, being slightly older, many are already married. And so Fran finds herself in what is called a "marriage squeeze."

Under these trying circumstances, you might expect that Jewish women would be so desperate that they'd settle for just about anybody. But they don't, and they won't. And that's the heart of the story, the part that doesn't show up in the charts and the tables. That's the part that has to do with women's evolving expectations, with the shortage not of men but of *mentschen*. The men who *are* around, if they're not married, gay, or otherwise unavailable, are often disappointing as people. However successful they may be in their working lives, they seem (to these women, at least) to be lacking in the personal realm. Their range of interests is often narrow; more important, there seems to be something missing. Their emotional resources and supportiveness, their willingness and ability to enter into a committed relationship— these all seem underdeveloped. What's missing, in short, is a set of qualities which women find so readily in other women.

Even those women who are eager to be married are often ambivalent. Sandy, 31, is a research scientist. "To give up being single," she
says, "is to give up a great deal. I couldn't imagine doing it lightly. It
used to be that single women couldn't wait to escape their fate. I wish
I had another twenty years of being 31 and single, now that I've finally
gotten good at it."[19]

The *good* news is that a generation of Jewish women staying single for
longer than any in the past has a unique opportunity to experience friendships in a powerful way that married women sometimes deny themselves.
Claudia Weill's 1978 film *Girlfriends* is based on this phenomenon. The
women's movement has tried to free all women from the competitiveness
over men that had characterized much of the contact between single
women in the past. Unattached women now have resources—both personal and financial—to enjoy themselves without a mate; prolonged or
permanent singlehood thus may define a whole new phase in women's
lives which will encourage friendships and women's activities in ways that
used to be available only in the prepuberty years. Recognizing this new
time together, some Jewish women choose to spend even their precious
evening hours in communal settings with other women. Especially in
urban centers, single women are the backbone of the evening groups of
Hadassah and other Jewish women's organizations. As they feel more
welcome, and have their single status validated and not pitied, more
women may choose to affiliate with Jewish organizations as a way of meeting and working with other Jewish women.

On the other hand, for some Jewish women, remaining single into their
late twenties and even later makes for a degree of dislocation from their
families of origin, as if we women cannot assume an adult role unless
we're attached to a man (and to a china pattern). "I feel like a superan-
nuated child when I'm with my parents. Somehow nothing I do is serious, compared with the life crises my married sister goes through," says
a psychologist from Washington, D.C. The problem is so widespread
that the 92nd Street Y in New York actually offered a lecture for singles
titled "Developing Adult Family Ties: You Can and Should Go Home
Again."

Novelist and short-story writer Nessa Rapoport has created a piece of
short fiction—a meditation of sorts—about an unmarried Jewish woman
who goes home, listens to "Her Mother and Aunt in the Kitchen" (the
title of the story), and measures her life against theirs.[20] Rapoport's
searching, spiritual, consciously Jewish single women—including the heroine of her novel *Preparing for Sabbath* and the narrator of this piece—are

struggling to integrate a separate, strong identity, sought and found with difficulty, with the traditional expectations and family values that the author calls "their mothers' birthright."

It's for single women more than for any others that the question is most distressing: "Is it possible to be Jewish without the Jewish family?" Women who are widowed (and usually beyond middle age) may have a Jewish community of other women through friendships or organizational ties, and sometimes widowed or divorced women have children to be Jewish "for." But unless a never-married Jewish woman or a divorced or widowed woman without children is going to "be Jewish" with her own parents, it's very hard for a woman to find a context in which to be a Jew, especially if she is not Orthodox.

A single Jewish man can walk into any synagogue anywhere in the world and know that he is going to be counted among the worshipers, that his identity as a Jew is never in doubt. For a single woman, unless she is living in a city with a large single population and belongs to one of the small havurah-style egalitarian worship groups, there's no ecological niche, no community, in which she can express her Jewish identity. There are sometimes single (or "career women") groups of Hadassah and other Jewish women's service organizations (see p. 454), but few other ways the single woman can be counted as part of the larger Jewish community.

For poet Diane Levenberg the link between her memories of an Orthodox childhood and her present single state is only an associational thread:

> Friday night then and now is
> Russian music   *challah* crumbs
>   . . . and I
> try to escape this 5,000 year old
> tradition in a grimy bar
> the only connection to my Friday night
> is that I'm still drinking wine[21]

For Orthodox single women the pressures are even greater. Early marriage is the norm in Orthodox communities, and Orthodox women have more stringent views of premarital sex (whether expressed by parents and others or already internalized), face an even smaller pool of eligible Jewish men than other single Jewish women, and have to contend with greater disapprobation from their communities. They're also highly visible as singles, even in a synagogue setting in which women sit separately from men: their hair is uncovered, unlike that of many Orthodox married women, who wear hats or wigs.

The Jewish Mating Game

There is a whole underground—and overground—movement to link up available Jewish single women and men. Maybe because people are living farther from their families of origin and from a natural pool of yentas who used to manage such things, or maybe because the number of mature Jewish singles has never before been so great, but whatever the reason, you can sense the ferment in the *shadchanut* (matchmaking) department. Mothers approach lecturers from other cities to ask about available Jewish men for their single daughters. Brothers ask around at social events, "So who d'you know for my sister?" The rumor is that one California rabbi who travels a lot keeps a notebook with names and addresses of all the single Jews he meets and gives them out to likely members of the opposite sex as he goes from town to town.

RESOURCES

The most successful programs and attempts at bringing single men and women together are the activities that are issue-oriented rather than the painful mixers everyone loves to hate. New York's 92nd Street Y has a Singles Lecture Series, featuring experts whose subjects range from taxes and the single person to "The Resurgence of Antisemitism." Shabbat meals and activities around holiday observances (including services for the High Holy Days) are also part of the Y's programming, which has been described as one of the few programs in which Orthodox men and women can meet.

Orthodox single women are now being helped in the search for mates by their (often married) sisters. For example, Amit Women, the religious women's Zionist organization, alerted to what they call "the plight of the many singles" in New York, has sponsored Saturday-evening programs for "traditional" singles at Congregation Prospect Park in Brooklyn.

Separate High Holiday services and meals for single people are sponsored by one Manhattan synagogue. The havurah of this synagogue also sponsors periodic all-singles Shabbatons—Saturday "retreats," with services, meals, and a controversial speaker guaranteed to incite people to speak out.

Sutton Place Synagogue
225 E. 51 Street
New York, NY 10021
(212) 593-3300

A highly successful program for Jewish singles, sometimes drawing as many as eight hundred participants, is an innovative Friday night synagogue service with guitar-playing singers (rather than cantor and choir) followed by a social hour. The rabbi who started the program says that he's trying to outdraw the local disco as a Friday night meeting place for unattached Jews.

Adas Israel Congregation
2850 Quebec Street, NW
Washington, DC 20008
(202) 362-4433

Other community institutions that become a magnet for single Jews at holiday times are university Hillel Foundations (call your local university and ask to speak to the Hillel director), where many people of postcollege age attend also. Other sources of holiday activity that attract singles and newcomers are services and festivities held at local Y's and Jewish community centers.

If you are a single Jewish woman and new in town, or newly eager to get in touch with a Jewish institution, try looking up the local synagogues in the Yellow Pages, and simply call and ask to speak to the rabbi. Tell him or her what you're looking for and ask if there are services or other programs that would fit your needs. Also look in the Yellow Pages to see if there is a Jewish weekly newspaper. These usually list local events, including special singles programs. The *Long Island Jewish World* in New York, for example, has a whole page of announcements called "The Singles Connection," and a Chicago Jewish paper, *The Sentinel,* runs a similar column on activities for singles. "Alternative" Jewish newspapers, such as Boston's *Genesis 2* and Jewish student newspapers, are also good sources of such listings.

New Jewish Agenda, an organization created by progressive Jews, sponsors groups and discussions for singles through its chapters around the country. Since local groups are in formation, contact the national office for information.

New Jewish Agenda
1123 Broadway, Room 1217
New York, NY 10010
(212) 620-0828

Here are some other programs for Jewish singles, useful if you live in one of these communities but also helpful if you want to set up a singles program and need models or advice.

The Society
Jewish Community Center
8201 Holmes
Kansas City, MO 64131

Jewish Singles Group
Jewish Federation of Lower Bucks County
1 Oxford Valley, Suite 602
Langhorne, PA 19047

Lo-La Jewish Singles
Box 254
Lathrup Village, MI 48076
(303) 356-0949

Almost every city with a Jewish Federation has under its aegis some kind of programming for singles. Call and ask. (See Listings of Federations in the Networking Directory.)

In addition to ongoing local programs, there are several tours—usually to Israel—organized expressly for Jewish singles. The American Jewish Committee and American Jewish Congress both sponsor travel for Jewish singles, and the United Jewish Appeal organizes special missions taking singles Jews to Israel.

UJA Singles Mission
Department of Overseas Programs
United Jewish Appeal
1290 Avenue of the Americas
New York, NY 10104

One woman who has done a careful analysis of programming for Jewish singles—and has run what some say are the most successful singles programs in the country—is Rita Tateel.[22] Tateel claims that "If all the programming is social, you only have them in the community for as long as they're single." She has set up a Young Professionals program in St. Louis which includes married couples. The advantage of such programs is obvious—they take the curse off "singles" events, which often attract more women than men, since for women the Jewish community is "safer" than a singles bar or, sometimes, a blind date. Sophisticated Jews—

women and men—often avoid Jewish singles gatherings, says Tateel, since they are uneasy about the stigma attached to the "meet-market" atmosphere. And "since our culture conveys the notion that people ideally should be able to find their own mates, attempts at matchmaking are often seen to imply at least some personal incompetence," says sociologist Mervin F. Verbit.[23]

Even with programs for singles based on the "interest-group" model, the women who seem to slip through the cracks are older women, whether newly single or never-married. Travel is often for "singles under forty," and groups are formed under such a rubric as "Young Jewish Adults Seminar." One woman writes to the *Jewish Week* in New York complaining: "I am not interested in the paltry few social functions offered for 'older' singles like me (late 50's). I find the dances and weekends demeaning and, yes, depressing—only a notch above the much condemned singles' bars. And since I do not intend to get married again I do not have the desire to join groups specifically designed to find spouses."

For such women one connection to the Jewish community might be through programs such as those now being planned for Jewish singles "40+" as part of New York Federation's Task Force on Jewish Singles, under the auspices of Rabbi Isaac N. Trainin. This committee wants to provide a role for an older Jewish singles group, perhaps with a specific fund-raising goal. The objectives of this group may not be as marriage-oriented as those of younger singles, and until now there have been fewer opportunities for them to participate actively in the Jewish community.

What else might you do if you're single, female, Jewish, and heterosexual and want to meet Jewish men (though there's no guarantee they'll be *mentschen*)?

1. Call Jewish organizations you already belong to and see what programs they sponsor that might interest you. National Council of Jewish Women, for example, has developed a program guide, available from NCJW headquarters, on programs for formerly married singles. (If you are a never-married Jewish woman, you are less likely to have joined these organizations in the first place.)

2. Approach the local Jewish Federation. Just call and ask whoever answers the phone if there are any programs for singles.

3. Start a group yourself. The Society, in Kansas City, a singles group that now has a list of four hundred Jewish singles in the area, was started by someone who went to the Federation with an idea. Try it.

4. Individual rabbis and community *machers* may be good bets. Let them know that you're available. Almost everybody likes to be a *shadchan*

(matchmaker), and rabbis often know more Jews in the community than anybody else does. There have been sad cases of rabbis' making a bad match, so don't assume that a rabbi's suggestion is a *hechsher* (seal of approval) on the relationship—it's just an introduction. A man may be a rat even if the rabbi has introduced him to you.

5. Try resort weekends and other gatherings. Certain kosher resorts, such as those in New York's Catskill Mountains, sponsor Singles Weekends, which have attracted large numbers of unattached Jews since the days of Marjorie Morningstar. Some of the events are organized by the hotels themselves, others by city-based singles groups, ranging from Orthodox singles organizations to such companies as Weekend Rendezvous, Inc., which asks in its ad in the *Long Island Jewish World*, "Looking for a Jewish Club Med?" The industrious people at Rendezvous also run telephone hotlines for party and matchmaking purposes.

The Jewish Singles Partyline
(212) 753-7282

Jewish Singles Date Phone
Men: call (212) 755-3009
Women: call (212) 755-3008

One caveat (at least one!): A recent caller noted that the smooth voice on the Partyline began, "Find out where all the good-looking Jewish singles are finding each other."

DATING SERVICES

At quite a remove from the matchmaker Yente in *Fiddler on the Roof*, dating services try to match eligible women and men on the basis of information the applicants provide. The qualifications of couples are then matched, either by studying the records or feeding them into a computer, to provide each participant with a certain number of prospects.

The Conservative movement has gotten in on the computer dating scene with:

Jewish Singles Introduction Service
Metropolitan NY Council
United Synagogue of America
155 Fifth Ave.
New York, NY 10010
(212) 533-7800

An Orthodox rabbi, unhappy with the high rate of intermarriages involving Jews, has begun a computer dating service that asks detailed questions about the applicant's level of religious observance and about what he or she would like/tolerate in a spouse. He brings compatible people together in groups of ten to twenty and tries to help the participants form social connections as well as matrimonial ones. For information:

Aish HaTorah
Jewish Computer Dating Service
1671 E. 16 Street, Suite 209
Brooklyn, NY 11229
(718) 336-7911

This service is run on a nonprofit basis, with any funds after expenses turned over to Jerusalem's Aish HaTorah Yeshiva.

A service sometimes mentioned in Jewish circles is one that doesn't specialize in Jewish singles and is a profit-making enterprise run by "a trained staff of college professionals":

Professional Dating Service
P.O. Box 181
Brooklyn, NY 11236
(718) 649-6624

Susan Peck, manager of the service, says that of the large numbers of Jewish singles they serve, the majority of women are middle-aged or older, while the majority of Jewish men are quite young.

There is a monthly publication for Jewish singles that also features coded advertisements in its personals column:

National Directory of Jewish Singles
1947 Ocean Avenue
Brooklyn, NY 11230

One nonprofit dating service started by a single Jewish woman and serving Jews only is Chutzpah Unlimited. For $25.00 and a short personal description based on answers to a questionnaire you can be listed in a thrice-yearly directory—blue for men, pink for women—which is sent out to all members of the opposite sex.

Chutzpah Unlimited
P.O. Box 2400
Chicago, IL 60690

CHOOSING WOMEN

The question is not whether lesbianism is a legitimate option for Jewish women—since sexual preference is probably not a matter of choice anyway—but, rather, how lesbian Jews feel about themselves as a subgroup within a larger Jewish context.

If common estimates are accurate, about 3 percent of all Jewish women are lesbians, yet Jewish lesbians have been almost totally invisible among other Jews. From some of the stories of I. B. Singer ("Zeitl and Rickel," for one) we can see lesbians in a Jewish historical context. These examples are few, however, and even among progressive Jews lesbianism is a hidden topic. For example, the most modern of Torah translations and commentaries, the first American translation, published by the Reform movement in 1981, speculates on the psychological groundings of male homosexuality, but says nothing at all about lesbians.[24]

In the Talmud, lesbianism is categorized as a lesser crime than male homosexuality, a mere misdemeanor. And according to Maimonides, the great twelfth-century codifier of Jewish law, a woman who has slept with another woman is not so besmirched that she is forbidden to a Cohen (member of the priestly class) or, if married, to her own husband.

While homosexuality is anathema to the Orthodox, there have been statements of support for homosexual rights from individual Conservative rabbis, and the Reform movement as a whole has been openly supportive of lesbian and homosexual Jews. In 1977 the General Assembly of Reform congregations issued their manifesto on the "Human Rights of Homosexuals." Other rabbis as well—Seymour Siegel and Herschel J. Matt among them—have made respectful comments on the subject, in tones ranging from advocacy to tolerance. While such Orthodox authorities as Maurice Lamm refuse to accept homosexuality in a Jewish context, others have said, with Leo Trepp:

"Homosexuality . . . cannot be regarded as a willful act of religious disobedience. Judaism as such cannot offer formal recognition to the bond that links homosexual persons, nor allow them any special privileges, but it also cannot deny them their Jewishness and the rights and privileges attached to it."[25]

Despite such well-meaning statements, however, many Jewish lesbians report feeling totally alienated, even with family and friends, partly be-

Spontaneous Mon. 10:00

25- Exploring ✡ ♀♀ (Lesbian's) relating to other ✡ Lesbians

Childcare: Issues of Mothers
Room Accessibility + Child[...]

2nd
Conference

CANCEL[...]

AFFINITY GROUPS ~

THESE A[...]
THE ROOM
AVAILABL[...]
SIGN UP FOR
THEM!

FOR MON AM 10:00

And... on stage The Dorothy Paper — Slide show

206 Red Diaper Babies
220 Zionist Caucus
224 Working Class OLDER WOMEN'S
201 Yiddishkeit [...]
[...] Cultural Workers, Artist & Writers OUTSIDE in 230
211 Jews by Choice
364 Livermore Action Block[...]
222 Israeli ♀
[...] 9 ✡ Lesbians with Gentile Lovers
[...] BISEXUAL
10 Fat Lesbians
208 Disabled Women
221 Raised w/o little ✡ Backgrou[...]
Back of And. Non-Zionist 9:30 PM

(© JEB Joan E. Biren)

cause of the male bias in Judaism, partly because of the emphasis of the culture on marriage and children. Some really fear that, as out-of-the-closet lesbians, they don't have a place in their own families or in a "straight" Jewish setting, despite the emergence of a Jewish support group of parents of lesbians and gays (see p. 402). A Jewish lesbian activ-

ist sees this exclusion as the reason for the existence of separate gay congregations: "I think that most gays involved in the shul community want
to be normal, average Jews but can't, because they aren't accepted in
straight shuls. . . . We have tremendous needs to form and maintain
extended families. A lot of us use the synagogue because we have lost our
own families through coming out. . . . If only the Jewish community
would realize that we are still their children."[26]

The alienation is no doubt a contributing factor to the feelings of marginality many Jewish lesbian women report. One such woman, addressing a 1974 conference on changing roles of Jewish women and men, as-
tonished her audience by comparing her outcast state as a lesbian to the
characteristic alienation of the Jews. "What's most lesbian about me is
also what is most Jewish about me."

Reality has reinforced these feelings of marginality and rejection,
proving them no fantasy. When the International Conference of Gay
and Lesbian Jews met in Israel in 1979, opposition came from individuals, from the rabbinate, and from the Jewish National Fund, which tried
to refuse the conference's gift of a large grove of trees.

While others have actively rejected the community that rejects them,
many Jewish lesbians continue to want to participate in Jewish life and
to identify as Jews. Some have expressed their Jewish connection as activists in a wide range of "alternative" Jewish institutions; others have
taken roles as visible Jews in the general women's movement, where
some say that they feel more exposed to anti-Semitism, since they represent a position more radical than that of heterosexual women.

Many lesbians report feelings toward the Jewish community similar in
focus and intensity to the reactions of heterosexual feminists. They feel
outraged not so much because of their invisibility as lesbians as because
of their oppression as women.[27]

Is there a special pain for Jewish women in "coming out" to their families as lesbians? First of all, there is the double whammy of telling parents
that not only is it unlikely that they will have grandchildren produced by
this daughter but, in addition, they'll have to come to terms with her own
sexual and affectional orientation, one totally different from that held up
as the ideal among Jews. If single heterosexual women and childless couples feel guilt and disapprobation from a community trying to reinforce
traditional "Jewish family" values, how much more painful it can be for
all parties when a lesbian reveals herself to her parents. The choice between maintaining no family ties and being less than honest with one's
parents is really a cruel one. One New York woman says that she tries

every year to reconcile herself to the fact that she has to bring her (female) lover to the family's Passover seder in disguise as "a friend."

It may be that, as the woman quoted earlier complains, lesbian and gay synagogues and other institutions are a substitute for what Jewish lesbians would ideally like to see as total support within and from their own families and the general Jewish community. Responses to these congregations from "mainstream" Jewish groups range from total acceptance (from the Reform movement, which has accepted as congregational members some of these synagogues) to official "support" (YM/YWHA's rent them space) to outright disapproval and condemnation. Rabbi Norman Lamm, representing the Orthodox position, has written that "it makes no more sense, Jewishly, than to suffer the formation of synagogues that cater exclusively to idol worshippers, adulterers, gossipers, tax evaders, or Sabbath violators."[28]

Ironically, although lesbians are free of an oppressive homophobic atmosphere in these synagogues, they are often faced with terrible sexism. One woman who some years ago left New York City's gay congregation says, "It was worse than in a traditional shul. These men had never had any friendly dealings with women, and they ran a synagogue that was more sexist than some 'straight' ones I've attended. The men were quite knowledgeable and dominated all the rituals, and even though I felt more at home as a lesbian, as a woman I found the atmosphere intolerable." Similar sentiments have been voiced by women across the country, and breakaway women's groups have emerged from the Chicago and San Francisco gay synagogues.

In some of these congregations, where men and women are not linked by the bonds of mutual attraction or marriage ties, the women—less fearful about breaking out of passive roles than they might be in a heterosexual congregation, and not as dependent on men for approval as heterosexual women—speak out against what they see as male domination of the ritual proceedings. Like other Jewish women, lesbians are angry at the patriarchal bias of the liturgy in the prayers used in some of these synagogues, but this seems to be a problem more amenable to correction or amelioration than the issue of who runs the show.

RESOURCES

For a listing of Jewish lesbian and gay congregations and action groups worldwide, see Networking Directory. See also *Nice Jewish Girls: A Lesbian Anthology*, ed. Evelyn Torton Beck (Persephone Press, 1982), and

Carole Mathews and Sandra Rubenstein, "Lesbian Jews: Reconciling a Dual Identity," unpublished M.A. thesis, Hebrew Union College and Univ. of Southern California, 1980.

Mathews and Rubenstein found that the greatest source of pain for most Jewish lesbians is the traditional attitude that *all* Jewish women are second-class Jews. The subjects of the study reported that they were more disturbed by gender-specific problems in Jewish life than by any Jewish condemnation of their lesbianism. They identified more strongly as Jewish feminists than as homosexuals, and expressed some of the same feelings of exclusion as single heterosexual Jewish women do.

8

◆

MARRIAGE

THE MARRIAGE LAWS

The centrality of marriage in Jewish life is an issue that has caused much friction in recent years between Jews who are single (by choice or by chance) and those who see unmarried Jews (especially those never married) as avoiding the basic obligations and expectations of Jewish peoplehood. Marriage is so much a part of Jewish people's expectations that the prayer said over a newborn child, and again for the Bat/Bar Mitzvah, is: "May s/he enter into Torah, the marriage canopy, and good deeds." This expectation—that marriage is part of a normal life—does have consequences. For example, Jews have higher marriage and remarriage rates and lower divorce rates than non-Jews.[1]

If and when a Jewish woman decides to marry, she may go through the traditional ceremony with less thought for the legal implications of the act itself than for the food or the flowers. This is a mistake. As we shall see, the Jewish marriage laws and ceremonies themselves create a legal connection between wife and husband that is more complicated and consequential than that created by an ordinary civil ceremony performed for non-Jewish marriage partners. And the consequences of the marriage contract are potentially much more radical for the Jewish woman than they are for her spouse.

Since Jewish identity is derived from one's mother, according to most present interpretations of Jewish law (paternity being susceptible to doubt), whom a woman marries, has intercourse with, or is divorced from has implications that the same actions do not have for Jewish men.[2]

באחד

On the first day of the week, the third day of the month of Elul 5742, corresponding to August 22, 1982, in Trenton, New Jersey, the groom, Harlan Mayer, son of George Joseph and Keeva Isaacs, and the bride, Fern Sandra, daughter of Max Solomon and Zelda Goodhart, entered into a covenant of marriage in accordance with the tradition of Moses and the people Israel, saying one to another: "Let us make a marriage covenant. Be my life's partner, and I will cherish you and honor you as is customary among the children of Israel. I will share with you the love of my heart, the substance of my dreams and the fruits of my labors. I will work for our sustenance and will strive with you to realize the best that is within us. Giving thanks to God whose gift of love has united us, let us sanctify our lives through reverence of the Divine, love of Torah, and the performance of good deeds. Behold with this ring you are consecrated unto me according to the law of Moses and the people Israel." In giving it to you, I pledge to you all of my love and devotion."

Bride _____ Groom
Witness _____ Witness
Rabbi _____ הרב

Egalitarian marriage contracts (ketubot) custom-made by calligrapher Betsy Platkin Teutsch. Each couple involved wrote their own contract, in which the bride and groom made reciprocal statements and pledges. (Beryl Goldberg)

On the first day of the week, the seventeenth of Elul 5742, corresponding to the fifth of September, 1982, in the city of Cambridge, Massachusetts, the bride Elizabeth Ann, the daughter of Barbara and Robert Lundeck, and the groom Gary Lloyd, the son of Elise and Jack Gerstle, entered into a covenant of marriage, saying one to another: "Let us make a marriage covenant. Be my life's partner, and I will cherish you and honor you. I will work for our sustenance and strive with you to realize the best that is within us in times of happiness and times of hardship. Let us build together a life of loving-kindness, tolerance, and understanding. With this ring you are consecrated unto me according to the tradition of Moses and the Jewish people. In giving it to you I pledge to you all of my love and my devotion."

Bride _____ Groom
Witness _____ Witness
Rabbi _____ Rabbi

Women examining Jewish marriage and divorce codes may find that their anatomy (or pregnability) is indeed viewed as their destiny. Adultery, for example, is a sin only when the woman involved is married. A married man having intercourse with an unmarried woman is not committing adultery. This is consonant with the idea of adultery as a property crime. One man is violating the property rights of another man, as in the Commandment: "Thou shalt not covet thy neighbor's wife, household, cattle . . ." Sexual relations between two unmarried people are frowned upon but are not associated with the same level of wrongdoing as adultery. (Under strict interpretation of Jewish law a man and a woman who have had intercourse are considered married to each other.)

Regardless of the forces that may enter into any woman's individual choice of spouse, Jewish law is very specific about which potential marriage partners are acceptable and which are not. Most of the laws have to do with maintaining healthy lineage, such as the incest-taboo laws forbidding marriages between close blood relatives, but others derive from a view of women as male property and have to do with keeping that property undefiled.

• A marriage in which either the man or the woman was previously

Joan Mesznik lettering a traditional marriage contract of her own design. (Marilynne Herbert)

married and hasn't obtained a Jewish divorce is not legal. Even if the former marriage was a civil marriage, it's necessary to obtain a Jewish divorce in order to have a Jewish ceremony the second time around. If you ignore this and have a *civil* ceremony for the second marriage, believing that you have thus sidestepped the issue, there may be consequences for any children from the second marriage (see "Divorce," p. 355).

• Children of an adulterous union, including children from the second marriage of a woman whose first marriage was not terminated by a Jewish divorce and who is hence considered to be still married to her first husband, are called *mamzerim*. *Mamzerim*, according to Halachah, cannot marry Jews (though they themselves were born Jewish) but for ten generations can marry only other *mamzerim* or converts to Judaism. The status of "bastard," which is the usual translation of *mamzer*, has nothing to do with being born out of wedlock. A *mamzer* is created only if the mother is pregnant from an adulterous union. No such complications arise in the life of a Jewish father who has not gotten a Halachic divorce, since the status and the legitimacy of the child derive only from the mother. As long as the man's next mate isn't married (that is, doesn't belong to another man), children of that liaison are considered full Jews.

The rabbinate in Israel and, some say, Orthodox rabbis in North America as well, allegedly keep "black books" of marriage and divorce records so that they can check on the legitimacy of newborn Jews.

• Mixed marriages (between Jew and non-Jew) are forbidden. The Jewish marriage contract is considered an agreement between Jewish man, Jewish woman, and God, so it's thought that the contract can't possibly make sense if one partner isn't Jewish. (For more on intermarriage and conversion, see p. 334 and p. 343.)

• A woman whose husband has disappeared without a trace is forbidden to remarry. She is an *agunah*, or chained woman. A man whose wife has disappeared and who wishes to remarry has several options. He can issue her a divorce decree *in absentia*, among other solutions (see Divorce, p. 356).

• A childless widow is not free to remarry without first performing a ceremony known as *chalitzah*, in which she releases her husband's brother from an obligation to marry her and continue the deceased man's line. Unless she performs the ceremony, which includes throwing a shoe at her brother-in-law and spitting at him, the widow is still considered bound to her late husband's family. If she doesn't go through the ceremony and remarries, the offspring of this second marriage are in the category of *mamzerim*.

The ramifications of this situation (created by the laws of levirate marriage), are explored in the film *I Love You, Rosa,* in which a young child-less widow must wait for her brother-in-law, only a child, to reach man-hood before she can release him from the obligation to marry her. Meanwhile she gets older and is neither wife nor single woman again. Al-though perhaps originally intended to help support the widow and keep the line going, the law itself reinforces women's dependent status.

• If the prospective groom is a Cohen, there are even more prohibi-tions. A Cohen was a priest at the holy Temple in Jerusalem, and still has certain ritual responsibilities in the synagogue today. Since one is a Cohen if one's father is/was a Cohen, there's an attempt to keep the line of de-scent very pure. Under Orthodox Judaism a male Cohen may not marry a divorced woman, or one who has been widowed and gone through the *chalitzah* ceremony, or a convert to Judaism, or a woman who has co-habited with a non-Jew or with a *mamzer,* or a woman who has been taken captive by non-Jewish soldiers (!). Some authorities say a Cohen may marry a woman who has had a lesbian relationship. A female Cohen (daughter of a Cohen) *may* marry a convert. Non-Orthodox Judaism permits the same marriages to Cohanim as to other Jews, since they are considered not to fulfill any actual priestly role in our time.

• Marriages arranged without the consent of the partners are forbid-den, though that has not stopped the subtle pressure on Jewish women to make marriages advantageous to the family. A tale told in many fami-lies is of a legendary relative, betrothed against her will, who ran away on her wedding night.

• People who are so incapacitated that they don't understand the mar-riage vows or contract cannot marry, nor can a eunuch or an impotent man, though sterile people may.

• All women (though only some men) are forbidden to marry if they are already married. Ashkenazi men, usually of European descent, are under a ban issued nearly a thousand years ago (and expiring in the year 2000) forbidding them to have more than one wife. The ban is not bind-ing on Sephardic men, who have often lived in countries where polygamy was practiced. (For example, Yemeni Jewish men had more than one wife even as late as the first half of this century.) By contrast, polyandry (having more than one husband) was never part of Jewish practice and has always been forbidden.

Interpretations of the law change as new circumstances create new questions. For example, in a collection of Reform responsa (rabbinic re-plies to queries about religious law), one rabbi was queried by another as to whether it was permissible to marry a couple where one member was a transsexual. (The response was as ambiguous as the sexuality.)

What are the implications of all these concepts for most contemporary Jewish marriages?

Nonobservant Jews not living in Israel may see the laws surrounding Jewish marriage and women as mere curiosities or examples of the ways in which women have been viewed through the ages. The problem is that they may affect their future lives in ways undreamed of now.

First of all, in Israel—where Orthodox Jewish law *is* the civil law code for Jews, and the only determinant of the laws of "personal status" such as marriage and divorce law—many couples whose marriages fall into the "prohibited" category must go out of the country to marry.

With the rising number of American Jews who are becoming more religious, and with the higher birthrate among the Orthodox, there's a greater likelihood than ever before that someone with "uncertain lineage"—for instance, one born of a mother who had not converted to Judaism before the birth (see Conversion, p. 344)—might want to marry an observant Jew. Because we hear so much more about those people who marry non-Jews, most of us haven't thought too much about the *legal* implications when a Jewish woman who has lived a fairly assimilated American existence—possibly with one or more marriages, one or more lovers before or after marriage—chooses to marry a man who is more Jewishly observant than she. The potential personal and legal conflicts are many. Women have described everything from terrible guilt at finding themselves in violation of laws most of them never even knew existed, with no chance of making "restitution" or undoing their own past, to fury at finding themselves culpable (and sometimes actually forbidden to marry) because of these violations.

Are all the pain and confusion and divisiveness among Jews necessary just to effect the enforcement of the marriage laws? That depends on your point of view. Maintaining the bonds one Jew must feel with another Jew is part of Judaism, along with the idea that being Jewish may require maintaining the purity and/or unity of the Jewish people. But if women are alienated in large numbers from mainstream Judaism, the greater good is *not* served by a rigid application of these laws.

MARRIAGE: THE PROCESS

In one book about Jewish law the section on marriage is entitled "Acquiring a Wife." In fact, the marriage contract is an act of acquisition by the man. Woman's passive and dependent role is continued in several aspects of the marriage contract and ceremony, as they are traditionally constituted. The man writes the woman a *ketubah*, or contract, in which he usually spells out what she has brought to the marriage and what will be returned to her if they divorce or if he dies first. It also makes explicit his obligation to support her.

In the ceremony itself the man gives the woman a gold ring (one without jewels, since the worth of jewels could not be determined easily) as part of the bargain. Double-ring ceremonies are not performed in Orthodox and usually not in Conservative ceremonies; the bride need not give the groom an object of value, because *he* is "acquiring" *her* in exchange for the ring, not the other way around.

Woman's dependency in marriage is demonstrated in another part of the ceremony also. Rabbi Daniel B. Syme discusses why a bride wears a veil in the traditional ceremony. "One beautiful interpretation asserts that just as one often covers one's eyes during the *Shema* as an expression of concentration upon and trust in God, so does a bride cover her eyes as a symbol of trust in her husband."[3] Needless to say, there is no parallel tradition of having the bridegroom put himself into such a completely dependent and helpless position!

One way around some of the inequities for women in the traditional marriage contract and ceremony is for couples to write their own. There is a long tradition of individualized marriage contracts in Judaism, with couples putting in clauses that usually had to do with the financial transactions preceding or accompanying the marriage. Increasingly, among Jews eager for their marriages to start off on an egalitarian footing, yet wanting to stay within some Halachic guidelines, conditions are being written into the standard Jewish marriage contract that eliminate some of the problems for women under Jewish marriage law. One such condition is the Berkovits *t'nai*, named after Rabbi Eliezer Berkovits, who initially developed it. If written into the standard Jewish marriage contract, Berkovits' clause eliminates the possibility that the wife might become an agunah and the problems of a woman whose husband refuses to issue her a Jewish divorce. A paraphrase of the operative clause states: "If we live separately for X years and no *get* [Jewish bill of divorcement] is forthcoming, or if either of us is not mentally capable of giving or receiving a *get* and we have not been in contact for X years, then this marriage contract is retroactively null and void."

Rabbi Irving Greenberg, Director of the National Jewish Resource Center and a leader in "modern" Orthodoxy, went so far as to suggest in the early 1970s that women should participate in the selection process of a congregational rabbi to make sure that he (and now she) would use the Berkovits contract when performing marriages.[4]

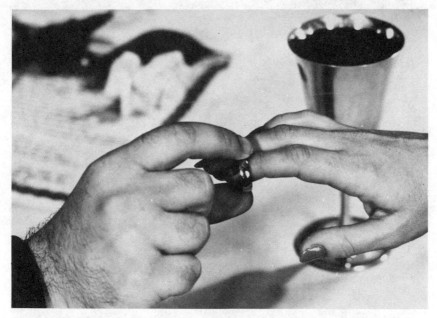

(from *A Seal Upon Thy Heart: Portrait of Modern Jewish Marriage*, Halcyon Films, a division of Spielman-Magilnick Communications, Inc.)

While signing a "conditional" marriage contract of this sort doesn't cancel out the problems in the law itself, it provides a way around the discriminatory aspects of marriage and divorce law as they are presently interpreted. The main problem is that most Orthodox rabbis refuse to use these conditional documents in a ceremony at which they officiate.

RESOURCES

Responding to the inherently inequitable language and structure of the marriage ceremony in all denominations of Judaism, couples and women rabbis themselves have taken to writing their own ceremonies. For copies of the ceremonies one rabbi has written, which she uses wherever possible, contact:

Rabbi Karen L. Fox
1155 South Alvira Street
Los Angeles, CA 90035
(213) 938-8120

For Jewish couples who want to personalize their marriage contract

A Jerusalem bride. (Barbara Gingold)

and embellish (or equalize, where possible) the traditional format, the Jewish Women's Resource Center in New York has an entire looseleaf file of "egalitarian" *ketubot*, including many in which the bride, flying in the face of custom, actually has a speaking role! Also at the Resource Center is an M.A. thesis by Susan Winter Young which will be useful to anyone researching the legal and traditional aspects of the *ketubah*: "An Annotated Bibliography of Books and Articles on the Jewish Marriage Contract" (1978).

If you would like to have a handwritten illuminated *ketubah* for your own wedding or as a gift for someone, you can contact many scribes and specialists in creating original Jewish marriage contracts. The creation of *ketubot* has been a burgeoning Jewish art form in the past decade, and a number of scribes, in various locations, advertise in local and national Jewish periodicals. Try to pick an artist near you so that you can see examples of her work before placing your order. Check Mae Shafter Rockland's *The New Jewish Yellow Pages* (New York: SBS Publishing, 1980) for names of scribes.

There is a very simple outline of marriage laws and customs, especially useful for delineating the different marriage ceremonies used in various branches of Judaism:

Marriage in Jewish Life and Tradition: A Mini-Course
by Rabbi Raymond A. Zwerin and Audrey Friedman Marcus
Alternatives in Religious Education
3945 South Oneida Street
Denver, CO 80237

THE MARRIED COUPLE

In religious Judaism the person who remains unmarried is considered to be less than a complete human being, since marriage, and sex according to medieval Jewish mystics, within marriage, unite male and female aspects of God. The married couple is not just an economic union or a child-producing operation.

Given this exalted view of marriage, the couple (especially the woman) is expected to make every effort to keep the relationship on an even keel, free from potential disruptions. In this context there are several specifically Jewish angles to the couple relationship in Jewish life:

Shalom Bayit—The Jewish Wife as Peacekeeper
Since the Jewish home is supposed to be the utopia where all oppression suffered in the outside world disappears, the concept of a peaceful home is crucial to understanding the expectations that Jewish culture has for the married couple. Even today, in rabbinic courts in America and Israel, women coming to rabbis with complaints about their husbands, or requesting assistance in getting a divorce, are told to return home for the sake of *shalom bayit* (the peace of the household). In an inadvertently funny transliteration of the Ashkenazic pronunciation, a pamphlet on marriage counseling issued by a Jewish agency talks about *"shalom bias."* There is indeed such a bias, not only in the customs but in the approach to marital difficulties traditionally taken by rabbis and Jewish organizations.

(Bill Aron)

The Partnership Model

The internal politics of a Jewish marriage are often quite different from the inequities of Jewish marriage laws, reflecting differences between day-to-day reality and the idealized, legalistic view of a married couple. This is not to say that Jewish marriages are free from the same inequalities that feminists have been pointing out in marriage generally. But more so than in some cultures, the relationship between wife and husband in Jewish law, tradition and—especially—practice is based on a partnership model.

The marriage contract and other writings on marriage spell out the husband's obligation to provide materially and sexually for his wife, while she is expected to provide household services, either by her own labor or through the servants she has brought with her. It's difficult to know whether or not the sexual obligations have been fulfilled. But the division of labor has, in twentieth-century North America at least, been very close to what was set out in the contract—right down to the power imbalance that is sometimes struck when one party has very specific duties ("make money; support your family") and the other party has to pick up the slack (and the socks).

Despite the open expression of conflict in many Jewish marriages (or perhaps because of it), there appears to be a fairly equal exchange on a verbal level, reinforcing the partnership concept as the model for Jewish married couples, at least for Jews of Eastern European descent. One of the paradoxes of Jewish marriages may be that even in families in which husband and wife abide by traditional role divisions, each sees the other as an equal. This perceived equality may, in fact, be a hallmark of many Jewish marriages.[5]

In *The Jewish Wife*, by Gwen Gibson Schwartz and Barbara Wyden, a 1969 study of Jewish wives based on anecdotal interviews, one of the recurring themes was that husbands and wives used each other as sounding boards, often discussed business or professional problems with each other, and appeared to be more supportive of each other in many ways than non-Jewish couples. By contrast, while Jewish women expect that their husbands will be their best friends, in "ethnic," non-Jewish working-class families women expect to have a network of women friends and most often do not expect friendship from their husbands.

Clearly the expectations for marriage are different for women of different backgrounds, and Jewish women, when asked what they would like in a prospective mate, answer, "Someone I can talk to."

One researcher reveals another difference in the marriages of Jewish women and other women. Italian and Slavic women place significantly higher value on caring for family as a source of self-worth than Jewish women: "The low percentage of Jewish women who report feelings of usefulness from caring for family indicates a devaluation of the family role among Jewish women. This devaluation has been noted by professionals and viewed as a probable source of conflict and of disruption in Jewish family life."[6]

On the other hand, more Jewish women rated marriage more important than career.

The growing number of Jewish two-career (as opposed to two-job) couples has made for a certain kind of strain on Jewish marriages. (For some insights into the consequences of this, see "Responding to the Childbearing Imperative," p. 374.)

Two-career marriage would seem to be the ideal partnership situation, with woman and man sharing all tasks and not dividing them up according to gender. In reality, there are certain undeniable conflicts. One woman, anxious and angry, stood up in the discussion session at a New Jersey conference on Jewish women's changing roles in the family and

(Gay Block)

said: "My husband makes so much more money than I do that his work takes on more importance than mine, *in both of our minds*, even though on the surface it seems that we agree that our careers are equally important. Like a lot of Jewish women, I guess, I got tracked into a career—social work—that just doesn't pay as much as my husband's. So it seems somehow reasonable, in a crazy way, that *I* should be the one to make most of the sacrifices—for instance, to rush away from work to pick up the kids in a crisis."

Jewish women, the recipients of at least some of the same conditioning as their brothers received, are now entering professional life (or at least graduate schools) in great numbers—in fact, informal reports suggest that nearly half the women at the nation's top professional schools (law, medicine, business) are Jewish. So the two-career-marriage phenomenon will be felt proportionally even more strongly among Jews than in the general population. One Jewish agency has already prepared a study on child-care alternatives for the two-career family (see "Responding to the

Childbearing Imperative," p. 394). Others have created programs dealing with the problems women and men face in this marriage situation. For example, a panel discussion titled "Two-Career Marriages—Making It Work," has both men and women as panelists, reinforcing the idea that the solutions to intrafamilial conflict will not have to be women's alone.

As roles change there is a "snowball" effect. Each couple able to make some progress toward equalizing their roles in a marriage gathers other adherents of equality; those who successfully integrate feminist values become role models for others. A male rabbi in a nurturing role with his wife or children will, one hopes, demonstrate attitudes and actions that will influence his congregants in a positive way. While the women's movement (and what are thought to be exclusively women's demands for equality) have been blamed in the past for causing disruptions in family life, in fact the dissolution of patriarchal or unrealistic expectations will more likely increase marital harmony, since a relationship founded on oppression wreaks its own havoc in resentment, withdrawal and depression.

At least one professional in the Jewish community is optimistic about the evolving nature of egalitarianism in Jewish marriages. Harry Graber, of the Philadelphia Jewish Family Service, says: "I am very sure that only in equality can couples find stability. I don't believe we can return to the traditional Jewish family model, because it no longer exists, but we can rediscover traditional Jewish values, like ethical human relations and mutual respect."[7]

RESOURCES

These are two films that deal with contemporary Jewish marriage itself, one from the point of view of tradition, and one from a more radical perspective:

A Seal Upon Thy Heart: A Portrait of Modern Jewish Marriage
Alden Films
7820, 20 Avenue
Brooklyn, NY 11214

This offers background material on the ceremonies of the traditional Jewish marriage, with personalized accounts through the preparations of a young Orthodox couple. According to its distributors, the film "provides us with the feeling for the Jewish wedding as an essential element in the planning and building of a successful Jewish marriage."

We Get Married Twice
Jewish Media Service
15 E. 26 Street
New York, NY 10010

Medium, the Jewish Media Service Newsletter, summarizes this film: "Two Jewish young people who have been living together for several years decide to get married in a private, personalized, highly eclectic fashion. A second, more traditionally Jewish wedding is then held to please their families, though for the couple it is a painful ordeal."

Jewish Support Systems for Couples

In almost every Jewish community there is counseling (usually much cheaper than private help) for individuals and for couples who are experiencing marital conflict and for people seeking clarification about issues that bother them in their marriages. To find out where to go for such support in your area, consult the Networking Directory for the listings of Jewish family and children's agencies across the continent. Here are highlights of some innovative programs for married couples.

A service dealing with the special problems of remarried couples, who may have "blended" families consisting of children from previous marriages, is used mainly by Jewish families ("from secular to Chassidic") but is open to everyone. It provides both educational/preventive and therapeutic programs. The educational supports include weekly discussion groups for remarried couples or those considering remarriage; there are also educational groups for whole families and for adolescents.

Remarried Consultation Service
Jewish Board of Family and Children's Services
120 W. 57 Street
New York, NY 10019
(212) 582-9100

Also in the category of "preventive psychiatry," is a course that focuses on "two major areas of concern and potential conflict in a relationship—sex and money."

"In Support of Marriage"
Group Services Division
92nd Street YM/YWHA
1395 Lexington Avenue at 92 Street
New York, NY 10028
(212) 427-6000

A parallel course, but broader in scope and open only to those planning marriage is:

Engaged Couples Seminar
Jewish Community Center
60 S. River Street
Wilkes Barre, PA 18701
(717) 824-4646

Los Angeles has become the first community in the United States to provide a program offering the opportunity for premarital support and education to all Jewish couples preparing to marry or recently married. The brochure has a very telling introduction: "You've been well trained for your career. But have you been taught the skills of 'husband' and 'wife'?" Run by a rabbi and a marriage counselor, the ten-session program discusses money, sex, career-family conflicts, in-laws, remarriage, the works.

Making Marriage Work
The University of Judaism
Department of Continuing Education
15600 Mulholland Drive
Los Angeles, CA 90024
(213) 476-9777

One encouraging factor in the counseling offered by secular Jewish agencies is the attempt now being made on the part of largely nonreligious Jewish social workers and psychologists to be sensitive to the family structure and needs of religious Jews who use their services. Religiously observant Jewish women need not fear, as they might have feared even five years ago, that they would be condemned by mental-health professionals or labeled neurotic because of their religious practices, such as adhering to the strict ritual role divisions in Orthodox religious practice or following the laws regulating sex in marriage (see "Our Bodies," p. 219).

A Jewish marriage "experience" that is definitely not run by professionals is the grass-roots Jewish Marriage Encounter. Geared to already married couples who "want to make a good marriage better," Jewish Marriage Encounter (like its Christian prototype), runs weekend encounters (Sunday-Monday, so as not to conflict with Shabbat), with the goal of helping couples improve communication. The encounter takes place within the context of Jewish symbols and values and is led by a rabbinic couple and a lay couple. For contact people from whom you can learn more about the process and the schedule of encounter weekends in your area, see the Networking Directory (p. 572).

INTERMARRIAGE

There's no doubt that the marriage of a Jew to a non-Jew is seen as a threat to Judaism and to the survival and growth of the Jewish people. Sociologist Egon Mayer calls intermarriage "the cardinal social offense that an individual Jew can commit against his [sic] family and community."[8] In fact, the offense may be more than merely symbolic, since couples of whom only one member is Jewish tend to do less in the way of Jewish observance and support of Jewish institutions than do all-Jewish couples. In addition, the birth rate among the intermarried is even lower, according to one study, than it is for the Jews as a whole—a reflection, perhaps, of the conflicts the marriage partners themselves see when they contemplate having children.

Intermarriage, even when the partners are a Jewish man and a non-Jewish woman, is a Jewish woman's problem for two reasons. First, more men than women marry "out," thereby reducing the pool of eligible Jewish men for Jewish women to marry. Secondly, the mother of the intermarrying child is often blamed for the "defection," or blames herself, since in Jewish family life it's the mother who allegedly transmits Jewish culture and values.

There's an additional, attitudinal, difference when it's Jewish women who are marrying out of the faith. There is a special category in Jewish law (and often in contemporary Jewish thinking as well) for a Jewish woman who has been involved with a non-Jewish man. Why is the contact between Jewish women and non-Jewish men seen as so threatening? Because women were and still are seen as the property of their families (read "fathers or husbands"), and the fear is that they will find the men of the majority culture more attractive. Since Jewish women who intermarry still have children who are considered halachically Jewish, and statistically do more to keep their homes Jewish than do Jewish men who intermarry, intermarriage by Jewish women represents not so much the potential loss of Jews but a loss of status and power to the ruling majority. This is why, despite the fact that for the Jewish birthrate it should be *less* distressing when a woman intermarries, the opposite is true.

Facing the fact that many of the men she was interested in were non-Jews and that no available Jewish men were on her horizon, one woman asked her rabbi's advice. His reply was: Date non-Jews, and when you find one you want to marry, have him convert. "That way you'll be creating another Jew."

Gratz College sociologist Rela Geffen Monson describes the situation of Jewish women who marry non-Jews as:

"The Case of the Reluctant Exogamists"

One striking example of the intermarriage statistics, whether from early in this century or the present day, is that between two and four times as many men marry out as women. Many authors have written about this trend, but few provide theoretical explanations for it. In most cases, it is dismissed with a few words, and where explained at any length is interpreted as a rejection of Jewish women by Jewish men.

These "blame the Jewish woman" explanations result partially from asking the wrong question. The analysts have asked, "Why is the intermarriage rate for Jewish men so high?" Then, after posing this incorrect question, they have gone on to blame Jewish women (mothers and potential wives) for what Jewish men do!

We should ask instead, "Why is the rate for women so low?" Posing *this* question, we can examine possible explanations of this important sex-linked difference, and then analyze the potential impact of the women's movement in the United States on the rate of female Jewish intermarriage.

At least two factors would lead the naïve observer to suppose that Jewish women would, in fact, be more prone to exogamy than Jewish men. First, the sex ratio among Jews in several age groups favors men in the marriage market; especially for ages 25–39 there are more women than men in the Jewish population. Since women have traditionally been more dependent upon marriage than men, both for their identity and their economic survival, we would expect that, faced with the probability of spinsterhood, they would choose intermarriage over the single life.

A second reason to suppose that Jewish women might marry out more than Jewish men is that, according to Jewish law, a child's religion is determined by the religion of the mother. Thus the fact that a woman marries out does not affect the Jewish affiliation of her children, while an exogamous Jewish man must have a spouse who has converted before the birth of their children, or must have the children formally converted after birth, for them to be considered Jewish. One would therefore expect stronger sanctions against exogamy for men than for women, whose out-marriage doesn't threaten group survival to the same degree.

Why is it then that Jewish women have been so reluctant to intermarry?

What are the structural and attitudinal factors built into their life experiences such that their intermarriage rate as a group is retarded? These impeding factors surely include the structure of the Jewish family together with the prevalence of traditional sex-role distinctions guiding the socialization process. *Sons* can fulfill their parents' expectations through educational and occupational success. The legend of "my son the doctor" and the sacrifices which parents make to assure the actualization of this dream are well known. Sons are also expected to marry and provide future "nachas" in the form of Jewish grandchildren, but parents find it difficult to abandon "my son the intermarried doctor," since he is still fulfilling parental expectations in other ways.

On the other hand, daughters are not necessarily expected to "make it" in the occupational world. "Success" for a nice Jewish girl has been defined as marriage to an educated Jewish man who could support her in the proper style, and close oversight of daughters in the courting years has effectively limited the possibility of their forming close relationships with non-Jewish men.

Further reinforcing daughters' early and suitable marriage is the fact that while it is generally difficult to function in the Jewish community as a single person, it is even harder for women.

Finally, the general closeness of daughters to their families was expected to carry over to married life. Intermarriage would therefore not only be a "failure" for the Jewish daughter but would also cut her off from anticipated and accepted future warm ties with her nuclear family. These ties are not projected as strongly for sons, who have been shown to extend their loyalty to the nuclear family into the broader community of all Jews.

As of 1971, the predominance of male exogamy still held in the American Jewish community. Fred L. Massarik and Alvin Chenkin, in reporting the findings of the *National Jewish Population Survey*, found that what had been true fifty and one hundred years ago was still the operative pattern: twice as many Jewish men marry "out" as Jewish women. (Recent figures suggest that the reservoir thus created of Jewish women who won't find Jewish men to marry is causing the difference to diminish.)

How about the impact of the women's movement on the future rates? We have traced much of the low incidence of intermarriage by Jewish women to sex-role definitions which are reinforced through familial and societal structures which limit women's paths to success and access to the outside social world. However, the legitimation of these sex-role differentiations has been challenged by the feminist movement.

With the exception of Orthodox institutions, the role of women in

Jewish communal structures, religious and secular, has broadened. Moreover, with three-quarters of Jewish women of college age in the university milieu—where the breakdown of sex-roles is greatest—it is highly unlikely that the traditional structural barriers restricting interaction with non-Jewish men will persist.

What of the strong parental expectations which so powerfully acted on Jewish women? We suspect that as women enter and succeed in the professional world in increasing numbers (as probably well over half of Jewish women in their late twenties are now doing), parents will reward that success more. More importantly, daughters will be less dependent on parental validation of their identity, and will thus be less susceptible to their push toward suitable marriage.

With the disappearance of the structural props minimizing the rate of intermarriage among Jewish women and the lessening of dependence upon suitable marriage as the sole validator of their worth, we can anticipate an increase in the Jewish wife/non-Jewish husband intermarriage rate. Egon Mayer and Carl Sheingold suggest in their summary report of a study of intermarried couples after their marriages [see below] that this process has already begun. Though their sample was not representative, their study shows equal numbers of male and female exogamists. . . .

It is certain that we can no longer take for granted the continuation of the historical phenomenon that Jewish *men* are more likely to intermarry. The low rate for women resulted from structural factors and traditional sex-role definitions and *not* from some innate attachment to Judaism unique to women.[9]

In one fictional Scottish Jewish family, here's what happened after the daughter eloped with a non-Jewish man: "Grandfather and Grandmother Perlson with all the six brothers then arranged the Sheeva, the week of mourning. . . . When people came to offer their sympathies, the family talked about their sister Helena as though she were dead. . . . They never saw Helena again. To them their daughter was literally dead."[10]

One woman, now married to a Jew, says that she would have married her non-Jewish college sweetheart except for her mother's reaction. "She said she'd put her head in the oven and turn on the gas if I married him." Another woman, entering college, says that her father insisted that she leave their small town, which has a fine university, to go to an East Coast college. "He said that our university was predominantly non-Jewish and, in his words, 'You can't marry someone you haven't met.' "

Not all parental responses are negative. After observing her daughter's single life for some time, one Jewish mother said: "She is better off married to a non-Jew than she would be if she had never married."[11] Inter-marriage may be less threatening—both to women and to their families—after a woman has reached the age of thirty-five. There are likely to be fewer children, if any, and the woman's own Jewish identity may be more secure than it was when she was younger.

Family responses to a daughter's intermarriage will vary, to be sure, but the strength of the disapprobation seems to vary inversely with the number of intermarriages the family has experienced intimately. For this reason, traditionalist rabbis often warn congregants to boycott such wedding celebration.

Some Jews take on personal responsibility for intermarriages in a larger fashion than just exercising sanctions against their own children who in-termarry. The hostess for a Shabbat dinner to which an intermarried couple was invited admitted that she would never have invited them if they hadn't already been married, because she wouldn't have wanted to cement the relationship and she wouldn't have wanted her children to think she sanctioned such a union.

What messages do the children of intermarriage get from their parents, even if they are being raised as Jews? That Judaism isn't good enough for Daddy? That Daddy isn't good enough for Judaism? An intermarriage in which the non-Jewish partner does not convert—sometimes called "mixed marriage"—certainly does dilute the strength of the children's connection with Judaism, no matter how hard the born-Jewish parent may try to provide a Jewish context. Sociologist Mervin Verbit says that the family's life and the community itself is weakened "by introducing a religious heterogeneity into both the nuclear and the extended family which keeps the family from being the context for full and enthusiastic transmission of Jewish life-styles."[12]

Since non-Jewish husbands of Jewish women are not likely to convert to Judaism, the Jewish woman who has intermarried has to bear the full responsibility of being the family's Jew—the educator, the sole adult Jewish presence in the household—and this while being a woman who in all likelihood never had much chance to get familiar with Jewish ritual herself. (For material on how to "do things Jewish" if you are the only Jewish parent, see "From Observer to Participant," p. 60, and "Rhythms and Cycles," p. 84.)

Who Marries "Out"?

Although any composite portrait of the Jewish woman who marries a non-Jew is not going to be accurate for every case, these are some broad observations of investigators in the field:

• Jewish women, like Jewish men, are more likely to marry non-Jews if they had little or no intensive Jewish education, experiences in Israel, or Jewish summer camps and youth movements. (But beware. Rabbi Richard Israel, Hillel rabbi in Boston, reminds parents that Herzl, Weizmann, and Ben-Gurion all had children who married non-Jews.)[13]

• Unlike Jewish men who intermarry, Jewish women who do don't necessarily have a history of dating non-Jewish men. Often the woman who intermarries is marrying the only non-Jewish man she has dated.[14]

• At least in North America, the Jewish woman marrying out is not also marrying up. She tends to marry a non-Jewish man of equal or similar education, economic level, and social class. The same is not true of Jewish men, who when they intermarry tend to marry women whose fathers, according to one study, have less education than the husbands and are usually of lower socioeconomic status.

• Although more Jewish men than women have traditionally married non-Jews, in one category Jewish women's rate of intermarriage exceeds that of men: more Jewish women than men marry blacks. Graenum Berger cites one study of black-white marriages in New York in which 50 percent of the white partners were Jews, most of them women.[15] In another study, this one of choices if one *had* to intermarry by race or religion, white Jewish men preferred to marry white Christians by a ratio 2 : 1, while white Jewish women split 50–50, with half preferring to marry black Jews and half white Christians.

• A special case are those Jews who have been divorced from Jewish spouses and who have remarried non-Jews. In some situations of this sort Judaism is rejected along with the rejected first spouse, and the sources of conflict in the first marriage are projected onto all Jewish men (or, in the case of a Jewish man in a second marriage, projected onto all Jewish women). Often the remarrying Jew imagines that the relationship with a non-Jew will be free of the difficulties that characterized the endogamous marriage.

Some of the same negative projections are found among Jews who are uncomfortable with their Jewishness, as the ethnotherapy work done by Dr. Judith Weinstein Klein has uncovered (see p. 439). In a videotape of the group sessions Klein has conducted, an unmarried Jewish woman announces that one of the reasons she was participating in the group was to find out "why Jewish men are not sexually attractive to me." Irving Levine, Director of the Institute on Pluralism and Group Identity of the American Jewish Committee, which has sponsored much of Klein's work, comments that "the most dramatic thing in the film is the sexual turning-off and its implications for intermarriage."

RESOURCES

The comprehensive study of the factors affecting intermarriage rates in a pluralistic society is Louis A. Berman, *Jews and Intermarriage: A Study in Personality and Culture* (South Brunswick, NJ, Thomas Yoseloff, 1968).

Other valuable resources on the mounting rates of intermarriage among Jewish women and some of the solutions proposed to deal with intermarriage among all Jews:

Intermarriage and the Jewish Future: A National Study in Summary
by Egon Mayer and Carl Sheingold
The American Jewish Committee, Institute of Human Relations
165 E. 56 Street
New York, 10022
$1.50

A companion to this is the 1983 pamphlet by Mayer, *Children of Intermarriage*.

One study of 446 intermarried couples around the U.S. resulted in some unexpected findings: intermarriage didn't seem to cause major disagreement and conflict between the spouses; extended family ties weren't cut; intermarried couples were less likely to give their children any formal Jewish education. How to respond to intermarriage is one of the subjects of:

"Intermarriage Among American Jews: Consequences, Prospects, and Policies"
by Egon Mayer
Policy Studies '79
National Jewish Resource Center
250 W. 57 Street, Suite 216
New York, NY 10019
$1.50

In this policy study, Mayer puts forth some provocative and original suggestions for community responses to intermarriage, including conversion outreach centers, greater involvement of Jewish grandparents with the children of an intermarried couple, and the "naturalization" (rather than conversion) of non-Jews married to secular Jews.

Women who are interested in discussing intermarriage have been assured of a sympathetic response by the:

Conversion Course Office
New York Federation of Reform Synagogues
838 Fifth Avenue
New York, NY 10021

Rabbis here do not officiate at intermarriages themselves but refer couples to rabbis who do.

Rabbi Burt Siegel, who teaches one of the conversion courses for the New York Federation of Reform Synagogues, says of intermarriage, "I do not see it as any kind of betrayal of Jewishness at all. As long as people take the trouble to seek out a rabbi, they should be treated kindly." His address:

Rabbi Burt Siegel
445 E. 65 Street, Apt. 4A
New York, NY 10021

If You Are Marrying a Non-Jew

There is no way at present that a marriage between a Jew and a non-Jew can be considered, in Halachic terms, to be a "Jewish" marriage. There is a great deal of debate in the Jewish community on how to deal with interfaith couples who approach a rabbi to marry them. Orthodox, Conservative, Reconstructionist, and most Reform rabbis will not perform such a ceremony. Other Reform rabbis state that being turned away from the *chuppah* (marriage canopy) turns the couple away from Judaism for life. These rabbis believe that every attempt should be made to keep the intermarried couple in the fold right from the start, particularly since about one-third of all converts in an intermarriage convert to Judaism after the marriage—leaving hope that if other Jews are receptive to the couple, conversion may occur at a later date.

Conversion of the non-Jewish partner before the marriage would solve the problem, but often someone who is considering marriage to a non-Jew isn't very religious and doesn't feel comfortable making what she might regard as a "hypocritical" demand of her fiancé. Conversion presents another problem: there is supposed to be no coercion involved, and if someone is converting for the sake of marrying a Jew, then the element of free choice is compromised. (For a discussion of the laws and process of Conversion, see p. 344.)

Some rabbis counsel against a Jewish marriage for an interfaith couple and say that the couple should not take personally the refusal of many rabbis to perform such a ceremony. The rabbis will always be available for counseling and approaches of any sort but just cannot perform the marriage. One rabbi suggests instead a completely secular marriage: "A couple civilly married can always adjust their religious allegiances, whereas a wedding performed by a rabbi may lull the couple into a sense of rightness that can preclude continued search and possible solution."[16] Well, of course that is the view of a rabbi who hopes that the search will continue. Many intermarried couples complain of feeling utterly rejected by Jewish religious authorities whom they've approached.

If your fiancé or fiancée is not converting, there are some ways you can arrange a wedding with some Jewish content or atmosphere. Such a ceremony will not wipe away the "invalid" nature of the marriage under Jewish law, but these suggestions at least keep the couple in a Jewish "holding pattern."

(Dennis Francis, courtesy *Long Island Jewish World*)

REFORM RABBIS

While the official position of Reform Judaism is that for a Jewish marriage both couples should be Jewish, there have been many accommodations made so that interfaith couples who do want to be married in a Jewish context, or even to have a Reform Jewish wedding, complete with rabbi, will not be turned away. There are individual Reform rabbis around the world who do perform intermarriages, although the criteria they use to decide whether or not to perform the ceremony vary from rabbi to rabbi and couple to couple. Some rabbis require that the non-Jewish partner take a conversion course, even if he or she does not intend to convert; others require the couple to promise to raise the children as Jews (one rabbi who used to require this pledge no longer does, feeling that couples can't really be held to it); still others will perform the ceremony only if the partners seem sincere in their desire for a Jewish wedding and are not planning it merely in the hope of, as one rabbi put it, "placating angry parents."

For an up-to-date list of Reform rabbis who will officiate at an intermarriage (annotated to let you know if there are specific requirements that must be filled before a given rabbi will perform the ceremony), write or phone:

Rabbi Irwin Fishbein
Rabbinic Center for Research and Counseling
128 E. Dudley Avenue
Westfield, NJ 07090
(201) 233-0419

In addition to sending the list with its 160 names, Rabbi Fishbein will respond to requests from people seeking rabbis in geographical areas not on the list, since there are Reform rabbis who are willing to officiate at an intermarriage but unwilling to be listed.

The caveat in all these situations is that intermarriages in which the non-Jewish partner hasn't converted are not recognized as Jewish marriages in other denominations, even if the ceremony has been performed by a Reform rabbi.

CIVIL MARRIAGE WITH A JEWISH JUDGE

Some women planning an intermarriage want the accouterments of a Jewish ceremony, but for a variety of reasons—objections from the fiancé or his family, disaffiliation from religious Judaism, or whatever—choose to have a secular marriage with a Jewish presence. Some do this by asking a Jewish judge to perform the ceremony. There are judges who do this only for friends; others refuse to perform an intermarriage out of personal conviction; still others make themselves generally available. To find out about which Jewish judges in your area might be approachable, see if there is a Jewish Bar Association nearby, check with faculty members at a local law school, some of whom may be Jewish, or ask a sympathetic rabbi, even if he or she is one who would not be willing to officiate at the wedding her/himself. The Wedding Announcements pages of the local newspaper can be a treasure trove for locating the names of Jewish judges who have officiated at intermarriages.

CANTORS

In some states, including New York, cantors are licensed to officiate at marriage ceremonies. First call your local marriage-license office to check on the laws in your state or province, then call local synagogues for the names of cantors. For names and addresses of women cantors, see Networking Directory.

THE NON-JEWISH WOMAN WHO MARRIES "IN": CONVERSION

Since far more women than men convert to Judaism in an intermarriage, the sometimes controversial issues surrounding conversion are *de facto* women's issues. For example, if you're a woman, the nature of your conversion—whether strictly Orthodox or not—may have consequences for your children in ways that have no parallel for a male convert.

The overwhelming majority of conversions to Judaism take place in connection with marriage to a Jew—either before the ceremony or at some time during the course of the marriage. Since a child is considered Jewish if the mother is Jewish, there's obviously more reason for the non-Jewish wife to convert than for the non-Jewish husband. Reform rabbi Alexander M. Schindler has called on Jewish authorities to recognize as Jewish any child with one Jewish parent—whether mother or father. Though this goes against the Halachic definition of a Jew, the committee that drew up the resolution, passed in March 1983, declared that under exclusively matrilineal descent Jewish fathers were being discriminated against. Now the Reform movement recognizes that "the child of one Jewish parent is under the presumption of Jewish descent," but provides that the Jewish identity of any young child must be affirmed through "appropriate and timely acts of identification with the Jewish faith and people," such as Bar or Bat Mitzvah and Torah study.[17]

Rabbi Helene Ferris at the ceremony marking a woman's conversion to Judaism. (Marilynne Herbert)

The Conversion Process
Jews have traditionally frowned upon proselytizing as historically un-Jewish, probably because it was practiced by the Christians among whom Jews lived, or out of fear that hostile surrounding populations would see

this activity as a threat. As a result of the long-standing discouragement of prospective converts (for about 1500 years proselytizing has been banned), conversion is still regarded as a difficult process to begin; in fact, some rabbis routinely turn away people seeking to convert and will teach only those who come back after a second rejection.[18]

Depending upon the practice of the individual rabbi, conversion may be complete after a period of study, including an exploration of the person's motivation for the conversion, and a ritual immersion in a mikveh or other body of water. For a more detailed description of the conversion process see: *The Third Jewish Catalog*, ed. Sharon Strassfeld and Michael Strassfeld (Jewish Publication Society, 1980), and Eliezer Berkovits, "Conversion According to Halachah," in *Crisis and Faith* (New York: Sanhedrin Press, 1976).

Converted Women Speak About Judaism

The great neglected area in conversion has not been in course material but in the emotional sequelae to conversion. What do women feel who, like Ruth in the Bible, leave their own people and take on another religious affiliation and/or identification? Most women who have converted to Judaism intend to take on a religious rather than a cultural or ethnic or national identity, so it's not surprising that several women, after conversion to Judaism, report finding themselves more religiously observant than their born-Jewish husbands. One woman, who had gone to church every week with her parents, assumed that when she converted to Judaism she and her husband would attend synagogue with similar frequency. Her assimilated, utterly nonreligious Jewish husband was at first discomforted, and then gradually found himself being drawn further and further into Jewish observance. The couple became strictly observant, and now they live in an ultrareligious community; she wears long sleeves, and dark stockings and he wears a black coat and hat.

Obviously this kind of transformation of both parties is the exception rather than the rule, but the experience of a woman converting to Judaism and then finding herself more religious than her spouse is not uncommon. There are other common experiences also, some of them having to do with feeling incompletely absorbed by the Jewish community or hurt by such comments as the one overheard in the lobby of a synagogue. A man, not knowing that a woman had converted to Judaism, said to her, "You know, you look just like a *shiksa*." Shoshana Lev of Los Angeles comments, "You continue to be called a convert by many Jews. Some indicate that they expect you to drop Judaism and flee, flying into the arms of Christianity when anti-Semitism touches you."[19]

While converts to Judaism cannot be expected to respond with the same sense of ingrained ethnic consciousness as do people born and raised Jewish, they are certainly considered halachically full Jews; in fact, some rabbis call intermarriages where the non-Jewish partner has converted "mitzvah marriages." Two women who have been the converted partner in such marriages tell of their responses to becoming Jewish:

I am aware of the concern that Jewish parents have when their sons or daughters marry someone who has converted. How committed is this person? Will he/she keep a Jewish home, or will my son/daughter be swayed away from our teachings? And what of our grandchildren— will they be raised as Jews, Gentiles, or something in between? These are legitimate, well-founded fears for *some* parents. However, I believe we need to give someone who has converted the benefit of the doubt. For many of us our conversion was not a meaningless formality intended to satisfy our in-laws and the conscience of our spouse, but rather a deeply spiritual life event.[20]

I used to think that conversion meant that you stopped being one thing in order to become something different, and for that reason I resisted it. But Adin Steinsaltz gave me a more organic metaphor. Conversion, he said, is like marriage. You are joined to a new community, but you bring to the union the strength and values that have been your foundation throughout your life.[21]

The most difficult aspect of being a convert to Judaism may well be in forging the synthesis of two different family backgrounds. What happens when Christmas rolls around, for example? What if the happy holiday celebration of one set of in-laws makes the other set of in-laws wild with anxiety? One woman whose daughter-in-law converted to Judaism says, "Every December I wait with trepidation to see if they'll have a Christmas tree, or if their children will want one because their other grandparents do." People who are involved in postconversion counseling suggest that if children are invited to celebrate Christmas or other non-Jewish holidays, they should do so in a way that makes it clear to all involved that they are there as Jewish guests, not as participating Christians.

Despite the splintering that an intermarriage or even a conversionary marriage causes the extended family, the Jewish community has a great deal to gain from conversions. Rabbi Wolfe Kelman, Executive Director of the national organization for conservative rabbis, the Rabbinical Assembly, has stated that the community will gain its future strength from *baalei tshuva* (Jews who have become more observant), women, and converts.

Rachel Cowan, a photographer and community activist who is now the Program Director of Manhattan's newly revitalized Temple Ansche Chesed, describes the path that led her to convert to Judaism after many years of marriage to a then non-observant Jewish man.[22]

Converting to Judaism at age 39, after 15 years of marriage and twelve years of motherhood, has been fascinating, difficult, and profoundly moving to me. I can see now that my life would have been emotionally simpler if I had converted before getting married. I would not have spent so many years caught between feeling like an outsider and insider. I would have been able to respond with more self-confidence when people called me a *shiksa*. And I would also have eased my children's acceptance into organized Jewish life by birthing them as traditionally defined Jews. But I would have missed a long struggle to discover what really attracted me to Judaism. I might never have learned that being Jewish was something important to me, not just another way of being a good wife and mother.

I didn't convert back then, before marriage, because it never occurred to me. My in-laws didn't urge it. They had sent Paul to an Episcopalian boarding school—one sign of their assimilation. Another was the way they celebrated Christmas and Easter, not Hannukah and Pesach. Conversion seemed meaningless. It couldn't make me a genetic Jew. Although Paul valued being Jewish, he had no level of Judaic education, tradition, or observance which would have inspired me to study.

Nevertheless, I suspect that Paul's being Jewish increased his already enormous attractiveness to me. As a child I had romanticized Jews. My parents, both atheists from Protestant families, taught us to fight bigotry. Then they moved us to an upper-class WASP suburb where I had frequent opportunities to challenge the anti-Semitism of my neighbors and classmates. I knew very few Jews, but in seeking to defend them, I read a lot. I envied them their history, and the ceremonies and traditions that gave their lives such a rich fabric.

Just after we were married, I bought the Ben Shahn Haggadah for Paul, though neither of us knew anything about seders. I must have been looking forward to setting up a Jewish home. Though Paul was always consciously proud of being a Jew, he had given no thought to leading a Jewish life. My interest in introducing ceremony into our home life was an impetus for him. I was helping to make a connection between the fact of his birth status and the traditions of the Jewish people, helping him to feel part of his people in a new way.

So it shocked me, then hurt me, when people saw me as a *shiksa*. I hated the word's implication—that I was a loathsome foreigner who had seized a helpless Jewish boy in order to turn him to my ways. I could understand it in old people—a friend's father chuckling that a *shiksa* should know the Shabbat blessings, or the woman in the elevator telling my bewildered son that he looked like a little *sheygetz*. But it stings when sophisticated people at dinner parties refer bitterly to "the *shiksas*" or at Jewish Federation meetings or Havurah gatherings tell jokes about "the *goyim*." I always knew how to counter an anti-Semitic remark, but felt defensive and inarticulate in the face of prejudice against non-Jews. I was afraid of being identified with anti-Semites, and frightened of disrupting a relationship where I felt that people accepted me somewhat provisionally.

There haven't been many of those painful encounters in my life, though. For the first eight years of our marriage I met few Jews who worried about *shiksas*. We lived on the Upper West Side of Manhattan, where I was involved with anti-war and feminist politics, day-care organizing, writing and photography. Many of the people I worked with were Jewish, but they didn't talk about it very much. We all saw ourselves relating to universal issues, not ethnic ones.

That changed in the early seventies. We grew to feel profoundly alienated from political allies who were not upset by the Munich massacre, who blamed Israel for many of the world's problems. People had become accustomed to Black people seeking meaning in their ethnic identity, and our friends began to talk about their feelings about being Jewish. I was an eager listener.

These discussions led to Hannukah parties and Passover seders. Our first ones were conducted from Arthur Waskow's Freedom Seder, which connected reassuringly with our political outlook. Some of us started a weekly Jewish after-school program for our kids. In the process, we created a consciousness-raising study group for ourselves.

Paul and I had to learn everything. Our first latkes were flavored with blood from scraped knuckles. The fish man stared incredulously when I ordered ground carp to make gefilte fish. Each year the seder grew larger, and we soon switched to a traditional Haggadah which we supplemented with storytelling, readings, music, and dramatic improvisations. Paul and I stopped going out on Friday nights, choosing to light candles and share a special meal with the children instead. I lost my desire to eat lobster and BLT's, once favorite foods. I loved the things I was learning, but I saw no reason to convert. I was happy to be helping my husband and children lead a Jewish life but felt it was not my birthright.

Soon, though, I began to be drawn to something more spiritual than a sense of history and celebration. Each year the High Holiday services at the New York Havurah, led by men and women, seemed less alien to me. The meditations connected with unexpected resonance to concerns I had been puzzling over. The intensity of the davening and the singing lifted my spirit in a way I had never experienced.

A few of us started a biweekly Shabbat morning group that reached minyan size only when we counted a baby as well as the Torah, but I began to learn to pray there.

As my spiritual connection to Judaism was consciously deepening, I was also forging an unconscious emotional identification with the Jewish people. I discovered its depth during a summer in Jerusalem. Faults and all, Israel was from then on a country to which I felt organically connected.

In Jerusalem I also experienced my first wave of doubt about the value of Judaism as a path for my search. One Shabbat morning I was leaning against the Western Wall in the small section reserved for women, trying to feel in the stones' rough warmth a sense of the power of such a holy place. But my concentration was not deep enough to blot out the conversation about shopping bargains being carried on by two Americans on my right. As I left to find a quiet, more distant spot, I passed a few women praying silently. Then I walked past a large cluster of women standing on benches, hanging over the dividing barrier to watch their sons or relatives becoming Bar Mitzvah on the men's side. From a distance it looked as if all the space, all the energy, all the vitality were allocated to the men. I started to cry. How could I join a religion with such ancient, innate sexism at its core? I thought of the thousands of years when men held the religious authority. My anger spilled over onto Paul when he came to find me, excited by his prayers at the Wall.

As I thought about it over time, I realized that for me the Wall was a historic site, not a spiritual locus. I had found a pathway to faith in the Havurah services and retreats, in moments of prayer and insight. I had been influenced by strong women who were struggling to find meaning and fight sexism within Judaism. I would try to do the same.

When we came back from Israel, it was finally obvious to me that I was deeply engaged with Judaism. It was no longer simply enough to identify with Jews, it was time to become one. The question was not whether to convert, but how.

Like many potential converts, I thought at first that I should have an Orthodox conversion, since that would imprint me with an indelible mark of authenticity. But as I talked with different rabbis, I couldn't find one whose view of the way I should be Jewish coincided with mine.

I respected the rabbis for the depth of their faith, and the honesty with which they talked with me. One remains a very important teacher. But I did not feel ready to promise that I would be *Shomer Shabbat,* obeying all the laws of Shabbat, or that I would impose strict laws of kashruth on my family, or that I would ever be able to accept the practice of "family purity" (going to the mikveh). Finally, though, the issue that convinced me that Orthodoxy was not the right form for my conversion was the separation of men from women during worship.

In 1980 I was converted by a *bet din* of three Conservative rabbis whom I like and respect greatly. A close friend came to the mikveh with me; I wanted her to be an integral part of the process. During the Minchah service which completed the conversion, my children opened the ark where the Torahs are kept. My mother sat in the congregation.

My converting so late has put my family in a religiously problematic situation in relationship to Conservative and Orthodox Jews and to the State of Israel. Technically, Paul and I are Jewish, but the kids are not. The debate is now on within the Conservative movement over whether Halachic interpretations could allow the children of a Jewish father and non-Jewish mother to be classified as Jews. Reform and Reconstructionist Jews have already made the change.

I think it's high time that Conservative Jews followed suit. The consequences are painful for many children of intermarriages. A Bryn Mawr student with tears in her eyes described to me studying for her Bat Mitzvah only to be told she couldn't perform the ceremony because her mother wasn't Jewish. Many kids like ours think it makes no sense that someone would think they weren't Jewish when they've had a Jewish education, and when they're more knowledgeable and observant than most of their friends with two Jewish parents. Converting, to them, means having to accept the premise that their own self-image is not correct.

At a time when fathers are becoming increasingly involved in child-rearing, they should be just as entitled as the mother to have their religious/ethnic identity conferred on their children. When Jews cry out in alarm because the numbers of self-identified Jews is dwindling, it makes no sense to hold apart children who want to be part of the fold.[23]

RESOURCES ON CONVERSION

One of the most promising developments in the wake of increasing intermarriage and conversion to Judaism is the emerging body of literature on conversion and the postconversion experience, and a growing awareness, on the part of rabbis and Jews-in-the-street, of the emotional as well as intellectual and spiritual needs of converts.

The Reform movement (the most liberal wing of Judaism) has created an "outreach" program to help reach and teach those people who are considering conversion to Judaism. The program includes weekends for Jews-by-choice and their "significant other," if relevant, in addition to providing course material for conversion classes and a wide range of audiovisual materials as well as organizing ongoing postconversion groups.

Outreach Program
Union of American Hebrew Congregations
838 Fifth Avenue
New York, NY 10021

In addition to her work with the Outreach Program of the Reform movement, Lydia Kukoff, herself a convert, has written *Choosing Judaism: A Guide for Jews-by-Choice*; available from UAHC—$10 cloth, $5.95 paperback.

The Outreach Program has also sponsored a study of several hundred converts to Judaism—two-thirds of them women—and the effect that conversion has had on their own identities and their relations with their birth family. Some of the converts feel they are on "permanent probation" as Jews, and simultaneously feel rejected by their own parents. The study recommends that conversion courses address the emotional aspects of the conversion process, that rabbis should stay in touch with converts even after the conversion has been formalized, and that born-Jews should be sensitized to understand the status of converts. See Dr. Steven Huberman, "New Jews: The Dynamics of Religious Conversion," Ph.D. thesis, Brandeis Univ., 1979; available from UAHC.

For a brochure for prospective converts, and a listing of materials available to individuals and groups, write:

Rabbi Sanford Seltzer
Task Force on Reform Jewish Outreach
1187 Beacon Street
Brookline, MA 02146

While conversion to Judaism may be quicker and simpler if performed by a Reform rabbi, Orthodox rabbis and some conservative ones will not recognize such a conversion. The consequences of a woman's Reform conversion may be experienced by her children, who may be refused Bar/Bat Mitzvah by Orthodox, Conservative, and Reform congregations until they convert formally, since their mother is considered a non-Jew.

If you are contemplating converting to Judaism and would like to explore a Halachic (strictly legal) conversion, contact:

Rabbi Steven C. Lerner
752 Stelton Street
Teaneck, NJ 07666
(201) 837-7552

A Conservative rabbi who has worked with converts for many years, Lerner has formed an organization for those people seeking rabbis to teach them and to officiate at Halachic conversions. Lerner is also sensitive to the issues raised by many women as they study for conversion to Judaism. Those women whose preliminary studies suggest to them an element of sexism in Judaism that they didn't suspect when their only contact was social or gastronomic Judaism would do well to consult him.

For support groups, or to discuss possible conversion, the local Hillel rabbi is often a good bet if you happen to live in or near a university community. Look up B'nai B'rith Hillel Foundation in the phone book or call the office of the university's Jewish chaplain. The Hillel Foundation at University of California at Berkeley has even sponsored groups for converts.

Two organizations devoting themselves to "missionary" work, though not specifically noted for their sensitivity in dealing with feminist issues raised by the women they assist with conversion:

National Jewish Hospitality Committee
201 S. 18 Street, Room 1519
Philadelphia, PA 19103
(215) 546-8293

National Jewish Information Service
5174 W. 8 Street
Los Angeles, CA 90036
(213) 936-6033

Both these organizations publish material explaining Judaism and making a positive effort to interest non-Jews in converting to Judaism.

A novel dealing with the identity problems of a Christian woman who converts to Judaism when she marries into a "modern" Orthodox family is Rhoda Tagliacozzo's, *Saving Graces* (St. Martin's Press, 1979).

For more on raising children in an intermarriage situation, see "The Jewish Mother's Survival Kit" (p. 401) and Sharon Strassfeld and Kathy Green, *The Jewish Family Book* (Bantam Books, 1981).

Rachel Cowan and her husband, Paul Cowan, speak to college and community groups around the country on intermarriage, conversion, and Jewish identity. They are especially sympathetic to couples with one non-Jewish partner and to situations created by interfaith marriages in which children's Jewish identity has been cast in doubt.

Rachel and Paul Cowan
285 Riverside Drive
New York, NY 10025

9

◆

DIVORCE

JEWISH DIVORCE LAW: A GUIDE FOR THE OPPRESSED

Judaism has always recognized that some marriages just don't work, and has always been liberal in permitting divorce. Despite the fact that the Talmud declares, "If a man divorces his first wife, even the altar sheds tears for him," divorce was instituted precisely to prevent couples from having to remain together in unendurable incompatibility and unhappiness. Since marriage is a contractual arrangement (rather than a sacrament, as it is in Catholicism), dissolving a marriage can be done in a manner similar to terminating any contract. There are, however, severe inequities in the laws and the process of Jewish divorce, and pitfalls especially, for women. If both parties are willing to act in accord, the hazardous issuance of a *get* (Jewish divorce) can be a mere formality. Where there is discord, the woman is entirely at the mercy of the man, since under traditional applications of Jewish law a husband has the sole power to dissolve the contract and terminate the marriage.

"Jewish men may make better husbands, but they make far worse *ex-husbands*," a battle-scarred woman reports at a Jewish women's conference. Though the Talmud says, "Just as one must respect the memory of one's widow, so must one respect one's divorcée," Jewish divorce law places women in such a powerless position that "today it provides husbands with the kind of powerful weapon of revenge which certainly is not intended by the Torah."[1]

With an increase in divorce among all segments of the Jewish population[2] comes a growing awareness on the part of women that they are not

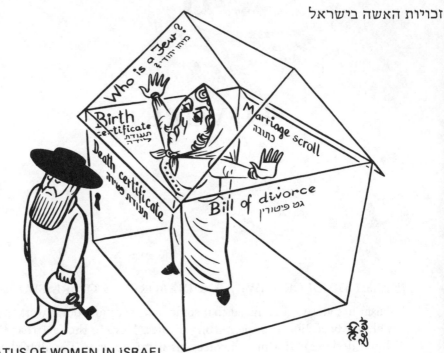

THE STATUS OF WOMEN IN ISRAEL

A 1979 *postcard distributed by a civil rights group in Israel, where women's personal status in such matters as divorce is wholly dependent on a strict interpretation of Jewish law; there is no civil divorce in Israel.* (courtesy the Fifth of Iyar Movement)

equal before the laws governing Jewish divorce. Not only do Jewish women who are divorcing risk some stigmatization in the community, as all women do, but they also come up against Halachah, many of them for the first time.

Along with the laws stating that women cannot give testimony (*edut*) in a rabbinic court (see p. 391) and that women cannot be counted in the quorum of ten necessary for communal prayer (*minyan*) (see p. 381), the laws of Jewish divorce rank among those most oppressive to women or, in less political terms, the most unjust in their inequality. Simply put, a man can issue a divorce decree to his wife, but she cannot issue such a decree to her husband. Although the law requires that the wife *accept* the divorce decree before it becomes final, it is not symmetrical. All power under the laws of Jewish divorce rest with the man. He has nothing to lose if he lives apart from his wife, and even if he chooses to father children with another woman, the children suffer no legal disadvantages. The wife, as we see from the Jewish marriage laws (p. 321), can neither remarry nor have children by another man (without serious legal consequences to the children) if she does not obtain a divorce. She is an agunah. Even if her husband has become insane, a wife has no recourse but to await a "period of lucidity" during which he might be able to authorize a *get;* a man whose wife is insane or for some reason incapable of accepting his *get* may petition one hundred rabbis for their permission to transcend the ban on polygamy and then may remarry. No such legal loophole is available to women.

The category of *agunot* includes not only those women whose husbands refuse to issue a divorce, or who cannot be found to give a divorce but also those whose husbands were killed at war, without witnesses, and whose bodies have never been recovered. (This was the case for many Is-

Chalitzah *scene in Holland, early eighteenth century; the old engraving conveys the antiquated nature of the laws which hold that a woman who is childless when widowed must perform a kind of divorce ritual with her brother-in-law if she is to be free to marry anyone else.* (courtesy New York Public Library Picture Collection)

raeli war widows, and also for women who survived the Holocaust and could only presume that their husbands had been killed.)

The situation of the *agunah* is tragic. She cannot ever remarry, according to Orthodox Judaism and also according to the marriage laws of Israel. To combat the awful situation of the war widows and the Holocaust survivors, Israeli rabbis were very compassionate, and arranged releases for many *agunot* based either on technicalities permitting annulment of the marriage, where applicable, or on the ground that a person who was sent directly to a death camp could be presumed dead as certainly as one who walks into the ocean (a circumstance for which there is Halachic precedent). The legal structure is less amenable to flexibility when the husband is alive and simply refuses to comply with Jewish law, using his power to withhold the *get* as a manipulative tool against his wife. Since the power to grant the divorce decree rests with the *man* under Orthodox and Conservative readings of Jewish law, the agunah is truly trapped. One source estimates that in New York City alone 15,000 women are fixed in the status of *agunah*.[3]

The power of these laws is so great that some Israeli men have even issued their wives a *get* (or have had a *get* written) before they go off to war, with the understanding that if they are killed in battle without a witness their wives can "accept" the *get* and not be left as *agunot*. Similarly, some Jewish Canadian and American soldiers during World War II issued their wives conditional bills of divorce so that if they were missing in action their wives could remarry.[4]

SAFE PASSAGE FOR WOMEN IN THE DIVORCE PROCESS

If both husband and wife agree to divorce, there is no impediment to their parting, nor do they have to invent a reason when going before the *bet din* (rabbinical court) to arrange the divorce. Compare this with the situation common until the 1970s in some states and provinces, where one party had to prove adultery or mental or physical cruelty on the part of the other before the marriage could be dissolved legally. Jewish law is far more understanding of the vagaries of human nature than are many civil laws, which, in some places, still require a person to perjure her/himself in order to terminate a marriage. Absence of affection is a perfectly justifiable cause for divorce according to Jewish law, although the intricate technicalities of writing the bill of divorcement itself were doubtless created to prevent precipitous divorces. Under Halachah, the couple (or an agent of each) must appear before the *bet din* for the proceedings; this was often an opportunity for the rabbis to try to persuade the couple to stay together, or to assure themselves that divorce was what both parties really wanted. Today, the *get* ceremony can be a formality with no personal delving on the part of the rabbis, depending on the community and the circumstances.

Traditionally, a *bet din* would be receptive to a woman's desire to divorce if the marriage suffered from one of several Talmudic criteria that meant automatic sanction of divorce: if either spouse is incapable of having children or prevents the other from observing *mitzvot*, if the husband has a noxious smell that is work-related and that won't go away (such as the smell of a tanner, says the Talmud), if the husband refuses to have sexual contact with the wife, or if he contracts a venereal disease. (If one spouse leaves Judaism this is also a ground for divorce; although the *bet din* is obviously powerless to compel the non-Jewish man to issue a divorce, some authorities suggest petitioning the Gentile authorities to press him to do so.)

If a woman is categorized by her husband as a "rebellious wife" (*more-det*), and if a *bet din* upholds his judgment, he can divorce her without

Antique chalitzah *slipper which the childless widow is required to throw at her brother-in-law as part of the ceremony releasing him from an obligation to marry her.* (courtesy of Christie's, New York)

paying her the money or property owed her under the terms of the marriage contract. A *moredet* may be a woman who has left her husband or who has done one of several things to disturb *shalom bayit* (peace in the home), including refusing to have sexual intercourse with him without what appears to a *bet din* to be good and sufficient reason. Some Jewish courts may, if they concur with the husband, cause her to forfeit custody of her children as well as her dowry. The very existence of such a category for women surely serves to keep some women from leaving or complaining about their marriages. And for a husband intent upon cheating his soon-to-be-ex-wife, the concept of *moredet* provides a convenient opportunity.

Since the husband is the party responsible for issuing the divorce, he is the active agent who must cause the divorce decree to be written. Usually the husband and wife go together to the rabbinical court, where they appear before a rabbi and two competent Jewish *male* witnesses. It is possible for a husband and wife to obtain a Jewish divorce even if they live in different cities; in such cases a rabbi usually acts as the agent of the absent party (with that party's consent, of course).

A scribe then writes the divorce document, which is highly stylized: it must be twelve lines long, written in Aramaic, and may contain no errors of spelling or address, to ensure that the document accurately describes the people who are divorcing. The operative phrase, directed to the wife, reads: "This shall be for you from me a bill of dismissal, a letter of release, and a document of freedom." The *get* is then put into the hands of the woman by the man, and she formally "receives" it. After the ceremony the *get* is sliced with a knife so that it can't be used again and is retained by the rabbi. The woman and man each receive a *petur*, or written statement of release, testifying that they have obtained a Jewish divorce.

Under Halachah a man is free to remarry immediately after the divorce decree has been issued by him and accepted by the woman, while the woman must wait ninety days to remarry, in case she might be pregnant by her former husband. In this case she could wait, give birth, and then remarry with no negative consequences to the child's status; the child would be presumed to be the offspring of the previous marriage. The existence of this device to ensure correct paternity is another reason why women who are receiving a civil divorce should know that time is of the essence in obtaining a Jewish divorce as well. A woman who becomes pregnant by a man other than her ex-husband after a civil divorce can be accused of adultery, since she is presumed under Jewish law to be still married. If a *get* is then issued, she is explicitly forbidden to marry the father of the child, since a woman cannot marry a man with whom she has had an adulterous relationship. No similar consequences await the husband in the period between civil and Jewish divorces, unless he should happen to cohabit with a married woman (see "Marriage," p. 320).

With the acceptance of larger numbers of women into the rabbinate, legal interpretation and practice will, one hopes, correct these confusions and inequities. There is ample precedent in Judaism for taking into account the unreasonable suffering that the assymetry in divorce laws causes women, and when women are empowered as legal authorities just as men are, we will not focus, as Rabbi Sandy Eisenberg Sasso has put it, "on the halachic pinhead, but rather on the nature of the fabric into which the pin has been woven."

"LET'S PART AS EQUALS": HOW TO CREATE JUSTICE

There is very little that a wife can do today to coerce her husband into giving her a divorce. Typically, in a traditional (very religious) community when a woman had difficulty in getting her husband to give her a divorce, communal sanctions could be applied: he would not be allowed to pray in his accustomed place, he would be denied synagogue honors, and other Jews would boycott his business. It has been reported that a group of Orthodox women in Montreal, in a *Lysistrata*-like move, refused to go to the mikveh (see p. 203)—which meant they were not sexually available to their husbands—until the men of the community persuaded their buddy to issue his wife a divorce decree. Another tactic rumored to be used today is the "hit-team" approach, whereby certain groups of ultra-Orthodox Jews send out thugs to frighten or threaten a man who refuses to grant his wife a divorce. (Even Maimonides sanctioned the use of corporal punishment as a coercion technique with husbands reluctant to issue a *get!*)

Where Jews are no longer living in closed communities, there are other solutions and pressure tactics that individuals and groups are trying, with varying degrees of success. They are all stopgap solutions, which halt short of changing the law itself to permit women as well as men to grant a Jewish divorce.

Since the process of legal decision-making in Judaism has been exclusively in the hands of men, the stories of individual women who have suffered under its inequities don't always reach the ears of the rabbinic decision-makers. Those who take a sympathetic view of the way rabbis handle most divorce cases claim that they *are* informed by what is going on in the community, and that they *are* responsive to the painful situations of women who are having difficulty obtaining divorces from recalcitrant husbands. However, those who are more skeptical (or more realistic) say that they find it hard to believe that male rabbis wouldn't find a way within Halachah to change the unequal laws themselves if they could only empathize with the inherent injustice and the great suffering that so many women undergo at the hands of these laws.[5] To begin this process, Aviva Cantor has suggested that women organize a speak-out on Jewish divorce law to which Orthodox rabbinical authorities are invited, so that there can be some exchange between those responsible for maintaining the legal structure and those who are helpless before it.

In fact, there have been changes in Jewish divorce law. For example, in the eleventh century, Rabbenu Gershom passed an enactment that the wife had to accept the *get* for it to be valid, involving her somewhat in the proceedings. And in Biblical times a man could cancel his *get* at will; now the *get* is delivered before witnesses and is assumed to be final. Judith Hauptman, instructor in Talmud at the Jewish Theological Seminary, has said that when this was the case, some women voluntarily assumed the status of *agunot* because of their fear that a cancellation of the *get* was coming at any time.[6]

At least *this* terrible uncertainty has been removed from the law, and there must surely be ways that this and other legal remedies to unfairness can act as precedents for altering the present interpretation of divorce laws. The major change necessary to equalize the law is never proposed by Orthodox rabbinical authorities today, despite the fact that there appears to be precedent for such a shift: from 500 c.e. to 1250 c.e. some sources reveal that women as well as men were permitted to issue divorces.[7]

Authorities now suggest that the *get* be arranged as part of the initial civil separation or divorce agreement, even before the civil divorce becomes final. This would obviate the common situation described by a Connecticut woman: "I've just been through a really awful civil divorce. Now I find out that while I was at it I should have gotten a religious one, too! We'd been married in a regular Jewish ceremony, but nobody ever told me I'd need a Jewish divorce. Now I find out I'm an *agunah!* My ex-husband is off in California someplace and nobody can even find him to make child-support payments, never mind to have him agree to a Jew-divorce."

Concerned women and men have tried to find remedies to ease the confusion and uncertainty for women under the different standards each denomination has for an acceptable Jewish divorce. Some of these measures have as their goal making changes in the law itself; others are used to make the situation slightly more tolerable for women until wider changes take place.

As things stand now, each denomination within Judaism has attempted its own solution. Unfortunately none of these is acceptable to the strictest Orthodox authorities. According to Orthodox feminist Blu Greenberg, these authorities see a need for preserving the male prerogative in divorce even though they know that "the only person whose hands are tied is the woman."[8]

Among the solutions that these rabbinic authorities reject is the Reform decision that the law of the land is the law governing such civil matters for Jews. The Reform movement has done away with Jewish divorces altogether, declaring that a civil divorce terminates a Jewish marriage. The Reconstructionist movement has not given up on *gittin* (plural of *get*), but has, true to its name, reconstructed the circumstances under which they are issued. Along these lines, in 1980, Reconstructionist rabbis arranged for the first Jewish divorce initiated by a woman and delivered to a man. Rabbi Ira Eisenstein, then dean of the Reconstructionist Rabbinical College, said: "If you enable her to divorce her husband in the presence of three rabbis, you are sparing her anguish for the rest of her life. No, you're not doing it within the framework of traditional Jewish law, but you are not ignoring Jewish law."[9]

In this vein Blu Greenberg suggests that the simplest and least divisive solution might be the adoption of a *takkanah* (addition) to the law, permitting a woman to serve a divorce document to her husband if he refused to grant one to her.[10]

Both Conservative and innovative Orthodox rabbis have put forth solutions to the *get* issue which are based on the use of a conditional marriage contract, such that the marriage is automatically annulled if the stated conditions are met (see "Marriage," p. 324). One set of conditions (*t'naim*) declares that if a civil divorce takes place and no Jewish divorce is granted by the husband within a certain length of time, he is liable to prosecution by the civil courts. Another solution, more commonly used in Conservative marriages, states that if the couple choose to live apart for a certain amount of time the marriage becomes invalid and could then be automatically annulled by a Jewish court. Orthodox and some traditionalist Conservative rabbis, however, object to a widespread use of annulment, which was employed historically, they say, only as an emer-

The divorce scene from Joan Micklin Silver's film Hester Street *vividly portrays a young woman's experience with an all-male court of judges when her husband divorces her.* (courtesy of Midwest Film Productions, Inc.)

gency measure; others object to the idea of signing the marriage contract conditionally.

Some Conservative rabbis will help a woman to free herself from a marriage if she can show proof that despite having granted her a civil divorce, her husband steadfastly refuses to issue a *get*. Then, without the use of any conditions in the marriage contract itself, a Conservative *bet din*, appointed by the Rabbinical Assembly, could declare the marriage null and void.

Along with the call of Blu Greenberg and others for a ruling that would give women and men equal powers to divorce a partner is the suggestion, originally made by Trude Weiss-Rosmarin, that decisions regarding Jewish divorce be taken out of the husband's hands and placed in the Jewish court.[11] An indirect application of this idea is the condition written into some Conservative marriage contracts in which the parties promise to go before a *bet din* if their marriage is dissolving. The idea is that once the man is before the *bet din* he will find it difficult to refuse to issue the *get* to his wife. An ancillary ploy with this condition is that if the husband refuses to go to a *bet din* he can be prosecuted in civil courts for violation of the marriage contract.[12]

Civil-Law Solutions to Jewish Divorce Dilemmas

The issue of enlisting the civil courts to settle a Jewish divorce case raises the specter of religion's interference in civil affairs, a situation that is anathema in the United States, which has constitutionally separated religious and secular affairs. Nonetheless, when a breach of contract is involved, the civil courts have stepped in and heard cases. The Jewish marriage contract, like any contract between two consenting adults, is enforceable in the civil courts.[13]

In a 1981 case, the New Jersey courts declared a Jewish marriage contract invalid, thereby annulling the marriage, because the parties signed the *ketubah* promising to be married "according to the laws of Moses and Israel." Since these laws forbid adultery, said the court, and since one of the parties to the marriage had committed adultery (this was the basis of the civil divorce suit, in fact), that partner had violated the conditions of the marriage contract, thus invalidating it.

Threading one's way through the maze of different contracts and the religious and secular enforcement of them is becoming more confusing as civil suits become more frequent. Several states and the Province of Manitoba have already been the scenes of civil suits, with varying decisions handed down, many of which were later challenged on Constitutional and other grounds by the higher courts. The potentially most useful utilization of the civil courts is one proposed in New York State in 1983, where a bill was signed into law denying a civil divorce to anyone who has failed to "remove all barriers" to a partner's remarriage. Jewish authorities are divided on this technique, with more liberal Jewish institutions typically opposing the law as breaching the wall between religion and state, and some right-wing (and Orthodox) authorities supporting the measure as a way of relieving the plight of women under Halachah without having to change Halachah itself.

Tools for Surviving Divorce

One of the tragedies in the current standstill on changing the divorce laws is that Jewish women, often less informed about Jewish matters than Jewish men, are at greater risk under the law. Yet, knowing less—in this case, about divorce law—they are doubly jeopardized, since they are also more helpless under that law. To learn more:

• A guide through the complexities of using the civil courts in what is essentially a religious issue is Irwin H. Haut, *Divorce in Jewish Law and Life* (New York: Sepher-Hermon, 1983). Haut, a New York attorney and an ordained rabbi, has prepared a superb handbook on Jewish divorce for lay readers, on civil law for rabbis and others interested in trying to apply it to Jewish matters, and on Jewish law for those lawyers who are now faced with making courtroom decisions on religious divorce. Haut's is also one of the clearest presentations of the options now available in preparing the marriage contract so as to eliminate some of the current problems with divorce. He endorses the rabbinic proposal that couples write a prenuptial agreement stating that in the event of a civil divorce the husband will automatically issue the wife a *get*. This contract is then enforceable by civil courts.

• If you would like a brief outline of the Orthodox position on divorce laws (which states that no other interpretation is permissible), you can order a four-page brochure:

"The Parting of Ways": Fundamentals of Jewish Divorce
Chicago Rabbinical Council
2735 W. Devon Avenue
Chicago, IL 60659

• A much more general presentation of the laws concerning Jewish divorce—in effect, a mini-course—also deals with the emotional issues involved for both the adults and their children:

Divorce in Jewish Life and Tradition
by Paulette Benson and Sherry Bissell
Alternatives in Religious Education
3945 S. Oneida Street
Denver, CO 80237

• To locate a *bet din* for a divorce, consult a local rabbi or contact either Orthodox or Conservative national organizations for a referral to local resources:

Bet Din
Rabbinical Council of America
    (Orthodox)
1250 Broadway, Suite 802
New York, NY 10001
(212) 594-3780

Bet Din
Rabbinical Assembly
(Conservative)
3080 Broadway
New York, NY 10027
(212) 749-8000

• Jewish sources are concerned, of necessity, with the legal implications of divorce, but few analysts have examined the feelings of Jewish divorced women. These feelings can include shame and guilt, especially among Orthodox women, for having taken a step considered threatening to the stability of one unit in the Jewish community. Some women, however, have expressed their desire to get closer to the Jewish community after a divorce. One study of divorced Jewish mothers found that "the upheaval of divorce caused [the Jewish women studied] to seek stability and community in their lives," and that they were more willing than before their divorces to involve themselves with the Jewish community.

"Divorced Jewish Mothers: A Study of the Effect Divorce Has upon Jewish Identity, Affiliation and Life Style"
Mona Panitz and Janis Plotkin
School of Jewish Communal Service M.A. Thesis (1976)
Hebrew Union College–Jewish Institute of Religion
3077 University Avenue
Los Angeles, CA 90007

While these Jewish women were drawn closer to the Jewish community after divorce, other women report having very negative Jewish associations after being divorced from a Jewish man. They are angry and they say that they don't want to marry Jews again. (See "Who Marries 'Out'?" p. 338.) "Lots of anger at individuals gets projected onto the group, often as a factor of the women's disappointment in the failure of their illusions about the 'good Jewish husband,'" says a Washington, D.C., therapist who works with divorced women.

• The Task Force on Marriage and Divorce of the Federation of Jewish Philanthropies of Greater New York has reached out to Jewish lawyers reminding them that when Jewish clients come to them to arrange a civil divorce they should propose—and even help to arrange, if possible—a religious divorce at the same time.[14]

• Another attempt to use a non-Halachic legal structure to alleviate the problems women have under Jewish divorce law is being made by the growing civil rights movement in Israel. The movement is attempting to create a civil law code for Israel, where at present all matters of personal status for Jews are governed by strict Jewish religious law. To keep abreast of changes in the Israeli law, contact:

American-Israeli Civil Liberties Coalition, Inc.
124 W. 79 Street
New York, NY 10024

• An Israeli organization that attempts to mediate between husband and wife so that they can agree to go before a *bet din* and arrange the divorce says that it acts as a "collective conscience" for those women who are victims of an unfair system or of cruel husbands. The usual tactic is face-to-face negotiations with the recalcitrant husband, but the group has also staged demonstrations and pickets against particularly unresponsive husbands.

Mitzvah
P.O.B. 506
Netanya, Israel 42104

• In the tactics and strategies department, the best news, short of the major push for Jewish divorce-law reform that is sorely needed, has been the formation in 1979 of a group known as G.E.T.—Getting Equitable Treatment. (The name is an obvious acronym for the Hebrew word *get*, meaning divorce document.)

The organization has the backing of many very well-known Orthodox groups and seeks support only from such groups. The founders believe, probably correctly, that the *get* issue is one that must be settled at the highest levels of Orthodoxy in order to have credibility in all branches of Judaism.

The tactics they employ to raise consciousness about the issue and to help bring about equitable divorce circumstances range from lecturing to Orthodox women's groups on inequities under the law to picketing in front of the house of a reluctant husband or his rabbi, or telephoning the husband's parents to try to elicit their help in encouraging him to give his wife a *get*.

G.E.T.
P.O. Box 131
1012 Avenue I
Brooklyn, NY 11230

• A group in Brooklyn offers discussion groups and support specifically for those women who are *agunot* and need relief under the law to change their status.

AGUNAH
c/o New York City Councilmember Susan Alter
463 E. 19 Street
Brooklyn, NY 11226

• Another consciousness-raiser in dealing with Jewish divorce has been the publication, in Hebrew and English, of a remarkable book that exposes the problems women have had with divorce law in Israel. The data come from Israeli court records, but the heartrending stories are illuminating for Jews everywhere as examples of the suffering of women under a law that keeps them in unsatisfactory and often physically abusive marriages because their husbands refuse to write them a divorce decree. The cases cited in this book on divorce reinforce the suspicions many women have had that the rabbinical courts often will send wives back into unhappy marital situations for the sake of maintaining *shalom bayit* (peace in the house). For information about its availability, write to the foundation that sponsored its initial publication:

Divorce in Israel: The Dead End
by Leah Ain Globe
c/o U.S./Israel Women-to-Women
4 Sniffen Court
156 E. 36 Street
New York, NY 10016

Several Jewish social-service agencies across the continent provide services for divorced women and their families. For example:
• Recently divorced women in Texas help cope with their situation via one-to-one counseling by trained volunteers who have themselves recently been divorced.

REWARDS Program
Jewish Community Center
7900 Northaven Road
Dallas, TX 75230
(214) 739-2737

• The Denver community runs six-week seminars for men and women who "have worked through the grieving process of divorce and now desire personal growth relationships with family, friends, colleagues and romantic partners."

"Growth Beyond Divorce"
Jewish Community Center
4800 E. Alameda Avenue
Denver, CO 80222
(303) 399-2660

• New York City's 92nd Street Y has offered a support group for separated and divorced people which includes child care while the sessions are taking place. The group has dealt with such topics as "Making a life of your own: How to know what's right in a time with rules" and "Dealing with the absent mate."

"Facing the Problems of Divorce"
YM/YWHA
1395 Lexington Avenue
New York, NY 10028

• In Philadelphia the Jewish community offers counseling for parents, children, and even grandparents who are trying to deal with the consequences of divorce in the family. (See also "Children and Divorce," p. 403.)

Jewish Family Service
1610 Spruce Street
Philadelphia, PA 19103
(215) KI 5-3290

10

◆

RESPONDING TO THE CHILDBEARING IMPERATIVE

TO HAVE OR HAVE NOT: FEMINISM, JUDAISM, AND OPTIONAL CHILDBEARING

The New York Times runs an editorial praising the fact that American women and men are marrying later and having the same number of children—two per family—as they did in the early 1970s. The population is being held at replacement level, and the editorial writers are happy. The same facts in the Jewish population are cause for demographic anxiety verging on alarm.[1] We're not even *at* replacement level! The goals of the Jewish community are clear: at the same time that Zero Population Growth is urging high school students to plan for one-child families, the Task Force on Jewish Population in New York is advocating that Jewish schools put up posters showing families with five children.

Some of the anxiety, even in America, realistically concerns politics. As our potential for growth shrinks, so does our political clout, making life in pluralistic America more difficult for those Jews who *are* around. In addition, with fewer babies being born, the population is shifting markedly toward older people, even more so among Jews than in American society at large.

The meaning and implications of having children obviously differ for Jewish women and men, as they do for Jews and non-Jews. Marriage is a necessary but not sufficient state for Jewish men and women. Once married, Jews are supposed to observe the mitzvah (obligation) of having children. (See "Our Bodies," p. 226, for Jewish laws and attitudes on controlling conception.)

Although the Biblical injunction to "be fruitful and multiply" is considered to apply only to men, Jewish women are now coming under considerable pressure to respond to this imperative to produce offspring. (Not that in past generations children appeared via parthenogenesis, but there was little choice involved in whether to have children, or when, or how many.) The pressure comes from religious authorities, community leaders, family members, and of course from people's own desires to fulfill a nurturing role. The perceived drop in Jewish population fuels much of the external pressure, while at the same time women's own goals out-

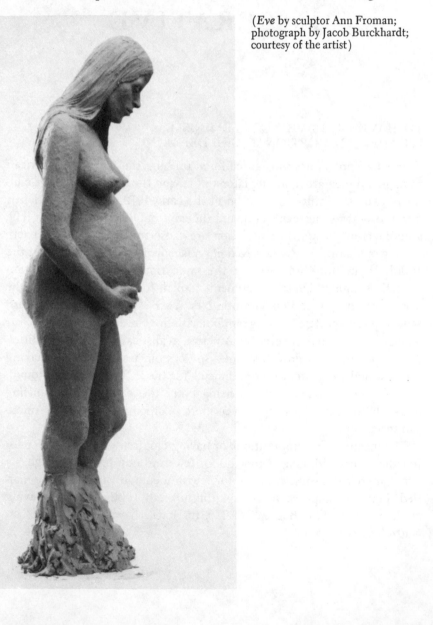

(*Eve* by sculptor Ann Froman; photograph by Jacob Burckhardt; courtesy of the artist)

side the family create for some a resistance to having children.

There probably isn't a single synagogue in North America that hasn't been the scene of a sermon in the last few years on the declining Jewish birthrate. The Las Vegas *Israelite* headlined one such story "Jews Should Have More Children," and a widely reprinted article by Steven Martin Cohen is titled "The Coming Shrinkage of American Jewry." In the face of these articles, it helps to remember that at many points in our past concern was voiced over Jews' lower birthrate—which has usually been about 60 percent of that of the general population.[2] We are, however, still around, and the current noises may do more harm than good if they turn off large numbers of young Jewish professional women who want their dilemma understood and do not want to be preached at by Jewish men who appear to have little sympathy for the conflicts childbearing can generate.

The fears of the demographers are not necessarily groundless; they're just distorted, as they try to assign blame for the present falling-off of the birthrate, suggesting that women jettison or modify their career goals just at a time when their professional lives are on an upward course.

A real possibility is that Jewish women who advance rapidly in their careers don't need children as a validation of their worth. Therefore, as soon as motherhood isn't automatic as a biological or social imperative, some of the reassurance that comes from "doing the right thing" is lost. Taking its place is ambivalence.

The single most crucial issue for women in the 1980s is no longer whether or not to work but whether or not to have children, asserts Betty Friedan.[3]

What used to be automatic in a woman's life—childbearing—has for the first time become optional. For many Jewish women, having this choice, plus having high expectations for themselves in every sphere, creates tremendous conflict. For the lucky others, there's just ambivalence. A woman in her thirties who isn't yet a mother can be faced with simultaneous one-time-only choices, which she may perceive as mutually exclusive: she has career options and a motherhood option, and she has to play them out at the same time, usually before the age of forty.

There's obviously no one attitude toward childbearing (and child rearing) that's typical for all Jewish women. Attitudes range from outright rejection of parenthood through ambivalence of varying degrees (for reasons explored below) all the way to positive affirmations of parenthood as validation that one is not only a "good woman" but also a "good Jew." The positions range from that of a woman in her late thirties who asked if she and her husband could visit with a friend's children to "test-drive" the family structure before deciding on offspring of their own to that of a California mother of five—not Orthodox—who has been angrily criticized by her Jewish friends active in the Zero Population Growth movement.

Demographers claim that Jews are a ZPG movement unto themselves; the Jewish birthrate in the United States is generally estimated to be lower than that of any other religious group in the country (with the exception of Hasidic and other Orthodox groups, for which very large families are the norm).

Why the low Jewish birthrate? What are the attitudes underlying the fact that Jews are now having no children or having fewer children or having their children later in life (thereby losing an entire generation every three decades)? The explanations vary according to whether or not one hears them from an "expert" analyst or a Jewish woman in her thirties contemplating parenthood. Nevertheless, regardless of who's talking, the choice about having children is always seen as the woman's.

Marshall Sklare accuses young women of hedonism, saying that Jewish women have fewer children because a large family "would mean continued subordination to the demands of others; it would interfere with self-realization."[4]

THE WORK VS. CHILDREN DICHOTOMY

The truth is that, given the present inequitable distribution of roles among the adults in the family, women are correct in predicting that the largest share of the burden will most probably be theirs. A professional woman in her late twenties tells a workshop full of women discussing their feeling about having children that "After years of work trying to create an egalitarian marriage, I am afraid of the loss of power that having a child would entail. I wouldn't be bringing in any money and I have a feeling that I would end up doing all the work." Sklare doesn't point out that few men perceive that they will be forced to make the same trade-offs—often forfeiting a hard-won professional identity—in order to have children.

One Jewish woman writes:

It may seem strange, but in most of the discussions of this burning issue of Jewish "fertility," there is little or no direct reference to the effects of the women's movement, even though it should be obvious that the number of children a woman chooses to have is likely to be re-

(courtesy of the 92nd Street Y Parenting Center)

lated to her aspirations and her achievements in other areas of life. One might conclude, from reading various articles, that most couples consult world population charts before deciding whether or not to have a baby, rather than consider who will be responsible for taking care of the child.[5]

Elsewhere, feminism *has* been blamed for the falling Jewish birthrate, as have the "me" concerns of the seventies generation and the lack of child-care facilities in the Jewish community. But very few commentators have bothered to look at or question or analyze the women who are choosing not to have the children.

For women now in college or in their twenties, forgoing career or meaningful work is just not an option—and this is true for educated women across the board. Women, especially those who have themselves been raised by at-home mothers, may not see a range of possibilities for their own future that would allow them to combine work and parenthood (short of being bionic), and so they are likely to push off into the distance making the choice to bear children, believing that it will involve serious, if not damaging, compromises with their work roles. And Jewish women, heirs to all the myths about the Jewish mother's paramount role in making and keeping the children Jewish, and believing that the Jewish mother is really on the front line of a battle for her children's souls and sanity, may really feel that a mother who is not on duty around the clock (as many of their mothers were) has failed in the mission of her lifetime.

Understanding all this, women are unlikely to get pregnant because of the warnings of the demographers, but they may be vulnerable to another kind of pressure to have children. Despite the fact that many young childless Jewish professionals are saying that instead of raising their own children they are doing good things for all Jewish children by their work in Jewish education or Jewish communal service, there are few role models in our past for the successful single or childless person. The Biblical images of childlessness all have to do with being "barren," bereft. And the stories we have of Jewish women who were, say, political activists in America or Israel, always stress their disappointment at not having been able to have children, or a richer family life, because of the demands of their work. Those women who were either single or without children (or who, like Golda Meir, had children but are portrayed as having neglected them) were to be pitied, so said their biographers.

The expectation that marriage and motherhood will be part of every Jewish woman's life hits hardest at Jewish women of the baby-boom generation born in the late 1940s and early 1950s, for whom the "marriage squeeze," in the phrase of journalist Bill Novak, means that there are not enough eligible Jewish men to marry (see p. 303). Faced with a choice of not marrying at all or marrying a man who either doesn't want children or who has children from a previous marriage, or both, Jewish women may choose to marry and remain childless.

Another form of pressure that results from the social structure of American Jewish life, rather than from any direct contact with preaching on the subject, comes from the mothers of this generation of childbearing-age women. Since a whole generation of American Jewish women lived almost entirely through their children (that is, women who didn't work outside their homes), there is much pressure from mother to daughter to see at least part of that way of life replicated. Many Jewish mothers, faced with the possibility of never being grandmothers, suffer a special kind of worthlessness. It goes like this: "If it's so terrible to have and raise children, why is it that I spent my whole life doing it?" This gets passed down to daughters, and sometimes daughters-in-law, as a persistent plea for another generation. Women may not respond positively to the suggestion, but the pressure is there nevertheless.

The alienation of daughter from mother over the issue of childbearing (see p. 276) may have implications for the relationships among other women as well. Social worker Vicki Rosenstreich of the New York Jewish Board of Family and Children Services comments that in past generations the potential for unity between mothers and daughters, while certainly not always fulfilled, was at least available through the common experiences of motherhood; she goes on to speculate on the consequences of this change:

Feminists (myself included) have argued that the new definitions of "woman" have expanded beyond her definition as a mother. Adult daughters have developed a heightened consciousness, a new appreciation of mothers and other women as multi-dimensional people, and this new, humanistic, intellectual and egalitarian perspective is supposed to supplement and compensate for the shift in female roles which postpones or eliminates childbearing. One consequence of this widely hailed shift has been that the formative, essential experiences of each woman's life are dissimilar from those of other women. Each person stands apart. Is the exchange of biological imperative for intellectual appreciation an even one? I think not. The extraordinary professional potential of "sisterhood" has been based on generations of shared biology that cuts across social and political lines. It is not in the banks of Wall Street or the halls of Ivy that women created bonds and harmonies that resonated through all walks of life. The nature of birthing and nursing and caring for dependent creatures shaped the nature of our relationships to each other and our gender capacities for empathy and sympathy. Can intellectual understanding bridge the gap when elements of each's woman's life are now potentially so dissimilar?[6]

In fact, the most divisive conflicts among Jewish women erupt over the question of *whether or not to have children.* The battle is drawn between hedonism and self-righteous responsibility, with a demographic controversy thrown in—a debate over how many Jews there will be in this country by the time America celebrates its tricentennial. (There are now about 5.2 million.)

COMPETENCY AND FEAR OF FAILURE AT MOTHERHOOD

A whole constellation of difficult personal issues arises out of these common personal and cultural concerns for Jewish women now in their twenties and thirties. Because of feelings of being part of a distinct cultural, religious, and ethnic group, Jewish women, in cross-cultural studies, do show a desire to marry, have children, and perpetuate the group. In one such study slightly more of the young Jewish women interviewed were married than their Italian American or Slavic American peers.[7] But this tropism toward marriage doesn't mean that Jewish women are traditionalists in any other ways; instead, there are built-in conflicts between this desire for marriage and family and other needs these women express. The Jewish women in this study were also the most vocal feminists, the best educated, and had the strongest feelings that *their self-esteem depended on work as well as marriage.*

There is an almost automatic conflict between work aspirations and home and family values, because both are so important for Jewish

(Bruce S. Schneider)

women, as they report them. The declining Jewish birthrate is one manifestation of this dual commitment. It's not that Jewish women care only
about careers and don't care about raising children; if this were the case
they might have the children anyway, just to yield to community and
social pressure. They want both.

Jewish women believe that they must be excellent mothers, super-
mothers. Many of us have been raised to believe that motherhood is our
most important task. And though we see it as time-limited, most of those
of us who have children see raising our children as the most valuable task
we'll do, and in the long run the most risky—more important ultimately
than the number of clients we see or how many sales we make in a day at
work and less easy to predict or to prepare for. Given the importance
placed on raising one's children "well," and given the fact that, paradoxically, Jewish women surveyed believed—along with Slavic and Italian
women—that mothers of preschool children should stay at home with
them,[8] many women who want to work or who must work may postpone
having children or choose not to have them at all.

These women may have negative feelings about their own performance
as mothers. For Jewish women the overriding concern about having children may revolve around competence. We are expected (and expect ourselves) to do well at everything.[9] But since most Jewish women growing
up in the 1940s and 1950s didn't come from large families themselves,
how could they have had the experience of seeing children being taken
care of? Tenement life had moved out to the suburbs, and we rarely even
saw our neighbors' children being cared for, much less had an active role
in child care ourselves. How to *do* it?

As Jewish women see themselves in roles of responsibility and competence in the business, professional, and academic worlds, they may be less
and less willing to risk incompetence in a new and scary experience. And
even if parents (now grandparents) are around as guides, their experiences and values may not seem relevant. One antidote to the mythologies
of the past—for example, that all Jewish mothers were supermoms until
the present generation—might be to talk to women who recall their own
mothers from the days of the shtetl in Eastern Europe. Another would be
to read some of the descriptions of Jewish family life in the Yiddish
novels from the turn of the century (before the sentimentalized view of
"the" Jewish family worked its way into the American Jewish literary
imagination). The truth is that many mothers were too busy scratching
for survival to spend much time with their children and that the conflicts
between work and family are nothing new for Jewish women. What's

new is only the expectation that it should be different. Psychoanalysis has taught us to blame our own parents, which puts an almost intolerable burden on *us* as parents. Our knowledge is sometimes more than we can bear.

The realities of parenthood are that by its very nature it offers little short-term feedback. If your child is going to turn out all right and get you points for being a good parent, you'll never know until she's grown up, or so the threat goes. The early returns—smiles, coos, good grades—may be inaccurate predictors of the end results. This makes parenthood a very risky business for a generation of potential parents accustomed to seeing regular signs of their own success: grades, money, regular promotions, or at least compliments on the pot roast or the kiwi tarts.

Three factors coalesce in contributing to women's fears of incompetence as mothers:

1. The American perfect-mom syndrome, still alive and well in the three decades since Philip Wylie coined "momism."

2. The Jewish mythological version of self-sacrificing motherhood inspired by a generation or two of American Jewish mothers who, not being permitted to work outside their homes, had to have perfection within them.

3. A growing understanding of the ideological perils of woman-centered parenting.[10]

One Jewish woman (after two children) says about her ambivalence toward being a mother: "I did not have the credentials for it. . . . I wish that in my eighth and ninth month, when I was getting ready to be terrific, that someone would have told me it was OK to say 'I don't know if I'm going to be terrific. This is my first day on the job, and I just don't know how I'll do.' "[11] And a Virginia woman admits, "I'm very glad that I had my children when I did, in the late sixties, when it wasn't really a choice. If I had to face the decision now as to whether or not to have children I'm not sure I'd be able to decide. Letting the biological clock decide for me might seem the only way out."

These choices exist for non-Jews also, and certainly have been taken up in the context of secular feminism—the conflicts over motherhood, the disputes between those women who see it as oppressive to women and those women who see it as a pleasure, though not without its difficulties. In a secular context, women who choose not to have children can at least make claims that the world is overpopulated anyway, that it's a bad place to raise children, and so on. For the Jewish woman self-identified as a Jew, such arguments are impossible. There is a whole burden of guilt and responsibility placed on Jewish women who choose not to have children or who postpone having children. It's as if the entire collectivity of the Jews were being threatened by this decision.

A SPECIAL CASE FOR THE JEWS: POST-HOLOCAUST PARENTHOOD

In the past the Jews have often been a very small minority, but our post-Holocaust consciousness, and the complexities of Israel-Diaspora relations, which seem to demand a large, strong American Jewish community, have probably made this population crisis more anxiety-provoking than those of the past. Historical reasons do play some part in people's decisions to have children—witness the baby boom after World War II in America, and the number of families that decided to have another child right after the 1967 Six Day War in Israel.

Particularly for women who have themselves been refugees from Hitler's Europe or who are the children of survivors of the camps or of pogroms, there is a strong imperative to have children to make up for those lost or never born. In fact, most Jewish-identified Jews living after the Holocaust see themselves as survivors. All feel some degree of fealty to Emil Fackenheim's "eleventh commandment": not to give Hitler any posthumous victories—which means that at least we must ourselves not contribute to the diminution of the Jewish people. Family size is an issue with implications that reach beyond the family itself.

These are some of the social, cultural, and historical reasons that Jewish women may feel that their having children, or having more children, matters in a way that goes beyond personal decision-making. *What's good for the Jews?* It's a question that other women don't ever have to ask, let alone answer.

LARGE FAMILIES: THE THIRD-CHILD QUESTION

For most Jews who have decided to have children the issue of family size is settled after the birth of the second child. The ZPG advocates are satisfied, the parents feel they haven't committed the "crime" of having an "only child," and the matter is closed. But this isn't the case for some Jewish couples. Women, particularly, have been wrestling with the third-child option—an especially difficult choice now that having *any* children is a decision some women feel they have to defend.

Inge Lederer Gibel, now a grandmother, describes her own choice as a "mistake": "I do have one terrible regret, that I didn't have more children. As a woman who worked originally, when my daughter and son were small, because our family needed my paycheck, and as a mother who in typical Jewish fashion wanted the best for her children—much of which it took money to buy—I convinced myself that two was a necessary limit. It is only in the last decade . . . that I have bitterly regretted that self-limiting choice."[12]

Elaine Shizgal Cohen of Teaneck, New Jersey, a Jewish community activist long involved in the havurah movement says:

We lived in Israel for two years and the experience changed me a lot. Israelis haven't lost the attitude that having a family is "natural." There's a joyful acceptance of children in the general culture. One sees less of that here in the States. Of course, there are complex motivations at play in that very different cultural and political environment: a widely shared commitment to nation-building, unspoken anxieties about the possibility of losing a child to war or terrorism, a post-Holocaust affirmation of Jewish destiny.

On some level, the decision to have a third child was connected for me with my identification as a Jew. It seemed to me an act of affirmation and of conscience after the Holocaust and in an age of widespread assimilation. I have heard other minority women express similar views, albeit in a different context, that we are being sold short by the image of the ideal American family (two children only, and preferably one of each), and are losing sight of our own interests in building our culture and strengthening our roots.[13]

On the other hand, there is the suggestion often made that a woman who continues, or returns to, childbearing is avoiding important career decisions. And what woman with career aspirations wants to hear that she is somehow betraying her own goals? Certainly not the well-educated Jewish woman who owns an apron that asks "For this I spent four years at college?" The same accusations are made to non-Jewish women, of course, as a cartoon in *The New York Times Magazine* demonstrates: A woman surrounded by children complains "I can't get to my career"— and she's pregnant again. The added dimension for Jewish women is that there is, from some quarters at least, a great deal of sanction and support for having "more" children at the same time that Jewish women's professional possibilities are widening.[14]

Vicki Rosenstreich describes her own choice when she and her husband decided to have their third child. "People in my women's group felt

I was sabotaging my career just when I was beginning to get recognition for my work. But I really felt—and told them—that I hope to have many years after 40 to be a well-regarded professional. Delaying the recognition for a few years wouldn't be so awful, but I wouldn't have a chance later to have another child. It wasn't so much a case of delayed gratification, but of substituting enormous personal gratification for an external, professional gratification."[15]

WHO CARES FOR THE CHILDREN? STRIVING FOR EGALITARIAN AND COMMUNAL CHILD REARING

The heated discussions about Jewish women's choices regarding childbearing are now—in the eighties—focusing on who will care for the children that are produced. One feminist, long legitimately cynical about the Jewish community's responses to women's needs, says: *"Now that there are no more Jewish children being born they have a conference to talk about child care!"*

While the explanations of the personal reasons that may keep Jewish women from responding to the childbearing imperative are interesting, and even useful insofar as they illuminate the dark corners of the conflicts many women feel, it is also unjust to claim that the problem is only a personal one and to leave it at that.

A group that suggests to its members that they take on a lifelong responsibility *for the good of the group* must provide some of the backup necessary to make the responsibility a shared one between the individual and the community being served. The Jewish community must provide facilities for parents and for the children they are being called upon to produce. These services range from all-day Jewish child-care facilities to sliding-scale tuitions in Hebrew day schools to making available more flexible working hours for employees of Jewish institutions.

The problem of how to care for Jewish children isn't new. Orphanages and other full-time institutions were sometimes the places of last resort for Jewish families in another era.[16] Sam Levenson's description of his placement in an orphanage when his father couldn't care for him after his mother's death and Tillie Olsen's short story "I Stand Here Ironing," from the collection *Tell Me a Riddle* (New York: Dell, 1956), provide only two examples among many of the pain with which parents confronted their child-care options in the past. There have always been Jewish families who needed communal support in this area. Only now are Jewish institutions addressing the need on a wide scale.

(courtesy of the 92nd Street Y Parenting Center)

In the 1950s there was a "build-a-better-basketball-court" mentality that pervaded Jewish communities across the continent. This was the era when Jewish community centers expanded and flourished and when every synagogue under construction had to have a fully equipped gymnasium. (Now all they need is a video arcade.) All this was being done in an attempt to "keep our young people"—by which was meant, of course, young male people, since the facilities were intended for them.

What's needed for the 1980s and 1990s is a commitment to "keeping our young people" that will mean providing services for men and women choosing to be parents. "Young" people ranging in age from their twenties through their forties and fifties need space—that isn't being used all day in synagogues and Jewish community centers—for drop-in child care and ongoing preschool programs for Jewish children which in many cities are available only through civic or church groups.

One woman from a New York suburb puts it very succinctly: "It's a real double bind. A rabbi gets up in his pulpit and says have four kids. (If you're Orthodox you do it even if you don't like it.) But—this choice is disallowed in the community. There's no day care to speak of, and often no part-time work available in Jewish agencies. And if you go to work full time, you don't exactly want to have four kids. The Jewish communities have all these commissions on family life, and then undermine it in other ways."

Jewish parents say that they want Jewish facilities for their young children not necessarily because a year-old child will learn to recite prayers or sing Hebrew songs but because there will be a certain ambiance in preparations for Shabbat, there will be candles and other concrete symbols and objects the child will learn to recognize. Positive Jewish experiences, even at this age, are crucial. Very important, especially to parents of a first child, are the associations that will be formed with other young Jewish families at a time when they will be creating communities and circles of friends in a family context for the first time; the milieu of the Jewish child-care facility provides a chance for the parents as well as the children to connect.

In an ideal world there would be many choices for Jewish parents:

• Ongoing listings of retired people maintained in synagogues and community centers—people who would like to act as surrogate grandparents to provide workday child care or to provide weekend and holiday "standby" help when the regular system isn't functioning. The Parenting Center at New York City's 92nd Street YM/YWHA maintains some lists, mostly in an informal fashion, but as it is now, many Jewish families in large cities advertise for help with their children in *The Irish Echo* or other, similar non-Jewish ethnic papers.

• Space in synagogues that is not usually used until after-school Hebrew classes arrive in the late afternoon could be converted into a whole array of day-care facilities. Many of these buildings have to be heated and maintained around the clock anyway. Some, especially in older sections of cities, are already centers for the Jewish elderly, who might welcome the chance to work as paid or volunteer assistants in the child-care programs.

Arguments against using synagogues or similar spaces for child care usually focus on the complex federal and local codes concerning the institutional care of very young children. But surely Jewish legal brains can find solutions to these red-herring difficulties, once synagogue authorities understand that on-premises child care is a way to get young Jewish families connected with the synagogue at least a dozen years before the Bat or Bar Mitzvah of their first child usually brings them in.

• Sliding-scale payments for Jewish day care and Jewish schools would be an inducement. Some families with two paychecks might be happy and willing to pay the going (high) rates if they were assured that they'd get quality child care in a Jewish setting. Other parents, equally eager, couldn't afford it; so subsidies must be found, perhaps by enlisting the help of Jewish organizations—men's as well as women's—to take on a local Jewish day-care project as a beneficiary. One section of the National Council of Jewish Women raised funds specifically for parents who needed "scholarships" to use Jewish day-care facilities.

• Baby-sitting services should be offered at every Jewish function. The argument for doing this is that parents can't maintain any involvement with the Jewish community if they are working and trying to take care of their children. And for parents who do not work full time this child care is also a necessary prerequisite if they are going to be involved in any volunteer activity. Women can take a stand by refusing to participate as speakers or performers or lecturers in Jewish programs that do not provide on-premises baby-sitting. The service may entail advance registration and an hourly fee, if necessary, but it should be there.

An available and highly visible positive communal response to the presence of Jewish children is in itself a sign to Jewish women (and men) that their children are of value to the whole community. It also shows Jewish people who have not yet decided to have children that there *are* communal support systems—a factor that can be especially reassuring to couples who have no family supports nearby.

• After-school programs at Hebrew day schools should be provided so that the children of working parents won't have to rely on private or *ad hoc* arrangements every day. The presence of good after-school programs (pick-up and delivery essential) would also be an incentive for parents to enroll their children in such schools.

• Family-style day care (which most working parents now rely on) would be staffed with trained child-care workers. Those who choose child care as their work would be trained free by the Jewish community. They could be satellites of a centralized child-care facility at a local YM/YWHA or synagogue, as they are in some cities now. Frankly, if child care were seen as a "status" job, or if it paid very well, more Jews would choose to do it. Children now being cared for eight to nine hours a day in non-Jewish homes could receive their care in a Jewish environment instead.

• Special scholarships for people intending to enter the child-care field —and assurances of placement in a Jewish child-care facility at a good salary—would draw both men and women into the field. In the ideal world, of course professional child care (like child rearing itself) would be seen not only as women's work but as equally suitable for men.

We all want the same ideal future for the Jewish population as Rabbi Norman B. Mirsky, who said, "I wish there could be myriads of Jewish infants without banishing Jewish women to the nursery and Jewish men to the petite bourgeois [sic]."[17] Well, women aren't going to be in the nursery, at least not all the time. They and their husbands will both be members of, if not the bourgeoisie, at least part of the paid labor force in some form.

To lessen the burden of guilt on those mothers who choose or are forced to work outside the home when their children are young, one need only listen to psychologist Alice Ginnott again, addressing a 1980 conference, "Who Cares for the Children: Alternatives in Jewish Child Care."[18] Ginnott advocates some form of day care for all children as a way of providing them with necessary variety of approaches. She states that not all parents are best with children at every stage of development; some are more comfortable with the very dependent stages of infancy, while others are more successful in relating to their children when they are older and more independent, for example. Ginnott goes on to claim that the Israeli *metapelet* system (in which a "helper" raises the child, either in a kibbutz children's house or in a private home as a part-time surrogate mother) is best for the child, since the person giving the care doesn't have the same vested interest in the child that the parents do. (For more on the Israeli system, see p. 392.)

Ginnott and others have expressed the feeling that the quality of the time the parent spends with the child is far more important than the quantity. Many Jewish mothers who have always worked outside the home would support that statement, agreeing with Ann G. Wolfe, who commented at a 1979 meeting of a Task Force on the Role of the Jewish Woman, "For heaven's sake! There are women who have been working for years and whose children are now old enough for the results to be in. Look at our kids—after all, they didn't turn out so badly."

Statistics support this: there seems to be no difference in the emotional life of children with mothers at home and children who've received good day care. Of course the problem then is how to provide the good day care. Ginnott also courageously told the child-care-conference audience she was addressing (a mixed group of men and women, some with high positions in various Jewish communal organizations): "*Men* create the atmosphere of power. Men have the money. Men will decide if Federation will change its policies and fund day-care centers. Until now, men have decided that *motherhood* will assure good care."

And where are the Jewish men in all this *angst?* The "problem" seems to belong only to women. Having children should be a shared decision and a shared responsibility for which both parents will make sacrifices and reap joy. But, as Paula Hyman points out, "The fertility boosters rarely call for men to assume a larger share of child care."[19]

Male rabbis can and often do sit on committees and make speeches about how frightening the "problem" is, but the fact that prospective mothers don't see Jewish men as prospective fatherhood material is never discussed. Perhaps if it were clear to a whole generation of Jewish women that the men they'll marry will share the responsibility of parenthood and not just sit on committees or play racquetball, they'd view motherhood more auspiciously.

The commandment to be fruitful and multiply applies Halachicly only to men. So while we are worrying about courses to help women air their ambivalence about motherhood, we should be starting training programs for young men on their responsibilities as fathers. Instead of such programs as "Investments, Wills and Estates," run for the men of the United Jewish Appeal Young Leadership Division (in the hopes of securing more dollars for the Jewish community in the future), why not such programs as "Why Parenthood Is a Joint Responsibility" or "Why Jewish Men Need to Be Prepared to Change Diapers and Stay Home with Sick Kids Too," in order to ensure that there will be Jews in the Jewish community of tomorrow and not just capital. In fact, with men and women prepared to perform similar tasks—sharing both breadwinning and nurturing—the family itself might be more stable, with less conflict than when the life's work is divided up tidily along gender lines.

What these and other suggestions revolve around are two basic assumptions that we must believe and act on:

1. Child care is not the exclusive responsibility of the parent who physically bears the child. She is only 50 percent of the parental couple.

2. Women have entered the paid labor force, and they will stay there. By 1990 only one in every four mothers in the U.S. with preschool children will be able to afford to stay home even if they all wanted to.

In our personal planning, and in the planning that the Jews do on a communal level, we have to consider these assumptions absolute and immutable. Otherwise we're acting on illusion, not reality.

We can hope that the new reality will reflect more of the attitude of men like Rabbi André Ungar, who described in his New Jersey temple's bulletin his feelings about the years when he had the major responsibility for caring for his children while his wife attended graduate school.

"He was a good mother." A middling rabbi, a so-so citizen, an un-even husband . . . but ah, yes, he was a pretty good mother. I hope they put it on my tombstone one of these days; not too soon; all in due time.

Let me count the benefits. For one thing, I got to know my own children far better than I ever had before. As a father, I used to have a short fuse and a limited amount of patience. As a mother, I could no longer afford that male chauvinist luxury. . . .

And I found out, on my own skin and soul, what being a housewife is like in actuality. How it simply never ends. How it can drain the last drop of energy, humor, tenderness, even sanity. How it consists of in-cessant traffic jams that make the George Washington Bridge on Monday at 9 a.m. seem like a tranquil meadow. How it can bewilder and exasperate and wring you out like a dishrag. (Please, please don't mention dishrags!) It gave me vast new respect for the people who are doing it and have over the generations been doing it, day after day, year in, year out, lifelong. The sheer enslavement of it all. The bleak horror. The outrage. The endlessness and hopelessness, especially for those who, unlike myself, had no other life, other work, for whom it was a life sentence.

Yet on the other hand, I also discovered . . . whole continents of unknown and unexpected joy also. Doing the daily chores I came to realize just how human, how personal, how creative so much of this kind of labor really was. Reading a story to—better still, with—a child is every bit as exacting and fulfilling as writing and publishing an article. Seeing a kid chomp away with relish at a meal I fixed gladdens me as much as watching an audience of hundreds absorbed in a lecture I give. Cheering up a boy after a blue day is more of a challenge to my imagination than parrying a critical committee meeting. To say that classical mothering, "woman's work," is hard is absolutely true. To say that it is degrading, demeaning, boring, worthless is utterly, shamefully false.

Like most other professions—medicine, law, accountancy, the rabbinate, bank robbery, window washing—mothering has its own balance of advantages and drawbacks. To force a person to do it against his—or her—own will is monstrously unfair. To dismiss it as less than intelligent or other than creative is a gross, cowardly insult. Personally, I believe that everybody ought to be doing it. For a few years anyway.[20]

Without falling into the sentimental and unrealistic glorification of a man who takes on what are merely his responsibilities (à la *Kramer vs. Kramer*), we *should* give credit to those men who are willing to go public as models for sharing the tasks of child rearing.

Visibility is an important factor in all these solutions, because the more that people see that having children and caring for them need not be done exclusively by the same people, namely the mothers, the more a climate of opinion is created that allows for more communal solutions. The personal *is* the political, but it has to be seen to have political impact.

If one father at home takes equal responsibility for his children, it doesn't change the attitudes of other fathers until the life-style is exposed to everyone. This is why it is especially useful to see men in child-care situations. Judith E. Zimmerman reports on her own family situation: "My husband is a congregational rabbi; therefore he works on weekends. He takes off on Tuesdays to be with our family. At nine each Tuesday morning he and our then year-and-a-half-old baby, David, arrived at

David's playgroup (Parkbench at New York's 92nd Street YM/YWHA). For the first few weeks, Shelly [Rabbi Sheldon Zimmerman] was the only father to attend, but now other fathers attend before going to work, or during holidays." The fact that one father made the effort to be with his toddler "had a profound ripple effect in other families as well."[21]

Granted, this attitude is rare. Despite their alleged "nurturing" role, many male rabbis demonstrate by their synagogue behavior that they view children as a nuisance, an attitude that can't help being transmitted to others.

A Pro-Family Workplace?

In addition to supporting those families that want alternatives to traditional gender-related child-care roles, leaders and institutions in the Jewish community can help ensure that communal organizations provide a workplace environment that helps employees to be better parents. One woman, an executive in a social-service agency says: "I think that the Jewish institutions—universities, hospitals, social-service agencies, community centers—should be in the *forefront* of developing alternative ways to organize the workplace so that Jewish women (and men) can work *and* raise their children. There should be flexible work hours, maternity *and* paternity leave, and some understanding that employees with children may not want or be able to stay late into the night attending meetings."

Responding to this need, a large Jewish family-service agency in the Northeast, with a woman in a top executive position (one of the few) now has a policy that encourages employees to take time off to be with a sick child or to attend a school play, and allows them to make up the time either from vacation leave, sick leave, or by coming in earlier and working later on another day. And the Jewish Board of Family and Children's Services of New York has been drawing up guidelines, "Pro-Family Policies for the Workplace," which include "Development of a work 'culture' which is approving of family needs, rather than covertly or overtly negative."

The changes that are taking place are few and far between, however, with the real needs of families with children often still going unnoticed. As an example, a wide-ranging two-day conference on ways to encourage Jewish population growth, held in New York in October 1983 under the sponsorship of a broad coalition of Jewish organizations, provided *no* facilities for participants with children, and offered no child care, even after the organizers were prodded on this issue. Judith Zimmerman, who attended with one of her children, expressed her outrage to reporters with the observation "I feel like I'm in Chelm!"

Women are slowly working to change their own realities in the workplace as they feel able to be more outspoken about their own needs and begin to see that they can use the community's "concern" for population issues as a lever in moving community agencies further along in related areas.

The emphasis on "family" issues on the agenda of women's organizations and Jewish bodies may have had one hidden benefit for women, who may now feel that they have permission to articulate their needs as workers *and* mothers. The attitude of this Washington, D.C., woman is a case in point: "I went to be interviewed for a job as a social worker at a Jewish family-service agency, and I told the interviewer that instead of only working one night a week, I'd prefer to leave at 3 p.m. each day to meet my three children when they come home from school and come back to work *two* nights a week. I decided that *this is my reality*, and the interviewer might as well know it. There's no sense pretending, as I might have a few years ago, that I don't have responsibilities—employers, especially in the Jewish community, will just have to understand."[22]

The Israeli Model
We can learn a great deal about the flaws in American patterns of child care by examining the Israeli model and its implications for mothers. Not only does Israel have a network of institutional and home-based day care for children from infancy on, but there also exists an underlying social attitude that approves of child care by people other than blood relatives (perhaps because other Israelis are viewed as part of an extended family). Whatever the reasons, Israeli families with young children generally have access to greater options in child care than do their American counterparts.

The Israeli six-day week, with six- or seven-hour workdays, means that even if a person works nearly full time, she/he can be at home by early to mid-afternoon and still have lots of time with the children. Under the American system parents arrive home after a full workday (which often includes lots of time spent commuting and picking up children from child-care facilities) and only begin to organize dinner at about 7:00 P.M. The Israeli system (which is now, alas, undergoing changes that would bring it closer to the American schedule) incorporates work and home life into each day in almost equal parts, as opposed to the North American division of time into work all week/leisure all weekend. (Although a serious flaw in the Israeli system is that school-age children end their day shortly after noon and are expected to return home for lunch, where, by some Houdini-like method, a mother is supposed to greet them with a hot meal although she is simultaneously supposed to be at her job at that time. The school schedule is often and correctly blamed for the fact that many Israeli women take only part-time jobs, so that while they don't face disapprobation for working outside the home, circumstances often dictate that they will not threaten men by advancing in full-time careers.)

But even with this reservation about the different diurnal rhythms of the two countries, there is a lot to be said for attitudes toward children and child care in Israel. It is clear that, in a population-poor country, each child is valued. Public policy reflects this, with grants to families for each child, regardless of the family's income. General responses suggest shared responsibility. No one who has traveled with children in Israel can help being struck by the number of people stopping to comfort a strange child who is crying, offering kind words, candy, and free advice.

After several months of living in Israel with a small child a returning American woman comments: "Every woman I met worked outside her home. One was a university instructor, another a teacher, another a student, another a secretary. All of these women had made adequate child-care arrangements and had *no guilt!!*"

Two lessons emerge:

1. Women most often hired a *metapelet* (literally, a care-giver) to care for the child at home when the child was very young. A transfer of this model to an American setting might have Jewish agencies serving officially as clearinghouses for college-age students to act as baby-sitters or care-givers on a regular basis, encouraging in-home child care as an appropriate and not demeaning part-time job. For example, the Jewish Federation Employment and Guidance Service in New York could set up and maintain training programs providing Jewish child-care workers to work in Jewish homes, obviating the necessity for having children raised by non-Jews, if this is an important value to the family and to the community.

2. Israeli families with children of play-group or nursery-school age— from about age two—send them to *gan*, a kind of institutionalized play group usually run by a woman in her own home. These arrangements are flexible, and sometimes go from 7:30 or 8:00 A.M. until noon, sometimes later. Their quality is uneven, but they do exist and in large enough numbers so that one can usually find one that is appropriate in services and location. These child-care options and the widespread pressure of women

in the work force are due partly to the need for workers in a labor-intensive economy (unemployment was virtually unknown in Israel until the late 1970s), partly to the fact that shared child rearing on the kibbutz has existed in Israel for decades and is a national custom, and partly to an inflation so severe that each family requires at least two paychecks.

Of course the entire sabra mythos is based on peer-group activity (with strong ties to one's school class and one's army group), so there is in fact much pressure *away* from the insular nuclear-family model which so many Israelis find antisocial when they first come to America.

RESOURCES

For a report on Jewish day-care programs around the country and a reading list, send for *Jewish Child Care: The Community Responds*, which is Vol. 1, No. 3 of:

The National Jewish Family Center Newsletter
Jewish Communal Affairs Department
American Jewish Committee
165 E. 56 Street
New York, NY 10022
$2.50 for an annual subscription

The American Jewish Committee has published a discussion guide for its members, *Changing Role of Men and Women in the Jewish Family*, which asks questions about the responsibility for child care. Also available from the committee is its *Jewish Family Impact Questionnaire*, intended for use by community organizations to determine—by analyzing data on flextime, number of evening meetings, and so on—whether their policies and practices meet the family needs of their workers and the people they serve.

A difficult problem for many Jewish parents is finding Jewish day care for very young children. Often maternity leave ends when the baby is three months old, and the parents are faced with either restructuring their work schedules or finding adequate care in a child-care facility. Few parents can afford the luxury of full-time help at home, and even some who can, worry that their child will be isolated in a home setting with no other children present. What to do? Many parents have taken advantage of church-run infant-care programs, and one such program in New York reports that parents sign up their children even before birth.

Pinpointing what may be a very important factor in the attractiveness of Jewish day-care facilities, Bea Paul notes that Jewish parents seem less uneasy, less guilt-ridden when they leave their children in Jewish facilities. However, Jewish institutions have been reluctant to establish child-care facilities for children who are very young—three months to three years old. Paul, director of one such center, says that when she first approached the community center and adjoining synagogue with her plan, the response of the men in charge was "You're not going to have *diapers* around, are you?" The innovative program Paul heads could be a model for others. Not only does it provide care for infants and toddlers but it also provides transportation to and from the local kindergarten for older children whose parents work all day. Write:

North Shore Jewish Community Center
4 Community Road
Marblehead, MA 01945
(617) 631-8330

Another community that has honored a commitment to provide adequate child care is Philadelphia. For a brochure describing a range of community-sponsored programs that will cause parents' mouths to water nationwide, write:

Federation Day Care Services
Jamison Avenue and Garth Road
Philadelphia, PA 19116

There are programs for preschool and school-age children, from 7:30 A.M. to 6:00 P.M., with full-day programs for school children on days when schools are closed for holidays and vacations, plus a variety of instructional, counseling and backup services.

Also in Philadelphia, the local chapter of the American Jewish Committee's Subcommittee on the Status of Women has published a report titled "Jewish Day-Care Facilities in Philadelphia," which includes some marvelous suggestions for filling the needs of parents and children. "The inevitable conclusion . . . is that the overwhelming majority of Jewish parents feel that good day care is of primary importance not only to shaping a child's Jewish identity, but to the health of the family."

The 92nd Street Y in New York has a Parenting Center with drop-in child care, a Parkbench Program for toddlers and parents, and counseling and classes. Many of the programs have become standard operating procedure for Y's. What's different here is that the Parenting Center sees itself also as a networking agency for meeting the diverse needs of Jewish parents. It maintains a baby-sitting registry, a clearinghouse for child-care and play-group information, a newsletter dealing with problems and solutions for parents, and is seen by many parents as the first line of defense, the place they turn to for information of all sorts. As a model for developing the centrality of the Jewish community center in the lives of women (as it once was in the lives of Jewish men a generation or so ago—with its handball courts and pool), the Parenting Center should be watched closely.

The Y has also been at the hub of a Jewish Family Day Care Network, providing training for Jewish women (why only women?) who will stay home and care for Jewish children in their homes rather than in an institutional setting. The goal, according to cofounder Arlene Bernstein, "is to provide affordable, quality services for infants ranging from one month to three years, within a Jewish home environment."

ADOPTION

One group caught in the crossfire between the attackers who harangue women to produce Jewish progeny and the defenders of women's right to remain child-free are those couples who want to have children and cannot. In response to the article "The Population Panic," *Lilith* magazine received this letter: "You write about the pressures on Jewish women to have babies. My husband and I can't conceive, but we want very much to bring children into our home and raise them as Jews. Where is the community which cries out for families to have more children when it comes to setting up a support system for those Jewish families who are trying to adopt?"

According to accounts in the Jewish press, some Jewish children have been placed in non-Jewish homes, either as adoptees or as foster children, even in areas in which Jewish homes for foster children exist.

For further information on becoming a foster parent, which can sometimes lead to adoption, or if you know of a child who might need temporary or permanent placement, get in touch with:

Rabbi Reuven Simons
Emergency Council of Jewish Families
2 Penn Plaza
New York, NY 10001
(212) 244-3100

Foster Homes/Adoption Information
Jewish Child Care Association
345 Madison Avenue
New York, NY 10017
(212) 490-9160

Louise Wise Services
12 E. 94 Street
New York, NY 10028
(212) 876-3050

The last agency also offers services such as counseling for unwed parents, residential care for women, a maternity residence and a residence for mothers and babies, plus adoption placement and postadoptive services for adoptees, birth parents, and adoptive parents.

There are statutes in most states requiring placement agencies to try to place adoptees and foster children in homes or institutions of their own religion; in some parts of the country officials claim that there are insufficient Jewish adoptive parents or foster parents for these children. The same woman who wrote that she would like to adopt suggests: "Considering the number of 'Jewish' names involved in publicity over so-called grey-market adoptions, perhaps this is a situation which lends itself to Jewish community involvement—connecting Jewish agencies with prospective adoptive Jewish parents."

For adoption of non-Jewish babies there are special conversion proce dures, which vary from converting the child at birth to waiting until Bar/Bat Mitzvah. Some rabbis believe that conversion cannot take place unless the child is an adult and can choose for her/himself. It is best to check with a local rabbi and/or one of the several texts on the Jewish laws concerning conversion.

Another dimension to the adoption issue for Jews is that while after the Korean and Vietnam wars Jewish families adopted Oriental children, these adoptions were more acceptable than adopting a black Jewish child or an interracial Jewish child, according to Graenum Berger in his study of black Jews. Berger also makes the point that Jewish families are losing out by this reluctance: "It is clear that the failure of white, black or mixed-color Jewish families to adopt interracial children, who are clearly Jewish by Halachic standards, results in a minor net loss to the Jewish census in a period of declining Jewish population."[23]

As a particular aside to the issue of sterility among Jews or the desire for Jewish couples to adopt, the suggestion has been made by various

groups concerned with "Jewish fertility" that the Jewish community provide counseling and/or subsidies for those women who can be persuaded
to give birth to a child that would be put up for adoption, rather than
have an abortion to terminate an unwanted pregnancy. This is a suggestion that has been made in non-Jewish circles as well, always by men.
What.is a married woman with other children going to tell her children
about the prospective "abandonment for adoption" of the baby growing
in her uterus? And what is the childless married or single woman supposed to tell her colleagues? This doesn't seem to be a suggestion with
much serious potential, but it's offensive in that it is made with so little
consideration of the feelings of the woman involved. When the same
suggestion was made by Israel's antiabortion forces, a Jerusalem obstetri-
cian replied, "The woman is not a child-bearing factory."[24]

An especially useful overview of the situation facing Jewish families
who want to adopt is a pamphlet published in 1981 by the organization
of Reform rabbis. The pamphlet deals with infertility, problems in both
civil and Jewish law concerning adoption, and suggestions for "living
with adoption."

A Rabbi's Guide to Adoption
Central Conference of American Rabbis
790 Madison Avenue
New York, NY 10021

Aside from the general medical and self-help organizations dealing
with infertility and the difficulties faced by couples trying to conceive,
there is a peer-counseling program now that provides a Jewish context for
women and couples dealing with miscarriage, stillbirths, and other heretofore almost unrecognized unhappy circumstances:

Pregnancy Loss Counseling
Jewish Women's Resource Center
National Council of Jewish Women—New York Section
9 E. 69 Street
New York, NY 10021

THE JEWISH MOTHER'S SURVIVAL KIT— RESOURCES FOR PARTICULAR SITUATIONS

Single Mothers

The women who are most in need of family supports are single mothers,
who have also commonly been the most powerless and invisible people in

the community. In a fairly typical head-in-the-sand routine, many Jewish agencies denied that there were families that conformed to anything but the two-parent model. The ostrich attitude is related to a fear also expressed in dealing with other phenomena (such as remaining single or being homosexual)—namely, if we admit that It's among us, does that look as if we're legitimizing It, and then will more and more people see It as a viable option within Jewish life?

Jewish women who are single because of widowhood or divorce face many of the same problems or situations in Jewish life that never-married single women do (see "To Be Single . . . ," p. 300, "Divorce," p. 355, and "When a Jewish Wife Becomes a Widow," p. 408). But for the single woman who is also a parent there are some additional problems.

First and foremost of these is the fact that single mothers are the new Jewish poor (see also "Displaced Homemakers," p. 484). Child-support payments are almost never generous, and enforcing payment is nearly impossible, so the people most in need of Jewish community support in the form of child-care subsidies, flexible work hours, and the like are single mothers. Since until recently Jewish agencies have done very little outreach to this population, most of these women may not even know about the services and supports that are available.

The angriest people at Jewish gatherings tend to be women who, through divorce or widowhood, have lost their role as half a couple and are at the same time in a situation of financial vulnerability. The Jewish community can—and does—become the target of this anger if the real needs of these women aren't met, especially in light of such proclamations as this one by Rabbi Sol M. Roth, Honorary President of the (Orthodox) Rabbinical Council of America: "The synagogue must preserve standards. It is concerned with norms, and a 'normal' Jewish life is not the single parent."[25]

The risk in not meeting the needs—not providing services for children, not making available single-parent supports in various ways—can mean that both these women and their children will be lost to the community. Although statistics predict that over 50 percent of divorced women will remarry within five years—meaning that single parenthood may be only a phase, with women reconnecting with the community if and when they remarry—their children may never get over their sense of alienation from Jewish life and institutions. Long marginal people in a community based on the couples model, single parents (about 95 percent of them women) are beginning to be recognized, partly because of a demographic panic, which is expressed as "We've got to pay attention to every Jew, so why not these?"

The needs of Jewish women raising children alone range from adequate child care to the kind of emotional and cultural buttressing pleaded for by a woman who interrupted a slow and dull PTA meeting on "Jewish values" with this *cri du coeur*: "How am I supposed to give my 10-year-old some Jewish values at home? How do I sit down with my macho son and say 'Let's sing'? The echoes reverberate all over the house! My ex-husband is a Marxist atheist who lives 3,000 miles away. I'm in town all alone without any family, so how do I do Shabbat with him? How can I be Jewish with him as a single parent? Why don't any of the other families in the school invite us to spend Shabbat with *them*?"

For suggestions and resources on how Jewish women can "learn" to do holidays and Shabbat celebrations without "a man in the house," see the section "Rhythms and Cycles," p. 84.

For some suggestions about appropriate community responses to the needs of single parents, see:

Single-Parent Families: A Challenge to the Jewish Community
by Chaim I. Waxman
American Jewish Committee Institute of Human Relations
165 E. 56 Street
New York, NY 10022
$1.00

The author's statements reflect the traditional bias in speaking of what is a growing and largely unserved population. Waxman says we "need to find ways of aiding the single-parent family while upholding the superiority of the two-parent family." The very useful suggestions in the booklet are somewhat undermined by this tone of grudging condescension, which seems to suggest that parents might willingly choose to raise their children alone rather than that they have to do so as a last resort after an unhappy marriage ends or as an inevitable consequence of the death of a spouse.

The Single Parent Family Center is a multiservice center for parents with children under eighteen at a YM/YWHA in Queens, New York. The center provides group events for parents and children and for single parents themselves, and legal advice, therapy groups, and rap sessions on such topics as "Can I or Can't I When the Kids are Home?"

Single Parent Family Center
YM/YWHA
45-35 Kissena Boulevard
Flushing, NY 11355

An Orthodox Single Parents Center (part of the new recognition of divorce as a reality even among observant Jews, at one time thought to be immune from such changes) deals with such special concerns as the "dual system of law"—Halachic and civil—under which single parents must operate. Its programs may be useful models for Orthodox groups elsewhere:

Orthodox Single Parents Center
Boro Park YM/YWHA
4912, 14 Avenue
Brooklyn, NY 11219
(718) 438-5921

In havurot a single parent would likely feel comfortable, as would her children. For havurot in your area, consult the National Havurah Coordinating Committee.

There is a program of "action, services and education" for Jewish single-parent families—Single Parent Awareness and Caring Exchange (S.P.A.C.E.)—sponsored by the National Council of Jewish Women in Los Angeles, Detroit, and other localities. For information, consult your local section or the NCJW national office (see Networking Directory).

In Boston there are programs geared to single parents of children under eighteen. For information call:

Jewish Family and Children Services
(617) 235-8997

Raising a Child Jewish When Your Husband Isn't

For parents trying to sort out their complicated feelings around children's Jewish identity in a mixed marriage, it helps to listen to the common experiences of others who have struggled over the same issue. "In many cases you don't know how committed you are to your religious roots, your cultural roots, until the children are born, until perhaps a parent dies and you are feeling all that guilt and all that need for continuity." Inge Lederer Gibel, speaking here, is one of five Jewish parents giving testimony in an article in *Lilith* on how they inculcated a sense of Jewishness in their young children, while the children also had to assimilate aspects of a non-Jewish parent's background.[26] Egon Mayer's study *Children of Intermarriage* (see p. 340) gives parents an idea of what to expect as children reach young adulthood.

For children going through the crisis of coming to terms with a mixed identity—a mixed heritage of being "half Jewish"—there are three books that treat the subject very intelligently and realistically. They're also useful for adults.[27]

Mixed-Marriage Daughter
by Hila Colman
(Morrow, 1968)

Are You There God? It's Me, Margaret
by Judy Blume
(Dell, 1970)

Kate
by Jean Little
(Harper and Row, 1971)

When Your Child Is Homosexual

This is a topic fraught with difficulty for Jewish parents because it evokes so much social and religious disapprobation (see "Lesbian Jews," p. 314). Evelyn Torton Beck, the editor of *Nice Jewish Girls: A Lesbian Anthology*, tells of how her mother was met with a wall of denial when she wanted to discuss her daughter's lesbianism: "My mother knows I am a lesbian but she obviously was looking for some kind of support from her rabbi. . . . She went to him and asked, 'Is it possible that Evie is a lesbian?' . . . Instead of giving her any kind of positive affirmation, he snapped at her and said: 'That is impossible!' "[28]

One place to write to for information about other families going through the same process of discovery and adjustment is National Federation of Parents and Friends of Gays:

National Federation
5715, 15 Street, N.W.
Washington, DC 20011

All parents, even those who believe that their children are completely "straight," should read the pages on homosexuality in Letty Cottin Pogrebin's *Growing Up Free: Raising Your Child in the 80's* (see Bibliography). Pogrebin points out that neither the parent's nor the child's ultimate success as a human being rests on whether the child is heterosexual or homosexual.

One woman has offered to act as a resource person for other Jewish parents of lesbians or gay men:

Charlotte K. Hoffman
3535 Chevy Chase Drive
Chevy Chase, MD 20815

Psychological Problems
If you suspect or know that your child is having real problems of an emotional/psychological nature, or if you're just worried and want to talk to someone in a nonthreatening setting, there is usually sliding-scale (sometimes free) qualified counseling available through the local Jewish Family and Children Services agency of the local Jewish Federation. (See Networking Directory.) Sometimes the local Y is an outpost for such counseling.

For children going through the crisis of bereavement, having lost a parent through death (or sometimes through divorce), a program has been developed that allows the children to express their grief and anger in a setting neutral enough to make them feel comfortable. For information:

Lilly Singer
Westchester Jewish Community Services
141 N. Central Avenue
Hartsdale, NY 10530
(914) 949-6761

Children and Divorce
There is a monograph that should be read by rabbis, educators, parents—and maybe even by the children themselves. It's titled *Children of Divorced Parent Households—Some Suggested Guidelines for School and Synagogue*. It is thoughtful, sensitive, and touches on material that is almost never talked about, much less published. Rabbi Sanford Seltzer, its author, rightly sees that schools, synagogues, even camps can be very supportive to the child whose parents are getting a divorce. They can equally be vehicles for exacerbating conflicts—such as when a model Sabbath or a model seder is planned and teachers take no account of the child who will come with only one parent, or when the class reads of idyllic family celebrations in textbooks that make no mention of divorce. Seltzer says: "The teacher should stress that the blessing over the Sabbath candles or the chanting of the Kiddush is not restricted to either parent, but can be performed by both depending upon the circumstances. Some children may respond, or feel, although reluctant to verbalize the feelings, that ritual observance at home merely reawakens hopes for reconciliation while simultaneously accentuating the loss of the intact family unit and the absent parent."

In addition to his useful suggestions on how to handle the subject of divorce in an open and sensitive way in various learning settings (textbooks, school, camp), he instructs teachers, rabbis, and administrators on how to deal with the needs of the noncustodial parent, with the sometimes agonizing Bar/Bat Mitzvah planning ("It is for many an event as much to be dreaded as anticipated"), and with the not uncommon situation of remarriage to a non-Jewish partner. Order the pamphlet from:

Program Perspectives
Union of American Hebrew Congregations
838 Fifth Avenue
New York, NY 10021

The time when parents divorce is a time of crisis for children's Jewish identity. Some children want to reject any Jewish affiliation altogether, perhaps seeing this as a way of punishing the parents. Others may become more religious, both for the support this affords and as a way of establishing an identity independent of the parents. This is a 1981 impressionistic study of the connections between divorce and children's Jewish identity:

Divorce and the Jewish Child
by Thomas Cottle, Ph.D.
The National Jewish Family Center
American Jewish Committee
165 E. 56 Street
New York, NY 10022
$2.00

Also from the same address, a 1983 report is available: Nathalie Friedman and Theresa F. Rogers, *The Jewish Community and Children of Divorce: A Pilot Study of Perceptions and Responses,* $2.00.

THREE

◆

POWER AND PARTICIPATION IN THE JEWISH COMMUNITY

◆

11

◆

JEWISH WOMEN IN CRISIS: COMMUNITY RESOURCES

A hallmark of every Jewish community on record is a desire and ability to "look after our own." Jewish loan funds, sick-benefit societies, welfare organizations, hospitals, and old-age homes in every community with a significant Jewish presence all attest to the responsibilities Jews take on, both for one another and for others in need in the general society—since many of these institutions serve a nonsectarian clientele.

Women are now trying to change the focus of Jewish community structures, causing organizations to recognize that there are new needs to be met among Jews and whole new needy constituencies. Once a primary focus was, for example, the Jewish hospital, providing kosher food for patients and internship training for Jewish doctors discriminated against in other institutions. Now the medical care of the Jewish population and the training of Jewish doctors take place in general institutions, and the Jewish-sponsored hospitals function just as all other hospitals do. Resources can now be channeled—and sometimes are being channeled—toward supports for Jewish women. As one might suspect, a large part of the impetus for these programs comes from Jewish women's groups (or individuals) and not from the larger Jewish organizations as a whole. Nonetheless, the very existence of resources for women in crisis situations augurs well for the development of community responses that give serious consideration to the needs of the female half of the Jewish population— older, poorer, and with fewer resources of every kind than Jewish men have had.

Some of these women are trying to handle life transitions that are

likely to affect most of us—widowhood, for example, or growing old.
Other crises, such as alcoholism and substance abuse, or physical abuse
at the hands of a spouse, are less common. In all these crises, however,
there are resources for help, usually within the Jewish community, or
resources for Jewish women that exist because of the feminist movement.

WHEN A JEWISH WIFE BECOMES A WIDOW

"Better a noodle for a husband than life as a widow," the Talmud tells
us. Yet if present life-span patterns continue, we can forecast that three
out of four married women will someday experience widowhood. Women
live longer than men—usually by about seven years. Despite this fact, the
woman alone, like the woman who has never married, goes unrecognized
in the Jewish community. She is often a rejected person, like the printing
term that bears her name: an incomplete line of type that takes up a
whole line of space at one end of a column, which must be moved to some
less conspicuous place or dropped entirely.

Like all widows, Jewish women whose spouses die must face this sense
of exclusion and dislocation from a wife-husband-kids family structure
idealized by the culture as a whole. And also like all widows, Jewish
women face the stressful adjustments to loss and grief, to a changing
financial situation, to rearrangements of relationships with children and
in-laws and friends. But for a Jewish woman becoming a widow may be
an even more stressful transition, because her self-image has been so
closely tied to marriage and family. Robin Siegel, a California social
worker who has studied Jewish widows, says, "The very values which
foster and promote Jewish family life are the same values which cause
the widow's transition period to be that much more difficult."[1]

The traditional virtues a Jewish woman is taught will ensure a happy
family life—keeping peace at home by subsuming her needs to the needs
of others, concerning herself with the care-giving and enabling tasks—are
precisely the attributes that defeat her when she becomes a widow. Jewish women report overwhelming feelings of uselessness after their husbands die. The survival skills of the Jewish wife become maladaptive
when the wife becomes a widow. One of the women Siegel interviewed
describes these feelings: "I would like to remarry, but I'm skeptical. I
would like to because I'm used to being a pair and sharing. To me life is
nothing if you don't share it with someone. . . . I'm not afraid of living
by myself, I'm afraid of living *for* myself. I have never lived just thinking
of me; I'm always used to thinking of someone else. Buying something

(Layle Silbert)

that someone else likes, and cooking something that someone else likes. In the widow's group they taught us to do things FOR ME, but I'm not that kind of a person."

For all grieving women there are certain especially stressful moments—meals alone, weekends without companionship. But for Jewish women there is the added pain and stress that may come from a culture that locates many religious and festival occasions in the home—holiday meals, for example, and Shabbat—which highlight on a regular basis the loss of a familiar presence around the table. One woman in Siegel's study mourns: "Nobody else notices that empty chair, but I do."

Widows may experience problems with their Jewish identity, as well as suffering from the primary loss of a spouse. Jewish women often receive a socialization that makes them dependent upon having a husband (and children) for the very foundation of their identity and their self-esteem. Some widows report that they do not even see themselves as Jews anymore after the death of their husbands. This may reveal the women's own tenuous connections to their Jewish identity even before widowhood, or it may be an expression of anger at bereavement, but it also suggests that for many women being Jewish is something they enabled their husbands and sons to do, and didn't see as something that was also a part of *their* identities and their lives as women alone.

Bereaved Jewish women are much less likely than men in the same position to seek solace from religious observance—from regular attendance in synagogue to say Kaddish, for example. Since in Judaism both ritual leadership and ritual participation have been male activities, Jewish widows often feel that they have no meaningful connection to religious life without men. One woman Siegel spoke with says her synagogue took away her seats after her husband died and gave them to "a family." She lost not only a loved one but also her roles: as respected community member, as part of a couple.

Paradoxically, one woman points out that the egalitarian seating patterns in Reform and Conservative synagogues (called "family worship")—with women and men sitting together—makes life harder for women alone. Rosa Felsenburg Kaplan says: "Now, when a widow or divorcee attends services, the joyful interaction of intact families in adjoining pews reminds her only too painfully that she lost her mate."[2]

Another woman in Siegel's study says she dropped her synagogue membership after her husband died when the rabbi didn't even call her after the *shiva*, even though her husband had for many years been on the synagogue board. Many women, such as this one, protest that their rabbis have had no training in counseling widows or even in showing their concern in a genuine way. "He kept telling me, 'You're a strong lady. I know you'll do fine.' I think he kept telling me that so he wouldn't have to help me."

During *shiva*, the traditional seven-day mourning period, mourners are not supposed to work, and relatives and friends bring in all meals. For a widow this usually means that all her roles vanish at once, with no ritual roles to replace them. It is customary to convene a *minyan* in the home in which mourners are observing *shiva*, so that no one has to leave the house to pray in synagogue. Regardless of practice at the synagogue of which the widow has been a member, many women complain bitterly that in their own homes they have been excluded from the *minyan*, with only men counting toward the quorum of ten needed for prayer. (For more on the rituals of mourning, see, "Death and Mourning," p. 143.)

The outsider status of a widow during *shiva*, even in her own home, may be a harbinger of exclusions to come. Many Jewish widows, like other women under the same circumstances, report changes in their relationship with married friends. "I feel like a fifth wheel," is a phrase that one widow uses over and over again. "If my friends' husbands ask me to dance at a *simcha* I feel they're only being charitable. If they don't ask me, I feel neglected and angry and hurt."

Couples and married men tend to lump widows together prejudicially. In Miami, where there are large numbers of Jewish women living alone, one frequently hears middle-aged Jewish men commenting, "Well, you know the restaurants will be crowded for early dinner because the widows go out to eat then," as if they would travel, by some instinct, in a pack. Or "Those widows are such picky shoppers," "such bad drivers," and other such negative stereotypes. The same kind of prejudice that we see directed toward women as a whole seems to have created a special category for those women—particularly older women—who are without men, allowing people to talk about them in sweeping and often denigrating or unsympathetic generalizations. Unlike a man whose spouse dies, a woman faces loss of caste status, loss of financial or class status, and a regrouping of friendships or a change in friendship patterns as she ends up spending time with other widows.

There are two situations in which widows, like women who experience a change of financial status through divorce, feel especially shunned: giving money and giving time. One woman tells: "I had less money to give after my husband died, and because I had to go out to work I also had less time for volunteer work. I really felt the community rejected me because I couldn't contribute at my previous level."

Professional fund-raisers often criticize the philanthropy of widows, expressing more anger than understanding. One, in a national position with the United Jewish Appeal, tells how "all those widows whose husbands gave generously still only give the relatively small 'extra gift' they gave before. They just aren't used to handling money." It might be more useful in the long run (and more humane) if the fund-raisers stopped and asked themselves what the woman's new reality is. The widow's reluctance to give at her late husband's high level may have less to do with naïveté about money than with a realistic anxiety over not having the regular source of income her husband provided.

Some women claim that the widows of men who were real *machers* (big shots) in the Jewish community are likely to be sought after still by organizations and individuals; but the widows of ordinary mortals feel shunned because they aren't keeping up their husbands' level of giving or participation.

Jewish women may suffer more from the shifts in socioeconomic status following the deaths of their husbands. The "status shock" of widowhood obviously affects middle-class and wealthy women more than others, and the majority of married Jewish women are middle-class when married. With financial supports diminished, and unable to collect substantial sums from Social Security or other pension plans because they have not been part of the paid labor force, many Jewish widows enter the ranks of the newly poor. Since for at least one or two generations in America the majority of middle-class Jewish women didn't work outside their homes, many have no equity for all the years they spent as *bale-bustes* (super-housewives).

Widows are also among the many Jewish women now considering themselves "displaced homemakers" in need of job training or retraining, counseling, or employment advice (see p. 482). Their previous financial dependency is reflected in the words of one Los Angeles widow: "I never in my life balanced a checkbook. My therapist taught me how."

Robin Siegel, whose Master's thesis at the Hebrew Union College-Jewish Institute of Religion was based on research with Jewish widows, can be reached:

c/o Jewish Family Service of Orange County
12181 Buaro Street, Suite G
Garden Grove, CA 92640

Here are some programs that will be helpful both to widowed Jewish women and as models for professionals in advisory services:

The Widow's Center
Temple Isaiah
10345 W. Pico Boulevard
Los Angeles, CA 90064
(213) 277-2772

Phyllis Solow (gerontologist)
20613 Callon Drive
Topanga, CA 90290

Solow is the designer of a widow-to-widow support group program in L.A. County and author of an unpublished 1978 M.A. thesis, "Survival Skills for Widows: A Study of a Feminist Intervention," California State Univ., 1978.

Widow-to-Widow
(for widows over 40)
Mayer Kaplan Jewish Community Center
5050 Church Street
Skokie, IL 60076
(312) 675-2200

Young Widows and Widowers of Westchester
Westchester Jewish Community Services, Inc.
172 South Broadway
White Plains, NY 10605
(914) 949-6761

This program includes regular discussions around a given topic, plus rap groups preceding the discussions for "newly widowed and those having trouble adjusting" and a counseling program to help children and adolescents cope with the death of a parent.

Institute on Remembering and Separating from a Loved One
Department of Senior Adult Services and Research
Jewish Y's of Philadelphia
401 S. Broad Street
Philadelphia, PA 19147
(215) 545-4400

Widow-to-Widow
YM/YWHA and NHS of Montreal
5500 Westbury Avenue
Montreal, Canada H3W 2W8
(514) 737-6551

Program services include self-help groups, social events, Jewish holiday events, and a weekend drop-in center.

ELDERLY JEWISH WOMEN

Unlike other crisis situations facing Jewish women, growing older will likely happen to us all. Although the majority of the Jewish elderly are women (by age eighty-five, nearly 65 percent of New York Jews are female), they are "invisible" in our mental image of aging Jews.[3] If you have ever been asked to conjure up a picture of an "old Jew," you will remember that your image is always of a Jewish man. Even the otherwise excellent section on the Jewish elderly in *The Third Jewish Catalog* is titled "World of Our Fathers." But the real pathos of the Jewish elderly is in the lives of elderly Jewish women, who may find themselves with no money, no comfort from study or communal prayer, few roles left, and no place to go.

Perhaps the men *are* more visible. They can congregate—those of them

Yudie, from the film of the same name by Mirra Bank, a portrait of a strong and self-sufficient older Jewish woman. (courtesy of Jewish Media Service)

who are mobile—around synagogues, where many of them have always felt at home. Some of them can even eke out a supplement to their meager support by getting paid as mourners or *minyan* members (not approved of by religious authorities, but practiced nonetheless). For elderly Jewish women there is no equally logical gathering place. Many of their roles are gone—parent, wife, consumer, friend; domesticity and the charitable organizations they may once have been involved with no longer provide the meaning they once did.

Despite these losses, Barbara Myerhoff, the anthropologist who has studied and reported on elderly Jewish women and men in California, concludes that Jewish women age more successfully than Jewish men, especially those women who have also known nondomestic roles in life. She speaks of the "underground role" of women aside from the idealized role of wife and mother: "With an ideal *and* contingent role available, women, it seems, had more options than the men, more flexibility, more opportunity to express their individuality and adapt to circumstances. And it was the contingent, the underground female role, prefiguring women's future accommodations in old age, that equipped them with the flexibility and pragmatism that ultimately served them so well. For these women, aging was a career."[4]

Because of the declining birthrate and relatively easy access to medical care, among other factors, Jews proportionally have more elderly than Americans as a whole. According to Gerald B. Bubis, Director of the Hebrew Union College School of Jewish Communal Service, "Median age of Americans is now 28 and the median age of Jews is 48. So now if we can speak of the greying of America, we can speak of the whitening of the Jews." Given these numbers, taking care of the needs of aging Jews, of which the majority are women, must become a priority of Jewish communities, just as it has become a priority for the middle-aged children of the elderly.

Not only are women the majority of elderly Jews, women have also traditionally been the primary care-givers for this group. Says one fifty-year-old woman, "I haven't been to a single social gathering in the past couple of years where the dominant subject for discussion among my contemporaries wasn't 'What are we going to do about our parents?' "

Although most of the care of the elderly takes place in private homes and not in institutions (where care can cost more than $35,000 per year), the proportion of the Jewish elderly in long-term care institutions is about twice that of non-Jews. About 5 percent of all America's elderly live in institutions as compared with 10 percent of Jews.[5] Jews in the middle generation (the children of the elderly) have tended to be professionals and managers, tend to relocate often, are committed to professional identities that take a great deal of their time, and hence just aren't present to care for aging parents.

Given the geographic and sometimes the emotional distance of Jewish daughters and mothers (see p. 268), and given the space limitations and the fact that there's now usually no full-time "wife" at home to provide care, a daughter facing the aging of an infirm mother often must consider institutional supports. That this is one of the most painful tasks of adult life for the middle-aged daughter is demonstrated by the fact that nearly half of the fiction manuscripts that are submitted by women to *Lilith* magazine deal in some way with conflicts over institutional care of an elderly relative.

The extensive network of "homes" for the Jewish elderly in North America indicates that the tradition of care may always have included provision for institutional care. Most Jewish communities have some system of Jewish institutions for the aged, usually under the auspices of the local Federation (see Networking Directory), though they may vary considerably in quality.

One such place makes it very clear that no applicant has to relinquish financial holdings in order to be admitted. There is also a democratic government, which, given what we know about Jewish women's need for independence, sounds like a part of the operation that should be included in every senior citizen's facility:

A Residents Council (government) has been organized at the Hebrew Home and Hospital to provide a means for residents to express their needs and participate in decisions which affect their lives. Too often trustees and staff of long-term care facilities make assumptions about the needs and aspirations of those they serve without consultation with the residents themselves. Membership on the council board is determined by election, but all residents are invited and encouraged to attend open meetings. The council provides a forum for residents of the Hebrew Home and Hospital to critique care and services and provide constructive suggestions for their improvement. We feel that the Residents Council is an important step in restoring a measure of self-determination and decision-making to our residents.[6]

National Council of Jewish Women sections have surveyed nursing-home facilities in various areas of the country and have published two nursing-home guides to help people select those that are appropriate for the elderly. "The guides are unique because they focus on the needs of the prospective nursing home residents themselves," claims NCJW. The volunteers who were trained to conduct the surveys have now become local advocates for nursing-home residents, to ensure that they are receiving adequate care.

One recent investigation into this area was also conducted under the auspices of the National Council of Jewish Women:

Options for Living Arrangements: Housing Alternatives for the Elderly
National Council of Jewish Women
Task Force on Aging
15 E. 26 Street
New York, NY 10010
$2.50

To find out about Jewish residential facilities across the country write:

National Association of Jewish Homes for the Aged
2525 Centerville Road
Dallas, TX 75228

We need new ways of identifying and serving this population. As the Jewish population gets older (the median age of Jews in North America rises steadily each year), we must insist that community organizations start thinking about appropriate housing. Communal funding should now be funneled into planning for the residential needs of Jews rather than for medical needs, which have largely been taken over by public facilities.

In the face of horrendous federal budget cuts in the early 1980s which affect the Jewish elderly in every way—from curtailment of kosher meals-on-wheels to cutbacks in Social Security—caring for the Jewish elderly will fall more heavily into the laps of Jewish voluntary organizations. Some of the most useful and creative programs have come not out of the traditional community structures but from young people who perceived the need and went to work answering it.

Dorot ("generations") is a project on New York's Upper West Side, connecting college students and other young people with the often homebound Jewish elderly in the neighborhood. Each young volunteer makes a weekly visit to an elderly friend, bringing Pesach and Purim and Chanukah food packages, arranging group holiday meals and other group programs.

Dorot
Temple Ansche Chesed
West End Avenue at 100 Street
New York, NY 10025
(212) 864-7410

Similar to Dorot is Project Ezra ("help"), which serves the elderly Jewish poor on the Lower East Side of New York. Many of these people feel uncertain about venturing forth into a neighborhood that was once a hub of Yiddish culture but is now crime-ridden and populated largely by non-Jews. Like Dorot, Ezra recruits young people to make regular visits helping the elderly with outings, shopping, and government bureaucracies, as well as reaching out to suburban synagogues to bring two disparate Jewish groups together for holidays and other events.[7]

An Ezra volunteer writes about her experiences:

(92nd Street Y archive photo)

For me, Ezra was a weekly visit with someone who opened up a window on the past. For Katie, it was a chance to share with someone her life and what she had learned, which most of the world didn't seem interested in: the guilt of living when all her brothers and sisters in Europe were killed; the anguish of realizing her mistake in deciding not to have children during the Depression because her husband didn't have a job; and now no husband, no children, no sisters or brothers; the joy of remembering funny stories—which are so funny she can hardly finish telling them—of how men used to chase her; the bitterness and acceptance of her physical ailments and the death of her husband.[8]

Project Ezra
197 E. Broadway
New York, NY 10002
(212) 982-3700

Another program model followed by Jewish women's groups in some communities involves less time from volunteers than a weekly visit. This is a telephone reassurance program in which volunteers make a daily phone call to an elderly person. The volunteer calls at a prearranged time each day to inquire after the elderly person's health and needs. If there is no answer or a prolonged busy signal, someone is dispatched to check. Aside from dispelling some of the anxieties of the homebound elderly (that they'll become ill and no one will know or care, or that they'll fall and be lying on the floor disabled for days before help comes), the daily call helps to combat the terrible loneliness of never hearing a human voice for days on end.

RESOURCES FOR THE ELDERLY AND THEIR FAMILIES

Central Bureau for the Jewish Aged
225 Park Avenue S.
New York, NY 10003

National Interfaith Council on Aging
298 Hull Street, P.O. Box 1924
Athens, GA 36603

Council for the Jewish Elderly
1015 W. Howard Street
Evanston, IL 60202

Synagogue Council of America
Project on Aging
432 Park Avenue S.
New York, NY 10016

(Layle Silbert)

Rabbi Sanford Seltzer
Union of American Hebrew Congregations Gerontology Program
1300 Boylston Street, Room 207
Chestnut Hill, MA 02167

Jewish Association for Service for the Aged
40 W. 68 Street
New York, NY 10023

Gray Panthers
3635 Chestnut Street
Philadelphia, PA 19104

Older Women's League
   (OWL)
3800 Harrison Street
Oakland, CA 94611
(Chapters are being formed around the continent.)

In addition to their nursing-home evaluation materials, National Council of Jewish Women has a wide variety of publications of interest to those working with the elderly, including guidelines on how to start a meals-on-wheels program, and the CAPS program for *Children of Aging Parents*.

Also addressing the needs of the "children" generation is a pamphlet published by the American Jewish Committee, *Your Aging Parent*, and such programs as the workshops sponsored by New York's 92nd Street Y, "You and Your Aging Relative."

For more resources on the painful dilemmas facing elderly Jewish women and their families, see Paula Gantz, "The Golden Years: You Should Live So Long!" *Lilith* #10.

Certain fictionalized accounts of the crises families face in dealing with aging are helpful in clarifying our own conflicts. Often books intended for children are the most direct. The issue of whether or not to institutionalize an old woman who is becoming senile is discussed by Rose Blue in *Grandma Didn't Wave Back* (New York: Franklin Watts, 1972). Our son Benjamin, then eleven, read it and wrote, "The book deals with a relationship between a 10-year-old girl and her grandmother, who at times thought she was the little girl she used to be. The only thing that separates them is a family that wants to '*put Grandma away*' somewhere."

Just as we have programs to help people integrate the changes they go through at other transitional times (adolescence, divorce, parenthood), there is a need for communities to provide a forum for the expression of the particular conflicts and resolutions of elderly Jewish women.

For short, pointed reviews of films relevant to the lives of older Jewish women, consult *Medium*, the newsletter of the Jewish Welfare Board's Jewish Media Service, which has published special issues on both women and aging.

Jewish Welfare Board
15 E. 26 Street
New York, NY 10010

JEWISH WOMEN ALCOHOLICS

A common thread runs through the fabric of Jewish life: the denial of problems most people refuse to acknowledge is associated with Jews. Since, like all Jews, women as a group have also had to "behave well" and deny problems, Jewish women have had to be doubly masked.

For centuries Jews have held themselves above certain problems that other groups faced, expressing in folk wisdom the feelings that such problems as alcoholism, beating of women and children, and abandonment of families didn't involve us. There was always sympathy for those who did actually suffer, but the mythology that "the Jewish family" immunized us against these maladies lingered on. Jewish men made better husbands because they didn't abuse their wives and were good providers was one myth. Because Jews use wine in a ritual context, Jewish children learn to drink wisely at an early age was another. The price has been that Jewish women especially have had to live with a great deal of guilt and secrecy for not having lived up to some illusory ideal of health and happiness.

The incidence of these crises (and others) among Jews is nothing new; even the Bible talks about drunkenness. The *response* to the problem is beginning to change, with truths displacing the myths. At some points in Jewish history it certainly must have been helpful for Jews to wear a public-relations halo of perfection, whether to buttress the feelings of being a people apart or to present a better image to the oppressive cultures at whose mercy the Jews often lived. Alcohol abuse has always been very *déclassé* in Jewish circles and also threatening, since for many Jews the image of the drunken Gentile wreaking havoc during a pogrom is only a generation or two in the past. But the denial of very real problems in the lives of Jewish women exacts too great a toll in internal anguish to be perpetuated in silence.

For example, a Minnesota woman in her forties tells:

> I went to my rabbi to speak to him about my alcoholism. I was in an Alcoholics Anonymous program, and one of the steps you have to go through on your way to recovery is to talk to a member of the clergy. So naturally I went to this rabbi, whom I had known for years. He told me that I couldn't possibly be an alcoholic, and when I tried to tell him that I needed to speak to him because I *was*, and that part of my recovery required talking to him, he claimed to have absolutely no idea what I was saying. So I ended up doing my "Step Five" with a minister.

This woman's story is not uncommon. What may be uncommon is that she has remained involved with the Jewish community. Others have taken their rejection personally and have left. One woman wrote to *Lilith* magazine that her husband, a prominent Jewish physician, had refused to let her get help for her alcoholism, saying that revealing her condition would damage his image. After his death several years ago she tried to get help from Jewish agencies and was rebuffed. She joined a church-based Alcoholics Anonymous group, recovered from alcoholism—and became a Unitarian.

Jewish women alcoholics bear a double burden of secrecy and invisibility. Jews, as a group, are thought not to be "prone" to alcoholism. Women, as a group, face terrible disapprobation (and also a lot of denial by others) if it appears that they have what is euphemistically called a "drinking problem." Until very recently there has been practically no recognition of alcohol abuse as a problem in the Jewish community. Drug abuse, on the other hand, especially among women, has been discussed more openly, perhaps because taking pills seems more socially acceptable, less reminiscent of *goyishe* acting-out, and more likely to be associated with medical therapeutics.

There are several signs that the issue is now open for discussion. The Federation of Jewish Philanthropies of New York has instituted a Task Force on Alcoholism, made up of professionals and volunteers, including recovered alcoholics. They hold retreats and other programs for Jewish recovered alcoholics. The Task Force has published a collection of articles in which there are pieces important for our understanding of the tremendous burdens on Jewish women alcoholics (of whom there are an estimated ten thousand in California's San Fernando Valley alone). The book also includes invaluable listings in its "Resources for Alcoholics" section.[9]

One article, "The Jewish Alcoholic Woman—Rara Avis?" by Dr. Sheila Blume and Dee Dropkin,[10] suggests that there are similarities between Jewish and non-Jewish women alcoholics, since all women incur more intense social disapproval and may have more opportunities for solitary drinking, which keep the problem hidden longer. Jewish women alcoholics also share with their Jewish male counterparts a feeling of stigmatization, but there are also some notable differences for Jewish women alcoholics:

1. The majority are single, while the majority of Jewish alcoholic men are married.

2. The women studied were able to pinpoint the specific incident in their lives that seemed to trigger the onset of their alcoholism—illness, loss, problems of various sorts. (This is not typical of alcoholic men.)

3. The Jewish women reported uneasiness at attending AA meetings held in churches and pain at hearing occasional anti-Semitic comments from non-Jewish alcoholics.

4. The parents and/or husbands of these women were "unusually nonsupportive" and could not accept their alcoholism and "its inappro-

priate stigma." The authors suggest that families of Jewish alcoholic patients should be involved in the treatment process also, to help provide some support for the women.

Ellen R. Bayer, one of the professionals instrumental in creating the retreats sponsored by the New York Federation, comments on the differences between Jewish women and Jewish men in this situation:

> Women who have attended retreat weekends for recovering Jewish alcoholics and their families have expressed some significant concerns about the need to reconcile alcoholism with being Jewish. They have attended these retreats in greater numbers than Jewish men, yet appear to harbor more conflicts about their own religious or spiritual identity.
>
> Those who have achieved recovery through Alcoholics Anonymous have found themselves accepting a program for living and survival which is largely spiritual in nature (the "12 Step" program) and which requires active acceptance of a "higher power." The supportive structure of A.A. and its spiritual philosophy have made the retreat participants more comfortable and braver about carrying out their "Jewish search." On the other hand, the "non-sectarian" but essentially Christian language and path of A.A. and Alanon leave many peripheral Jews with a sense of alienation. The development and implementation of specialized support programs like the retreat and groups or networks seem to fill this critical need.
>
> Many Jewish women, in their isolation, have felt as if each was, as one woman put it, the "only Jewish woman alcoholic in the world," and therefore had to have been "a Christian masquerading in a Jewish body." This sense of alienation caused women to be both propelled to and repelled from participation in a "Jewish" event. Many were sure that their identity fears would be confirmed. They felt sure that rejection they'd felt in the past by the Jewish community would be repeated.
>
> Women more than men seemed to feel a "spiritual vacuum" when it came to looking toward Jewish sources for strengthening their recovery process.
>
> Why? They express a deep sense of emptiness when it comes to drawing on their Jewish identity for strength. This is not surprising considering that Jewish women have had, by and large, significantly less Jewish training and education than men and thus cannot look to their "background" for sustenance. One man described his sense of identity as follows: "When I hit bottom and fell down, I was like a sick tree—but when a tree falls down its roots remain attached." However, Jewish women at the retreats almost uniformly felt detached from

their heritage and community. Paradoxically, despite the lacks they perceive in the community, women have been more open to the search—overcoming anger and frustration—to find a warm and loving framework within Judaism to strengthen their recovery.

Rabbis and other Jewish institutional representatives need to be sensitized to the presence and needs of Jewish alcoholics, especially women, in their communities. Jewish women differ little from all other alcoholics in succumbing to and recovering from the disease of alcoholism; one difference seems to be in their willingness to search for spiritual and communal belonging and understanding.[11]

RESOURCES

For the book *Alcoholism and the Jewish Community* and information about weekend retreats for recovering Jewish alcoholics (men and women), which attract people from all over the country, assure anonymity, and have facilities for the accommodation of "significant others," contact:

Task Force on Alcoholism
Commission on Synagogue Relations
Federation of Jewish Philanthropies
130 E. 59 Street
New York, NY 10022

An article outlining the historical dimensions of the problem and some of the present-day social realities for Jewish women alcoholics (including comments from Jewish women professionals and community leaders who are recovered alcoholics): Marcia Cohn Spiegel, "Jews and Booze: The Wrath of Grapes," *Hadassah Magazine* (Nov. 1980). One of the few works that specifically treats Jewish women and alcohol is Spiegel's Master's thesis, "The Heritage of Noah: Alcoholism in the Jewish Community Today," Hebrew Union College-Jewish Institute of Religion, School of Jewish Communal Service (1979).

One of the earliest books to deal with the subject is: Charles R. Snyder, *Alcohol and the Jews* (Free Press, 1958).

What the Jewish woman alcoholic probably needs least is a duplication of all the services of various recovery programs available everywhere. (Alcoholics Anonymous chapters are listed in the phone book of almost every city.) What *is* necessary, and what the New York Task Force on Alcoholism and other groups are trying to do, is to sensitize professionals and lay people to the issue so that the wraps of secrecy and denial can be lifted, even by such simple means as opening synagogues to A.A. groups. In addition, support groups (such as the retreats) have the advantage of allowing Jewish women to see that they are not alone with their problem.

Beth Israel Alcoholism Treatment Center
307 Second Avenue
New York, NY 10012
(212) 533-5700

There is a special program for women alcoholics at:

Brunswick House
Alcoholism Treatment Center
366 Broadway
Amityville, NY 11701
(516) 264-5000 (ext. 361)

A rabbinical group now also offers services to Jewish alcoholics and recovered alcoholics:

JACS Foundation, Inc.
(Jewish Alcoholics, Chemically dependent persons and Significant others)
c/o New York Board of Rabbis
10 E. 73 Street
New York, NY 10021

Sensitive discussions of some of the problems facing minority women alcoholics in general are found in: Marian Sandmaier, *The Invisible Alcoholics: Women and Alcohol Abuse in America* (McGraw-Hill, 1980), and Edith Lynn Hornik, *The Drinking Woman* (Association Press, 1977).

BATTERED JEWISH WOMEN

The last taboo in Jewish life may be domestic violence. And it's being broken. There has been a lot of finger-pointing along with the claim that *other* men beat their wives. There's also what one journalist has called "subcategories of ostriches"—those who say that the problem exists only in ultra-Orthodox families in which there are many children and little money and therefore much stress; others say that it's only assimilated Jews, far from such Jewish traditions as the "sanctity of the home," who are violent.

(courtesy National Council of Jewish Women)

The reality is that both of these "kinds" of Jews, and many others, are the kinds who commit violent acts against members of their own families. The emerging case histories of battered Jewish women don't differ much from those of women generally, except for the problem of having to deal with massive community denial that beatings take place. We know from studies of wife abuse, largely carried out in the last decade as an outgrowth of the women's movement, that domestic violence cuts across all racial, religious, ethnic, and class differences. There are very few groups or locales that can claim a lower incidence, though one California study found more abuse in upper-middle-class Jewish homes than in other socioeconomic groups of Jews.

The way domestic violence is reported is more surreptitious among Jews. For example, a Jewish woman would not be likely to go to the police with a report that her husband had abused her physically. She might, in an Orthodox community, tell the *rebbetzin*, the rabbi's wife, who often acts as a counselor for troubled women looking for a sympathetic female with some access to (male) authority. A Jewish woman who belongs to a less observant community might go to a distant hospital to be treated, so that she won't be identified, or might go to her own doctor but say that the injuries were the result of an accident. Anecdotal reports from rabbis and social workers suggest that Jewish women, whether Orthodox or nonobservant, are likely to report domestic violence only if or when it involves their children.

There is a parallel in Jewish law to the outdated and erroneous belief of some police departments that cases of wife abuse are merely domestic quarrels in which the long arm of the state has no right to interfere. Some rabbinical courts, in which women have tried to cite physical abuse as evidence to obtain a divorce from a reluctant husband, have sent the women home to patch things up (and to face more beatings), as if the family must be preserved regardless of the cost to its members.[12]

Actually, the issue of domestic violence is crucial to the survival of Jewish families, but in a way exactly opposite to the view held by some rabbis. Since all the studies of domestic violence show that young people who see physical abuse in their families grow up to be abusive in their own homes (or, in the case of girls who see their mothers being abused, grow up expecting to be beaten in their own marriages), the earlier the problem is recognized and intervention and cure take place, the less likely it is that the pattern of battering will be transmitted to the next generation.

RESOURCES

One-third of all American couples will see a domestic quarrel degenerate into violence this year, so here are selected resources that attempt to combat or respond to domestic violence among Jews:

A shelter sponsored by the Associated YM/YWHA's of Greater New York provides facilities with kosher kitchens for battered women and their children. It's the first kosher shelter in the country. "Abused Jewish women should feel free to contact the Transition Center," says Barbara Harris, director of the domestic-violence program. "The location of the shelter will not be publicized, for their protection."

Call: (212) 377-7660.

In Milwaukee, a group of women of various faiths have formed a committee to sensitize clergy to the problems of battered women. Many victims had complained that religious advisers often would send them back into the abusive situations, causing the victims to feel guilty or responsible if the abuse continued; some victims even felt that it was a religious duty to stay in their marriages, regardless of threats to their safety. Rabbi Dena Feingold, the Jewish representative on the committee, cites Genesis—"Her desire shall be toward her husband and he shall rule over her"—and says, "some victims take those passages literally: stand by your man, no matter what. . . . How do we counsel women to recognize that it may be better to terminate a marriage, while, at the same time, showing we value the institution of marriage?"[13]

The Milwaukee group is developing "tools for counselors" who must deal with these religious issues raised by domestic violence victims, and its umbrella organization, the Milwaukee Task Force on Battered Women, staffs a 24-hour crisis line.

RUTH
    (Religions United to Help)
Milwaukee Task Force on Battered Women
1228 W. Mitchell
Milwaukee, WI 53204
(414) 643-5455

Largely through the efforts of a few concerned professionals and activists, the subject of battered women has actually appeared on the agendas of several conventions and conferences of both lay and professional leaders, reinforcing the Jewish community's understanding of the reality of wife abuse among Jews.

Women are beginning to research the extent of family violence in the Jewish community, and as their reports receive publicity, there's additional validation for those women who have thought theirs were unique situations. Two theses at the Hebrew Union College-Jewish Institute of Religion School of Jewish Communal Service in Los Angeles deal with different aspects of the problem.

Ellen Goldsmith and Betsy Gillen investigated intrafamilial violence in the Los Angeles Jewish community in the late 1970s and found that people responded very openly to a questionnaire circulated with the help of local rabbis. Family violence in a Jewish context tended to be less sadistic (there was no reported use of instruments and no burning) than among other groups, but there were reported cases of sexual abuse of children among the responses. The 209 questionnaires turned up 118 cases of child abuse, 20 cases of wife abuse, and 2 of abused husbands. The study also indicated that a higher-income family was more violence-prone.

Mimi Scarf, also at HUC-JIR, conducted another study by advertising in the Jewish and general press for American-born Jewish women battered by their husbands. Scarf's findings suggest that the battered women's view of the Jewish family as a "sacred institution" kept them from reporting their attacks. Rather than seeing the problem as a political one, some of the Jewish women felt that they were personally to blame for not managing to have perfect households.

There is a half-hour film by Canadian filmmaker Gail Singer on the subject of wife abuse and the difficulties one woman encounters when she tries to leave the abusive situation:

Loved, Honoured and Bruised
National Film Board of Canada
1251 Avenue of the Americas
New York, NY 10036

National Council of Jewish Women has prepared a remarkable booklet dealing with how women around the country can combat family violence and how Jewish women's organizations can set up programs addressing the issue. The booklet reviews existing community services, and gives a very helpful bibliography:

Domestic Violence: An NCJW Response
National Council of Jewish Women
15 E. 26 Street
New York, NY 10010

For case histories of battered Jewish women and the particular conflicts they experience, see Jane Biberman, "Violence in the Modern Home," *Inside*—quarterly magazine of the *Philadelphia Jewish Exponent*—(Spring 1981) and Melanie Shimoff, "Battered Women: A Problem for the Jewish Community," Women's American ORT *Reporter*, March/April 1981.

There is now a telephone hotline for battered Jewish women, staffed twenty-four hours a day by Jewish women who have been specially trained:

Shiloh Hotline
P.O. Box 6031
North Hollywood, CA 91603
(213) 784-6894

In Toronto, Canada, Doreen Lichtenstein and Barbara Waisberg have organized Koach, which means "strength" in Hebrew, to lobby for kosher facilities in a shelter being planned in a suburb with a large Jewish population and to raise money for shelters in Israel.[14]

Koach
Box 245
Station K
Toronto, Ontario M4P 2G5

Two resources available to all women who are victims of abuse are a book by Dr. Albert R. Roberts, *Sheltering Battered Women—A National Study and Service Guide* (Springer Pub. Co., 1981), and a grass-roots coalition of services for battered women, including shelters and counseling:

National Commission Against Domestic Violence
1728 N Street, NW
Washington, DC 20007

Pioneer Women/Na'amat, the Women's Labor Zionist Organization, has opened a shelter in Tel Aviv for "battered spouses." According to a pamphlet distributed by the organization, the shelter provides counseling services for the batterer as well as the victim, and sees as one of its roles to function as a liaison between the family and the community resources available. (A cynical observer of the American Jewish scene, upon hearing of this project, commented, "It's always easier to support something that's far away from home. What are they doing for the battered Jewish women right in their own organization?")

The Na'amat Counseling Center for the Problems of Violence in the
   Family
Tel Aviv, Israel
(03) 235-922 and (03) 231-675

There are now several shelters for battered women in Israel not under the aegis of any government agency or major organization. All have been started and are largely staffed by women volunteers who responded to what they saw as a crisis situation of overwhelming proportions. According to Ruth Rasnic, founder and director of the shelter in Herzliya, near Tel Aviv, there are sixty thousand cases of wife abuse in Israel each year.[15]

The shelters can be contacted in ways that will not endanger the women living in them:

"Women for Women"
P.O. Box 4667
Haifa, Israel
(04) 662114

Carmela Nakash Women's Aid Center
c/o "LO"
   ("NO"—Combatting Violence Against Women)
68 Sokolov Street
Herzliya, Israel
(052) 86629/83856

Beit Zipporah
c/o Women to Women
P.O. Box 10403
Jerusalem, Israel

JEWISH WOMEN BEHIND BARS

When photojournalist Marilynne Herbert suggested in 1978 that *Lilith* publish an article on the Jewish women inmates at a New York State prison, there had been almost no coverage of Jewish women prisoners in any of the media. The same blackout of denial was thrown over them as over other "deviant" Jewish women.

After the piece ran in *Lilith* in 1979,[16] letters came in from around the country offering to correspond with prisoners, offering to buy *Lilith* subscriptions for them, and describing efforts that were being made by Jewish women's groups to initiate visiting programs at local prisons in which there might be Jewish women.

Not all the experiences of the Jewish women in jail are the same, of course. Some feel terrified at being for the first time in the white minority of a prison population largely nonwhite. Some find themselves confronting anti-Semitism (or ignorance about Judaism) for the first time. Others find that they create alliances with Black women because of their shared perceptions of oppression on many levels, and with Black Muslim women on the issue of kosher food.

One Jewish woman felt more threatened and more oppressed being a Jew in the prison system: "If you're a Jew in jail, you're treated worse— by the guards and by the prisoners. They think that if you're Jewish you

Rabbi Ya'acov Rone with one of the Jewish prisoners he serves at a women's prison in New York State. (Marilynne Herbert)

must have money, and you must think you're better. But it's not like that." Another, educated on three continents, asked us not to mention this when writing about her: "You know—the Patty Hearst syndrome. Don't talk about my background, because the more sophisticated you are in prison, the more they say, 'She deserves it.'"

Although their numbers aren't great (an estimate by the Jewish Welfare Board is five thousand Jewish prisoners in federal, state, and local prisons in the United States), the coverage given the issue is very important for several reasons.

1. It brings us, again, to the realization that Jewish women are in many respects like other women—sometimes the victims of an unfair judicial system, sometimes the perpetrators of violent crimes, sometimes victimized by their relationships with men (as was the case with several of the women we interviewed at Bedford Hills prison in New York State).

2. For Jewish women on the outside who have trouble identifying with suffering unless it's Jewish suffering ("Were there any Jewish names in the list of victims from that airline crash?"), discussions of Jewish women

The Jewish chaplain on the prison grounds with a group of Jewish women prisoners and volunteers. Suggesting the sense of identity the volunteers feel with the women they visit is the fact that the two sets of women are virtually indistinguishable from each other. (Marilynne Herbert)

prisoners allow them to identify with and therefore become involved with certain civic issues that affect all of society—prison reform, reform of unfair laws and sentencing requirements, and other such causes. Unfortunately the existence of Jewish women prisoners may provide the only "way in" to these issues for women who would not otherwise take notice of them.

3. The demonstrations of concern that follow an article such as the one that appeared in *Lilith,* and some of the follow-up articles in other publications, assure the women prisoners that they are not forgotten as Jews, whatever the nature of their crimes. The existence of a Jewish communal support system—whether through rabbis, volunteers, or social-change activists—helps these women to endure incarceration without feeling totally abandoned and worthless.

RESOURCES

B'nai B'rith has a program of Community Volunteer Services that educates the Jewish community concerning prison visits to and communications with Jewish women and men in prison. In keeping with the goal of rehabilitation, B'nai B'rith has been encouraging members to offer "friendship, time and personal commitment to prisoners while they are in prison and after their release." They suggest helping with Jewish study groups and holiday observances, plus shopping for gifts for prisoners' families and transporting family members to the prison for visits. They provide basic rules to follow and a listing of resource materials:

A Guide for Volunteers Working with Prisoners
Commission on Community Volunteer Services
B'nai B'rith
1640 Rhode Island Avenue, N.W.
Washington, DC 20036

Since in most prisons there's a "religious connection" via a local rabbi as the Jewish prison chaplain, you can usually find out if there are any Jewish women inmates in your area by tracking down the prison rabbi and asking her or him. The local Jewish Federation should be able to tell you whom to contact, or you can query:

Rabbi Allen Kaplan
New York Board of Rabbis
10 E. 73 Street
New York, NY 10021

or

Chaplaincy Program
Jewish Welfare Board
15 E. 26 Street
New York, NY 10010

Some chapters of the National Council of Jewish Women have become involved not only in contacting local women prisoners but also in providing child-care facilities for people visiting prisoners. For information:

National Council of Jewish Women
15 E. 26 Street
New York, NY 10010

The Jewish chaplain at the Bedford Hills facility in New York State has, with a group of women volunteers, created programs for the Jewish women prisoners that are models of *mentschlichkeit* (humane feeling):

Rabbi Ya'acov Rone
Congregation Bet Torah
60 Smith Avenue
Mount Kisco, NY 10549

CULT MEMBERS AND THEIR FAMILIES

Since figures for some cult groups indicate that as many as 50 percent of their members are Jewish (while Jews make up only about 3 percent of the total American population), the pull of cults is obviously of considerable concern. Until recently some observers of the Jewish community thought that the anxieties expressed by rabbis and communal leaders over cults were a deflection of energies that should be going into other community needs. But in the past few years the situation has become so distressing that one New York City woman tells, "I stopped being a skeptic when I realized that at every suburban party I've been to for the past several months someone knows at least one family who's had a child in a cult."

Counseling and discussion groups are particularly helpful to mothers because they are the ones who "suffer quite a bit more shame and guilt" than other family members, according to Arnold Markowitz, who directs the first cult clinic in North America, sponsored by New York's Board of Family and Children Service. The clinic serves the parents of children who have joined cults and provides counseling for people who have left various cults. The staff doesn't do deprogramming (helping cult members to separate from the cult), but they do have long- and short-term contact with ex-members. Most of the parents who have come to the clinic since its opening in 1981 have been from "intact" families in which the mother hasn't been working outside the home, has spent a good deal of time and energy on child rearing, and feels responsible in part for the child's involvement with a cult. Often other relatives too, see the mother as the person responsible for the child's defection. Young Jewish women attracted to the cults, Markowitz suggests, show some interest in Jewish observance before joining, although most are from secular homes in which this interest is typically anomalous.

RESOURCES

24-hour Cult Clinic Hot Line
(212) 860-8533

A series of "counterinformation packets" designed to give young people answers to some of the questions missionary groups raise about Judaism is available from:

Jews for Judaism
17720 N. Bay Road, Suite 60
Miami Beach, FL 33160
$5.00 donation

A young woman's story of her engagement with and disengagement from a California cult is told by Elsa Solender in "The Making and Unmaking of a Jewish Moonie," *National Jewish Monthly* (Dec. 1978). It is available from:

B'nai B'rith
1640 Rhode Island Avenue, NW
Washington, DC 20036

A Jewish mother's pained acceptance when her son "dropped out" and joined a cultlike group appears in the touching memoir *Starting in the Middle,* by the late writer Judith Wax (New York: Holt, Rinehart & Winston, 1979).

Coffeehouses for Jewish students have become a popular antidote to cult recruitment on college campuses. For a list and details of those in the Metropolitan New York area, write:

Task Force on Missionary Activity
Jewish Community Relations Council of New York
111 W. 40 Street
New York, NY 10018

A picture of those who join the cults, with helpful guidelines for parents (how to respond—for example: don't cut off contact), plus listings of anticult organizations nationwide, appear in James and Marcia Rudin, *Prison or Paradise: The New Religious Cults* (Fortress Press, 1980).

Two important contacts for relatives or friends who are concerned over their children's involvement:

Philip Cushman
West Coast Jewish Training Project
   (Deprogramming)
190 Denslowe Drive
San Francisco, CA 94132
(415) 563-7820

Rabbi Maurice Davis
Jewish Community Center
252 Soundview Avenue
White Plains, NY 10606
(914) 949-4717

Rabbi Davis has been involved for several years in counseling the families of cult members and in helping to deprogram the young people themselves.

PSYCHOLOGICAL STRESS

Despite the growing acknowledgment of Jewish women's involvement in alcoholism, in crime, or in other forms of non-normative behavior, society, especially Jewish society, is much more disapproving of women who step out of line than of men. Both as women and as Jews we have put the brakes on the full expression of our anger, and our needs.

When they do address these needs, or seek to explore the ways in which they find themselves deviating from the elusive "norm" of Jewish womanhood, Jewish women as a group are more likely to seek professional psychological help than either other women or other Jews. First, women are greater users of mental-health facilities in general than men are. Second, Jews as a group have less resistance to psychiatry than Protestants or Catholics. Judaism emphasizes health and life over rigid adherence to religious law, and there is little conflict for most Jews between religious proscriptions and seeking help for emotional pain.

Perhaps one of the reasons that Jewish women are often portrayed in pop culture as the apotheosis of neurotic, self-conscious womanhood stems from this double predisposition to seek help from mental-health professionals. However, there are psychological issues peculiar to—or especially evident in—Jewish women's lives: role strain, low self-esteem, depression, among others.

There are several approaches to Jewish women's therapeutic mental-health needs, addressing them from different points on the Jewish feminist spectrum.

Low Self-Esteem
In work based on the explorations of blacks in the late sixties Judith Weinstein Klein has studied the effects of Jewish identification on the self-esteem of Jewish men and women. Klein, an ethnotherapist in

Berkeley, California, was trained in working with minority ethnic groups to help them to see what attitudes toward themselves (usually negative) they'd absorbed from the majority culture.

In her groups of Jewish men and women Klein discovered that for Jewish *men*, the more strongly identified they were as Jews, the higher their self-esteem (based on measures of whether or not their closest friends were Jewish, among other parameters). Conversely, for many Jewish women, the more strongly they identified as Jews, the lower their sense of self-worth. Apparently, negative attitudes toward women in Jewish families, and toward Jews in the larger society, were absorbed by these women in such a way that the more Jewish they felt, the less self-esteem they had. (For some of Klein's observations on how Jewish women and Jewish men see each other, see p. 293.)

Jewish Identity and Self-Esteem: Healing Wounds Through Ethno-therapy
by Judith Weinstein Klein, Ph.D.
American Jewish Committee
165 E. 56 Street
New York, NY 10022

Klein is also in private practice and trains other therapists in her techniques. She can be reached at:

921 The Alameda
Berkeley, CA 94707

Two resources that give some insights into the mental health (or lack of it) among Jews in general, though without specific focus on Jewish women, are nevertheless useful. One is *The Ethno-Cultural Factor in Mental Health*, by Joseph and Grace Pineiro Giordano. This literature review and bibliography gives an overview of the work being done in an effort to understand the role ethnicity plays in mental health: the perception of illness, cultural barriers in treatment, and many other factors. It is available from:

Institute on Pluralism and Group Identity
American Jewish Committee
165 E. 56 Street
New York, NY 10022
$2.25

(Also ask to receive the catalogue that lists all the institute's materials.)

The second work is: *Ethnic Groups of America: Their Morbidity, Mortality, and Behavior Disorders* (*Volume I—The Jews*), ed. A. Shiloh and Ida Cohen Selavan (Charles C. Thomas, 1973).

Conflicts with the Expectations of Others

New York psychotherapist Aphrodite Clamar, like several other women in her field, believes that women raised in traditional religious structures generally—including Catholics and Fundamentalist Protestants—have similar problems. These derive from their having very few options within their own groups, while maintaining a strong commitment to some of the values of these groups.

In a paper, "Torah-True and Feminist Too," Clamar encourages action rather than introspection for her patients, who, if they are Orthodox, tend to seek help because what they encounter in the outside world challenges the beliefs they've been raised with. Of the patient Clamar says: "She will need to gain inner strength . . . to work creatively and positively for change within the confines of Halakhah . . . to learn how to change power relationships within the family and within marriage." The feminist therapist treating the Orthodox woman "faces the challenge of reconciling her commitment to the dignity of her patient—including her heritage, beliefs and customs—with an allegiance to the Women's Movement principles of liberation and growth."[17]

Sara Silver Bunim, a Brooklyn-based Orthodox social worker with a largely Orthodox female clientele, has been examining in her work the conflicts Orthodox women feel when they experience what she calls "role strain."[18] The usual Orthodox mode of resolving perplexity or conflict is to consult a rabbi. Women's part in the healing or solving process has to do partly with how much actual knowledge they bring to their "problem" in order to present their case to the rabbinical authority.

While the initial approach to the therapist—in this case a psychologically oriented social worker—may be the same as for a non-Orthodox woman, the resolution may go beyond the internal and psychological; it may also involve bringing problems non-Orthodox women would consider "personal" to a higher authority. Decisions about family size or career path are not always, in these cases, the individual's to make. This process, whereby women's life situations are affected by Jewish law, is one unfamiliar to most non-observant Jewish women.

For most Jewish women engaged in difficult struggles for self-definition the biggest hurdles are not those of religious law and tradition *per se*. They are, rather, those that women face within their own families—

which can be the source of the greatest support and also the potential locus for the greatest oppression. (See "Women and the Jewish Family," p. 255.)

"Superwoman" Stress

Jewish women feel more conflict over competing roles than do many other women: they want both careers and families and need very much to excel in both spheres (see "Responding to the Childbearing Imperative," p. 371). Even many non-Orthodox Jewish women, especially those who are married and have children still living at home, say that they are torn between their desire for individual achievement and their need to maintain their "traditional" role as enabler, fulfilling the needs of others rather than their own. One woman, a writer and a mother of five, suggested that "we need a conference dealing with just this problem," since it affects so many women so severely. She says that of the women she knows who are juggling home and career, not one is free from anxiety, guilt, extreme fatigue, and the sense of frustration that comes from feeling that no task has been done adequately "because of the pressures of all those *other* tasks."

Freud expressed the view that the two essentials for happiness are love and work. Maybe for Jewish women the presence of both in one life is almost unbearable, because we have inherited (or been conditioned to want) competing standards of excellence in both areas. For some women, however, the conflict may be disabling, bringing with it the fear of losing the love of spouse or children if the woman doesn't conform to a fantasy ideal of Jewish womanhood.

In response to the pressures these women feel, Jewish feminist conferences all across the country schedule workshops with titles like this one from Philadelphia: "The Two-Career Family and What the Community's Responses Should Be"; or from Kansas City: "Changing Life-Styles and Stress in the Jewish family." And for those women who are parents alone there's the very real conflict when one is the primary care-giver and *also* the primary wage-earner (see "Single Mothers," p. 398).

However the dichotomy is expressed, many Jewish women report feeling torn apart by conflicting needs—theirs and those of the people around them. The Jewish superwoman is no myth; the only allusion is that she is able to fill all roles at no personal cost.

For places that offer help in coping with specific family problems, see "Divorce" (p. 355), "Single Mothers" (p. 398), and "When a Jewish Wife Becomes a Widow" (p. 408).

Crises in Mothering

Much of the literature of Jewish women's psychological patterning deals with their relationships within the family—mainly with their roles as mother or with the mother-daughter dyad. Consider, for example, Pauline Bart's work on how Jewish women feel when their children leave home, and the inner problems "working" women have when their professional responsibilities conflict with the "good-parent" values they themselves have and which are also enforced so strongly by the Jewish community.

Martha Wolfenstein, in "Two Types of Jewish Mothers,"[19] sees that the American-born Jewish mother who has problems in her relations with a child is not as personally involved with the child as her European-born counterpart. She desires and fosters greater independence in the child and can express more anger both at the child and at her own mother. For this mother, quarrels with the child don't have the component of murder but are usually about order and control.

The European-born mothers she has treated denied any hostile feelings toward their children, just as they denied any such feelings toward their own mothers. The child is both totally helpless (even when no longer a baby) and at the same time very powerful ("You're going to kill me!"). Every quarrel or disagreement is potential murder. Wolfenstein posits that model for this contradiction is childbirth, when a child is both helpless and can indeed harm the mother. Wolfenstein's next step is more complicated; she states that this mother is unsatisfied sexually, and so chidlbirth is her most powerful genital experience. Therefore she "recreates" it in relation to her child but in a masochistic way.

A special situation exists with those European-born mothers who survived World War II and its aftermath. Yael Danieli, a New York–based psychologist who has pioneered in work with Holocaust survivors and their families, says that mothers who are survivors themselves feel great grief when their children leave home. In these families, for obvious reasons, there is enormous interdependence of the two generations, and the conflict for mothers may not be internal so much as it is societal: the family itself values closeness and dependency more than the more assimilated, or "secure," American Jewish family.

Yael Danieli, Ph.D., Director
The Group Project for Holocaust Survivors and their Children
345 E. 80 Street
New York, NY 10021
(212) 737-8524

Many stories of women, both as survivors and as daughters, appear in Helen Epstein's *Children of the Holocaust* (Bantam, 1979). There are now groups of survivors' children forming around the country to discuss, among other things, relationships with their parents. For information:

ZACHOR
National Jewish Resource Center
250 W. 57 Street
New York, NY 10019

Depression
One subset of Jewish women are anxious about the conflicting needs of family and self: they have too many hats (or aprons) to wear. For another group (usually a generation older) the presenting problem for which they want psychological help or emotional support is that they don't have enough roles. Their most important role, as mother to their children, dissolves when their children leave home, making them the victims of the "empty nest" syndrome. They are depressed; and Jewish women, especially those with European-born mothers, are more likely than other women to be hospitalized for depression.

Sociologist Pauline Bart titles one version of her pioneering work on the subject of depression in middle-aged Jewish women "Portnoy's Mother's Complaint." Bart's description of the classic pre-illness history of "involutional depressives" sounds like the caricatures of Jewish mothers: "a history of martyrdom with no payoff (and martyrs always expect a payoff at some time) to make up for the years of sacrifice, inability to handle aggressive feelings, rigidity, a need to be useful in order to feel worthwhile, obsessive, compulsive supermother, superhousewife behavior and generally conventional attitudes."[20]

The women Bart interviewed, hospitalized for depression, felt their children didn't need them, didn't respect them, didn't call or visit often enough.

These are people who have had one source of primary gratification in their adult lives: their children. They are women who have invested "too much" in their children by current standards but who were, essentially, doing what society had taught them to do—fulfill themselves through their families. The very same society, however, provides no guidelines to help these women once their children become adults; the marriage or leave-taking of a child was often what precipitated their depression. Bart says: "There is no bar mitzvah for menopause. . . . One can think of these women as overcommitted to the maternal role and then, in middle age, suffering the unintended consequences of this commitment."[21]

Typically, women who suffer from severe depression at menopause, or when their children leave home and their official maternal role is *de facto* over, have thought of themselves as one-dimensional, precisely the opposite of the "role-diffusion" women who are striving to reconcile a multiplicity of roles. In each case the women are absorbing and taking very seriously the directives of their societies.

Usually the women suffering most at the "empty nest" stage are women who have had to invest their energies exclusively in their children, since so few other avenues were open to them—not even gainful employment. The sign of the rapid advancement of the Jewish middle-class family was not only the move to the suburbs but also, perhaps especially, the incarceration of the wife and mother in the home. Even in the second generation of affluence, women express the limits of this role, although the emphasis for nonworking women today in their twenties and thirties seems to be on the "creative" use of their own leisure time. A Long Island woman responded angrily to a discussion of feminism with the comments: "My husband has made me a completely liberated women. I do whatever I want. I just have to turn into a pumpkin at 4 p.m. when the children come home." Now the children are the tether to the home rather than being the *raison d'être* for keeping the woman in it.

Are women such as this one happy, or emotionally healthy? An imaginative study of depressive symptoms in a nonclinical population of Jewish women reveals a connection between feminist values and mental health. Laura B. Wolf, in looking at more than six hundred women reached through a Houston Jewish Community Center, found that "as adult Jewish women's feminist attitudes increased, so too did their self-esteem; as their self-esteem began to rise, their depressive symptoms began to decrease." She concludes that "feminism decreases depressive symptoms by increasing self-esteem."[22]

The study suggests ways that Jewish community agencies can help foster feminist attitudes, "defined as the elimination of stereotypical role prescriptions." Wolf proposes that the gap between Judaism and feminism can be narrowed by validation of nontraditional as well as traditional family roles and by helping Jewish men adapt to more flexible roles in the family and at work.

12

◆

GIVING TIME
AND MONEY

THE DIVISION OF POWER IN
THE JEWISH COMMUNITY

One of the salient characteristics of women in the North American Jewish community is that they have tended to band together in volunteer organizations—especially Jewish organizations—at rates that far outstrip the rate of affiliation of non-Jewish women. According to one set of statistics, 45 percent of Jewish women "join," compared with 30 percent of their non-Jewish sisters,[1] and Jewish women join and participate even more than Jewish men. Why do these women choose to affiliate thus? And what do they do once they're in? Is this good for the Jews? For the women themselves? In the wake of the women's liberation movement, how are they reshaping the organizations and the community?

If the Jewish religious structure can be seen as the legislative branch of Judaism, the myriad "secular" groups (see Networking Directory) are the ones that make and execute the public policy of North American Jews. These groups include the large, visible national bureaucracies (the ones whose leaders are approached by journalists for relevant comments on any late-breaking "Jewish" news) and the alternative grass-roots, issue-oriented organizations. Women are more visible in these diverse communal structures than in the institutions of religious Judaism, but the greater activity does not necessarily mean that women have wielded more real power on this front, nor that their work is valued equally with that of their male counterparts.

The women's liberation movement has had an effect here, though the knife cuts both ways: some Jewish women are now searching for more power and responsibility within organized Jewish life, while others feel that their feminist consciousness precludes their participation in what they see as a discriminatory social structure. Some women want more pie; others are rejecting the pie outright. The women who see a "bigger slice" solution to women's lack of visibility or power are trying to make changes both in the organizations themselves and in the ways the organizations act to meet women's specific needs. (Some of the response to these needs appears in the chapter "Jewish Women in Crisis," p. 407.)

The organizations that form what we think of as "the Jewish community" range from local community centers for social and recreational activity, to Israel-oriented groups, to large national service or policy organizations ostensibly created to meet the "public" needs of North American Jews.[2] Since affiliation with any of these groups is purely voluntary, as is any Jewish affiliation, and since, therefore, enforcement of any standards is considered impossible because of the organizations' different constituencies, there is no real democracy or constitution for North American Jewish life.

(courtesy United Jewish Appeal—Young Women's Leadership Division)

The modern Jewish "community"—this network of social-service, welfare, fraternal (sic), and religious organizations that make up what is jokingly referred to as the "alphabet soup" of Jewish life—holds no broad elections in which every self-identified Jewish woman votes for who will represent her, whether as the Jewish voice in the White House or the titular head of the American Jewish religious groups. Councils of leaders tend to be self-perpetuating, in what California social worker Rosa Felsenberg Kaplan calls a "Farmer-in-the-Dell" selection process.

Aviva Cantor, a *Lilith* editor, author, and activist, takes issue with this structure: "From a feminist perspective it is no accident that American Jewry is dominated by a small group of wealthy assimilationist men and their hired male hacks. These men harvest the Jewish people's money, and allocate it to projects that enhance their power and status. They speak and act in our name without our having selected either them or their policies. There's no 'recall' in the Jewish community; no accountability, no democracy; there's not even the concept of a 'loyal opposition' or of open criticism of policy or politics. Thus the majority of American Jews, women and men, are disenfranchised."[3]

Unlike the kibbutz model or the structures of radical Jewish political and Zionist organizations of Eastern Europe at the turn of the century, the North American and Western European Jewish communities have not even made a pretense of equalizing the roles and the power of women and men. There has been only limited change since the New York Federation Women's Division was honored thus: "As a 'token of appreciation' of [the Federation Women's Division's] work in the 1918 fundraising drive a woman had been placed on the list of Federation officers."[4]

More than sixty years later, with women continuing to work actively in fund-raising campaigns, their labors are often still given merely token recognition by the Jewish community, with real power remaining in the hands of men, who lead all but one of the mixed-gender major Jewish organizations.

In his 1976 sociological study, *Community and Polity: The Organizational Dynamics of American Jewry*, Daniel J. Elazar analyzes the status of women volunteers in this larger "coed" context, confirming the segregation of women in separate-sex organizations but also pointing out that women in the larger sphere do have "custody" of a range of social-welfare or cultural activities—typically areas of women's concern. "This central role is due to the fact that 'culture' is defined as a leisure-time activity in American society and hence is the province of women. To the extent that living Jewishly as a whole is increasingly being defined as a leisure-time activity, the role of women in other spheres of Jewish life is also growing."[5]

Elazar does not make clear that Jewish men, regardless of whether or not they view Jewish activity as a leisure-time pursuit, do have a vested interest in maintaining their own positions of power in Jewish communal organizations. For the ones who have made it (usually the wealthy), the status and contacts so acquired would be hard to replace in another milieu. It is for this reason as well as because of a traditional religious restriction of women's roles (transmitted osmotically into the secular realm) that men will not soon (or at least not easily) give up the reins of power in the volunteer sector of the Jewish community (see "Affirmative Action," p. 492).

Even those men who would like to see changes in personal and communal life don't hear what women are saying about how to make these changes. Here is one example. A Chicago Anglo-Jewish newspaper ran a forum criticizing the lack of adequate, visionary Jewish leadership—a problem that radical and not so radical Jewish women and men have been protesting for years. The forum featured only male critics. The editor wrote: "Almost alone among the entire Jewish press we have always fought for the real equality of women. . . . The truth—whether one likes it or not—is that most women are content to leave things as they are: in the hands of an inept and self-satisfied male leadership. . . . That is why there were no females on our panel."[6] Clearly this is a false perception. There are women who are actively involved in trying to change the shape and even the focus of Jewish organizations, some from within and some by creating new instruments.

The battles fought by German Jewish feminist Bertha Pappenheim in the first decade of the twentieth century sound chillingly familiar today to women who are trying to make the North American Jewish community more nearly egalitarian. Pappenheim, according to historian Marion Kaplan, "met with strong male resistance when she demanded that women participate in decision-making positions on the boards of Jewish charities. She warned that the leaders of the Jewish community welfare boards are losing some of their best women, who were turning to German feminism as an outlet for their energies."[7]

Just as women's work is worth less in the paid economy than men's, so it is in volunteer life. While women often do a substantial part of fund raising, and know their communities intimately, especially the needs of the groups sometimes unnoticed by the male *machers* ("honchos") who sit on boards, these women are not often nominated to sit on the com-

(courtesy United Jewish Appeal—Young Women's Leadership Division)

mittees that disburse the money they've helped raised, and their expertise is ignored. Women volunteers, like their professional counterparts in Jewish life, are most likely to serve in children's and "family" agencies, institutions for the elderly, cultural organizations, but not, say, on the long-range planning committee.

One woman protested: "When I make a suggestion in a meeting where men are present, the conversation simply continues where it left off. The men don't even respond to my comments. It's like the pond smoothing over again after a pebble drops into it—the smooth surface of the meeting is never disrupted by what I have to say."

We have documentation of even less subtle discrimination against Jewish women even in the very communal organizations that their energies are helping to run. Here are a few examples:

• In 1980 the New York Federation of Jewish Philanthropies surveyed

Jewish community agencies nationwide. They found that, parallel to the discrimination against women employees, there is a paucity of women in key decision-making capacities on the volunteer side. Where women do have leadership positions in co-ed organizations or agencies they tend to be in traditional "women's areas," such as children's agencies or care of the elderly. There are a few notable exceptions to this pattern, usually on the east and west coasts, but the rule is that the larger the community or organization, the smaller the opportunity for women to participate at the highest levels.

• The National United Jewish Appeal decided in the mid-1950s to create a "Young Leadership Cabinet," primarily to attract and keep within the philanthropic fold the children of older "big givers." Along the way the founders of the elite cabinet managed to exclude the daughters of the wealthy. The cabinet now consists of young (under-forty) male community "leaders" from around the country, and activities feature retreats, Jewish education, and grooming sessions to create the next generation of Jewish "leaders." Obviously the intent was that none of these would be of the female persuasion.

In the mid-1970s, after protests from women who felt that their talents (and often their money) ought to be similarly recognized as part of future leadership pool of the Jewish community, and from male supporters of this position, a vote was taken to include women in the cabinet. "Somehow" the decision was never implemented, and instead UJA set up a separate Young Women's Leadership Cabinet (often featuring the wives of the men in the male cabinet).[8] Whether this two-track system will actually bring women into key lay leadership positions in a generation or so remains to be seen. What we do know is that the very idea of a co-ed leadership pool was very threatening to some people in power, and the men's-club atmosphere of the male cabinet continues.

• Even the establishment Jewish organizations have now created special committees to examine the status of women in Jewish life (for listing, see "Affirmative Action," p. 492). In April 1980 the American Jewish Committee and the National Council of Jewish Women collaborated on a survey of women's involvement in the Pittsburgh Jewish community and reported that there have been more women visible in the community in the past few years but that change is slow in coming. Those women who do achieve officer status are usually still in "enabling" positions: vice-presidents, secretaries, recording secretaries, assistant treasurers. "Twenty-six organizations reported male presidents; only one woman served as president of a Jewish communal organization."

The survey examined the scant representation of women on executive committees of organizations, particularly the five largest communal institutions, where women make up from 2 to 18 percent of the executive-committee members. Even these few women often have little effect on policy. The analysts of the survey say: "Women have been consistently excluded from the centers of power in Pittsburgh's Jewish community, for policy making is not generally decided at a full meeting of the board of directors. Rather, decisions are often made by executive committees under the leadership of the president of the organization."[9]

• Jacqueline Levine, now head of the National Jewish Community Relations Advisory Council, active in several organizations in her local community and nationally, has made it a point to insist that more women be placed on the nominating committees that preselect candidates for leadership in co-ed organizations. (The elections themselves are usually a rubber-stamp process.) Only with women in place on these committees will the community be able to plug into the talent bank of capable women in every region.

• A group of women in Milwaukee, noticing that the few women on the local Federation board were often ignored at meetings, put together a cadre of local Jewish professional and business women to conduct a "skills workshop" for teaching the city's Jewish women leaders all about certain business terms and practices that male leaders had spent a lifetime learning in the course of their work experience. Thus armed, the women lay leaders were able to use all the right "buzz words" when discussing the Federation's budget at board meetings, knew how to deal with personnel contacts, and generally upgraded both their performance and their image.

There is a difference of opinion on how change is to come about. One opinion holds that changes giving women volunteers equal access to leadership positions or more power in the community will come only because those now in power (usually male) recognize the ecological benefits of a community that makes full use of all of its members. This is the approach that puts its faith in the enlightened self-interest of those now at the top. Others believe that only by direct challenge—whether through Jewish feminist organizations, through legal challenges, or by other means—will the community be forced to democratize.

The "different pie" approach to making change for women in the Jewish community is exemplified by the Bay Area Jewish Women's Collective in Berkeley, California, which in the late 1970s consisted of committed Jewish feminists who taught courses on Jewish women's issues to local organizations, gave lectures, planned conferences, and generally acted as an alternative Jewish feminist voice and resource in the community. Their very presence made it clear that not all Jewish women are content with reformist solutions to the inequities in the Jewish community.

A new organization, composed of both women and men volunteers, created as an alternative to the perceived priorities of the established Jewish organizations, is New Jewish Agenda, which tries to create a model for an egalitarian Jewish organization through its feminist task force and the progressive orientation of its local chapters. Its first leaders were men, and women involved with the organization remain vigilant to ensure that the phenomenon of male dominance familiar from Old and New Left political groups isn't replicated here.

New Jewish Agenda
1123 Broadway
New York, NY 10010
(212) 620-0828

(courtesy United Jewish Appeal—Young Women's Leadership Division)

The Task Force on Women of the Coalition for Alternatives in Jewish Education (CAJE) has become another rallying point for women who want to be active in the Jewish community but aren't drawn to the more traditional volunteer organizations.

Coalition for Alternatives in Jewish Education
468 Park Avenue South
New York, NY 10016
(212) 696-0740

Although there is no longer any national Jewish feminist organization (there was a short-lived J.F.O. in the mid-70s), there are independent women's groups operating in cities around the continent. Many of these are now religious in orientation (see Networking Directory). The New Jewish Agenda has grass-roots groups addressing women's issues, and *Lilith* magazine has become a clearinghouse for information on the sometimes ephemeral change-oriented Jewish feminist groups.

Here are contact points outside North America for locating other Jewish feminists:

London Jewish Feminist Group
c/o Margaret Green
Flat 7, Callcott Court
Callcott Road
London NW 6, England

Monique Chalude
177 Avenue Armand Huysman
1050 Brussels, Belgium

Deborah, The Jewish Women's Group
c/o WIZO
Dwarslaan 18
126 B.B. Blaricum
Amsterdam, The Netherlands

There are two good American sources for information on feminist groups in Israel: U.S./Israel Women-to-Women (see p. 471) and

Coalition for Women in Israel
35-24 78th Street, Apt. B-39
Jackson Heights, NY 11372

The Israeli feminist magazine would be a good contact point for a North American wanting to meet Israeli feminists:

Noga
P.O. Box 21376
Tel Aviv, Israel

AN ANATOMY OF THE JEWISH WOMEN'S ESTABLISHMENT

Aside from general Jewish organizations open to both men and women (such as the American Jewish Committee or Americans for a Progressive Israel or a number of educational and cultural and Zionist groups), here are the "establishment" Jewish women's organizations. All have national offices and vary enormously on the local level. Depending on who is drawn to which organizations in any given community, the local programs can vary from a social, clublike orientation to those which are educational or sometimes even strongly feminist in focus. On a local level it's possible in almost all these organizations to have some influence on programs, if not directly on policy. However, the rise to national office (and with it the opportunity to make large-scale policy decisions) usually comes to those women who have money or access to their husband's money and the leisure time that money can buy.

The "women's division" organizations themselves are concerned with keeping the co-ed entity attractive to large numbers of women if separate divisions are phased out, and with any drop in fund-raising for good works if women slip into larger categories where they will simply append their names to their husbands' gifts. Fund-raisers worry that the money women now give on their own—sometimes referred to as "pin-money gifts" or "plus giving"—through their own structures would thus be lost.

Here is a listing of major national Jewish women's organizations. With the exceptions of Hadassah and the National Council of Jewish Women, all are affiliated with some parent organization.

Amit Women
817 Broadway
New York, NY 10003
(212) 477-4720
(A religious women's Zionist organization.)

B'nai B'rith Women
1640 Rhode Island Avenue, N.W.
Washington, DC 20036
(202) 857-6670
(Community service and education programs; women's affiliate of B'nai B'rith.)

Brandeis University National Women's Committee
Brandeis University
Waltham, MA 02254
(617) 647-2194
(Financial support of Brandeis University library; study groups in local communities that use faculty-prepared syllabi.)

Hadassah, the Women's Zionist Organization of America
50 W. 58 Street
New York, NY 10019
(212) 355-7900
(The title is self-explanatory, but local chapters also have social and educational programs for members, in addition to raising money for the Hadassah Medical Organization in Israel, Youth Aliyah, and Young Judaea.)

National Council of Jewish Women
15 E. 26 Street
New York, NY 10010
(212) 532-1740
(Strong on social-welfare programs, especially for women and children.)

National Federation of Temple Sisterhoods
838 Fifth Avenue
New York, NY 10021
(212) 249-0100
(The women's organization for Reform congregations.)

Pioneer Women/Na'amat
200 Madison Avenue
New York, NY 10016
(212) 725-8010
(Women's Labor-Zionist organization. Supports social services for women in Israel through Na'amat, its Israeli counterpart and women's issues in American life.)

Union of Orthodox Jewish Congregations—Women's Branch
84 Fifth Avenue
New York, NY 10011
(212) 929-8857
(The umbrella group for sisterhoods of Orthodox congregations.)

Women's American ORT Federation
315 Park Avenue S.
New York, NY 10016
(212) 505-7700
(Women's branch of the American ORT Federation; supports vocational training for Jews around the world.)

Women's Division, Council of Jewish Federations and Welfare Funds
575 Lexington Avenue
New York, NY 10022
(212) 751-1311
(C.J.F. is the umbrella group for eight hundred Jewish Federations in the United States and Canada, giving advice on programs, fund raising, community organizing, and more.)

Women's Division, United Jewish Appeal
1290 Avenue of the Americas
New York, NY 10019
(212) 757-1500
(Fund raising for a variety of local and Israeli projects, plus Jewish programming for women. UJA also sponsors a Young Women's Leadership Cabinet, which tries to identify up-and-coming Jewish women leaders.)

Women's League for Conservative Judaism
48 E. 74 Street
New York, NY 10021
(212) 628-1600
(Umbrella for sisterhoods of Conservative synagogues in the U.S. and Canada.)

Who are the members of these women's organizations? Without blurring the differences based on group ideology—some groups with, say, a Zionist orientation will often attract women different from those drawn to associations with a domestic social-action focus—what are the "types" of women drawn to organized Jewish life?

All of them are women who first and foremost are looking for a way to identify as Jews. Those who join traditional Jewish organizations may or may not also belong to synagogues; although one study indicates that religious participation is often a precursor to community involvement,[10] it would seem that this would be a more likely path for men than for women, who are often not full participants in synagogue life to begin with.

For most non-Orthodox Jews in North America the strongest tie to their religious and ethnic roots is through this sometimes elusive sense of community with other Jews, expressed privately through friendship patterns[11] and publicly by affiliation. For Jewish women of all degrees of religious observance Jewish organizations have become their shul, the place where they can go to stand up and be counted as Jews.

With a high percentage of Jews in geographically mobile occupations and professions, Jews certainly make up some of the 20 percent of Americans who move every year. Women facilitate this transplantation and socialization process when they join a Jewish women's organization; they gain instant community, access to potential friendships, and share familiar goals. Organizational affiliation is a way of finding "like" in a situation in which one is confronted with many alien "others." Women who are thus transplanted seem to join Jewish organizations for motives different from men's; according to sociologist Marshall Sklare, men are looking for "conviviality" rather than for a "seriousness" of Jewish involvement.[12]

Women also tend to give more time and energy to Jewish organizations—even when they're single and/or working—than men do; witness all the single women involved in "young professional" chapters of Jewish women's organizations nationwide. There is no parallel setup or enrollment of young unmarried Jewish men.

What are the characteristics of the women who do join? They fall into one of two categories: leaders and followers (queens and drones). As one high-profile Jewish woman leader tells it:

> There are two kinds of people involved: "volunteers," who are relatively powerless, and "lay leaders," who are part of the organization's decision-making process. It's hard to say exactly at what point you can go from the first category into the second. It's largely an intangible matter of self-perception. Knowledge and understanding do make a difference. It helps if you know where the money in your community is buried, and how to turn it on. You have to establish that you have valuable and/or unique knowledge, entree into the right places, and so on.[13]

Obviously "knowing where the money is buried" is less a mystery in a chapter-based membership organization such as Hadassah or Amit Women and more important in such community-wide fund-raising operations as Federation of Jewish Philanthropies or United Jewish Appeal. But the distinction between those in the know and those who are the foot-soldier volunteers holds throughout. The ordinary volunteer usually has less money and/or time to give and is also not as personally invested in the processes of the organization. The leaders, supervolunteers, are likely to describe themselves as "career volunteers" or "professional volunteers" and to sit on the board of more than one Jewish organization or committee.

For "career volunteers," their long hours of work in the community may consume as much time as a paying job would, but these women don't reveal the conflict over the time away from their families often expressed by women who are working for a living. They see themselves as very competent, capable people who often have their families' approval for their volunteer activity. "The simple fact that . . . women in high-level volunteer jobs universally experience themselves as free to choose home over job is enough to liberate them from the painful conflicts that dominate the lives of so many women who work for pay. The volunteers can claim their competence, acknowledge their abilities, say it out loud for the world to hear. Not for them the fears that come to women who move toward a world where they'll compete with men."[14]

These women's organizations, although clearly not equal even while remaining separate, do serve important purposes for some women. In a women-only group, just as at all-women's colleges, women have to take the lead. Similarly in organizations: women rise to the top, assume leadership, take responsibility, all in ways that might be denied them (or that they might be shy of assuming) in a co-ed context. Since the organizations usually put no restrictions on how much one participates, they can provide a way for women to learn skills and gain confidence and recognition for something other than strictly domestic tasks. Women also get an opportunity to perform in roles that might be closed to them in the paid labor force because of age or lack of formal training or experience.

Volunteer activity at its finest gives women a sense of competence and instrumentality—the ability to take action and make change—that is often lacking in other areas of life. For example, a group of Jewish women in a New York City suburb organized an annual "shared seder" for the first night of Passover. The seder now draws people from all over the city and suburbs—those newly bereaved, single parents, students, hospital patients, even small families that couldn't hold their own seders. These women saw people with unmet needs and reached out to them. So did members of the National Council of Jewish Women who volunteered to accompany through the courts women who were pressing wife-abuse cases and who might have been afraid to testify without the comforting support of another woman.

However fine these actions are, they do cast into relief two problems:

(1) they involve activities for which women can and do get paid—social-welfare planning and advocacy in the courts—so that volunteer activity in these areas may cause paid jobs (usually held in these areas by women) to disappear and contribute to the illusion that Federal budget cuts have no effect; (2) they are, alas, merely superficial solutions, leaving uncorrected the basic problems of rootlessness that cause people to be lonely and without communities at holiday times, and that give men the idea that it's their right to harm other people just because they happen to be married to them.

Certainly there are kinds of volunteer activity that will always make a difference and help create a better world. As Gloria Steinem has put it, "It has always been acceptable to volunteer—but not for our *own* revolution. Now it's time to start." Jacqueline Levine, in 1981 the first woman to chair the American Jewish Congress National Governing Council and long an advocate of women's greater participation in leadership roles in Jewish life, has great faith in the social-change potential of volunteer activity: "I agree with de Tocqueville that volunteers are the hallmark of a democratic society. Volunteers are unfettered by bureaucracy and can allow new ideas to grow and thrive."[15]

Doris Gold, in a landmark article, "Voluntarism," warns that women collude in masking certain real social problems that would otherwise be the responsibility of government, or of society as a whole, when they try to correct serious social ills through piecemeal volunteer efforts. She also notes that sometimes "do-gooder," bandage-rolling types of volunteer work take paid jobs away from poor women who have no marketable skills.[16] This isn't necessarily true of the Israel-oriented work of some Jewish women's organizations, but it might well be the case for direct-service volunteers who serve in schools, or act as paralegal counselors, or staff thrift shops without pay.

Obviously, despite even the good intentions of leaders and rank-and-file members alike, there are certain pitfalls in volunteer activity, as there are with much paid work in the nonprofit sector. Volunteer work has few criteria for self-evaluation. There's no economic motivation for greater efficiency, and many of the volunteers are unfamiliar with businesslike style because of their own lack of exposure to the work world. Therefore many Jewish organizations, especially women's organizations—which have come to depend on a now-shrinking pool of volunteers with limitless time—tend to take too long in making decisions, and foster inefficiency in many ways. A woman active in Women's American ORT moaned: "We have four large meetings every year, and each meeting takes several days. This is crazy. Two meetings would be more than enough. Not very much happens that needs to be decided on every three months, so the same material is gone over each time. We heard all about it at the last meeting but have to listen again. Nobody wants to offend anyone else, so there's endless checking back and forth. It's a real time-waster."

Aviva Cantor provides a worst-case analysis of Jewish women's volunteer style in "The Sheltered Workshop," in which she argues, in part:

> What Jewish women volunteers find in these organizations is a distorted form of occupational therapy. . . . In this set-up, it is not the end product but the working (the process) that is [each] organization's real agenda. It is for this reason that the organizations' issue content is thin and marginal (unlike that of volunteer organizations dedicated to changing society, where members' commitments are to the issues). The *Jewish* content is also minor and *pareve* [middle-of-the-road].
>
> The work process itself is reminiscent of housework, with boring scutwork, plus interminable meetings. Instead of preparing women for work in the "real world," in which people even get fired from jobs, the volunteer organizations are an alternative *un*real world. The volunteers, in short, are programmed for permanent servitude in a kind of sheltered workshop.
>
> The vast majority of Jewish women, however, are neither physically nor mentally handicapped; nor are they, for the most part, even educationally deprived. And if they are temperamentally unsuited to "the outside," it is largely because of their lack of self-confidence and self-esteem, a lack reinforced by these organizations' work habits that foster dependency and inefficiency.
>
> Women's volunteerism is thus a form of warehousing, of keeping women safely busy at harmless tasks that do not threaten their husbands or challenge the other power relationships in the Jewish community.
>
> The upper-class leaders of the women's organizations know that, given the patriarchal structure of American Jewish society, they could not hold down the same positions or be rewarded with the same status in a co-ed organization or as paid workers. But without their mass base, the leaders would not have the power and prestige they hold: like the nobles at Versailles, they derive their power from the *corvée* of the laborers. Therefore it is in their interest to keep the women members from defecting. . . .
>
> With the prime responsibility for the organization in the hands of a few women at the top, and the main administrative work done by paid professionals, the majority of the members become infantil-

ized. . . . As currently practiced, volunteer work reinforces rather than heals the damage society has already done to women—accentuating women's fear of making decisions ("Selma, tuna salad or salmon salad for the luncheon, I can't decide"), a lack of discipline ("Honey, I don't think I'll come in today, I'm a bit tired from that big dinner party we had last night, you do understand, don't you?"), and terror of making a mistake, God forbid ("Girls, let's go over this again just one more time, it can't hurt to make sure we've covered every angle").

Many women feel ashamed of joining an organization mainly to seek the sense of self-worth missing in their lives, believing that their problems are personal rather than political. The leaders know that if they can offset this feeling, the members are theirs forever. And offset it they do, with massive doses of organizational chauvinism.

The trick is to make the members believe that they are needed rather than needy, that what they are doing is necessary, invaluable and, of course (the standard, hallowed unchallengeable argument), Good For The Jews, and that only *their* organization can Do The Job. . . .

Organizational chauvinism serves the leaders well because it distorts the fact that all the organizations are basically interchangeable and often duplicate each other's work (and even membership lists). Members most often join not out of commitment to the organization's vague goals but by chance—because the organization is nearby, the one a friend belongs to, or one perceived as the most prestigious group around.

Organizational chauvinism also keeps the women active in the different organizations apart from each other. Women are thus triply isolated: first, by men into the women's volunteer ghetto; second, by the leaders into organizational mini-ghettos; and third, into loneliness fostered by competitiveness—over donations, home furnishings, clothing worn to organization functions. . . .

The women's volunteer organizations arose to give women some way to cope with their crushing lack of self-worth engendered by patriarchy, but they ultimately reinforce that lack of self-esteem.[17]

When Cantor's article first appeared, some critics claimed that she had exaggerated both the trivializing of women's work and the extent of the chauvinism. But reality-testing has borne out her analysis.

I myself was skeptical of Cantor's analysis of organizational chauvinism, but I had all the proof I needed when in 1978 leaders of American Jewish women's organizations were invited by Virginia Snitow, a past president of the Leadership Conference of American Jewish Women's Organizations,[18] to a meeting to discuss crises for women in Israel—including issues of wife abuse, rape, and health care. The leader of each organization claimed that *her* organization represented the best interests of Israeli women and that there were no needs of women in Israel unmet. The core group of women who had called this meeting with Snitow finally decided to form an independent entity for the express purpose of investigating and funding feminist projects in Israel, addressing needs to which the established women's organizations were blind precisely because of the organizational chauvinism Cantor protests.

Where do we go from here? A danger on the horizon (though an odd complaint to make at this stage, perhaps) is that the Jewish women's movement has become too "kosher" too fast, making of a struggle for justice and equality (which is fully in accord with the highest precepts of Judaism) merely another fad, which is being co-opted by Jewish estab- lishment organizations eager to justify their existence and seeking to be seen in step with what's new and "trendy." In nearly every Jewish orga- nization in every community there has been a meeting or conference on the subject of women in Judaism. After the meeting or conference is over, are the real questions and conflicts any closer to being resolved or eliminated? Or is it that women's issues are seen as safe "radical" topics, giving the community or organization the illusion of being part of a movement for social change without having to actually make any real changes? More precisely, the specific danger is that the *hechsher*, the seal of approval, of the Jewish community structure, bestowed on the pro- liferation of *ad hoc* committees and task forces, may actually subvert the very real goals of Jewish women. These goals are full equality in Jewish life and the opportunity to choose how we want to define ourselves as Jewish women. Just as advertisers use hip street talk to sell cars, some of the specific demands of the Jewish women's movement may be co-opted as symbolic tokens by Jewish organizations, thus giving a veneer of progress to a structure still male-dominated.

What are the real conflicts often glossed over in these gatherings? First, the basic patriarchal structure of the whole Jewish community is not addressed: a focus, for example, may be on the status of women under Jewish law, but lacking any discussion of who made and makes the law and by what contemporary mechanism the laws concerning women can be changed. No conference run by a major Jewish organization has yet addressed the role division at the root of much of the injustice being described—namely, that the men have the power and the women are the classic "enablers," making it possible for the men to use their power un- fettered by such concerns as who'll serve the lunch. Even when women speak among themselves of their status in Jewish life they tend to undervalue the work they do. For example, the Union of American Hebrew Congregations held a conference in New York in 1980 titled "Feminists of Faith," to which women of different faith groups came to share their experiences and goals. The meeting was scheduled for a full day, and the conference fee included coffee and dessert, but *the women were expected to bring their own brown-bag lunches!* Would *any* Jewish organization planning a conference for *men* of different faiths ever ask them to *bring lunch?*

The conferences and meetings on Jewish women's issues take up many woman-hours in their planning and execution—most of those woman-hours unpaid. Are those conferences being designed to shore up the status quo? To conclude that there is, indeed, a "delicate balance" between feminism and Jewish concerns? That eternal vigilance is necessary to combat the erosion of so-called traditional family values? Or do we as Jewish women have the power to shape our own agenda and decide what kinds of conferences we want, what kinds of services our Jewish communities need to provide for us, what strategies and tactics we think best?

RECLAIMING OUR OWN IDENTITIES
IN THE COMMUNITY

Even if the worst criticism of women's traditional volunteer activity is valid, women alone cannot be blamed.

Men, of course, have contributed to the trivializing and undervaluing of women's volunteer work. They have seen it as less threatening to their own needs and status than women's paid work would be—otherwise why would they encourage their wives to be active in community organizations while often actively discouraging them from going "out to work"? Volunteer work has been one of the sanctioned activities for Jewish women otherwise confined to their homes by custom or social pressure. For men of a certain generation and mind-set to have a wife at work for pay insults their capabilities as breadwinners (see "Jewish Women and the World of Work," p. 475). Yet the same men claim to be pleased by their wives' volunteer accomplishments, which often take as much time out of the home as paid work would but don't create a competing breadwinner.

The fact that many men take pleasure in their wives' communal involvement is only partly explained by natural pride in the accomplishments of a family member. Vicariously, the men have also basked in communal glory when women are not even known by their own names but are referred to in speeches, programs, and community newspapers as the female components of their husbands' identities. "Mrs. Sam Cohen" rather than "Judy Cohen" did something wonderful that was written up in the local Jewish paper, and even strangers find out that someone attached to the family of Sam Cohen has done something that reflects well on the patriarch of the family. A woman who lectures before Jewish audiences comments: "A member of the audience spoke out on the name issue when I mentioned it in a talk. One woman said, 'My husband is very proud of my accomplishments, and he *likes* to see me referred to by his name. It's part of his pride in what I do.' Great, I said, but when your husband writes scientific papers, does he use your name so that you can be equally proud of being linked to him?"

Women's organizations and those which are co-ed are equally reprehensible in allowing this practice to continue. The executive director of New York's Federation of Jewish Philanthropics announced with pride at a 1980 women's conference that the new president of the Federation was "Mrs. Lawrence Tisch." The outraged women in the hall, whose consciousness was considerably higher than his, interrupted him, calling out, "Who? Who?" He repeated "Mrs. Lawrence Tisch." It was only after women hollered, "What is *her* name?" that the man finally got the point. "Oh. She's Billie Tisch." Mazel tov. When Jewish organizations finally break down and have women in positions so important that they must be listed on the letterhead, they're still often listed under their husbands' names—and therefore still invisible in their own right.

To help correct this situation some women have taken to writing notes of protest to any organization sending out letters or publications addressing women by their husbands' names. Others have circulated petitions in women's organizations for women to "take back our names." Meanwhile the National Council of Jewish Women, clearly one of the most progressive of Jewish women's organizations when it comes to women's rights, still asks for "husband's name" on its enrollment card. What about all the single women they are allegedly trying to draw in? To say nothing of those married women who would just as soon have nothing to do with an organization that takes a Siamese-twin approach to husbands and wives? Hadassah's membership form at least has a box you can check saying "List me under my own first name."

Using our own names, in whatever form, seems only a small change, but we know how great is the power of naming. How we identify ourselves has an impact on how we perceive ourselves and on how others regard us. In the Jewish community, women are beginning to emerge from behind the scrim of their husbands' identities, suddenly appearing on their own recognizance.

"BEYOND THE VALLEY OF THE SHMATTES"

As women value themselves more, they place a higher value on their time as well.

Recent changes in some women divisions—such as the 1982 decision that American Jewish Congress would phase out its women's branch and that women and women's issues would be part of the organization as a whole—indicate some of the ferment over how women participate in organized Jewish life. For years the leaders of women's organizations have bemoaned a "crisis in volunteerism," with women lessening their commitment, though usually retaining their affiliations. There are several reasons for these shifts, among them that women are entering or reentering the work force—out of economic necessity or to achieve personal goals, or both—and that they are reevaluating the status and usefulness of much of the volunteer work they and/or their mothers did in the past. Out of this careful scrutiny is emerging an agenda for change that bodes well for creating a more nearly egalitarian Jewish community.

The great strength of the Jewish women's organizations today may in fact lie not in their direct provision of social services, but in their power for advocacy. They represent hundreds of thousands of North American women, and with these numbers can put a great deal of weight behind the opinions they voice to American and Canadian legislators and opinion-makers. *Ms.* editor and author Letty Cottin Pogrebin asked the fifteen or twenty Jewish women leaders at a New York Federation of Jewish Philanthropies meeting in 1981: "Do you realize how powerful you are? Please go around the room and estimate, each of you, how many women you speak for." The women, reticent at first, were surprised at the tally—a hundred thousand women were represented although not by democratic vote. Thus there is considerable value in making visible resolutions and statements on women's issues, in an effort to shape national policy (to say nothing of policy within the Jewish community). One method is that of Pioneer Women Na'amat, which published and distributed a list of resolutions for 1983–1985 detailing the organization's pro-choice position on reproductive freedom, its support of the true feminist agenda of the U.N. Decade of Women, its advocacy of economic equality for women, and its stand in favor of adequate public and private child care. The National Council of Jewish Women and several of the other organizations listed have similar, if less comprehensive, position statements. Examining them would be a useful way of comparing the organizations' up-to-the-minute policies on matters of concern to women.

One change for the better is the new professional approach to volunteer work exemplified by a 1980 reference booklet published by the Women's Council of the Federation of Jewish Agencies in Philadelphia. (Although the introduction to the booklet is signed by a president of the Women's Council who goes by her husband's name, it is to be hoped that this will not cast a shadow on the book's usefulness, both to potential volunteers and to other communities.) The booklet goes through Philadelphia, agency by agency, with a page for day schools, another for Y's, another for kosher meals-on-wheels, and so on. For each agency there's a description of the kinds of general volunteer services it can use, plus a section on the professional skills needed (teachers, speech therapists, social workers), so that people with specialized skills or retired people eager to be useful don't have to feel that they can contribute to the Jewish community only by stuffing envelopes or setting the table for a senior citizen's luncheon. And for each agency there is the name and number of the person to call "for an interview." The professionalization of volunteer work (and even those women who work full time often like to be involved in some types of volunteer work) has arrived, at least in one city.

One example of women's changing self-perception speaks for many. Asked to come and sort through donations for a rummage bazaar at her child's Hebrew day school, a Manhattan woman protested:

The amount of money ultimately raised was insignificant—no more than a few hundred dollars. Yet dozens of women were spending money on baby-sitters and taxicabs to go over to the school in the evenings and sort through old linens and broken toys and assorted *shlock*, debating about pricing the items, arranging tables for the bazaar. The social needs that were being met by the bazaar might have been met in a more valuable or appropriate way—through parents' group discussions, or a party in one of the parents' homes, but somehow the "excuse" of doing good while socializing was very important to these women. If each one had given half a day's pay, or donated the cost of child care and cab fare instead of giving unremunerated time to the bazaar, the school could have come out ahead. Or if the women had come up with some more creative ways of raising the money so that they wouldn't have felt like ragpickers themselves, the male rabbi who headed the school and his all-male board of directors would have been a little more respectful of their efforts.

An ancillary benefit that women could reap from following these suggestions would be tax deductibility. You can't deduct time given to a nonprofit organization, but you can deduct goods or money. Since time is traditionally what women have had more of than money, they've been faced with situations in which even the IRS denies the value of what they are giving. In 1980, for example, women's voluntary work in the United States was valued at $18 *billion, none of it tax-deductible!*[19] Men usually give money, which is tax-deductible and therefore somehow real, while women's work, usually not quantified in the same way, is "invisible" and unrecognized.

Although women often claim that they do receive community recognition for their unpaid labor, we can see from the comments of those women who have tried to reenter the paid labor force on the strength of volunteer work and skills (see p. 486) that this "value" only exists as long as nobody actually has to pay for it.

Most of the women I meet speak of the personal benefits gained from volunteer work, it's true, but they also understand the costs. They know that volunteerism exploits them and their skills, that it helps to reinforce their second-class status by relegating some of the most talented among them to unpaid jobs that have little power and prestige. They know that their unpaid labor has been a gift to society—a gift responsible for large economies in both the public and private sectors. And they know, too, that their gift has been poorly appreciated, inadequately repaid.[20]

THE MONEY CONNECTION

Since much of the structure of secular American Jewish life is predicated on giving, getting, and disbursing money, we need to examine how Jewish women's attitudes to money are connected with our relative lack of power in the community (although, of course, this isn't the only reason for women's powerlessness).

"A tale popular in my family," says a woman from Canada, "has it that on Fridays, my great-grandfather in his small village in Russia would steal a loaf or two of the breads my great-grandmother had baked for Sabbath, so he could give them to poor families. The story goes that my great-grandmother, known also for other incidents of a less-than-generous sort, was furious at the thefts."

The story may be an unfortunate paradigm of sorts for the attitude Jewish women have had toward their family's giving. Even in folk tales

A contemporary tzedakah *(charity) box with a women's motif.* (courtesy In the Spirit gallery, New York)

and children's stories, the *bobbe* is the hardheaded practical one and the *zayde* is the dreamer, willing to risk.[21] Women have probably been less secure over their own ability to support the family, if need be, and more directly responsible for the family's physical survival, and so they measured out charity by what would cause no loss to their first unit of responsibility, the family. Which is not to say that Jewish women haven't been known for charitable work in one form or another—the Talmud says that women give more direct *tzedakah*—but their attitude toward money itself, particularly the giving of money, has been colored by anxieties about their own and their dependents' futures. One sign of this is that professional fund-raisers in Jewish community organizations often despair when a big male donor dies. Their fear, borne out by experience, is that the widow of the donor will not see the necessity of carrying on her husband's large financial contribution. (See "When a Jewish Wife Becomes a Widow," p. 408.)

In organized Jewish life, giving money—or having lots potentially to give—is one of the access routes to power. (The other ways are hard work, and achieving status in some field of endeavor so that the communal organizations want the luster of your name on their letterheads.) Some women know this already. For example, there are those career women who do not want to be counted as part of the UJA-Federation Women's Division but want instead to make their "gift" through one of the many business and professional divisions—lawyers, accountants, department-store executives, and so on. They want the same access to business connections and status that professional men's contributions bring their donors. The reason that the separate occupational divisions were started in the first place was that there was a feeling (proved valid) that people will give more generously when solicited by their business associates, both as a way of establishing goodwill among suppliers, clients, and peers and as a way of demonstrating financial success to their competitors. Many women now want the same opportunity to mix good works and professional advancement.

Daniel J. Elazar discusses the centrality of giving money in American Jewish life (what critics have called "checkbook Judaism"), suggesting that of the 25 to 30 percent of American Jews who aren't affiliated with the Jewish community, "many . . . have such limited incomes that they cannot develop more formal or lasting attachments in a context that makes financial expenditure a binding factor in the associational process."[22] Since many Jewish women have incomes limited by inadequate education, or discrimination, and others are newly poor through divorce or widowhood, they are among those closed out of the "associational process." For other women, having power through having money to give can lead to their taking the few leadership positions open to women. In other words, the wealthy advance whereas the less affluent are underrepresented at the top.

Just as women are beginning to understand that their financial support of certain political candidates gives them a greater voice in government or greater access to those with voices, so women wanting a decision-making role in Jewish community life see (for better or for worse) that where they put their money, and in what quantities, will make a difference in their personal status and in the power they are allowed to wield. Large gifts of money do not necessarily ensure power, but capable women will advance faster in the community if they understand early on that *visible* donations are important to their rise.[23]

Jewish giving in general has declined since the substantial sums raised after the 1973 Yom Kippur War, with more Jews entering salaried professions and fewer choosing to work as independent entrepreneurs. This means that the Jewish fund-raising apparatus in each community will have to reach out to women, especially salaried professional women, more than they have, looking to more people, who will give smaller gifts.[24] In an attempt to connect with these often unaffiliated Jewish women, Federations have been organizing groups for "Business and Professional Women" around such alluring topics as "Managing Your Investments—A Guide for Women" and "Money and the Working Woman's Attitude Toward It," in the hope of bringing professional women out of the woodwork and onto the rolls of donors.

Many women (and men) feel that Federations and the larger Jewish communal organizations aren't doing enough on women's issues either through programming or in their organizational structures. There are, then, two ways to put your "gift" to work to help make change. Either give to the traditional organizations and make clear your areas of interest, insisting that your money be earmarked as a vote for change, or give your money to (or through) alternative Jewish organizations.

Giving Through Traditional Channels—but with a Difference

If you decide to give to the traditional Jewish (and non-Jewish) causes, whether Federation, United Way, whatever, here are some important political considerations and guidelines:

• When making a "family" contribution, give one-half the amount in the name of the wife, one-half in the name of the husband. "This will make a big difference in the perception of women's roles," one woman asserts.

• If you can, try to earmark your gift so that it goes to a women's project, or a project with input from women as directors or trustees.

• Make sure you, as a woman, are visible in other ways too. If the money you are giving comes out of a family foundation or some kind of charitable trust, make sure that your name appears along with that of the foundation. Do not be an anonymous benefactor. Let the organization know who's responsible for the gift. This will give much more weight to any suggestions you might make. Granted, Maimonides puts anonymous giving on a higher rung than a gift from a known donor, but if *any* name is going to be attached to a gift you are responsible for giving, try to have it be *yours*.

• Make sure that if members of your family are making *tzedakah* contributions of a substantial part of the family income, and you assume that this takes care of your giving obligation too, you know what use the money will be put to. Remember that giving *tzedakah* is an obligation of every Jew. We may have differing attitudes toward God and organized religion, but those mitzvot that concern our relationship to other people are those with which we should have no theological difficulties.

Where to Give

In her article on Jewish women's organizations in *Lilith*'s premiere issue Doris Gold proposes a Jewish Women's Community Chest to support Jewish feminist projects. Until this becomes a reality, here are some places to put your *tzedakah* contribution so that it can support Jewish women's causes (all tax-deductible):

New Israel Fund
22 Miller Avenue
Mill Valley, CA 94941
(415) 383-4866

NIF supports social-change projects in Israel, and one of its five areas of commitment is women's rights in Israel.

U.S./Israel Women-to-Women
4 Sniffen Court
156 E. 36 Street
New York, NY 10016

This is a foundation started in the late seventies by "women of independent means" who wanted to channel some of their *tzedakah* to feminist projects in Israel. Anyone who gives $100 per year is a voting member. They have funded a film on the status of women in the Israeli army, a shelter for battered women, university-level women's studies programs, a book on abuses under Israel's divorce law (see p. 369), and other "controversial" women's projects that would certainly not have received funding from traditional American channels.

On the domestic scene there is:

Lilith Magazine
250 W. 57 Street
New York, NY 10019
(212) 757-0818

The nation's only independent Jewish women's magazine, which looks with a feminist eye at all aspects of Jewish life (religious, political, communal, personal), has been sustained since 1976 almost exclusively by the *tzedakah* of committed Jewish women (and men).

Women's Institute for Continuing Jewish Education
4079, 54 Street
San Diego, CA 92105
(619) 442-2666

This is an academy of sorts for Jewish women, offering everything from career counseling and rap groups to courses on Jewish women's history. It is an important resource and "place to connect with being Jewish" for women on the West Coast (see "Our Minds for Ourselves," p. 188).

For other women's projects worthy of and needing financial support, see the Networking Directory listings of shelters for battered women, rape crisis centers and hotlines, and educational institutions, among others.

A unique resource for women concerned about maximizing the impact of their philanthropy is an organization created by a woman who spent many years as a volunteer in Jewish and general community organizations:

Betty Lieberman
Philanthropic Focus, Inc.—Consultants in Charitable Giving
10701 W. North Avenue
Milwaukee, WI 53226
(414) 453-8282

Finally, we have a guide to the myriad worthy Israeli charities, listing everything from agencies that provide "religious help by telephone" to organizations for the handicapped. Several of the Israeli feminist organizations listed in the Networking Directory appear here, plus a useful section on how a potential donor can evaluate the organizations listed. The book is Eliezer B. Jaffe, *Giving Wisely: The Israel Guide to Non-Profit and Volunteer Social Services* (Jerusalem: Koren, 1983). In America it is available through the offices of the *Jerusalem Post*.

How to Give
In the 1950s Jewish women in some towns got together once a week to play cards, then turned the weekly winnings over to charity. Their children often had a hard time figuring this out, but there is some lesson to be distilled, perhaps based on the "wages of sin" theory. In any case, it's

possible for almost any social engagement that might involve money or gambling to be used to further a greater end. Perhaps in the breaks from the card games the women discussed which worthwhile women's projects should be supported with the kitty.

On the same theme, but a little more sophisticated, are the women who form investment clubs, pooling their funds, deciding how to invest them, and donating their profits to charity. The advantage of this method over the card playing is that the women involved gain the opportunity to inform themselves a little about financial realities in the Big World, which may even turn them into financial wizards, to the ultimate benefit of the projects they support.

Some women, rather than investing in North American companies, invested their money in Israeli firms, among them a publishing house run by women and devoted to publishing Hebrew translations of feminist books. (Such books are not widely accessible in the original to the large numbers of Israeli women who don't read English well.) The house has published *Against Our Will; Our Bodies, Ourselves;* and other books of crucial importance to women.

The Second Sex Publishing Company
55 Rechov Shenkin
Givatayim, Israel 53298

Tzedakah collectives have become increasingly popular over the past decade (see Sharon Strassfeld and Michael Strassfeld, *The Third Jewish Catalog*). Their big advantage is that they provide a forum in which to discuss one's giving priorities, and because of the number of members, individual worthy projects can be investigated more thoroughly than would be possible by an individual donor. *Tzedakah* collectives usually work on the principle that members will contribute a percentage of their gross income to the pool. Decisions on what to fund are made by the group as a whole. Consider starting a Jewish women's *tzedakah* collective in your community, one that, like Women-to-Women, would have as its goals the funding of women's projects, either here or in Israel. Of course, standard allocation of 3 percent of one's income to the collective still leaves some money to each woman for giving to other worthy projects. The collective provides a context for discussion and a resource for finding out what projects are around—both to use and to support. Some women report that when they sit down to pay their monthly bills they make it a point to write out at least one *tzedakah* check at the same time. If you have children who receive a regular allowance, encourage them to put money into a *tzedakah* box when they get their funds. And tell your daughters and sons what you support with your *tzedakah* and why.

Other women say that in honor of any special occasion involving a female relative—birthday of a mother or an aunt, Bat Mitzvah of a daughter—they make a *tzedakah* contribution in her honor to a women's charity. "I like to mark special events this way, and my mother likes to get a card telling her that a gift has been made in her honor, and she likes to feel she's in touch with new projects, and then the organization has someone else who knows about them, and they can send her mailings and ask her for funds directly when they do a fund-raising drive, so I figure this gift does a lot of different kinds of good." (One member of a Jewish audience was so impressed with hearing a lecture by Blu Greenberg, Orthodox feminist author and educator, that she sent a check to *Lilith* magazine "as *tzedakah* in honor of Blu Greenberg.")

Remember also that anyone traveling is supposed to travel under special protection when she is doing a mitzvah. So give a friend a contribution to be made to a Jewish women's project at her destination, and she becomes a *shlichat mitzvah*, one who is the messenger of a mitzvah—in this case, the mitzvah of *tzedakah*. This is especially nice to do when someone is traveling to Israel, but the mitzvah credit is also valid for domestic travel.

Traditional "women's" holidays are good times to give to Jewish women's projects, such as Purim, which celebrates the story of Queen Esther, Rosh Chodesh, the new-moon celebration (see religion, p. 95), or any other holiday when *tzedakah* is traditionally given. Try to remember on Purim, for example, that it is especially fitting to take *shalach manot* (Purim delicacies or snacks) to women in Jewish homes for the aged (to the men, too, of course, but the majority of Jewish elderly are women; see p. 414). Remember on these women's holidays to give to projects that support the needs of all women—shelters for homeless or battered women, political-action groups that support the civil and constitutional rights of women. We need to remember, even while we stress the *Jewish* women's projects in need of support, that there are plenty of worthwhile general women's endeavors that benefit us all.

If you are giving your money to women's causes, try to give to those organizations or agencies that are most likely to put your dollars to use to create change. An organization already on its way may need your funds also, but try to strike a balance in your giving so that you can support both more established women's projects and also those high-risk ventures that would not survive without the support of women.

13

◆

JEWISH WOMEN
AND THE WORLD
OF WORK

◆

CHANGING JEWISH ATTITUDES
ON WOMEN AND WORK

Ann G. Wolfe remembers being asked by her mother, when she was five or six, what she wanted to be when she was grown up. "I answered what most little girls would have then—a nurse or a teacher. My mother said, 'I hope you'll also choose to be a mother. But one thing you must never forget: a woman has to be able to take care of herself.'" And Aviva Cantor quotes her own mother as saying, "Your education and your career are the dowry you bring to your marriage."

Echoing a combination of these sentiments are all the Jewish mothers who have told their daughters: "You should prepare yourself to work *in case you ever have to*." On the off chance that there might be times in your life when a man won't be supporting you (usually intended to mean "if, God forbid, you are left a penniless widow"), you should be prepared—as a teacher, nurse, social worker, bookkeeper. The numbers of Jewish women who find themselves in their middle years as unemployable, displaced homemakers (see "Jewish Women in Crisis," p. 407) lead one to believe that many Jewish women paid more attention to the promises of total support from their husbands than to the veiled warnings of their mothers.

While the Talmud stresses that a Jewish father must teach his son a trade (and that not to do so is tantamount to teaching him to steal), daughters were to be not so much instructed as groomed for their fated occupation. "A father must provide for his daughter clothing and covering and must also give her a dowry so that people may want to woo her and to marry her," says the Talmud. Many communities even today have special funds to provide dowries and weddings for poor or orphaned young women—though not to educate them or teach them a trade (see "Our Minds for Ourselves," p. 149).

Yet work was once considered something that everyone did for mere survival. It wasn't something one planned for, necessarily; it was simply part of daily life, as it is rapidly becoming again for American Jewish women. Hear what is said about the legendary Eyshet Chayil—the woman of valor—whose description in Proverbs every religious Jewish man is supposed to quote to his wife on Sabbath eve: The lines include these: "She considers a field, and buys it." "She perceives that her merchandise is good." "She makes linen garments and sells them; And delivers linen girdles to the merchant." Nothing is said about raising the children, doing the laundry, or participating in any volunteer organizations, except that "She stretcheth out her hand to the poor."

According to Emily Taitz and Sondra Henry in *Written Out of History*, Jewish women have been warriors, scholars, entrepreneurs, printers, and politicians—to say nothing of labor organizers and philosophers.[1] The path of the Jewish businesswoman in America is an especially interesting one to follow, because she sounds a lot like the typical Eyshet Chayil. By 1840 in America, with relative prosperity, women of every ethnic group stayed at home and out of the workplace if they could afford it. This was certainly true among Sephardim, who made up the majority of Jews in America then. But with the influx of German Jews in the middle of the nineteenth century, the picture changed. Out of necessity, these Jewish women became peddlers, merchants, and artisans. They worked until their husbands could afford to become more settled—as shopkeepers, say—and then these German Jewish women, like their Sephardic sisters before them, stayed at home too, eager to comply with the "American" concept of woman's role.

Following the large-scale migrations to America of Eastern European Jews (1881–1924), the pattern repeated itself, with women working now in factories or sweatshops. A difference here is that many Jewish women, especially those from socially conscious backgrounds in Russia, saw their work not only as a way to earn a living but also as a way of bringing about changes in society.[2]

Jewish women were active in the early days of the labor movement in the United States, and the changes in working conditions in the wake of the tragic 1911 Triangle Shirtwaist Fire, for example, were brought about

A Jewish family working as garment makers, photographed by Lewis Hine, 1910.
(Library of Congress)

primarily by Jewish women such as Rose Schneiderman (1882–1972), a longtime organizer for the International Ladies Garment Workers Union and president of the Women's Trade Union League. Women of this caliber—activists, workers, revolutionaries—have provided more vivid models for many American Jewish women of the sixties through the eighties than some of our own mothers. The work lives of these women present a strong counterweight to the more passive stay-at-home women of the intervening generations. As one Jewish woman, a faculty member at Vassar College, put it, "Jewish women like me don't model ourselves after the Jewish mother but after [nineteenth-century suffragist] Ernestine Rose." Diane Balser of Boston says, "The whole thrust of the twentieth-century working women's movement was Jewish," and that at a recent convention of the Coalition of Labor Union Women, "it was really interesting to see women who were much less abashed about being powerful Jewish women. I can't explain it, but there's a power to them that you just don't see in our generation."[3]

Aside from their greater social consciousness, Jewish women of earlier generations believed their work had different meaning for their personal lives than did Italian immigrant women, for instance. Jewish working women saw work as a route to independence within their families. As "autonomous adults," they would often keep portions of their wages—however small—for their own use, and they themselves often determined how much of the money they earned should be given to their families. In contrast to young Italian women of the same generation, who may have identified more with their parents and who turned over their entire salaries to them, young Jewish working women, although they too lived at home, "saw themselves as active agents with control over their own lives." Paid work had given them their sense of autonomy and self-worth.[4]

This generation of Jewish working women worked to provide for their families. The satisfaction of being able to contribute to the support of the families was what gave the work value—it wasn't necessarily inherently interesting work in itself. It was often backbreaking, exhausting, unsafe, dirty, and boring, whether it took place in factories (where there

Archival footage from the documentary film Free Voice of Labor: The Jewish Anarchists, *which documents Jewish women's contributions to the fledgling labor movement in the United States. (*Free Voice of Labor: The Jewish Anarchists, *directed by Steve Fischler and Joel Sucher)*

was the added hazard of sexual harassment) or at home (where even children were pressed into service and privacy was eliminated entirely when women took in boarders for the extra income).[5]

Present-day stereotypes to the contrary notwithstanding, not all Jewish women in America were part of the bourgeoisie. They were, and considered themselves, "workers." The daughters of these women, the second generation in America, often didn't work at all and thus had to find satisfaction in other ways—from the successes of husband and children and from a sense of being needed for useful volunteer work in the community. New York writer Elenore Lester remembers that her grandmother "was passionately Orthodox, raised five children, ran a grocery store, and bought up local real estate. My mother, a nonreligious woman, chose to give up a career as a buyer in the garment industry in order to devote herself to home and family. To her it was a luxury to stay home."

For third-generation Jewish women the work motives are considerably more complex. It's clear that financial necessity is still a big factor. But so is the desire for self-actualization and accomplishment through the nature of the work task itself. (This is, of course, true for third-generation Jewish men too; the sons of entrepreneurs go into the salaried professions. The income goes down but the status goes up. Downward earning capacity is not as threatening to them as it would be if their work in itself didn't promise satisfaction and power.)

Working-class Jewish men in America in the forties and fifties, dependent (as most of us are in the eighties) on two incomes to support their families, often felt as if this made them failures.[6] And we have no evidence about the extent to which such an attitude follows younger Jewish men into their family lives today, nor do we know how many of them measure their own success or failure by the degree to which their wives' salaries are viewed as "pin money" or how many wish that they could support their wives in the way their fathers supported their mothers. The amount of distress for Jewish women (and sense of failure for Jewish men) associated with women's working is as yet unanalyzed. But it would not be surprising if at least some of them identified with Marie Jastrow, reminiscing about her childhood in America fifty years ago. Her mother went to work and her father said, "Do as you wish, but understand that when you hire out, I am shamed," so she quit the job she desperately needed.[7]

Ethnologist Corinne Azen Krause speaks of her own previous nonworking status and that of other women: "Our presence at home and in charitable activities announced to the Jewish community that our husbands had made good."

Just as Krause's generation had to make a big leap from the work ethic of their mothers to the enforced leisure of their own lives, so the "daughters" generation now has to overcome a lot of built-in ambivalence toward work. One woman, now in her thirties, working full time and with two young children, described to her women's consciousness-raising group how her life differs from her mother's:

> When I was growing up, my mother and all the women around her didn't work for pay. One day my mother came home and announced that she'd been offered a job acting in a television commercial. (She'd always done amateur theatricals.) I was really upset at the embarrassment of having a mother who would be in a paying job, and one that was so visible! And when my girlfriends and I decided that it might be fun to apply for work at the local drug store, we also decided that it just wouldn't look right if we took the jobs. We had such *ladylike* views of what women should be doing! And now all of us are killing ourselves working hard at our jobs, plus raising our families, with less money, relatively, than our parents had, and certainly with less help. How did we change?

Part of the change came when the new generation of working women, influenced by the feminist movement, began looking to women other than their own mothers as role models. A woman in Washington, D.C., says that when she led discussion groups of older Jewish women, she learned from them: "They were old Labor Zionist women; they had all worked when their children were little."[8]

Even this older generation wasn't free from some conflicts over working when there were children at home. In the film *Joyce at 34*, the mother of filmmaker Joyce Chopra and a group of her friends, all retired, confess to having felt very guilty all the years they worked; one reports her daughter saying, "Mama, I'm sorry you're sick today, but I'm glad that you'll be here when I come home from school."

Many women report changes in the dynamics of their families when they begin to work after having been at home for some years.

"If you're contributing to the family's economy, that shifts the balance of power," notes clinical social worker Sarah Silver Bunim. Bunim predicts that the fact that more and more women, even those with young children, will have to enter the paid labor force will make a difference in women's status within the family. In fact, she sees that this shift is already happening, even among the Orthodox families who are her clients. Sociologist Rela Geffen Monson, commenting on the estimate that nearly two-thirds of Jewish women with elementary-school-aged children are employed outside the home, notes that "The most significant changes in the Jewish family may not be those of structure visible to the outside observer—changes such as those resulting from widowhood or the rising divorce rate. Rather, in all probability, it is the changing roles and relationships between husbands and wives *in intact families* which constitute the most radical shifts in Jewish family life."[9]

What makes things hard for Jewish women (especially those with children at home) is the emphasis on the primacy of women's role in the home and the recent public emphasis on the "necessity" for Jewish women to have more children (see "Responding to the Childbearing Imperative," p. 371).

Obviously Jewish women aren't alone in feeling the conflicts. A 1981 Yankelovich study of attitudes about women and work reports that the public believes "Freedom to work outside the home extracts a heavy price from women in the form of strains on family life, stress from carrying a double load and difficulties in redefining relationships with men."

Two women sitting side by side in a meeting of an Orthodox women's group in Long Island exemplify this stress. One got up to speak, beginning with a caveat: "I want you to know first of all that my children—I have three—are very well taken care of. I am trained as an art teacher, and I've gone back to work in the local Hebrew day school three mornings a week. But I feel *very* guilty to be leaving my three young children those mornings." The woman next to her rose. "I can't believe what I'm hearing. We went to school together, I also have three small kids, and I am writhing with guilt *staying at home!* I keep feeling that I should be out there using my education!" Both women obviously felt not only guilty about their choices—whichever path they chose—but also fearful about being judged by the rest of the group.

Another variation on this theme comes from a Jewish woman who is a physician and whose mother was also a doctor. She has two children, ages eight and five, and says that she and her husband *never* go out together in the evenings because she feels her children are deprived of parents all day long when they are at home with a housekeeper. So the husband and wife go to movies or meetings separately, with one parent always at home with the children after dinner. The woman feels too guilty over working to have any social life and too responsible to her medical education (and too drawn to her identity as a doctor) to give up her career and stay home with the kids full time.

Women aren't inventing the conflicts, of course. Individual men and institutions are feeding right into them. One example speaks for many: a recent issue of the National Jewish Family Center Newsletter, discussing how women with large families balance career, family, and personal needs, is titled "Careers and Motherhood: Can Women Have Both?" The Technical Advisory Committee to the Center, set up in part to help plan for the needs of working Jewish mothers, consists of four women and thirteen men!

In some ways the Jewish woman's official role as commander of the home has made working women believe that we have diversified our investments, as it were. If we have families, we do have the opportunity to obtain satisfactions—ego gratification—from a source other than the workplace. What that means is that if you've had an awful day at work, you needn't be totally devastated—there's still the home front, still a place where you may be useful and valued. The Jewish home functions in this way as an ego salve for women much more so than for men, because women are more instrumental in the home (still) and less the passive recipients of its balm, as men often are.[10] In an ideal future men also, by way of their shared involvement and competence in all aspects of domestic life, could have an alternative arena in which to function and in which to see themselves as worthy human beings, instead of having their egos totally bound up in their work lives alone. Paid work—and having a work role—keeps a woman mentally healthy (even if anxious), according to recent reports on feminism and mental health.[11] One woman says: "I *like* being more than one person, having more than one major source of my identity." This pleasure is the positive side of the anxieties created by having to keep all the oranges in the air at once.

ENTERING OR REENTERING THE JOB MARKET

One form of Jewish machismo in America has been Man as Provider (or Husband as Sugar Daddy). Even in times when Jewish husbands frequently deserted their wives, such as in the early years of the immigration to America when there was even a Desertion Bureau to track them down, the macho myth persisted: the Jewish husband supports the family. Women, especially over fifty, often report that their husbands were not supportive either of their working early in the marriage or of their reentering the work force when the children were grown. Some women have gone out to work anyway; others—so-called "women in transition"— are trying to ease their way out of the house and into the workplace by degrees.

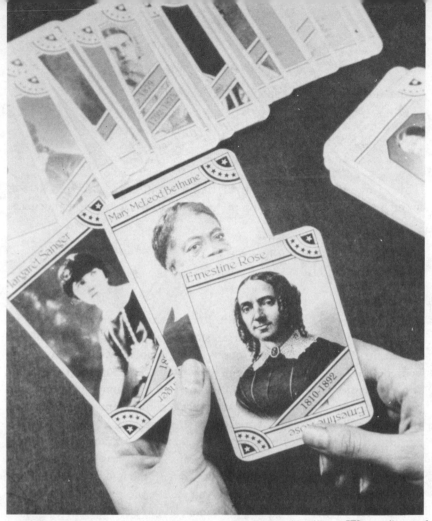

Jewish women are among the movers and shakers featured in "Great Women," a card game developed by Miriam Hipsch to celebrate the lives and achievements of American women who have made history. (courtesy Great Women Card Company, New York)

Addressing the needs of these women are short-term career guidance and training centers that have been set up in local Jewish communities—for example:

Women's Institute for Self-Enrichment (WISE)
Community Center of Southern New Jersey
2393 W. Malton Pike
Cherry Hill, NJ 08002
(609) 662-8800

Here women can get career counseling, learn to set priorities, and receive the support necessary to make the leap out of their homes and into the workplace.

Federation Employment and Guidance Service
  (FEGS)
114 Fifth Avenue
New York, NY 10011
(212) 741-7110

This agency provides employment training and counseling and acts as
an employment agency, placing its trainees in Jewish and other agencies.

The Women's Career Center
Bramson ORT Technical Institute
New York, NY 10010
(212) 677-7420

The center was designed especially for women who are considering returning to the work force after a substantial absence or want to enter it
for the first time. Conceived as "a service for women seeking careers," the
center offers "individual and group counseling, workshops, and a resource
service of information and referrals. Since ORT around the world specializes in vocational training programs, technical and otherwise, you
might consult your local chapter or the national office to see what new
facilities there might be for reentry women in your community.

One of the most useful aspects of counseling for a woman reentering
the workplace, especially if there is no clear-cut financial need, is helping
her combat what might be great resistance on the part of her husband
and children. As if her own ambivalence weren't enough, there will be
plenty of people coming out of the woodwork (all of them employed
males) to ask, "Tell me, is it really so much more satisfying to be selling
stockings [real estate, handicrafts] than to be staying home, where your
time is your own?" Counseling or a work support group can give you am-
munition to fight against these entrenched attitudes.

Displaced Homemakers

Displaced homemakers are women who have been catapulted into the
work world by some cataclysmic event. These are women who, through
separation, desertion, divorce, or widowhood have lost their sole means
of support—their men. Because the pattern for two generations in North
America has been that Jewish women were at least partially (and usually
wholly) financially dependent on their husbands, women suddenly without husbands providing this support become overnight the new poor in
the Jewish community.

This isn't even comparable to the situation of a man who finds himself suddenly fired from a job; he at least may qualify for unemployment compensation, Social Security, union benefits, severance pay, and the like. For the growing numbers of women who've lost their jobs as "homemakers" and are left without support (usually through divorce), there are no such social/financial safety nets, since their work in the house has been unpaid. Especially if there are dependents now depending on her, the plight of the displaced homemaker is exactly that described by a middle-class woman in the Midwest, solely responsible for the care of her five children: "Every woman with a child is only one man away from Welfare."[12]

The typical homemaker thus "displaced" is a woman without readily marketable skills (or who thinks she has none), who hasn't been in the paid labor force for two years or more (in many cases, much longer). Every kind of service is needed for these women—from support groups and personal counseling through assertiveness training, job-training programs, and help with résumé writing or coaching for the interview process.

One program, started in 1980 by an Orthodox organization but serving all Jewish women who need its services, defines its goals thus: "The situation of a displaced homemaker is that she is faced with a financial crisis precisely at the time she is most vulnerable, having just gone through a major life crisis. Before a homemaker can be successfully placed in a job, there is a need for a transition period when she can receive an introduction to the world of work, an orientation to the present employment market, evaluation of her own skills and aptitudes, and financial and legal advice."

Most of the job training is in clerical work, because "that's where the jobs are," says director Risa Schmookler. But the program is highly individualized. "If a woman wants to be a carpenter, we can train her for that too." About 80 percent of the women served are Jewish, and the main outreach is to Orthodox women. For further information about services provided:

Fresh Start Training Program
Project COPE
A Division of Agudath Israel of America
813 Avenue H
Brooklyn, NY 11230
(718) 434-8098

Since many of the problems displaced homemakers face have to do with legislation—such as the fact that there is no Social Security for housework and no real means of enforcing child-support or alimony payments, influencing government officials is an effective way of improving the situation at the macro level. To stay abreast of how legislation is proceeding, contact:

Displaced Homemakers Network
755, 8 Street, N.W.
Washington, DC 20001
(202) 347-0522

It is particularly important for a Jewish women's organization to be visible on such an important women's issue, both because many Jewish women are affected and because women's issues provide an area for coalition building between Jews and non-Jews.

An example of how the women of the organized Jewish community have addressed the issue—taking themselves to Washington and presenting the problem before legislators, volunteers, and other interested parties—is the Conference on the Displaced Homemaker held in Washington in 1979 under the sponsorship of the American Jewish Congress Women's Division (now phased out). The topics examined obviously are not relevant only to Jewish women but affect the status of all women in American society. For a copy of the report that came out of the conference, write:

American Jewish Congress
15 E. 84 Street
New York, NY 10028

Another path for community involvement in solving the problems of displaced homemakers has been put forth by Brenda Shapiro of Miami. Shapiro has proposed that Federations give scholarships or stipends to such women to enable them to learn a trade to support themselves.[13] This would be more efficient than providing the vocational supports themselves.

Abigail S. Moore is working on a dissertation (Department of History, Rutgers University) dealing with some historical background of the current "displaced homemaker" issue, focusing on marital desertion.

An excellent film on the economic and emotional devastation middle-aged women feel when they lose their roles as homemakers through divorce:

Who Remembers Mama?
Produced by Cynthia Salzman Mondell and Allen Mondell
Jewish Media Service
Jewish Welfare Board
15 E. 26 Street
New York, NY 10010

National Council of Jewish Women has a pamphlet on assistance programs for women facing these displacements:

ESHA (Each Sister Helps Another): Women in Transition
National Council of Jewish Women
15 E. 26 Street
New York, NY 10010

For further resources, including listings of centers, programs, and projects providing services to displaced homemakers, consult Laurie Shields, *Displaced Homemakers: Organizing for a New Life* (McGraw-Hill, 1980).

Recycling Volunteer Experience
One of the arguments put forth in favor of women's volunteer work is that volunteers are gathering basic skills and experience that will give them greater marketability if they decide to reenter the paid labor force "once the children are a little older." To some extent this argument is valid. Women do acquire experience in volunteer work that they might not get if they were "merely" at home managing their families. But can women transfer these skills into the marketplace, especially when so much of "women's work" is devalued to begin with, and especially in a time when jobs are scarce? Amy Swerdlow replies: "Just as the Emperor had no clothes, the housewife/mother has no worth. Her résumé listing decades of budgeting, mediating, managing, creating, decision making, nurturing, and physical and mental exertion in the home, school and community elicits from the job interviewer a sentence that chills the soul 'Aha, I see you haven't worked in twenty years.' "[14]

To bolster their volunteers' sense of the worth of their experience, National Council of Jewish Women has developed a kit that will help women keep track of and evaluate their volunteer experience, with an eye to packaging it in some form that might make them attractive to an employer in the future. Other groups offer such lectures as "Using Volunteer Skills as a Preparation for a Career."

It might work. But many women are skeptical. One, who tried to make the transition into a paying job within the organization for which she had been a respected volunteer (or so she thought), recounts her experience and comments, "All of a sudden, when I wanted to get paid for the work, I wasn't Mrs. Wonderful anymore."[15] And Elie Faust-Lévy, editor of the Women's American ORT *Reporter* says: "Women who have achieved leadership positions in these organizations can't then turn around and go to work in some low-status job. And the higher up the women go as volunteers, the harder it is to make the transition into the labor force. What about those women who get to the top in a volunteer post, travel around the country and to Israel, and have sat at head tables with Golda Meir? How do they make the change to being somebody's paid secretary?" One might call these women displaced Presidents.

In contrast, another woman professional working in a Jewish organization insists that an incentive for many Jewish women to enter the workplace is their failure to ascend to positions of power and status in volunteer life.

Lots of "reentry" women who have had volunteer experience in the Jewish community decide to get academic training to do some of the same kinds of work for money that they've been doing without payment—organizing, programming, direct service volunteering. Many are going back to get social-work degrees or degrees in Jewish communal service in the attempt to "professionalize" their skills. (Some institutions—New York's Fordham University is one—offer "Life Experience Credit" for volunteer work.) Programs that offer such degrees in serving the Jewish community are the Wurzweiler School of Social Work at New York's Yeshiva University, the Hornstein Program at Brandeis University, and the School of Jewish Communal Service at the Hebrew Union College–Jewish Institute of Religion in Los Angeles.

CASUALTIES OF THE WORKPLACE: THE POOR AND THE HOMELESS

JEWISH WOMEN AND THE FEMINIZATION OF POVERTY

Jewish women struggling with poverty face the same appalling discrimination as all other women in America. The "gender gap" in wages means that women earn, on average, fifty-nine cents for every dollar men earn. In other words, women must work nine days to earn what men earn in five. (Here's another good reason for the Jewish community to support legislation ensuring equality under the law—including equality in the labor force—for women. See "Affirmative Action," p. 492.)

(Marilynne Herbert)

Since Ann G. Wolfe first wrote "The Invisible Jewish Poor" in 1971[16] and lectured on the subject—casting light on the lives of people most middle-class American Jews had believed didn't exist—Jewish organizations have had to deal with the facts and to recognize that most of the Jewish poor are women. These women are both the solitary elderly and the young-to-middle-aged who are the sole support of dependent children. Single-parent families, almost all headed by women, make up half the total of Jews living in poverty.

Both these groups of women can't afford life in the affluent suburbs, to which many American Jews moved after the Second World War, where they built the Jewish community centers and other facilities that their comfortable incomes allow them to support. The elderly poor, especially, tend to live in pockets of abandonment in older parts of large cities such as Miami's South Beach and New York's South Bronx and Lower East Side (see "Elderly Jewish Women," p. 414), a geographic segregation which causes a degree of blindness in some who work in more affluent parts of the Jewish community.

For single women raising children, the status shock of divorce may include a forced relocation because of straitened circumstances. Several grandparents have reported postponing the sale of a home when grandchildren and a divorced daughter needed a place to live; the newly poor daughter and her family thus obviously have an impact on the financial status (and often the retirement plans) of the older generation. Studies of divorce and the "new" poverty of its surviving women and children have not yet taken into account the financial consequences for grandparents as well.

In the wake of Ann Wolfe's writings, there is now at least one large-city agency focusing on the needs of the Jewish poor:

Metropolitan New York Coordinating Council on Jewish Poverty
15 Park Row, Room 2425
New York, NY 10038

For women with short-term financial needs the local Hebrew Free Loan Society, which exists in almost every city with a sizable Jewish population, is a good place to turn to. Many offer, as the name implies, interest-free loans. The local Jewish Federation should be able to refer you. (See Networking Directory: Financial Aid.)

Much of the material in this book which deals with the elderly, displaced homemakers, single parents and other human conditions also touches on the issue of Jewish women in poverty. In addition, see some of the biographical accounts (though most are about men) in Thomas Cottle, *The Hidden Survivors: Poor Jews in America* (Prentice-Hall, 1980), and Loretta Schwartz-Nobel, *Starving in the Shadow of Plenty* (Putnam, 1981).

HOMELESS JEWISH WOMEN

Some Jewish women are not precisely displaced homemakers. They are in fact without any home to make. These are "shopping-bag ladies," women who for a number of reasons—poverty, emotional instability, trauma, uncertainty—are wandering the streets—sometimes sleeping on them, sometimes camping out in all-night bus and train stations or other "public" facilities, sometimes staying for a short time at one of the very few shelters for homeless women that exist in various cities. They are rarely captured in the net of Jewish and other organizations that could serve them, although outreach workers from a church group are reported to have held a Passover seder for some of these women in the women's washroom of Manhattan's Pennsylvania Station, where many seek shelter.

There is no count of how many homeless women wandering the streets of North America are Jewish, but some are, we know from reports of volunteers at various shelters and from street encounters. And the problem is likely to worsen as redevelopment and gentrification of the city neighborhoods force older, poorer people (mostly women) out of their homes and apartments and into a housing market where they have no hope of surviving. This is becoming the case on New York's Upper West Side as many single-room-occupancy hotels—as they are called—are being demolished, "dumping" their residents, many of whom are older Jewish women, into the streets.

One male Federation executive stated that he was sure there were no Jewish homeless women ("shopping-bag ladies"), because none had ever come to the doorstep of "his" community centers looking for shelter. It hadn't even occurred to him that these homeless women might be wandering the streets of the inner city, far from well-equipped suburban Jewish centers, or that they might not even know of the existence of such centers.

Rabbis and workers in urban synagogues and other facilities have begun to provide shelter for some of these women in unutilized space. Why can't a mitzvah corps be organized? Like the Lubavitch mitzvah mobiles telling Jews about candlelighting and daily prayers, this one could go out into the streets of older neighborhoods to try to identify these homeless women (for whom there are only one tenth as many shelter beds as for men) and help them to get in touch with agencies that might be able to help, such as local health and welfare organizations, the Jewish Board of Family and Children's Services, or some similar social-service agency (see listings in Networking Directory).

New York editor Esther Cohen has written that "Somehow a woman on the street is more shocking. Because she is female, we all feel that she should be taking care of someone else, or at the very least be taking care of herself."[17]

A New York City–based group that has encouraged synagogues and churches to house the homeless while at the same time lobbying for increased government support for shelters is:

Partnership for the Homeless
208 W. 13 Street
New York, NY 10014
(212) 807-6653

THE QUALITY OF THE WORKPLACE:
AFFIRMATIVE ACTION AND JEWISH WOMEN

For Jewish women who have access to education, training, or jobs, the battle for equality has just begun. Often, women's professional advancement, or the struggle for equal opportunity to compete for advancement, has met with resistance from Jewish men. Even in the face of government intervention to combat past discrimination—in the form of equal-opportunity legislation and affirmative-action programs—many men have claimed that women need no mechanism under the law to ensure that they won't be discriminated against in the workplace.

Evan Bayer, a Director of Field Services with the American Jewish Congress in New York, has analyzed the Jewish community's responses to these attempts at legislating equality in the workplace and in educational institutions:

"Affirmative action" refers to special efforts, above and beyond "standard operating procedure," that can be initiated in order to remedy the effects of past discrimination because of sex, color, religion, or national origin.

Jewish men often claim that all that affirmative action has meant is the lowering of standards, and reverse discrimination against white males. Some minorities which have traditionally been discriminated against in this country, such as Jews and Italians, aren't included as "suspect categories," so Jewish men think that all Jews are hurt by affirmative action. *What about Jewish women?* Affirmative action has opened the doors of law schools and medical schools of the United States to Jewish women, providing all kinds of opportunities that were previously unavailable.

Most people know of affirmative action because of the U.S. Supreme Court cases that have received wide public attention. *De Funis* v. *The University of Washington* and *Regents of the University of California* v. *Bakke* dealt with the issue of quotas in academic admission. In the *De Funis* case (1974)[18] Jewish organizations split their support for and against the voluntary use of quotas to ensure racial and ethnic diversity. (There is disagreement among Jewish organizations as to whether the University of Washington actually used a *quota* or *goals and timetables*.) The National Council of Jewish Women (NCJW) and the Union of American Hebrew Congregations (UAHC) supported the University's right to give special preference to certain minority groups (black, Chicano, American Indian, Philippine American) in order to increase their numbers admitted to the law school. The American Jewish Committee, American Jewish Congress, Anti-Defamation League

(ADL), and Jewish Labor Committee filed *amicus* briefs supporting De Funis' claim of reverse discrimination. The U.S. Supreme Court, however, in finding the case moot, avoided resolving this controversial issue.

The 1978 decision in the *Bakke* case was, therefore, the first U.S. Supreme Court case to cast light on the question of voluntary quotas in academic admissions. No Jewish organization supported the University of California's quota system. However, several Jewish organizations joined in two separate *amicus* briefs in support of Bakke's claim of reverse discrimination. Neither the UAHC or NCJW entered briefs in this case. The complex decision outlawed fixed racial quotas in college and university admissions, but left the way open for other, less rigid affirmative action programs to promote the admission of racial and ethnic minorities and women.

Although these cases did not specifically involve women, the effect of the decisions and the general acceptance of the need for affirmative action programs to insure equal opportunity opened previously restricted avenues to women as well. The numbers of women accepted to medical and law schools increased dramatically, as did opportunities for promotion in business and educational institutions.

Some of the national Jewish organizations that had been active in the civil rights struggles of the 1950's and 1960's supported affirmative action. But, as realistic implementation of the concept developed, differences in philosophy among Jewish groups as well as between Jewish and Black organizations began to emerge. These differences are reflected in their position statements.

ADL opposes "quotas, preferential treatment, proportional representation, and the use of race as an absolute qualification for any post, as inconsistent with the principle of equality of opportunity." American Jewish Committee, on the other hand, calls for "the granting of special consideration to those applicants from among those discriminated against or disadvantaged who are substantially equal in qualifications to others being considered" and "carefully and sensitively developed goals and timetables" as a means of monitoring the effectiveness of an affirmative action program. American Jewish Committee, however, still completely rejects the concept of quotas as undermining "the concept of individual merit and the principle of equal opportunity." Women's American ORT advocates the "full measure of support for affirmative action in practice including the employment of quotas in cases where evasion or defiance of the laws against discrimination are established."

Until recently there seems to have been little recognition that affirmative action, and even quotas where deemed necessary, could have a positive effect on the ability of Jewish women to overcome past discrimination. The expressed concern over the quota concept was always how it would affect Jewish men. Jewish women were ignored. Even in the strong Women's American ORT statement supporting "Affirmative Action as a vehicle for combatting discrimination against minorities," women are not specifically mentioned.[19]

Ironically, Jewish women have been in a unique position to benefit from affirmative action programs, being relatively well educated. The argument cannot be made legitimately that they are ill prepared for graduate school admissions or hiring or promotion, as is sometimes the case with minority-group men.

Job Discrimination Against Women— How Does the Jewish Community Respond?

Many Jewish organizations, even those that have been in the forefront of the civil rights movements and other struggles for greater equality for all peoples, fail to make sufficient efforts to recognize inequality under their own roofs. As the title of an article by Amy Stone puts it, "The Jewish Establishment is NOT an Equal Opportunity Employer."[20]

Women's caucuses and task forces within various Jewish organizations have conducted surveys of women's positions on the "job ladder" (as well as looking at what their status is on the volunteer side of the office), and the results are scandalous. One survey, conducted by Ellen Friedland-Moulton in 1981 for the New York Federation's Task Force on the Role of the Jewish Woman in a Changing Society, demonstrated dramatically that women are primarily "line workers" in Jewish Federations across the country, while men are the bosses. Even in such a "women's" area as services to families and children, where the ratio of women employees to men is more than two to one, there are no women executive directors, and 60 percent of assistant directors around the country are men. In the fund-raising field, where a great deal of the community's power resides, there are, as one would suspect, fewer women than men employed, and no women executive directors, no women assistant directors; 60 percent of the supervisors and department heads are men.

One male executive optimistically predicts that this situation will change in the next few years, since "So many men are turned away from Jewish communal service, because the pay scale is generally so low, that women are going to have to move into executive positions—there just won't be any men left to fill them."

Even considering the relatively low scale paid all workers in Jewish agencies, there is a marked difference in salaries paid to men and women. As of June 1980, despite the fact that women have usually been employed for longer than their male counterparts, they were paid less at the same positions. Nearly 9 percent of male employees across the country made over $40,000. Only *half of 1 percent* of women made this amount. Another survey, conducted at the same time by the Committee on Opportunities for Women of the National Conference of Jewish Communal Service, shows that at every salary level from $25,000 a year up, only a tiny fraction—less than 5 percent—of women are earning in the same range as men. In the moderate salary range ($20,000–$25,000) even in a field where there are twice as many women as men employed, less than 18 percent of the female employees make as much as this. Remember—nationwide, women earn only fifty-nine cents for every dollar men earn. And in the Jewish community it's no better, and may be worse.

There is high irony in the fact that the national office of the American Jewish Committee sponsored a conference on "pay equity" to address the fact that women's work has always been undervalued, and to publicize the "59¢ wage gap." In fact, women employees of this same organization have complained privately for years that they were passed by as less able men were promoted, and that in pension, general benefits, and salary itself they had been discriminated against. But the organization looked good as it "addressed" the issues before the public at a well-attended conference.

The situation for women employed in the Jewish community is so bad that with each survey documenting what women already know, there's uneasiness about whether or not to make the results known. One cautious professional woman asked, "Do you think we are going to do our cause more harm than good if we go public with these numbers? I think we have to find some *positive* way to present the data to the executive directors, so this thing won't backfire." A less timid approach was advocated by Naomi Levine, former executive director of American Jewish Congress, now a vice-president of New York University. The only woman ever to direct a major national co-ed American Jewish organization, Levine, a lawyer, suggests: "Maybe women should consider taking the Jewish organizations to court. Their employment practices seem to be in direct violation of the Equal Employment Opportunity laws."

Individual women have discussed using the law to advance women's rights, but never on a large scale. Evan Bayer comments on the discrimination against women within the Jewish community:

"Your shekel is worth less. Are you worth less?" To highlight discrimination in salaries of working women, Pioneer Women/Na'amat distributed this advertisement throughout Israel. From the evidence women have uncovered in the United States, many Jewish organizations are contributing to the "gender gap" in salaries. (courtesy Pioneer Women/Na'amat)

For the women who are paid inequitably and who are restricted in their career movement, the answer may have to be to resort to the American legal system through a discrimination suit. Several legal actions have already been initiated and more will probably be forthcoming. On the other hand, Jewish communal employers claim that there is a dearth of women at the appropriate levels for promotion to executive positions. Time (and a special effort) is needed to identify, train and promote women to the job levels from which executives are selected. As more women move into mainstream careers in Jewish communal service, however, this argument is becoming less credible.

Sometimes women themselves contribute to continued inequality in the Jewish community. We bring the values and traditions of patriarchy, which stress the role of "helper" for women rather than "leader" and "initiator." These sometimes contradictory roles work to hinder Jewish women's movement toward equality.

Jewish communal workers, men and women alike, are acting in a traditional woman's role when they "serve" the Jewish community. The functions now carried out by professionals were once carried out exclusively by women volunteers. Those who choose to work for the Jewish community are doing so at least partly out of commitment and other intrinsic rewards, since the organizations' non-profit status precludes the high financial rewards of the profit-making sector. It is, therefore, very difficult for women, who have been socialized to that "giving" role, to demand high salaries or bring suit against a Jewish institution. Jewish men, on the other hand, are better socialized to fight for what they deserve, thus exacerbating the salary disparities that already exist. Many of the young, competent, career-oriented women coming into Jewish communal service become frustrated by the inequities in salary and status and leave for the private sector, where the opportunities that have been opened up by affirmative action are greater.

A related phenomenon beginning to occur is "devaluation" of the field as increasing numbers of women come into Jewish communal service. This is not just a problem in the Jewish community, but has occurred in all areas of work since the Industrial Revolution. As women become the majority in any occupation, the salaries and status of that occupation are deflated. (This was especially evident during World War II when salaries dropped as women took over jobs previously done by men. Those same salaries were raised when the men came home from war and returned to their jobs.)

Although women's traditional behavior patterns can be a barrier to their own equality in the Jewish community, systematic discrimination has long existed and continues to restrict equal opportunities for women in professional and lay leadership roles. Affirmative action programs could do much to improve the situation quickly, if they were undertaken seriously by Jewish organizations and institutions.

What has been happening, however, is that Jewish women are beginning to see equal-opportunity and affirmative-action legislation as issues that put them into direct conflict with many Jewish men (see "Jewish Women and Jewish Men," p. 286), since Jewish women stand to benefit (indeed, many have already benefited) under the programs set up to implement the legal guidelines.

The Volunteers and the "Professionals"

One factor that has impeded action on this front has been the sometimes unspoken conflict between volunteer women and the paid staff ("professionals," as they are termed in the Jewish community).

Granted, the two groups of women also have much in common—including a shared oppression by the male-dominated communal leadership structure. Volunteers and professional women suffer from being closed out of certain powerful "cabinets" and committees. But there are very real and painful (and often hidden) differences in class and status between the volunteers and the professionals. By definition the full-time volunteers are women who can afford not to work. They are either the wives or daughters (sometimes both) of wealthy men. They often travel in different circles (particularly in larger cities) from those of the women professionals. This creates an especially wide gulf among women, since male employees of Jewish agencies, if they are at the executive level, are often paid salaries that allow them to live very nearly as well as the wealthy men who work with them as volunteers. Nor do the men of both categories spend much time together; male volunteers have businesses to run and have secretaries who can do much of the communicating with the agency professionals. Recognizing this, a Ft. Wayne woman confessed that she had turned down a high leadership position as a volunteer—not because of any deep-rooted female "fear of success," but because "the men in the community have reached the level in their careers where they have staffs at work who can help them with their volunteer activities. I'm not at that point yet, professionally, and I was not about to do all that scut work myself!"

When a woman takes on a major volunteer (or "lay leadership") position, especially with a national Jewish organization but even with large organizations locally, everyone assumes that it will be a full-time volunteer position, sometimes necessitating moving to New York or another headquarters city, and almost invariably with her own office in headquarters. (This never happens with male volunteer leaders, since how could a man be expected to give up business or professional commitments for an eight-hour day in a voluntary position?) Because the lines are thus somewhat blurred between the female volunteer leader and the (sometimes female) paid professional staff of the organization, the situation is ripe for conflict unique to women's volunteer activity.

Who is pulling whose strings? The lay leader is in reality the employer of the professional; yet the professional knows more and may wield more day-to-day power as the tenured civil servant who outlasts many different rulers. Even for women volunteers who are not married into the ruling class it's not clear how volunteer and professional roles are distinct, since boards that are created for fund-raising purposes often try to give members the illusion that their presence is needed for decision-making also. "I was asked to serve on the Board of Jewish Education," says one New York woman, "and I really can't tell, after half a dozen meetings, what the volunteer leaders are expected to do. It seems to me that the real decisions must be made by the professionals, who have the day-to-day responsibility for the agency and really know what's going on."

In Los Angeles the National Council of Jewish women has commissioned a study to be done by the School of Jewish Communal Service at Hebrew Union College–Jewish Institute of Religion to examine and try to correct what one woman long active as a volunteer in that community calls "the deterioration" of relations between volunteers and professionals. An M.A. thesis by Fred Rothstein suggests a "positive and effective" partnership between these groups: "Professional and Volunteers: Partners in Helping," Hebrew Union College–Jewish Institute of Religion (Los Angeles), School of Communal Service (1980).

One longtime "career" volunteer calls on lay leaders to act as advocates for women professionals in Jewish organizations, ensuring salary equity, advancements, and an end to discrimination in hiring and placement. Peggy Tishman says: "I watched for years in a rather detached way what was happening to professional women in [UJA-Federation in New York], but somehow I needed to be galvanized into action. . . . This happened when I realized that three volunteer leaders headed the most important committees at Federation and yet not one professional woman was among the top executives. The president of Federation frequently boasted about his sex blindness, but I should have realized that only volunteers qualified for his type of myopia!"[21]

The relationship between volunteers and professional women working in the Jewish community has been affected by the community's positions on affirmative action in general. The fact that equal opportunity for women was an issue in the larger sphere set the scene for changes in women's status in the Jewish community as well. Evan Bayer notes this:

> At the same time that affirmative action positions were being developed by national Jewish organizations in the mid-1970's, women of the organized Jewish community began to question their relationship to the male-dominated power structure and the Jewish community's internal discrimination against women. The Women's Division of the Council of Jewish Federations (CJF), the national umbrella for Jewish community organizations, did a survey on the status of women among the lay leadership of the Federations around the country. They found that women were most heavily represented in the least powerful positions. The Committee on Opportunities for Women of the Conference of Jewish Communal Service (CJCS), a loose-knit group of professional associations for people who work in Jewish communal agencies and organizations, did a statistical analysis on the status of women who work for the Jewish community and found that women were well represented in the entry-level positions but extremely few women held positions of Assistant Executive or Executive Director of an agency. Salaries paid to men and women were glaringly unequal, even for the same positions.

One study, conducted in Pittsburgh in 1980, tried to create change more directly. The Pittsburgh study, a joint effort of NCJW and American Jewish Committee, surveyed the status of lay and professional women in Jewish agencies, organizations and synagogues. Then they published the results in a pamphlet and called on each agency or organization to endorse publicly a series of affirmative action guidelines (see below) which would help redress some of the inequities that had been discovered. The results of the study and the list of endorsing organizations were then published in the local Jewish newspaper.

The development of these affirmative action guidelines was an important and unique step in the follow-up process to earlier consciousness-raising efforts. *These guidelines represent the first time that the organizations' own policies on affirmative action have been interpreted for use within the organization* as well as the broader Jewish community. Already there has been some tangible evidence of success because of the guidelines.

Principles Regarding the Nomination and Appointment of Lay Leaders

1. We will strive to have our nominating committee consist of an equal number of qualified women and men. The nominating committee will be charged to seek and consider women as well as men for every elective board position and office.

2. Our president or chairperson will actively seek and consider women as well as men for every committee chair and appointed lay position.

3. We will actively seek and recruit women as well as men for leadership training programs.

Principles Regarding the Employment and Promotion of Professional Leaders and Staff

1. We will vigorously seek and recruit women as well as men for professional positions.

2. As a first step to filling professional positions, we will advertise vacancies in appropriate national and regional professional publications as well as the [local Jewish paper], which is read by potential candidates in the [local] area. Advertisements for positions will include a statement that we are an equal opportunity employer and will consider candidates without regard to sex.

3. We will publicize and provide equal access to all professional training opportunities for employees regardless of sex. We will encourage qualified women to take advantage of professional training opportunities.

4. We will include women on every search committee organized to fill professional vacancies.

5. We will provide equal salaries and benefits to employees who hold substantially equal positions, regardless of sex.

There is written information available about affirmative action as well as the community and/or agency audits that have been conducted on the status of women in lay leadership and professional positions in the Jewish community.[22] The best way, however, to learn more about what's going on in the Jewish community in this area is to be in touch with the network of people who work on this issue within Jewish agencies.

AGENCY POSITIONS ON AFFIRMATIVE ACTION

Statement on Affirmative Action (1977)
American Jewish Committee
165 E. 56 Street
New York, NY 10022
(212) 751-4000

Resolution on Quotas and Affirmative Action (1974)
American Jewish Congress
15 E. 84 Street
New York, NY 10028
(212) 879-4500

Policy on Discrimination and Affirmative Action (1977)
Anti-Defamation League of B'nai B'rith
823 United Nations Plaza
New York, NY 10017
(212) 490-2525

Position on Affirmative Action (1975)
National Jewish Community Relations Advisory Council
443 Park Avenue S.
New York, NY 10016
(212) 684-6950

COMMUNITY OR INSTITUTIONAL AUDITS

The Status of Women in Jewish Communal Service
c/o Sophie Engel
Council of Jewish Federations
575 Lexington Avenue
New York, NY 10022
(212) 751-1311

*Survey of the Status of Women in Professional and Lay Leadership
Positions in Jewish Community Relations Agencies*
National Jewish Community Relations Advisory Council
443 Park Avenue S.
New York, NY 10016
(212) 684-6950

The Status of Women in AJC & WF (1979)
c/o Gail Chalew
Associated Jewish Charities and Welfare Fund
319 W. Monument Street
Baltimore, MD 21201
(301) 727-4828

The Status of Women in Jewish Organizations of Greater Pittsburgh
    (1980)
c/o American Jewish Committee
Pittsburgh Chapter
128 N. Craig Street
Pittsburgh, PA 15213
(412) 683-7927

Where Women Are in Federations
c/o Sue Stevens, Director
Council of Jewish Federations
Women's Division
575 Lexington Avenue
New York, NY 10022
(212) 751-1311

Women in Jewish Schools (1979)
Jewish Education Service of North America, Inc.
114 Fifth Avenue
New York, NY 10011
(212) 675-5656

*Bringing Women In: A Survey of the Evolving Role of Women
    in Jewish Organizational Life in Philadelphia* (1977)
c/o American Jewish Committee
Philadelphia Chapter
1411 Walnut Street, Suite 1004
Philadelphia, PA 19102
(215) LO 4-2460

Women in Jewish Communal Roles
c/o Emily Fink Bauman, Director
Jewish Community Relations Council
Jewish Federation of Greater Dallas
7800 Northaven Road, Suite A
Dallas, TX 75230
(214) 369-3313

OTHER RESOURCES

Evan Bayer
American Jewish Congress
15 E. 84 Street
New York, NY 10028
(212) 879-4500

Task Force on the Jewish Woman in a Changing Society
Federation of Jewish Philanthropies of Greater New York
130 E. 59 Street
New York, NY 10022
(212) 980-1000

Task Force on Equal Opportunities for Women
National Jewish Community Relations Advisory Council
443 Park Avenue S.
New York, NY 10016
(212) 684-6950

Task Force on Women and Minorities
Commission on Social Action of Reform Judaism
Union of American Hebrew Congregations
838 Fifth Avenue
New York, NY 10021
(212) 249-0100

14

◆

RECONCILING
JEWISH AND FEMALE

There have been times in the "decade of change" (now almost fifteen years) since the beginning of the contemporary women's liberation movement when Jewish women—even those who consider themselves committed feminists—have felt a sense of the dissonant identities we can all recognize if we are honest with ourselves; sometimes we have experienced what seems like an inherent conflict between our interests as women and our interests as Jews.

In this trying and energizing time, depending on individual background and the complexities of circumstance, some Jewish feminists have been more active in the secular women's movement, while others have been trying to make changes in Jewish life. Depending on the arena of the struggle, these women have on occasion perceived the conflict differently, with each group insulated from some of the concerns of the other.

Judaism and Feminism
Studies show Jewish women identify more with feminist goals than many other women do. Jewish women, themselves in the forefront of the general women's movement, saw an injustice that affected them and brought to bear on this the Jewish drive toward social justice and equality. In a 1976 interview in the premiere issue of *Lilith*, Betty Friedan claimed that her passion for equality for women "was really a passion against injustice, which originated from my feelings of the injustice of anti-Semitism."

In the late sixties and seventies, at the same time that women were

lobbying for change and raising their own and others' consciousness in the world at large, Jewish women, in women's discussion groups and synagogue sisterhoods, in Judaic-studies programs and around the family seder table, were bringing the lessons of the general women's movement into their lives as Jews. The struggle continues.

Just as there are still Conservative synagogues that refuse to count women in a prayer quorum (*minyan*) despite the fact that this is permitted by the Conservative movement (see "From Observer to Participant," p. 60), so there are Jewish situations in which women are denied access to the seats of power, or are called only by their husbands' names, or are automatically assigned to making coffee, not policy. But the war has been brought home, and some changes have already been made, either through a bloodless process of natural evolution or, sometimes, after women have done battle to win enfranchisement and empowerment in their own Jewish communities.

Despite the fact that the effects of the women's movement have been so strongly felt in Jewish life, Jewish feminists share a disappointment in the organized Jewish community's responses. For example, several major Jewish conventions and conferences were held in states that had failed to ratify the Equal Rights Amendment at precisely the time when feminists were calling for a boycott of those states. Small wonder that many Jewish women say they feel alienated from Jewish institutions. One activist asks: "Why is it that when there's some crisis with Israel, or Soviet Jews, or when something bad happens over civil-rights gains, the American Jewish organizations are right in there protesting—press conferences, statements, the whole works—yet when the Equal Rights Amendment was threatened, or abortion rights, the 'major' Jewish organizations were virtually silent, with no public protests. Don't they realize that *we're* part of *them?*"

While feminists who are Jewish can agree on many issues—including the need to combat anti-Semitism and to support a broad range of women's issues—there are real or perceived conflicts between the women's movement and what has passed for normative Jewish life in America. Women are still not valued equally with men. Sociologist Steven Martin Cohen writes on "American Jewish Feminism": "Just as contemporary Jewry leaves much to be desired in the eyes of modern feminists, so has feminism been viewed suspiciously by many conventional American Jews. Perhaps the paramount reason for this hostility is feminism's image as an opponent of the family, of population growth and of volunteerism, all of which are heartily endorsed by contemporary Jewish survivalists. Moreover, any ideology imported from the non-Jewish world is bound to be viewed with suspicion by an ethnic community fearful of succumbing to assimilation."[1]

But North American Jews began to assimilate the moment they stepped onto these shores. That the "survivalists" are choosing this particular issue as one on which they must stand firm (rather than concerning themselves with the failures of Jewish education, for example, or the erosion of Jewish identity among alienated Jewish women) suggests more hysteria than genuine concern about the quality of the Jewish life we are trying to preserve.[2]

After interviewing ten women responsible for expanding women's roles in Jewish life, Cohen tries to delineate what he views as the built-in conflicts between Judaism and feminism. It's useful for us to examine his views not because he is ill-intended—he's not—but because he is so well meaning,[3] yet sees feminism as a kind of primitive selfishness rather than recognizing the highest goals of feminism as the achievement of an interdependent, egalitarian structure *not* based on any kind of individual or partiarchal tyranny. ". . . feminism extols self-fulfillment, self-actualization, self-assertion; it calls upon communal institutions to accommodate individual needs. Judaism is communitarian in its approach; ultimate fulfillment revolves upon the historic community rather than the individual. . . . Yet despite the wide gulf between normative Judaism and contemporary feminism, a number of women have achieved a synthesis of the two systems strong enough to lay the groundwork for many . . . substantive changes in Jewish life."[4]

The feminist motto Sisterhood Is Powerful certainly stresses the communal aspect of feminism rather than any kind of selfish self-actualization, yet the alleged "selfishness" of feminism is often cited by those looking for ways to discredit the women's movement in the Jewish community. And in having to defend ourselves against these charges, we become isolated from one another and from non-Jewish women as well.

There arc, of course, real differences among Jewish women and not merely artificial distinctions imposed from without.

(courtesy National Council of Jewish Women)

Some Jewish groups are almost always opposed to everything on the so-called Women's Agenda (for example, ultra-Orthodox groups who oppose all aspects of the abortion-rights or sexual-preference platform); others have jeopardized women's interests by such thoughtless and damaging acts as holding large conferences in states that didn't ratify the Equal Rights Amendment. Other groups—such as the National Council of Jewish Women, one of the most liberal Jewish women's organizations—have consistently supported a wide range of women's issues (abortion rights, affirmative-action programs, legal aid for battered women) and are just beginning to act on the Jewish front.

Forging Alliances

The relationship between Jewish women's organizations (and individual Jewish women) and the general women's movement has sometimes been an uneasy one. This alliance has been threatened by anti-Semitic sentiments from our sisters in the movement—sometimes out of ignorance or insensitivity, sometimes from the same kind of misguided and manipulated joining of Israel's political behavior with a condemnation of all things Jewish.

Two of the most obvious links between anti-Semitism and the international women's movement have been forged, not surprisingly, at United Nations–sponsored conferences. "Mexico City" and "Copenhagen" have come to mean to some Jewish feminists what "Bay of Pigs" meant to American radicals in the sixties. Mexico City was the scene of the passage of the heinous Zionism-as-racism plank at the 1975 United Nations conference on women; Copenhagen was the setting for widespread anti-Semitism (often masked as anti-Zionism) that shocked so many of the Jewish (and some of the non-Jewish) women at the UN Mid-Decade Conference on Women in 1980. Novelist E. M. Broner writes: "We women acted as separate nations, not as ourselves, not out of our shared experiences. If Israel were not in our midst, the nations seemed to say, there would be no wife-beating, no child abuse, no sexual slave trade, no illiteracy, no malnutrition, no refugees. And no war."[5]

Some Jewish women have on occasion gone along with condemnation of "Zionism" as if they were afraid of being judged impure feminists if they supported Israel. Other women have allied themselves with anti-Semites by succumbing to their own self-hatred. These women are like the wicked child of the Passover seder, who denies the reality of Jewish experience by echoing with scorn the question of the man who asked, "Do you mean to tell me that you really believe *Jewish* women have been oppressed? That's a joke!"

Not knowing much about Jewish history but feeling uneasy over what they mistakenly assume is some unearned "white, privileged status" of all Jews, these Jewish women have been willing to prove their radical feminist credentials by allying themselves with the enemy.

A group of committed Jewish feminists decided to respond to the growing number of incidents of anti-Semitism in the women's movement. The group made its debut at an important conference of feminist educators, the National Women's Studies Association conference in 1981. The focus of the conference was on "racism," but originally there was no mention of the racism directed at Jewish women. The Jewish feminist group, calling itself Feminists Against Anti-Semitism, presented a panel at the conference: "Anti-Semitism, the Unacknowledged Racism." In one of the panel's presentations historian Paula Hyman, Dean of the Jewish Theological Seminary's College of Jewish Studies and a longtime activist in Jewish feminist affairs, said, "Both of us, Jews and women, seek to define *ourselves* and not be bound to a definition imposed on us by others."

Feminists Against Anti-Semitism, which Batya Bauman, Paula Hyman, Letty Cottin Pogrebin, and several other women steer, has as its statement of purpose words that echo Hyman's, plus the powerful con-

Logo of the Bay Area Jewish Women's Collective in San Francisco. (courtesy of Jane Litwoman)

clusion that "anti-Semitism pits women against women. It divides those of us who should be allied in our struggle for women's liberation throughout the world."

Feminists Against Anti-Semitism
P.O. Box BB 694
Cathedral Station
New York, NY 10025

Also in response to anti-Semitism from some parts of the women's movement, women long active in Jewish affairs and drawn to the movement formed an *ad hoc* caucus prior to the National Women's Conference at Houston in 1977. It was meant to serve the special interests of Jewish women in connection with international aspects of the women's movement, and to emphasize that Jewish women are not a single-issue group. Composed of active feminists, the caucus meets only occasionally, at meetings of the National Women's Conference Committee and at government and nongovernment conferences dealing with women's issues on a national and international level.

Jewish Women's Caucus
Betty K. Shapiro, Chairperson
3001 Veazey Terrace, N.W., #1604
Washington, D.C. 20008

By facing together the "Jewish" issue of anti-Semitism, and by facing together the challenges to women's legislative gains (in the form of the antichoice legislation proposed by conservative legislators, for example), "general" feminists are becoming more involved with aspects of the Jewish community, while more Jewish-oriented feminists are struggling to move Jewish organizations to put their weight behind women's issues. A cross-fertilization has begun to take place, with some women drawn to feminism by first recognizing inequalities in Jewish institutions and practices, while others look at Jewish life through an already well-polished feminist filter.

Jewish women from different points on the spectrum are making common cause around these issues. The great challenge we now face outside our own community is in building and strengthening coalitions with women of other religions and ethnic groups, and with feminist organizations.

(drawing by Laurie Sucher)

"Equal Access and Equal Value"

Women have great hopes for the future of the synthesis of feminism and Judaism. To speak of "a delicate balance" between Judaism and feminism—as the proposed title for a Federation-sponsored conference did—is to suggest that the balance can tip very easily into some undesirable state. This is a real misapprehension. Feminism is *good* for the Jews. The Jewish women's movement has been one of the most enriching developments in every aspect of Jewish life—religious, communal, personal, spiritual—giving affiliated Jewish women a new sense of self-worth and participation, and giving unaffiliated women, who may never before have identified as Jews, an entranceway into Jewish life.

The secular women's liberation movement, with its emphasis on women's right to equality, self-actualization, and an end to oppression by men and male-dominated institutions, has probably been the single most powerful influence on the Jewish community structure since the 1967 Six-Day War, which brought both female and male "closet" Jews out into the open. Suddenly, with the advent of the women's movement, half of the Jewish population saw itself as newly entitled to shape the community.

And there is no shortage of goals (or fantasies). When *Lilith* asked several Jewish women to create a scenario for the kind of progress they'd like to see in the next twenty years, the replies were swift and fascinating:[6] a women's synagogue; family life free of gender stereotyping; an egalitarian communal structure; the "mainstreaming" of Jewish women's experience into all Judaic-studies curricula. Is this what a post-feminist Judaism will look like?

The biggest problem Jewish women face is the built-in ambivalence of wanting to restructure a sexist, oppressive culture and yet at the same time feeling bound to this culture as it is presently constituted by ties too strong to break. Jewish women feel simultaneously an integral part of Jewish life and yet quite alienated from it. The challenges we now must deal with fall into two categories: changing the facts (as in the 1983 decision of the Conservative movement to ordain women as rabbis) and changing the attitudes (Will the women rabbis so ordained be hired by Conservative congregations?). Historian Paula Hyman has formulated an elegant phrase which captures these two distinct tasks that await us. She calls on Jewish women to attain both "equal access and equal value" in Jewish life. Our work is now to make women's experiences and perceptions a part of normative Jewish life.

It's easy enough to look back on the changes that have taken place since the early 1970s and declare that once the remaining battles are won (reform of the divorce laws, burying the nasty stereotypes, rewriting Jewish texts to include *our* history) all will be well. Unless we can resist burn-out, which allows us to accept inequities in Jewish life with the comforting excuse that "change comes gradually," we'll enter the 1990s at the same point we've reached today.

We may have to teach each other some new skills and strengths to be able to weave a seamless fabric out of these two skeins of our identities. There will probably always be issues that cry out to us to rally specifically as Jews or as women. But for those of us engaged in the struggle to learn and to weave, there is the faith that we are acting in accord with a shared goal—shared with all Jews and all feminists—of repairing and improving the world.

(drawing by Laurie Sucher)

To create a community that values all Jews, women as much as men, we women are responsible for living out the changes that we and others have struggled to bring about. This means not standing by as observers but springing forth as active participants, willing to take risks, be visible, act on what we *know* about the necessity for equality, even if we run the risk of offending the occasional Jewish male. Now that we are seeing a whole generation of women raised to speculate "Should I be a rabbi or a doctor?" we have to make sure that we don't stop before we have created an entire Jewish community that is true both to a renewed Judaism and to feminism's high goals for women.

The women's movement has been powerfully served by Jewish women's energy, and women's strength and self-awareness have changed Jewish life in so many ways that a return to men-only Judaism is out of the question to us now. The transformation of much public religious life, of personal prayer and celebration, of communal institutions, of the ways we view ourselves and other women and men, are real and permanent. We have chosen to make them so, as women, as Jews.

THE JEWISH WOMAN'S NETWORKING DIRECTORY

Information in the Directory is the most recent available. There may be changes in address, additions or deletions that came to the author's attention too late to be included in this edition of *Jewish and Female*. To suggest changes for future editions, please write to:

Susan Weidman Schneider
Lilith magazine
Suite 1328
250 West 57 Street
New York, NY 10019

Here is a guide to the topics covered in this Directory.

ALCOHOLISM

Al-Anon and Alateen Family
   Intergroup of New York
115 E. 23 Street
New York, NY 10010
(212) 475-6110

Alcoholics Anonymous
   (worldwide)
468 Park Avenue S.
New York, NY 10010
(212) 686-1100

Beth Israel Alcoholism Treatment
   Center
307 Second Avenue
New York, NY 10012
(212) 533-5700

Brunswick House
Alcoholism Treatment Center for
   Women
366 Broadway
Amityville, NY 11701
(516) 264-5000, ext. 361

JACS Foundation, Inc.
   (Jewish alcoholics, chemically
   dependent persons)
c/o New York Board of Rabbis
10 E. 73 Street
New York, NY 10021
(212) 879-8415

Jewish Family Service of
   Philadelphia
   (Northwest district office)
Benjamin Fox Pavilion, Suite 507
Foxcroft Square
Jenkintown, PA 19046
(215) 545-3290

National Council on Alcoholism
730 Fifth Avenue
New York, NY 10019
(212) 756-0990

Task Force on Alcoholism and
    Substance Abuse
Commission on Synagogue
    Relations

Federation of Jewish Philanthropies
130 E. 59 Street
New York, NY 10022
(212) 980-1000

Women for Sobriety
Box 618
Quakertown, PA 18951
(215) 536-8026

BATTERED WOMEN

Beit Zipporah
c/o Women-to-Women
P.O. Box 10403
Jerusalem, Israel

La Casa de las Madres
P.O. Box 27236
San Francisco, CA 94127
(415) 469-7650

Carmela Nakash Women's Aid
    Center
c/o LO
68 Sokolov Street
Herzliya, Israel 46380
(052) 86629-83856

Koach (strength)
Box 245
Station K
Toronto, Ontario M4P 2G5
Canada

National Commission Against
    Domestic Violence
1728 N Street, N.W.
Washington, DC 20007
(202) 347-7017

Religions United to Help
    (RUTH)
Milwaukee Task Force on Battered
    Women
1228 W. Mitchell St.
Milwaukee, WI 53205
(414) 643-5455

A Safe Place
P.O. Box 275
Oakland, CA 94604
(415) Bus. off. 444-7255
    crisis line 536-7233

Siloh Hotline for Battered Jewish
    Women
(See Hotlines)

Transition Center
    (kosher women's shelter)
    (address unlisted)
New York City
(212) 327-7660

Women for Women
P.O. Box 4667
Haifa, Israel 31046
04-662114

(See also Hotlines; Rape and
    Violence Against Women and
    Children)

BOOKSTORES

Charis: Books & More
419 Moreland Avenue, N.E.
Atlanta, GA 30307
(404) 524-0304

Everywoman's Books
641 Johnson Street
Victoria, British Columbia V8W
    1M7
Canada
(604) 388-9411

Goodman's Hebrew Books and
    Gifts
2305 University Boulevard W.
Wheaton, MD 20902
(301) 949-8100

I.C.I.–A Woman's Place
4015 Broadway
Oakland, CA 94611
(415) 547-9920

Israel Book Shop Inc.
410 Harvard Street
Brookline, MA 02146
(617) 566-7113

Jane Addams Bookstore
5 S. Wabash Avenue, 15th floor
Chicago, IL 60603
(312) 782-0708

The Jewish Museum Bookshop
1109 Fifth Avenue
New York, NY 10028
(212) 749-3770

J. Levine Company
58 Eldridge Street
New York, NY 10002
(212) 966-4460

Modern Times Bookstore
968 Valencia Street
San Francisco, CA 94110
(415) 282-9246

Oscar Wilde Memorial Book Shop
15 Christopher Street
New York, NY 10014
(212) 255-8097

J. Roth Bookseller
9427 W. Pico Boulevard
Los Angeles, CA 90035
(213) 557-1848

Sistermoon: Feminist Bookstore &
    Art Gallery
2128 E. Locust
Milwaukee, WI 53211
(414) 962-3323

Stavsky Hebrew Book Store
147 Essex Street
New York, NY 10002
(212) 674-1289

Toronto Women's Bookstore
85 Harbord Street
Toronto, Ontario M5S 1G4
Canada
(416) 922-8744

Womanbooks
201 W. 92 Street
New York, NY 10025
(212) 873-4121

Womansplace Bookstore
425 S. Mill Avenue
Tempe, AZ 85281
(602) 966-9276

Woman's Voice
99 Hanassi Avenue
Haifa, Israel

CANTORIAL SCHOOLS FOR WOMEN

Cantors Institute
Jewish Theological Seminary
3080 Broadway
New York, NY 10027
(212) 678-8000

Gratz College
M.A. Program in Jewish Music
10 Street and Tabor Road
Philadelphia, PA 19141
(215) 329-3363

Herzliah–Jewish Teachers Seminary
Music Division
69 Bank Street
New York, NY 10014

School of Sacred Music
Hebrew Union College-
Jewish Institute of Religion
1 W. 4 Street
New York, NY 10012
(212) 674-5300

CANTORS (WOMEN)

Nancy Abramson
Congregation Sons of Israel
1666 Pleasantville Road
Briarcliff Manor, NY 10510
(914) 762-2700

Vicki Axe
Temple Emanu-El
455 Neptune Blvd.
Long Beach, NY 11561
(516) 431-4060

Sheri Blum
Temple Emanuel
280 May Street
Worcester, MA 01602
(617) 755-1257

Phyllis P. Cole
North Shore Synagogue
83 Muttontown Road
Syosset, NY 11791
(516) 921-2282

Emilie Coopersmith
Temple Shalom
815 W. 7 Street
Plainfield, NJ 07063
(201) 756-6447

Mindy J. Fliegelman
Nassau Community Temple
  Beth-El
240 Hempstead Avenue
West Hempstead, NY 11556
(516) 485-1811

Mimi Frishman
7 Jeffrey Place
Monsey, NY 10952
(914) 352-2849

Donna Goldfarb
Temple Beth Jacob
67 Broadway
Concord, NH 03301

Nancy S. Hausman
Temple Beth Orr
P.O. Box 8242
2151 Riverside Drive
Coral Springs, FL 33065
(305) 753-9081 or 9082

Regina Y. Heit
Temple Adath B'nai Israel
3600 Washington Avenue
Evansville, Indiana 47715
(812) 477-1577

CANTORS (WOMEN) *(continued)*

Anita Hockman
Congregation M'Kor Shalom
Church and Fellowship Roads
Mt. Laurel, NJ 08054
(609) 235-0590

Gail I. Posner Karp
Temple Beth El
920 Bay Street
Santa Cruz, CA 95060
(408) 423-3012

Jan Mahler
Temple Beth Torah
35 Bagatelle Road
Dix Hills, NY 11746
(516) 643-1200

Ellen Stettner Math
Stephen Wise Free Synagogue
30 W. 68th Street
New York, NY 10023
(212) 877-4050

Emily Sleeper Mekler
Sinai Temple
1100 Dickinson Street
Springfield, MA 01108
(413) 736-3619

Jane Myers
Germantown Jewish Center
Lincoln Drive at Ellet Street
Philadelphia, PA
(215) 844-1507

Martha Novick
Temple Emanu-El
100 James Street
Edison, NJ 08817
(201) 549-4442

Barbara Ostfeld-Horowitz
Temple Beth-El
5 Old Mill Road
Great Neck, NY 11023
(516) HU 7-0900

Helene Reps
Temple Israel
1000 Pinebrook Boulevard
New Rochelle, NY 10804
(914) 235-1800

Linda Rich
Temple Beth Zion
5555 W. Olympic Boulevard
Los Angeles, CA 90036

Janice L. Roger
The Indianapolis Hebrew
     Congregation
6501 N. Meridian
Indianapolis, IN 46260
(317) 255-6649

Sue Romer
Congregation Beth Am
Silver Spring, MD
(301) 340-6818

Aviva Kligfeld Rosenbloom
Temple Israel of Hollywood
7300 Hollywood Boulevard
Los Angeles, CA 90046
(213) 876-8330

Judith K. Rowland
6700, 192 Street, #1405
Fresh Meadows, NY 11365
(718) 454-2584

Sarah J. Sager
Fairmount Temple
23737 Fairmount Boulevard
Cleveland, OH 44122
(216) 464-1330

Galit Pinsky Sassower
Temple Beth Shalom
Highland at Webster
Needham, MA 02194
(617) 444-0077

Judith Blanc Schiff
Temple Beth Israel
1931 N.W. Flanders Street
Portland, OR 97209
(503) 222-1069

Michal Schiff
Temple Israel of Northern
    Westchester
Glengary Road
Croton, NY 10520
(914) 271-4705

Elaine Shapiro
Temple Beth-El
2815 N. Flagler Drive
West Palm Beach, FL 33407
(305) 833-0339

Robin Sherman
Temple Emanuel
Cherry Hill, NJ 08034
(609) 665-0888

Linda Shivers
119 S. 1 Street
Highland Park, NJ 08904

Rita Shore
Temple Judea
1407 14 Lane
Lake Worth, FL
(305) 439-5642

Faith R. Steinsnyder
509 W. 110 Street, #5E
New York, NY 10025
(212) 864-3391

Jodi Sufrin
Temple Beth Elohim
10 Bethel Road
Wellesley Hills, MA 02181
(617) 235-8419

Dana S. Troupp
Temple Beth El of Westchester
220 Bedford Road
Chappaqua, NY 10514
(914) 238-3928

Ellen Sussman Vaida
Temple Shalom
5 Ayrmont Lane
Aberdeen, NJ 07747
(201) 566-2621

Women Cantors Network
c/o Cantor Deborah Katchko-
    Zimmerman
Congregation Beth El
109 East Avenue
Norwalk, CT 06851

CHARITY

Joint Passover Association
33 W. 60 Street
New York, NY 10023
(212) 586-2900

New Israel Fund
22 Miller Avenue
Mill Valley, CA 94941
(415) 383-4866

Philanthropic Focus, Inc.
Consultants in Charitable Giving
10701 W. North Avenue
Milwaukee, WI 53226
(414) 453-8282

U.S./Israel Women-to-Women
4 Sniffen Court
156 E. 36 Street
New York, NY 10016
(212) 684-7614

(*See also* Financial Aid)

CHILD CARE

(All-day facilities for preschool-age children)

Arizona
Phoenix Hebrew Academy
515 East Bethany Home Road
Phoenix, AZ
(602) 277-4016

Jewish Community Center
3822 E. River Road
Tucson, AZ
(602) 299-7933

California
Berkeley/Richmond Jewish
    Community Center
1414 Walnut Avenue
Berkeley, CA 94709
(415) 848-0237

Bureau of Jewish Education
2351 Wyda Way
Sacramento, CA 95825
(926) 485-4151

Contra Costa Jewish Community
    Center
Bayit Ha-Yeladim
1355 Creekside Drive
Walnut Creek, CA 94596
(415) 938-7800

Jewish Community Center
Hollywood/Los Feliz
1110 Bates Ave.
Los Angeles, CA 90029
(213) 663-3843

Jewish Community Center
3801 E. Willow
Long Beach, CA 90815
(213) 426-7601

Juvia Preschool
Temple Menorah (Reform)
1101 Camino Real
Redondo Beach, CA 90277
(213) 316-8997

Temple Adat Avi El
5540 Laurel Canyon Blvd.
No. Hollywood, CA 91607
(818) 766-6375

Temple Adat Shalom
3030 Westwood Blvd.
Los Angeles, CA 90034
(213) 470-1969

Temple B'nai David Judea
9017 W. Pico Blvd.
Los Angeles, CA 90035
(213) 274-1250

Valley Cities Jewish Community
    Center
13164 Burbank Blvd.
Van Nuys, CA 91401
(818) 786-6310

Vista del Mar Child Care Service
3200 Motor Avenue
Los Angeles, CA 90034
(213) 836-1223

Westside Jewish Community
    Center
5870 W. Olympic Blvd.
Los Angeles, CA 90036
(213) 938-1531

Connecticut
Jewish Community Center of
    Greater New Haven
1156 Chapel Street
New Haven, CT 06511
(203) 865-5181

Colorado
Jewish Community Center
4800 East Alameda
Denver, CO 80222
(303) 399-2660

Delaware
Jewish Community Center
101 Garden of Eden Road
Wilmington, Delaware 19803
(302) 478-6200

District of Columbia
Toddler Day Care
3935 Macomb St. NW
Washington, D.C. 20016
(202) 328-8087

Florida
Jewish Community Center
4200 Biscayne Blvd.
Miami, FL 33137
(305) 576-1660

Georgia
Jewish Children's Service
   (regional childcare service)
1430 W. Peachtree Street, N.W.,
   Room 303
Atlanta, GA 30309
(404) 892-0503

Jewish Community Center
1745 Peachtree Rd. N.E.
Atlanta, GA 30309
(404) 875-7881

Illinois
Gan Yeladim
Niles Township Jewish
   Congregation
4500 W. Dempster
Skokie, IL 60076
(312) 675-4141

Jewish Community Centers of
   Chicago
1 South Franklin
Chicago, IL 60606
(312) 346-6700

Moriah Child Care Center
Moriah Congregation
200 Hyacinth Lane
Deerfield, IL 60015
(312) 948-8930

Therapeutic Family Day Care
Jewish Children's Bureau
One S. Franklin
Chicago, IL 60606
(312) 346-6700

Virginia Frank Child Development
   Center
Jewish Family and Community
   Service
3033 W. Touhy Avenue
Chicago, IL 60645
(312) 761-4550

Indiana
Jewish Community Center
   Association
6701 Hoover Road
Indianapolis, IN 46260
(317) 251-9467

Kansas
Jewish Community Center
8301 Lamar
Overland Park, KS 66207
(913) 649-4848

Kentucky
Jewish Community Center
3600 Dutchman's Lane
Louisville, KY 40205
(502) 459-0660

Maryland
Gan Yeladim (Garden of Children)
6300 Park Heights Avenue
Baltimore, MD 21215
(301) 764-7646

Rockville Jewish Day Care
6125 Montrose Rd.
Rockville, MD 20852
(301) 881-0100

Shaarei Zion Day Care Center
Shaarei Zion Congregation
6602 Park Heights Avenue
Baltimore, MD 21215
(301) 764-6810

CHILD CARE (*continued*)

Massachusetts
Jewish Community Center
633 Salisbury St.
Worcester, MA 01609
(617) 756-7109

Leventhal–Sidman Jewish
  Community Center Preschool
333 Nahanton Street
Newton Centre, MA 02159
(617) 965-7410

North Shore Jewish Community
  Center
4 Community Road
Marblehead, MA 01945
(617) 631-8330

Yal-Day-New Day Care Center
62 Green Street
Brookline, MA 02146
(617) 232-6019

Michigan
Jewish Community Center of
  Metropolitan Detroit
6600 W. Maple Road
W. Bloomfield, MI 48033
(313) 661-1000

Minnesota
Adath Jeshurun
3400 Dupont Ave. S.
Minneapolis, MN 55408
(612) 824-2685

Minneapolis Jewish Community
  Center
3440 S. Cedar Lake Rd.
Minneapolis, MN 55416
(612) 377-8330

Missouri
Jewish Community Centers
  Association
2 Millstone Campus
St. Louis, MO 63146
(314) 432-5700

New Jersey
Green Lane Child Development
  Center
Jewish Community Center
Green Lane, Union, NJ 07083
(201) 289-8112

YMHA
25 Adelaide Ave.
Highland Park, NJ 08904
(201) 249-2221

YM/YWHA of Metro
760 Northfield Ave.
West Orange, NJ 07052
(201) 736-3200

Shalom Yeladeem
JCC of Atlantic County
501 N. Jerome Ave.
Margate, NJ 08402
(609) 822-1167

New York
Bronx House at Co-op City
100A Aldrich Street
Bronx, NY 10475
(212) 379-6763

Central Queens YM/YWHA
67–09 108th Street
Forest Hills, NY 11375
(718) 268-5011

Child Care Center for Jewish
  Community Workers
National Council of Jewish Women
9 E. 69 Street
New York, NY 10021
(212) 535-5900

Educational Alliance Co-op
  Nursery
197 East Broadway
New York, NY 10002
(212) 475-6200

Gustave Hartman YM/YWHA
710 Hartman Lane
257 B. 17th Street
Far Rockaway, NY 11691
(718) 471-9600

Jewish Center
2640 North Forest Road
Getzville, NY 14068
(716) 688-4033

Jewish Community Center
5655 Thompson Road
P.O. Box 29
Dewitt, NY 13214
(315) 445-2630

Jewish Community Center
1200 Edgewood Ave.
Rochester, NY 14621
(716) 461-2000

Jewish Community Center
2565 Balltown Road
Schenectady, NY 12309
(518) 377-8803

Jewish Community Center of
   Staten Island
475 Victory Boulevard
Staten Island, NY 10301
(718) 981-1500

Kings Bay YM/YWHA
3495 Nostrand Avenue
Brooklyn, NY 11229
(718) 648-7703

Mid-Island YM–YWHA
45 Manetto Hill Road
Plainview, NY 11803
(516) 822-3535

Mosholu–Montefiore Community
   Center
3450 DeKalb Avenue
Bronx, NY 10467
(212) 882-4000

Northern Westchester
   YM/YWHA
129 Plainfield Avenue
Bedford Hills, NY 10507
(914) 241-2064

Parenting Center Daycare Network
92nd Street YM/YWHA
1395 Lexington Avenue
New York, NY 10028
(212) 427-6000

Pripetshik Program
   (Yiddish play group for
   preschoolers)
3328 Bainbridge Avenue
Bronx, NY 10467
(212) 654-8540

Samuel Field YM/YWHA
58–20 Little Neck Parkway
Little Neck, NY 11362
(718) 225-6750

Shorefront YM/YWHA
3300 Coney Island Avenue
Brooklyn, NY 11235
(718) 646-1444

Starrett City Early Learning Center
1325 Pennsylvania Avenue
Brooklyn, NY 11239
(718) 642-8724

Stephen Wise Free Synagogue
Jewish Day Care Program
30 W. 68 Street
New York, NY 10023
(212) 877-4050

Suffolk YM/YWHA
74 Hauppauge Road
Commack, NY 11725
(516) 462-9800

Yaldenu Jewish Day Care Center
Temple Ansche Chesed
251 W. 100 Street
New York, NY 10025
(212) 865-0600

YM/YWHA of Washington
   Heights–Inwood
54 Nagle Avenue
New York, NY 10040
(212) 569-6200

CHILD CARE (*continued*)

Ohio
Dayton Jewish Community Center
4501 Dehlinger Road
Dayton, OH 45426

Jewish Children's Bureau/Jewish
   Day Nursery
21811 Fairmount Boulevard
Cleveland, OH 44118
(216) 932-2800

Jewish Community Center
1580 Summit Road
Cincinnati, OH 45237
(513) 761-7500

Jewish Community Center
6465 Sylvania
Sylvania, OH 43560
(419) 882-5096

Jewish Early Learning Cooperative
3101 Clifton Avenue
Cincinnati, OH 45220

Leo Yassenoff Jewish Center
1125 College Avenue
Columbus, OH 43202
(614) 231-2731

True Sisters Day Care Center
True Sisters
3205 Fairmount Blvd.
Cleveland, OH 44118
(216) 321-6744

Pennsylvania
Federation Day Care Services
Jameson and Garth Roads
Philadelphia, PA 19116
(215) 676-7550

   Branch offices:
   Downtown Children's Center
   366 Snyder Avenue
   Philadelphia, PA 19148
   (215) 389-1018

Samuel Paley Day Care Center
Strahle and Horrocks Streets
Philedelphia, PA 19152
(212) 725-8930

Jewish Community Center
5738 Forbes Avenue
Pittsburgh, PA 15217
(412) 521-8010

South Carolina
Little Community Pre-School and
   Kindergarten
Jewish Community Center
P.O. Box 6968
Columbia, SC 29260
(803) 787-2023

Texas
Jewish Community Center
7900 Northaven Rd.
Dallas, TX 75230
(214) 739-2737

Jewish Community Center
405 Mardi Gras
El Paso, TX 79912
(915) 584-4437

Jewish Community Center
6801 Dan Danciger Rd.
Ft. Worth, TX 76133
(817) 292-3111

Jewish Community Center
   Educational Center
5601 South Braeswood
Houston, TX 77096
(713) 729-3200

Solomon Schechter Preschool
Solomon Schechter Academy
7111 Starbuck
Dallas, TX 75252
(214) 248-3032

Teenok/K'Tantan
Akiba Academy
6210 Churchill Way
Dallas, TX 75230
(214) 239-7248

Temple Emanu-El Pre-school and
    Extended Care Center
Temple Emanu-El
8500 Hillcrest
Dallas, TX 75230
(214) 368-3613

Virginia
Jewish Community Center
7300 Newport Ave.
Norfolk, VA 23505
(804) 489-1371

No. Va. Jewish Community Center
8822 Little River Turnpike
Fairfax, VA 22031
(804) 323-0880

Washington
Jewish Community Center
3801 East Mercer Way
Mercer Is., WA 98040
(206) 232-7115

Jewish Community Center
11051 34th N.E.
Seattle, WA 98125
(206) 364-6655

Pooh Corner Educare
5244 South Morgan
Seattle, WA 98118
(206) 725-0641

Canada
Gan Yiladim
c/o Beth Emeth-Bais Yehuda
    Synagogue
100 Elder
Toronto, Ontario
Canada M3H 5G7
(416) 633-3838

Ganeynou
Ecole Primaire
6920 Rue Lavoie
Montreal, Quebec H3W 3G9
(514) 733-8851

Garderie Beth Rivkah
Beth Rivkah
5001 Vezina
Montreal, Quebec H3W 1C2
(514) 731-3681

Toronto Jewish Congress
4600 Bathurst Street
Willowdale, Ontario M2R 3V2
(416) 638-7800

CHILDREN: EDUCATION

California
Bureau of Jewish Education
2351 Wyda Way
Sacramento, CA 95825
(916) 485-4151

Bureau of Jewish Education
639, 14 Avenue
San Francisco, CA 94118
(415) 751-6983

CHILDREN: EDUCATION (*continued*)

Jewish Education Council
3245 Sheffield Avenue
Oakland, CA 94602
(415) 533-7032

Jewish Education Service of
  Orange County
12181 Buaro
Garden Grove, CA 92640
(714) 537-2424

Los Angeles Bureau of Jewish
  Education
6505 Wilshire Boulevard, Suite 710
Los Angeles, CA 90048
(213) 852-1234

Rhea Hirsch School of Education
(213) 749-3424
Hebrew Union College/Jewish
  Institute of Religion
3077 University Avenue
Los Angeles, CA 90007

San Diego Bureau of Jewish
  Education
5511 El Cajon Boulevard
San Diego, CA 92115
(619) 583-8532

Colorado
Central Agency for Jewish
  Education
300 S. Dahlia Street, #207
Denver, CO 80222
(303) 321-3191

Connecticut
Committee on Jewish Education
Hartford Jewish Federation
333 Bloomfield Avenue
West Hartford, CT 06117
(203) 233-2774

Department of Jewish Education
New Haven Jewish Federation
1162 Chapel Street
New Haven, CT 06511
(203) 562-3163

Florida
Central Agency for Jewish
  Education
4200 Biscayne Boulevard
Miami, FL 33137
(305) 576-4030

Georgia
Atlanta Bureau of Jewish Education
1745 Peachtree Road, N.E.
Atlanta, GA 30309
(404) 873-1248

Illinois
Associated Talmud Torahs of
  Chicago
2828 W. Pratt Boulevard
Chicago, IL 60645
(312) 973-2828

Board of Jewish Education of
  Metropolitan Chicago
618 S. Michigan Avenue
Chicago, IL 60605
(312) 427-5570

The Kohl Jewish Teacher Center
161 Green Bay Road
Wilmette, IL 60091
(312) 256-6056

Indiana
Bureau of Jewish Education
6711 Hoover Road
Indianapolis, IN 46260
(317) 255-3124

Kansas
Jewish Education Council of
    Greater Kansas City
2210 W. 75 Street, Suite 12
Shawnee Mission, KS 66208
(913) 722-2922

Kentucky
Bureau of Jewish Education
3600 Dutchman's Lane
Louisville, KY 40205
(502) 459-0798

Maryland
Board of Jewish Education
5800 Park Heights Avenue
Baltimore, MD 21215
(301) 367-8300

Board of Jewish Education of
    Greater Washington
9325 Brookville Road
Silver Spring, MD 20910
(301) 589-3180

Massachusetts
Bureau of Jewish Education
824 Boylston Street
Chestnut Hill, MA 02167
(617) 277-3100

Michigan
United Hebrew Schools of
    Metropolitan Detroit
21550 W. 12 Mile Road
Southfield, MI 48076
(313) 354-1050

Missouri
Central Agency for Jewish
    Education
10957 Schuctz Road
St. Louis, MO 63141
(314) 862-0606

Jewish Teachers Resource Center
225 Meramec, Suite 405
St. Louis, MO 63105

Nebraska
Department of Jewish Education
333 S. 132 Street
Omaha, NB 68154
(402) 334-8200

New Jersey
Bureau of Jewish Education
1 Pike Drive
Wayne, NJ 07470
(201) 595-0560

Bureau of Jewish Education of
    Southern New Jersey
2393 W. Marlton Pike
Cherry Hill, NJ 08002
(609) 662-6300

Department of Jewish Educational
    Services
Jewish Education Committee
United Jewish Community of
    Bergen County
111 Kinderkamack Road
P.O. Box 176, North Hackensack
    Station
River Edge, NJ 07661
(201) 488-6800

Jewish Education Association
1 Henderson Drive
West Caldwell, NJ 07006
(201) 575-6050

New York
Board of Jewish Education of
    Greater New York
426 W. 58 Street
New York, NY 10019
(212) 245-8200

Bureau of Jewish Education
50 Chestnut Street
Rochester, NY 14604
(716) 546-1468

Bureau of Jewish Education of
    Greater Buffalo, Inc.
2640 N. Forest Road
Getzville, NY 14068
(716) 689-8844

CHILDREN: EDUCATION (*continued*)

Coalition for Alternatives in Jewish
   Education
468 Park Avenue South
New York, NY 10016
(212) 696-0740

Equal Play Magazine
Women's Action Alliance, Inc.
370 Lexington Avenue
New York, NY 10017
(212) 532-8330

Abraham Joshua Heschel School
   (egalitarian Hebrew day school)
270 W. 89 Street
New York, NY 10024
(212) 595-7087

Jewish Education Service of North
   America, Inc.
114 Fifth Avenue
New York, NY 10011
(212) 675-5656

Melton Research Center
Jewish Theological Seminary
3080 Broadway
New York, NY 10027
(212) 678-8031

Torah Umesorah
   (national society for Hebrew day
   schools)
229 Park Avenue S.
New York, NY 10003
(212) 674-6700

Union of American Hebrew
   Congregations
838 Fifth Avenue
New York, NY 10021
(212) 249-0100

Ohio
Bureau of Jewish Education
1580 Summit Road
Cincinnati, OH 45237
(513) 761-0203

Cleveland Bureau of Jewish
   Education
2030 S. Taylor Road
Cleveland, OH 44118
(216) 371-0446

Commission for Jewish Education
3970 Logan Way
Youngstown OH 44505
(216) 759-0452

Toledo Board of Jewish Education
2727 Kenwood Boulevard
Toledo, OH 43606
(419) 531-8969

Pennsylvania
Hebrew Institute of Pittsburgh
6401-07 Forbes Avenue
Pittsburgh, PA 15217
(412) 521-1100

Rhode Island
Bureau of Jewish Education of
   Rhode Island
130 Sessions Street
Providence, RI 02906
(401) 331-0956

Texas
Commission for Jewish Education
5603 S. Braeswood Boulevard
Houston, TX 77096
(713) 729-7000

Washington
Jewish Education Council of
   Greater Seattle
516 Securities Building
Seattle, WA 98101
(206) 625-0665

Wisconsin
Milwaukee Association for Jewish
  Education
4650 N. Port Washington Road
Milwaukee, WI 53212
(414) 962-8860

Canada
Winnipeg Board of Jewish
  Education
301-365 Hargrave Street
Winnipeg, Manitoba R3B 2K3
Canada
(204) 949-1482

Board of Jewish Education
22 Glen Park Avenue
Toronto, Ontario M6B 2B9
Canada
(416) 781-4687

Department of Education and
  Culture
Canadian Jewish Congress
150 Beverley Street
Toronto, Ontario M5T 1Y6
Canada
(416) 977-3811

Jewish Education Council of
  Greater Montreal
5151 Côte Ste. Catherine Road,
  Room 201
Montreal, Quebec H3W 1M6
Canada
(514) 735-3541

CHILDREN'S RESOURCES

Association for Jewish Children
1301 Spencer Street
Philadelphia, PA 19141
(215) 549-9000

Jewish Big Brother and Big Sister
  League
5750 Park Heights Avenue
Baltimore, MD 21215
(301) 466-9200

Jewish Big Brother/Sister
  Association
31 New Chardon Street
Boston, MA 02114
(617) 367-5818

Jewish Child Care Association of
  New York
345 Madison Avenue
New York, NY 10017
(212) 490-9160

Jewish Children's Bureau
1 S. Franklin Street
Chicago, IL 60606
(312) 346-6700

Jewish Children's Regional Service
P.O. Box 15225
New Orleans, LA 70175
(504) 899-1595

Jewish Family & Children's Bureau
Atlanta Jewish Welfare Federation
1753 Peachtree Road, N.E.
Atlanta, GA 30309
(404) 873-2277

Jewish Family & Children's Service
Jewish Federation
505 Gypsy Lane
Box 449
Youngstown, OH 44501
(216) 746-3251

Rebecca Gratz Club
  (residential program for
  adolescent girls)
532 Spruce Street
Philadelphia, PA 19106
(215) 925-1573

(*See also* Family Resources)

CONVERSION

Rabbi Stephen C. Lerner
752 Stelton Street
Teaneck, NJ 07666
(201) 837-7552

National Jewish Hospitality
  Committee
201 S. 18 Street, Room 1519
Philadelphia, PA 19103
(215) 546-8293

National Jewish Information
  Service
5174 W. 8 Street
Los Angeles, CA 90036
(213) 936-6033

Outreach Program
Union of American Hebrew
  Congregations
838 Fifth Avenue
New York, NY 10021
(212) 249-0100

Rabbi Sanford Seltzer
Task Force on Reform Jewish
  Outreach
1187 Beacon Street
Brookline, MA 02146

COUNSELING AND PSYCHIATRIC SERVICES

Rachel Adler
Sagaris Women's Therapy
  Collective
2617 Garfield Avenue S.
Minneapolis, MN 55408

Association for Women in
  Psychology
P.O. Box 31449
Wallingford Station
Seattle, WA 98103

Bellefaire
  (for children)
22001 Fairmount Boulevard
Cleveland, OH 44118
(216) 932-2800

B'nai B'rith Career and Counseling
  Service
1405 Locust Street, Suite 1507
Philadelphia, PA 19102
(215) 545-1455

Coalition for Human Rights and
  Against Psychiatric Oppression
Box 396, F.D.R. Station
New York, NY 10022

Jewish Child and Family Services
(Contact your local Federation of
  Jewish Philanthropies office.)

Jewish Counseling and Service
  Agency
161 Milburn Avenue
Milburn, NJ 07041

Jewish Counseling Service
60 S. River Street
Wilkes-Barre, PA 18701
(717) 823-5137

Jewish Family and Children's
  Bureau
1753 Peachtree Road, N.E.
Atlanta, GA 30319

Judith Weinstein Klein, Ph.D.
  (ethnotherapy)
921 The Alameda
Berkeley, CA 94707

Women Against Psychiatric Assault
2054 University Avenue, Room 406
Berkeley, CA 94704
(415) 548-2980

Philadelphia Psychiatric Center
Human Development Center
  (Northeast division)
Outpatient Clinic
Smylie Times Building
Rhawn and Roosevelt Boulevard
Philadelphia, PA 19115
(215) 332-2000

Irving Schwartz Institute for
  Children and Youth
Ford Road and Monument Avenue
Philadelphia, PA 19131
(215) 877-2000

Rabbinical Alliance of America
156 Fifth Avenue, Room 810
New York, NY 10010

Rabinical Center for Research and
  Counseling
128 East Dudley Avenue
Westfield, NJ 07090

Shiloh Hotline
(*See* Hotlines)

Valley Beth Shalom Lay Counseling
15739 Ventura Boulevard
Encino, CA 91436

Westchester Jewish Community
  Services
2 Gramton Avenue
Mount Vernon, NY 10500
and
598 Tuckahoe Road
Yonkers, NY 10700
and
20 South Broadway
Yonkers, NY 10700

(*See also* Family Resources)

CULTS

B'nai B'rith Cult Program
1640 Rhode Island Avenue, N.W.
Washington, DC 20036

Philip Cushman
West Coast Jewish Training Project
190 Denslowe Drive
San Francisco, CA 94132
(415) 563-7820

Rabbi Maurice Davis
Jewish Community Center
252 Soundview Avenue
White Plains, NY 10606
(914) 949-4717

Emergency Council of Jewish
  Families
(*See* Parenting)

Jews for Judaism
17720 N. Bay Road, Suite 6D
Miami Beach, FL 33160

National Institute for Campus
  Ministries
885 Centre Street
Newton Centre, MA 02159

Sanctuary
P.O. Box 4591
Boulder, CO 80306
(303) 443-1486

Task Force on Missionary Activity
Jewish Community Relations
  Council of New York
111 W. 40 Street
New York, NY 10018
(212) 221-1535

24-Hour Cult Clinic Hot Line
(*See* Hotlines)

DISPLACED HOMEMAKERS

Displaced Homemakers Network
755, 8 Street, N.W.
Washington, DC 20001
(202) 347-0522

Fresh Start Training Program
Project COPE
  (Division of Agudath Israel of
  America)
813 Avenue H
Brooklyn, NY 11230
(718) 434-8098

Jewish Vocational Service Displaced
  Homemaker Program
25900 Greenfield Road, Suite 242
Oak Park, MI 48237
(313) 967-0500

(*See also* Employment)

DIVORCE

AGUNAH
c/o Councilwoman Susan Alter
463 E. 19 Street
Brooklyn, NY 11226

American-Israeli Civil Liberties
  Coalition
124 West 79 Street
New York, NY 10024

G.E.T.
  (Getting Equitable Treatment)
P.O. Box 131
Brooklyn, NY 11230

Jewish Community Center
4800 E. Alameda
Denver, CO 80222
(303) 339-2668

Jewish Family Service of
  Philadelphia
1610 Spruce Street
Philadelphia, PA 19103
(215) K15-3290

Mitzvah
P.O. Box 506
Netanya, Israel

National Jewish Commission on
  Law and Public Affairs
  (COLPA)
71 Broadway
New York, NY 10006
(212) 269-0810

Rewards Program
Jewish Community Center
7900 Northaven Road
Dallas, TX 75230
(214) 739-2737

Task Force on Marriage and
Divorce
Commission on Synagogue
Relations
Federation of Jewish Philanthropies
of Greater New York
130 E. 59 Street
New York, NY 10021
(212) 980-1000

YM/YWHA "Facing the Problems
of Divorce" Support Group
1395 Lexington Avenue
New York, NY 10028
(212) 427-6000

EDUCATION: INSTITUTIONS

Bais Chana
Women's Institute of Jewish
Studies
Lubavitch House
15 Montcalm Street
St. Paul, MN 55116

Drisha Institute
122 W. 76 Street
New York, NY 10023
(212) 595-0307

Dropsie College
Broad and York Streets
Philadelphia, PA 19066
(215) 229-1566

Gratz College
10 Street and Tabor Road
Philadelphia, PA 19141
(215) 329-3363

Hebrew Union College–
Jewish Institute of Religion
(See Rabbinical Schools)

Herzliah–Jewish Teachers Seminary
69 Bank Street
New York, NY 10014

Hornstein Program in Jewish
Communal Service
Brandeis University
Waltham, MA 02254

Jewish Foundation for the
Education of Women
(See Financial Aid)

Jewish Theological Seminary
(See Rabbinical Schools)

Makhon Hannah
1367 President Street
Brooklyn, NY 11225

National Council of Beth Jacob
Schools
1415 E. 7 Street
Brooklyn, NY 11230

San Diego Women's Institute for
Continuing Jewish Education
4079, 54 Street
San Diego, CA 92105
(619) 442-2661

Spertus College of Judaica
618 S. Michigan Avenue
Chicago, IL 60605
(312) 922-9012

Touro College
30 W. 44 Street
New York, NY 10036
(212) 575-1090

EDUCATION: INSTITUTIONS (*continued*)

Wurzweiler School of Social Work
Yeshiva University
55 Fifth Avenue
New York, NY 10003
(212) 790-0241

Yeshiva University
Stern College for Women
245 Lexington Avenue
New York, NY 10016
(212) 960-5400

Yeshiva University High School for
  Girls
425 Fifth Avenue
New York, NY 10016
(212) 481-3746

(*See also* Women's Prayer and
  Study Groups)

EDUCATION: RESOURCES

Academy for Jewish Studies
  Without Walls
165 E. 56 Street
New York, NY 10022
(212) 751-4000

Agudath Israel of America
Girls' Division—Bnos Agudath Israel
5 Beekman Street
New York, NY 10038
(212) 791-1800

Alternatives in Religious Education
3945 S. Oneida Street
Denver, CO 80237

American Jewish Historical Society
2 Thornton Road
Waltham, MA 02154

Blaustein Library
American Jewish Committee
165 E. 56 Street
New York, NY 10022
(212) 751-4000

B'nai B'rith Department of Adult
  Jewish Education
and
B'nai B'rith Hillel Foundation
1640 Rhode Island Avenue, N.W.
Washington, DC 20036
(202) 857-6600

Coalition for Alternatives in Jewish
  Education
468 Park Avenue South, Room 904
New York, NY 10016

Datrix Thesis Search
University Microfilms International
300 N. Zeeb Road
Ann Arbor, MI 48106
(800) 521-3042
In Canada: (800) 268-6020

Jewish Education Service of North
    America
114 Fifth Avenue
New York, NY 10011
(212) 675-5656

Jewish Foundation for the
    Education of Women
(See Financial Aid)

Rabbi Miller
Jewish Education Program
425 E. 9 Street
Brooklyn, NY 11218

National Academy for Adult Jewish
    Studies
155 Fifth Avenue
New York, NY 10010

National Association of Temple
    Educators
838 Fifth Avenue
New York, NY 10021
(212) 249-0100

National Committee for
    Furtherance of Jewish Education
824 Eastern Parkway
Brooklyn, NY 11213
(718) 735-0200

Publications Department
Sex Desegregation Program
New York Board of Education
110 Livingston Street
Brooklyn, NY 11201

Speakers Bureau
Lilith Magazine
250 W. 57 Street, Suite 1328
New York, NY 10019
(212) 757-0818

*TABS: Aids for Ending Sexism in
    the School*
(*See* Periodicals)

Women and the Holocaust Project
The Institute for Research in
    History
432 Park Avenue S.
New York, NY 10016
(212) 689-1931

Women's Studies Section
Association for Jewish Studies
Widener Library
Harvard University
Cambridge, MA 02138
(617) 495-2985

YIVO Institute for Jewish Research
1048 Fifth Avenue
New York, NY 10028
(212) 535-6700

ELDERLY WOMEN

California
JFS Drop-In Center for
    Dysfunctional Seniors
2930 Copley Avenue
San Diego, CA 92116
(714) 295-0555

Older Women's League (OWL)
3800 Harrison Street
Oakland, CA 94611

ELDERLY WOMEN *(continued)*

United Jewish Community Centers
(services to the elderly)
3195 California Street
San Francisco, CA 94115
(415) 929-1986

District of Columbia
(*Greater Washington area*)
Jewish Council for the Aging of
Greater Washington, Inc.
6111 Montrose Road
Rockville, MD 20852
(301) 881-8782

Jewish Social Service Agency
6123 Montrose Road
Rockville, MD 20852

Florida
Southeast Multi-Purpose Center for
Seniors
2838 Hollywood Boulevard
Hollywood, FL 33020
(305) 921-6511

Georgia
National Interfaith Coalition on
Aging, Inc.
P.O. Box 1924
298 S. Hull Street
Athens, GA 30603

Illinois
The Ark
3509 W. Lawrence Avenue
Chicago, IL 60625

Council for Jewish Elderly
1015 W. Howard Street
Evanston, IL 60202
(312) 974-4105

Massachusetts
Union of American Hebrew
Congregations Gerontology
Program
1300 Boylston Street, Room 207
Chestnut Hill, MA 02167

New Jersey
Jewish Older Adult Services of
Atlantic County
5321 Atlantic Avenue
Ventnor, NJ 08406
(609) 823-8061

Branch offices:
H.G. Rosin Senior Citizens
Center
906 Pacific Avenue
Atlantic City, NJ 08401
(609) 345-3057

Senior Chelsea Office Outreach
Project (SCOOP)
10 S. Chelsea Avenue
Atlantic City, NJ 08401
(609) 345-1367

Senior Citizens Medical Clinic
906 Pacific Avenue
Atlantic City, NJ 08401
(609) 345-8409

New York
Central Bureau for the Jewish Aged
80 Fifth Avenue
New York, NY 10011
(212) 929-3999

Dorot
Temple Ansche Chesed
251 West 100 Street
New York, NY 10025
(212) 864-7410

The Jewish Association for Services
  for the Aged
  (JASA)
40 West 68 Street
New York, NY 10023
(212) 724-3200

    Branch offices:
Bronx Borough Service Center
2488 Grand Concourse
Bronx, NY 10458
(212) 365-4044

Brooklyn Borough Service Center
2211 Church Avenue
Brooklyn, NY 11226
(718) 693-7606

Nassau-Suffolk District Service
  Center
158, 3 Street
Mineola, NY 11501
(516) 742-2050

Queens Borough Service Center
97-45 Queens Boulevard
Rego Park, NY 11374
(718) 263-4700

National Action Forum for Older
  Women
c/o Jane Porcino

School of Allied Health Professions
Health Sciences Center
SUNY at Stony Brook
Stony Brook, NY 11794
or
c/o Nancy King
Center for Women Policy Studies
2000 P Street, N.W.
Washington, DC 20036

92nd Street YM/YWHA
1395 Lexington Avenue
New York, NY 10028
(212) 427-6000

Project Ezra
197 E. Broadway
New York, NY 10002
(212) 982-3700

Project on Aging
Synagogue Council of America
10 E. 40 Street
New York, NY 10016
(212) 686-8670

Pennsylvania
Gray Panthers
3635 Chestnut Street
Philadelphia, PA 19104
(215) 382-3300

Northeast Walk-In Service for the
  Elderly
  (administered by Jewish Family
  Service)
6445 Castor Avenue
Philadelphia, PA 19149
(215) 338-9800

Texas
National Association of Jewish
  Homes for the Aged
2525 Centerville Road
Dallas, TX 75228
(214) 327-4503

Canada
Coordinated Services to the Jewish
  Elderly
3995 Bathurst Street
Downsview, Ontario M3H 5V0
Canada
(416) 635-2860

Creative Living Centre
15 Hove Street
Downsview, Ontario M3H 4Y8
Canada
(416) 630-3200

Golden Age Association
5700 Westbury Avenue
Quebec, Montreal H3W 3E8
Canada
(514) 739-4731

ELDERLY WOMEN (*continued*)

Golden Age Club
410 Pritchard Avenue
Winnipeg, Manitoba
Canada
(204) 582-4256

Jewish Senior Citizen's Drop-In
  Centre
10052, 117 Street
Edmonton, Alberta T5K 1X3
Canada
(403) 488-4241

EMPLOYMENT

California
Advocates for Women
414 Mason
San Francisco, CA 94102
(415) 391-4870

Career Math
National Council of Jewish Women
543 N. Fairfax Avenue
Los Angeles, CA 90036

Jewish Vocational and Career
  Counseling Service
870 Market Street, Room 872
San Francisco, CA 97102
(415) 391-3595

Jewish Vocational Service
6505 Wilshire Boulevard, Suite 303
Los Angeles, CA 90048
(213) 655-8910

Tradeswoman, Inc.
P.O. Box 40664
San Francisco, CA 94140

Union WAGE
  (Women's Alliance to Gain
  Equality)
P.O. Box 40904
San Francisco, CA 94140

District of Columbia
B'nai B'rith Career and Counseling
  Service
1640 Rhode Island Avenue, N.W.
Washington, DC 20036
(202) 393-5284

Coalition for the Reproductive
  Rights of Workers
1917 Eye Street, N.W., Suite 201
Washington, DC 20006

Federation of Organizations for
  Professional Women
2000 P Street, NW, Suite 403
Washington, DC 20036

Florida
Jewish Vocational Service
318 N.W. 25 Street
Miami, FL 33127
(305) 576-3220

Georgia
Jewish Vocational Service
Atlanta Jewish Welfare Federation
1745 Peachtree Road, N.E.
Atlanta, GA 30309
(404) 876-5872

Illinois
Jewish Vocational Service
1 S. Franklin Street
Chicago, IL 60606
(312) 346-6700

Maryland
Vocational Services of Sinai
    Hospital
2440 W. Belvedere Avenue
Baltimore, MD 21215
(301) 367-4041

Massachusetts
B'nai B'rith Career and Counseling
    Service
1000 Worcester Road
Framingham, MA 01701
(617) 879-3301

Jewish Vocational Service
31 New Chardon Street
Boston, MA 02114
(617) 723-2846

Vocations for Social Change
P.O. Box 211
Essex Station
Boston, MA 02112

Michigan
Jewish Vocational Service
Community Workshop
4250 Woodward Avenue
Detroit, MI 48201
(313) 833-8100

Minnesota
Jewish Vocational Service
6715 Minnetonka Boulevard
Minneapolis, MN 55462
(612) 927-6524

Jewish Vocational Service
1821 University Avenue, Suite 369
St. Paul, MN 55104
(612) 645-9377

Missouri
Jewish Employment and Vocational
    Service
1727 Locust Street
St. Louis, MO 63103
(314) 241-3464

Jewish Vocational Service
1516 Grand Avenue
Kansas City, MO 64108
(816) 471-2808

New Jersey
Jewish Vocational Service of
    Metropolitan New Jersey
111 Prospect Street
East Orange, NJ 07017
(201) 674-6330

Women's Institute for Self-
    Enrichment
    (WISE)
Community Center of Southern
    New Jersey
Cherry Hill, NJ 08002

New York
American Women's Economic
    Development Association
1270 Avenue of the Americas
New York, NY 10019
(212) 397-0880

Catalyst (women's career
    development)
14 East 60 Street
New York, NY 10021
(212) 759-9700

Coalition of Labor Union Women—
    N.Y.C. Chapter
386 Park Avenue S., Room 603
New York, NY 10016
(212) 697-0765

EMPLOYMENT (*continued*)

Committee on Opportunities for
  Women
Conference of Jewish Communal
  Service
15 E. 26 Street
New York, NY 10010
(212) 683-8056

Employment Bureau
National Council of Young Israel
3 W. 16 Street
New York, NY 10011
(212) 929-1525

Federation Employment and
  Guidance Service
114 Fifth Avenue
New York, NY 10011
(212) 741-7110

National Association of Jewish
  Vocational Services
386 Park Avenue S.
New York, NY 10016
(212) 685-8355

Non-traditional Employment for
  Women
  (NEW)
105 E. 22 Street
New York, NY 10010
(415) 420-0660

Women in the Trades
198 Forsyth Street, Room 313
New York, NY 10002
(212) 625-3776

(*See also* Political Action (for
  affirmative-action groups)

Women's Career Center
Bramson ORT Technical Institute
New York, NY 10010
(212) 677-7420

Ohio
Jewish Vocational Service
1660 Sternblock Lane
Cincinnati, OH 45237
(513) 631-2400

Jewish Vocational Service
13878 Cedar Road
Cleveland, OH 44118
(216) 321-1381

Pennsylvania
Jewish Employment and Vocational
  Service
1624 Locust Street
Philadelphia, PA 19103
(215) 893-5900

Texas
Jewish Vocational Counseling
  Service
7800 Northaven
Dallas, TX 75230
(214) 369-4211

Washington
Association for Women in
  Psychology
(*See* Counseling and Psychiatric
  Services)

Wisconsin
Jewish Vocational Service
1339 N. Milwaukee Street
Milwaukee, WI 53202
(414) 272-1344

Canada
Jewish Vocational Service
74 Tycos Drive
Toronto, Ontario M6B 1V9
Canada
(416) 787-1151

Jewish Vocational Service and
  Sheltered Workshop
5151 Côte Ste. Catherine Road
Quebec, Montreal H3W 1M6
Canada
(514) 735-4217

(*See also* Political Action for
  affirmative-action groups)

FAMILY RESOURCES

Arizona
Jewish Family and Children's
  Service
2033 N. 7 Street
Phoenix, AZ 85006
(602) 257-1904

Jewish Family Service
102 N. Plumer Avenue
Tucson, AZ 85719
(602) 792-3641

California
Jewish Family and Children's
  Services
1600 Scott Street
San Francisco, CA 94115
(415) 567-8860

　　　Branch offices:
490 El Camino Real #A 208
Belmont, CA 94002
(415) 591-8991

1330 Lincoln Avenue
San Rafael, CA 94901
(415) 456-7554

Jewish Family Service
3801 E. Willow Avenue
Long Beach, CA 90815
(213) 427-7916

Jewish Family Service
3355 Fourth Avenue
San Diego, CA 92103
(619) 291-0473

Jewish Family Service
2075 Lincoln Avenue, Suite C
San Jose, CA 95125
(408) 264-7140

Jewish Family Service North
  County Office
2725 Jefferson Street
Carlsbad, CA 92008
(714) 434-4043

Jewish Family Service of Alameda
  and Contra Costa Counties
3245 Sheffield Avenue
Oakland, CA 94602
(415) 532-6314

Jewish Family Service of
  Los Angeles
6505 Wilshire Boulevard
Los Angeles, CA 90048
(213) 852-1234, ext. 361

Jewish Family Service of Orange
  County
8100 Garden Grove Boulevard,
  Suite 2
Garden Grove, CA 92644
(714) 898-0023

Jewish Family Service of Santa
  Monica
1424, 4 Street, Room 303
Santa Monica, CA 90401
(213) 393-0732

Colorado
Jewish Family and Children's
  Service of Colorado
300 S. Dahlia Street
Denver, CO 80222
(303) 321-3115

Connecticut
Jewish Family and Children's
  Service
1020 Country Club Road
Waterbury, CT 06720
(203) 758-2441

Jewish Family Service
2370 Park Avenue
Bridgeport, CT 06604
(203) 366-5438

Jewish Family Service
152 Temple Street
New Haven, CT 06510
(203) 777-6641

FAMILY RESOURCES (*continued*)

Jewish Family Service
302 State Street
New London, CT 06320
(203) 444-6333

Jewish Family Service
1035 Newfield Avenue
Stamford, CT 06905
(203) 322-6938

Jewish Family Service
740 N. Main Street
West Hartford, CT 06117
(203) 236-1927

Delaware
Jewish Family Service
3717 Silverside Road
Wilmington, DE 19803
(302) 478-9411

Florida
Gulf Coast Jewish Family Service
8167 Eubow Lane N.
St. Petersburg, FL 33710
(813) 381-2373

Jewish Family and Children's
    Service
1790 S.W. 27 Avenue
Miami, FL 33145
(305) 445-0555

Jewish Family and Children's
    Service
2411 Okeechobee Boulevard
West Palm Beach, FL 33409
(305) 684-1991

Jewish Family and Children's
    Services
1415 LaSalle Street
Jacksonville, FL 32207
(904) 396-2941

Jewish Family Service of Broward
    County
2500 N. State Road
Fort Lauderdale, FL 33319
(305) 735-3394

and

Jewish Family Service of Broward
    County
1909 Harrison Street
Hollywood, FL 33020
(305) 927-9288

Jewish Family Services
Box 1508
851 N. Maitland Avenue
Maitland, FL 32751
(305) 645-5933

Tampa Jewish Social Service
2808 Horatio Street
Tampa, FL 33609
(813) 251-0083

Georgia
Social Service Committee of Jewish
    Council, Inc.
5111 Abercorn Street
Savannah, GA 31405
(912) 355-8111

Illinois
Jewish Family and Community
    Service
1 S. Franklin Street
Chicago, IL 60606
(312) 346-6700

Indiana
Jewish Community Services of the
    Jewish Federation
2939 Jewett Street
Highland, IN 46322
(219) 972-2250

Jewish Family and Children's
Services
1717 W. 86 Street, Suite 450
Indianapolis, IN 46260
(317) 872-6641

Iowa
Jewish Family Service
910 Polk Boulevard
Des Moines, IA 50312
(515) 277-6321

Kentucky
Jewish Family and Vocational
Service
3640 Dutchman's Lane
Louisville, KY 40205
(502) 452-6341

Louisiana
Jewish Family and Children's
Service
5342 St. Charles Avenue
New Orleans, LA 70175
(504) 899-1595

Shreveport Jewish Family and
Children's Services
2030 Line Avenue
Shreveport, LA 71104
(318) 221-4129

Maine
Jewish Family Services
57 Ashmont Street
Portland, ME 04103
(207) 773-7254

Maryland
Jewish Family and Children's
Service
5750 Park Heights Avenue
Baltimore, MD 21215
(301) 466-9200

Massachusetts
Jewish Family and Children's
Service
31 New Chardon Street
Boston, MA 02214
(617) 227-6641

Jewish Family Service
430 N. Canal Street
Lawrence, MA 01840
(617) 683-6711

Jewish Family Service
564 Loring Avenue
Salem, MA 01970
(617) 745-9760

Jewish Family Service
646 Salisbury Street
Worcester, MA 01609
(617) 755-3101

Jewish Family Service of Greater
Framingham
76 Salem End Road
Framingham, MA 01701
(617) 879-3303

Jewish Family Service of Greater
Springfield
184 Mill Street
Springfield, MA 01108
(413) 737-2601

Michigan
Jewish Family Service
24123 Greenfield Road
Southfield, MI 48075
(313) 559-1500

Minnesota
Jewish Family and Childrens'
Service
811 LaSalle Court Suite
Minneapolis, MN 55402
(612) 338-8771

Jewish Family Service
1546 St. Clair Avenue
St. Paul, MN 55105
(612) 698-0767

JEWISH
FAMILY
NETWORK

FAMILY RESOURCES (*continued*)

Missouri
Jewish Family and Children's
   Service
9385 Olive Boulevard
St. Louis, MO 63132
(314) 993-1000

Jewish Family and Children's
   Services
1115 E. 65 Street
Kansas City, MO 64131
(816) 333-1172

Nebraska
Jewish Family Service
333 S. 132 Street
Omaha, NB 68154
(402) 334-8200

Nevada
Jewish Family Service Agency
1555 Flamingo Road
Las Vegas, NV 89109
(702) 732-0304

New Jersey
Jewish Counseling and Service
   Agency
161 Milburn Avenue
Milburn, NJ 07041
(201) 467-3300

Jewish Family and Children's
   Service
601 Grand Avenue, Suite 502
Asbury Park, NJ 07712
(201) 774-6886

Jewish Family and Children's
   Service of North Jersey
1 Pike Drive
Wayne, NJ 07470
(201) 595-0111

Jewish Family and Counseling
   Services of Jersey City and
   Bayonne
1050 Kennedy Boulevard
Bayonne, NJ 07002
(201) 436-1299

Jewish Family Service
2393 W. Marlton Pike
Cherry Hill, NJ 08002
(609) 662-8611

Jewish Family Service
100 Menlo Park, Suite 101–102
Edison, NJ 08817
(201) 494-3923

Jewish Family Service
Jewish Federation of Community
   Services, Bergen County,
   N.J., Inc.
20 Banta Place
Hackensack, NJ 07601
(201) 488-8340

Jewish Family Service
2 S. Adelaide Avenue
Highland Park, NJ 08904
(201) 246-1905

Jewish Family Service
31 S. Surrey Avenue
Ventnor, NJ 08406
(609) 822-1108

Jewish Family Service Agency of
   Central New Jersey
500 Westfield Avenue
Elizabeth, NJ 07208
(201) 352-8375

Jewish Family Service of Greater
   Mercer County
51 Walter Street
Trenton, NJ 08628
(609) 882-9317

Jewish Family Service of Morris-
Sussex County
500 Route 10
Ledgewood, NJ 07852
(201) 584-1850

Jewish Family Service of Passaic-
Clifton and Vicinity
199 Scoles Avenue
Clifton, NJ 07012
(201) 777-7638

New York
Federation-Jewish Community
Council Service Center of the
Rockaways
20-38 Mott Avenue
Far Rockaway, NY 11691
(718) 327-0112

Jewish Board of Family and
Children's Services
120 W. 57 Street
New York, NY 10019
(212) 582-9100

Jewish Community Services of
Long Island
97-45 Queens Boulevard
Rego Park, NY 11374
(718) 896-9090

Jewish Family Service
96 Hawley Street
Binghamton, NY 13901
(607) 724-3141

Jewish Family Service
456 E. Main Street
Rochester, NY 14604
(716) 232-5440

Jewish Family Service Bureau, Inc.
601 Midtown Plaza
700 E. Water Street
Syracuse, NY 13210
(315) 474-4249

Jewish Family Service of Erie
County
615 Sidway Building
775 Main Street
Buffalo, NY 14203
(716) 853-9956

Jewish Family Services
930 Madison Avenue
Albany, NY 12208
(518) 482-8856

Westchester Jewish Community
Services
172 S. Broadway
White Plains, NY 10605
(914) 949-6761

Ohio
Jewish Family Service
305 W. Market Street, #102
Akron, OH 44313
(216) 967-3388

Jewish Family Service
1710 Section Road
Cincinnati, OH 45237
(513) 351-3680

Jewish Family Service
1175 College Avenue
Columbus, OH 43209
(614) 231-1890

Jewish Family Service
Division of the Jewish Federation
of Greater Dayton, Inc.
4501 Denlinger Road
Dayton, OH 45426
(513) 854-2944

Jewish Family Service
6525 Sylvania Avenue
Sylvania, OH 43560
(419) 885-2561

Jewish Family Service Association
of Cleveland
2060 S. Taylor Road
Cleveland, OH 44118
(216) 371-2600

FAMILY RESOURCES (*continued*)

Oregon
Jewish Family and Child Service
316 Mayer Building
Portland, OR 97205
(503) 226-7079

Pennsylvania
Jewish Family and Children's
  Service
234 McKee Place
Pittsburgh, PA 15213
(412) 683-4900

Jewish Family Service
3332 N. 2 Street
Harrisburg, PA 17110
(717) 233-1681

Jewish Family Service
Laurel and Hemlock Streets
Hazelton, PA 18201
(717) 454-3528

Jewish Family Service
1610 Spruce Street
Philadelphia, PA 19103
(215) 545-3290

Jewish Family Service of Jewish
  Federation
702 N. 22 Street
Allentown, PA 18104
(215) 435-3571 / 821-8722

Jewish Family Service of
  Lackawanna County
615 Jefferson Avenue
Scranton, PA 18510
(717) 344-1186

Jewish Family Service of Lower
  Bucks County
115 Mill Street
Bristol, PA 19007
(215) 788-9269

Rhode Island
Jewish Family and Children's
  Service
229 Waterman Avenue
Providence, RI 02906
(401) 331-1244

South Carolina
Charleston Jewish Social Service
1645 Millbrook Drive
P.O. Box 31298
Charleston, SC 29407
(803) 571-6565

Tennessee
Jewish Family Service
6560 Poplar Avenue
Memphis, TN 38138
(901) 767-5156

Jewish Family Service
3500 West End Avenue
Nashville, TN 37205
(615) 269-4927

Texas
Jewish Family Service
7800 Northaven Road
Dallas, TX 75230
(214) 696-6400

Jewish Family Service
405 Mardi Gras
El Paso, TX 79912
(915) 581-3256

Jewish Family Service
4131 S. Braeswood
Houston, TX 77125
(713) 667-9336

Jewish Family Service of San
  Antonio
8438 Ahern Drive
San Antonio, TX 78216
(512) 349-5481

Jewish Social Service
750 Everhart Road
Corpus Christi, TX 78411
(214) 855-6239

Virginia
Jewish Family Service of Tidewater
7300 Newport Avenue
Box 9503
Norfolk, VA 23505
(804) 489-3111

Jewish Family Services
Village Shopping Center
7027 Three Chopt Road, 2nd floor
Richmond, VA 23233

Washington
Jewish Family Service
1214 Boylston
Seattle, WA 98101
(206) 447-3240

Wisconsin
Jewish Family and Children's
    Service
1360 N. Prospect Avenue
Milwaukee, WI 53202
(414) 273-6515

Jewish Social Services of Madison,
    Inc.
310 N. Midvale Boulevard, #325
Madison, WI 53705
(608) 231-3426

Canada
Alberta
Jewish Family Service
5720 MacLeod Trail S.
Calgary, Alberta
Canada
(403) 252-8136

Jewish Family Services
606 McLeod Building
10136, 100 Street
Edmonton, Alberta T5J 0P1
Canada

British Columbia
Jewish Family Service Agency
950 W. 41 Avenue
Vancouver, British Columbia
    V5Z 2N7
Canada

Manitoba
Jewish Child and Family Service
304-956 Main Street
Winnipeg, Manitoba
Canada
(204) 589-6343

Ontario
Family Service Department of the
    Jewish Community Centre
1641 Ouelette Avenue
Windsor, Ontario N8X 1K9
Canada
(519) 254-7558

Jewish Family and Child Service
3101 Bathurst Street, 5th floor
Toronto, Ontario M6A 2A6
Canada
(416) 781-1592

Jewish Social Service Agency of
    Ottawa-Carleton
151 Chapel Street
Ottawa, Ontario K1N 7Y2
Canada
(613) 238-6351

Jewish Social Services
57 Delaware Avenue
Hamilton, Ontario L8M 1T6
Canada
(416) 528-8579

Quebec
Jewish Family Services of the Baron
    de Hirsch Institute
5151 Côte Ste. Catherine Road
Montreal, Quebec H3W 1M6
Canada
(514) 731-3882

FEDERATIONS

Alabama
Birmingham Jewish Federation
P.O. Box 9157
Birmingham, AL 35213
(205) 879-0416

Jewish Community Council
3960 Montclair Road
Birmingham, AL 35223
(205) 879-0411

Jewish Federation of Montgomery,
    Inc.
P.O. Box 1150
Montgomery, AL 36101
(205) 263-7674

Mobile Jewish Welfare Fund, Inc.
1 Office Park, #404C
Mobile, AL 36609
(205) 343-7197

Tri-Cities Jewish Federation
    Charities, Inc.
Route 7
Florence, AL 35623

Arizona
Greater Phoenix Jewish Federation
1718 W. Maryland Avenue
Phoenix, AZ 85015
(602) 249-1845

Jewish Community Council
102 N. Plumer
Tucson, AZ 85719
(602) 884-8921

Arkansas
Jewish Federation of Little Rock
221 Donaghey Building
Main at 7th
Little Rock, AR 72201
(501) 372-3571

California
Jewish Community Federation
    (sponsors United Jewish Welfare
    Fund)
3801 E. Willow Avenue
Long Beach, CA 90815
(213) 426-7601

Jewish Federation-Council of
    Greater Los Angeles
    (sponsors United Jewish Welfare
    Fund)
6505 Wilshire Boulevard
Los Angeles, CA 90048
(213) 852-1234

Jewish Federation of Greater San
    Jose
1777 Hamilton Avenue, Suite 201
San Jose, CA 95125
(408) 267-2770

Jewish Federation of Orange
    County
    (sponsors United Jewish Welfare
    Fund)
12181 Buaro
Garden Grove, CA 92640
(714) 530-6636

Jewish Federation of Sacramento
P.O. Box 254589
Sacramento, CA 95865
(916) 486-0906

Jewish Federation of the Greater
    East Bay
3245 Sheffield Avenue
Oakland, CA 94602
(415) 533-7462

Jewish Welfare Federation of Palm
    Springs—Desert Area
611 S. Palm Canyon Drive
Palm Springs, CA 92262
(714) 325-7281

Jewish Welfare Federation of San
Francisco, Marin and Sonoma
Counties and the Peninsula
121 Steuart Street
San Francisco, CA 94105
(415) 777-0411

San Bernardino United Jewish
Welfare Fund, Inc.
Congregation Emanu-el
3512 N. "E" Street
San Bernardino, CA 92405

Santa Barbara Jewish Federation
P.O. Box 6782
Santa Barbara, CA 93111
(805) 962-0770

Stockton Jewish Welfare Fund
5105 N. El Dorado Street
Stockton, CA 95207
(209) 477-9306

United Jewish Federation of San
Diego County
4797 Mercury Street
San Diego, CA 92111

Ventura County Jewish Council
Temple Beth Torah
7620 Foothill Road
Ventura, CA 93003
(805) 647-4181

Colorado
Allied Jewish Federation of Denver
300 S. Dahlia Street
Denver, CO 80222
(303) 321-3399

Connecticut
Greater Hartford Jewish Federation
333 Bloomfield Avenue
West Hartford, CT 06117
(203) 236-3278

Jewish Community Council of
Greater New London
302 State Street
New London, CT 06320
(203) 442-8062

Jewish Federation of Greater
Danbury
54 Main Street
Danbury, CT 06810
(203) 792-6353

Jewish Federation of Greater
Norwalk
Shorehaven Road
East Norwalk, CT 06855
(203) 853-3440

Jewish Federation of Waterbury,
Inc.
1020 Country Club Road
Waterbury, CT 06708
(203) 758-2441

Meriden Jewish Welfare Fund, Inc.
127 E. Main Street
Meriden, CT 06450
(203) 235-2581

New Haven Jewish Federation
1162 Chapel Street
New Haven, CT 06511
(203) 562-2137

United Jewish Council of Greater
Bridgeport, Inc.
4200 Park Avenue
Bridgeport, CT 06604
(203) 372-6504

United Jewish Federation
1035 Newfield Avenue
Stamford, CT 06905
(203) 322-6935

Delaware
Jewish Federation of Delaware, Inc.
101 Garden of Eden Road
Wilmington, DE 19803
(302) 478-6200

District of Columbia (Greater
Washington area)
United Jewish Appeal—Federation
of Greater Washington, Inc.
7900 Wisconsin Avenue
Bethesda, MD 20814
(301) 652-6480

FEDERATIONS (*continued*)

Florida

Greater Miami Jewish Federation,
  Inc.
4200 Biscayne Boulevard
Miami, FL 33137
(305) 576-4000

Jacksonville Jewish Federation
10829-1 Old St. Augustine Road
Jacksonville, FL 32223
(904) 262-2800

Jewish Federation of Greater Fort
  Lauderdale
8358 W. Oakland Park Boulevard
Ft. Lauderdale, FL 33321
(305) 748-8400

Jewish Federation of Greater
  Orlando
851 N. Maitland Avenue
P.O. Box 1508
Maitland, FL 32751
(305) 645-5933

Jewish Federation of Palm Beach
  County, Inc.
501 S. Flagler Drive, Suite 305
West Palm Beach, FL 33401
(305) 689-5900

Jewish Federation of Pinellas
  County, Inc.
302 S. Jupiter Avenue
Clearwater, FL 33515
(813) 446-1033

Jewish Federation of South
  Broward, Inc.
2719 Hollywood Boulevard
Hollywood, FL 33020
(305) 921-8810

Pensacola Federated Jewish
  Charities
1320 E. Lee Street
Pensacola, FL 32503
(904) 438-1464

Sarasota Jewish Federation
2917 Ringling Boulevard
Sarasota, FL 33577
(813) 365-4410

South County Jewish Federation
336 N.W. Spanish River Boulevard
Boca Raton, FL 33431
(305) 368-2737

Tampa Jewish Federation
2808 Horatio
Tampa, FL 33609
(813) 875-1618

Georgia

Atlanta Jewish Federation, Inc.
1753 Peachtree Road, N.E.
Atlanta, GA 30309
(404) 873-1661

Augusta Jewish Federation
P.O. Box 3251—Sibley Road
Augusta, GA 30904
(404) 736-1818

Jewish Welfare Federation of
  Columbus, Inc.
P.O. Box 6313
Columbus, GA 31907
(404) 563-4766

Savannah Jewish Council
5111 Abecorn Street
Savannah, GA 31405
(912) 355-8111

Idaho

Southern Idaho Jewish Welfare
  Fund
1776 Commerce Avenue
Boise, ID 83705
(208) 344-3574

Illinois

Central Illinois Jewish Federation
3100 N. Knoxville, Suite 17
Peoria, IL 61603
(309) 686-0611

Decatur Jewish Federation
c/o Temple B'nai Abraham
1326 West Eldorado
Decatur, IL 62522
(217) 429-5740

Elgin Area Jewish Welfare Chest
330 Division Street
Elgin, IL 60120
(312) 741-5656

Champaign-Urbana Federation
503 East John Street
Champaign, IL 61820
(217) 367-9872

Jewish Federation of Metropolitan
   Chicago
1 S. Franklin Street
Chicago, IL 60606
(312) 346-6700

Jewish Federation of Peoria
3100 N. Knoxville, Suite 17
Peoria, IL 61603
(309) 686-0611

Jewish Federation of Southern
   Illinois
6464 W. Main, Suite 7A
Belleville, IL 62223
(618) 398-6100

Jewish Federation of the Quad
   Cities
224, 18 Street, Suite 511
Rock Island, IL 61201
(309) 793-1300

Jewish Federation of Volusia and
   Flagler Counties, Inc.
P.O. Box 5434
504 Main Street
Daytona, IL 32018
(904) 255-6260

Jewish United Fund of Metropolitan Chicago
(See Jewish Federation of Metropolitan Chicago, above)

Joliet Jewish Welfare Chest
250 N. Midland Avenue
Joliet, IL 60435
(815) 741-4600

Rockford Jewish Community
   Council
1500 Parkview Avenue
Rockford, IL 61107
(815) 399-5497

Springfield Jewish Federation
730 E. Vine Street
Springfield, IL 62703
(217) 528-3446

Indiana
Evansville Jewish Community
   Council, Inc.
P.O. Box 5026
Evansville, IN 47715
(812) 476-1571

Federated Jewish Charities
P.O. Box 676
Lafayette, IN 47902
(317) 742-9081

Fort Wayne Jewish Federation
227 E. Washington Boulevard
Fort Wayne, IN 46802
(219) 422-8566

The Jewish Federation, Inc.
2939 Jewett Street
Highland, IN 46322
(219) 972-2251

Jewish Federation of St. Joseph
   Valley
804 Sherland Building
South Bend, IN 46601
(219) 233-1164

FEDERATIONS (*continued*)

Jewish Welfare Federation, Inc.
615 N. Alabama Street
Indianapolis, IN 46204
(317) 637-2473

Michigan City United Jewish
　　Welfare Fund
2800 Franklin Street
Michigan City, IN 46360
(219) 874-4477

Muncie Jewish Welfare Fund
c/o Beth El Temple
P.O. Box 2792
Muncie, IN 47302
(317) 284-1497

Iowa
Jewish Federation
525, 14 Street
Sioux City, IA 51105
(712) 258-0618

Jewish Federation of Greater
　　Des Moines
910 Polk Boulevard
Des Moines, IA 50312
(515) 277-6321

Jewish Welfare Fund of Linn
　　County
115, 7 Street, S.E.
Cedar Rapids, IA 52401
(319) 366-3553

Waterloo Jewish Federation
c/o Congregation Sons of Jacob
411 Mitchell Avenue
Waterloo, IA 50702

Kansas
Mid-Kansas Jewish Welfare
　　Federation, Inc.
400 N. Woodlawn, Suite 8
Wichita, KS 67206
(316) 686-4741

Topeka–Lawrence Jewish
　　Federations
3237 S.W. Westover Road
Topeka, KS 60604
(913) 357-4244

Kentucky
Jewish Community Federation of.
　　Louisville, Inc.
P.O. Box 33035
3630 Dutchman's Lane
Louisville, KY 40232
(502) 451-8840

Louisiana
Jewish Federation of Greater Baton
　　Rouge
P.O. Box 80827
Baton Rouge, LA 70898
(504) 769-0561

Jewish Federation of Greater New
　　Orleans
1539 Jackson Avenue
New Orleans, LA 70130
(504) 525-0673

The Jewish Welfare Federation and
　　Community Council of Central
　　Louisiana
1261 Heyman Lane
Alexandria, LA 71301
(381) 442-1264

Shreveport Jewish Federation
2030 Line Avenue
Shreveport, LA 71104
(318) 221-4129

United Jewish Charities of North-
　　east Louisiana
2400 Orrel Place
Monroe, LA 71201
(318) 387-0730

Maine
Jewish Community Council
28 Somerset Street
Bangor, ME 04401

Jewish Federation Community
   Council of Southern Maine
57 Ashmont Street
Portland, ME 04103
(207) 773-7254

Lewiston–Auburn Jewish
   Federation
74 Bradman Street
Auburn, ME 04210
(207) 786-4201

Maryland
Annapolis Jewish Welfare Fund
601 Ridgley Avenue
Annapolis, MD 21401

Associated Jewish Charities and
   Welfare Fund, Inc.
101 W. Mt. Royal Avenue
Baltimore, MD 21201
(301) 727-4828

Massachusetts
Combined Jewish Appeal of
   Holyoke
378 Maple Street
Holyoke, MA 01040
(413) 534-3369

Combined Jewish Philanthropies
   of Greater Boston, Inc.
72 Franklin Street
Boston, MA 02110
(617) 542-8080

Greater Framingham Jewish
   Federation
76 Salem End Road
Framingham Centre, MA 01701
(617) 879-3301

Haverhill United Jewish Appeal,
   Inc.
514 Main Street
Haverhill, MA 01830
(617) 372-4481

Jewish Federation of the Berkshires
235 East Street
Pittsfield, MA 01201
(413) 442-4360

Jewish Community Council of
   Greater Lawrence
580 Haverhill Street
Lawrence, MA 01841
(617) 686-4157

Jewish Federation of Fitchburg
40 Boutelle Street
Fitchburg, MA 01420
(617) 342-2227

Jewish Federation of Greater New
   Bedford, Inc.
467 Hawthorn Street
North Dartmouth, MA 02747
(617) 997-7471

Jewish Federation of the North
   Shore, Inc.
4 Community Road
Marblehead, MA 01945
(617) 598-1810

Leominster Jewish Community
   Council, Inc.
268 Washington St.
Leominster, MA 01453
(617) 534-6121

Springfield Jewish Federation, Inc.
1160 Dickinson
Springfield, MA 01108
(413) 737-4313

Worcester Jewish Federation, Inc.
633 Salisbury Street
Worcester, MA 01609
(617) 756-1543

FEDERATIONS (*continued*)

Michigan

Flint Jewish Federation
120 W. Kearsley Street
Flint, MI 48502
(313) 767-5922

Greater Lansing Jewish Welfare
    Federation
P.O. Box 975
East Lansing, MI 48823
(517) 351-3197

Jewish Community Fund of Grand
    Rapids
1410 Pontiac, S.E.
Grand Rapids, MI 49506
(616) 452-6619

Jewish Welfare Federation of
    Detroit
Fred M. Butzel Memorial Building
163 Madison
Detroit, MI 48226
(313) 965-3939

Kalamazoo Jewish Federation
c/o Congregation of Moses
2501 Stadium Drive
Kalamazoo, MI 49008
(616) 349-8396

Northeastern Michigan Jewish
    Welfare Federation
1125 Orchard Road
Essexville, MI 48732
(517) 893-7779

Saginaw Jewish Welfare Federation
1424 S. Washington Avenue
Saginaw, MI 48601
(517) 753-5230

Minnesota

Jewish Federation and Community
    Council
1602 E. 2 Street
Duluth, MN 55812
(218) 724-8857

Minneapolis Federation for Jewish
    Services
811 La Salle Avenue
Minneapolis, MN 55402
(612) 339-7491

United Jewish Fund and Council
790 South Cleveland
St. Paul, MN 55116
(612) 690-1707

Mississippi

Jewish Welfare Federation
1210 Washington Street
Vicksburg, MS 39180
(601) 636-7531

Jackson Jewish Welfare Fund
P.O. Box 123929
Jackson, MS 39211
(601) 944-0607

Missouri

Jewish Federation of Greater
    Kansas City
25 E. 12 Street
Kansas City, MO 64106
(816) 421-5808

Jewish Federation of St. Louis
12 Millstone Campus Drive
St. Louis, MO 63146
(314) 432-0020

United Jewish Fund of St. Joseph
509 Woodcrest Drive
St. Joseph, MO 64506
(816) 279-7154

Nebraska

Jewish Federation of Omaha
333 S. 132 Street
Omaha, NB 68154
(402) 334-8200

Lincoln Jewish Welfare Federation,
Inc.
P.O. Box 80014
Lincoln, NB 68501
(402) 464-0602

Nevada
Jewish Federation of Las Vegas
1030 E. Twain Avenue
Las Vegas, NV 89109
(702) 732-0556

New Hampshire
Jewish Federation of Greater
Manchester
698 Beech Street
Manchester, NH 03104
(603) 627-7679

New Jersey
Bayonne Jewish Community
Council
1050 Kennedy Boulevard
Bayonne, NJ 07002
(201) 436-6900

Federation of Jewish Agencies of
Atlantic County
5321 Atlantic Avenue
Ventnor City, NJ 08406
(609) 822-7122

United Jewish Federation of
Metro-West
60 Glenwood Avenue
East Orange, NJ 07017
(201) 673-6800

Jewish Federation of Central New
Jersey
Green Lane
Union, NJ 07083
(201) 351-5060

Jewish Federation of Cumberland
County
629 Wood Street
Vineland, NJ 08360
(609) 696-4445

Jewish Federation of Greater
Monmouth County
100 Grant Avenue
Deal Park, NJ 07723
(201) 531-6200

Jewish Federation of Greater
Passaic-Clifton
199 Scoles Avenue
Clifton, N.J. 07012
(201) 777-7031

Jewish Federation of Northern
Middlesex County
1775 Oaktree Road
Edison, NJ 08820
(201) 494-3920

Jewish Federation of North Jersey
1 Pike Drive
Wayne, NJ 07470
(201) 595-0555

Jewish Federation of Raritan
Valley
2 S. Adelaide Avenue
Highland Park, NJ 08904
(201) 246-1905

Jewish Federation of Somerset
County
2 Division Street
Sommerville, NJ 08876
(201) 725-6994

Jewish Federation of Southern
New Jersey
2393 W. Marlton Pike
Cherry Hill, NJ 08002
(609) 665-6100

Ocean County Jewish Federation
301 Madison Avenue
Lakewood, NJ 08701
(201) 363-0530

United Jewish Appeal
604 Bergen Avenue
Jersey City, NJ 07304
(201) 433-4200

FEDERATIONS *(continued)*

United Jewish Federation of Bergen
  County
111 Kinderkamack Road
River Edge, NJ 07661
(201) 488-6800

New Mexico
Jewish Community Council of
  Albuquerque, Inc.
12800 Lomas N.E.
Albuquerque, NM 87112
(505) 292-1061

New York
Elmira Jewish Welfare Fund, Inc.
P.O. Box 3087
Grandview Road
Elmira, NY 14905
(607) 734-8122

Federation of Jewish Philanthropies
  of New York
130 E. 59 Street
New York, NY 10022
(212) 980-1000

Glens Falls Jewish Welfare Fund
P.O. Box 177
Glens Falls, NY 12801
(518) 792-6438

Greater Albany Jewish Federation
350 Whitehall Road
Albany, NY 12208
(518) 459-8000

Jewish Community Council of
  Utica, N.Y., Inc.
2310 Oneida Street
Utica, NY 13501
(315) 733-2343

Jewish Community Federation of
  Rochester
441 East Avenue
Rochester, NY 14607
(716) 461-0490

The Jewish Federation of Broome
  County
500 Clubhouse Road
Binghamton, NY 13903
(607) 724-2332

Jewish Federation of Greater
  Buffalo, Inc.
787 Delaware Avenue
Buffalo, NY 14209
(716) 886-7750

Jewish Federation of Greater
  Kingston, Inc.
159 Green Street
Kingston, NY 12401
(914) 338-8131

Jewish Federation of Greater
  Schenectady
2565 Balltown Road
Schenectady, NY 12309
(518) 393-1136

Jewish Federation of Orange
  County
360 Powell Avenue
Newburgh, NY 12550
(914) 562-7860

Jewish Federation of Niagara Falls,
  N.Y., Inc.
Temple Beth Israel Building #5
College and Madison Avenue
Niagara Falls, NY 14305
(716) 284-4575

Jewish Welfare Fund of Dutchess
  County
110 Grand Avenue
Poughkeepsie, NY 12603
(914) 471-9811

Jewish Welfare Fund of Hudson,
N.Y., Inc.
Joslen Boulevard
Hudson, NY 12534
(518) 828-6848

Syracuse Jewish Federation, Inc.
P.O. Box 510
2223 E. Genesee
Syracuse, NY 13214
(315) 422-4104

Troy Jewish Community Council,
Inc.
2500, 21 Street
Troy, NY 12180
(518) 274-0700

North Carolina
Charlotte Jewish Federation
P.O. Box 13369
Charlotte. NC 28211
(704) 372-4688

Durham-Chapel Hill Jewish
Federation and Community
Council
1509 Crestwood Lane
Chapel Hill, NC 27514
(919) 933-6810

Federated Jewish Charities of
Asheville, Inc.
236 Charlotte Street
Asheville, NC 28801
(704) 253-0701

Greensboro Jewish Federation
713A N. Green Street
Greensboro, NC 27401
(919) 272-3189

High Point Jewish Federation
1308 Long Creek
High Point, NC 27260
(919) 431-7101

Winston-Salem Jewish Community
Council
471 Archer Road
Winston-Salem, NC 27106
(919) 773-2532

Ohio
Akron Jewish Community
Federation
750 White Pond Drive
Akron, OH 44320
(216) 867-7850

Columbus Jewish Federation
1175 College Avenue
Columbus, OH 43209
(614) 237-7686

Federated Jewish Charities of Lima
District
2417 W. Market Street
Lima, OH 45805
(419) 224-8941

Jewish Community Council
P.O. Box 472
Steubenville, OH 43952
(614) 282-9031

Jewish Community Federation of
Canton
2631 Harvard Avenue, N.W.
Canton, OH 44709
(216) 452-6444

Jewish Community Federation of
Cleveland
1750 Euclid Avenue
Cleveland, OH 44115
(216) 566-9200

Jewish Federation
3893 E. Market Street
Warren, OH 44483

Jewish Federation of Cincinnati
1811 Losantiville
Suite 320
Cincinnati, OH 45237
(513) 351-3800

Jewish Federation of Greater
Dayton
4501 Denlinger Road
Dayton, OH 45426
(513) 854-4150

FEDERATIONS *(continued)*

Jewish Federation of Youngstown,
   Ohio, Inc.
P.O. Box 449
Youngstown, OH 44501
(216) 746-3251

Jewish Welfare Federation of
   Toledo, Inc.
6505 Sylvania Avenue
Sylvania, OH 43560
(419) 885-4461

Oklahoma
Jewish Federation of Greater
   Oklahoma City
3022 N.W. Expressway #116
Oklahoma City, OK 73112
(405) 949-0111

Jewish Federation of Tulsa
2021 East 71st Street
Tulsa, OK 74136
(918) 495-1100

Oregon
Jewish Federation of Portland
6651 S.W. Capitol Highway
Portland, OR 97219

Pennsylvania
Butler Jewish Welfare Fund
148 Haverford Drive
Butler, PA 16001
(412) 287-3814

Federation of Jewish Agencies of
   Greater Philadelphia
226 S. 16 Street
Philadelphia, PA 19102
(215) 893-5600

Federation of Jewish Philanthropies
1308, 17 Street
Altoona, PA 16601
(814) 944-4072

Jewish Community Council
Laurel and Hemlock Streets
Hazelton, PA 18201
(717) 454-3528

Jewish Community Council of
   Easton, Pa., and Vicinity
16th and Bushkill Streets
Easton, PA 18042
(215) 253-4235

Jewish Community Council of Erie
701 G. Daniel Baldwin Building
1001 State Street
Erie, PA 16501
(814) 455-4474

Jewish Federation of Allentown
702 North 22nd
Allentown, PA 18104
(215) 435-3571

Jewish Federation of Delaware
   Valley
20-28 N. Pennsylvania Avenue
Morrisville, PA 19067
(215) 736-8022

Jewish Federation of Greater
   Wilkes-Barre
60 S. River Street
Wilkes-Barre, PA 18701
(717) 824-4646

Jewish Federation of Lower Bucks
   County
1 Oxford Valley, Suite 602
Langhorne, PA 19047
(215) 757-0250

Jewish Federation of Reading, Pa.,
   Inc.
1700 City Line Street
Reading, PA 19604
(215) 921-2766

Scranton-Lackawanna Jewish
   Council
601 Jefferson Avenue
Scranton, PA 18510
(717) 961-2300

Shenango Valley Jewish Federation
840 Highland Road
Sharon, PA 16146
(412) 346-4754

Untied Jewish Appeal of New
  Castle, Pa.
3218 Plank Road
New Castle, PA 16105
(412) 654-7438

United Jewish Charities
2300 Mahantongo Street
Pottsville, PA 17901
(717) 622-5890

United Jewish Community Council
  of Lancaster, Pa., Inc.
2120 Oregon Pike
Lancaster, PA 17601
(717) 569-7352

United Jewish Community of
  Greater Harrisburg
100 Vaughn Street
Harrisburg, PA 17110
(717) 236-9555

United Jewish Federation
406 W. Main Street
c/o Jewish Community Center
Uniontown, PA 15401
(412) 438-4681

United Jewish Federation of
  Greater Pittsburgh
234 McKee Place
Pittsburgh, PA 15213
(412) 681-8000

United Jewish Federation of
  Johnstown
1334 Luzerne Street
Johnstown, PA 15905
(814) 255-1447

York Council of Jewish Charities,
  Inc.
120 E. Market Street
York, PA 17401
(717) 843-0918

Rhode Island
Jewish Federation of Rhode Island
130 Sessions Street
Providence, RI 02906
(401) 421-4111

South Carolina
Charleston Jewish Federation
1645 Raoul Wallenberg Boulevard
Charleston, SC 29407
(803) 571-6565

Columbia United Jewish Welfare
  Federation
4540 Trenholm Road
Columbia, SC 29206
(803) 787-2023

South Dakota
Jewish Welfare Fund
National Reserve Building
Sioux Falls, SD 57102
(605) 446-2880

Tennessee
Chattanooga Jewish Welfare
  Federation
5326 Lynnland Terrace
Chattanooga, TN 37411
(615) 894-1317

Jewish Federation of Nashville and
  Middle Tennessee
801 Perry Warner Boulevard
Nashville, TN 37205
(615) 356-3242

Jewish Welfare Fund, Inc.
6800 Deane Hill Drive
P.O. Box 10882
Knoxville, TN 37919
(615) 693-5837

FEDERATIONS (*continued*)

Memphis Jewish Federation
6560 Poplar Avenue
P.O. Box 38268
Memphis, TN 38138
(901) 767-7100

Texas
Beaumont Jewish Federation of
   Texas, Inc.
P.O. Box 1981
Beaumont, TX 77704
(713) 833-5427

Corpus Christi Jewish Community
   Council
750 Everhart Road
Corpus Christi, TX 78411
(512) 855-6239

Federation of Jewish Welfare
   Funds
P.O. Box 934
Tyler, TX 75710

Galveston County Jewish Welfare
   Association
P.O. Box 146
Galveston, TX 77553
(409) 744-8295

Jewish Community Council of
   Austin
11713 Jollyville Road
Austin, TX 78759
(512) 331-1144

Jewish Federation of El Paso, Inc.
405 Mardi Gras
P.O. Box 12097
El Paso, TX 79912
(915) 584-4437

Jewish Federation of Fort Worth
   and Tarrant County
6801 Dan Danciger Road
Fort Worth, TX 76133
(817) 292-3081

Jewish Federation of Greater Dallas
7800 Northaven Road, Suite A
Dallas, TX 75230
(214) 369-3313

Jewish Federation of Greater
   Houston, Inc.
5601 S. Braeswood Boulevard
Houston, TX 77096
(713) 729-7000

Jewish Federation of San Antonio
8434 Ahern Drive
San Antonio, TX 78216
(512) 341-8234

Jewish Welfare Council of Waco
P.O. Box 8031
Waco, TX 76710
(817) 776-3740

Utah
United Jewish Council and Salt
   Lake Jewish Welfare Fund
2416 E. 1700 S.
Salt Lake City, UT 84108
(801) 581-0098

Virginia
Jewish Community Council
P.O. Box 1074
Roanoake, VA 24005
(703) 774-2828

Jewish Community Federation of
   Richmond, Inc.
5403 Monument Avenue
P.O. Box 8237
Richmond, VA 23226
(804) 288-0045

Jewish Federation of Newport
   News–Hampton, Inc.
2700 Spring Road
P.O. Box 6680
Newport News, VA 23606
(804) 595-5544

Portsmouth Jewish Community
Council
Dominion National Bank Building,
Room 430
Portsmouth, VA 23704
(804) 393-2557

United Jewish Federation, Inc., of
Norfolk and Virginia Beach, Va.
7300 Newport Avenue
P.O. Box 9776
Norfolk, VA 23505
(804) 489-8040

Washington
Jewish Community Council of
Spokane
521 Parkade Plaza
Spokane, WA 99201
(509) 838-4261

Jewish Federation of Greater
Seattle
Securities Building, Suite 5101
Seattle, WA 98101
(206) 622-8211

West Virginia
Federated Jewish Charities
P.O. Box 947
Huntington, WV 25713
(304) 523-9326

Federated Jewish Charities of
Charleston, Inc.
P.O. Box 1613
Charleston, WV 25326
(304) 346-7500

United Jewish Federation of
Ohio Valley, Inc.
20 Hawthorne Court
Wheeling, WV 26003

Wisconsin
Jewish Welfare Council of
Sheboygan
1404 North Avenue
Sheboygan, WI 53081

Kenosha Jewish Welfare Fund
6537 Seventh Avenue
Kenosha, WI 53140
(414) 658-8635

Madison Jewish Community
Council
310 N. Midvale Boulevard,
Suite 325
Madison, WI 53705
(608) 231-3426

Milwaukee Jewish Federation, Inc.
1360 N. Prospect Avenue
Milwaukee, WI 53202
(414) 271-8338

Racine Jewish Welfare Board
944 Main Street
Racine, WI 53403
(414) 633-7093

United Jewish Charities of
Appleton
3131 N. Meade Street
Appleton, WI 54911
(414) 733-1848

Canada
Allied Jewish Community Services
5151 Côte Ste. Catherine Road
Montreal, Quebec H3W 1M6
Canada
(514) 735-3541

Calgary Jewish Community Council
1607, 90 Avenue, S.W.
Calgary, Alberta T2V 4V7
Canada
(403) 253-8600

FEDERATIONS *(continued)*

Edmonton Jewish Community
 Council, Inc.
7200, 156 Street
Edmonton, Alberta T5R 1X3
Canada
(403) 487-5120

Hamilton Jewish Federation
57 Delaware Avenue
Hamilton, Ontario L8M 1T6
Canada
(416) 528-8570

Jewish Community Council
1641 Ouellette Avenue
Windsor, Ontario N8X 1K9
Canada
(519) 254-7558

Jewish Community Council of
 Ottawa
151 Chapel Street
Ottawa, Ontario K1N 7Y2
Canada
(613) 232-7306

Jewish Community Fund and
 Council of Vancouver
950 W. 41 Avenue
Vancouver, British Columbia
 V5Z 2N7
Canada
(604) 266-8371

London Jewish Community
 Council
536 Huron Street #24
London, Ontario N5Y 4J5
Canada
(519) 673-3310

United Jewish Welfare Fund of
 St. Catharines
c/o Jewish Community Centre
Church Street
St. Catharines, Ontario
Canada

Winnipeg Jewish Community
 Council
370 Hargrave Street
Winnipeg, Manitoba R3B 2K1
Canada
(204) 943-0406

FILMS (SOURCES)

Alden Films
7820, 20 Street
Brooklyn, NY 11214
(718) 331-1045

American Jewish Committee
165 E. 56 Street
New York, NY 10022
(212) 751-4000

Audio Brandon Films
34 MacQueston Parkway South
Mount Vernon, NY 10550
(914) 664-5051

Ilana Bar-Din
c/o Film Arts Foundation
490, 2 Street
San Francisco, CA 94107

Cine Information
419 Park Avenue S.
New York, NY 10016
(212) 686-9897

International Women's Film
   Project
3518, 35 Street, NW
Washington, DC 20017
(202) 996-0260

Jewish Media Service
Jewish Welfare Board
15 E. 26 Street
New York, NY 10010
(212) 532-4949

National Association of Lesbian and
   Gay Filmmakers
301 W. 19 Street
New York, NY 10011
(212) 691-7497

National Center for Jewish Film
Lown Building, #102
Brandeis University
Waltham, MA 02254
(617) 899-7044

National Film Board of Canada
1251 Avenue of the Americas
New York, NY 10036
(212) 586-5131

New Day Films
P.O. Box 315
Franklin Lakes, NJ 07417

Pacific Film Archives
(See Libraries and Archives)

Pacific Street Films
22, 1 Street
Brooklyn, NY 11231
(718) 875-9722

Phoenix Films
470 Park Avenue S.
New York, NY 10016
(212) 684-5910

Rutenberg and Everett Yiddish
   Film Library
Lown Building, #102
Brandeis University
Waltham, MA 02254

United Synagogue of America
Department of Education
155 Fifth Avenue
New York, NY 10010
(212) 260-8450

Women Make Movies, Inc.
100 Fifth Avenue
New York, NY 10011
(212) 929-6477

World Zionist Organization
Department of Education and
   Culture
515 Park Avenue
New York, NY 10022
(212) 752-0600

(See also Media)

FINANCIAL AID

Arizona
Hebrew Free Loan Association
4005 Palomar Drive
Tucson, AZ 85711
(602) 325-3403

Jewish Free Loan Association
1718 W. Maryland
Phoenix, AZ 85015

California
Federation Free Loan Association
3801 E. Willow Avenue
Long Beach, CA 90815
(213) 427-7916

Free Loan Fund
3245 Sheffield Avenue
Oakland, CA 94602
(415) 532-6314

Gay Academic Union Scholarship
Fund
P.O. Box 927
Hollywood, CA 90028

Hebrew Free Loan Association of
San Francisco
703 Market Street
San Francisco, CA 94103
(415) 982-3177

Jess Abramovitz Student Loan
Funds
3245 Sheffield Avenue
Oakland, CA 94602
(415) 533-7462

Jewish Free Loan Association
6505 Wilshire Boulevard
Los Angeles, CA 90048

Connecticut
Hebrew Free Loan
55 Lexington Avenue
Waterbury, CT 06710

Hebrew Free Loan Association
360 Autumn Ridge Road
Bridgeport, CT 06611

District of Columbia
Hebrew Free Loan Association
4501 Connecticut Avenue
Washington, DC 20008
(301) 953-2960

Florida
Greater Miami Hebrew Free Loan
Association
1545 Alton Road
Miami Beach, FL 33139
(305) 532-5421

Georgia
Free Loan Agency (Hebrew
Gemilath Chesed Society)
5111 Abercorn Street
Savannah, GA 31405

Maine
Hebrew Free Loan
341 Cumberland Avenue
Portland, ME 04101

Maryland
Hebrew Free Loan Association
5752 Park Heights Avenue
Baltimore, MD 21215
(301) 358-4406

Massachusetts
Hebrew Free Loan Society
2 Atwater Street
Worcester, MA 01602

Michigan
Hebrew Free Loan Association
21550 W. 12 Mile Road
Southfield, MI 48076
(313) 559-1500

New Jersey
Hebrew Free Loan Association
c/o Temple Emanuel
151 E. 33 Street
Paterson, NJ 07514

Hebrew Free Loan Association
1418 W. State Street
Trenton, NJ 08618
(609) 393-8256

New York
Hebrew Benevolent Loan
    Association
787 Delaware Avenue
Buffalo, NY 14209

Hebrew Free Loan Society
205 E. 42 Street
New York, NY 10017
(212) 725-8444

Jewish Foundation for the
    Education of Women
120 W. 57 Street
New York, NY 10019
(212) 265-2565

Ohio
Free Loan Agency
Jewish Family Service
5151 Monroe Street
Toledo, OH 43623

Frances Grabow Goldman
    Memorial Fellowship
    (in advanced Judaic studies)
Dean, Graduate Studies
Hebrew Union College–Jewish
    Institute of Religion
3101 Clifton Avenue
Cincinnati, OH 45220

Hebrew Free Loan Association
338 The Arcade
Cleveland, OH 44114
(216) 771-7349

Oklahoma
Hebrew Free Loan Committee
Jewish Community Council
3314 E. 51 Street
Tulsa, OK 74135

Pennsylvania
A. B. Cohen Free Loan Society
601 Jefferson Avenue
Scranton, PA 18510

Gus and Lena Weinberger
    Academic Scholarship Fund
601 Jefferson Avenue
Scranton, PA 18510

Texas
Hebrew Free Loan
701 N. Chaparral
Corpus Christi, TX 78401

Hebrew Loan Association
5330 W. Bellfort, #3
Houston, TX 77035

Hebrew Free Loan Association
431 Isom Road #117
San Antonio, TX 78216

Virginia
Free Loan Society
P.O. Box 537
Newport News, VA 23607

Hebrew Ladies Charity Society
    (Free Burial and Loan Service)
908 Armfield Circle
Norfolk, VA 23505
(804) 489-2947

Canada
Hebrew Free Loan Association
5775 Victoria Avenue
Montreal, Quebec
Canada

(*See also* Charity)

GENERAL JEWISH ORGANIZATIONS

American Jewish Committee
165 E. 56 Street
New York, NY 10022
(212) 751-4000

American Jewish Congress
15 E. 84 Street
New York, NY 10028
(212) 879-4500

Anti-Defamation League of
  B'nai B'rith
823 United Nations Plaza
New York, NY 10017
(212) 490-2525

Council of Jewish Federations
575 Lexington Avenue
New York, NY 10022
(212) 751-1311

(*See* Federations *for individual
cities*)

Jewish Welfare Board
15 E. 26 Street
New York, NY 10010
(212) 532-4949

United Jewish Appeal–Federation
  of Jewish Philanthropies
  Campaign, Inc.
130 E. 59 Street
New York, NY 10022
(212) 980-1000

United Jewish Appeal of Greater
  New York, Inc.
130 E. 59 Street
New York, NY 10022
(212) 980-1000

HAVUROT

Federation of Reconstructionist
  Congregations and Havurot
270 W. 89 Street
New York, NY 10024
(212) 496-2960

National Havurah Coordinating
  Committee
  (for referrals to individual
  havurot in your area)
270 W. 89 Street
New York, NY 10024
(212) 496-2960

(*See also* Synagogues; Women's
  Prayer and Study Groups)

HEALTH

American Cancer Society
777 Third Avenue
New York, NY
(212) 371-2900

American Physicians for Human
  Rights
also Bay Area Physicians for Human
  Rights
P.O. Box 14546
San Francisco, CA 94114
(415) 673-3189

Berkeley Women's Center Health
  Collective
2908 Ellsworth
Berkeley, CA 94704
(415) 843-6194

California Lesbian Physicians
  Association
1815 Chestnut
Berkeley, CA 94702

Canadian Abortion Rights Action
  League
Box 935, Station Q
Toronto, Ontario M4T 2P1
Canada
(415) 961-1507

Center for Science in the Public
  Interest
1755 S Street, NW
Washington, DC 20009
(202) 332-9110

Chelsea Women's Health Team
188 Eighth Avenue
New York, NY 10011
(212) 243-9336

Coalition for the Medical Rights
  of Women
1638B Haight Street
San Francisco, CA 94117
(415) 621-8030

Committee for Abortion Rights and
  Against Sterilization Abuse
  (CARASA)
17 Murray Street, 5th floor
New York, NY 10007
(212) 964-1350

Elizabeth Blackwell Health Center
  for Women
112 S. 16 Street
Philadelphia, PA 19102
(215) 563-7577

Emma Goldman Clinic
715 North Dodge
Iowa City, IA 52240
(319) 337-2111

Feminist Health Works
487A Hudson Street
New York, NY 10014
(212) 929-7886

Feminist Women's Health Center
540 West Brevard Street, Suite C
Tallahassee, FL 32301
(904) 224-9600

Guttman Breast Diagnostic
  Institute
3 W. 35 Street
New York, NY 10001
(212) 689-9797

HealthRight
c/o Health/PAC
17 Murray Street
New York, NY 10007

Herpes Resource Center
c/o American Social Health
  Association
P.O. Box 100
Palo Alto, CA 94302

Hot Flash
(*See* Periodicals)

HEALTH (*continued*)

Jewish Vocational Service Nutrition
    Program
920 Alton Road
Miami Beach, FL 33139
(305) 673-5106

Lesbians in Health Care
P.O. Box 1278
Rockefeller Station
New York, NY 10185
(212) 787-4101

National Abortion Rights Action
    League (NARAL)
825, 15 Street, N.W.
Washington, DC 20005
(202) 317-7774

National Foundation for Jewish
    Genetic Diseases
609 Fifth Avenue, Suite 1200
New York, NY 10017
(212) 753-5155

National Women's Health Network
224, 7 Street, S.E.
Washington, DC 20003
(202) 543-9222

New Hampshire Feminist Health
    Center
38 S. Main Street
Concord, NH 03301
(603) 225-2739

Planned Parenthood
810 Seventh Avenue
New York, NY 10019
(212) 541-7800

Post-Mastectomy Counseling
    Program
92nd Street YM/YWHA
1395 Lexington Avenue
New York, NY 10028
(212) 427-6000

Post-Mastectomy Program Guides
National Council of Jewish Women
15 E. 26 Street
New York, NY 10010

Pregnancy Loss Peer Counseling
    and Telephone Counseling
Lamaze Prepared Childbirth Classes
Jewish Women's Resource Center
9 E. 69 Street
New York, NY 10021
(212) 535-5900

St. Mark's Women's Health
    Collective
    (for lesbians, older women, and
    women-identified women)
9 Second Avenue
New York, NY 10003
(212) 228-7482

Santa Cruz Women's Health
    Center
250 Locust Street
Santa Cruz, CA 95060
(408) 427-3500

HOTLINES

Abused Women's Aid in Crisis
    Hotline
New York, NY
(212) 686-1676

Federation Information and
    Referral Service
4200 Biscayne Boulevard
Miami, FL 33137
(305) 576-4000

Jewish Center Hot Line
1125 College Street
Columbus, OH 43209
(614) 237-8894

Jewish Information and Referral
    Service
130 E. 59 Street
New York, NY 10022
(212) 753-2288

Jewish Information Service
2030 S. Taylor Road
Cleveland Heights, OH 44118
(216) 371-3999

New York City Gay/Lesbian
    Anti-Violence Project Hotline
New York, NY
(212) 772-0404

New York Women Against Rape
    Hotline
(212) 777-4000

Pregnancy Loss Telephone
    Counseling
(*See* Health Resources)

Shiloh Hotline
    (for battered Jewish women)
P.O. Box 6031
North Hollywood, CA 91603
(213) 784-6894

24-Hour Cult Clinic Hot Line
1651 Third Avenue
New York, NY 10028
(212) 860-8533

Valley Beth Shalom Counseling
    Center Hot Line
15739 Ventura Boulevard
Encing, CA 94136
(213) 784-1414

WOMEN USA
Women's News Hotline
New York State: (212) 344-2431
Elsewhere in U.S.A.: (800) 221-
    4945

Youth Hotline
240 E. 31 Street
New York, NY 10016
(212) 683-4388

(*See also listings under* Battered
    Women; Rape and Violence
    Against Women and Children)

IMMIGRANT SERVICES

Hebrew Immigrant Aid Society
1 S. Franklin
Chicago, IL 60606
(312) 346-6700

Hebrew Immigrant Aid Society
5750 Park Heights Avenue
Baltimore, MD 21215
(301) 466-9200

Hebrew Reestablishment Services
152 Beverley Street
Toronto, Ontario M5T 1Y6
Canada
(416) 869-3811

IMMIGRANT SERVICES (continued)

Jewish Immigrant Aid Service of
  Canada
5151 Côte Ste. Catherine Road
Quebec, Montreal H3W 1M6
Canada

Jewish Immigrant Aid Services
152 Beverley Street
Toronto, Ontario M5T 1Y6
Canada

National Council of Jewish Women
  Immigration and Naturalization
633 Salisbury Street
Worcester, MA 01609
(617) 791-3438

New York Association for New
  Americans
225 Park Avenue S.
New York, NY 10003
(213) 674-7400

Rescue and Migration Service
National Council of Jewish Women
4200 Biscayne Boulevard
Miami, FL 33137
(305) 576-4747

Resettlement Service
24123 Greenfield Road
Southfield, MI 48075
(313) 559-1500

Russian Resettlement Program
850 Washington Avenue
Miami Beach, FL 33139
(305) 445-0555

INTERMARRIAGE GROUPS

Rachel and Paul Cowan
285 Riverside Drive
New York, NY 10025
(212) 866-0888

Rabbi Irwin Fishbein
Rabbinic Center for Research and
  Counseling
128 E. Dudley Avenue
Westfield, NJ 07090
(201) 233-0419

Conversion Course Office
New York Federation of Reform
  Synagogues
838 Fifth Avenue
New York, NY 10021

Dr. Egon Mayer
903 Park Avenue
New York, NY 10021

Rabbi Burt Siegel
445 E. 65 Street, Apt. 4A
New York, NY 10021
(212) 570-9047

marriage encounter

JEWISH FEMINIST ORGANIZATIONS

U.S.A.
Ezrat Nashim
924 West End Avenue, Apt. 45A
New York, NY 10025

Jewish Feminist Collective
900 Hilgard Avenue
Los Angeles, CA 90024

Jewish Women's Open Discussion
    Group
c/o Cambridge Women's Center
46 Pleasant Street
Cambridge, MA 02139

Belgium
Monique Chalude
177 Avenue Armorie Huysman
1050 Brussels, Belgium

England
London Jewish Feminist Group
c/o Margaret Green
Flat 7, Callcott Cosa
Callcott Road
London N.W. 6, England

The Netherlands
Deborah, the Jewish Women's
    Group
c/o WIZO
Pwarslaan 18
126 B.B. Blaricum
Amsterdam, The Netherlands

(*See also* Prayer and Study Groups;
    Lesbian and Gay; Political Ac-
    tion; Women in Israel. For new
    groups you may be able to get
    information from the women's
    center or bookstore nearest you.)

JEWISH WOMEN'S ORGANIZATIONS

Amit Women
817 Broadway
New York, NY 10003
(212) 477-4720

B'nai B'rith Women
1640 Rhode Island Avenue, N.W.
Washington, DC 20036
(202) 857-6670

Brandeis University National
    Women's Committee
Brandeis University
Waltham, MA 02254
(617) 647-2194

Hadassah, The Women's Zionist
    Organization of America
50 W. 58 Street
New York, NY 10019
(212) 355-7900

Lubavitch Women's Organization
770 Eastern Parkway
Brooklyn, NY 11213
(718) 774-2060

National Council of Jewish Women
15 E. 26 Street
New York, NY 10010
(212) 532-1740

National Federation of Temple
    Sisterhoods
838 Fifth Avenue
New York, NY 10021
(212) 249-0100

Pioneer Women/Na'amat
200 Madison Avenue
New York, NY 10016
(212) 725-8010

JEWISH WOMEN'S ORGANIZATIONS *(continued)*

Women's American ORT
315 Park Avenue S.
New York, NY 10010
(212) 505-7700

Women's Branch
Union of Orthodox Jewish
    Congregations of America
84 Fifth Avenue
New York, NY 10016
(212) 929-8857

Women's Division
American Jewish Congress
15 E. 84 Street
New York, NY 10028
(212) 879-4500

Women's Division
Jewish Labor Committee
25 E. 78 Street
New York, NY 10021
(212) 535-3700

Women's Division
United Jewish Appeal
1290 Avenue of the Americas
New York, NY 10019
(212) 757-1500

Women's League for Conservative
    Judaism
48 E. 74 Street
New York, NY 10021
(212) 628-1600

Women's League for Israel
1860 Broadway
New York, NY 10023
(212) 245-8742

Young Women's Leadership
    Cabinet
1290 Avenue of the Americas
New York, NY 10019
(212) 757-1500

LEGAL

AGUNAH
(See Divorce)
Bet Tzedek Jewish Legal Services
163 S. Fairfax Avenue
Los Angeles, CA 90036
(213) 938-6271

Feminist Law Collective
1197 Valencia Street
San Francisco, CA 94103
(415) 647-0836

G.E.T. (Getting Equitable
    Treatment)
(See Divorce)

Legal Defense and Education Fund
National Organization for Women
132 W. 43 Street
New York, NY 10036
(212) 840-1335

Lesbian Rights Project
1370 Mission Street
San Francisco, CA 94103
(415) 621-0675

National Center for Women and
    Family Law
799 Broadway, Room 402
New York, NY 10003
(212) 674-8200

National Jewish Commission on
    Law and Public Affairs
(*See* Divorce)

Women's Rights Law Reporter
(*See* Periodicals)

LESBIAN AND GAY

Alabama
Birmingham, Alabama, Group
c/o Keith Scribner
1926, 16 Avenue S.
Birmingham, AL 35205

California
Congregation Beth Chayim
    Chadashim
6000 W. Pico Boulevard
Los Angeles, CA 90035
(213) 931-7023

Congregation Sha'ar Zahav
P.O. Box 5640
San Francisco, CA 94101
(415) 921-7612

Council on Religion and the
    Homosexual
P.O. Box 11021
San Francisco, CA 94101
(415) 921-0134

Women's Building of the Bay Area
    (headquarters for diverse lesbian
    and feminist groups)
3543, 18 Street
San Francisco, CA 94110
(415) 863-5259

Jewish Lesbian Feminists
c/o Ocean Park Community Center
245 Hill Street
Santa Monica, CA 90405

Lesbian and Gay Jewish Activists
511 Capp Street
San Francisco, CA 94110

Lesbian Task Force of N.O.W.
P.O. Box 1404
Sacramento, CA 95807

The Lost Tribe
c/o Naphtali Offen
863 Waller Street, #1
Can Francisco, CA 94117
(415) 863-3202

Robin Tyler
c/o West Coast Women's Music
    Festival
1195 Valencia Street
San Francisco, CA 94110
(415) 641-4892

Colorado
Hatikvah HaShalom
c/o Gerald Gerash
1360 Corona
Denver, CO 80218
(303) 831-6144
(303) 861-0700

District of Columbia
    (greater Washington area)
Bet Mischpachah
P.O. Box 1410
Washington, DC 20013
(202) 544-3434

Jewish Gays of Baltimore/
    Washington Area
P.O. Box 34038
Washington, DC 20034

LESBIAN AND GAY (*continued*)

Jewish Lesbian Group
c/o Glad Hag Books
P.O. Box 2934
Washington, DC 20013

Jewish Parents and Friends of Gays
(*See* Parenting)

National Federation of Parents and
    Friends of Gays   .
5715 15 Street, NW
Washington, DC 20011

Florida
Congregation Etz Chaim
Metropolitan Community
    Synagogue of Greater Miami
19094 W. Dixie Highway
North Miami Beach, FL 33180
(305) 324-0180

Illinois
Chicago Jewish Lesbians
c/o Women and Children First
913 W. Armitage Street
Chicago, IL 60614
(312) 871-7417

Congregation Or Chadash
c/o Second Unitarian Center
656 W. Barry Street
Chicago, IL 60657
(312) 248-9456

Havurat Ach'yot
P.O. Box 14066
Chicago, IL 60614

Indiana
Havurah Or B'Emek
P.O. Box 11041
Fort Wayne, IN 46855

Iowa
Kosher Gay Farming
Synagogue B'nai Or Torah
c/o Randall L. Sly
1510 Ninth Avenue West
Oskaloosa, IA 52577

Louisiana
Lambda Chai—New Orleans
Box 73622
Metairie, LA 70033-3622

Maryland
Jewish Gays of Central Maryland
c/o Gay Community Center
P.O. Box 74
Baltimore, MD 21230

Massachusetts
Am Tikva
P.O. Box 11
Cambridge, MA 02138
(617) 628-3986
(617) 524-1617

International Congress of Lesbian
    and Gay Jews
c/o Larry Sorgmyn
44 Gartland Street
Jamaica Plains, MA 02130

Michigan
Lambda Chai
P.O. Box 351
Farmington, MI 48024
(313) 867-1347

Minnesota
Etz Hayyim Fellowship
P.O. Box 14258
Dinkytown Station
Minneapolis, MN 55414

Womyn's Hagadah/Jewish Lesbian
    Feminist Newsletter
3305 Clinton Avenue South
Minneapolis, MN 55408

Missouri
St. Louis Gay Havurah
P.O. Box 9235
St. Louis, MO 63117
(314) 721-4028
(314) 862-7961

New York
Congregation Beth Simchat Torah
P.O. Box 1270, G.P.O.
New York, NY 10116
(212) 929-9498

Lesbian and Gay Rights Task Force
New Jewish Agenda
150 Fifth Avenue
New York, NY 10011
(212) 620-0828

Women's Center
   (Jewish lesbian events)
243 W. 20 Street, 3rd floor
New York, NY 10011
(212) 741-9114

Lesbian Herstory Archives
Lesbian Herstory Educational
   Foundation, Inc.
P.O. Box 1258
New York, NY 10116
(212) 874-7232

Lesbian Switchboard
New York, NY
(212) 741-2610

National Gay Task Force
80 Fifth Avenue
New York, NY 10011
(212) 741-5800

New York City Parents of Lesbians
   and Gay Men
Box 553
Lenox Hill Station
New York, NY 10021
(212) 662-6700

Zionist Union of Gays, New York
c/o CBST
P.O. Box 1270, G.P.O.
New York, NY 10116

Pennsylvania
Congregation Beth Ahavah
P.O. Box 7566
Philadelphia, PA 19101
(215) 922-3872

Havarim
P.O. Box 59104
Pittsburgh, PA 15210

Texas
Beth Chaim
c/o Robbins
219 Marshall, #201
Houston, TX 77006

Washington
Congregation Tikvah Chadashah
P.O. Box 2731
Seattle, WA 98111

Kadima
P.O. Box 7
2420 First Avenue
Seattle, WA 98121

Seattle Jewish Lesbian Group
c/o Judith Klain
1516, 18 Avenue
Seattle, WA 98122
(206) 324-6394

Wisconsin
Jewish Lesbian Group
c/o A Room of One's Own
   Bookstore
317 W. Johnson Street
Madison, WI 53703
(608) 257-7888

Canada
CHAI
CP 596 Haute-Ville
Quebec PQ Canada
GIR 4R8

Ha-Chug
P.O. Box 69406
Vancouver, British Columbia V5K
   4W6
Canada

Naches—GJDG
P.O. Box 298, Station H
Montreal, Quebec H3G 2K8
Canada

LESBIAN AND GAY (*continued*)

Toronto GSH
c/o Henry Wiseberg
15 Arrowstock Road
Willowdale, Ontario M2K 1K1
Canada

Australia
Beth Chaverim
P.O. Box 90
Balwyn, Vic 3103
Australia

Chutzpah
c/o Martin Smith
94 Surrey Street
Darlinghurst, NSW 2010
Australia

Chutzpah
c/o Gottlieb
Unit 5, 19 Glen Avenue
Randwick, NSW 2031
Australia

Congregation Beth Simcha
11/75 O'Brien Street
Bondi Beach, NSW 2026
Australia

England
Jewish Gay Group
Timothy Goldard
BM JGG
London WC1V 6XX, England

France
Beit Haverim
B.P. 397
75626 Paris Cedex 13
France

Beit Haverim
c/o Rev. Joseph Douce
3 bis, rue Clairaut
75017 Paris, France
627.49.36

Israel
Society for the Protection of
    Personal Rights
P.O. Box 16151
Tel Aviv, Israel 61160
(03) 246-063
(03) 221-721

The Netherlands
Sjalhomo
Postbus 2536
1000 CM Amsterdam
The Netherlands

LIBRARIES AND ARCHIVES

American Jewish Archives
Hebrew Union College–Jewish
  Institute of Religion
3101 Clifton Avenue
Cincinnati, OH 45220
(513) 221-1875

American Jewish Women of
  Achievement Collection
William E. Wiener Oral History
  Library
American Jewish Committee
165 E. 56 Street
New York, NY 10022
(212) 751-4000

Blaustein Library
American Jewish Committee
165 E. 56 Street
New York, NY 10022
(212) 751-4000

Central Archives for the History of
  the Jewish People
Hebrew University—Givat Ram
  Campus
P. O. Box 1149
Jerusalem, Israel

Jewish Women's Resource Center
  Library
c/o National Council of Jewish
  Women
9 E. 69 Street
New York, NY 10028
(212) 535-5900

Jewish Women's Resource Library
National Council of Jewish
  Women, Los Angeles Section
543 N. Fairfax Avenue
Los Angeles, CA 90036
(213) 651-2930

Lesbian Herstory Archives
(See Lesbian and Gay)

Library of the Jewish Woman
190 Apple Drive
Exton, PA 19341
(215) 363-8644

National Yiddish Book Exchange
(See Yiddish and Ladino
  Organizations)

Pacific Film Archive
University Art Museum
2625 Durant Avenue
Berkeley, CA 94720
(415) 642-1124

Philadelphia Jewish Archive Center
625 Walnut Street
Philadelphia, PA 19106
(215) 923-2729

YIVO Institute for Jewish Research
1048 Fifth Avenue
New York, NY 10028
(212) 535-6700

MARRIAGE

Engaged Couples Seminar
Jewish Community Center
Wilkes-Barre, PA 18701
(717) 824-4646

Rabbi Karen L. Fox
  (for innovative marriage
  contracts and ceremonies)
Temple Isaiah
10345 W. Pico Boulevard
Los Angeles, CA 90064
(213) 277-2772

MARRIAGE (*continued*)

Jewish Marriage Encounter
c/o Laurie and Bob Brussel
365 Woodmere Boulevard
Woodmere, NY 11598
(516) 374-6430

"Making Marriage Work"
The University of Jerusalem
Department of Continuing
    Education
15600 Mulholland Drive
Los Angeles, CA 90024
(213) 476-9777

Remarried Consultation Service
Jewish Board of Family and
    Children's Services
120 W. 57 Street
New York, NY 10019
(212) 582-9100

MEDIA

Jewish Student Press Service
15 E. 26 Street
New York, NY 10010
(212) 679-1411

Jewish Telegraphic Agency
165 W. 46 Street
New York, NY 10036
(212) 575-9370

Media Information Bulletin
Commission on Jewish Life and
    Culture
American Jewish Congress
15 E. 84 Street
New York, NY 10028

Pacifica Program Service
Pacifica Foundation
5316 Venice Boulevard
Los Angeles, CA 90019
(213) 931-1625

Women Against Pornography
358 W. 47 Street
New York, NY 10036
(212) 307-5055

Women's Institute for Freedom
    of the Press
3306 Ross Place, N.W.
Washington, DC 20008
(202) 966-7783

(*See also* Films; Periodicals)

MIKVEH

International Mikveh Directory
Armis Publications
118 W. 79 Street
New York, NY 10024

North Shore Mikveh Association
c/o Great Neck Synagogue
26 Old Mill Road
Great Neck, NY 11023

Los Angeles Mikvah Society
9548 W. Pico Boulevard
Los Angeles, CA 90035
(213) 550-9124

The Riverdale Mikveh
3708 Henry Hudson Parkway E.
Bronx, NY 10473
(212) 549-8336

Valley Mikvah Society
12800 Chandler Boulevard
North Hollywood, CA 91607
(213) 506-0996

MINYANIM

California
Aquarian Minyan
P.O. Box 7224
Berkeley, CA 94707

Library Minyan at Temple Beth Am
1039 S. La Cienega Boulevard
Los Angeles, CA 90035

District of Columbia
Farbrengen
4500 Connecticut Avenue, N.W.
Washington, DC 20008

Illinois
Upstairs Minyan
c/o University of Chicago
5715 S. Woodlawn
Chicago, IL 60637

Massachusetts
Havurat Shalom
113 College Avenue
Somerville, MA 02144

Minnesota
Twin Cities Women's Minyan
c/o Bet Hillel
150A University Avenue
Minneapolis, MN 55455

New Jersey
Teaneck Prayer Group
c/o Task Force on Jewish Woman
P.O. Box 1062
Teaneck, NJ 07666
(201) 836-3098

New York
Einstein Minyan
c/o Jackson
1579 Rhinelander Avenue
Bronx, NY 10461
(212) 828-6557

Jewish Theological Seminary
   Conservative Women's Minyan
Office of Student Activities
3080 Broadway
New York, NY 10027
(212) 678-8000

Minyan Mi'at
and
Upper West Side Minyan
c/o Congregation Ansche Chesed
251 W. 100 Street
New York, NY 10025
(212) 864-6637

MINYANIM (*continued*)

Pennsylvania
Germantown Minyan
c/o Germantown Jewish Center
Lincoln Drive and Ellet Street
Philadelphia, PA 19119

Philadelphia Free Minyan
c/o Hillel
202 South 36 Street
Philadelphia, PA 19136

Israel
Mevakshei Derekh
c/o Rehavia Gymnasia
Keren Kayemet 18
Jerusalem, Israel 92428

(*See also* Women's Prayer and
    Study Groups; Synagogues—
    Egalitarian)

MUSIC AND DANCE

Hora
(*See* Periodicals)

Israeli Folk Dance Institute
American Zionist Youth
    Foundation
515 Park Avenue
New York, NY 10022

The Jewish Family Music Bank
Martin Steinberg Center
American Jewish Congress
15 E. 84 Street
New York, NY 10028

Klez-meydlekh
    (Women's klezmer band)
c/o Leuchter
245 West 107 Street
New York, NY 10025
(212) 864-4574

National Foundation for Jewish
    Culture
122 E. 42 Street
New York, NY 10168
(212) 490-2280

Star Publications
P.O. Box 7768
Long Beach, CA 90807
(213) 422-3710

Women's Music Archives
208 Wildflower Lane
Fairfield, CT 06430
(203) 255-1348

NEIGHBORHOOD SOCIAL SERVICE CENTERS

Bronx Neighborhood Service
    Centers
1130 Grand Concourse
New York, NY 10456
(212) 293-1200

Free Synagogue Social Service
30 W. 68 Street
New York, NY 10023
(212) 877-4050

Jewish Community Development
  Corporation
60 Glenwood Avenue
East Orange, NJ 07017
(201) 673-6800

Lower Eastside Service Center
The Educational Alliance
197 E. Broadway
New York, NY 1002
(212) 475-6200

Selfhelp Community Services
300 Park Avenue S.
New York, NY 10010
(212) 533-7100

Theresa Grotta Center for
  Restorative Services
20 Summit Street
West Orange, NJ 07052
(201) 736-2000

PARENTING

Association of Jewish Family and
  Children's Agencies
200 Park Avenue S.
New York, NY 10010
(212) 674-6800

Foster Homes
Jewish Child Care Association
345 Madison Avenue
New York, NY 10017
(212) 490-9160

Jewish Parents and Friends of Gays
Charlotte K. Hoffman
3536 Chevy Chase Drive
Chevy Chase, MD 20815

Louise Wise Services
  (or unwed Jewish mothers and
  others)
12 E. 94 Street
New York, NY 10028
(212) 876-3050

National Alliance for Optional
  Parenthood
3 N. Liberty Street
Baltimore, MD 21201

National Federation of Parents and
  Friends of Gays
(*See* Lesbian and Gay)

*National Jewish Family Center
  Newsletter*
(*See* Periodicals)

New York City Parents of Lesbians
  and Gay Men
(*See* Lesbian and Gay)

Parenting Center
92nd Street YM/YWHA
1395 Lexington Avenue
New York, NY 10028
(212) 427-6000

Pregnancy Loss Peer Counseling
  and Lamaze Prepared Childbirth
(*See* Health)

Rabbi Reuven Simons
Emergency Council of Jewish
  Families
  (anticult)
2 Penn Plaza
New York, NY 10001
(212) 244-3100

PERIODICALS

Agada: Jewish Literary Tri-annual
2020 Essex Street
Berkeley, CA 94703

American Jewish History
American Jewish Historical Society
2 Thornton Road
Waltham, MA 02154

Conditions
P.O. Box 56
Van Brunt Station
Brooklyn, NY 11215

Council Woman
National Council of Jewish Women
15 E. 26 Street
New York, NY 10010
(212) 532-1740

Feminist Studies
c/o Women's Studies Program
University of Maryland
College Park, MD 20742

Genesis 2
233 Bay State Road
Boston, MA 02215

Hadassah Magazine
50 W. 58 Street
New York, NY 10019
(212) 355-7900

Heresies
P.O. Box 766
Canal Street Station
New York, NY 10013

Hora
American Zionist Youth
  Foundation
515 Park Avenue
New York, NY 10022

Hot Flash
School of Allied Health Professions
Health Sciences Center
State University of New York
Stony Brook, NY 11794

Jewish Arts Newsletter
Martin Steinberg Center
(*See* Ritual Objects

Jewish Folklore and Ethnology
  Newsletter
YIVO Institute for Jewish Research
1048 Fifth Avenue
New York, NY 10028

Jewish Student Press Features
Jewish Student Press Service
(*See* University-Affiliated
  Resources)

Journal of Women and Religion
Center for Women and Religon
2465 Le Conte Avenue
Berkeley, CA 94709

Kolenoe
  Jewish women's monthly
  magazine (in Dutch)
Maardblad Voor de Bewust Joodse
  Vrow
Postbus 70371
(Postgiro 187744 Van de Rabobank
  Te)
10007 KJ Amsterdam

Lilith—The Jewish women's
  magazine
and
Lilith Networking Newsletter
250 West 57 Street
New York, NY 10019

Midstream: A Monthly Jewish
  Review
515 Park Avenue
New York, NY 10022
(212) 752-0600

Moment
462 Boylston Street
Boston, MA 02116

Ms.
119 W. 40 Street
New York, NY 10018
(212) 719-9800

National Jewish Family Center Newsletter
Jewish Communal Affairs Department

American Jewish Committee
165 E. 56 Street
New York, NY 10022

New Menorah: The B'nai Or Journal of Jewish Renewal
Beyt B'nai Or
6723 Emlen Street
Philadelphia, PA 19119

Noga
(quarterly Israeli feminist magazine) (in Hebrew)
P.O. Box 21376
Tel Aviv, Israel

Off Our Backs
1841 Columbia Road, N.W. #22
Washington, DC 20009

Paper Pomegranate
The Pomegranate Guild of Judaic Needlework
1 Fanshaw Avenue
Yonkers, NY 10705

Pioneer Woman
200 Madison Avenue
New York, NY 10016
(212) 725-8010

Present Tense
165 E. 56 Street
New York, NY 10022
(212) 751-4000

Reconstructionist
15 W. 86 Street
New York, NY 10024

Resources for Feminist Research Documentation sur la recherche féministe
Department of Sociology
Ontario Institute for Studies in Education
252 Bloor Street W.
Toronto, Ontario M5S 1V6
Canada

Response: A Contemporary Jewish Review
610 W. 113 Street
New York, NY 10025

Shehechiyatnu
1027 Sherman Street
Madison, WI 53703

Shifra
(British Jewish feminist magazine)
Box 2
c/o 59 Cookridge Street
Leeds 2, Yorkshire, England

Signs: Journal of Women in Culture and Society
5801 Ellis Avenue
Chicago, IL 60637

TABS: Aids for Ending Sexism in the School: A Quarterly Journal
744 Carroll Street
Brooklyn, NY 11215
(718) 788-3478

Womanews
P.O. Box 220
Village Station
New York, NY 10014
(212) 989-7963

Women's American ORT Reporter
1250 Broadway
New York, NY 10014
(212) 594-8500

Women's League Outlook
48 E. 75 Street
New York, NY 10021
(212) 628-1600

PERIODICALS (*continued*)

Women's Rights Law Reporter
Transaction Periodicals Consortium
Department 2000
Rutgers The State University
New Brunswick, NJ 08903

Women's Studies Quarterly
Box 334
Old Westbury, NY 11568

Womyn's Braille Press, Inc.
P.O. Box 8475
Minneapolis, MN 55408

*Yugntruf: A Yiddish Student
    Quarterly*
3328 Bainbridge Avenue
Bronx, NY 10467
(212) 654-8540

POLITICAL ACTION

Chutzpah Women's Group
P.O. Box 60142
Chicago, IL 60660
(312) 871-3598

Center for Sexual Equality
American Jewish Commitee
165 E. 56 Street
New York, NY 10022
(212) PL1-4000

The Israel Women's Caucus
c/o American Jewish Congress
3 Mapu Street #4
Jerusalem, Israel 94189
(02) 245810

National Abortion Rights Action
    League (NARAL)
(*See* Health)

National Commission on Women's
    Equality of the American Jewish
    Congress
c/o American Jewish Congress
15 East 84 Street
New York, NY 10028
(212) 879-4500

National Jewish Community
    Relations Advisory Council
111 W. 40 Street
New York, NY 10018
(212) 221-1535

National Organization for Women
425, 13 Street, N.W.
Washington, DC 20004

New Jewish Agenda
Feminist Task Forces
1123 Broadway
New York, NY 10010
(212) 620-0828

Religious Action Department
New York Federation of Reform
    Synagogues
838 Fifth Avenue
New York, NY 10021
(212) 289-0100

Religious Coalition for Abortion
    Rights
100 Maryland Avenue, N.E.
Washington, DC 20002

Student Struggle for Soviet Jewry
210 W. 91 Street
New York, NY 10024
(212) 799-8900

Task Force on Equality of Women
    in Judaism
New York Federation of Reform
    Synagogues
838 Fifth Avenue
New York, NY 10021
(212) 289-0100

Task Force on Equal Opportunities
   for Women
National Jewish Community
   Relations Advisory Council
443 Park Avenue S.
New York, NY 10016
(212) 684-6950

Task Force on the Role of Women
   in a Changing Society
New York Federation of Jewish
   Philanthropies
130 E. 59 Street
New York, NY 10022
(212) 980-1000

Task Force on Women and
   Minorities
Commission on Social Action of
   Reform Judaism
U.A.H.C.
838 Fifth Avenue
New York, NY 10021
(212) 249-0100

Women's Action Alliance, Inc.
370 Lexington Avenue
New York, NY 10017
(212) 532-8330

Women's Issues Task Force
National Council of Jewish Women
15 E. 26 Street
New York, NY 10010
(212) 532-1740

POVERTY

Metropolitan New York Coordinating Council on Jewish Poverty
15 Park Row
New York, NY 10007
(212) 267-9500

(*See also* Charity; Financial Aid;
   Employment; Elderly; Displaced
   Homemakers)

PRISONERS

B'nai B'rith Prisoner Outreach
   Program
1640 Rhode Island Avenue, N.W.
Washington, DC 20036

Books for Prisoners
Box A
92 Pike Street
Seattle, WA 98101

Books for Women in Prison
c/o ICI/A Woman's Place
   Bookstore
4015 Broadway
Oakland, CA 94611
(415) 547-9920

Chaplaincy Program
Jewish Welfare Board
15 E. 26 Street
New York, NY 10010

Jewish Prisoners Assistance
   Foundation
c/o Congregation Kol Ami
233 E. Erie Street
Chicago, IL 60611

Justice for Children Task Force
National Council of Jewish Women
15 E. 26 Street
New York, NY 10010
(212) 532-1740

PRISONERS *(continued)*

Rabbi Allen Kaplan
New York Board of Rabbis
10 E. 73 Street
New York, NY 10021
(212) 879-8415

National Council of Jewish Women
  (information on Jewish
  prisoners)
15 E. 26 Street
New York, NY 10010
(212) 532-1740

Prison Subscription Program
Lilith magazine
250 W. 57 Street
New York, NY 10019
(212) 757-0818

Shalom Sisterhood
California Institution for Women
Frontera, CA 91720

PUBLISHERS

Alternatives in Religious Education
3945 S. Oneida Street
Denver, CO 80237

Biblio Press
P.O. Box 22
Fresh Meadows, NY 11365

Bobbeh Meisehs
Judith Stein
137 Tremont Street
Cambridge, MA 02139

Chadish Media Press
78 Courtelyou Avenue
Staten Island, NY 10312
(718) 356-9495

Human Relations Press
American Jewish Committee
165 E. 56 Street
New York, NY 10022
(212) 751-4000

Jewish Publication Society of
  America
117 S. 17 Street
Philadelphia, PA 19103

KAR-BEN Copies
11713 Auth Lane
Silver Spring, MD 20902

Publications Department
Central Conference of American
  Rabbis
790 Madison Avenue
New York, NY 10021

The Second Sex Publishing
  Company
55 Rechov Shenkin
Givatayim, Israel 53298

RABBINICAL SCHOOLS ORDAINING WOMEN

Hebrew Union College–Jewish
Institute of Religion
1 W. 4 Street
New York, NY 10012
(212) 674-5300

Jewish Theological Seminary
3080 Broadway
New York, NY 10027
(212) 678-8000

Reconstructionist Rabbinical
College
Church Road and Greenwood Ave.
Wyncote, PA 19095
(215) 576-0800

RABBIS (WOMEN)

Reconstructionist
Dr. Rebecca T. Alpert
Dean of Students
Reconstructionist Rabbinical
College
Church Road and Greenwood
Avenue
Wyncote, PA 19095

Rabbi Devorah Bartnoff
Congregation Am Kaskalah
903 North 18 Street
Allentown, PA 18104

Rabbi Susan Frank
Reconstructionist Rabbinical
College
Church Road and Greenwood
Avenue
Wyncote, PA 19095

Rabbi Nancy Fuchs-Kreimer
Reconstructionist Rabbinical
College
Church Road and Greenwood
Avenue
Wyncote, PA 19095

Rabbi Linda Holtzman
Beth Israel Congregation
5th Avenue and Harmony Street
Coatesville, PA 19320

Rabbi Bonnie Koppell
Jewish Fellowship of Davis
1821 Oak Avenue
Davis, CA 95616

Rabbi Cynthia Kravitz
7400 Roosevelt Blvd., Apt. F 201
Philadelphia, PA 19152

Rabbi Joy Levitt
B'nai Keshet
87-89 Valley Road
Montclair, NJ 07042

Rabbi Hava Pell
Director, Women's Division
Jewish Federation of Southern
New Jersey
Marlton Pike
Cherry Hill, NJ 08002

Rabbi Ruth Sandberg
871 N. Easton Road, Apt. 8A1
Glenside, PA 19038

Rabbi Sandy E. Sasso
Beth El Zedek Congregation
600 West 70th Street
Indianapolis, IN 46260

Rabbi Ilene Schneider
114 Country Farms Road
Marlton, NJ 08053

RABBIS (WOMEN) (*continued*)

Rabbi Susan Schnur
61 West Broad Street
Hopewell, NJ 08525

Rabbi Gail Shuster-Bouskila
HaNerd Street 191B
Jerusalem, Israel

Reform
WOMEN'S RABBINIC
  NETWORK:
  (umbrella group for Reform
  women rabbis)

Rabbi Ellen Dreyfus
  (Midwest Region)
Temple B'nai Israel
600 Harrison Avenue
Kankakee, IL 60901
(815) 933-7814

Rabbi Rosalind A. Gold
  (past coordinator)
Northern Virginia Hebrew
  Congregation
1441 Wiehle Avenue
(703) 437-7733

Rabbi Patricia Karlin-Neumann
  (West Coast Region)
Hillel Council of U.C.L.A.
900 Hilgard Avenue
Los Angeles, CA 90024
(213) 208-3081

Rabbi Lynne Landsberg
  (Mid-Atlantic Region)
Temple House of Israel
15 North Market Street
Staunton, VA 24401
(703) 886-4091

Rabbi Ellen Lewis
  (co-coordinator)
Temple Sinai
208 Summit Avenue
Summit, NJ 07901
(201) 273-4921

Rabbi Carole Meyers
  (Southwest Region
Congregation Beth Israel
5600 North Braeswood
Houston, TX 77036
(713) 771-6221

Rabbi Mindy Portnoy
  (co-coordinator)
3511 Davenport Street, N.W.
  #312
Washington, DC 20008
(202) 362-6755

Rabbi Julie Wolkoff
  (Northeast Region)
Congregation Berith Sholom
167 Third Street
Troy, NY 12180
(518) 272-8872

Rabbi Marjorie Yudkin
  (New York Metropolitan
  Region)
Congregation Emanu-El of
  Westchester
Westchester Avenue
Rye, NY 10580
(914) 967-4382

Independent
Rabbi Lynn Gottlieb
295 La Plata N.W.
Albuquerque, NM 87107

RAPE AND VIOLENCE AGAINST WOMEN AND CHILDREN

Abused Women's Aid in Crisis
  Hotline
  (New York City)
(*See* Hotlines)

Bay Area Women Against Rape
P.O. Box 240
Berkeley, CA 94701
(415) 845-RAPE

Center for Victims of Family
  Violence (sponsored by
  Na'amat)
Tel Aviv, Israel
(03) 235-922
(03) 231-675

Domestic Violence Committee
Women's Issues Task Force
National Council of Jewish Women
15 E. 26 Street
New York, NY 10010

Marital Rape Clearinghouse
2325 Oak
Berkeley, CA 94705

LO ("No")—Combatting Violence
  Against Women
Sokolov 68
Herzliya, Israel
(852) 83856

New York Women Against Rape
(212) 477-0819
(For NYWAR Hotline, see
  Hotlines)

San Francisco Women Against
  Rape
3543, 18 Street
San Francisco, CA 94110
(415) 647-RAPE

Support for family members testifying in domestic-violence cases:
National Council of Jewish
  Women—New York Section
9 E. 69 Street
New York, NY 10021
(212) 535-5900

Support for Orthodox Victims of
  Rape and Incest
Call: Victims Service Agency
  54 Nagle Street
  New York, NY 10040
  (212) 567-5008
They will forward calls to SOVRI.

Women Against Rape—South
  Alameda County
P.O. Box 662
Hayward, CA 94543
(415) 582-RAPE (6 P.M.–6 A.M.)

Women, Inc.
  (for battered women)
2940, 16 Street
San Francisco, CA 94103
(415) 864-4722

(See also Battered Women;
  Hotlines)

RELIGIOUS ORGANIZATIONS

Jewish Reconstructionist
  Foundation
31 E. 28 Street
New York, NY 10016
(212) 316-3011

Union of American Hebrew
  Congregations (Reform)
838 Fifth Avenue
New York, NY 10021
(212) 249-0100

RELIGIOUS ORGANIZATIONS *(continued)*

Union of Orthodox Jewish
   Congregations of America
45 W. 36 Street
New York, NY 10018
(212) 563-4000

United Synagogue of America
   (Conservative)
155 Fifth Avenue
New York, NY 10010
(212) 533-7800

(See also Havurot; Jewish Women's
   Organizations; Minyanim;
   Women's Prayer and Study
   Groups; Women's Religious
   Organizations)

RITUAL OBJECTS

Ita Aber
   (needlework)
1 Fanshaw Avenue
Yonkers, NY 10705
(914) 968-4863

Fern Amper
   (ceramics)
65-50 Wetherole Street
Rego Park, NY 11374

In the Spirit Gallery
460 E. 79 Street
New York, NY 10021
(212) 861-5222

Martin Steinberg Center for Jewish
   Art and Artists
American Jewish Congress
15 E. 84 Street
New York, NY 10028
(212) 879-4500

Betsy Platkin Teutsch
   (wedding contracts)
989 West End Avenue, 9-C
New York, NY 10025
(212) 866-5448

SCHOLARS AND SCHOLARSHIP

Rachel Adler
1408, 6 Street, S.E.
Minneapolis, MN 55414

Councilwoman Susan Alter
463 E. 19 Street
Brooklyn, NY 11226

Sarah Silver Bunim
1195 Channing Road
Far Rockaway, NY 11691

Blu Greenberg
4620 Independence Avenue
Riverdale, NY 10471

Feminist Studies
(*See* Periodicals)

Judith Hauptman
Jewish Theological Seminary
3080 Broadway
New York, NY 10027

Rivka Haut
852 E. 13 Street
Brooklyn, NY 11230

Paula Hyman
Dean of the College
Jewish Theological Seminary
3080 Broadway
New York, NY 10027

National Women's History Project
P.O. Box 3716
Santa Rosa, CA 95402

Resources for Feminist Research
(*See* Periodicals)

*Signs: Journal of Women in Culture
and Society*
(*See* Periodicals)

Dr. Trude Weiss-Rosmarin
Jewish Spectator
P.O. Box 2016
Santa Monica, CA 90406

Women's Studies Quarterly
(*See* Periodicals)

(*See also* Women's Prayer and
Study Groups; Periodicals;
Education)

SINGLE PARENTS

California
Single Parent Awareness and Caring
Exchange
(SPACE)
National Council of Jewish
Women—Los Angeles
543 N. Fairfax Avenue
Los Angeles, CA 90036

Colorado
Single Parents Group
Temple Sinai
8050 E. Dartmouth Avenue
Denver, CO 80231
(303) 750-3006

New York
Gustave Hartman Y
710 Hartman Lane
Far Rockaway, NY 11691
(718) 471-0200

Jewish Community House of
Bensonhurst
7802 Bay Parkway
Brooklyn, NY 11214
(718) 331-6800

National Jewish Family Center
American Jewish Committee
165 E. 56 Street
New York, NY 10022
(212) 751-4000

Single Parent Center
YM/YWHA of Boro Park
4910 Fourteenth Avenue
Brooklyn, NY 11219
(718) 439-5921

Single Parent Family Center
Dora and Abraham Felt Building
YM-YWHA of Greater Flushing
45-35 Kissena Boulevard
Flushing, NY 11355
(718) 461-3030

Single Parents Group
Central Queens Y
108-05, 68 Road
Forest Hills, NY 11375

Single Parent Support Group
Mid Island YM-YWHA
45 Manetto Hill Road
Plainview, NY 11803

SINGLE WOMEN: PROGRAMS AND RESOURCES

Colorado
Denver Jewish Singles Council
Jewish Community Center
4800 E. Alameda
Denver, CO 80222
(303) 399-2660

District of Columbia
Singles Program
Adas Israel Congregation
2850 Quebec Street, N.W.
Washington, DC 20008
(202) 362-6295

Illinois
Center Singles
Bernard Horwich Jewish
    Community Center
3003 W. Touhy
Chicago, IL 60645
(312) 761-9100

Central Synagogue Singles
30 E. Cedar
Chicago, IL 60611

Chutzpah Unlimited Personals
P.O. Box 2700
Chicago, IL 60670

Ezras Israel Singles
Congregation Ezras Israel
7001 N. California
Chicago, IL 60645

Opportunities Unlimited for Jewish
    Singles
B'nai B'rith Women
P.O. Box 11846
Chicago, IL 60611
(312) 966-7910

Sentinel
    (singles listings)
323 S. Franklin Street
Chicago, IL 60606

Sholom Singles
Temple Sholom
3480 Lake Shore Drive
Chicago, IL 60657

South Suburban Young Jewish
    Singles
South Suburban Jewish Community
    Center
18600 Governors Highway
Flosmoor, IL 60422

Maryland
Shalom Adventure
Box 2132
Wheaton, MD 20902

Massachusetts
Genesis 2
    (personals column)
(*See* Periodicals)

Michigan
Lo-La Jewish Singles
    ("for him—for her")
Box 254
Lathrup Village, MI 48076

Missouri
The Society
Jewish Community Center
8201 Holmes
Kansas City, MO 64131

New York
Aish HaTorah
Jewish Computer Dating Service
1671 E. 16 Street, Suite 209
Brooklyn, NY 11229
(718) 336-7911

Bilu Coffee House
3833 Jerusalem Avenue
Seaford, NY 11783
(516) 643-5012

B'nai Zion Singles
Temple Emanuel of Great Neck
150 Hicks Lane
Kings Point, NY 11023
(516) 482-5701

Brunch for Singles
Beach YM-YWHA
310 National Boulevard
Long Beach, NY 11561
(516) 431-2929

Club for Singles
Central Queens YM-YWHA
108-05, 68th Road
Forest Hills, NY 11375
(718) 268-5011

Congregation Beth Israel of Boro
  Park
Physically Handicapped Jewish
  Singles
5602, 11th Avenue
Brooklyn, NY 11219
(718) 854-1620

Council of Jewish Federations Task
  Force on Singles (nationwide)
575 Lexington Avenue
New York, NY 10022
(212) 751-1311

Handicapables–Social Group for
  Physically Handicapped Jewish
  Single Adults
Temple Sinai
425 Roslyn Road
Roslyn Heights, NY 11577
(516) 484-1545

Havura Singles Affiliates
Sutton Place Synagogue
225 E. 51 Street
New York, NL 10022
(212) 593-3300

Hillel Coffee House
Adelphi University
Chaplain Center
Earle Hall
Garden City, NY 11530
(516) 294-8700, ext. 7623

Jewish Adult Penmate Center
P.O. Box 207
Monticello, NY 12701

Jewish Singles Date Phone
Women call (212) 755-3008

Jewish Singles Introduction Service
Metropolitan New York Council
United Synagogue of America
155 Fifth Avenue
New York, NY 10010

Jewish Singles Partyline
(212) 753-7282

Long Island Jewish Singles
Dix Hills Jewish Center
Vanderbilt Parkway and De Forest
  Road
Dix Hills, NY 11746
(516) 499-6644

Metropolitan Almanac Personals
80 E. 11 Street
New York, NY 10003

New Jewish Agenda
  (singles groups)
(*See* Political Action)

New York Federation Task Force
  on Jewish Singles
130 E. 59 Street
New York, NY 10022
(212) 980-1000

North Shore Singles Rap Group
Temple Judaea
Searingtown Road
Manhasset, NY 11030

Sinai Singles of Roslyn
Temple Sinai
425 Roslyn Road
Roslyn Heights, NY 11577
(516) 621-6800

SINGLE WOMEN: PROGRAMS AND RESOURCES
(*continued*)

Singles Programs
Group Services Department
92nd Street YM/YWHA
1395 Lexington Avenue
New York, NY 10028
(212) 427-6000

South Shore YM/YWHA
Jewish Singles Helping Singles
   Group
806 Merrick Road
Baldwin, NY 11510
(516) 623-9393

UJA Singles Mission to Israel
Department of Overseas Programs
United Jewish Appeal
1290 Avenue of the Americas
New York, NY 10104

Young Adults of Temple Israel
Singles Programs
Temple Israel of New Rochelle
1000 Pinebrook Boulevard
New Rochelle, NY 10804
(914) 476-9167

Pennsylvania
Congregation Shaare Shamayim
9768 Verree Road
Philadelphia, PA 19115
(215) OR 7-1600

Contemporary Jewish Dating
   Service
Box 14333
Philadelphia, PA 19115

Jewish Family Service
(*See* Family Resources)

Rodeph Sholom Singles Again
615 N. Broad Street
Philadelphia, PA 19123
(215) 627-6747

Israel
Communication for Jewish Singles
   Worldwide
Shiluv Organization
P.O.B. 6190
Tel Aviv, Israel

(*See also* Federations; Family
   Resources; Single Parents;
   University-Affiliated Resources)

SPEAKERS' BUREAUS

Feminist Voices
Batya Bauman Enterprises
315 Riverside Drive
New York, NY 10025
(212) 866-6422

B'nai B'rith Adult Education
   Lecture Services
1640 Rhode Island Avenue, N.W.
Washington, DC 20036

Jewish Welfare Board Lecture
   Bureau
15 E. 26 Street
New York, NY 10010
(212) 532-4949

Lilith Magazine Speakers Bureau
250 W. 57 Street
New York, NY 10019
(212) 757-0818

SPORTS

Brooklyn Women's Martial Arts
421 Fifth Avenue, 2nd floor
Brooklyn, NY 11215
(718) 788-1775

Women's Karate Committee
Jewish Karate Federation of
   America, Inc.
1609 Kings Highway
Brooklyn, NY 11229

Women's Martial Arts Center
16 W. 30 Street
New York, NY 10001
(212) 685-4553

Brandeis
University
National
Women's
Committee

SURVIVORS AND THEIR CHILDREN

One Generation After
   (awareness group)
c/o Ruth Bork
Zionist House
17 Boylston Street
Boston, MA 02167

Zachor
National Jewish Resource Center
250 W. 57 Street
New York, NY 10019

SYNAGOGUES: EGALITARIAN (CONSERVATIVE, ORTHODOX, OR INDEPENDENT)

Congregation Beth Torah
   (Conservative)
810 Lookout
Dallas, TX
(214) 234-1542

Hebrew Institute of Riverdale
   (Orthodox)
3700 Henry Hudson Parkway
Riverdale, NY 10463

Lincoln Square Synagogue
   (Orthodox)
200 Amsterdam Avenue
New York, NY 10023
(212) 874-6105

Temple Ansche Chesed
   (Conservative)
100 Street and West End Avenue
New York, NY 10025
(212) 865-0600

Tri-Sulom
   (Orthodox)
4634 W. 14 Street
Denver, CO 80204
(303) 623-8466

(*See also* Havurot; Women's
   Prayer and Study Groups)

UNIVERSITY-AFFILIATED RESOURCES

Barnard Women's Center
Barnard Hall
3009 Broadway
New York, NY 10027
(212) 280-2067

B'nai B'rith Hillel Council of
    Metropolitan Boston
233 Bay State Road
Boston, MA 12215
(617) 266-3882

B'nai B'rith Hillel Foundation
    (international)
1640 Rhode Island Ave., N.W.
Washington, DC 20036
(202) 857-6560

B'nai B'rith Hillel Foundations of
    Greater Miami
1100 Stanford Drive
Coral Gables, FL 33146
(305) 661-8549

B'nai B'rith Hillel Foundations of
    Montreal
3460 Stanley
Montreal, Quebec H3A 1R8
    Canada
(514) 845-9171

B'nai B'rith Hillel Foundations of
    Northeastern Ohio
11291 Euclid Avenue
Cleveland, OH 44106
(216) 231-0040

B'nai B'rith Hillel Foundation
College Age Youth Services
    (CAYS)
1 S. Franklin Street
Chicago, IL 60606
(312) 346-6700

Hillel Foundation—Jewish Student
    Union
750 Spadina Avenue
Toronto, Ontario M5S 2J2
Canada
(416) 923-9861

Intercollegiate Women's Coalition
    (Boston area)
Box 672
Brandeis University
Waltham, MA 02254

Jewish Association for College
    Youth
130 E. 59 Street
New York, NY 10022
(212) 688-0808

Jewish Campus Activities Board
2129 F Street, N.W.
Washington, DC 20037
(202) 333-5923

Jewish Campus Centers
5742 Montezuma Road
San Diego, CA 92115
(714) 583-6080

Jewish Student Press Service
15 E. 26 Street
New York, NY 10010
(212) 679-1411

Los Angeles Hillel Council
900 Hilgard Avenue
Los Angeles, CA 90024
(213) 208-6639

Masada Hillel
1103 W. Franklin Street
Richmond, VA 23220
(804) 353-6477

North American Jewish Students
    Network
1 Park Avenue
New York, NY 10016
(212) 689-0790

WIDOWS

Department of Senior Adult
  Services and Research
JYC of Philadelphia
401 South Broad Street
Philadelphia, PA 19147

Robin Siegel
c/o Jewish Family Service of Orange
  County
12181 Buaro Street, Suite G
Garden Grove, CA 92640

Phyllis Solow, Gerontologist
20613 Callon Drive
Topanga, CA 90290

The Young Widowed of
  Westchester
c/o Mrs. Lilly Singer
Westchester Jewish Community
  Services
172 S. Broadway, Dept. L
White Plains, NY 10605
(914) 949-6761

Widow-to-Widow
Mayer Kaplan Jewish Community
  Center
5050 Church Street
Skokie, IL 60076
(312) 675-2200

Widow-to-Widow
YWHA and NHS of Montreal
5500 Westbury Avenue
Montreal, Quebec H3W 2W8
Canada
(514) 737-6551

(*See also* Family Resources)

WOMEN IN ISRAEL

Coalition for Women in Israel
35-74, 78 Street
Apt. B-39
Jackson Heights, NY 11372

International Institute of Women's
  Studies in Israel
Box 601
1230 Grant Avenue
San Francisco, CA 94133
(415) 931-6973

Israel Programs Office
3950 Biscayne Boulevard
Miami, FL 33137
(305) 576-4000

The Israel Women's Caucus
(*See* Political Action)

LO—Combatting Violence Against
  Women
(*See* Battered Women)

Mitzvah—League for Family Rights
  in the Courts
P.O. Box 506
Netanya, Israel
(053) 44413

The Second Sex Publishing
  Company
(*See* Publishers)

SHILO Pregnancy Advisory Service
34 Abarbanel Street
Jerusalem, Israel

WOMEN IN ISRAEL (*continued*)

Society for the Protection of
   Personal Rights
(*See* Lesbian and Gay)

U.S./Israel Women-to-Women
(*See* Charity)

Woman's Voice
(*See* Bookstores)

Women's Social Service for Israel
240 W. 98 Street
New York, NY 10025
(212) 666-7880

(*See also* Battered Women;
   Hotlines)

WOMEN'S CENTERS

Barnard Women's Center
(*See* University-Affiliated
   Resources)

Jewish Women's Resource Center
Jewish Community Center
4800 East Alameda
Denver, CO 80206
(303) 399-2660

Jewish Women's Resource Center
c/o NCJW New York Section
9 E. 69 Street
New York, NY 10021

Women's Building of the Bay Area
3543, 18 Street
San Francisco, CA 94110
(415) 863-5259

Women's Center
National Council of Jewish
   Women—Los Angeles Section
Council Building
543 N. Fairfax Avenue
Los Angeles, CA 90036
(213) 651-2930

Women's Center
243 W. 20 Street
New York, NY 10011
(212) 741-9114

(*See also* University-Affiliated
   Resources)

WOMEN'S PRAYER AND STUDY GROUPS

Barnard College Women's Services
c/o Newman
620 W. 116 Street
New York, NY 10027
(212) 316-2360

Congregation Ohav Sholom
   Women's Minyan
New Krumkill Road
Albany, NY 12208
(518) 489-4706

Council of Jewish Organizations
Rabbi Ruth Sohn
105 Earl Hall
Columbia University
New York, NY 10027
(212) 280-5111

Creative Jewish Women's Alliance
c/o Marcia Spiegel
4856 Ferncreek Drive
Rolling Hills Estate, CA 90274

Einstein Minyan
(*See* Minyanim)

Flatbush Women's Davening
   Group
c/o Sacks
466 Argyles Road
Brooklyn, NY 11218
(718) 287-8939

Jewish Feminist Ritual Group
c/o Weinberg
6909 Greene Street
Philadelphia, PA 19119
(215) 849-5584

Jewish Feminist Study Group
c/o Charlotte S. Waisman, Ph.D.
Route 3, Box 491 AK
Texarkana, TX, 75503
(214) 792-5813

Jewish Women's Organization
Rabbi Patrice Karlin
Hillel Council at UCLA
900 Hilgard Avenue
Los Angeles, CA 90024
(213) 208-3081

Kol Nashim
c/o Kaplan
1717 Wroxton Court, #1
Houston, TX 77005

Lincoln Square Rosh Chodesh
   Services
c/o Joselet Weissman
441 West End Avenue
New York, NY 10024

Midtown Women's Service
c/o Wagschal
155 W. 68 Street
New York, NY 10023
(212) 580-8071

Minyan Mi'at
(*See* Minyanim)

Riverdale Women's Tefilah
Hebrew Institute of Riverdale
3700 Henry Hudson Parkway
Riverdale, NY 10463

Rosh Chodesh Group
Penina Villenchik
37 Drew Road
Belmont, MA 02178

Task Force on Jewish Woman
   (umbrella for women's prayer
   and study groups)
Box 1062
Teaneck, NJ 07666

Twin Cities Women's Minyan
c/o Bet Hillel
150A University Avenue
Minneapolis, MN 55455

WOMEN'S PRAYER AND STUDY GROUPS
(*continued*)

Washington Heights Women's
  Service
c/o Brandriss
360 Cabrini Boulevard, Apt. 8M
New York, NY 10040
(212) 928-4177

Women's Minyan of Baltimore
c/o Siegman
3406 Labyrith Road
Baltimore, MD 21215

Women's Rosh Chodesh Services
4894 St. Kevin
Montreal, Quebec
Canada

Women's Tefilah Group of Chicago
c/o B'nai B'rith Hillel Foundation
  at The University of Chicago
5715 Woodlawn Avenue
Chicago, IL 60615
(312) 667-4792

Women's Tefilah Group of
  Teaneck
c/o Janet Hoffman
430 Winthrop Road
Teaneck, NJ 07666
(201) 837-0449

Women's Torah Study Group
Beth Israel Synagogue
1007 Sinclair Street
Winnipeg, Manitoba R2V 315
Canada

(*See also* Havurot; Jewish Feminist
  Organizations; Lesbian and Gay;
  Rabbis; Scholars and Scholarship;
  University-Affiliated Resources;
  Women's Religious
  Organizations)

WOMEN'S RELIGIOUS ORGANIZATIONS

Feminists of Faith
  (interreligious)
c/o Annette Daum
Union of American Hebrew
  Congregations
838 Fifth Avenue
New York, NY 10021
(212) 249-0100

Feminist Theological Institute
198-01 56th Avenue
Bayside, NY 11364

Institute of Women Today
  (interreligious spiritual and
  social-action group)
1307 S. Wabash Avenue
Chicago, IL 60605
(312) 341-9159

YIDDISH AND LADINO ORGANIZATIONS

Adelante!—The Judezmo Society
4594 Bedford Avenue
Brooklyn, NY 11235

Committee for Jewish Culture in
  Israel
228 Bnei Ephraim Street
Maoz Aviv, Tel Aviv, Israel 69017

CYCO Publishing House and
  Bookstore
25 E. 78 Street
New York, NY 10028
(212) 535-4320

IKUF—Yidishe Kultur-Farlag
80 Fifth Avenue, Room 906
New York, NY 10011
(212) 477-9084

Jewish Labor Bund
25 E. 78 Street
New York, NY 10028
(212) 535-0850

National Yiddish Book Exchange
P.O. Box 969
Amherst, MA 01004

Pripetshik Program
  (Yiddish play group for
  preschoolers)
(See Child Care)

Workmen's Circle—Education
  Department
45 East 33 Street
New York, NY 10016
(212) 889-6800

YIVO Institute for Jewish Research
1048 Fifth Avenue
New York, NY 10028
(212) 535-6700

Yugntruf—Youth for Yiddish
3328 Bainbridge Avenue
Bronx, NY 10467
(212) 654-8540

YOUTH ORGANIZATIONS AND RESOURCES

Association of Jewish Sponsored
  Camps, Inc.
130 E. 59 Street
New York, NY 10022
(212) 751-0477

B'nei Akiva
  (religious Zionist youth
  movement)
25 W. 26 Street
New York, NY 10010
(212) 338-7247

B'nai B'rith Youth Organization
1640 Rhode Island Avenue, N.W.
Washington, DC 20036
(202) 857-6600

Gay and Young
Youth Aid and Advocacy Program
240 E. 31 Street
New York, NY 10016
(212) 684-5865

Jewish Welfare Board
15 E. 26 Street
New York, NY 10010

N.F.T.Y. (National Federation of
  Temple Youth)
  (Reform)
838 Fifth Avenue
New York, NY 10021

United Synagogue Youth
155 Fifth Avenue
New York, NY 10010

Young Judaea
50 W. 58 Street
New York, NY 10019

Yugntruf—Youth for Yiddish
(See Yiddish and Ladino
  Organizations)

(See also University-Affiliated
  Resources)

NOTES

Introduction

1. "I've Had Nothing Yet So I Can't Take More," *Moment*, Sept. 1983, p. 23.

2. "Judaism—Where Does the Feminist Go?" *Humanistic Judaism* (Winter 1981), p. 3.

3. "Woman-Identified Women in Male-Identified Judaism," in *On Being a Jewish Feminist: A Reader*, ed. Susannah Heschel (New York: Schocken, 1983), pp. 132–33.

4. From a 1980 lecture at a conference on "Feminists of Faith," sponsored by a coalition of groups including the American Jewish Committee and the Union of American Hebrew Congregations.

Chapter 1   Law and Leadership

1. For a thoughtful (though not feminist) précis on the Talmud and the way it has shaped laws and attitudes, see Adin Steinsaltz, *The Essential Talmud* (New York: Bantam, 1980).

2. Rachel Adler, "The Jew Who Wasn't There: Halacha and the Jewish Woman, *Response*, Summer 1973, p. 82.

3. The wedding ring he gives her is not to have any jewels in it but is to be as plain as possible so that its value may be determined easily; it is part of the "payment" she receives for becoming his bride. Dr. Trude Weiss-Rosmarin reminds us that *kiddushin*, the Hebrew word for the Jewish marriage ceremony, "does not really stand for 'sanctification' but . . . signifies 'setting apart,' in this context setting apart, or aside, the bride as the *legal* personal property of the groom, of which only he can dispose with a bill of divorcement" (*Proceedings of the 1979 Rabbinical Assembly Convention*, p. 223).

Weiss-Rosmarin says elsewhere (*The Jewish Spectator*, Oct. 1970): "The legal reasoning is that marriage is an act of acquisition (*kinyan*, literally 'purchase') and thus the owner of 'the possession' cannot be dispossessed by court action. He, and only he, can issue the writ of divorcement."

4. From "The Jewish Woman," a pamphlet "adapted from the works of Rabbi M. M. Schneerson," Lubavitch, 1974.

5. In Israel, of course, Halachah is the civil law code for Jews for marriage, divorce, and personal-status issues. This means that to obtain a divorce a woman must operate under the limitations Jewish law places on her appearing as a witness. And in Israel there is no recourse to civil marriage or divorce (see p. 36), so a woman who might choose to cannot simply ignore the inequalities of religious law, as she might in another country.

6. "The Status of Women in Halachic Judaism," in *The Jewish Woman: New Perspectives*, ed. Elizabeth Koltun (New York: Schocken, 1976), p. 122.

7. Address at the 79th annual convention of the Rabbinical Assembly, in *Proceedings of the 1979 Rabbinical Assembly Convention*, Vol. XLI, 1979.

8. Paula Hyman, in *The Jewish Woman: New Perspectives*; Rachel Adler, *op. cit.*; Nessa Rapoport, in *Lilith* #6 (1979).

9. Richard M. Yellin, "A Philosophy of Jewish Masculinity," *Conservative Judaism* (Spring 1976), p. 93.

10. "Notes Toward Finding the Right Question: A Vindication of the Rights of Jewish Women," *Lilith* #6 (1979), p. 28.

11. The rabbinic responses to individual or group need have formed the basis of Jewish legal codes. Immanuel Jakobovits explains part of the mechanism in his discussion of recent medical developments in contraception and the rabbinical responses to them: ". . . none of these verdicts represents *ex cathedra* pronouncements or impersonal edicts for general application. In contrast to the formulation of moral attitudes by other faiths or legislatures, the responsa are usually authentic replies to personal enquiries, submitted by individuals who seek to govern their lives in consonance with Jewish law, and answered by rabbis aware of their grave responsibility. . . ." *Jewish Medical Ethics* (New York: Bloch, 1975), p. 268.

12. "The issue is of particular concern to Orthodox women with young children, because within the eruv they are able to carry their children or wheel them in carriages to visit friends." In Lawrence, Long Island (New York), a community of Orthodox Jews has strung a nylon cord across utility poles and considers this an *eruv*. "A Nylon Cord Is a Constitutional Issue," *The New York Times*, May 10, 1983, p. B1.

13. From a talk on her book *Voices of Wisdom: Jewish Ideals and Ethics for Everyday Living* (Pantheon, 1980) delivered at a B'nai B'rith Anti-Defamation League "Book and Author" luncheon, 1980.

14. *Conservative Judaism*, Vol. XX, No. 1 (Fall 1965), p. 53.

15. Susan Grossman, a member of the first class at the Jewish Theological Seminary to admit women as rabbinical students, prepared this material especially for inclusion in *Jewish and Female*.

16. Blu Greenberg, in *Face to Face*, a newsletter published by the B'nai B'rith Anti-Defamation League (Spring 1981), p. 10. The demands of Ezrat Nashim in 1972 did include a plank that women be declared fully obligated.

17. *Op. cit.*, p. 94.

18. *Op. cit.*, *loc. cit.*

19. "Our Readers Speak: Women as Rabbis," *Moment*, May 1980, p. 34.

20. Robert Blair Kaiser, "Drive Pressed for Ordaining Female Rabbis," *The New York Times*, March 23, 1980, p. 40.

21. Quoted in Marta Berl Shapiro, "Changing Role for Women in Conservative Synagogues," *Long Island Jewish World*, April 18, 1980, p. 12.

22. "Women in the Rabbinate—A Personal Reflection," prepared for publication in *Outlook*, March 1984.

23. See reporting by Reena Sigman Friedman in *Lilith*: "The Politics of Ordination," #6, p. 9, and "Conservative Rabbis Endorse Women's Ordination," #7 (1980), p. 6.

24. *Judaism: A Quarterly Journal of Jewish Life and Thought*, Vol. 30, No. 4 (Fall 1981), p. 426.

25. "Woman Assumed Pulpit," *American Jewish Outlook*, Jan. 19, 1951, p. 7.

26. *Unorthodox Judaism* (Columbus: Ohio State Univ. Press, 1978), p. 79.

27. *The Jewish Spectator* (Feb. 1972), pp. 6–8.

Chapter 2   From Observer to Participant

1. "The Status of Women in Halachic Judaism," *The Jewish Woman: New Perspectives*, ed. Elizabeth Koltun (New York: Schocken, 1976), pp. 121–122.

2. For detailed descriptions of the ways in which one family observes these "women's" mitzvot, see Blu Greenberg, *How to Run a Traditional Jewish Household* (New York: Simon and Schuster, 1983).

3. Rachel Gershon, "Women and Mitzvot: An Experiential Approach," *Bechol Zot*, p. 23.

4. *Women and Judaism* (Garden City, NY: Doubleday, 1980), p. 103.

To counter the ugly notion that women are dangerous and need to be kept quiet and isolated, the news section of *Lilith* magazine is entitled "Kol Ishah," with this explanation: "Traditionally, the voice of the Jewish woman was not to be heard in public, lest it arouse men. No more. These pages are for news about Jewish women, usually in their own strong voices." The very phrase that has been used to signal women's removal from the public sphere announces here that women are participating in it with great energy.

5. Frayda Siller Turkel, "I Was Asked to Read from the Torah," *Sh'ma*, 11/209, March 6, 1981, p. 65.

6. *Face to Face* (Spring 1978), p. 17.

7. April 18, 1980, pp. 12–14. Both rabbis insisted on anonymity.

8. Ann Braude, "The Jewish Woman's Encounter with American Culture" in *Women and Religion in America: Volume I: The Nineteenth Century*, ed. Rosemary Radford Ruether and Rosemary Skinner Keller (San Francisco: Harper & Row, 1981), p. 155.

9. Quoted by William Novak in "From Somerville to Savannah . . . and Los Angeles . . . and Dayton," *Moment*, Vol. 6, No. 2 (Jan.–Feb., 1981), p. 22.

10. Personal communication.

11. Richard M. Yellin, "A Philosophy of Jewish Masculinity," *Conservative Judaism* (Spring 1976), p. 92.

12. *Humanistic Judaism* (Winter 1981), p. 25.

13. Reported on at the Conference on Jewish Women and Men, New York, April 1974.

14. "Female God Language in a Jewish Context," *Womanspirit Rising: A Feminist Reader in Religion,* ed. Carol P. Christ and Judith Plaskow (New York: Harper & Row, 1979), p. 171.

15. Ibid., p. 167.

16. *Beyond God the Father: Toward a Philosophy of Women's Liberation* (Boston: Beacon Press, 1973).

17. Robert Gordis, "Women's Rights in Jewish Life and Law," *United Synagogue Review* (April 1977), p. 30.

Speculating on the attitude that might have been behind the creation of this prayer in its original form, Jewish Family Life Education specialist Vicki Rosenstreich speculates that men need to define themselves here by what they're *not*—that is, by differentiating themselves from their surroundings, especially from women. While women know that they can safely identify with their (usual) earliest care-giver, their mother, men may need to reassure themselves of their differentiated identity by saying that they are *not* Mother.

Chapter 3   Rhythms and Cycles

1. Lynn Gottlieb, in "It's Called a Calling: Interview with Lynn Gottlieb," *Moment*, Vol. 4, No. 5 (May 1979), p. 36.

2. *Guide to Shabbat* (New York: National Jewish Resource Center, 1981), p. 48.

3. *Leviathan* (Spring 1981); also, Roselyn Bell, "The Rising of the Moon: A Women's Holiday," Jewish Student Press Service, Feb. 1978.

4. Moshe Meiselman, *Jewish Woman in Jewish Law* (New York: Ktav, 1978), p. 54.

5. Jewish Chronicle News Service, Nov. 1980.

6. Letty Cottin Pogrebin, *Growing Up Free: Raising Your Child in the 80's* (New York: McGraw-Hill, 1980), p. 522.

7. From a letter to the editors of *Lilith*.

8. Quoted in Gloria Hayes Kremer, "It's Tough to Be Jewish Alone," *Inside*—quarterly magazine of the *Philadelphia Jewish Exponent*—(Spring 1981), p. 19.

9. For a look at how women's experience can create a distinct "women's theology," see Valerie Saiving, "The Human Situation: A Feminine View," a 1960 essay, rp. in *Womanspirit Rising*, ed. Carol P. Christ and Judith Plaskow (New York: Harper & Row, 1979).

10. *Face to Face*, a newsletter published by the B'nai B'rith Anti-Defamation League (Spring 1981), p. 8.

11. *Womanspirit Rising*, p. 14.

12. I am grateful to Dr. Nechama Liss-Levinson for calling this prayer to

my attention. It can be found in the collection of the Jewish Women's Resource Center, New York.

13. *How to Run a Traditional Jewish Household* (New York: Simon and Schuster, 1983), p. 225.

14. Lucy Robins Lang, *Tomorrow Is Beautiful* (New York: Macmillan, 1948), p. 1.

15. Ashkenazi Jews are usually those from Central or Eastern Europe. Sephardic Jews are, strictly speaking, the descendants of those Spanish Jews who fled Spain for Holland, Germany, Italy, and other countries in the wake of the Inquisition of the fifteenth century. The term is used now to refer also to Jews from Mediterranean countries, the Middle East, and/or the Levant.

16. Ruth Koffler on the Sephardic baby-naming ceremony, *Lilith* #3, p. 23. These early ceremonies were not necessarily a glorification of womanhood; among the spirits warned against was Lilith.

17. Mary Gendler, in a provocative article, "Sarah's Seed," *Response* (Winter 1974–75), has proposed a piercing of the girl's hymen as an equivalent "opening" to the boy's circumcision. E. M. Broner, in an interview in *Lilith* #4, makes a similar point, describing a scene from her novel *A Weave of Women* (Bantam, 1980): "A baby girl is born: on the eighth day, which is the time of the circumcision, they pierce the baby girl's hymen—there's a hymenotomy, so that all orifices are open, so that she will be delivered intact to no man."

Ethiopian Jews, the Falashas, sometimes perform ritual clitoridectomy on newborn girls, a tradition deriving perhaps from the practice of this genital mutilation in surrounding cultures rather than from Jewish tradition. See the novel by Moris Farhi, *The Last of Days* (Crown, 1983).

Some of the anxieties both men and women express around the issue of circumcision as mutilation are discussed in Zalman Schachter-Shalomi, with Donald Gropman, *The First Step: A Guide for the New Jewish Spirit* (New York: Bantam, 1983), and by Barbara Cohn, "Circumcision: A Mother's Ambivalence," *Sh'ma*, Feb. 5, 1982.

18. As did *Jewish Catalog* editors Sharon and Michael Strassfeld. See Amy Stone, "Ceremonial Welcoming for a Newborn Jewish Daughter," *Lilith* #2, p. 22.

19. The rabbis are Rebecca Trachtenberg Alpert, Nancy Fuchs-Kreimer, Linda Holtzman, Sandy Levine, Joy Levitt, Deborah Prinz, Ruth Sohn, Marjorie Yudkin, and Deborah Zecher. The ceremony was brought to my attention by Rebecca Trachtenberg Alpert.

20. For help in figuring out correspondences between Hebrew and English names, see Alfred J. Kolatch, *The Name Dictionary: Modern English and Hebrew Names* (New York: Jonathan David, 1967).

21. I am grateful to Dr. Nechama Liss-Levinson for calling my attention to this ceremony, and for sharing her copy with me.

22. From an unpublished paper, "Possibilities and Problems of Creating a Jewish Feminist Theology."

23. From an undated broadside distributed by Bat Kol in the mid-1970s.

24. Yael (June 1980) and Raquel (December 1982), the daughters of

Mierle and Jack Ukeles. Two other girls in the Riverdale Orthodox community have marked Bat Mitzvah in similar ceremonies.

25. At a panel discussion at New York's 92nd Street YM/YWHA in March 1982. The program was titled by its male organizers "The Promise and Limits of Jewish Feminism."

26. For a psychological approach to the responses of Israeli women at mid-life, see Nancy Datan, Aaron Antonovsky, and Benjamin Maoz, *A Time to Reap: The Middle Age of Women in Five Israeli Subcultures* (Baltimore: Johns Hopkins University Press, 1981).

27. For a discussion of the sexist nature of the traditional Ashkenazi prayer service for a deceased woman, see Sibyl Cohen, "Over My Dead Body . . . ," *Lilith* #7 (1980), p. 29.

28. "On Saying Kaddish: A Letter to Haym Peretz, New York, September 16, 1916," *Response*, Vol. VII, No. 2 (Summer 1973), p. 76.

29. *Lilith* #2 (Winter 76/77), p. 4.

30. "The Mourning Minyan," *Lilith* #7 (1980), p. 28.

31. At a consultation on the roles of women in Jewish religious life, sponsored by the American Jewish Committee in 1983, the issue of women's full participation in mourning rituals emerged as a petition demanding (along with the demand for ordination of women as rabbis and cantors) that "women be counted equally and fully in *all* minyanim, especially for Shiva and Kaddish." In addition, one of the liveliest exchanges at the session occurred when women shared information about which congregations around the country were especially welcoming to women mourners.

Chapter 4   Our Minds for Ourselves

1. Adin Steinsaltz, *The Essential Talmud* (New York: Bantam, 1977), p. 137.

2. Yitzchak Leib Peretz, "A Woman's Wrath," translated from the Yiddish by Zora Zagrabelna, *Lilith* #1, p. 29.

3. Mary Cahn Schwartz, "The High Price of Failure," *Lilith* #1, p. 22.

4. Isaac Metzker, ed., *A Bintel Brief: Sixty Years of Letters from the Lower East Side to the Jewish Daily Forward* (Garden City: Doubleday, 1971), pp. 109–10.

5. "Culture and Radical Politics: Yiddish Women Writers, 1890–1940," *American Jewish History*, Vol. LXX, No. 1 (Special Issue on American Jewish Women), p. 73.

6. *America's Jews* (New York: Random House, 1971), p. 81.

7. Corinne Azen Krause, *Grandmothers, Mothers and Daughters: An Oral History of Ethnicity, Mental Health, and Continuity of Three Generations of Jewish, Italian, and Slavic-American Women,* (New York: The Institute on Pluralism and Group Identity of the American Jewish Committee, 1978), p. 143.

8. Mary Cantwell, "Books: Role Models," *The New York Times*, August 6, 1982, p. C22.

9. Dr. Elizabeth E. Seittelman, "The Contributions of Jewish Women to

Education in the United States: Part I—In the Nineteenth Century," *The Principal*, Vol. XXI, No. 1 (Sept. 1975), p. 7.

10. Mary Helen Washington, "Working at Single Bliss," *Ms.* (Oct. 1982), p. 56.

11. *On Women and Judaism: A View from Tradition* (Philadelphia: Jewish Publication Society, 1982), p. 26.

12. This and other stories of women whose lives can serve as role models come from Emily Taitz and Sondra Henry, *Written Out of History* (New York: Biblio Press, 1983).

13. "Notes Toward Finding the Right Question," *Lilith* #6 (1979), p. 22.

14. Beth Zuriel, "Nehama Liebowitz's Fifth Book of the Bible," *Israel Scene* (April 1980), p. 34.

15. New York: E. P. Dutton, 1978, p. 90.

16. For more on how Jewish women's intellectual development fared in this period, see: Hannah Arendt, *Rachel Varnhagen: The Life of a Jewish Woman* (New York and London: Harcourt Brace Jovanovich, 1974); Adolf Kober, "Emancipation's Impact on the Educational and Vocational Training of German Jewry," *Jewish Social Studies*, Vol. 16, No. 1 (January 1954), pp. 3–32; Bertha Meyer, *Salon Sketches: Biographical Studies of Berlin Salons of the Emancipation* (New York: Bloch, 1938); and Michael Meyer, *The Origins of the Modern Jew: Jewish Identity and European Culture in Germany, 1749–1824* (Detroit: Wayne State University Press, 1967).

17. Deborah Weissman, "Bais Yaakov: A Historical Model for Jewish Feminists," in *The Jewish Woman: New Perspectives*, ed. Elizabeth Koltun (New York: Schocken, 1976), p. 142.

18. Rabbi Selig Korolnek, "Jewish Women Are Responsible for Survival of the Jewish People," *Canadian Jewish News*, March 19, 1981, p. 10.

19. "Bertha Pappenheim: Founder of German-Jewish Feminism," in Koltun, *The Jewish Woman: New Perspectives*, p. 162.

20. Personal communication from the Jewish Education Service of North America. This figure is consonant with those that have emerged from other studies—for example, a survey on Jewish education conducted by the Conservative movement, reported in *United Synagogue Review* (Spring 1980), p. 9.

21. Gerhard Lang, Maureen Carroll, and Leslie Liebman, "Women in Jewish Schools," in *Jewish Education*, Vol. 46, No. 3 (Fall 1978).

22. This study was prepared by the Reform movement's Religious Action Center in Washington. See also Susan Wall, "Non-Sexist Jewish Education," *In the Profession*, Philadelphia Board of Jewish Education (Feb. 1975), and Susan Rosenblum Shevitz, "Sexism in Jewish Education," *Response* (Summer 1973).

23. In the "Proceedings" of the Consultation, available from the Jewish Communal Affairs Department, American Jewish Committee, New York.

24. *Lilith* #2 (Winter 1976/77), p. 17.

25. "A Family Affair: Rachel and David Ebner, Married Students to Receive Degrees in Advanced Jewish Studies from Bernard Revel Graduate School," Yeshiva University press release, June 23, 1980.

26. Quoted in Eillene Leistner, "You've Come a Long Way, Stern College," *Long Island Jewish World*, October 31, 1980, p. 19.

27. "It's Called a Calling: Interview with Lynn Gottlieb," *Moment*, Vol. 4, No. 5 (May 1979), p. 34.

28. Various treatments of the Lilith story: Lilly Rivlin, "Lilith," *Ms.* (Dec. 1972); Judith Plaskow Goldenberg, "Applesource," in "The Jewish Feminist: Conflict in Identities," *Response*, Vol. VII, No. 2 (Summer 1973); Aviva Cantor Zuckoff, "The Lilith Question," *Lilith* #1; Pamela White Hadas, "The Passion of Lilith" (poem), from her collection *In the Light of Genesis* (Philadelphia: Jewish Publication Society of America, 1980).

29. In a paper, "The Unethical and the Unspeakable: Toward a Feminist Interpretation of the Holocaust," presented in New York in 1981 at an interfaith meeting on Women and the Holocaust.

30. From a talk given at the second annual National Women's Studies Association convention, Bloomington, Ind., May 1980.

Chapter 5 Our Bodies

1. See Rabbi Alan S. Green, *Sex, God and the Sabbath: The Mystery of Jewish Marriage* (Cleveland: Temple Emanu El, 1979); also see Zalman Schachter-Shalomi, with Donald Gropman, *The First Step: A Guide for the New Jewish Spirit* (New York: Bantam, 1983).

2. *Birth Control in Jewish Law* (New York: New York Univ. Press, 1968), p. 74.

3. Leonard Swidler, *Women in Judaism: The Status of Women in Formative Judaism* (Philadelphia: Scarecrow Press, 1978).

4. Gila Berkowitz, a Palo Alto–based writer, has just completed a book on Jewish sexuality and a novel entitled *Dirty Diamonds*. Her contributions here on sexuality and mikveh observance were written specially for *Jewish and Female*.

Berkowitz' comments on the mikveh revival are borne out by others. Nechama Liss-Levinson reports that the North Shore Mikveh Association on Long Island in New York now holds dinners honoring publicly the women who have been active in supporting the local mikveh, whereas a few years ago the very existence of a mikveh in Great Neck, New York, was something of an embarrassment in the community.

5. Leo Trepp, *The Complete Book of Jewish Observance: A Practical Manual for the Modern Jew* (New York: Behrman House/Summit, 1980), p. 296.

6. "Women and Change in Jewish Law," *Conservative Judaism*, Vol. XXIX, No. 1, Fall 1974, pp. 10, 11.

7. Michael Asheri, *Living Jewish: The Lore and Law of the Practicing Jew* (New York: Everest House, 1978), p. 62.

8. "Ritual Bath Claim Is Questioned," *Jerusalem Post*, international edition, Dec. 9–15, 1979.

9. "Mikveh Is Not a Viable Mitzvah," *Sh'ma*, Vol. 11, No. 205, Jan. 9, 1981, p. 39.

10. "Let's Reappropriate Mikveh," *Sh'ma*, Vol. 11, No. 212, April 17, 1981, p. 95.

11. Philadelphia: Jewish Publication Society, 1981.

12. "Integrating Mikveh and Modernity," *Sh'ma*, Vol. 11, No. 205, Jan. 9, 1980, p. 37.

13. "Mikva Dreams—A Performance," *Heresies* #5 (1979), pp. 52–54.

14. Jewish Student Press Service, March 1981.

15. Sharon Strassfeld and Michael Strassfeld, eds. (Philadelphia, Jewish Publication Society, 1976), pp. 96–99.

16. New York: Schocken, 1970.

17. As we have learned from Susan Brownmiller's *Against Our Will: Men, Women and Rape* (New York: Bantam, 1976).

18. *Sh'ma*, Vol. 11, No. 205, Jan. 9, 1980, p. 38.

19. See Pauline Bart, "Portnoy's Mother's Complaint: Depression in Middle-Aged Women," in *The Jewish Woman: New Perspectives*, ed. Elizabeth Koltun (New York: Schocken, 1976), and Alexander Grinstein, "Profile of a Doll—A Female Character Type," *Psychoanalytic Review*, Vol. 50, No. 27 (1963), pp. 161–174.

20. "I've Had Nothing Yet So I Can't Take More," *Moment*, Sept. 1983, p. 25.

21. Columbus: Ohio State Univ. Press, 1978, p. 176.

22. Perigee, 1981.

23. "Prostitute's Progress," a review of *The Maimie Papers*, *Lilith* #7, 1980, pp. 40–41.

24. Ruth Rosen, historical ed., Sue Davidson, textual ed. (Old Westbury, NY: The Feminist Press, in cooperation with the Schlesinger Library, Radcliffe College, 1977).

25. Friedman, "Prostitute's Progress," p. 40.

26. "Bertha Pappenheim: Founder of German-Jewish Feminism," in Koltun, ed., *The Jewish Woman: New Perspectives*, p. 157. See also Marion Kaplan, *The Jüdischer Frauenbund* (New York: Columbia Univ. Press, 1979).

27. Quoted in Immanuel Jakobovits, *Jewish Medical Ethics* (New York: Bloch, 1975), p. 165.

28. Marshall Sklare, *America's Jews* (New York: Random House, 1971), p. 80.

29. I am indebted to William Kavesh, M.D., of Boston for calling my attention to the ritual behavior prescribed after an abortion, which involves practices similar to the purification after menstruation, and, in earlier times, also involved sacrificial offerings. In the English Soncino edition of the Talmud, see *Niddah*, pp. 139–219, and *Keritoth*, pp. 53–62.

30. Quoted in Julie Liedman, "Abortion: A Painful Jewish Dilemma," *Jewish Exponent*, Jan. 9, 1981, p. 5.

31. Quoted in "Abortion—A Fundamental Right in Jeopardy," a report of the American Jewish Congress Commission on Law and Social Action, March 1981.

In Canada, attempts to liberalize restrictive abortion laws (historically formulated by the powerful Catholic Church) are often characterized by the right wing as "Jewish" movements. This is partly the result of the visibility in the abortion-reform movement of Dr. Henry Morgentaler, a Jew and a survivor of Auschwitz. Morgentaler is a Montreal-based gynecologist who has opened abortion clinics in the provinces of Quebec and Manitoba to challenge the laws that restrict women's access to abortion. Protests against Morgentaler's abortion stand have almost always been marked by anti-Semitic pickets, one such demonstration in Winnipeg, in the spring of 1983, reportedly being accompanied by the taped music of "If I Were a Rich Man," from *Fiddler on the Roof*.

33. In *The Woman Who Lost Her Names*, ed. Julia Wolf Mazow (San Francisco: Harper & Row, 1980).

34. *Jerusalem Post*, international edition, Dec. 9–15, 1979, p. 369A.

35. Private communication to the author.

36. See Dov I. Frimer, "Grounds for Divorce Due to Immoral Behavior (Other than Adultery) According to Jewish Law," Ph.D. thesis (in Hebrew), Hebrew Univ., Jerusalem, 1980, p. 47 (also on file at Yeshiva Univ. NY). Historical facts are culled from the Introduction and Chap. 8 (pp. 45–137).

37. Ibid. The only Biblical allusion to hair-covering occurs in the case of the adulteress, where the High Priest uncovers the head of the woman as a sign of her degradation. Those Halachic authorities who consider the obligation to cover the hair to be of Biblical origin base themselves on this allusion.

38. Ibid., pp. 48–49. Practices varied in the Babylonian Exile and in Palestine.

39. Ibid., p. 59.

40. The definition of *tzniut* is derived from Moshe Meiselman, *Jewish Women in Jewish Law* (New York: Ktav, 1978), p. 215.

41. Giti Bendheim, a psychologist, lives in Riverdale, NY. Her remarks on hair covering were written especially for *Jewish and Female*.

42. Saul Berman, in *The Jewish Woman: New Perspectives*, says: "The fact that Jewish women are relieved of the obligations of putting on *tallit* and *tefillin*, of praying at fixed times of the day, and even of covering their heads prior to marriage, and have traditionally been discouraged from voluntarily performing these acts, has left them largely devoid of actively symbolic means of affirming their identities as observant Jews.

"An interesting byproduct of this absence of covenant affirming symbols is the emphasis which Orthodox outreach groups have placed on dress standards. Not wearing slacks has been treated as if it were a revealed *mitzvah*, equivalent to *tzitzit* as a sign of one's commitment" (p. 115).

43. Deuteronomy, XXII, 5.

44. Leo Trepp, *The Complete Book of Jewish Observance* (New York: Behrman House/Summit Books, 1980), p. 267.

45. Chana Forse, "Throwing Off the Old 'Pushover' Stereotype," *Lilith* #4 (Fall/Winter 77/78), p. 31.

46. "Female Humanity," *Judaism* (Spring 1981).

47. Gloria Averbuch, "Ten Women Tell . . . The Ways We Are," *Lilith* #2 (Winter 76/77), p. 7.

48. Interviewed in *Lilith* #2, p. 25.

49. See Anna Sequoia's distressingly popular *J.A.P. Handbook* (New York: Plume, 1982), in which are discussed the "styles" of various plastic surgeons operating on Jewish women.

50. See "Ethnotherapy with Jews," a videotape of therapy groups conducted by Judith Weinstein Klein (see p. 438). In one session Klein and several group members try to convince one woman who is defending her "nose job" that she might be oppressed by negative feelings about being Jewish. They remind her that it is not common for non-Jewish women to endure a similar rite of passage to ensure social acceptability.

51. Garden City, NY: Doubleday, 1979. See Chap. 30, "The Subject Was Noses," pp. 161–73.

52. Even Yiddish popular music treats issues of health and disease in a clinical manner. One such is "Mentshen-fresser" (Man-Eaters), a waltz-tempo song about tuberculosis popular in the early years of the twentieth century. The very first verse of the song refers to "bacilli and microbes." See Mark Slobin, *Tenement Songs: The Popular Music of the Jewish Immigrants* (Urbana: Univ. of Illinois Press, 1982), p. 148.

53. Since the health professionals tend to be male, there is an imbalance of power here overlying the already unequal relationship between the dependency of a sick or suffering person and the person with the specialized knowledge to cure or succor. Two extraordinarily informative and analytical pamphlets discuss this and other feminist health issues that affect all women: Barbara Ehrenreich and Deirdre English, *Witches, Midwives and Nurses: A History of Women Healers* and *Complaints and Disorders: The Sexual Politics of Sickness* (Glass Mountain Pamphlets Nos. 1 and 2, Old Westbury, New York: The Feminist Press, 1973).

54. Baruch Modan, "Cancer," in *Genetic Diseases Among Ashkenazi Jews*, ed. Richard M. Goodman and Arno G. Motulsky (New York: Raven Press, 1979), pp. 372–373.

55. Schneir Levin, "Breast Feeding: Religious Influences," *Journal of Psychology and Judaism*, Vol. 3, No. 3 (Spring 1979), pp. 195–200.

Chapter 6   Jewish Women in the Nuclear Family and Beyond

1. For an overview of some of the recent cross-cultural research into family life, see Andrew J. Cherlin and Carin Celebuski, *Are Jewish Families Different?* (New York: The William Petschek National Jewish Family Center, American Jewish Committee, 1982). The monograph states, "the premise that Jewish family life is different, or distinctive, does not rest on a solid empirical foundation."

2. *Single-Parent Families: A Challenge to the Jewish Community* (New York: American Jewish Committee, 1981).

3. At a conference, "Women's Roles and the Family," 1980.

4. Judith G. Rabkin and Elmer L. Struening, in *Ethnicity, Social Class and Mental Illness* (New York: American Jewish Committee, 1976).

5. "An Exclusive Interview with Dr. Phyllis Chesler," *Lilith* #2, Winter 76/77, pp. 26–27.

6. From an address delivered at the 1979 Jewish Educators Assembly convention.

7. From a speech before the American Jewish Congress in the mid-1970s.

8. "The Ties that Choke [*sic*]," *Perspectives*, U.S. Commission on Civil Rights Quarterly (Spring 1980), pp. 39–43.

9. Marshall Sklare, *America's Jews* (New York: Random House, 1971), p. 95.

10. For an analysis of the unique patterns American Jews have developed for connecting with their relatives, see William E. Mitchell, *Mishpokhe: A Study of New York City Jewish Family Clubs* (The Hague: Mouton, 1978).

11. Myrna Silverman, "Jewish Family and Kinship in Pittsburgh," Ph.D. thesis, Univ. of Pittsburgh, 1976.

12. Anti-Semitic because certain general characteristics are defined simultaneously as negative and Jewish.

13. "The Real Jewish Mother," *Congress Monthly* (June 1977); see also Zena Smith Blau, "In Defense of the Jewish Mother," in *The Ghetto and Beyond*, ed. Peter I. Rose (New York: Random House, 1969).

14. For expansion of the subject of the changes immigrant and second-generation Jewish women have gone through, see Charlotte Baum, Paula Hyman, and Sonya Michel, *The Jewish Woman in America* (New York: Dial, 1976).

15. New York: Harper & Row, 1979, pp. 134–135.

16. James West, *Plainville, U.S.A.* (New York: Columbia Univ. Press, 1961).

17. Cathy N. Davidson and E. M. Broner, eds. *The Lost Tradition: Mothers and Daughters in Literature* (New York: Frederick Ungar, 1980), p. 191.

18. P. 232.

19. *Of Woman Born: Motherhood as Experience and Institution* (New York: Bantam, 1977), p. 237.

20. See Shulamit Firestone's astonishing, brilliant essay *The Dialectic of Sex* (New York: Bantam, 1972) for an analysis of how daughters and sons betray their mothers as they grow up.

21. *Op. cit.*, pp, 237, 238.

22. *Grandmothers, Mothers and Daughters* (New York: American Jewish Committee, 1978). See Bibliog.

23. There are distinct differences here between Jews and other groups. Among blacks in America, for example, who may have lived in poverty for several generations, it is assumed that children with any degree of economic stability will support not only their nuclear family but also the parents of the working adult(s). For more on the cross-cultural differences and similarities among families of different ethnic backgrounds, see *Ethnicity and Family Therapy*, ed. Monica McGoldrick, John K. Pearce, and Joseph Giordano (New York: The Guilford Press, 1983).

24. Harold J. Wershow, "The Older Jews of Albany Park—Some Aspects of a Subculture of the Aged and Its Interaction with a Gerontological Research Project," *The Gerontologist*, 4 (1964), pp. 198–202, cited in Bart, "Depression in Middle Aged Women: Some Sociocultural Factors," Ph.D. thesis, UCLA, 1967.

25. "What Is a Jewish Mother?" *Lilith* #4, Fall/Winter 77/78, pp. 18–20.

26. New York: Persea Books, 1978 (rpt. of 1925 ed.).

27. *Lilith* #1, Fall 1976, pp. 27–29.

28. *Women's League Outlook* (Spring 1982), p. 7. See also a 1977 discussion guide published by the American Jewish Committee, "Changing Roles of Men and Women in the Jewish Family."

29. See Margaret Hennig and Anne Jardim, *The Managerial Woman* (Garden City, N.Y.: Doubleday, 1977).

Chapter 7   Whom We Choose and Why

1. Quoted in the *Baltimore Jewish Times*, Oct. 22, 1976.

2. Charlotte Baum, Paula Hyman and Sonya Michel, *The Jewish Woman in America* (Dial, 1976), p. 14.

3. From a paper presented at a conference, "The Evolving Jewish Family," sponsored by the American Jewish Committee and Queens College (New York) in June 1981.

4. Gloria Averbuch, "The Ways We Are," *Lilith* #2, Winter 76/77, p. 7.

5. From "World of Our Brothers," an unpublished paper originally prepared for *Jewish and Female*.

6. Remarks made at a conference on the Jewish family, Kansas City, Nov. 1981.

7. Of course there was survival value in the attractiveness of intellectual men for Jewish women. Such partnerships select for bright offspring. One study of inherited IQ (in Goodman and Motulsky's *Genetic Diseases Among Ashkenazi Jews*—see Bibliog.) points out that since rabbis and scholars were considered good matches for the daughters of learned men, people of high intelligence were sorted out for each other, and these couples might have known more about hygiene—and therefore had more surviving children—than people of a less intellectual bent. In some other situations, notably among Catholics, the best and the brightest young people were encouraged to enter the priesthood, or a convent, and remain celibate. Not so in Judaism, which encouraged the marriages between bright men and the most eligible women.

8. From a talk delivered at the founding convention of the New Jewish Agenda, Washington, DC, Dec. 1980.

9. Aviva Cantor Zuckoff, "The Lilith Question," *Lilith* #1 (Fall 1976), pp. 5 ff. *For Men Against Sexism: A Book of Readings*, ed. Jon Snodgrass, and Bob Lamm, "American Jewish Men: Fear of Feminism," *Lilith* #1, Fall 1976, p. 23 ff.

10. From a talk at the New Jewish Agenda convention (see n. 8), "Jewish Men and Feminist Visions."

11. There are specific areas in which Jewish women and Jewish men will be on the opposite side of certain issues almost automatically. Two examples are:

Affirmative action. Jewish women have benefited greatly by affirmative-action programs and guidelines that gave them access to certain professional schools and employment opportunities. At the same time large numbers of Jewish men have opposed affirmative action, claiming that it would obliterate the gains (male) Jews have made under a strict merit system (see p. 492). When the opponents of affirmative action argue their case they invariably neglect to mention the benefits gained by Jewish women by virtue of their being *women*. If Jewish *men* don't gain, their reasoning has it, it's bad for the Jews.

American political platforms. In the 1980 American presidential election Jews supported the Republican candidate, Reagan, in unprecedented numbers. Women supported the Democratic platform, by and large, preferring the Democratic planks on women's issues, such as the Equal Rights Amendment and abortion legislation. Many Jews (read "Jewish men") thought Reagan would be "better for Israel." Many Jewish women, however, voted with other women for the candidate they thought would be "better" on women's issues. One woman etched the conflict very clearly when she said, "For the first time I had to ask myself, 'Is my primary identity as a Jew or as a woman?' "

There is a parallel to this in the voting patterns of Jewish women and Jewish men in the 1952 presidential election, When Jewish men, who tended to be more assimilated by virtue of being out in the business world, went along with the general trend and supported Eisenhower. Jewish women voted for Stevenson. (Of course the split in 1952 was not along Jewish/feminist lines.)

In social and political attitudes, Jewish women are generally more liberal than either Jewish men or non-Jewish women and men. For a fascinating analysis of the data that confirms what many of us had intuited, see Geraldine Rosenfeld, *Jewish College Freshmen: An Analysis of Three Studies*, American Jewish Committee, 1984.

12. *The Majority Finds Its Past: Placing Women in History* (New York: Oxford Univ. Press, 1979), p. 41.

13. Letty Cottin Pogrebin, "Anti-Semitism in the Women's Movement," *Ms.* (June 1982).

14. New York: Schocken, 1948, pp. 48–49.

15. "What Kind of Way Is That for Nice Jewish Girls to Act?: Images of Jewish Women in Modern American Drama," *American Jewish History*, Vol. LXX, No. 1 (Sept. 1980), p. 107.

See also Livia Bitton-Jackson, *Madonna or Courtesan?: The Jewish Woman in Christian Literature* (New York: Seabury Press, 1982). This book is a chilling compendium of the particular stereotyping, often in the form of anti-Semitic misogyny, that has run through the writings of Christian men (and some women) from medieval times onward.

16. "Bloodroot," *Lilith* #5 (1978), p. 39.

17. The theme of the evil that can come about when a Jewish woman marries a non-Jew appears in the writings of I. B. Singer. There is, however, hardly any parallel opprobrium for the Jewish man attracted to a non-Jewish woman.

18. Mary Helen Washington, "Working at Single Bliss," *Ms.*, Oct. 1982, p. 56.

19. *Moment*, Vol. 5, No. 2 (Feb. 1980); excerpted here with permission of *Moment*.

20. Read at The Jewish Museum, New York City, Feb. 7, 1982.

21. From "Friday Night," *Out of the Desert* (Garden City, N.Y.: Doubleday, 1980), p. 30. Reprinted with the kind permission of the author.

22. Tateel's M.A. thesis in social work is titled "In Research of the Jewish

Single." A précis is available from the School of Jewish Communal Service, Hebrew Union College–Jewish Institute of Religion, 3077 University Ave., Los Angeles, CA 90007.

23. "The Jewish Family in America: Today and Tomorrow," a paper circulated at a 1980 conference on the Jewish family, sponsored by National Council of Jewish Women, New York (unpaginated).

24. Almost all of the current books dealing with Jewish views on observance, ethics or sexuality avoid mentioning lesbianism even when they speak of male homosexuality, perhaps because there is no specific Biblical sanction against it. An exception to the general invisibility of the subject is Maurice Lamm's *The Jewish Way in Love and Marriage* (New York: Harper and Row, 1982), p. 69, where "no genital intercourse" and "no wasting of seed" are the reasons Lamm gives for why lesbianism is "not considered a perversion of God's intent."

25. *The Complete Book of Jewish Observance* (New York: Behrman House/Summit, 1980), p. 267.

26. Quoted in Judy Rosenfeld, "A Jewish Minority Speaks Up for Its Rights," Jewish Student Press Service, Aug. 1981.

27. See Batya Bauman, "The Ways We Are," *Lilith* #2 (Winter 76/77), p. 4, and Janet Myers, "Diaspora Takes a Queer Turn," *Dyke* #5 (Fall 1977), pp. 12–14. Evelyn Torton Beck's anthology of Jewish lesbian writing (see p. 317) provides other insights, as does Beck's analysis of I. B. Singer's attitudes toward women, especially the lesbian themes in the short stories "Yentl the Yeshiva Boy" and "Zeitl and Rickel." See her critique, "I.B. Singer's Mysogyny," *Lilith* #6 (1979), pp. 34–36.

28. "Judaism and the Modern Attitude to Homosexuality," *Encyclopedia Judaica Yearbook 1974*, p. 205. Lamm takes a strictly Halachic view, condemning homosexuality and calling for it to be defined again as an illness.

Chapter 8   Marriage

1. Mervin F. Verbit, "The Jewish Family in America: Today and Tomorrow," a paper circulated at a 1980 conference on the Jewish family, sponsored by National Conference of Jewish Women, New York (unpaginated).

2. The 1983 decision of the Reform movement to consider any self-identified Jew born of one Jewish parent (whether mother or father) as Jewish (see p. 344) has caused great controversy and fracturing in the Jewish community at large. Critics of the decision claim that Conservative and Orthodox authorities will now look with suspicion on anyone calling herself or himself a Jew. (See n. 17, below.)

For a discussion of the confusing definitions of Jewish family identity—sometimes matrilineal and sometimes patrilineal—see Trude Weiss-Rosmarin, "The Mother's Child," *Jewish Spectator*, Vol. XXXVII, No. 3 (March 1972).

3. "The Jewish Wedding: The Modern Ceremony," *Reform Judaism* (Dec. 1981), p. 14.

4. At a talk at the 1974 National Conference on Jewish Women and Men held in New York.

5. Exceptions to this may be found in marriages between Jews of German descent or of Syrian or other Middle Eastern background, in which very traditional, patriarchal role distinctions prevail between husband and wife. One statistical comparison of German Jewish marriages in Portland, Oregon, and those of Eastern European immigrants shows that "Eastern European women, though subordinate to their husbands in law and lore, were not part of a patriarchal tradition. Indeed, patterns of age at marriage, age differentials between wife and husband, size of family and female employment suggest a more assertive female role and a sharing of responsibility between wife, husband and children which we would call 'mutuality,' " (William Toll, "The Female Life Cycle and the Measure of Social Change: Portland, Oregon, 1880–1930," *American Jewish History*, Vol. LXXII, No. 3 [March 1983], p. 318).

6. Corinne Azen Krause, *Grandmothers, Mothers and Daughters* (New York: American Jewish Committee, 1978), p. 121. See Bibliography.

7. Quoted in Jane Biberman, "Violence in the Modern Home," *Inside* (Spring 1981), p. 54.

8. "Intermarriage Among American Jews: Consequences, Prospects, and Policies," National Jewish Conference Center Policy Studies, 1979, p. 1.

9. This piece, in somewhat different form, first appeared in the *Gratz College Annual*, 1976. Reprinted by permission. Rela Geffen Monson is Professor of Sociology at Gratz, and Chair of the Faculty.

10. Evelyn Cowan, *Portrait of Alice* (New York: Taplinger, 1979), p. 38.

11. In Betty Steck, "The Jewish Family in the 80's," *Inside*, (Summer 1980), p. 32. For other, perhaps more pathological responses to a child's intermarriage, see Edwin H. Friedman, "The Myth of the Shiksa," in Monica McGoldrick, John K. Pearce, and Joseph Giordano, eds. *Ethnicity and Family Therapy* (New York: Guilford Press, 1982).

12. "The Jewish Family in America." See also the personal accounts in "Raising Kids Jewish in an Intermarriage," *Lilith* #11 (Fall/Winter 1983), pp. 26 ff.

13. Reported by Ben Gallob, "No Guaranteed Method to Prevent Intermarriages," *The Sentinel* (Chicago), March 12, 1981.

14. Fred Massarik, *Intermarriage: Facts for Planning* (New York: Council of Jewish Federations National Population Study, n.d.), p. 7.

15. *Black Jews in America: A Documentary with Commentary* (New York: Commission of Synagogue Relations, Federation of Jewish Philanthropies, 1978), p. 122.

16. Leo Trepp, *The Complete Book of Jewish Observance* (New York: Behrman House/Summit Books), p. 291.

17. "Reform Rabbis Change Rule on Who Is a Jew," *New York Times*, March 17, 1983, p. A17. For Schindler's own evaluation of the consequences of the change, see Neil Barsky, "Reform Welcome Resolution on Jewish Identity," *Long Island Jewish World*, May 13–19, 1983, p. 8. (See also n. 2, above.)

18. In fact, some rabbis will steadfastly refuse to convert anyone who wants to marry a Jew, claiming that the conversion might at some level have an ulterior motive and therefore be invalid.

19. "The Convert's Dilemma: How Do I Live in Two Cultures at One Time?" *Direction* (Dec. 1980), p. 8.

20. Sandra Ariela Schachar, "Jew—Not Convert," *Moment* (Dec. 1979), p. 63.

21. From Rachel Cowan's speech at the ceremony marking her conversion to Judaism, 1980. Privately circulated.

22. Rachel's husband, Paul Cowan, has documented his own journey from assimilation to an embracing of his Jewish identity in *An Orphan in History: Retrieving a Jewish Legacy* (Garden City, N.Y.: Doubleday, 1982).

23. Rachel Cowan's discussion of her conversion was written for *Jewish and Female.*

Chapter 9   Divorce

1. Trude Weiss-Rosmarin, "There Is a 'Panacea' for the Agunah," *The Jewish Week*, May 20, 1983, p. 31.

2. Chaim I. Waxman, *Single Parent Families: A Challenge to the Jewish Community* (New York: Institute of Human Relations, American Jewish Committee, 1980), p. 3. American Jews are only slightly less likely to divorce than white American non-Jews. Divorce is, however, on the rise even among the Orthodox. See Bernard Weinberger, "The Growing Rate of Divorce in Orthodox Jewish Life," *Jewish Life* (Spring 1976), p. 9.

3. Irwin H. Haut, *Divorce in Jewish Law and Life* (New York: Sepher-Hermon, 1983), p. 101. Haut notes also that the figure 150,000, cited in *The New York Times* (July 5, 1982, p. 40) is a misprint.

4. Oscar Z. Fasman, "After Fifty Years, an Optimist," *American Jewish History*, Vol. LXIX, No. 2 (Dec. 1979), p. 163.

5. See, for example, Blu Greenberg, *On Women and Judaism: A View from Tradition* (see Bibliography) and "Jewish Divorce Law: If We Must Part, Let's Part as Equals," *Lilith* #3 (Spring/Summer 77), p. 26.

6. In a lecture at New York's 92nd Street Y, March 1982.

7. The woman could not terminate the marriage herself, however, but had to petition a *bet din* to issue the *get*. See Irwin H. Haut, *op. cit.*, pp. 51–52.

8. *On Women and Judaism: A View from Tradition*, pp. 141–42.

9. Quoted in Cissy Carpey, "A Woman and Judaism," *Inside* (Summer 1982), p. 67.

10. "Women's Liberation and Jewish Law," *Lilith* #1 (Fall 1976), p. 17.

11. *Op. cit.* Weiss-Rosmarin has for years been calling for a transfer of executive power for the *get* from the husband to the *bet din*. In this article she sets forth her case in response to recent civil-court "solutions" to the *agunah* problem.

12. David Margolick, "Court Rules New York Can Enforce Jewish Marriage Contract," *New York Times*, Feb. 18, 1983, p. B1.

13. Madeline Kochen, "Constitutional Implications of New York's 'Get' Statute," *New York Law Journal*, Oct. 27, 1983, p. 1. I am grateful to Edith Gross for calling this article to my attention.

14. Supporting the thrust of the Task Force proposal to lawyers, Richard

Kurtz, a Manhattan attorney who has handled many *get* cases, advises: "If the lawyer tells you there's nothing you can do about it, change lawyers. . . . There are always things the husband wants . . . in exchange for which he'll give a *get*. . . . But after the civil divorce . . . forget about it. There's no further relationship between the parties, and you'll never be able to negotiate a *get*." (Quoted in Bracha Osofsky, "Progress on the Get Problem," *Lilith* #10 (Winter 1983), p. 5.

Chapter 10   *Responding to the Childbearing Imperative*

1. Steven Martin Cohen, "The 1981–1982 National Survey of American Jews," *American Jewish Yearbook 1983* (New York: American Jewish Committee; Philadelphia: Jewish Publication Society, 1983), pp. 89–110.

2. Fred Massarik, "Assessing Jewish Survival: Considering the Evidence, 1971–81," a report presented to the Federation of Jewish Philanthropies of New York, Jan. 1983, pp. 50–52. A study by the American Council on Education shows that non-Jewish college graduates who were in their late twenties in 1980 were far more likely to have at least one child than were the Jews in the same population. "Of non-Jews, 24 percent of men and 28 percent of women were parents; of Jews, only three percent of men and six percent of women," according to Geraldine Rosenfield, *Jewish College Freshmen: An Analysis of Three Studies* (American Jewish Committee, 1984), p. 17.

3. In Lillian Wachtel, "Betty Friedan: On the Realities of Feminist Writing," *Womensweek* (Nov. 1979), p. 18.

4. *America's Jews* (New York: Random House, 1971), p. 83.

5. Shirley Frank, "The Population Panic: Why Jewish Leaders Want Jewish Women to Be Fruitful and Multiply," *Lilith* #4, p. 15.

6. Rosenstreich prepared these observations for inclusion in *Jewish and Female*.

7. Corinne Azen Krause, *Grandmothers, Mothers and Daughters* (New York: American Jewish Committee, 1978), p. 13.

8. Ibid., p. 73.

9. A spate of books, many written by Jewish women, tell women's own tales about the pleasures and despair they have known and have seen in others who are experiencing childbearing and child rearing. This truth-telling and "speaking bitterness" probably doesn't affect our choices about parenthood directly, but probably does feed into some women's preexisting ambivalence. Among the books: Phyllis Chesler, *With Child: A Diary of Motherhood* (New York: Crowell, 1979); Jane Lazarre, *The Mother Knot* (New York: McGraw-Hill, 1976); Adrienne Rich, *Of Woman Born: Motherhood as Experience and Institution* (New York: Bantam, 1977).

10. Learned from such analyses as Nancy Chodorow, *The Reproduction of Mothering: Psychoanalysis and the Sociology of Gender* (Berkeley: Univ. of California Press, 1978) and Doroth Dinnerstein, *The Mermaid and the Minotaur: Sexual Arrangements and Human Malaise* (New York: Harper and Row, 1976).

11. Symposium on motherhood, *Women: A Journal of Liberation* (Summer 1980), p. 7.

12. Remarks made at a "Women of Faith" conference, Philadelphia, Nov. 1980, sponsored by Women's Interreligious Dialogue on the Middle East.

13. Cohen's personal observations were prepared especially for inclusion in *Jewish and Female*. See also Rebecca Trachtenberg Alpert, "Survival Imperatives after the Holocaust," *Reconstructionist*, April 1977.

14. See also Judith E. Zimmerman, "Or Should I Have a Third Child?" in *Jewish Population: Renascence or Oblivion*, ed. Zimmerman and Barbara Trainin (New York: Commission on Synagogue Relations, Federation of Jewish Philanthropies, 1978).

15. Personal communication.

16. Reena Sigman Friedman, "Orphanages and Other Child-Care Institutions in the Jewish Community, 1900–1920," Ph.D. dissertation in progress, Dept. of History, Columbia Univ.

17. "Mixed Dating, Mixed Mating, Mixed Message," *Moment* (Oct. 1980), p. 63.

18. Sponsored by the Commission on Synagogue Relations of the New York Federation of Jewish Philanthropies and the New York Board of Jewish Education.

19. "We Need Quality More Than Quantity," in *Jewish Population: Renascence or Oblivion*, p. 215.

20. Newsletter of Temple Emanuel of Pascack Valley (N.J.), May 1980, p. 1. Reprinted by permission.

21. From "The Impact of Feminism on the Jewish Family," presented in Dec. 1980 to a National Council of Jewish Women district leadership meeting in New York City.

22. Reported to the author by Vicki Rosenstreich.

23. *Black Jews in America* (New York: Commission on Synagogue Relations, Federation of Jewish Philanthropies, 1978), p. 117.

24. Dr. Palti, *Jerusalem Post*, international edition, Nov. 14–20, 1982.

25. "The State of Orthodoxy," *Tradition*, Vol. 20, No. 1 (Spring, 1982).

26. "Raising Kids Jewish in a Mixed Marriage," *Lilith* #11 (Fall/Winter '83), pp. 27–33.

27. All three of these books deal with half-Jewish *girls*. Where's the literature for boys? There are two possible explanations for the lack:

Girls are the ones for whom, under Jewish law, the question of identity becomes important, since the official "Jewishness" of their children will depend on whether or not they themselves are Jewish (born of a Jewish mother or themselves converts to Judaism), according to Conservative and Orthodox authorities.

Girls are thought to be more in touch with their feelings than boys, as is evidenced by the spate of novels dealing with all sorts of sensitive topics from a girl's point of view: sexual awakening, divorce, homosexuality. Maybe it's just because most authors of children's books are women and tend to model their books after themselves. At any rate, the issues are live ones for "half-Jewish" boys too, so don't hesitate to suggest these books to them, especially *Mixed-Marriage Daughter*.

28. "Lilith Interview: Evelyn Torton Beck," *Lilith* #10 (Winter 82–83), p. 12.

Chapter 11   Jewish Women in Crisis: Community Resources

1. M.A. thesis, "When a Jewish Wife Becomes a Widow," Hebrew Union College–Jewish Institute of Religion School of Jewish Communal Service, 1979, p. 73.

2. "The Noah Syndrome," in *On Being a Jewish Feminist: A Reader*, ed. Susannah Heschel (New York: Schocken, 1983), p. 213.

3. Bernard Warach, *The Status of the Jewish Elderly of Greater New York*, 1981, a study available from the Jewish Association of Services for the Aged, New York.

4. *Number Our Days* (New York: Dutton, 1978), pp. 245, 251.

5. Warach, *op. cit.*

6. From a booklet describing the Hebrew Home and Hospital in Hartford, Connecticut.

7. The article on Project Ezra in Strassfeld and Strassfeld, *The Third Jewish Catalog* (see Bibliography), gives many useful suggestions on how to start such a program in your own community.

8. Toby Brandriss, quoted in a Project Ezra brochure.

9. *Alcoholism and the Jewish Community*, ed. Rabbi Allan Blaine (New York: Commission on Synagogue Relations, Federation of Jewish Philanthropies, 1980).

10. *Op. cit.*, pp. 275–293.

11. Ellen Bayer prepared this material specially for inclusion in *Jewish and Female*. She is now Director of the Speakers Bureau and Campaign Affairs for UJA/Federation in New York.

12. For harrowing tales of women's plight under Jewish divorce laws, with no recourse even in violent situations, see Leah Ain Globe, *The Dead End: Divorce in Israel*, privately pub., 1982 (distributed in America by Bloch). See also "Divorce," p. 355.

13. Ben Gallob, "Woman Rabbi Finds Battered Jewish Wives Seek Help." *Intermountain Jewish News*, Dec. 9, 1983, p. 24.

14. "Wife Beating Also Occurs among Jews," *Canadian Jewish News*, June 17, 1982, p. 10.

15. "According to Menahem Amir, Director of Hebrew University's Institute of Criminology, the high incidence of battered wives in Israel is not the result of drunken spouses, as in most other countries, but a direct function of the male chauvinist society that exists in Israel," *Jewish Week*, April 30, 1978, p. 9.

16. Susan Weidman Schneider, "A Jewish Women's Community—Behind Bars," *Lilith* #5 (1978), pp. 10–15.

17. "Torah-True and Feminist Too: A Psychotherapist's View of the Conflict Between Orthodox Judaism and the Women's Movement," *Journal of Jewish Communal Service*, no. 4, 1980, pp. 297–300.

18. Role and role strain in Orthodox women are the main foci of Bunim's Ph.D. thesis, now in progress.

19. In *Childhood in Contemporary Cultures*, ed. Margaret Mead and Martha Wolfenstein (Chicago: Univ. of Chicago Press, 1955).

20. "Portnoy's Mother's Complaint: Depression in Middle Aged Women," *Response* (Summer 1973), p. 131.

21. Ibid., p. 132.

22. "The Relationship Between Feminism and Depression in Adult Jewish Women," M.A. thesis, Graduate School of Social Work, Univ. of Houston, 1982. I am grateful to Julia Wolf Mazow for bringing Wolf's work to my attention.

Chapter 12   Giving Time and Money

1. Doris B. Gold, "Beyond the Valley of the Shmattes: A Meditation on Jewish Women's Organizations," *Lilith* #1 (Fall 1976), p. 30. See also Corinne Azen Krause, *Grandmothers, Mothers and Daughters: An Oral History of Ethnicity, Mental Health, and Continuity of Three Generations of Jewish, Italian, and Slavic-American Women* (New York: American Jewish Committee, 1978). In this study, more than 70 percent of the Jewish women belonged to a "service or fraternal ethnic organization" compared with 28 percent of the Italian and 45 percent of the Slavic women (p. 33).

2. For comprehensive listings of general Jewish organizations, in which women usually play some role as volunteers, see the annual *American Jewish Yearbook*, published jointly by the American Jewish Committee (New York) and the Jewish Publication Society of America (Philadelphia).

3. From a Dec. 1980 speech before the New Jewish Agenda, Washington, D.C.

4. Deborah Dash Moore, *At Home in America: Second Generation New York Jews* (New York: Columbia Univ. Press, 1981), p. 157.

5. Philadelphia: Jewish Publication Society, 1976.

6. A debate taken up in several issues in the Chicago *Sentinel* in the fall of 1981.

7. For the history of how earlier Jewish women confronted some of the same problems we face today over whether to join forces with other women's movements or to identify totally with the Jewish community, see Kaplan's, *The Jewish Feminist Movement in Germany: The Campaigns of the Jüdischer Frauenbund, 1904–38* (Westport, CT: Greenwood Press, 1979).

8. Amy Stone, "The Locked Cabinet," Lilith #2, p. 17.

9. This study was issued as a pamphlet, *The Status of Women in Jewish Organizations of Greater Pittsburgh*.

10. Marshall Sklare, *America's Jews* (New York: Random House, 1971).

11. See Krause, *op. cit.*, and Judith Weinstein Klein, *Healing Wounds Through Ethnotherapy* (New York: American Jewish Committee, 1979) for data on how Jewish-identified Jewish women tend to have "best" friends who are Jewish.

12. Sklare, *op. cit.*

13. Private communication to the editors of *Lilith*, "not for attribution."

14. Lillian B. Rubin, *Women of a Certain Age: The Midlife Search for Self* (New York: Harper & Row, 1979), p. 66.

15. From Levine's statement upon taking office, quoted in an American Jewish Congress press release.

16. In *Women in Sexist Society*, ed. Vivian Gornick and Barbara K. Moran (New York: Basic Books, 1971).

17. Excerpted from *Lilith* #5 (1978), with permission.

18. The umbrella organization for the major Jewish women's organizations. Under the aegis of this group much of the Jewish planning for the U.N. Decade of Women took place, as has other important planning and discussion, yet the *American Jewish Yearbook* (see note 2, above) does not even list it.

19. Phyllis Chesler and Emily Jane Goodman, *Women, Money and Power* (New York: Morrow, 1976), p. 171.

20. Lillian Rubin, *Women of a Certain Age*, p. 162.

21. See, as one example of many, Linda Heller, *The Castle on Hester Street* (Philadelphia: Jewish Publication Society, 1983). From a press release describing this children's book: "Grandpa Sol is given to tall tales about the journey from Russia. . . . Grandma Rose, ever the realist, wants Julie to hear 'only the truth.'"

22. *Community and Polity*, p. 73.

23. Some men, on the other hand, are a little late in seeing this. With women a rising force in Jewish philanthropy—making more money than ever before and controlling it as widows and daughters of wealthy men—Marc Lee Raphael, in *Understanding American Jewish Philanthropy* (New York: Ktav, 1979), has included in twenty-two articles only one written by a woman about women. This is Amy Stone's "The Locked Cabinet," about the UJA's men-only Young Leadership Cabinet (see n. 6 above).

24. Professional fundraisers in the Jewish community say that at present 80 percent of the money comes from 20 percent of the donors. The more cynical claim that 90 percent comes from 10 percent of the donors.

Chapter 13   Jewish Women and the World of Work

1. Fresh Meadows, NY: Biblio Press, 1983. See also Mark Wischnitzer, *A History of Jewish Crafts and Guilds* (New York: Jonathan David, 1965).

2. See Tillie Olsen, *Tell Me a Riddle* (New York: Dell, 1976), for a portrait of a woman from this background growing old in America. Meredith Tax's historical novel *Rivington Street* (New York: Bantam, 1983) also features a radical European-born Jewish woman struggling to change working conditions in early twentieth-century America.

3. Quoted in Ellen Stone, "Lilith Resurrected: The Emerging Consciousness of Jewish Women," *The Second Wave* (Summer 1981), p. 42.

4. Sydney Stahl Weinberg, "Working Daughters," *Lilith* #8 (1981), pp. 20–23. See also Rose Pastor Stokes, "Voice from the Sweatshop," *Lilith* #8, pp. 24–25.

5. Alice Kessler-Harris, *Out to Work: A History of Wage-Earning Women in the United States* (New York: Oxford Univ. Press, 1982), documents some of the occupations of Jewish immigrant women, pp. 123–28.

6. We know this from anecdotal reports and oral histories of Jewish women. A description of this phenomenon in several American subcultures appears in

Lillian B. Rubin, *Worlds of Pain: Life in the Working-Class Family* (New York: Basic Books, 1976).

7. *A Time to Remember* (New York: Norton, 1979).

8. Quoted in Linda Gordon Kuzmack and George Salomon, *Working and Mothering: A Study of 97 Jewish Career Women with Three or More Children* (New York: American Jewish Committee, 1981).

9. "Jewish Macho in the 80s," *Women's League Outlook*, Spring 1982, p. 7.

10. Aviva Cantor, on reading this paragraph in manuscript form, commented in the margin, "I'd rather be the passive recipient of balm," a statement which suggests strongly that no matter the positive feelings we as women may have about our domestic roles, we are still filling the classic "enabler" role when we claim to be "in charge" on the domestic scene.

11. Laura B. Wolf, "The Relationship Between Feminism and Depression in Adult Jewish Women," M.A. thesis, Graduate School of Social Work, Univ. of Houston, 1982.

12. A remark sometimes attributed to one or another well-known feminist leader, most often to Gloria Steinem; according to the *Ms.* research department, however, the anonymous woman cited here gets the credit.

13. I am grateful to Aviva Cantor for bringing Shapiro's suggestion to my attention.

14. *Feminist Perspectives on Housework and Child Care* (Bronxville, NY: Sarah Lawrence College, 1978). Proceedings of a conference by the same name.

15. Lillian B. Rubin, *Women of a Certain Age: The Midlife Search for Self* (New York: Harper & Row), p. 162.

16. In the proceedings of the annual meeting of the Chicago chapter of the American Jewish Committee. The address was reprinted in the *Journal of Jewish Communal Service*, Spring 1972, pp. 259–65.

17. "Homeless Women," Women's American ORT *Reporter*, Sept./Oct. 1980.

18. De Funis is a Sephardic Jew.

19. This material and the other quotations from Evan Bayer on affirmative action and the Jewish community were prepared specially for inclusion in *Jewish and Female*.

20. *Lilith* #4 (Fall/Winter 77/78), pp. 25–26.

21. "An End to Exploitation of Women in the Jewish Establishment," *Lilith* #8 (1981), p. 48.

22. "Affirmative Action in the 1980's: Dismantling the Process of Discrimination," A Proposed Statement of the United States Commission on Civil Rights, Clearinghouse Publication 65, Jan. 1981; Cardin, Nina, "Bakke, The Jews and Affirmative Action," *Sh'ma*, 8/147 (Feb. 3, 1978); Marx, Robert J., "Affirmative Action as a Jewish Mandate," *ibid.*, pp. 58–59; Pearlstein, Mitchell B., "Jewish leaders of Affirmative Action," *Sh'ma* 10/199 (Oct. 17, 1980), pp. 148–49; Rabinove, Samuel, "Jews, Blacks and the Quest for Justice," *ibid.*, pp. 146–48; Wasserman, Lois D., "Quotas, No–Special Consideration, Yes," *ibid.* (Oct. 17, 1980).

Chapter 14   Reconciling Jewish and Female

1. *American Behavioral Scientist*, Vol. 23, No. 4 (March–April, 1980), p. 522.

2. Religious Judaism is in fact probably the least rigid of Western religions. A heavy investment in the status quo seems to surface only when women's issues challenge it. Susannah Heschel sums up this attitude of reverence toward the past: "Ultimately, since the Jewish history we know is the history of Jewish men, it is precisely that historical consciousness that is invoked by Conservative leaders when they want to oppose any changes in the status of women." *On Being a Jewish Feminist: A Reader* (New York: Schocken, 1938), p. 28.

3. However, Cohen, in an important 1983 report on what American Jews think about Israel, prejudice, Judaism, and other topics, was not sensitive to the fact that many Jewish women slipped through the holes in his net and were not captured by his sampling techniques, claimed to be among the most sophisticated used in making Jewish demographic analyses. At a press conference sponsored by the American Jewish Committee in October 1983, the analysis (now called by some "The Cohen Report") was said to derive from samplings of Jews across the United States; these Jews were identified by their having Jewish surnames, which would omit those Jewish women married to non-Jews whose names they had taken (intermarried men were still captured, of course), and from lists of car owners (many women drive cars registered in their husbands' names) or from telephone listings (ditto). So a survey purporting to tell us how American Jews think is in reality telling us how American Jewish men think, without making this distinction explicit.

4. Cohen, "American Jewish Feminism," p. 523.

5. Quoted in Letty Cottin Pogrebin, "Anti-Semitism in the Women's Movement," *Ms.*, June 1982.

6. "How to Get What We Want by the Year 2000," *Lilith* #7 (1980), pp. 18–22.

SELECTED
BIBLIOGRAPHY

Adler, Rachel. "The Jew Who Wasn't There." *Response*, No. 18 (Summer 1973), pp. 77–82.

Asheri, Michael. *Living Jewish: The Lore and Law of the Practicing Jew*. New York: Everest House, 1978.

Bart, Pauline. "Depression in Middle-Aged Women: Some Sociocultural Factors." Ph.D. thesis, UCLA, 1967.

Baum, Charlotte, Paula Hyman, and Sonya Michel. *The Jewish Women in America*. New York: Dial, 1976.

Beck, Evelyn Torton, ed. *Nice Jewish Girls: A Lesbian Anthology*. Watertown, MA: Persephone Press, 1982.

Benson, Paulette, and Joanne Altschuler. *The Jewish Family: Past, Present and Future*. Denver: Alternatives in Religious Education, 1979.

Benson, Paulette and Sherry Bissell. *Divorce in Jewish Life and Tradition*. Denver: Alternatives in Religious Education, 1979.

Berger, Graenum. *Black Jews in America*. New York: Commission on Synagogue Relations, Federation of Jewish Philanthropies, 1978.

Bitton-Jackson, Livia. *Madonna or Courtesan: Jewish Women in Christian Literature*. New York: Seabury, 1983.

Blaine, Allan, ed. *Alcoholism and the Jewish Community*. New York: Task Force on Alcoholism, Federation of Jewish Philanthropies, 1980.

Blume, Judy. *Are You There God? It's Me, Margaret*. New York: Dell, 1970.

Borowitz, Eugene. *Choosing a Sex Ethic*. New York: Schocken, 1970.

Brin, Ruth F. *The Shabbat Catalogue*. New York: Ktav, 1978.

Broner, E. M. *Her Mothers*. New York: Holt, Rinehart & Winston, 1975.

———. *A Weave of Women*. New York: Holt, Rinehart & Winston, 1978.

Brownmiller, Susan. *Against Our Will: Men, Women and Rape*. New York: Simon and Schuster, 1976.

Bubis, Gerald B. *Serving the Jewish Family*. New York: Ktav, 1977.

Cantor, Aviva. *The Jewish Woman: 1900–1980. An Annotated Bibliography.* Fresh Meadows, NY: Biblio Press, 1981.

Chesler, Phyllis. *Women and Madness.* Garden City, NY: Doubleday, 1972.
———— and Emily Jane Goodman. *Women, Money and Power.* New York: Morrow, 1976.

Christ, Carol P., and Judith Plaskow, eds. *Womanspirit Rising: A Feminist Reader in Religion.* San Francisco: Harper & Row, 1979.

Cohen, Jessica Lynn. "A Comparison of Norms and Behaviors of Childrearing in Jewish and Italian Mothers." Ph.D. thesis, Syracuse Univ., 1977.

Cohen, Steven Martin. "The 1981–82 National Survey of American Jews," in *American Jewish Yearbook 1983.* New York: American Jewish Committee, 1983.

Colman, Hila. *Mixed-Marriage Daughter.* New York: Morrow, 1968.

Cone, Molly. *Hear, O Israel: The Storybooks About Learning.* New York: Union of American Hebrew Congregations, 1971.

Cottle, Thomas. *Divorce and the Jewish Child.* New York: American Jewish Committee, 1981.
————. *The Hidden Survivors: Poor Jews in America.* New York: Prentice-Hall, 1980.

Cowan, Evelyn. *Portrait of Alice.* New York: Taplinger, 1979.

Daly, Mary. *Beyond God the Father: Toward a Philosophy of Women's Liberation.* Boston: Beacon Press, 1973.

Davidson, Cathy N., and E. M. Broner, eds. *The Lost Tradition: Mothers and Daughters in Literature.* New York: Frederick Ungar, 1980.

Dinnerstein, Dorothy. *The Mermaid and the Minotaur: Sexual Arrangements and Human Malaise.* New York: Harper and Row, 1976.

Directory of Jewish Health and Welfare Agencies. New York: Council of Jewish Federations, 1983.

Directory of Jewish Homes for the Aged. Dallas: National Association of Jewish Homes for the Aged, 1982.

Domestic Violence: An NCJW Response. New York: National Council of Jewish Women, 1981.

Donin, Rabbi Hayim Halevy. *To Pray as a Jew.* New York: Basic Books, 1980.
————. *To Raise a Jewish Child: A Guide for Parents.* New York: Basic Books, 1977.

Dworkin, Andrea. *Pornography: Men Possessing Women.* Perigee, 1981.

Elazar, Daniel. *Community and Polity: The Organizational Dynamics of American Jewry.* Philadelphia: Jewish Publication Society, 1976.

Elwell, Ellen Sue Levi, and Edward R. Levenson. *The Jewish Women's Studies Guide.* Fresh Meadows, NY: Biblio Press, 1982.

Epstein, Helen. *Children of the Holocaust.* New York: Bantam, 1979.

Feldman, David M. *Birth Control in Jewish Law: Marital Relations, Contraception, and Abortion as Set Forth in the Classic Texts of Jewish Law.* New York: New York Univ. Press, 1968.

Firestone, Shulamit. *The Dialectic of Sex.* New York: Bantam, 1972.

Fisher, Anne E. *Women's Worlds: NIMH Supported Research on Women.* Rockville, MD: National Institute of Mental Health, 1978.

Frank, Blanche. "The American Orthodox Jewish Housewife: A Generational Study in Ethnic Survival." M.A. thesis, City Univ. of NY, 1975.

Friedan, Betty, *The Feminine Mystique*. New York: Norton, 1974.

Frimer, Dov I. "Grounds for Divorce Due to Immoral Behavior (Other than Adultery) According to Jewish Law." Ph.D. thesis (in Hebrew), Jerusalem: Hebrew Univ., 1980 (also on file at Yeshiva Univ., NY).

Gittelman, Sol. *From Shtetl to Suburbia: The Family in Jewish Literary Imagination*. Boston: Beacon Press, 1978.

Gittelsohn, Roland B. *Love, Sex and Marriage: A Jewish View*. New York: Union of American Hebrew Congregations, 1980.

Globe, Leah Ain. *Divorce in Israel: The Dead End*. Israel: privately pub., 1982; U.S. distributor, Bloch, New York.

Gold, Doris B. "Women and Voluntarism," in *Women in Sexist Society*. Vivian Gornick and Barbara K. Moran, eds. New York: Basic Books, 1971. Pp. 384–400.

Goldenberg, Naomi. *Changing of the Gods: Feminism and the End of Traditional Religions*. Boston: Beacon Press, 1979.

Goodman, Richard M., and Arno G. Motulsky, eds. *Genetic Diseases Among Ashkenazi Jews*. New York: Raven Press, 1979.

Gordis, Robert. *Love and Sex: A Modern Jewish Perspective*. New York: Farrar, Straus & Giroux, 1978.

Gornick, Vivian, and Barbara K. Moran, eds. *Women in Sexist Society: Studies in Power and Powerlessness*, New York: Basic Books, 1971.

Greenberg, Blu. *How to Run a Traditional Jewish Household*. New York: Simon & Schuster, 1983.

———. *On Women and Judaism: A View from Tradition*. Philadelphia: Jewish Publication Society, 1981.

Hadas, Pamela White. *In Light of Genesis*. Philadelphia: Jewish Publication Society, 1980.

Hamelsdorf, Ora, and Sandra Adelsberg. *Jewish Women and Jewish Law: A Bibliography*. Fresh Meadows, NY: Biblio Press, 1981.

Haut, Irwin H. *Divorce in Jewish Law and Life*. New York: Sepher-Hermon Press, 1983.

Heschel, Susannah, ed. *On Being a Jewish Feminist: A Reader*. New York: Schocken, 1983.

Himmelfarb, Milton, and David Singer, eds. *American Jewish Year Book*. New York and Philadelphia: The American Jewish Committee and The Jewish Publication Society of America; published annually.

Hirsch, Marilyn. *The House on the Roof*. New York: Bonim Books, 1976.

Hite, Shere. *The Hite Report: A Nationwide Study of Female Sexuality*. New York: Macmillan, 1976.

Hoffman, Nancy, and Florence Howe, eds. *Women Working: An Anthology of Stories and Poems*. Old Westbury, NY: The Feminist Press, 1979.

Hornik, Edith Lynn. *The Drinking Woman*. New York: Association Press, 1977.

Kaplan, Marion A. *The Jewish Feminist Movement in Germany: The Cam-

paigns of the Jüdischer Frauenbund, 1904–38. Westport, CT: Greenwood Press, 1979.

Kessler-Harris, Alice. *Out to Work: A History of Wage-Earning Women in the United States.* New York: Oxford Univ. Press, 1982.

Klagsbrun, Francine. *Voices of Wisdom: Jewish Ideals and Ethics for Everyday Living.* New York: Pantheon, 1980.

Klein, Judith Weinstein. *Healing Wounds Through Ethnotherapy.* New York: American Jewish Committee, 1979.

Koltun, Elizabeth, ed. *The Jewish Woman: New Perspectives.* New York: Schocken, 1976.

Kramer, Sydelle, and Jenny Masur, eds. *Jewish Grandmothers.* Boston: Beacon Press, 1976.

Krause, Corinne Azen. *Grandmothers, Mothers and Daughters: An Oral History Study of Ethnicity, Mental Health, and Continuity of Three Generations of Jewish, Italian, and Slavic-American Women.* New York: American Jewish Committee, 1978.

Kukoff, Lydia. *Choosing Judaism: A Guide for Jews-by-Choice.* New York: Union of American Hebrew Congregations, 1982.

Kuzmack, Linda Gordon, and George Salomon. *Working and Mothering: A Study of 97 Jewish Career Women with Three or More Children.* New York: American Jewish Committee, 1981.

Lacks, Roslyn. *Women and Judaism: Myth, History, and Struggle.* Garden City, NY: Doubleday, 1980.

Lamm, Maurice. *The Jewish Way in Love and Marriage.* New York: Harper & Row, 1980.

Lang, Lucy Robins. *Tomorrow Is Beautiful.* New York: Macmillan, 1948.

Lerner, Anne Lapidus. *"Who Hast Not Made Me a Man": The Movement for Equal Rights for Women in American Jewry.* New York: American Jewish Committee, 1977.

Lerner, Gerda. *The Majority Finds Its Past: Placing Women in History.* New York: Oxford Univ. Press, 1979.

Lebeson, Anita. *Recall to Life: The Jewish Woman in America.* New York: Yoseloff, 1970.

Levenberg, Diane. *Out of the Desert.* Garden City, NY: Doubleday, 1980.

Marcus, Jacob Rader. *The American Jewish Woman: A Documentary History.* New York: Ktav, 1981.

Mathews, Carole, and Sandra Rubenstein. "Lesbian Jews: Reconciling a Dual Identity." M.A. thesis, Los Angeles: Hebrew Union College and Univ. of Southern California, 1980.

Mayer, Egon. *Intermarriage Among American Jews: Consequences, Prospects and Policies.* New York: National Jewish Resource Center, 1979.

——— and Carl Sheingold. *Intermarriage and the Jewish Future: A National Study in Summary.* New York: American Jewish Committee, 1979.

Mazow, Julia Wolf, ed. *The Woman Who Lost Her Names: Selected Writings of American Jewish Women.* San Francisco: Harper & Row, 1980.

McGoldrick, Monica, John K. Pearce, and Joseph Giordano, eds. *Ethnicity and Family Therapy.* New York: Guilford Press, 1982.

Meiselman, Moshe. *Jewish Women in Jewish Law*. New York: Ktav, 1978.

Mirsky, Norman B. *Unorthodox Judaism*. Columbus: Ohio State Univ. Press, 1978.

Moore, Deborah Dash. *At Home in America: Second Generation New York Jews*. New York: Columbia Univ. Press, 1980.

Myerhoff, Barbara. *Number Our Days*. New York: E. P. Dutton, 1978.

Options for Living Arrangements: Housing Alternatives for the Elderly. New York: National Council of Jewish Women, 1981.

Paige, Karen Ericksen, and Jeffrey M. Paige. *The Politics of Reproductive Ritual*. Berkeley: Univ. of California Press, 1981.

Parent, Gail. *Sheila Levine Is Dead and Living in New York*. New York: Bantam, 1973.

Piercy, Marge. *Small Changes*. Garden City, NY: Doubleday, 1972.

Pinzer, Maimie. *The Maimie Papers*. Ruth Rosen, historical ed., Sue Davidson, textual ed. Old Westbury, NY: The Feminist Press, in cooperation with the Schlesinger Library of Radcliffe College, 1977.

Pogrebin, Letty Cottin. *Getting Yours: How to Make the System Work for the Working Woman*. New York: Avon, 1975.

————. *Growing Up Free: Raising Your Child in the 80's*. New York: McGraw-Hill, 1980.

Raphael, Marc Lee. *Understanding American Jewish Philanthropy*. New York: Ktav, 1979.

Reifman, Toby Kishbein, with Ezrat Nashim. *Blessing the Birth of a Daughter: Jewish Naming Ceremonies for Girls*. Englewood, NJ: privately pub., 1978.

Reimer, Jack. *Ethical Wills*. New York: National Jewish Resource Center, 1978.

Rich, Adrienne. *Of Woman Born: Motherhood as Experience and Institution*. New York: Bantam, 1977.

Rubin, Lillian B. *Women of a Certain Age: The Midlife Search for Self*. New York: Harper & Row, 1979.

Rudenstein, Gail M., Carol Farley Kessler, and Ann M. Moore. "Mothers and Daughters in Literature: A Preliminary Bibliography," in Cathy N. Davidson and E. M. Broner, eds. *The Lost Tradition: Mothers and Daughters in Literature*. New York: 1980. Pp. 309–322.

Rudin, James, and Marcia Rudin. *Prison or Paranoia? The New Religious Cults*. Philadelphia: Fortress Press, 1980.

Ruether, Rosemary Radford, ed. *Religion and Sexism: Images of Women in the Jewish and Christian Traditions*. New York: Simon and Schuster, 1974.

Ruether, Rosemary Radford, and Rosemary Skinner Keller, eds. *Women and Religion in America, Volume 1: The Nineteenth Century*. San Francisco: Harper & Row, 1981.

Sandmaier, Marian. *The Invisible Alcoholics: Women and Alcohol Abuse in America*. New York: McGraw-Hill, 1980.

Sasso, Sandy Eisenberg. *Call Them Builders*. New York: The Reconstructionist Foundation, 1978.

Saypol, Judyth R., ed. *Jewish Life on Campus: A Directory of B'nai B'rith*

Hillel Foundations and other Jewish Campus Agencies with Information on Jewish Enrollment, Jewish Studies, and Kosher Dining. Washington, DC: B'nai B'rith Hillel Foundation, 1982.

Schachter-Shalomi, Reb Zalman, with Donald Gropman. *The First Step: A Guide for the New Jewish Spirit.* New York: Bantam, 1983.

Schaeffer, Susan Fromberg. *Falling.* New York: Macmillan, 1973.

Seaman, Sylvia S. *How to Be a Jewish Grandmother.* Garden City, NY: Doubleday, 1979.

Sheraton, Mini. *From My Mother's Kitchen: Recipes and Reminiscences.* New York: Harper & Row, 1979.

Shields, Laurie. *Displaced Homemakers: Organizing for a New Life.* New York: McGraw-Hill, 1980.

Shiloh, A., and Ida Cohen Selavan, eds. *Ethnic Groups of America: Their Morbidity, Mortality, and Behavior Disorders, Volume One: The Jews.* Springfield, IL: Charles C. Thomas, 1973.

Shulman, Alix Kates. *Memoirs of an Ex-Prom Queen.* New York: Knopf, 1972.

Siegal, Richard, Michael Strassfeld, and Sharon Strassfeld, eds. *The Jewish Catalog: A Do-It-Yourself Kit.* Philadelphia: Jewish Publication Society, 1973.

Sisters of Exile: Sources on the Jewish Woman. New York: Ichud Habonim Labor Zionist Youth, undated.

Sklare, Marshall. *America's Jews.* New York: Random House, 1971.

Snodgrass, Jon, ed. *For Men Against Sexism: A Book of Readings.* Albion, CA: Times Change Press, 1977.

Sochen, June, ed. *American Jewish Women,* Vol. LXX, No. 1 of *American Jewish History* (Sept. 1980).

Solow, Phyllis. "Survival Skills for Widows: A Study of a Feminist Intervention." M.A. thesis, Dominguez Hills, CA: California State Univ., 1978.

Stern, Arlene L. *International Mikvah Directory.* New York: Armis Publications, 1979.

Stern, Chaim. *Gates of Prayer: The New Union Prayerbook.* New York: Central Conference of American Rabbis, 1975.

Stimpson, Catharine R., and Ethel Spector Person, eds. *Women: Sex and Sexuality.* Chicago: Univ. of Chicago Press, 1980.

Strassfeld, Michael, ed. *A Shabbat Haggadah.* New York: American Jewish Committee, 1981.

Strassfeld, Sharon and Kathy Green. *The Jewish Family Book.* New York: Bantam, 1981.

Strassfeld, Sharon, and Michael Strassfeld, eds. *The Second Jewish Catalog: Sources and Resources.* Philadelphia: Jewish Publication Society, 1976.

————, eds. *The Third Jewish Catalog: Creating Community.* Philadelphia: Jewish Publication Society, 1980.

Swerdlow, Amy, ed. *Feminist Perspectives on Housework and Child Care.* Bronxville: NY: Sarah Lawrence College, 1978.

————, Renate Bridenthal, Joan Kelly, and Phyllis Vine. *Household and Kin: Families in Flux.* Old Westbury, NY: The Feminist Press, 1981

Swidler, Leonard. *Women in Judaism: The Status of Women in Formative Judaism.* Philadelphia: Scarecrow Press, 1978.

Taitz, Emily, and Sondra Henry. *Written Out of History.* Fresh Meadows, NY: Biblio Press, 1983.

Taking the Fruit: Modern Women's Tales of the Bible. San Diego, CA: Women's Institute for Continuing Jewish Education, 1982.

Tateel, Rita. "In Research of the Jewish Single." M.A. thesis, Los Angeles: Hebrew Union College, 1978.

Tax, Meredith. *The Rising of the Women: Feminist Solidarity and Class Conflict 1880–1917.* New York: Monthly Review Press, 1980.

Tonner, Leslie. *Nothing but the Best: The Luck of the Jewish Princess.* New York: Ballantine, 1975.

Trepp, Leo. *The Complete Book of Jewish Observance: A Practical Manual for the Modern Jew.* New York: Behrman House/Summit, 1980.

Tufte, Virginia, and Barbara Myerhoff, eds. *Changing Images of the Family.* New Haven: Yale Univ. Press, 1979.

Vetaher Libenu. Sudbury, MA: Congregation Beth El of the Sudbury River Valley, 1980.

Waskow, Arthur. *Seasons of Our Joy: A Handbook of Jewish Festivals.* New York: Bantam, 1982.

Waxman, Chaim I. *Single Parent Families: A Challenge to the Jewish Community.* New York: Institute of Human Relations, American Jewish Committee, 1980.

Wenig, Maggie, and Naomi Janowitz. *Siddur Nashim.* Brooklyn, NY: privately ptd., 1980.

Wolf, Laura B. "The Relationship Between Feminism and Depression in Adult Jewish Women." M.A. thesis, Houston: Univ. of Houston, 1982.

Wolfenstein, Martha. "Two Types of Jewish Mothers," in Margaret Mead and M. Wolfenstein, eds. *Childhood in Contemporary Cultures.* Chicago: Univ. of Chicago Press, 1955.

Yezierska, Anzia. *Bread Givers: A Struggle Between a Father of the Old World and a Daughter of the New.* New York: Persea Books, 1978 (rpt. of 1925 ed.).

Young, Susan Winter. "An Annotated Bibliography of Books and Articles on the Jewish Marriage Contract." M.A. thesis, 1978, on file at Jewish Women's Resource Center, New York.

Zimmerman, Judith, and Barbara Trainin, eds. *Jewish Population: Renascence or Oblivion.* New York: Federation of Jewish Philanthropies, 1979.

Zborowski, Karl, and Elizabeth Herzog. *Life Is with People: The Culture of the Shtetl.* New York: International Universities Press, 1952.

Zwerin, Rabbi Raymond A., and Audrey Friedman Marcus. *Marriage in Jewish Life and Tradition: A Mini-Course.* Denver: Alternatives in Religious Education, 1978.

INDEX